S0-CPC-254

LOOKING BACKWARD
A Reintroduction to American History

LOOKING BACKWARD
A Reintroduction to American History

Lloyd C. Gardner
Professor of History
Rutgers University

William L. O'Neill
Professor of History
Rutgers University

McGraw-Hill Book Company
New York St. Louis San Francisco Düsseldorf Johannesburg
Kuala Lumpur London Mexico Montreal New Delhi
Panama Paris São Paulo Singapore Sydney Tokyo Toronto

LOOKING BACKWARD
A Reintroduction
to American History

Copyright © 1974 by McGraw-Hill, Inc.
All rights reserved. Printed in the United States of America.
No part of this publication may be reproduced,
stored in a retrieval system, or transmitted,
in any form or by any means, electronic, mechanical,
photocopying, recording, or otherwise, without
the prior written permission of the publisher.

1234567890VHVH7654

This book was set in Helvetica Light by Black Dot, Inc.
The editors were Stephen D. Dragin and Helen Greenberg;
the designer was Jo Jones;
the photo editor was Juanita James;
and the production supervisor was Leroy A. Young.
Von Hoffmann Press, Inc., was printer and binder.

Library of Congress Cataloging in Publication Data

Gardner, Lloyd C   date
    Looking backward.

    Includes bibliographies.
        1. United States—History. I. O'Neill, William L.
II. Title.
E178.1.G2 1974   973   73-12191
ISBN 0-07-022841-8 (pbk.)

To our parents
Lloyd and Hazel
John and Helen

CONTENTS

PREFACE

This book differs from the usual text in several ways. We decided at the outset to write chiefly about what interests us, to poke around in unfamiliar places when necessary to satisfy ourselves on a given question. This meant leaving out many subjects usually covered in surveys of American history. We also decided to emphasize interpretation and to retain our own voices. Most of O'Neill's chapters deal with social and cultural history, Gardner's with diplomatic history and foreign policy. Both authors cover some political history. Although we feel that our views on most topics are not dissimilar, we do not agree on everything and have made no effort to harmonize our opinions.

We hope that this approach will reduce the tyranny of the printed word. We also hope the result has been a book more lively, readable, and interpretative than is customary, yet sufficiently inclusive to be used as a basic text. If we have succeeded even partway, this will not be the kind of survey that the instructor may safely assign and forget. It is going to raise questions that will have to be dealt with in class. There are omissions that the instructor must himself discuss in lectures or through other readings. We do not consider this a drawback but rather an opportunity for teachers to organize a provocative course. We hope the instructor will find that our treatment of (or the lack of) various problems will encourage him or her to build on them in class, supplementing our material, taking issue with it, or both.

We believe the principal weakness of survey courses is their tendency to make students think of American history as a finished subject, one in which all questions have been answered and all verdicts agreed on. We found that not to be the case while writing the book, and we have consciously tried to dispel that impression by setting forth our conclusions clearly enough so that teachers can work against as well as with our book. This is a reintroduction to American history, then, not in the sense of acquainting the student with what is familiar (and probably known), but with what isn't.

We would like to thank the many people who assisted us in one way or another. They include James Mirrielees, Robert R. Rainier, and Helen Greenberg of McGraw-Hill, and the following scholars who read portions of the manuscript: Eugene Carraher, Prince George's Community College; John Demos, Brandeis University; Thomas V. DiBacco, American University; David Grimsted, University of Maryland; George C. Herring, Jr., University of Kentucky; George Lowin, University of Maryland; George B. Oliver, Randolph-Macon College; Robert C. Pierce, Foothill College; Stanley K. Schultz, University of Wisconsin; Robert Sklar, University of Michigan; Earl E. Thorpe, North Carolina Central University; and Jacqueline B. Tusa, University of Maryland. Finally, we would like to thank our parents, to whom this book is dedicated.

Lloyd C. Gardner
William L. O'Neill

ONE

European Origins

Period covered: 1415 to the present
Emphases: Politics and diplomacy
Major events: Portuguese attack on Ceuta, 1415
Columbus sails for the East Indies, 1492
Vasco da Gama rounds Africa, 1497
Cortés conquers Mexico, 1519
Magellan goes around the world, 1520
Navigation Acts, 1660–1673
Glorious Revolution, 1688
Anglo-Portuguese Commercial Treaty
(Methuen Treaty), 1703
American Revolution, 1776
American Civil War, 1861
War in Vietnam begins, 1961

Most historians now agree that the Norsemen came to America first. The Irish have their advocates, who insist that St. Brendan reached Newfoundland, the West Indies, Mexico, and even the Ohio River in the second half of the seventh century. There is no real evidence to support any of these tales. But there were Irish settlements on Iceland when the Vikings landed there and took possession in the ninth century. The Viking seafarers used Iceland as a base for further probes as far west as Greenland, Labrador, and Newfoundland. Yet the rest of Europe remained largely ignorant of these early discoveries.

Rumors of the Norse explorations may have reached a few curious ears, but they did not spark any great enthusiasm among peoples whose main interest was fixed on Eastern problems and opportunities. Beginning in 1096, Christian Europe had embarked on a series of Crusades to restore the "Holy Lands" to the control of true believers. The Crusades lasted for nearly 200 years, and failed in their original objective. Nevertheless, they changed Europe. Crusaders' tales of the opulence they had seen in the East and, later, Marco Polo's famous account of his overland journey to China and twenty-year stay at the court of the Emperor stimulated explorers to take to the sea to find an easier route to the fabled riches of Cathay.

The Crusades had diffused knowledge of the Indian Ocean trade routes throughout Europe. At the same time, however, they centered the increasingly valuable Eastern trade (spices, silks, perfumes, etc.) in the hands of Italian middlemen—many of whom grew rich by supplying the army of Crusaders with European provisions. Why should the Italians have it all, asked explorers—and their financial backers?

There were other ways in which the Crusades stimulated the imagination of Europeans toward commercial production for an international market. One order of knights returned from the struggle against the infidels with the most up-to-date technological know-how on the refining process for sugar cane, which they then introduced into Sicily. Like the sons of Christian missionaries who went to Hawaii in the nineteenth century, the knights found commerce more profitable than conversion. In both instances, others were quick to learn.

The growth of international commerce was a key factor in the breakdown of the ideological foundations of the Middle Ages. Like the Gothic cathedral, the Crusades represented a world view: religious zeal, feudalism, Christian internationalism, and chivalry. When they finally came to an end around 1300, a new world view had already begun to spread across Europe, an outward-looking attitude which replaced the closely ordered medieval life. The world of the Gothic cathedral could not, after all, move out beyond Europe and yet remain the same.

The holy war against Islam, which the Crusades had epitomized, did succeed in removing Mohammedan power from Spain and Portugal—thus freeing those countries to begin the race for empire. From the eighth century, Arabs had controlled the whole of North Africa and large portions of Spain and Portugal. During the centuries of Mohammedan occupation, however, both Spanish and Portuguese seamen had benefited greatly from Arab advances in the fields of geography, astronomy, and shipbuilding. In the fifteenth century, after chasing out the anti-Christian intruders from their midst, a new breed of seagoing crusaders were ready to put to use what they had learned from their enemies in the search for Christians and spices.

Seagoing Crusaders

In 1415, King John I of Portugal ordered an attack on Ceuta, a Mohammedan fortress across the Mediterranean in North Africa. A more important decision, however, was John's determination to hold the place with a Portuguese garrison and to use it for the systematic exploration and development of trade with Africa. From the very beginning, therefore, religion and commerce went together in European explorations. John put Prince Henry, his brother, in charge of these operations. Delighted with his assignment, Prince Henry promptly assembled a group of seamen, cartographers, and instrument makers to aid him in his work.

Any expansion of Christian power against Islam was considered a matter for great rejoicing, but Henry's ultimate objective soon became nothing less than the discovery of an alternative route to the Indian Ocean around the southern tip of Africa. The continuing high cost of Asian products which had passed through the hands of Arab shippers and Italian middlemen justified the search and promised its discoverers great riches and power. Added to these expected benefits was the intangible incentive shared by all great explorers: the fascination of the unknown.

Under Henry's able direction, Portuguese ships set sail southward along the coast of Africa—but it took fourteen years for his captains to round Cape Bojador, the first major landmark on the West African coastline. Not only did they encounter navigational difficulties, but the sailors held back at the least sign of trouble, afraid that what they had heard from old sailors was true: the tropical sea was boiling hot and the tropical sun would change them all into black Africans! Once around the Cape, in 1434, their fears disappeared and exploration could go on at a much faster pace.

Fears that Henry's explorations would prove unprofitable also disappeared with the rounding of Cape Bojador. In 1441 a Portuguese caravel returned from the coast south of the Cape with a small parcel of gold dust and a few African captives, the first appearance of "black gold" in the Atlantic trade. Over the next five years Portuguese ship captains brought back more than a thousand slaves, either captured or purchased from coastal chiefs. The African trade, despite early moral questionings about slaves, became so extensive that in 1448 Prince Henry ordered the construction of a fortress-warehouse on Arguim Island, located in the bay formed by the curve of Cape Blanco. This warehouse provided a model for hundreds to come over the next centuries.

Henry's business acumen was not limited to the building of ships and warehouses. He secured monopoly rights from his brother on the African coastal trade and then applied to the Pope for a similar monopoly on the work of converting inland Africans to Christianity. His foresight enabled Portugal to become the first of the great European empires. Henry died in 1460, but his imprint, the Portuguese empire in Africa, has now lasted more than 500 years. Even after World War II, when the British and French finally began liquidating their formal empires (under considerable pressure from African nationalists and world opinion), the Portuguese have managed to retain Angola and Mozambique. The first to arrive, the Portuguese seem determined to be the last to leave.

They pioneered the development of the Atlantic slave trade (the consequences of which were profound in colonial politics and are still felt today), and they practiced in Africa an informal imperialism in territories not under their actual political control. After World War II this relationship would be called neocolonialism, but the basic features had already taken shape in the early sixteenth century. In a famous document, the Regimento of 1512, the Portuguese agreed to help the King of the Congo reorganize his realm on a more efficient basis. It was agreed that the Europeans would introduce their legal system into the Congo and train the Congolese in European methods of warfare; in return, the Congolese were expected to fill Portugal's ships with valuable cargo. The King of Portugal explained in delivering the Regimento to his emissary:

This expedition has cost us much; it would be unreasonable to send it home with empty hands. Although our principal wish is to serve God and the pleasure of the King of the Congo, none the less you will make him understand, . . . what he should do to fill the ships, whether with slaves or copper or ivory.

Nearly 500 years later, pacts between advanced industrial nations and underdeveloped countries still followed the same pattern. Military security and protection are still exchanged for economic dependence. The language of military assistance agreements in the cold war, while not so crude perhaps, covers the same points. Article VII of a 1952 pact with Ecuador, for example, makes it clear that the cost of American military aid and advice was easy access to raw materials:

In conformity with the principle of mutual aid . . . the Government of Ecuador agrees to facilitate the production and transfer to the Government of the United States of America for such period of time, in such quantities and upon such terms and conditions as may be agreed upon of raw and semi-processed strategic materials required by the United States of America as a result of deficiencies or potential deficiencies in its own resources, and which may be available in Ecuador. Arrangements for such transfers shall give due regard to reasonable requirements for domestic use and commercial export of Ecuador.

Ironically, Portugal itself would become part of England's informal empire as the competition for riches and power developed in the seventeenth and eighteenth centuries, but its first great rival was Spain.

The Spanish join in the race

Once the profitability of the Portuguese venture had been established, Spain eagerly took to the sea. In 1497, Vasco da Gama, a Portuguese, set out on the voyage that would take him all the way to India, the first successful trip around Africa. Five years earlier, however, Spain had sent Christopher Columbus sailing off to the west in search of a better route across the Atlantic. Newly united under Ferdinand and Isabella, the Spanish outfitted their explorer with a small three-vessel flotilla for the voyage to the Indies and eagerly awaited his return.

Actually, Columbus had first approached Portugal with his plan back in 1484, but that country had turned him down, preferring to stick with Prince Henry's original plan. If Columbus succeeded, if there was a better route, then a century of effort (except for the

African trade itself) would have been wasted.

Columbus set sail from Spain late in the summer of 1492. It was a lucky voyage, with unusually favorable weather conditions providing a fair wind the whole way out. After thirty-three days of uneventful sailing, the three ships arrived in the outer cays of the Bahamas Islands. If these islands were, as Columbus wrongly supposed, part of the Japanese archipelago, then the next step was to find Japan. Instead, the expedition found Cuba and Hispaniola (the island shared today by Haiti and the Dominican Republic), enough gold to stimulate the interest of the Spanish crown in further voyages, and natives who seemed willing to trade on European terms. He kidnapped a few of these natives, calling them "Indians" to lend substantiation to his claim that he had indeed found an easy route to Asia, and returned to Spain. On three subsequent voyages, he explored the Venezuelan and Central American coast, still looking for a passage to India—apparently having given up on ever finding Japan. He also looked for more gold, forcing the "Indians" to pan for it in the streams of Hispaniola. His characterization of the natives as "fit to be ordered about and made to work" typifies the attitudes of those who came after to conquer not only the West Indies but Mexico and Peru as well.

Columbus's first voyage, meanwhile, had sparked a serious rivalry between Spain and Portugal, which was settled by papal intervention and the Treaty of Tordesillas in 1494. According to this pact, Portugal retained sole rights to explore the African route to Asia and to whatever conquests she made along the way, while Spain was granted the same privilege west of a demarcation line in the Atlantic Ocean. Once that was settled, the work of Christianizing the world—as well as the search for this world's material ameni-

ties—could go on without further hindrance. But Spain and Portugal were unable to establish a joint monopoly. Despite protests from the Spanish Ambassador, Henry VII of England commissioned John Cabot, in 1496, to explore the North Atlantic in the hope that the passage to India would be found there. Cabot did not find the passage, nor did he find any gold, but he did return with news of a teeming fishery which would figure greatly in British colonial policies and politics and which would become an issue in early American politics after independence.

Spain even hired Ferdinand Magellan, a Portuguese, to find the way around America (named for Amérigo Vespucci because of the popularity of his published accounts of voyages to the New World) and thus duplicate Vasco da Gama's great feat in finding the way around Africa. Magellan left Seville in September 1519 with five heavily laden caravels. He found the way around South America all right, but the passage through the straits that bear his name took thirty-eight terror-filled days. That experience was followed by an interminable crossing of the Pacific, which reduced the ships' companies to a diet of rats and leather. Then, in the Philippine Islands, Magellan and forty of his men were killed in a local war. His navigator took over and began the return trip with the remaining two vessels, stopping off long enough in the spice islands to load a precious cargo. One ship was sent back toward South America; the other set out across the Indian Ocean. The first was captured by the Portuguese; but the battered *Victoria* finally made it back to Spain. Aside from the crown's natural rejoicing that one ship, at least, had returned, there was not much for the Spanish to be happy about. The voyage had taken three years. Prospects for sending more trading caravels through the

Straits of Magellan were not highly regarded, as returns were not likely to be great enough to justify the outlay of royal funds. In sum, Magellan's achievement was of no immediate practical use to the King. The Portuguese would still control the Indian trade.

The conquest of the New World

Simultaneously with Magellan's departure from Seville in 1519, Hernándo Cortés left Cuba on a much shorter voyage to Mexico. In the years after Columbus's first trip, a considerable number of Spaniards had settled in Cuba and Hispaniola. They imported cattle, horses, and black Africans to serve as slaves to replace the dwindling native tribes, whose contacts with the white man were already leading to their destruction. These settlers were not really very settled men; soldiers of fortune, they would jump at the least rumor of gold, leaving everything behind to investigate the source of the tale, however remote. A persistent story in the Indies had the Aztecs of Mexico in possession of gold and other wealth beyond calculation. It was enough to persuade Cortés to find out for himself.

Cortés had 600 men, a few small cannons, 13 muskets, and 16 horses when he landed near what is now Vera Cruz. In Mexico the Aztecs ruled over other peoples with brutality and arrogance. Their main control mechanism was human sacrifice. Cortés took full advantage of the hatred and fear among Aztec subjects to gain their passive loyalty for his successful effort to conquer Mexico. Eight years later Francisco Pizarro, another adventurer, repeated the feat by conquering the Inca civilization in Peru. By 1550 all the chief centers of settled population in tropical America were in Spanish hands—but not those of the *conquistadores.* Useful in their moment of glory, Cortés and Pizarro (and all the rest) were shunted aside by the administrators of empire.

Magellan's brillant failure—for that was what it amounted to in practical terms for the sixteenth century—had focused attention on the New World itself. The situation had changed dramatically; henceforth the struggle for supremacy would take place *in* America (all of it), not around or through imagined sea passages to the Orient. Small quantities of gold had been found in the West Indies; rumors of the yellow metal had led Cortés and Pizarro to the continent; but the real mineral wealth of Mexico and Peru was found to be in silver. In 1545 the Spanish discovered the silver mines of Potosí. With that discovery began the exploitation of the riches of the New World and the labor of its native peoples. Between 1503 and 1660 some 16 million kilograms of silver arrived in Seville, enough to triple the existing silver resources of Europe. The Indian population of Central Mexico, which supplied the labor for the mines, declined in this same period from 25 million to 1 million.

This was no business for two-bit lances like Cortés or Pizarro. To ensure that it received the royal share of the treasure, the Spanish court excercised close control over the colonies; it could not risk everything on the organizational ability of a few adventurers whose only accomplishments lay in defeating the Indians. From this simple assumption grew a theory of empire which dominated European thinking about the New World throughout the colonial period. As the Spanish practiced it, the theory could best be described as bullionism. The full-blown theory as later developed by the Dutch, French, and English came to be known as mercantilism. One thing, or attitude, remained constant under bullionism and all later forms of mercantilist political economy: the belief that the wealth of the entire world was limited.

That belief defined the limits of imperial thought and shaped the structure not only of the Spanish silver empire but also that of the fur-trading empire founded by the French in Canada as well as that of the more complex empire the British developed along the coast of North America. International relations were, in the words of modern strategic thinking, a zero-sum game. One king's gain was another's loss. The sum of the gain and the loss always added up to zero. War and its variants—such as piracy—were, therefore, the natural order in relations among nations. When the North American colonies revolted against English rule in 1776, their leaders charged that the mother country had involved them in continuous wars with Britain's rivals. As stated, the charge was somewhat misleading since the colonists often instigated conflicts in disputes over the American hinterland, but it was an accurate description of the mercantilist world order and world view.

The British success story

Spanish bullionists treated ore as the most valuable product of the New World. The crown claimed a one-fifth share of all metal produced there; and it sought by all possible means to encourage gold and silver mining and to enforce payment of the bullion tax. Viceroys brought order to the mining areas, adjusted rival claims between local entrepreneurs, and supervised the draft of Indian labor, the *mitas*, to work the mines. The forced *mita* labor added significantly to what historians Stanley and Barbara Stein have called "one of the most disastrous demographic declines in world history." Indians were replaced where necessary and when possible by African slaves purchased from Portuguese middlemen. The Spanish were never independent of other European nations in managing their empire, but they persisted in believing that their control of bullion from the mines to Seville was the only thing that really mattered.

To protect the precious ore, the Spanish organized a convoy system across the Atlantic. Beginning in 1564, two armed fleets were dispatched from Spain each year, one to Mexico and the other to the Isthmus of Panama. They wintered in America and returned to Spain the following spring. The sailings were predictably regular, enough so that privateers could lay in wait for them along what became known as the Spanish Main. At least one or two ships were lost each year. Elizabeth I of England encouraged English privateers in this dark business and even invested royal funds in the ventures upon occasion. When the Spanish protested the activities of Francis Drake, who not only attacked Spanish ships but plundered settlements in Spanish America as well, the Queen responded by conferring knighthood upon him.

The exploits of Drake and his dashing companions have been told and retold in history books and romantic novels and most recently in Hollywood color extravaganzas of the 1940s. One can still catch sight of Errol Flynn late at night on television reruns of those great old movies. Cutlass in hand, he leaps from his ship onto the deck of a Spanish galley to confront the villainous captain. These scenes are a clue to England's success story, but not because they portray the brave deeds of Sir Francis and his goodly crew of "sea dogs." To heighten the drama and justify Drake's piracy, the Spanish captain always seems to ooze evil through his ornate costume covered with brocade and other finery. Flynn, of course, wears the simplest cloth outfit, the proper garb for any real fighting man.

Figure 1-1 Elizabeth the Queen. Her shrewd management of limited resources enabled England to survive an armada and prosper in the new world. *(Culver Pictures)*

Another clue is hidden in the riddle proposed by a Spanish writer in 1660: "The fact that there is neither money, gold nor silver in Spain, is because there *is*; and the fact that Spain is not rich, is because she *is*; making two true and contradictory statements about one subject, Spain." The answer to the riddle is this: despite British raids, the convoys served the purpose intended by the Spanish authorities and were maintained for a century and a half. The real loss of bullion came after the metal arrived in Seville, to pay for finery imported from other countries—thus the real-life situation shown symbolically in the Spanish sea captains' movie costumes.

It can be argued that the discovery of the silver riches of the New World was the worst thing that could have happened to Spain at the beginning of the modern era. The same might be said for Portugal, whose Brazilian gold flowed almost directly to England in the eighteenth century. The influx of American ore perpetuated an archaic form of monarchy in those countries more suited to the feudal era than to the needs of modern nations, inflated the Iberian price structure more rapidly than that of trading partners and rivals, and ruined the few industries which had developed by 1550 to meet the demands of the home and colonial trade.

Other nations were quick to take advantage of these conditions and attitudes to make the Iberian peninsula an economic dependency of commercially forward-looking powers. The Netherlands and England profited most. "The cloth trade is England's Indies," asserted a later writer, meaning simply that the British reaped great profits by supplying others with elementary needs and luxuries, while at the same time developing their supremacy on the seas. The British colonial empire in North America was structured (after an initial failure to find gold) to serve the needs of the cloth trade and the growing commerce occasioned by imperial expansion.

During the seventeenth century a long revolution took place in England, which ended when a mercantile elite and associated groups established their hegemony in Parliament. The process also saw the elimination of all major obstructions to the economic development of a modern capitalist society as well as the establishment of mechanisms, such as the joint stock company, necessary to the continued growth of the colonial trade. The textile trade with Spain and Portugal, much of it intended for reexport to the New World, brought England more gold and silver than Sir Francis Drake and the sea dogs ever brought back in tow from the West Indies.

These funds provided a credit base to support a great navy and merchant fleet, and a large capital reserve to subsidize joint stock companies such as the Royal East India Company and the Royal West India Company. Thus launched on an upward spiral, England grew rich and powerful.

A relative latecomer to empire, her explorers not only finished the work to be done in North America but also planted outposts in Africa and Asia. But the crucial work of economic empire was done closer to home, where in 1703, when John Methuen, the diplomat son of a rich clothier, negotiated a commercial treaty with Portugal. The treaty was the last in a series of pacts by which England entered into political alliance with Portugal and gained economic advantages for its trade in return. "Since our Treaty with Portugal," asserted *The British Merchant* in 1713, "we have exported yearly to that country prodigious quantities of our Woollen Manufactures vastly greater than we ever did before; vastly greater than we ever did to France." Payment was made in port wine— and gold. "From this time the drinking of Port was regarded as a patriotic duty by the English squire."

Methuen was well aware of the treaty's impact on Portugal:

This agreement will have this consequence in Portugal that all their own manufactures, which at this time make a vast quantity of ill cloth and dear, will be immediately laid down and totally discontinued; and the cloth or stuffs of no other nation will be able to come into competition with those of England, of which the duties payable here are likewise very advantageously settled by the Treaty of Commerce. . . .

The North American colonies were found-

ed and nurtured on a similar theory, which became known as mercantilism. Just as some Portuguese statesmen objected to the situation thus created between their country and England, so the American colonial leaders would conclude (after a time) that military protection was not worth the price of subservience. Colonial manufactures were not always prohibited—some were very definitely encouraged—but the decisions were made in London. And it was in London that the philosophers of empire developed mercantilist theory in its most complex form.

The structure of British mercantilism

The first serious English philosopher of the political economy of mercantilism was Thomas Mun, whose *England's Treasure by Forraign Trade* appeared in 1664, although much of it had been written as early as 1628. "The main thing," Mun declared, "is to possess goods; if you have them you will get money." A simple bullionist outlook would not have suited a country like England, lacking mines at home or in the colonies, but Mun's statement marked an advance in economic thinking. "The ordinary means therefore to increase our wealth and treasure is by foreign trade, wherein we must ever observe the rule to sell more to strangers yearly than we consume of their value."

With the "Restoration" of Charles II in 1660, the English monarchy was transformed into something like a modern executive department of government. The executive was charged with the enforcement of the basic mercantilist navigation acts pertaining to the colonies. These were:

The Navigation Act of 1660, which provided that goods should be imported into Great

Britain and the American colonies only on British ships (including those built in the colonies, a great boon to colonial shipbuilding) and which listed certain goods such as tobacco, sugar, and cotton that could be sent only to England or another colony.

The Staples Act of 1663, which provided that all goods intended for the colonies must be shipped from England.

The Plantations Duties Act of 1673, which provided for export duties on intercolonial trade.

The attempt to enforce these acts in the colonies was frustrating; fortunately England had a number of leaders who realized how unwise it would have been always to press for the letter of the law. At home the effect of the laws was something else. They were so important as to be called the Magna Carta of the Sea. They provided, in truth, the basis of English sea power, whether or not they were strictly enforced in the colonies.

One commentator characterized the Navigation Act of 1660 as "a true way to enlarge dominions throughout the world, the most easy for conquests, and the least costly for appropriating the property of others." As British wealth grew, sophisticated institutions took the place of gold-hoarding individuals or companies. Banks and other credit institutions were chartered by the King. Limited competition between joint stock companies was encouraged. The final modernization of the monarchy into an executive department took place in the "Glorious Revolution" of 1688, although the power shift was not complete until Queen Victoria's time. By then the monarch herself had become a symbol; real power rested in an executive, the Prime Minister and his advisers, who were fully responsible to Parliament. Between Elizabeth and Victoria, England's two greatest queens, the empire was created and the monarchy put in its place.

The real meaning of the Glorious Revolution of 1688 emerged with the creation of the Board of Trade in 1696, which henceforth managed the day-to-day affairs of the empire. Mercantilism was, however, more than navigation acts and boards of trade. It was a whole way of life. Feudal obligations had become national obligations. The responsibility for poor laws, welfare, subsistence wages, and such all fell to the state.

The problem of law and order at home and abroad became more than one of locking up wrongdoers. England's new rulers needed a justification for their revolution which would attract former enemies in the landed classes and demonstrate to all the potential of the new system. John Locke accepted the task of providing such a rationalization for Parliament's supremacy over the King. The Glorious Revolution was justified, Locke argued, because the stockholders in the enterprise—that is, all Englishmen—had found themselves being deprived of their natural God-given rights to private property by the King's actions in attempting to personalize the executive department to the detriment of the company. In making this argument, however, Locke also revealed a serious tension within mercantilist theory between the general welfare and private property. In this instance, the monarch's erratic behavior had clearly not been synonomous with the general welfare. But suppose, just suppose, that the executive developed a serious view of the general welfare and was determined to enforce his will regardless of property rights? Or suppose that, at a later date, the poor collectively asserted that their natural rights to property were being denied by either the executive or the legislative? What then?

Locke could explain this (to himself) by asserting that though Man in the abstract was rational, workingmen were somewhat less rational—and some propertyless souls actually depraved. Society was actually a pyramid, therefore, in which all did not share equally. Larger shareholders in society had special obligations and deserved special privileges. Locke's emphasis on the superiority of property rights and their close connection to rational behavior led him to the conclusion that the general duty of government was to prevent conditions from deteriorating to a point where revolution became the only way left for rational (or irrational) men. To the argument that all the property in England was taken up, leaving no way for those who lacked property to gain it except by taking it from others, Locke replied, "full as the World seems," a man may still find enough and as good land in "some in-land, vacant places of *America.*"

Less than a hundred years later Jefferson put the Lockean doctrine of natural rights into the words and spirit of the Declaration of Independence. The colonists offered their Declaration to the opinions of mankind, so certain were they that their resort to arms against an executive—George III and his ministers—who had distorted the empire for the benefit of some against the natural rights of others (themselves Englishmen) fulfilled Locke's criteria.

Here was paradox on a grand scale: to enjoy their rights as Englishmen, the colonists had to cease being Englishmen and become Americans. But it did not end there. Within the lifetime of the Founding Fathers of the new nation, its citizens discovered that their "Empire of Liberty" had not resolved the central tension in Locke's theory. Once again the central government's ability and willingness to treat all individuals and their property rights equally were in question—as was the issue of property rights itself. The slave system in the South was the most visible evidence of the tension, but it existed elsewhere as well. The result was the Civil War. A second American Revolution some called it, a new beginning.

Still the dilemma persisted. Finally it became a world dilemma. Americans had broken free from England but found themselves reliving the American Revolution in each generation without ever resolving the Lockean puzzle of unequal property rights and equal political rights in a democratic society. New frontier followed new frontier, finally into the swamps of Southeast Asia. At a time when it still seemed possible that the elusive missing piece might be found there, an American military commander in Vietnam summed up 200 years of searching this way:

I am reminded of our own Revolution. It took eight years to get through our Revolution, and then we ran into some of the toughest guerillas that we ever want to run into any place— the American Indians. We started what we call in Vietnam today an "oil spot" moving across the country. The last Indian war was 1892, over a hundred years after we started our Revolution. There is a social revolution going on now in Vietnam. They are not at the stage to say "We the people," but when they do get to that stage, then things will be fine. . . .

Frustrated explorers once regarded the North American land mass as an obstacle blocking the way to the riches of Asia. European-Americans finally got there, and found only their history.

Selected references

Special studies and general works on exploration and conquest, and on mercantilist theory and practice are almost without number. Three books of special help in preparing this chapter were J. H. Parry, *Europe and a Wider World* (1949), Sandro Sideri, *Trade and Power: Informal Colonialism in Anglo-Portuguese Relations* (1970), and Stanley and Barbara Stein, *The Colonial Heritage of Latin America* (1970). England's rise to power is the subject of Charles Wilson's excellent study of the Anglo-Dutch Wars, *Profit and Power* (1957), while Spain's decline is related by J. H. Elliott in *Imperial Spain, 1469–1716* (1964). Mercantilism has its students, most notably Eli F. Heckscher, *Mercantilism* (1962), in two volumes, and John Locke his many biographers, including M. W. Cranston, *John Locke* (1957). Locke's dilemma receives the full treatment in C. B. MacPherson, *The Political Theory of Possessive Individualism* (1962).

Readers who survive the heavy going in MacPherson will never be quite the same again, and they will find accounts of the explorations a welcome respite. The journey now begun by Samuel Eliot Morison, *The European Discovery of America: The Northern Voyages* (1971), is the best thing that can happen to a reader interested in the explorers; it will be concluded in a similar volume on the southern voyages. For the broad sweep, William H. McNeill, *The Rise of the West* (1963), supplies all the background one could want. Looking ahead, one might want to plunge into David Potter's *People of Plenty* (1954), Louis Hartz's *The Liberal Tradition* (1955), and William Appleman William's *The Contours of American History* (1961). Score one point for each book on this list; anything above three (before you graduate) is excellent.

TWO

Colonial Life

Period covered: 1609–1776

Emphases: First settlements. Political, economic, and cultural development.

Major events: Settlement of Jamestown, 1609

The Puritan Great Fleet arrives in Massachusetts Bay, 1630

The Salem witchcraft begins, 1692

The Great Awakening, 1739

The French and Indian War, 1756–1763

Virginia

The first colonies in what would become the United States of America were settled by people who ran risks and experienced hazards, both mental and physical, that are scarcely to be believed. The London Company sent 144 colonists to Virginia late in 1606. Of these, 39 died at sea before their three ships reached the coast in April. By mid-September Jamestown had been established at the cost of 46 more deaths, mostly from starvation. When the next supply from England arrived in January 1608, only 38 persons were still alive. They owed their survival to Captain John Smith, a controversial figure who was first stripped of power and then, in the fall of 1608, made president of the governing council. Smith was a hard man who got results. In the winter of 1608–1609, only 12 died, because Smith could make men work. All the same, he was replaced by a new governor in 1609 and, having been wounded, returned to England. New settlers brought the population up to about 500, but without Smith all but 60 died in the "starving time" the following winter. Thereafter, the death rate fell, yet Jamestown remained a warning that subsequent colonists ignored at their peril. Men died in Jamestown of many causes— illness, accident, the Indians—but mostly of famine. This, in turn, was not so much because food was hard to get but because lack of discipline and organization allowed men to escape gathering it. Some spent their time quarreling or searching for gold. Others died of despair. The wilderness inspired a terror that was no less deadly than the wilderness itself.

Strong motives were needed to overcome such appalling obstacles. New Englanders had a sense of mission, Virginians only the hope of gain. Jamestown's survival was evidence that the profit motive worked even where there was no profit. The London Company finally went bankrupt, though not before it tried an ingenious set of experiments. Most of these too failed, but in the process the essential conditions of Southern life were established. At first the company expected to prosper by discovering valuable minerals and trading with the Indians. These aims attracted gentlemen more than farmers and workers. Of the sixty-seven members of the first Jamestown expedition whose names we know, twenty-eight were gentlemen. The dreadful times that followed were partly a consequence of this imbalance. The gentlemen would not work and could not lead. Once this fact was grasped, the company changed its program.

Thomas Dale, governor of the colony in 1610, assigned military ranks and developed a rigid, hierarchical system of command. This worked in the sense that Jamestown stayed alive, but so disagreeably that few could be persuaded to join it. All had to attend church twice a day and live in barracks. When a group attempted to escape in 1612, Dale had them shot, hanged, and broken on the wheel according to their degree of guilt. When it became clear that such a program discouraged emigration, the system was modified and then, in 1619, revised. Under the new plan colonists got generous land grants and often married and lived in their own homes. These incentives brought 5,000 new settlers in the next six years (three-fourths of whom died), about twice as many as had come over in the previous twelve years. But while the incentive system worked, it was fatal to the company's organization. Landownership created a new status that was separate from rank in the company, though related to it at first. Social position involved wealth, while wealth was partially a function of tenure. All other things being equal, those who arrived first had the most land and the highest status, though gentlemen who came later were able to buy land too. Increasingly, rank in the company counted for less in Virginia, while landholdings and length of residence counted for more. The company's reward for its successful incentive plan was the destruction of its organization, an irony that did not so much ruin the company as compound misfortunes already underway.

The company's chief problem was that nothing it did brought in enough money to meet expenses. When gold was not found, the company tried manufacturing; but labor costs were so high in Virginia—four or five times what they were in England—that the finished products were priced out of the English market. Tobacco saved the colony though not the company. John Rolfe proved that it could be grown in 1614. Three years later, 20,000 pounds were shipped to England. By 1627 Virginia was sending half a million pounds of leaf to the mother country. This was desirable inasmuch as it saved Virginia and kept bullion within the British Empire. Previously the English had had to buy all their tobacco from Spain, a violation of the mercantile economic principles then in fashion which held that imports from outside an imperial system were bad. But the company did not want Virginia saddled with a one-crop economy, nor did the crown. Moreover, the Stuart kings thought tobacco smoking a great vice—James I wrote a famous treatise attacking the "sotweed," as it was called—and did what they could to discourage it. All the same, as there seemed no immediate alternative, tobacco became the mainstay of Virginia's economy.

When the company went bankrupt in 1623, it left behind a colony that, if not exactly flourishing, was still well launched. It had a cash crop, a hardy core of "ancient" settlers who had survived the starving times and the great Indian war of 1622, and a system of government providing for considerable local autonomy through an elected assembly. It also left an essentially two-class system in which everyone was either a planter or a laborer. This, together with the overdependence on tobacco, settled the future of Virginia—though not immediately. At first a substantial number of indentured servants (who contracted to serve an employer for six or seven years in return for passage to America) became landowners. At their peak these small yeomen with plantations of a few hundred acres constituted 90 percent of the landowning population. As early as 1632 at least six of the thirty-nine members of the House of Burgesses had been indentured servants, and this proportion continued for several decades. Perhaps 30 to 40 percent of the landowners between 1630 and 1660 had come over as indentured servants. Thus, while family counted for much in Virginia as everywhere in the seventeenth century, the system allowed for much more social and economic mobility than there was in England.

But Virginia was not destined to have a broadly based, independent yeomanry like the North. As the production of tobacco mounted, its price fell and markets outside the British Empire became crucial. After 1660, when the restored Stuart monarchy began regulating it more strictly, trade with Europe became difficult. The tobacco industry was depressed and many small planters were driven out of business. After 1682 trade revived, but the price per pound did not go up, so that small producers were not greatly benefited. The great planters met the situation by expanding their acreage and reducing production costs. This was accomplished chiefly by moving from an indentured servant to a slave labor system. In the seventeenth century, tobacco was raised mostly by the planter and his servants. But indentured servants were expensive. Their transportation to Virginia was costly, as was their maintenance. And when their contracts expired, usually after seven years, the planter had to make a new capital expenditure to replace them. The capital spent on buying a slave was not a net loss, as with indentured servants, but an investment. It was good for the slave's lifetime, recoverable by the slave's sale if necessary and multiplied when the slave reproduced. And the cost of maintaining a slave was only a quarter to half that of keeping an indentured servant, whose contract guaranteed his standard of living. So the logic of the market made itself felt. In 1670 only 5 percent of the people in Virginia were black. In 1730 slaves made up 26 percent of the population. In this casual manner was the stage set for the most tragic and momentous drama in American history.

This shift in labor policies created a planter aristocracy which dominated the tidewater in the eighteenth century and captured the imagination of white Southerners for generations thereafter. The great planter had a dual character. On the one hand he managed a large enterprise; on the other he was an aristocrat. As a manager the planter was responsible for what was in effect an agricultural factory with a large work force, extensive acreage, and transatlantic commercial relationships. Few planters could afford to neglect their interests for, given the social primacy of landholders, men of ability usually secured land of their own or emigrated. There was no managerial class for the planter to employ. Since they had to do so much of their own work, planters did not enjoy in practice all the leisure convention dictated, nor— given their involvement in large international trade combinations—was the distinction be-

tween planter and merchant so clear in fact as it was in principle. The successful planter was a businessman despite himself.

But the planter's role as aristocrat was not mere pretense. Though inhabiting a very different economic world than the English country gentry, Virginia planters copied them all the same. This created its own reality, as imitation always does. And the aristocratic image was further reinforced when some English gentlemen came to Virginia in the late seventeenth century. Certain planter families could honestly claim cavalier forebears, though perhaps only a minority of those who made the boast. Intermarriage reinforced the ties among great planters and helped make them something of a caste as well as a class. And their political and religious institutions further cemented them together. The House of Burgesses was planter-controlled; so was the parish, a unit of the Church of England which was frequently the same size as the county and which had both civil and religious functions. The vestry of each parish (board of directors) selected its own minister, who could be fired at will as there was no higher ecclesiastical authority in Virginia. The vestry also had police powers and the authority to tax, among other responsibilities. It was the principal social welfare agency for the common people. The rich had their own welfare office—the House of Burgesses. When John Robinson, Speaker of the House, died in 1766, it was found that he had distributed £100,000 (in today's money perhaps $2,500,-000) of public money to distressed friends. The sums ranged from £15,000 (William Byrd, III) to £11 (Patrick Henry, not an aristocrat but a comer). Few were surprised or upset by this revelation.

Given the harmony between their social, economic, religious, and political institutions, it was hardly remarkable that the planter class had such confidence in representative government and the church. The church was ideologically undemanding, a broad umbrella under which most men of good will could find shelter. The parish was an administrative and political convenience as well, and a training ground which prepared young members of the aristocracy for larger public services. The political structure, though genuinely representative, was controlled by the planter class and would no doubt have been run by them even if the suffrage had not been restricted when the old yeomanry declined. As the planters dominated every area of Virginia life, they had little to fear from elections in which votes were cast publicly.

The surprising thing about this tightly knit patriarchy was that it produced such brilliant leaders. A society where many were poor and few rich, with no towns to speak of, no real educational system below the college level, no printing presses or book shops, striving to emulate the English gentry, based on human slavery and riddled with guilt because of it, yet managed to produce not only a Jefferson, which would have been enough, but a Washington, a Madison, and a Monroe—to name only the most famous members of an oligarchy fabulously rich in talent. One can hardly think of another ruling class so narrowly based (perhaps only a few hundred families strong) that had so many men of high ability. This paradox is not easily resolved, though Virginia was hardly the first social dung heap to raise brilliant flowers. Ancient Athens was based on human slavery too. Imperial England rested on sweated labor in mine, mill, and warship. There seem to be no fixed rules that govern the creation of notable elites, only times when certain elements fall into favorable alignment. Virginia in the eighteenth century was peaceful. The ruling class had some leisure and a degree of cultivation,

often improved by trips to England. Good connections alone did not ensure advancement. These facts do not explain much. The origins of Virginia's brilliant ruling class remain obscure.

The causes of its fall are easier to name. An economy based on a single crop is always vulnerable. After the Puritan revolution the tobacco market declined, ruining the Virginia economy and destroying much of the wealth on which the planter aristocracy depended. Diversification later revived Virginia's economy, but not before the old planter class was irreparably damaged. What tobacco began, slavery completed. As slavery came under heavier attack, everything was sacrificed to its defense, including the expansive open-mindedness and liberality that characterized the old aristocracy at its best. Consequently, Jefferson and Madison left no heirs. Theirs was the last great generation that Virginia would produce.

Maryland

All the Southern colonies except Virginia were proprietorial for two reasons. First, merchants declined to subsidize more colonies after the London Company failed. Second, Stuart kings hoped to strengthen the royal party by making land grants to deserving noblemen. George Calvert, who became Lord Baltimore, was the first Southern proprietor. Calvert was the only Catholic proprietor and the only one whose family profited enormously from colonization, thus proving it was possible to get rich even without the Protestant ethic. The royal charter of 1632 gave Baltimore more power in "Mary Land" than the king enjoyed in England. But in practice the second Lord Baltimore, who planted the first colony in 1634, discovered that free Englishmen would not give up their rights what-ever the charter said. Colonists early de-manded and got an assembly with some legislative powers, and they made life dif-ficult for the Calverts ever after. This was partly because colonists always quarreled with their governors and partly because Prot-estants as well as Catholics came to Mary-land, which enjoyed religious freedom out of necessity more than conviction. Protestant England would not tolerate a purely Catholic province. If Catholics were to worship freely, Protestants had to be free also. This arrange-ment did not satisfy the Puritan colonists who fretted under Catholic rule. They seized power briefly in the 1650s after Charles I was beheaded and the Commonwealth estab-lished in England. Baltimore, who had im-portant Puritan friends, retrieved the province in 1658, and the family kept it until the Glori-ous Revolution of 1688, which made the mon-archy Protestant for all time. A royal governor was sent to Maryland, though the Calverts kept their revenues and land titles. All else having failed, the fourth Lord Baltimore turned Protestant and regained control of Maryland, which stayed in the family until 1776.

Though a great burden, Maryland was worth the trouble. It brought the tenacious Calvert family an income comparable, in modern money, to $350,000 a year. This was because Maryland had much the same cli-mate and resources as Virginia, and since it was established later, profited from Virginia's mistakes. There was no starving time. Careful planning enabled colonists to begin growing crops soon after settling in. Maryland devel-oped political institutions similar to Virginia's and an even more homogenous ruling class. Though dictatorial when allowed to be, the Calverts were shrewd. Most of the important

families in Maryland were allied with them through blood or marriage. Thus, despite insurrections and Protestant discontent, Maryland flourished and the Calverts did too.

North and South Carolina

Carolina was founded by eight noble adven-turers who secured a generous charter from Charles II in 1663. They thought to make money on the cheap by luring settlers already in the New World to Carolina. The proprietors supposed that religious toleration, free land, a popular assembly with legislative powers, and other fringe benefits would do the job. Where they erred was in not realizing that Virginia offered many of the same advantages plus established institutions, lines of com-merce, and lower landrents. Few settlers came to Carolina, and those who did settled on small farms in the North. There they traded through Virginia, which had the nearest har-bor.

In 1669 the proprietors reluctantly financed an expedition from England and began sub-sidizing agriculture in Carolina on the theory that if trade improved, more land would be settled, bringing in more rents. The Earl of Shaftesbury and his friend, physician, and secretary John Locke, the great philosopher, drew up an elaborate constitution and plan of settlement for what became South Carolina. It was widely disregarded. Instead of settling in orderly patterns as they were supposed to, people moved along the waterways. Southern Carolina prospered accordingly. Its pork, lumber, cattle, corn, and later rice were ship-ped from Charlestown to Barbados, and the profits were used to buy manufactured goods in England that were then resold in Carolina. This triangular trade meant that South Carolina had few contacts with other American colonies. Unlike Virginia, Carolina had easy access to its back country, and the west provided Charleston with furs and Indian slaves. Carolina never developed local government like the Chesapeake Bay colonies, with their vestries, sheriffs, and justices. The back country was ruled from Charleston, which neglected it.

North Carolina remained oriented toward Virginia. It had its own governor and assembly. North Carolina was settled mainly by farmers, though it was also the largest colonial exporter of naval stores—tar, pitch, and turpentine—in the eighteenth century. There were very few slaves. North Carolina lacked anything resembling a distinct culture and was looked down on by Virginians. William Byrd called it "lubberland." All the same, North Carolinians were politically active and the proprietors, despairing equally of peace and profits, sold out to the crown in 1729. It awarded more large land grants, and the struggle between large and small holders and between inland and coastal counties got worse. The back country felt victimized by corrupt officials, high court costs, high rents, tithes to the established Anglican Church, a lack of roads and bridges, and underrespresentation in the assembly. In 1771 it revolted, but the "Regulators," as the insurgents were called, were put down at the battle of Alamance. This was a brief, nearly bloodless (9 men were killed on each side out of some 2,000 combatants), and decisive engagement.

South Carolina was dominated in the eighteenth century by a handful of planters whose enormous wealth came from rice and indigo, the source of a popular blue dye. That it could be grown in America was discovered by Eliza Lucas Pinckney (1773–1793). She contributed more to South Carolina's prosperity than any man or group of men. These planters were the largest, richest, most dissipated group in colonial America, which was not quite what Shaftesbury and Locke had in mind. But they did want an aristocratic society and, in American terms, that is what they got. The great planters spent winters on their inland estates and summers in the cooler climate of Charleston, an agreeable pattern flawed only by malaria, which was universal, and the fear of slave uprisings. Slaves outnumbered whites by three to one in the colony as a whole and by fifty to one in some areas. They did rise up in 1739 and, though crushed, gave whites nightmares ever after. The tidewater elite dominated government as well as business, and though the assembly secured the right to appoint the governor in 1719, political rights did not extend to the back country. As the back country had no voice and the elite was agreed on all essential matters, South Carolina gave the appearance of perfect unity.

This was misleading. Back-country men had no courts and few roads or schools, yet they paid the same tax per acre as the tidewater planters did on their more valuable lands and were underrepresented in the assembly. Worst of all, they got little protection from the government against roving bands of outlaws. In 1767 an "association" was created for "regulating" back-country affairs. Charleston, aware of its shortcomings and unable to remedy them—partly because of standing royal instructions that, for example, forbade enlarging the assembly—looked the other way. In two years the Regulators cleaned up their territory and then, when individuals began to abuse their power, disbanded. The Regulators' South Carolina uprising was a conservative movement, designed as much to secure government as to correct abuses. It changed the balance of power in South Carolina hardly at all.

Georgia

Georgia demonstrated that given adequate funds, good organization, and careful planning, it was still easy to fail. Though a proprietorial colony, Georgia was more the work of the English people than any colony since Virginia. It was conceived by General James Edward Oglethorpe, M.P., both as a refuge for imprisoned debtors and a barrier against Spanish incursions from Florida. Subscriptions were raised in churches from people inspired by the plan's humanitarian aspect. Parliament, grasping its defensive value, appropriated the enormous sum of £136,608 (approximately $3,400,000 in modern money) to get Georgia started. The charter of 1732 was granted to twenty-one "trustees" who were to hold the land for twenty-one years, after which it would become crown property. Oglethorpe himself led the first settlers to Georgia in 1732. They worked communally at first, under military discipline. At the end of a year male settlers received land, livestock, and equipment. A limit of 500 acres was placed on all grants to prevent large plantations from arising. Land was not held outright but subject to conditions imposed by the trustees. Trade was closely regulated and strong spirits prohibited throughout the colony.

These sensible rules discouraged settlement. South Carolina flourished because plans were ignored; Georgia failed because they were not. The whole point of taking chances in a new colony was to become rich or free or both, neither of which was easy or even possible in Georgia. In 1738 restrictions on land holdings were eased and landrents reduced. A ban on black slavery was lifted in 1750, settlers were allowed to buy and sell land freely, and alcohol was legalized. These concessions came too late, and in 1751 the trustees confessed failure and returned Georgia to the crown two years ahead of schedule. Georgia remained thinly populated for years afterward, proof once again that if the hope of gain rather than the fear of God led people to colonize, there should not be too many restrictions on enterprise. After William Penn, Oglethorpe was the most high-minded proprietor, the most disinterested, and perhaps the least successful. Georgia survived his good intentions anyway and in the nineteenth century finally became a typical Southern state.

Puritanism and the New England colonies

Except for slavery and the plantation system, Puritanism was the most important feature of colonial life in the seventeenth century. Though as a system of beliefs it perished in the eighteenth century, it left a residue of convictions that lives still. This gives us a dim sense of the force generated by Puritanism in its own time. It began as an expression of the Calvinist impulse. Sixteenth-century English Puritans believed in predestination, salvation by God's grace alone, and the equality of all men in their fallen state. They denied the value of doing works except as a sign of virtue. The most controversial aspect of Puritanism was its opposition to the Church of England's structure. Puritans thought that the church was supposed to be the city of God, the kingdom of Christ on earth. The Church of England, however, was in effect an arm of the state. Its bishops were appointed by the secular power. Its supreme authority was the crown. Puritans believed that the church was coequal with the state and that the church ought to be led by an assembly of elected representatives. If enacted, this would have destroyed the constitution of England. Accordingly, Puritans were treated as subversives—which indeed they were—by Queen Elizabeth.

But while denied many public rights, Puritans remained free to discuss these issues with one another. As with all radical movements which must substitute speech for action, the word became paramount. Puritans were intensely ideological and, inevitably, sectarian. These sects encouraged fissioning, as did the Puritan theology. Each man's views were presumably as good as any other's, since all had the same access to revealed truth. Every man was potentially his own sect. This made for enormous tension. To remain a coherent force, Puritans could not tolerate separation, that is, the formation of independent churches. Yet to remain theologically pure while they were in the minority, they had to separate. There was no way of reconciling these convictions, which in the seventeenth century led repeatedly to separations and to fights against them.

By the seventeenth century Puritans had roughly divided into three groups. On the right were Presbyterians who wanted to organize the church by synods, regional organizations with authority over congregations. In the center were Independents who favored stricter requirements for church membership and more autonomy for preachers and congregations. These later became known as Congregationalists and were chiefly responsible for the settlement of New England. On the left were groups like the Diggers and Levellers who professed radical, often egalitarian doctrines abhorrent to the great majority of Englishmen, whether Puritan or not. Later generations have sometimes admired these utopians, but in their own time

they were seen mainly as horrible examples of what dissent led to.

Predestination might possibly have inspired people to rest on their moral oars. If God had already decided whom to save and whom to damn, what reason was there to pursue virtue? Puritans avoided this pitfall by believing that the mark of salvation was evident. It consisted of an unrelenting war against sin. Those who were to be saved, the elect, were not free of weakness but struggled constantly against it. Who fought sin to the end was assured of salvation; who faltered was not. This was a mighty psychological engine which drove the Puritan to labor heroically for truth and virtue as he saw it. Added to it was another principle that made Puritanism a vital force in economic affairs. Traditional Christianity taught that some activities were more blessed than others. Puritans believed that God called all men to fruitful labor. Virtue consisted not in seeking out professions endowed with special grace, as Catholics did, but in prospering at the occupation God called you to. All callings were morally equal. The trick was to succeed at what one did. Wealth was not to be esteemed for its own sake; quite the contrary. Pomp and display were evidence of damnation. But wealth together with frugality, industry, and like attributes was proof of election. This doctrine, which we call "the Protestant ethic," sanctified the profit motive and released energies that had much to do with the development of modern capitalism. In a debased form it survives today in the equation of wealth with virtue and poverty with vice. No other aspect of Puritanism proved so durable.

The Pilgrims

Most English Puritans remained at home, but a venturesome minority did not. The first of these are now called Pilgrims. They were Congregationalists who had separated. Believing that they could not secure the moral health of themselves and their children in England, they moved first to tolerant Holland and then, when it seemed that their descendants might become Dutch, to New England. This was partly by accident, as they had apparently meant to settle on the Hudson River. But having reached Cape Cod after a difficult voyage, they remained, undergoing the usual privations. Half of them died during the winter of 1620–1621. The Pilgrims were later much admired for being less aggressive than their fellows in Massachusetts Bay and for having invented Thanksgiving. But their colony, while interesting to historians, was unimportant. Though well led, they suffered from a crushing debt that took seventeen years to repay, since the interest amounted to as much as 45 percent a year. Their unscrupulous backers—led by Thomas Weston, a shady hardware dealer—were among the few investors to profit directly from the early settlements. Their obscurity did not trouble the Pilgrims. They had no great sense of mission and came to New England only to practice their religion in peace, which they did.

Massachusetts

The early history of New England is, therefore, mostly the history of Massachusetts. The Bay Colony was sponsored, like Virginia, by a stock company that aimed to make money. The difference was that the stockholders were Puritans who meant also to create a place where true religion could flourish. They were determined to build the holy commonwealth that England denied. "We shall be as a city upon a hill," said John Winthrop once the great fleet was at sea, and "the eyes of all people are upon us . . . ," a sentiment which has moved Americans ever since. Massachusetts was founded by people borne up by a vision of the "wilderness Zion" they would construct according to God's plan. As the political situation in England deteriorated, the Massachusetts Bay Company wisely removed its charter and leadership to Boston, so that the company and the colony were united. Between 1630 and 1640 some 20,000 Englishmen came to Massachusetts to serve God and escape Charles I and Archbishop Laud, who were trying to reform the Church of England by purging it of Puritans.

The gifted men who led the Bay Colony devised very successful institutions. The basic unit of society was the covenanted church, so called because the members and the minister made a contract with each other and with God to establish a congregation. The unit of government was the town, a civil institution designed to secure the aims of the church. The town was an agricultural community governed by a meeting, which elected selectmen and other officers. It raised taxes, enforced the laws, supported the school if there was one, paid the minister's salary, and provided most public services. The General Court of the Massachusetts Bay Company, originally the body of stockholders, evolved into a representative legislative assembly over time. In the seventeenth century it probably had more authority over the towns than after 1691, when the colony's charter was revoked. The towns then became largely autonomous on a day-to-day basis, and the life of most colonists was little affected by the General Court or by the governor and his council.

The town

In theory the town and the congregation were identical, both being composed of saints. Citizens were expected to live within walking distance of the meeting house, as the church was called. This enhanced community solidarity and made it easy for the authorities to monitor individual conduct. The town provided physical and psychological security, promoted uniformity, ensured the common good, and harmonized the interests of God and man. Most saints were farmers of approximately equal substance. Land was apportioned according to need and social rank. The Puritans were not levellers. They maintained the distinction between gentlemen and commoners as in England. But while differences in rank were clearly defined, they were not marked by great disparities in wealth. Provincial government was dominated by gentlemen, local offices by the more prosperous and educated. Massachusetts had an equitable rather than an egalitarian social and political system. It aimed to promote fairness, not equality. Nonetheless, it has been rightly admired by posterity for being perhaps the most broadly based system of ordering human affairs in the seventeenth century.

Though the town was a brilliant solution to Puritan problems, it could not of itself meet every need. The town, like the Bay Colony, was inflexible. Both worked well as long as uniformity of behavior and belief obtained. Profound disagreement, not to mention dissent, was unthinkable because insoluble. When it arose, Puritans commonly responded in physical ways. If a town could not reach agreement on a fundamental matter, the minority seceded and founded another town. Troublesome individuals were exiled.

Roger Williams

Roger Williams was the most famous of these. He came to Massachusetts in 1630 and was soon esteemed as minister and man. All the same, he was banished in 1635 for, in effect, heresy and subversion. He did not believe that God meant Israel to be a model for later states, though Massachusetts supposedly re-created this holiest of all governments. Worse still, he believed in the separation of church and state—not, as liberals would later argue, because the church corrupted the state but rather the opposite. This was a direct challenge to the Puritan constitution and reason enough for exile. But Williams's infamies did not end there. He opposed compulsory worship and favored religious freedom. While he despised Quakers and other deviants as much as any Puritan, he insisted that it was no business of the state to define truth. God alone knew who was right and who wrong. Men were free to entertain views, but it was God's right alone to sanction them. Even the Bay Colony saints were sometimes in error, though believing themselves infallible. The saints had no choice but to remove him, for to tolerate such notions was to jeopardize their holy experiment. Today, Williams is honored for his libertarian positions, though his reasons for taking them were different from our own, being based on obscure and sometimes eccentric religious principles. But the conclusions he reached were the only ones possible for the heterogeneous civilization then beginning in America.

The "hivings out," as they were called, did not end when Williams began his own settlement in Rhode Island. What became Exeter, New Hampshire, was founded when Anne Hutchinson's followers were expelled from Massachusetts for doctrinal reasons. The col-

Figure 2-1 Matthew Hopkins, English witch finder, with two witches and their familiar spirits. *(The Granger Collection)*

ony of New Haven was established by Puritans who found Massachusetts too lax and secular for their taste. Others, like Connecticut, were as much products of ambition as of theological discontent. Massachusetts did not relish the competition, yet these new colonies were not only inevitable but essential. Rigid societies require safety valves. Massachusetts needed Rhode Island more than she knew.

All the Bay Colony's problems could not be hived out, unfortunately. Religious passion is more often an acquired than an inherited trait, and it tends to fade with time. The Puritans could not raise their children to feel as deeply about religion as they did themselves. The

ebbing of belief made it harder to determine who the elect were and reduced church membership. Their city on a hill required that all citizens be saints. As the number of unchurched increased, the number who were unfranchised did also. This made for discontent and weakened the civil order on which congregationalism rested. The clergy thought to remedy this in 1662 by means of the Half-Way Covenant. This opened church membership to people who were not clearly saints but who led upright lives. Though meant to revive the church, this agreement weakened it further. The children of the elect became church members, and the church itself became less important. Membership no longer symbolized election but only rectitude. Many new farms were located too far from the meeting house for it to control them. The Protestant ethic worked too well for its own good. As Massachusetts became, by contemporary standards, an affluent society, corruptions resulted. The merchant class flourished and secularism gained at the expense of piety. The worldly habits of Restoration England spread. The optimism that was characteristic of Puritanism deteriorated into smugness. The saint's unflagging intensity of purpose gave way to thoughtless habit. In this way what were Puritanism's chief virtues became the petty vices of later generations.

The Salem witch hunt

The old order gave way slowly. What was left of it suffered a mortal blow in 1691, when the charter was revoked and the source of government returned to England. Yet even afterward the Puritan impulse still found expression. The Salem witch hunt was one such outburst of defensive piety and the Great Awakening another. There have been many explanations offered for the Salem madness, including one argument that the accused in fact practiced witchcraft. But whether guilty or no, it seems clear that the magnitude and intensity of the phenomenon was a function of clerical desperation. It began in 1692, a year after the charter was lost, at a time when the holy experiment was obviously finished and Massachusetts sinking, as it appeared to the clergy, into secularism and vice. Preachers had warned that God would punish the colony for its sinful ways. Now that day had come, bringing with it a rebirth of faith and restoration of clerical authority. The rationalist tide would at last be turned back and a new respect for the supernatural would be inspired. These feelings must have been largely unconscious, for though the saints could be cruel, they were not unscrupulous. Most clergymen close to the scene had mixed feelings about the witch hunt. They hoped it would be good for religion, but they feared it was unwarranted and would do the church harm. Hope prevailed for some time after two children of the Reverend Samuel Parris accused his West Indian slaves of bewitching them. The contagion spread quickly throughout the Bay Colony. At first the possessed were chiefly hysterical adolescent girls, but in time some forty people claimed to have been bewitched. The first executions took place in June 1692. By the end of September, 20 witches were dead (14 women and 6 men), and 150 more were in prison awaiting trial.

At this point doubts became widespread. The possessed were now accusing eminent people, including the Governor's own wife, Lady Phipps. The General Court called an assembly of ministers to rule on the admissibility of "spectral" evidence. This was information obtained by the witnesses from voices and apparitions. Without it, no witches would have been convicted. The ministers declared that spectral evidence was too uncertain a basis for conviction. Even Increase Mather, the great divine whose writings on witchcraft and other supernatural manifestations had done much to create a psychological climate favorable to witch hunting, and who still believed in spectral evidence, agreed. Governor Phipps secured the release of many accused witches, a few of them only children. All the same, trials and accusations dragged on through the winter. In May 1693, the Governor ordered all who were still in jail released. Some, however, were unable to pay their costs, for all prisoners, whether innocent or not, were charged room and board for their time in jail and could not go free until they paid. One old woman died in prison. Others escaped only when farms were mortgaged to pay costs that sometimes had been accumulating for over a year. The toll of ruined fortunes and wrecked lives was incalculable.

This laid a terrible weight upon the colony's conscience, which was made all the heavier when witnesses began to confess they had lied. January 15, 1697, was set aside by the colony as a day of fast and repentance for wrongs done during the witchcraft, as these events were called. One judge confessed his error on that day, as did many jurors. In 1711 Massachusetts paid damages to the victims and their survivors. About $15,000 in our money was disbursed, more as an admission of responsibility than an effort at redress. Full compensation would have cost many times that amount. All the same, it was remarkable to see such efforts made. American history is full of incidents like the Salem witch trials, but only rarely have confession and restitution followed. In 1741 New York was gripped by fears of a great slave conspiracy. When it was over, four whites had been hanged and eighteen blacks. Thirteen blacks were burned to death and seventy shipped out of the colony. There is no evidence that New Yorkers later thought this response hasty or ill conceived.

But repentance, though notable and impressive, was not enough to save Puritanism from the consequences of Salem. The clergy's prestige was irreparably damaged; the rise of secularism and rationalism was ensured. The supernatural lost something of its hold on the minds of men. In the seventeenth century the invisible world seemed as real as the visible. Educated, even scientific men had as much confidence in the one as the other. An intimate relation with the supernatural was one of the keystones of Puritan intensity. Science and rationalism gradually eroded it. Salem gave it another blow. Thereafter belief in the invisible world tended to degenerate into superstition among the unlettered. Religious faith among the educated became more formalistic.

The Great Awakening

There would be only one more attempt to save the Puritan impulse. The Great Awakening began in 1739 when George Whitefield, greatest of the eighteenth-century preachers, began what was to be an unprecedentedly successful tour of the colonies. His way had been paved by a series of revivals which since 1720 had helped people reject the formalism of established churches, especially Presbyterian and Congregational ones. In most colonies only a minority were church members. Even in New England perhaps 75 percent of the people were outside the fold. Church membership no longer signified election but only a kind of probity. People went to church mainly to be lectured by an increasingly mediocre clergy. In 1699, when the

Brattle Street Church was established, it did away with the testimony of individual religious experiences—not to save new members from embarrassment but because members had little experience to relate. Revivals attempted to broaden church membership through emotional appeals to the unlettered. Puritans had come to think that religion was a matter of the mind as well as the heart, hence the need for an educated ministry, a class of experts who could interpret and explain the complex word of God. Revivalists, though often educated themselves, believed that religion was a matter of direct contact between God and man. They were contemptuous of doctrine and of distinctions between sects. They gave what were intoxicatingly emotional sermons by our standards though staid enough when measured against nineteenth-century revivals. They tended toward salvation through faith. Thus their message was simple, direct, and confident. By 1740 the revival was an established form and the need for it was clearly demonstrated.

The tinder was ready: it only remained for Whitefield to strike the spark. His great tour of 1739–1740 converted thousands and began a series of revivals under other preachers that affected all the colonies. The Awakening burned out in 1743, but by then the essential character of the Protestant experience was changed. At first the revival produced schisms and discord everywhere. The clergy resented Whitefield for his doctrine—or lack of it—and for his scathing attacks on them. They mistrusted the fainting, weeping, and other excesses that revivalists inspired. Puritans mistrusted "enthusiasm"—excessive zeal—as much as they hated godlessness. Whitefield explained his success in New England by saying that congregations had been dead before because "dead men preach to them." In time evangelical religion came to dominate American Protestantism. During the Enlightenment this meant the creation of new colleges—Brown, Dartmouth, Princeton, and the University of Pennsylvania—and the separation of church and state. The efforts of one faction or another to engage government in its quarrels compelled ministers to begin accepting Roger William's view of the secular power. The Awakening helped make possible the American Revolution, which was based in part on propositions congenial to evangelicals. It destroyed what was left of Puritanism and made Calvinism, once dominant in the colonies, a minority influence. Of the denominations that emerged from the post-Awakening ferment, Baptists and Methodists gained the most. In time the anti-intellectualism natural to teachings that glorified impulse at the expense of academic training became uppermost. The Enlightenment, that great age of reason, restrained this development for a while. But in the nineteenth century, aided by the frontier spirit of later revivals, it became irresistible.

Pennsylvania

As the Enlightenment flowered, Philadelphia replaced Boston as the colonies' intellectual capital. There was some irony in this development, for William Penn had built his city with quite a different goal in mind. Pennsylvania, like Massachusetts earlier, was to be a model society where true religion might flourish. Quakers found the practice of their religion to be exceptionally difficult both in England and the colonies. Though part of the Puritan movement, their teachings were far too radical for most Puritans. They did not take oaths, defer to authority, or recognize

distinctions among men. They practiced a degree of egalitarianism in an age when rank and station were still carefully defined. They carried the idea of a direct relationship between God and man to the point of dispensing with ministers altogether. In the Quaker meeting, one spoke only when moved by the holy spirit. They were harassed everywhere save Rhode Island, but especially in Massachusetts, where they were branded, whipped, and hung. At least one woman, Mary Dyer, was nearly hung twice. On her first visit to Massachusetts she was sentenced to death and the rope placed around her neck. She was then let go and warned never to return again. She did come back and was duly executed. Their enthusiasm was one of the reasons why Quakers were hated so.

William Penn, whose father had been an admiral in the British Navy, decided to found a colony where Quakers might live in peace. He secured a great land grant in lieu of debts owed his father by the crown. In 1682 he arrived in Philadelphia, which had already been laid out. Pennsylvania was truly a model colony. It prospered from the start, thanks to a superb location and generous management. Served by the Schuykill and Delaware Rivers and surrounded by fertile lands, Philadelphia had every physical advantage and soon was a major port. The Delaware Valley became the agricultural and manufacturing capital of North America. Its natural advantages were enhanced by a policy of religious toleration and liberal legislation that attracted German as well as English, Welsh, and Scotch-Irish immigrants. Land was widely owned. Ambitious Quakers, being limited to a thousand acres each, went in for trade. They too viewed work as a calling, and their honesty was proverbial. Because of these many advantages, Pennsylvania prospered more than

Massachusetts. There was no Indian problem at first, for the local Delawares were eager to be protected against the dominating Iroquois. Penn further ensured the colony's future by dealing honestly with them.

Yet the Quaker experiment failed all the same, for several reasons: The increase in wealth was not distributed equally, and there were further differences between Quakers and the other groups which, thanks to Quaker tolerance, multiplied. Then too, the popular assembly fought the proprietors, as all colonial assemblies did. The Quakers held power by gerrymandering and other devices long after they were a minority of the population. And, less successfully, they used this power to safeguard their principles. In time their laws came more to resemble those of other colonies. They owned slaves like other colonists, and they were forced to abandon pacifism, though slowly. Usually, they conceded in practice what they denied in principle. Thus, in the 1690s they voted money for "the relief of the distressed Indians of the Six Nations," knowing that it was in fact a war levy. These expedients began collapsing in 1756, when the French and Indian War put great pressure on the Assembly. Indians raided the aggressive Scotch-Irish settlers on the frontier, but even sober, peaceable Germans in the interior demanded protection. The bodies of slaughtered families were brought to Philadelphia and publicly exhibited. Finally, the Assembly voted a large sum for defense, after agonized debate and the resignation of nine Quaker assemblymen. Many other Quakers abandoned politics. This weakened the Quaker party, though skillful maneuvering by Benjamin Franklin kept it in power until 1763, when the Pontiac War completed its ruin. Chief Pontiac had rallied the tribes to prevent England from occupying Canada, which France had just ceded. Colonists demanded a stronger defense against the Indians than the Quaker party was thought ready to make, and so it lost control of the assembly at the next election. This ended the great attempt to keep the colony at peace in a warring world, though some Quakers remained politically active until the American Revolution.

Though, like all such experiments, the Quaker effort ultimately failed, it was notable anyway. It proved that treating the Indians fairly paid off. Had it not been for the combination of imperial politics and Scotch-Irish maltreatment of Indians, Pennsylvania might have stayed at peace. The Quaker program of tolerance and prosperity made Pennsylvania the best colony for the average man to live in and produced in Philadelphia an outstanding cultural life. And the Quakers offered a great example when, faced with a choice between abandoning their beliefs or losing power, they stood on principle. Even failure had some useful consequences. Freed of the awful strain that defense measures put on their consciences, Quakers were able to improve their spiritual life and make their meetings a force for peace and brotherhood that persists even today. Power had had the usual corrupting effect on Quakers. The hypocrisy of spending money for war in the name of peace bothered them more than it does politicians today. The maneuvers necessary to keep them in office when they were such a small minority (only one-ninth of the whole population) were debilitating also. They had restricted the suffrage to substantial property holders in the east while limiting representation from the new western districts. The rotten boroughs of Pennsylvania were nearly as bad as those of England. Their fall did them good. What they lost in influence they gained in grace. Hence, they survived as a notably virtuous and productive segment of the population and left Pennsylvania a splendid legacy that would take generations to run through.

New York and New Jersey

Both these colonies were notably discordant, though for different reasons. In New Jersey the struggle mostly concerned land titles. Jersey was originally part of New Netherlands but was given to Lord John Berkeley and Sir George Carteret after being taken from the Dutch. Berkeley sold out to Quakers, who thus acquired West Jersey. They later bought East Jersey at auction after Carteret's death. When Pennsylvania was founded, Quakers lost interest in Jersey and it had various owners thereafter. In the eighteenth century Scotch-Irish squatters occupied much land and politics became chiefly concerned with disputes over land ownership. Jersey had no port and little identity—East Jersey was oriented toward New York, West Jersey toward Philadelphia—but it was a fortunate colony all the same. Its farmers prospered. Because it had no towns, there was no conflict between town and country, as elsewhere. There were no provincial taxes either, as the government paid its own way through interest charges on the bills of credit it issued. These blessings were offset by endless battles over land ownership, which paralyzed government and reduced Jersey at times to a state of near anarchy except when hatred of the governor brought assemblymen briefly together. Jersey politics were a disgrace, and they still are. Today it maintains the colonial tradition and is both prosperous and poorly governed. The state of New Jersey, like the colony, never escaped the pressure exerted by New York and Philadelphia and remains, as Benjamin Franklin said, a keg tapped at both ends.

The first Dutch settlement in New York was at Albany in 1624. Two years later Peter Minuit, director-general of the colony, bought Manhattan Island, then called New Amsterdam, for $24 worth of trinkets, a good deal for the Manhate Indians who were selling land they had no claim to. New Netherlands never amounted to much because the Dutch West India Company, which owned it, was more interested in the lucrative Indies. The company awarded large grants of land to individual "patroons," who had feudal powers and were supposed to bring over emigrants and spend whatever was necessary to make the economy prosper. Most of the patroonships failed and New Netherlands had only about 8,000 inhabitants, many from New England, when it was captured during the second Anglo-Dutch War in 1664. It was then renamed New York, after James, Duke of York, its new proprietor. The Dutch left New York their alliance with the Iroquois, the patroon system, parochial schools, and a tradition of animosity between ethnic and religious groups that would last and last. Puritans resented the elite Dutch families who dominated the colony even after it became English. Puritans and Anglicans were at odds as usual. Most people, again as usual, resented the proprietor who ran the province without an assembly for twenty years.

When James became King, he united New England, New York, and New Jersey into the Dominion of New England, which perished when he was overthrown by the Glorious Revolution. An interregnum followed during which control of New York was seized by Jacob Leisler, a wealthy immigrant who had the support of most small farmers and craftsmen and even of some great families. When the royal governor arrived, Leisler handed over his power too slowly, giving his enemies time to discredit him. Leisler and his son were convicted of treason and butchered, as was the gruesome custom. Later Parliament reversed their conviction. This did the Leislers no good and failed to bind up any wounds. For years afterward pro- and anti-Leisler sentiments disrupted New York politics.

New York was further divided by a weird mixture of economic rivalries, ethnic-religious hostilities, family feuds, personality conflicts, and sectional differences. The shape of these struggles stemmed from rivalry between two great families, the Livingstons and the DeLanceys. Each of these led powerful contending factions, though their membership changed frequently depending on what was at issue. New York had the most complicated political alignments of any colony. This was one reason why it did not grow as much as some. Another was that the port of New York failed to capture the vital rum trade from Boston or the trade in foodstuffs from Philadelphia. Landlords preferred to rent land rather than sell it, which made New York less attractive than New Jersey. A body of German immigrants were abused by landlords early in the eighteenth century, and thereafter Germans went to Pennsylvania instead of New York. Bad luck and bad leadership combined to make New York a mediocre colony. Few could have guessed then that while its problems would continue, New York would become great anyway, thus proving that intolerable social and political problems were no barrier to enterprise.

The colonial family

It used to be thought that the colonial family was extended (that is, composed of several generations and perhaps collateral relatives), that life expectancies were short, that families had many children, and that infant and maternal mortality rates were high. Only recently have historians begun looking at the demographic data, chiefly in New England, but their work already suggests that domestic life in the colonial era was closer to modern patterns than people think. John Demos has found that in Plymouth Colony the average family size was from four to six persons, though women did have more children than now, giving birth every two years as a rule. Nuclear families (parents and children only) were the most common. It was unusual to have other relatives in the household except, sometimes, an aged grandparent. The life expectancy for a male at age twenty-one was about seventy, for a woman, sixty-three. This reflected the higher maternal mortality rate. Death in childbirth accounted for 20 percent of the deaths of adult women and of course a much higher proportion of those who died during the childbearing years. (By comparison, the life expectancy of a twenty-year-old man in 1945 was 68.6 years and a woman's 72.9.) The chances of a child dying before the age of twenty-one were one in four. This was a much higher figure than now, but it is low by the standards of most preindustrial societies. Adults usually married only once. Among a sample of 700 individuals gathered by John Demos, 60 percent of the men and 75 percent of the women had but a single spouse.

There were differences between the Puritan family and the modern family. Some children were apprenticed out, but most (around 90 percent in Bristol, Rhode Island, according to Demos) lived at home. There were some servants, but not many (13 percent of the population in Bristol) and they were concentrated in a few households (two-thirds of the families in Bristol had no servants, and only a handful had more than one). The family had more responsibilities in the way of education, employment, social welfare, religion, and so forth than now. On the other hand, family life was natural, taken for granted, tied together with shared tasks on the farm or in the shop.

Another difference was that in the eighteenth century there were no adolescents. A person moved smoothly from childhood to adulthood, without the long intervening period that exists today. Children, though loved, were seen as miniature adults, victims of original sin, prey to man's evils, and less able to resist them than older people. Great weight was placed on the conversion of children and on protecting them from temptation. Their recreation was supposed to be "Lawful, Brief, and Seldom."

The Puritan family was like the modern family in being male-dominated and nuclear but unlike it in having no adolescents, in producing more children, in making fewer allowances for immaturity, and in functioning as a unit of production rather than consumption. Most families were engaged in subsistence farming and provided for their own needs. Broadly speaking, this seems to have been the family pattern throughout New England and the Middle Colonies where English-speaking Calvinists predominated. It was less true of the frontier and the South.

People in the eighteenth century still believed that the wilderness turned men into beasts. Family life on the frontier was thought tainted by looseness and promiscuity. Since there was little religion on the frontier, there were fewer marriages. People lived together out of wedlock for years, from choice or necessity. Women were scarce and hence sometimes shared. The travelers' accounts on which this material is based are not entirely reliable. But there is reason to suppose that family life suffered from exposure to the wilderness, especially where the settling was done by small groups or individuals. Morality was less of a problem in western New En-

gland, where the frontier was opened a town at a time.

The little evidence available suggests that the plantation family was more primitive also. On the plantation the nuclear family, relatives, friends, visitors, and slaves all lived together, isolated in varying degree from the world. Because they were cut off from ordinary social intercourse so much of the time, planter families made a great event of visiting and entertaining. A major celebration might go on for weeks, with relatives and visitors sharing the family's beds. Even William Byrd II, one of the greatest landowners in Virginia, shared his mattress with male visitors on such occasions. This was a purely social, not a sexual, arrangement. But he did have intercourse with his female servants when he could, and being a pious man (by Anglican standards) felt guilty afterward. Religion was not as great a restraint on men as in the North. Slavery discouraged modesty because, being thought less than human, slaves were not dressed or treated according to the rules governing white society. Plantation society was pleasure-loving, secularized, and relatively tolerant. Its family life was, therefore, somewhat reactionary by Northern standards, a throwback to the looser, more promiscuous family type that seems to have existed before the Protestant Reformation. Southerners worried less about their children. Family discipline was less severe, though for girls etiquette was often more formal. It was not until evangelical religion overcame Anglicanism in the nineteenth century that the Southern family approximated the national norm.

Cultural and intellectual life

As the colonies matured, they began to have a cultural and intellectual life of their own, even though this was derived from England

Figure 2-2 Stratford, one of the most splendid remaining great houses of colonial Virginia. *(Wide World Photos)*

and France. That it existed at all was something of a feat. Most Americans were farmers with little or no education. There were but five towns of consequence, and of these only Boston and Philadelphia had a real cultural life. Yet they proved sufficient for the colonies' most pressing needs. Both provided schools, printers, and some patrons of the useful arts. Americans were not much interested in abstractions for their own sake. The Enlightenment opened their minds to new ideas without altering their taste for the practical. This is best illustrated by Benjamin Franklin, who, though hardly typical, displayed traits enlightened colonials thought admirable, as did Thomas Jefferson.

Philadelphia in Franklin's day was a place of schools and books and men who read

them. Whether Quaker or not, its chief figures traveled to Europe, bought fine furniture and works of art, built lovely Georgian homes, and practiced philanthropy. Philadelphia was the second largest city in the British Empire then, and no place in the Western world had a comparable array of private charitable agencies and public services. The Philosophical Society that Franklin organized made it a center of practical scientific inquiry too. The intersection of Quaker and Enlightenment values produced a rich provincial culture that, even if not terribly original, helped build American self-confidence. It contributed something to the sense of nationality. It demonstrated that light and learning would not die if the colonies decided to go their own way.

The future Revolutionary leaders, being steeped in the Enlightenment, were the first generation raised in America that is comprehensible to moderns. Cool, rational, suspicious of passion, and believers in common sense, they were often wrong by later standards but their values and goals were enough like our own to be understood. Still, they were men of the eighteenth and not the twentieth century, as a brief survey of their fundamental assumptions may make clear. The great principle which their system of thought depended on was the nature of the physical universe. All creation was perfectly organized; everything showed the hand of the planner. The perfection of Nature's design was a function of economy and uniformity. Since neatness was the creator's most salient trait, redundant or exceptional phenomena were disturbing. Swamps, marshes, and the presense of seashells on mountains seemed at odds with the great design. But men were convinced that all had a place in Nature's scheme if properly understood. Philadelphia's Dr. Benjamin Rush, a brilliant physician and intellectual, believed that aging was Nature's way of preparing man for death by making life progressively more unpleasant. Jefferson argued that it also made death easier by blunting man's faculties.

Their anthropology was physically based. Women were physically inferior to men, hence socially and intellectually as well. The equality of man was demonstrated by the uniformity of men's bodies. Where they differed, it was for practical reasons. Hair, skin, stature, and so forth varied according to environment. In theory then, no race was unequal—only different. In practice, it did not quite work out that way. Racial prejudices were already sufficiently embedded that even so egalitarian a philosophy as this could not erase them. Jefferson believed that the Indi-

an's inferior civilization was evidence not of the Indian's own inferiority but only of the different problems he faced. Yet Jefferson was unable to apply this same rule to blacks. If his thought was to be consistent, he had to admit that blacks and whites were equally endowed by nature, but as a slave owner he could not. So his remarks on blacks were evasive and contradictory. This was true of most intellectuals then, though not of Rush. He tried to find a physical explanation for the peculiar attributes of blacks as he saw them—dark skin, thick lips, immunity to pain, strong sexual appetites, and the like. He decided these were the consequences of a congenital leprosy with which all blacks were infected. When a cure to it was found, the race would vanish. This seems insulting and ignorant now, but it was an honest effort by an exceptionally troubled and conscientious man to square the theory of equality with the facts of black degradation. Had he known of the cultures of black Africa, he would not have needed to reach so far for an explanation of why slaves were as they were. Nearly everyone believed that black inferiority was the reason for slavery; hardly anyone understood that the opposite was true. Lacking reliable information from Africa, there was no empirical evidence to support an argument for black equality and much to disprove it. Rush's leprosy theory was both the measure of his decency and proof of the harm done to whites as well as blacks by slavery.

Enlightened colonists believed that thought had physical origins. Men's ideas were a function of the size, shape, and configuration of their brains. Such a straightforwardly materialistic an explanation pretty well ruled out the soul, but it promoted tolerance—since the errors of men were understood to be caused not by their evil characters but by their physical brains. While this did not keep literate men from trying to convert or proscribe those who disagreed with them, it did make for a more open and relaxed intellectual climate than had obtained earlier.

Morality was equally matter-of-fact. Justice was necessary if men were to live peacefully together; therefore, man was endowed with a sense of justice. Virtue was socially desirable and therefore to be sought. Vice was antisocial and hence to be cured or at least contained. But vice was a sickness and its practitioners were more to be pitied than condemned, though that too if necessary.

Religion was admired for its benefits in the same manner as morality. Enlightened men were typically not pious or doctrinaire, but they believed in the existence of a creator and in the social advantages of Christianity. Tom Paine, the great infidel, was far from being an atheist. He attacked the churches and the Bible in his *Age of Reason* for making God seem capricious and misanthropic when in fact Paine knew God to be benevolent, rational, intelligible, and benign. These complaints were not unique to Paine, though on balance most prominent colonists respected Christianity for teaching men to love their neighbors and practice the golden rule. Other religions were applauded to the degree they did this also. Enlightened men admired the historical Jesus as a reformer and philosopher like themselves.

This hardly exhausts the list of things American leaders and intellectuals believed in, but it does illustrate the habits of mind they brought to public questions. When war came, they fought it as best they could in the same rational, tolerant, open-minded, common-sense way. There were excesses during the war. The Enlightenment did not abolish fear, ambition, greed, and other unfortunate human traits. To make great efforts, men must be greatly roused—a state not always consistent with the values enlightened men tried to live by. Loyalists were sometimes persecuted and their property was confiscated. Local quarrels were often marked by great viciousness. All the same, it is hard to think of another civil war, which in large measure the Revolution was, conducted in a more sane and responsible manner. This was, perhaps, the greatest blessing conferred on America by the Enlightenment.

Selected references

Here, as throughout, only those works will be cited which influenced this chapter or are pertinent to it. For a complete guide to all the published literature on American history written before 1951, see Oscar Handlin et al. (eds.), *Harvard Guide to American History* (1954). For more recent materials, students will have to consult the standard authorities.

A good textbook history of the colonial period is David Hawke, *The Colonial Experience* (1966), which includes an excellent bibliography. The classic work is Charles M. Andrews, *The Colonial Period of American History* (1934–1938), in four volumes. Also useful is Wesley Frank Craven, *The Southern Colonies in the Seventeenth Century* (1949). An intriguing discussion of first settlements, together with documents, is a pamphlet in the Berkeley Series edited by Sigmund Diamond, *The Creation of Society in the New World* (1963). On early American slavery, see the monumental study by Winthrop D. Jordan, *White over Black* (1968).

Perry Miller's books *Orthodoxy in Massachusetts* (1935) and *The New England Mind: The Seventeenth Century* (1939) are brilliant but frequently obscure. A valuable account written in the eighteenth century is Thomas Hutchinson, *History of the Colony and Province of Massachusetts Bay* (1936), in three volumes. See also Thomas J. Wertenbaker, *The Puritan Oligarchy* (1947), and the very sympathetic Samuel Eliot Morison, *Builders of the Bay Colony* (1930). The Protestant ethic is a controversial concept which some deny ever existed in reality, at least as described by Max Weber in *The Protestant Ethic and the Spirit of Capitalism* (many editions). His work remains the point of departure for anyone wishing to pursue the subject. A fine discussion of Puritan contradictions is

Edmund S. Morgan, *The Puritan Dilemma: The Story of John Winthrop* (1958). See also Ola Elizabeth Winslow, *Master Roger Williams* (1957). A lively account of the great witchcraft is Marion L. Starkey, *The Devil in Massachusetts* (1950). Edwin S. Gaustad, *The Great Awakening in New England* (1957), is concise and readable.

On the early history of Pennsylvania see Edwin B. Bronner, *William Penn's "Holy Experiment": The Founding of Pennsylvania, 1681–1701* (1962). Frederick B. Tolles, *Meeting House and Counting House: Quaker Merchants of Colonial Philadelphia* (1948), is most interesting. Carl and Jessica Bridenbaugh, *Rebels and Democrats: Philadelphia in the Age of Franklin* (1942), is excellent cultural history.

A charming study of colonial family life is Edmund S. Morgan, *The Puritan Family* (1944). Of late, demographic historians have greatly enhanced our knowledge of early American domestic life. John Demos, *A Little Commonwealth: Family Life in Plymouth Colony* (1970), is fascinating. See also Philip J. Greven, Jr., *Four Generations: Population, Land, and Family in Colonial Andover, Massachusetts* (1970). The data on Bristol in the text comes from John Demos, "Families in Colonial Bristol, Rhode Island: An Exercise in Historical Demography," *William and Mary Quarterly* (January 1968). Carl Bridenbaugh, *Myths and Realities: Societies of the Colonial South* (1952), is provocative and illuminating on family life in the South and on the frontier. Louis B. Wright and Marion Tinling (eds.), *The Secret Diary of William Byrd of Westover, 1709–1712* (1941), is wonderfully revealing, as is Maude Woodfin and Marion Tinling (eds.), *Another Secret Diary of William Byrd of Westover, 1739–1741* (1942). Everyone interested in the family must begin with Philippe Ariès, *Centuries of Childhood: A Social His-*

tory of Family Life (1962), which, though about France, is a rich source of ideas on the origins of modern family life.

The classic study of colonial towns is Carl Bridenbaugh, *Cities in the Wilderness* (1938). A stimulating new book is Michael Zuckerman, *Peaceable Kingdoms: New England Towns in the Eighteenth Century* (1970). The standard work on American intellectual history is Merle Curti, *The Growth of American Thought*, 3d ed. (1964). A provocative analysis of the Enlightenment is Daniel J. Boorstin, *The Lost World of Thomas Jefferson* (1948).

THREE

Benjamin Franklin and the Achievement of American Independence

Period covered:	1750–1783
Emphases:	Diplomacy and politics
Major events:	Albany Congress, 1754
	French and Indian War, 1754–1763
	Stamp Act, 1765
	Declaratory Act, 1766
	Townshend Acts, 1767
	Boston Tea Party, 1774
	Quebec Act, 1774
	Continental Congress convenes, 1774
	Invasion of Canada, June 1775
	Common Sense appears, January 1776
	Declaration of Independence, 1776
	French Alliance, 1778
	Battle of Yorktown, 1781
	Treaty of Paris, 1783

If someone had asked George III of England to name the most improbable revolutionary in America, he might well have replied: "That ungrateful old reprobate Benjamin Franklin!" And so might Franklin himself; at least he would have agreed that he was an unlikely revolutionary. In 1776 he was seventy years old. He had risen on the ladders of colonial politics to a lofty position of power and influence—His Majesty's Deputy Postmaster for the Colonies. His son William, also a beneficiary of royal preferment, was Governor of New Jersey. Such families usually do not produce revolutionaries, especially not revolutionary fathers and loyal sons as in the case of the Franklins.

More than secure economically as well, Franklin no longer practiced the frugality he still recommended to his fellow Americans through *Poor Richard's Almanac*, a sort of handbook and guide to mercantilist economic theory he had devised for the common man. Generations of schoolboys yet unborn would first come to know Franklin in Poor Richard's guise, repeating his homely aphorisms—"Early to bed, and early to rise, makes man healthy, wealthy, and wise"—with the same lack of enthusiasm they felt for the spoonfuls of spring tonic their elders measured out each morning. In general, Poor Richard stayed with them longer—well into adulthood—even when they tried to ignore the work ethic.

Poor Richard was, however, only one of Franklin's many creations to outlast the colonial era. By all accounts, Franklin was the first man of science in the colonies. His papers on electricity and other subjects were published in the annual reports of the Royal Society, the most prestigious academy of learning in the empire. He was an elected member of the Royal Society as well as a contributor to its

publications, a rare honor for any man, let alone a colonial. After the Revolutionary War, a French admirer declared that Franklin, the American scientist, had "wrested fire from heaven and the scepter from the tyrants." That was a poetic way of putting what Franklin himself believed, not about his accomplishments necessarily (although he may have believed that too) but about the close connection between the natural world and the political world.

It was the Age of Reason, and Franklin, like other colonial leaders, approached political questions in the same spirit as he did natural phenomena. Both situations involved comparing appearances with reality. His famous rainy-day experiment demythologized the "heavenly bolts" of lightning, taking away their supposed supernatural character. What was true in physics, concluded the scientist Franklin, must also be true in the laws of politics. Or, the political theorist Franklin would argue, it must be made so. Here was a clue to Franklin the revolutionary that George III had missed.

Of all the colonial leaders, Franklin had given the most thought to foreign affairs and imperial relationships. He thoroughly understood mercantilist theory (the basic rationale of the empire), had applied it to America, and had gone beyond its limits. Just how far he had gone amazed him when he gave the matter some thought. Franklin had developed through his political writings a comprehensive rationale for separation and independence. Of course he had not originally intended that his writings should be used for such a purpose by himself—or by anyone else for that matter. Franklin always said that he was interested in promoting the interests of the British Empire in North America and those of his friends and himself within that empire. It did not demean political theory to use it for practical gain, any more than it demeaned natural law to find some practical use for electricity. That assumption was part of the Age of Reason too.

Still, Franklin was surprised at the outcome. "I never had heard in any Conversation from any Person drunk or sober," he was to write late in life (in Franklin's case *very* late, because he was still writing peace treaties at the age of seventy-seven), "the least Expression of a wish for a Separation, or Hint that such a Thing would be advantageous to America."

How did it happen then that Franklin and other upper-class men, Massachusetts lawyers and Virginia planters, came finally to see no alternative to separation? what allied them with radicals who also wanted to change things in the colonies? Just because it was so improbable, Franklin's rapid evolution at an advanced age from king's trusted deputy to determined revolutionary suggests some answers to both questions. It was a fascinating story to his contemporaries as well, even to those who entered caveats about Franklin's central role in the saga of American independence. "The history of our Revolution will be one continued Lye from one end to the other," John Adams would complain. "The essence of the whole will be *that Dr. Franklin's electrical Rod smote the Earth and out sprung General Washington. That Franklin electrified him with his rod—and thence forward these two conducted all the Policy, Negotiations, Legislatures and War.*"

Adams was wrong. If anything, Franklin's role has been played down by historians. And that is unfortunate, not only because it is typical and critical to the movement for independence, but also because it is an interesting story.

Figure 3-1 That ungrateful old reprobate Benjamin Franklin! In 1776 he was seventy years old. A beneficiary of royal preferment, Franklin was hardly a revolutionary "type." His conversion to the cause of independence tells much of the revolutionary tale. (*John Trumbull,* Benjamin Franklin, *Yale University Art Gallery*)

Working through the imperial "system"

Perhaps the first doubt passed through Franklin's mind when Parliament passed the Iron Act of 1750, making it illegal to build ironworks in the colonies except for those producing crude iron for shipment to England. He wrote a pamphlet on the question, which, in a gentle but firm manner (as if dealing with a somewhat slow pupil), pointed out the error. "A vast demand is growing for British Manufactures, a glorious market wholly in the Power of Britain. . . . Therefore Britain should not too much restrain Manufac-

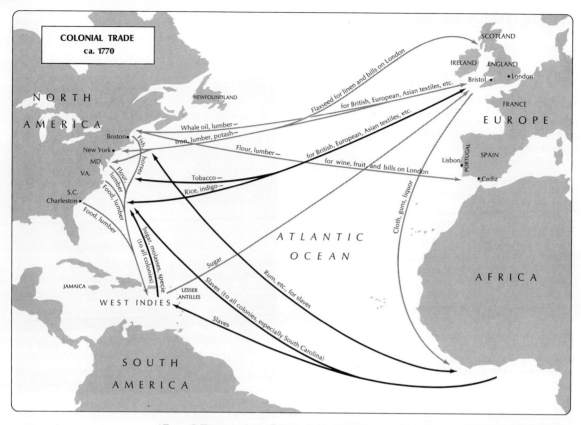

COLONIAL TRADE
ca. 1770

SCOTLAND

IRELAND ENGLAND
Bristol • • London

NEWFOUNDLAND

NORTH

AMERICA

FRANCE

EUROPE

Flaxseed for linen and bills on London

for British, European, Asian textiles, etc.

Whale oil, lumber—
Boston• Iron, lumber, potash—

New York •
MD. Flour, lumber—
VA.

for British, European, Asian textiles, etc.

Fish, horses

Flour, lumber

SPAIN
Lisbon

PORTUGAL

Tobacco—
Rice, indigo—

S.C.
Charleston •

Food, lumber

Food, lumber

for wine, fruit, and bills on London

• Cadiz

Cloth, guns, liquor

ATLANTIC

OCEAN

Sugar, molasses, specie
(to all colonies)

Sugar

AFRICA

JAMAICA

LESSER
ANTILLES

Rum, etc., for slaves

Slaves (to all colonies, especially South Carolina)

WEST INDIES

Slaves

SOUTH

AMERICA

(From A History of the American People *by Graebner, Fite and White. Copyright* ©
1970 by McGraw-Hill, Inc. Used with permission of McGraw-Hill Book Company)

tures in her colonies. A wise and good Mother will not do it. To distress, is to weaken, and weakening the Children weakens the whole Family."

The fate of would-be American iron-mongers was of less concern to Franklin than other tendencies he saw in the law. On several occasions, down to the eve of the Revolution, he would defend the Navigation Acts against their enemies. Franklin argued that they formed an integral part of the imperial defense system. It was all the more important, therefore, that the Navigation Acts should not be manipulated by special interest groups in Parliament to the obvious detriment of the

colonies. The Iron Act, by laying a foundation for future exploitation, was a bad sign. One could not tamper with the "system" without endangering the empire as a whole.

Of more immediate concern to the whole empire and to Franklin individually was the unfolding struggle between England and France to control the rich lands between the Allegheny Mountains and the Ohio River. As he gazed westward, the Philadelphia printer perceived three possible threats to imperial expansion: (1) French advances out of Canada, (2) intercolonial rivalry, and (3) malfunction of the British imperial system at its highest levels. Indeed, all three seemed to be materializing in the 1750s. Speculators associated with Virginia's colonial hierarchy had organized the so-called Ohio Company and had successfully petitioned the king for a grant of 200,000 acres "near the forks of the Ohio." Efforts to occupy the royal grant led the Ohio Company into direct conflict with French and Indian claimants.

These doings disturbed leading Pennsylvanians, but the Governor and Assembly of that colony divided over what kind of response they should (or could) make. Meanwhile, Governor Robert Dinwiddie of Virginia went ahead, sending a small force of militia under newly commissioned Lieutenant Colonel George Washington, then just twenty-two years old, to drive the French out before they could establish a strong point at Fort Duquesne. Washington's subsequent defeat prompted demands from Virginia for war. But London instructed the royal governors instead to send representatives to parley with Indian leaders at Albany, New York. Nothing came of the talks, but the Albany meeting produced a plan for colonial union. Its author was Ben Franklin.

The Albany Plan

Before the surprised delegates, Franklin unveiled his plan for a grand council to be selected by each of the colonial assemblies. Presiding over the council, as he envisioned it, would be a president-general appointed by the crown. Together the council and president-general would exercise sole power over questions of war and peace with the Indians, of the Indian trade, and of purchases or land grants outside existing colonial boundaries. To this end, the intercolonial council could build forts, raise armies, equip fleets, and levy taxes.

A central government could also, so Franklin intended, put a close rein on Virginia's western activities—thus preventing the Ohio Company or any successor group from reaping the lion's share of the disputed territory and reducing the rest to arguing among themselves like jackals over the leavings. Delegates from the eight colonies north of the Potomac River approved the plan, but the colonial assemblies and the Board of Trade in London both said no. Here was an early indication, by the way, that any future American government would have difficulty arriving at (and enforcing) decisions binding on all sections.

The Albany Plan was later charged against Franklin as proof of a long-harbored desire for an independent North American empire. Such a charge was bad history. He had desired to reduce intercolonial bickering, yes, and to secure equal opportunities for Pennsylvanians, and to promote the expansion of the British Empire. But the *rejection* of the Albany Plan was what put new ideas in his mind.

Never one to put his eggs in a single basket, Franklin had linked private and public interests in a variety of ways. He could happily devote the rest of his life, he once wrote the Methodist evangelist George Whitefield, to a project for establishing new colonies north of the Ohio River. Colonies planted in that wilderness would redound to the greater glory of God, offer new security to the older colonies, and increase the people, territory, strength, and commerce of the empire. Having once tried to curb the Ohio Company, Franklin and William, his son, soon joined forces with a transatlantic group of politicians and speculators to form the Vandalia Company. The company offered the crown a huge sum of money for the right to acquire and develop 10 million acres in the

Ohio Valley, an area roughly equivalent to that of New Jersey.

Rival land companies joined in the scramble, but none received the king's favor. Between the idea and its realization grew up an alliance of fur traders and British manufacturers. The manufacturers feared the growth of colonial rivals and population shifts, while the fur traders were eager to maintain good relations with their Indian suppliers.

The spokesman for these groups on the Board of Trade declared in 1763 that as the number of Americans increased they should emigrate instead to Nova Scotia or to southern provinces, "where they would be useful to their Mother Country instead of planting themselves in the Heart of America, out of reach of Government where from the great difficulty of procuring European commodities, they would be compelled to commerce and manufactures to the infinite prejudice of Britain. . . ."

Disappointment in London

Franklin welcomed the opportunity to dispel what he still regarded as erroneous notions about colonial ambitions when he went to London as the Pennsylvania Assembly's agent to represent its interests at the seat of empire. He soon found that he could not catch up with events or changing attitudes. At the conclusion of the French and Indian War, the crown issued the Proclamation of 1763, restricting all western settlements to a line along the Appalachian Mountains. The proclamation line was supposed to be a temporary measure, lasting only until a permanent policy could be developed. But there were growing indications that a broad change in imperial attitudes was taking place.

This fear of American manufactures—even textile products—was clearly getting out of hand, thought Franklin. His remonstrance of 1764 was not so gentle as the comment he had made on the 1750 Iron Act:

[A]s to our being always supply'd [with cloth] by [England], 'tis folly to expect it. Only consider the rate of our Increase, and tell me if you can increase your Wooll in that Proportion, and where, in your little Island you can feed the Sheep. Nature has put Bounds to your Abilities, tho' none to your Desires.

Franklin's mood had changed. The atmosphere in London had changed. Which had changed first? Which had changed the most? Historians still ponder these questions, but one thing was certain. There was now an "Amercan Question" in British politics which went beyond the matter of western settlement or colonial manufactures. There was, to begin with, the problem of taxation and revenue. Who was to pay for empire defense? In 1765 Parliament passed the Stamp Act to raise funds for the maintenance of a 10,000-man defense force in America. Colonial leaders became aware that this army was also to be charged with enforcing the Proclamation of 1763. Aha! That added up to conspiracy, a plot to keep Americans from their share of the empire.

Given this focus, the new Stamp Act was bound to generate controversy and to center attention, as no earlier measure had, on the common fate of all colonials: the fact that they lacked direct representation in Parliament. The act required everyone who used legal and commercial papers to purchase special stamps and to affix these to the documents. A man could not marry without first pasting a stamp on his marriage license, nor could he

EUROPEAN CLAIMS IN NORTH AMERICA · 1763

England
France
Spain
Disputed

Proclamation Line, 1763
Boundary by proclamation, 1763
Boundary of Quebec Act, 1774

(From A History of the American People by Graebner, Fite and White. Copyright © 1970 by McGraw-Hill, Inc. Used with permission of McGraw-Hill Book Company)

circulate a complaint about the law without first sticking one of the blasted things on it. Rich and poor alike were affected, but hardly to the point of impoverishment in either instance.

Conservative colonial leaders were just as vexed about the Stamp Act as anyone, but how could they make an effective protest without weakening respect for the structure of the law and property rights? Many doubtful conservatives would finally be brought over to independence by an argument that Parliament and the King, by their foolish behavior from the time of the Stamp Act, were endangering law and order in the colonies. It was straight from John Locke, and it would succeed with some where other appeals to direct economic advantage had already failed.

The Stamp Act crisis saw the creation of farmers' and workers' societies known as the "Sons of Liberty." The Sons were considerably less polite about their protests and more direct in their methods. Stamp distributors were threatened by mobs, driven out of town, and even manhandled. A rioting crowd broke into the home of Massachusetts Lieutenant Governor Thomas Hutchinson, destroying the furnishings and much of his famous library.

The powers of the British ruling class had been challenged, but also the prerogatives of those governing within the colonies. Where did the Sons of Liberty draw the line, if they did? More important, said others, where could colonial leaders draw a distinction which would restrain their British rulers while protecting the colonial governments? Perhaps things could not be set right in the colonies—and kept right—until the imperial question was resolved. But how, and when?

It was a very worried group of men who assembled in New York during October 1765 for what became known as the Stamp Act Congress. Caught between the coolly arrogant tyranny of Parliament and King and the noisy outbursts of the Sons of Liberty, they needed a way out. Under considerable pressure, the delegates to the Stamp Act Congress arrived at a twofold solution: they would petition George III for repeal and call for a colonial boycott on British imports until it was granted. The other part of the solution was ideological and has an interesting rationale. According to the Congress, Parliament had the right to impose external taxes, such as duties on imports and exports. But it had no right to levy internal taxes without the consent of the colonial assemblies. Such an argument was obviously designed not only to delineate separate responsibilities but also to enhance the status of the colonial assemblies in the face of the radical challenge at home. Otherwise the elaborate reasoning that had gone into its formulation was just so much wasted effort.

The strategy worked—in part. Within a few months a clamor arose among the British merchants demanding repeal. Just at this moment Franklin again took center stage. His friends in England, who agreed with him at least in part that Parliament was headed in the wrong direction in its dealings with the colonies, arranged things so that he could testify before the House of Commons concerning the effects of the Stamp Act. But the eminent Dr. Franklin also took this opportunity to explain his theory on the proper governance of a great empire and to speculate on what might happen should Parliament foolishly decide to ignore his precepts.

When one impatient questioner asked if an external tax on the necessities of life would not have the same practical effect as an internal tax, thus exposing the weakness in the colonial argument, Franklin riposted, "I do not know a single article imported into the

Northern Colonies, but what they can either do without, or make themselves."

That was not an answer. It was a challenge which led his questioner off in a direction Franklin wanted him to go. Franklin was then asked, "Don't you think cloth from England absolutely necessary to them?"

Franklin: "No, by no means absolutely necessary; with industry and good management, they may very well supply themselves with all they want."

His questioner proved persistent, if nothing else saying: "Will it not take a long time to establish that manufacture among them? And must they not in the mean while suffer greatly?"

Franklin, now in full command of the situation, replied "I think not. They have made surprising progress already. And I am of the opinion, that before their old clothes are worn out, they will have new ones of their own making."

And there the questioner was left to draw his own conclusion.

At the crossroads of empire

Repeal brought congratulations from Franklin's Philadelphia friends and supporters. Joseph Galloway, for example, was a powerful figure in Pennsylvania politics and a future loyalist who had hoped only to strengthen ties with England by protesting the Stamp Act. From him Franklin heard that "Our friends" (the conservative elite of Philadelphia) had patrolled city streets to prevent the celebration from spilling over into "indecent Marks of Triumph and Exultation." Galloway predicted that discontent in America would now subside, although it was clear to him that certain people wanted something "further than a Repeal, and even wished it might not take Place,

in order to furnish them with a Pretext for other Designs." He took comfort that their number remained comparatively small.

So did Franklin. Now he could settle back to his own affairs, and those of the Vandalia Company, in the hope that the crisis had finally aroused the King's ministers to the danger of ignoring the rightful claims of the colonials: their inalienable rights as citizens. But on the same day that the King signed the repeal, he also assented to the Declaratory Bill reaffirming Parliament's absolute power to enact binding laws for the colonies. Without meaning to, the crown had thereby reduced the options open to its friends in America, including some of the men who had so carefully devised the internal-external tax hypothesis at the Stamp Act Congress. A future crisis would almost certainly get out of hand.

Franklin was disturbed, moreover, by the attitude he now observed during his accustomed London routine of coffee house discussions. "Every man in England," he wrote a Scotch friend early in 1767, "seems to consider himself as a Piece of a Sovereign over America; seems to jostle himself into the throne with the King, and talks of *OUR Subjects in the Colonies.*" England and the colonies were fast approaching a crossroads. Soon those who felt as he did, who considered themselves British citizens, would have to decide whether they would go along with Parliament and King or choose the unknown path to separation. Parliament speeded things up by enacting new revenue measures, the so-called Townshend Acts. For a time His Majesty's Government did restrict itself to external duties on paper, glass, lead, and tea; but, even so, and indeed because the colonials had forced the issue, the Townshend Acts dissolved the imaginary distinction between internal and external taxes.

What was real—and permanent—was the nature of the colonial relationship itself.

It was real all right, and suddenly visible everywhere. When New York refused to comply with the Quartering Act of 1765 by supplying provisions and housing for British troops still stationed there, Parliament suspended the colony's legislative privileges. That action left even the most conservative colonial leaders stranded without civil government to protect their interests and themselves from the wrath of the Sons of Liberty, who were soon out rioting again. Parliament was forcing a choice on them—independence or anarchy—with every new measure it enacted. Seemingly oblivious to the plight of these friends in America, the King's ministers redoubled their determination to bring the Colonies to heel.

The Boston Massacre

Tensions erupted in Boston early in March 1770 when British soldiers fired into a crowd which had gathered outside the customs house to protest the new duties. Three men were killed and several others wounded. A vast mob poured out into the streets demanding removal of all British troops. Governor Hutchinson managed to quell the raging storm of citizenry, and a general lull settled over the colonies when the Townshend Acts were repealed. Parliament continued only the tea duty as a symbol of its undiminished authority.

What more could the colonials want? Even Franklin seemed satisfied that things would now take their natural course. Hold your tempers and stick to your principles, he wrote a friend in Boston. By the newspapers, he noted, "there seem to be among us some violent spirits. But I trust the general pru-

dence of our country will see, that by our growing strength we advance fast to a situation in which our claims must be allowed; that by a premature struggle we may be crippled, and kept down another age. . . . [E]very encroachment on right is not worth a rebellion."

Not so, said Samuel Adams, Boston's most outspoken advocate of independence. Not so at all. Things had gone too far. With the help of a few friends disguised as Indians, who dumped the East India Company's tea chests into Boston Harbor, Adams forced things along even farther. The Boston Tea Party was well reported in London newspapers. Franklin was discouraged by the accounts he read: "I suppose we never had since we were a people, so few friends in Britain," he wrote from London. "The violent destruction of the tea seems to have united all parties here against us."

Amid shouts for even stronger action, Parliament enacted the Boston Port Bill, which forbade imports except food and firewood and curtailed civil government until the city fathers agreed to pay for the tea. Having dealt with the rioters and hooligans, the British legislators turned back to a more difficult problem they had postponed to settle that outrageous business in Massachusetts. Franklin regarded this other question, which resulted in the Quebec Act of 1774, as far more ominous.

The Quebec Act

Individuals might succumb to temptation or prejudice; they might lack talent for governing. That could happen on both sides of the Atlantic; it could produce situations like the Boston Tea Party and what followed. The strength of the system lay in its supposed self-correcting balances. Aberrations even served as reminders that a sound governmental plan took into account the many weaknesses shared by all mankind.

But what if the system itself was irrational? Viewed from an American perspective, the Quebec Act signaled the triumph of the irrational. It shut off the West to Americans but protected the special interest groups, speculators, wild Indian tribes, and French Catholics in Canada. What the law said was that Quebec province would be extended northward to Hudson Bay, westward to the Mississippi, and southward to the Ohio. Within that huge area, French civil law and the Roman Catholic Church were to be given official recognition. Massachusetts voices were now heard to say that the next step would be the establishment of the Church of England as the state church for their colony. If the colonists did overreact, it was easy to understand why.

In Massachusetts, the scene of already so much violence, the Quebec Act seemed to provide the clergy with a reason for joining those urging revolution. But the thought of moral regeneration through separation was not limited to the clergy. "By 1776," writes Gordon Wood, "it seemed to many of the ministers that decades of corrupt and vicious social behavior had at last caught up with the Americans, that now, here in this crisis with Britain, was the providential opportunity, not to be lost, for 'a reformation in principles and practices,' involving 'a change of mind, and our entertaining different thoughts of past conduct.'" Yet the spirit of change uplifted Sam Adams, too. America would become "the *Christian* Sparta."

More than the Stamp Act even, the Quebec Act drew the colonies together out of common concern. Compared to the fears of the heavily mortgaged planters, Franklin's ventures in land speculation and his vision of a future North American empire encompassing Canada must have seemed but the fancies of an old man's idle hours. He was serious about them, but not desperate. For the planters, however, the West offered the best, and indeed the only, way out of a vicious circle of debts and soil depletion. Their plight was to be repeated in the decade before Lincoln's election: both times the planters chose war rather than submit to what they feared would be slow strangulation. Even more consciously than their Northern counterparts, the Virginians measured freedom by the acre.

Washington, for example, had long eyed the Ohio Valley as a new beginning, a place where he and his neighbors could "increase our export of wheat, gently lead our people off from tobacco, as well as render a vast extent of back country useful to trade." Jefferson proclaimed the Quebec Act to be the final defeat of the planters' hopes. By making the acquisition of land more difficult, the act meant, said Jefferson, that "the population of our country is likely to be checked."

That was the crucial point, thought Franklin. He and others had once believed it was only a matter of waiting until "our growing strength" prevailed. But the Quebec Act convinced him that George III and his ministers, as well as America's many enemies in Parliament, would never allow nature to take its course or willingly turn over the reins of empire to the upstart Americans.

New York's Alexander Hamilton summed up the situation in a way which could have a powerful appeal to sober conservatives who had little sympathy for Sam Adams and less for the methods of the Sons of Liberty: "We are already suspected of aiming at Independence, and that is one principal cause of the severity we experience. The same cause will always operate against us, and produce an unfair severity of treatment."

The Continental Congresses

Hamilton's point covered the grievances of both the merchant and planter classes: every protest would now be taken as evidence of sedition and rebellion. What was there left to do? The First Continental Congress, which met on Septermber 5, 1774, revived the tactics of the Stamp Act crisis. But even as they drafted new petitions, there was a growing feeling amount the delegates that they faced, at best, an unending series of crises or, if the worst happened, the imposition of permanent martial law.

In the months that followed these fears were confirmed. Warrants were issued for the arrest of Sam Adams and John Hancock; the colonials began storing arms at Concord, Massachusetts, and other depots; and Parliament declared that colony was in open rebellion. Franklin returned to Philadelphia just in time to take his seat in the Second Continental Congress in May 1775. His presence gave the deliberations enhanced legitimacy in the eyes of fellow delegates: Here was no rabble-rouser or leveller but a transatlantic figure of great accomplishments in everything he had undertaken.

Franklin had no intention of becoming a trophy for others to display, however, whether radicals or conservatives. As the discussions wandered from one question to another, he offered the following resolution:

Whereas altho the Conquest of Canada, and Louisiana, was effected . . . by the joint Force and Expense of America and Britain, the latter hath seized the whole acquired Territory as its own, excluding us from any share in the Property, without the least regard to Equity or Justice.

Resolved, that in case such satisfaction as aforesaid is refused, all the lands in America claimed by the Crown, and all the Quit rents now unpaid to the same, shall be considered as liable to an appropriation for that purpose.

Franklin's resolution took into account the possibility of eventual reconciliation, but in spirit it and the plan he submitted for confederation of the colonies ruled out such an option. His draft for a new confederation even provided for the incorporation of the British West Indies, Canada, and Florida into the new empire. Florida, of course, was part of the Spanish empire. What he offered to the delegates was, therefore, a plan for an independent empire encompassing all of colonial North America!

The delegates put aside Franklin's confederation plan to concentrate on securing Canadian support, first by flattery and cajolery, then by military invasion in June 1775. Neither worked. In February 1776, Franklin and two other delegates traveled through winter storms to Canada in a futile effort to initiate negotiations for that colony's adherence to the plans of the Continental Congress. Americans feared that without the Canadians at their side the only chance for success rested in securing the aid of another European empire. That could be dangerous. If the worst happened, the colonials would have succeeded only in trading an English King for a French one; at best the colonials would have to limit their ambitions for an independent North American empire and bargain for everything they got politically and territorially.

Common Sense

The Continental Congress was, to put it bluntly, in a hell of a predicament. The way out, many had been saying for months, was to declare independence first, then seek foreign aid. The final push for independence was aided by Thomas Paine's *Common Sense*, which first appeared in January 1776. Within three months the pamphlet had become a major topic of conversation in and out of Congress. A recent emigrant from England, Paine had brought with him letters of introduction to Philadelphia printers signed by Franklin himself. Paine listened to the delegates as they came and went and then laced the threads of the strongest arguments for independence into his own powerful prose style.

Common Sense was the very sort of pamphlet Poor Richard would have written. The author's argument began by drawing the cause of all mankind into the American dispute with Great Britain, a not uncommon fixture in later American state papers. The British constitutional system, said Paine, was "noble for the dark and slavish times in which it was erected. . . ." But it no longer sufficed for American needs in a more complex era. England's system could not be America's; its interests were no longer America's. England's future was limited; America's was not:

In this extensive quarter of the globe, we forget the narrow limits of three hundred and sixty miles [England's extent] and carry our friendship on a larger scale; we claim brotherhood with every European Christian, and triumph in the generosity of the sentiment.

Nowhere in nature, Paine continued, had the satellite been made larger than its primary planet. England and America *in their present relations* thus reversed the natural order. That could not continue. Those who persisted in prolonging this error would bear full responsibility for letting loose forces in America which would sweep away all the liberties they now professed to cherish. If Congress failed to establish a government for America by reasoned arguments, it could expect to see some future demagogue lay hold of popular disquietudes and establish a tyranny. "Ye that oppose independence now, ye know not what ye do; ye are opening a door to eternal tyranny."

The sweep of Paine's logic took one's breath away, so swiftly had he moved from one question to another, knocking down all the arguments for delay. There was more. To many proseparation conservatives Paine was a positive danger with all this talk about revolution and liberty, but his warning that Congress should take heed to the signs of "popular disquietudes" hit home. To those who raised economic objections to independence, he had an even better comeback. American products were in demand throughout Europe. America's barrenness of gold and silver would protect it from invaders and ensure Europe's desire to have the new country as a free port. As long as America stayed clear of political connections with rival powers, there could be no danger economically in independence. "The commerce by which she has enriched herself, are the necessaries of life, and will always have a market while eating is the custom of Europe."

"We have it in our power to begin the world over again," Paine exclaimed. "A situation, similar to the present, hath not happened since the days of Noah until now. The birthday of a new world is at hand, and a race of men, perhaps as numerous as all Europe contains, are to receive their portion of freedom from the events of a few months. The reflection is awful, and in this point of view, how trifling, how ridiculous, do the little paltry cavilings of a few weak or interested men appear, when weighed against the business of a world."

How to win friends and influence people, especially in France

How ridiculous, how paltry indeed—except that it had never been done. France was the most logical place to seek aid, but also the most ironic. Ten years before Americans had rejoiced at the British victory over French arms and cheered the removal of the French menace from Canada; now they were hoping to impress Louis XVI, an absolute monarch, with their revolutionary cause. After the Declaration of Independence was signed on July 4, 1776, the Continental Congress assigned this crucial mission to Franklin, who sailed for France in October with instructions to negotiate a treaty of alliance and commerce. His most important task, however, was to persuade the French to open their treasury to the needy American revolutionaries.

Franklin was a good choice, for, despite what Paine had written about Europe's keen interest in seeing America set free politically and economically, Old World diplomacy did not run on the same principles. Franklin would have to convince French officials on other grounds—mercantilist principles—of the wisdom of aiding the American rebellion. Adept in any role, Franklin more than fulfilled the expectations of Congress—and enjoyed it all to the fullest.

He pleased and charmed French intellectuals, and the ladies of the court, by appearing in homespun and a fur hat which he wore originally to conceal a skin ailment. He did not disabuse his admirers of their notion that the costume was "natural man's contribution" to Old World manners and styles. Franklin frequented the French Academy of Sciences,

where he accomplished much with unofficial diplomacy. On one occasion the famous philosopher Voltaire was present. As word spread through the Academy, there arose a demand that the two should be formally introduced. They took each other by the hand, but this was not enough. The tumult subsided, observed John Adams dourly, only after they had embraced in the French manner. Adams's description of the incident reflects not a little envy of his countryman's great success: "The two aged Actors upon this great Theatre of Philosophy and frivolity then embraced each other by hugging one another in their arms and kissing each others cheeks. . . . And the cry immediately spread throughout the whole Kingdom and I suppose over all Europe. . . . How charming it was! Oh! it was enchanting to see Solon and Sophocles embracing!"

Meetings with the Count de Vergennes, the French Foreign Minister, were more frequent and decidedly less emotional. It was all business on those occasions. Vergennes wanted to be as certain as he could that the outcome would not find France facing England alone once again while the chastened colonies, reunited to the mother country, jeered from the sidelines. Franklin's original instructions had called for a treaty of alliance without political commitments of any kind to the French monarch and with specific prohibitions against any claims Louis XVI might want to make for any territory on or near the North American continent. He was left to his own devices to find a way to perform these feats.

Agile as he was, Franklin could not quite make that leap. The alliance came high. The United States agreed to make common cause with France should the latter be forced to go to war, and they pledged to continue fighting until both parties agreed that their objectives had been achieved. French possessions in

North America, moreover, were explicitly recognized in the treaty, as were still unnamed additions Vergennes might win at the peace table.

No one had to tell Franklin that the alliance was a mixed blessing. He himself had opposed any plan for treaties which included political commitments to other nations. But before America could be an empire unto itself, it had to achieve independence for the thirteen colonies. With the treaty that could be accomplished; without it there was little hope. Besides the direct military assistance the United States received under the treaty of 1778, Franklin squeezed out of a depleted French treasury more than $8 million in loans and subsidies.

Franklin's ever-active mind was already at work on postwar problems posed by the French treaty, the danger that America's financial obligations to Louis XVI would be used to limit the new nation's freedom of action or that the French would maneuver the treaty with the other powers to limit the United States territorially. He was especially alert to the possibility that Vergennes might try to strengthen Spain's position in the American hinterland by refusing American claims to the Mississippi River. In keeping with eighteenth-century Old World traditions and his own private interests, Franklin kept up an active correspondence with various British "acquaintances" and former associates in the Vandalia Company. Someday the war would be over and the race for Western lands would begin again. But there was always a larger purpose to be served. Franklin allowed Vergennes to know just enough about these exchanges to keep him concerned about what he did not know. That was all part of the diplomatic game. But the Foreign Minister did not know anything about Franklin's proposal to David Hartley, a Member of Parliament, that England accept an Anglo-French-American treaty recognizing the independence of the United States. It would be even better, Franklin slyly confided to Hartley, if, upon signing such a treaty, England would grant more than it could be compelled to cede—"all that remains in North America; and thus conciliate and strengthen a young power, which she wishes to have a future and serviceable friend."

Franklin thus implied that the French Treaty of Alliance with the United States was an emergency measure, and could, if things were handled just right, be dispensed with after the war. Congress had instructed its ambassadors in Europe to settle for nothing less than full and equal navigation rights on the Mississippi and an equal right to the fisheries off Newfoundland. The Mississippi was for the South, the fisheries for the North. The former wanted an outlet for its staples, the latter assurance that sea harvests would continue to provide a base for New England commerce. At one point, when the war's outcome seemed to hang in the balance, Congress offered to renounce its claims, for the time being, to the lower Mississippi if Spain would loan the new nation badly needed funds to purchase supplies. The idea of bartering away navigation claims on that key waterway for a few thousands in gold or an alliance of dubious value with a declining power horrified Franklin. "Poor as we are," he warned a colleague, "yet as I know we shall be rich, I would rather agree with them to buy at a great price the whole of their right on the Mississippi than sell a drop of its waters. A neighbor might as well ask me to sell my street door."

Alliance or no, Franklin was determined to achieve the imperial vision to its fullest limits. He was aided by factors beyond his control, or beyond the vicissitudes of Congressional policymaking. What the American peace commission lacked the wherewithal to accomplish, was done for it by British military blunders. If one sought more proof that the imperial system was out of kelter, even damaged beyond repair, there was the conduct of the war.

Diplomatic gamesmanship

Great Britain's generals botched the war fully as much as its statesmen had mishandled the colonies in the critical pre-Revolution years. In the fall of 1776, General Sir William Howe captured New York, which the British held throughout the war. He failed, however, to finish off Washington's retreating army, which escaped into Pennsylvania. Gentlemen did not wage war after the temperature fell, so Howe settled down with his mistress to enjoy the warmer pursuits of a long winter's dalliance. That bounder, Washington, interrupted his pleasure by striking back across the Delaware at British forces holding Trenton. The battle was hardly a decisive encounter, but it convinced skeptics of the colonial army's determination to stay in the fight after being driven from New York and through the long winter of 1776–1777.

The Saratoga campaign, which ended with an American victory in October 1777, was another early turning point in the war. It was proof enough even for Vergennes that the Americans might just pull it off. After Trenton, doubtful colonials signed up with Washington; after Saratoga, the French were ready to sign a treaty with the Continental Congress. French naval aid at the decisive battle of Yorktown in October 1781 played a very large part in Cornwallis's defeat. Yorktown was the last really significant military engagement of the war. Actual peace negotiations did not

begin for several months, but the victory made them inevitable. George III all but acknowledged defeat by appointing officials committed to ending the conflict.

"The English seem not to know either how to continue the war, or to make peace with us," Franklin complained to Washington in early 1782. He was anxious to see if George III's new ministers would pick up hints the peace commissioners had been dropping since the change in advisers to the throne. The hints the Americans were so busy dropping implied even more pointedly than before that American independence would not mean continued dependence upon France. Yet Franklin was careful to warn his British correspondents that *they* should not expect to divide France and America. His objective was to keep both London and Paris off stride and to forestall separate Anglo-French negotiations, which, in the European custom, could endanger America's claims and spoil everything.

Informal negotiations began in April 1782 when Franklin met with "Richard Oswald, Esquire," who had been recommended to him by Lord Shelburne as a "pacifical man" better suited for the business at hand than "any person of higher rank." Franklin set out to test Mr. Oswald's pacifical temperament, and his diplomatic acumen, by raising again the subject of Canada. Taking note of Oswald's chance comment that France's surrender of Canada at the end of the last war had proved to be a politic act, weakening ties between England and the other American colonies, Franklin moved right into the opening and "spoke of the occasions of future quarrel that might be produced by [England's] continuing to hold it; hinting at the same time, but not expressing too plainly, that such a situation, to us so dangerous, would necessarily oblige us to cultivate and strengthen our union with

France." Lord Shelburne failed to see the Canadian question in that light; nor was he willing to include a precise statement of American independence in the peace treaty. As to boundaries, he suggested returning to lines established in 1763. Despite a mutual desire to end the fighting, Great Britain and America were still far apart.

At this point Franklin was taken ill, and the major burden of the negotiations with Oswald fell to John Jay. His information and his intuition told the New Yorker that the Canadian diversion was unwise. While Franklin had been distracted by its charms, Count Vergennes was busy preparing to bargain with Shelburne for a quick peace that would keep the Americans well east of the Mississippi. Jay moved quickly to prevent that misfortune by informing the British negotiator that if his government agreed to a preamble naming the "Thirteen United States of America" as the other party, that would suffice. England would save face, and the new nation would gain independence. "And more than that," the emissary reported to London, "they would not be long about it; and perhaps would not be over hard upon us in the conditions." A draft treaty was signed on November 3, 1782, stipulating the Mississippi River as America's western boundary and providing for equal navigation rights. The United States was also given guarantees concerning fishing rights off Newfoundland. Shelburne had obvious reasons for supporting American claims to the Mississippi, among them Great Britain's continued rivalry with old world powers in North America, but even so the treaty was a diplomatic triumph for the new nation.

Vergennes was amazed at all the Americans obtained in the peace treaty—and more than a little annoyed at their behavior. Franklin was somewhat uneasy himself about Jay's overly cavalier attitude concerning American

obligations under the French alliance, but the plan for playing off the two great powers to America's best advantage had been in his mind from the beginning. He hoped to avoid giving Vergennes any added cause for irritation, quite simply because there was still something to be gained from the French. The chagrined Foreign Minister demanded an explanation for the negotiations which had been concluded "without any communication between us" and added with great indignation that he wished to know how Franklin, especially, proposed to fulfill America's obligations "which are due to the King."

In his best "Poor Richard" guise Franklin began a letter to Vergennes by saying that no prince was ever more beloved and respected by his own subjects than the French king was by the people of the new nation. Then came this: "*The English, I just now learn, flatter themselves they have already divided us. I hope this little misunderstanding will therefore be kept a secret, and that they will find themselves totally mistaken.*" What could Vergennes say or do? Stymied by this New World ambassador's audacity and genuinely fearful of an Anglo-American reconciliation, the Foreign Minister not only agreed to the treaty but facilitated yet another loan from his king's near-empty treasury!

A new empire

"I must soon quit this scene," Franklin had written Washington on March 5, 1780,

but you may live to see our country flourish, as it will amazingly after the war is over; LIKE A FIELD OF YOUNG Indian corn, which long fair weather and sunshine has enfeebled and discolored, and which in that weak state, by a thunder gust of violent wind, hail, and rain, seemed to be threatened with absolute destruction; yet the storm being past, it recovers fresh verdure, shoots up with double vigor, and delights the eye, not of its owner only, but of every observing traveller.

Rhapsodic in his predictions of America's future greatness on this occasion, Franklin remained an eminently practical man. Not a popular leader like Sam Adams or Patrick Henry, he became a revolutionary on purely pragmatic grounds, having concluded that developments on both sides of the Atlantic left those interested in enjoying the rights of Englishmen with no other choice. He always considered those rights to extend throughout North America—and beyond. In short, he was first a British imperialist of extraordinary talents and great vision and then a revolutionary. He pursued the same goals in each instance.

One night long before, in August 1767, Franklin had dined with one of England's leading statesmen. The conversation turned to the subject of the Illinois country, with Franklin expounding as usual on the advantages to be gained from putting a settlement there. These included, "furnishing provisions cheaper to the garrisons, securing the country, retaining the trade, raising a strength there which on occasion of a future war, might easily be poured down the Mississippi upon the lower country, and into the Bay of Mexico, to be used against Cuba, or Mexico itself, &c."

The "&c" held a great fascination for Franklin. It was with that in mind that he had advanced a plan for union back in 1754, proposed resolutions to the Continental Congress twenty years later, and undertaken the French mission in 1776. It took a long time and a war of independence, but he was satisfied with the results.

In this chapter the emphasis has often been on those conservative colonial leaders who became revolutionaries. Perhaps the word *separatists* could be used to describe them, but it would fail to suggest the complexity of the issues involved. Quite clearly, however, separation was an answer for many who feared the tension between the mother country and the Sons of Liberty would destroy them all. And the Revolution against British mercantilism did involve empire builders on this side of the ocean who had their own vision of an American mercantilism. It also included antimercantilists who harked to a different tradition, the radical levellers of England's past. Sometimes a man became one or the other and sometimes he became both, in sequence or even at the same time. Tom Paine was an antimercantilist in 1776, yet his arguments appealed to American mercantilists, and by 1783 he was himself calling for an American-style mercantilism. Each time, moreover, he spoke in the name of "common sense."

It is this constantly shifting perspective which makes any revolutionary period so fascinating to historians—and to contemporaries. The real conservatives, or nonseparatists, those called Tories by contemporaries, remained loyal to the King. Unhappy with the prospect of independence, and fearful that their rash friends had no idea of the proper way to govern an empire, they returned (or were forced) "home" to the shelter of the mother country. Conservative in politics, they were also conservative in temperament.

Once involved in the liberation struggle, even high Whigs like New York's John Jay got carried away to some extent by what they were doing, discovering rather like Dickens's Scrooge the delights of a noble cause. "It was nothing less than the weight of the entire

Christian tradition," observes Hannah Arendt sagely, "which prevented them from owning up to the rather obvious fact that they were enjoying what they were doing far beyond the call of duty." If it was not exactly "Revolution for the Hell of It," neither was it totally devoid of genuine converts to democratic thinking, certainly more democratic than Tories wished to endure.

To this one would only add that it was a lot easier to take such a view once the war began, because it was only then that the cause of separatists and Sons of Liberty were fully reconciled. And if conservatives still shuddered a bit when that Tory down the road lost his home and fields, at least the violence now had a focal point and the Sons of Liberty were now under army discipline. For a time internal tensions were submerged, and when they did emerge again an independent America would be better able to deal with them.

Selected references

For a starter on the problem of ideology and power in the revolutionary equation try Hannah Arendt, *On Revolution* (1963). The best study of Ben Franklin's impact on early American foreign policy is Gerald Stourzh, *Benjamin Franklin and American Foreign Policy* (1954). The atmosphere of rising empire is covered in Richard W. Van Alstyne, *The Rising American Empire* (1960), and the best integration of the Western problem remains Thomas Perkins Abernathy, *Western Lands and the American Revolution* (1937).

On the ideology of the revolutionaries themselves, see Bernard Bailyn, *Ideological Origins of the American Revolution* (1967), and Gordon S. Wood, *The Creation of the American Republic* (1969). Elisha P. Douglass, *Rebels and Democrats* (1955), is an eminently readable discussion of social change and institutions in conflict during the Revolution. Neglected today, but still suggestive, is J. Franklin Jameson's little book, *The American Revolution Considered as a Social Movement* (1926). Even older is Arthur M. Schlesinger's *The Colonial Merchants and the American Revolution* (1918), but it still is the last on that subject. Carl Becker's *The Declaration of Liberty* (1922) is of the same vintage and quality. The Navigation Acts are explored fully in O. M. Dickerson's *The Navigation Acts and the American Revolution* (1952), while the diplomacy of gamesmanship has found its historian in Richard B. Morris, *The Peacemakers* (1965). A world perspective is supplied by R. R. Palmer's *The Age of the Democratic Revolution* (1959). The Sons of Liberty await full treatment.

FOUR

Making a Nation

Period covered: 1776–1800
Emphases: Economic conditions. The American Revolution.
The Federal system. Organizing the new territories.
Major events: The Declaration of Independence, 1776
Lord Cornwallis surrenders at Yorktown, 1781
Treaty of peace ratified, 1783
Northwest Ordinance, 1787
The Constitution takes effect, 1789

The colonies revolt

On the eve of rebellion the American colonists were well off by European standards. In the North subsistence farming prevailed. Except for the Dutch estates on the Hudson, there were few large landholdings and many small-to-middling ones. Wealth was more concentrated in the cities, as Jackson T. Main has shown. In Boston 30 percent of the estates left by deceased males were worth more than $1,250, as against 8 percent in the country. In the North about one-third of the population was truly poor, including indentured servants; another 10 percent owned too little land to be much better off; the rest were adequately provided for. Men of substantial property, worth at least $50,000, made up 10 percent of the population and owned 45 percent of the wealth (while today the top 10 percent owns nearly 60 percent of the wealth).

Southern property was not so well distributed. Commercial one-crop farming rather than subsistence farming took root early, and with it the tendency to accumulate land. Speculators acquired huge tracts, especially on the frontier, so physical expansion did not have an egalitarian effect, as in the North. In certain counties only 30 percent of the adult white males owned land and in some a handful of men owned 70 percent or more of the land. In the whole South, one-fifth of the white males were landless laborers. If slaves were included, the landless amounted to one-third of the total. About 40 percent of white men were small farmers who enjoyed a lower standard of living than their counterparts in the North. The top 10 percent of wealth holders owned half the wealth and one-seventh of the population.

American class and status lines were fluid by European standards, even in the South.

Agriculture was the preferred occupation. Although small farmers ranked ahead of professional men in theory, this meant little in fact, as the wealth and offices held by professionals showed. There were three main social classes: a lumpenproletariat of slaves, servants, and landless workers at the bottom; a very broad middle class of farmers, artisans, tradesmen, and professionals; and an upper class of great landowners and merchants. This group is sometimes called aristocratic, though mainly out of courtesy. There was no nobility in the European sense, only an element of the bourgeoisie that did better than the rest. Outside the South this was an easy class to join. In 1787, 90 of the 100 richest Virginians had inherited their wealth, while perhaps 40 percent of the leading merchants of Boston and New York were self-made men. As a rule, whatever one's occupation, success in it led to respect and community leadership.

In modern times great revolutions are commonly thought to have profound social origins. This seems not to have been true of the American Revolution. A society where 70 percent of the free men are self-employed property holders can hardly be called inequitable. And as most property owners voted, it could not be called unrepresentative either except by women and blacks. Per capita taxation in the colonies was, at most, 4 percent of what Englishmen paid. The colonies had flowered under British rule. There seemed to be more reasons for preserving the imperial connection than for severing it. If England had not tried to make the colonies pay a larger share of the costs of their own administration and defense there would probably have been no Revolution. But England did try to tighten up the imperial system and make colonial practices square more with British theories. And when that was resisted,

London responded in ways which convinced many colonists that a conspiracy was afoot to deprive them of their ancient liberties. Though untrue, this was so widely believed as to make no difference. What began as a struggle to maintain the status quo ended as a holy crusade against political tyranny and moral corruption.

The Puritans had relished adversity, mistrusted blatant displays of affluence, and revered what were always seen as the more virtuous days of old. As Edmund S. Morgan has shown, these habits persisted even after Puritanism was dead and played an important role in conditioning men's minds for the battle to come. In 1764–1765 sermons hailed the nonimportation acts more for the blessings they would bring America than the harm they would do England. They would improve the colonial character and set the austere past against the luxurious and dissipated present. Thus liberty became associated with virtue and plain living. This line did not appeal to merchants. There was no profit for them in self-denial. Nonimportation undermined their will to resist England and so made them all the more unpopular as a class. Commerce as such was attacked for being an incitement to luxury. Manufacturing was hailed as a morally attractive substitute for trade as well as a means of freeing colonists from their dependence on English goods. The new taxes were damned for penalizing colonial industry and thrift. England, once so admired for the perfection of her public institutions, came to be seen as the classic example of a great country laid low by power and prosperity. When England sent over customs commissioners, this was viewed as proof that she meant to export her vices to America, to burden the colonies with a swarm of "placeholders" such as infested London. The ocean was no longer a barrier against the English

blight. Only independence would keep America virtuous.

These extravagant suspicions were vital to the Whig or patriot cause. Until 1774 and perhaps not even then, what Britain did was not enough to persuade most reasonable men that the imperial connection should be broken. To nerve themselves for such drastic action, colonists had to believe that everything most dear to them—religion, character, personal liberty—was threatened. Those who lacked a stake in English rule were most easily persuaded. Small farmers, being largely self-sufficient, had no strong ties with England. Sailors hated the Royal Navy for impressing (kidnapping) them into what was no better, though more dangerous, than a slave's life. Southern planters were often in debt to English factors and limited by the Navigation Acts, which required them to trade only within the British Empire. They therefore had little love for Britain. Land speculators resented the British attempt to limit Western expansion. On the other hand, merchants and professional men relied on Britain for trade and credit, as did public men for offices. Back-country men remained loyal for the most part, maybe because they were politically undeveloped and could not follow or comprehend seaboard politics, or because they wondered who would help them fight Indians when the British Army was gone.

But while the Revolution had no important social causes, it had profound social consequences outside the ports. The population was divided in complex ways; power, property, and positions changed hands accordingly. One hundred thousand Tories, or loyalists, mostly business and professional families from the middle colonies, left the country. This was a larger percentage than escaped from France after the French Revolution. Most of their estates were confiscated and sold to

Whigs. The distribution of wealth did not change much; but the wealth holders did. A whole new class of speculators, profiteers, and entrepreneurs was raised up. Bruce G. Merritt has illustrated this in the case of Deerfield, Massachusetts. It was 100 years old and had a population of 800 when the Revolution broke out. The line between loyalist and patriot that was drawn then had less to do with income than with occupation. Of the ten men with the most real property (land) in 1772, five were Whigs. Of the ten with most personal property, three were Whigs. However, while farmers made up three-quarters of the town's population, they comprised only one-third of the Tory party. On the other hand, the commercial class—merchants, artisans, professionals—was almost solidly Tory.

Men of business supported the crown for more than economic reasons though. The Tory faction revolved around a core of old families, two especially, which had dominated town affairs for most of the previous century. When the Revolution broke out, this elite held eleven of sixteen militia commissions and all eight royal appointments as sheriff, justice of the peace, and so on. The faction was stripped of these offices immediately because most selectmen were Whigs. Thus, much political power had already passed out of the elite's hands even before 1776. The group that became the Tory party had a majority of selectmen from 1750 to 1765, but from 1766 on Tories were in the minority. This was a consequence of the rise to local power of big farmers, who represented the new farmer majority. The Tories hung on for a time only because the provincial government allowed them to monopolize crown appointments. What the Revolution in Deerfield amounted to, then, was wrapping up a transfer of power that was already well advanced. This was doubtless the case else-

where in Massachusetts, where most towns supported the Revolution, especially after the Intolerable Acts of 1774 which abolished the elective jury and forbade town meetings except when authorized by the royal governor. The towns would not give up their traditional prerogatives without a fight or tolerate local officeholders with higher or more ambiguous loyalties. Elsewhere, Tories and Whigs divided along different lines. But Deerfield illustrates the general rule that the people who became Tories identified themselves or their interests with the empire while those who became Whigs had more homely concerns.

Deerfield also shows nicely how war restructured the upper class. Tories naturally paid a heavy price for their politics. Among the most wealthy, the proportion of loyalists declined sharply between 1772 and 1784. Interestingly enough, however, the Whigs lost ground too. Of eight Whigs who were among the twenty leading real property holders in 1772, seven declined in wealth, though only one among them died or moved. In 1784, twelve of the top twenty real property holders were Whig, but only three were carryovers from 1772. Personal property holdings tell the same story. The number of Whigs in the top twenty rose from nine in 1772 to eleven in 1784, but only five were on both lists (two having died or moved in the interim). Thus while the Whig party flourished on account of the war, the original Whig leadership suffered. Those who profited most were the *noveaux riches* who made money from the Revolution. This seems to have been true of other places. The struggle for independence destroyed many old elites, both Whig and Tory, while creating new ones. This doubtless came as a great shock to some Whig leaders. It took no great prescience to know that Tories would suffer from confiscations and loss of business. Those who replaced them would

Figure 4-1   Federal Hall, Wall Street, New York City. (*Wide World Photos*)

obviously gain. The war's other effects were harder to anticipate.

Congress issued paper money that declined rapidly in value, creating many opportunities for currency speculators and giving birth to the phrase "not worth a Continental [dollar]." The Navy was unimportant, but 20,000 men served in privateers that captured 2,000 British ships and cargoes worth $450 million in our money. Legalized piracy was a gold mine for those who financed and sailed these ships and for the traders who marketed their prizes. The merchants, frequently profiteers of the worst sort, who serviced the Continental Army did very well too. Even farmers, 90 percent of the population, prospered. The Army was a steady consumer of their surplus all through the war. Apart from Tories, only wage earners were really hurt by the struggle. Clerks, craftsmen, the clergy,

schoolteachers, and such were victimized by inflation. Wages rose, but not so rapidly as prices. The troops suffered most of all. Profiteering and Congressional and state ineptitude, not to say corruption, kept them short of food, clothing, and munitions throughout the war. Officers had to pay their own expenses. Officers and men alike were paid in Continental dollars and so suffered three ways: from a declining currency, rising prices, and fixed wages. Washington said rightly that "the long and great suffering of this army is unexampled in history."

As this suggests, the American Revolution was not a social revolution in which one class seizes power from another but a war of independence, a national liberation struggle, to use the modern term, aimed mainly at political autonomy. There was no real aristocracy to overthrow as in France, and most great landowners either led the rebellion or came to terms with it. But the war had profound effects all the same. Power changed hands in many places; so did wealth. The locus of power was brought home and imperial authority, a stabilizing, even conservatizing force, destroyed. This brought new men to the fore and democratized government in most places. The state constitutions usually provided for an upper house or senate, and those upper houses were more like the lower houses of the prewar era than the governors' councils they replaced. Democracy in this limited sense did not so much mean universal, white manhood suffrage, though it led to that, as it did having access to the decision-making process, now a much more localized, clearly defined phenomenon. With the Tories gone, innovation became easier, though at first it was infrequent. The war for independence was a great transforming experience psychologically more than anything else. So the country that emerged from it was different in many respects from the old colonies even though the distribution of wealth and power seems to have remained fairly constant.

The Constitution

Since their fight was waged, as they saw it, to destroy tyranny, public men in the postwar era were naturally most concerned with preventing its reappearance. This was the central political question of the time, and it was recognized as such by everyone, whether Federalist or Anti-Federalist. They differed mainly in the degree of power the central government ought to have and also over where threat to liberty originated. Those who joined the Federalists, the party of Washington and Hamilton, wanted less local autonomy and a stronger central government.

Partly this was to facilitate trade and partly to check democratizing tendencies (which they saw as the chief threat to liberty) that were thought to be strongest at the grass roots. Federalists tended to be merchants, professionals, and townsmen. They were especially strong on the seaboard which, after the war as before it, was the seat of power and wealth. Anti-Federalists, the party of Jefferson and Madison, feared centralized power more than they did local democracy. They were more concerned with preserving agriculture than with encouraging trade. They idealized farmers and distrusted towns and townsmen.

The result of these competing fears and ambitions was an ingenious compromise that worked because it secured, or conceded, the chief interests of both sides. Small states, where sentiment for confederation was strongest, were protected by equal representation in the upper house. Large states, where nationalists were concentrated, would dominate the lower house. The Chief Executive was given enough authority to satisfy most nationalists, and Congress was provided with enough checks on this authority to reassure confederationists. Slavery was protected in several ways so as to accommodate the South, which had the most coherent objectives of any region. Where agreement could not be reached, as over the admission of new states, the problem was postponed for later resolution by the new Congress.

The Constitution that emerged is more a patchwork quilt than a seamless web and owes more to practice than theory. Later generations have admired it extravagantly for such principles as the separation of powers and the checks and balances system. In fact, the apparatus leaves much to be desired. The separation of powers makes it hard for government to develop national programs. Congress has proved to be invincibly parochial.

The Executive's broader perspective does him little good at home because Congress has the power, frequently exercised, to block him. On the other hand, congressional power tends to stop at the water's edge. The President, so hamstrung on the national scene, is Commander in Chief of the Armed Forces and has broad authority over the conduct of foreign affairs. The result is a Congress that is obstructive at home and impotent abroad, and, conversely, a President with imperial power over foreign affairs by comparison with other popularly elected heads of state, but less influence domestically than the typical Prime Minister.

The best thing to be said about this system of government is that it works, which is saying a great deal. Since 1789 the world has seen many new states created. Few have managed to ensure representative government and protect the rights of minorities—much less those of critics of the administration—while providing for the orderly transfer of power. The American system has done this since the very beginning. As always, luck played its part. The country was fortunate to have as its first Chief Executive a man of great restraint who conferred his immense personal prestige on the new form of government without at the same time bending it excessively to serve his own personal and political interests. In modern times perhaps only Charles de Gaulle has resembled George Washington in bringing such rectitude and force of character to the problem of establishing constitutional government. Mainly, however, the American experiment succeeded because the federal system was solidly based on the realities of American life. Its architects were not revolutionaires, ideologues, or even intellectuals in many cases, though they were frequently well versed in political theory. They had all been influenced to a degree by the rhetoric and

sometimes high principle that accompanied the war for independence. But mostly they were bargainers, willing to trade off a point there for a point here. Since the key elements of American life were represented, however unequally, at the convention, what emerged was a settlement that reflected the facts of American life.

The states, like the colonies they succeeded, desired local autonomy above all things. Hence they agreed on the Federal system, which alone could accommodate the need for both strong local and strong central governments. This passion for local control survives even today and is, for better or worse, one of the chief legacies of the colonial era to our own times. Besides being parochial, American communities were also diverse. This made Federalism all the more desirable and ruled out a national policy on religion, education, and other matters. Religious freedom, ethnic toleration, and such principles were not adopted out of enthusiasm but from necessity. Americans, like most peoples, did not admire variety for its own sake. In the eighteenth century as now, most lived in homogenous communities among people who went to the same church and spoke the same language as themselves. But there were too many different churches and too many ethnic enclaves to decree uniformity, however much it may have been admired. Forty percent of the white population in 1790 was not English. America became a pluralistic society because the colonial experience made any other kind impossible. And, with a continent to fill up and proved techniques for coping with diversity at hand, there was little reason to restrict immigration and much to encourage it. Few thought heterogeneity desirable for its own sake. Americans did not then, as they would later, make a virtue of necessity by proclaim-

Figure 4-2 A camp meeting. (*The Bettmann Archive*)

ing the country to be a melting pot in which base alien metals contributed to a superior native alloy. But they knew that immigrants were essential, and on this basis formulated a generous immigration policy.

The colonial era made other contributions to the new nation: an Indian policy that combined theft with genocide for one, slavery for another. The treatment of women was a scandal, though it was seldom recognized as such except by women. They had few rights even over their own property. In some areas there were competing traditions, and it was not until the Federal period that it became clear which would prevail. Land disposition is a case in point. There were two main ways of allocating land. The Northern way was to encourage an orderly expansion based on small holdings. The Southern way was to open vast tracts for speculation. In the eighteenth century the concept of social planning

as exemplified by Puritans and Quakers declined. Independence, by removing the imperial perspective, removed also the last authority with continental vision, some degree of objectivity, and—if not a plan—at least the sense that one might be useful. This assured the triumph of speculation, as the Northwest Ordinance of 1787 demonstrated.

At first Congress thought to provide immediately self-government for settlers in the immense territory beyond the mountains. In 1784 it enacted Jefferson's plan, which had that effect. In 1785 it passed a Land Ordinance that attempted to impose order on the settlement process. The Northwest Territory was to be surveyed into ranges 6 miles wide. These were to be divided into townships 6 miles square, which would be subdivided into thirty-six sections of 640 acres each. The land would be sold at public auctions in the

East, where no unit smaller than a section would be sold. Bidding was to begin at a dollar an acre. This admirable plan collapsed almost at once. Few settlers could afford to pay $640. Squatters began trickling into the area. Congress desperately needed money, and when tempted by land speculators, it succumbed to them. The Land Ordinance was set aside and 6 1/2 million acres were sold to two private companies at a price that worked out to be 8 cents an acre in hard money.

The greed and resentment of the squatters, "licentious people" according to Congress, led to a fast reversal of the earlier policy and enactment of the Northwest Ordinance. It withdrew self-government from the territory, which became a kind of colonial empire. The settlers would be ruled by an appointed governor with an absolute veto over the territorial legislature until it had 60,000 people and was qualified for admission as a state. Suffrage was restricted to men who owned at least 50 acres. On the other hand, once admitted to the union, each new state (no less than three or more than five) in the Northwest would be equal to the older states. This meant that the public domain was made a protected hunting ground for land speculators, whose rights were guaranteed by appointed officials. But the ordinance also assured the settlers political liberties (a bill of rights was attached to it), prohibited slavery, guaranteed religious freedom, and promised the territories future equality with the other states of the union. It thus embodied the best and the worst features of the new American nation. The great continental empire that seemed in those days an inexhaustible resource was to be plundered rather than developed in terms of any public interest. On the other hand, its white male inhabitants would be free and equal, at least in theory and often in fact, to all other citizens.

Far more tragic was the new nation's attitude toward slavery. At first it seemed that the war for independence might end slavery along with British rule. Enlightened men were never entirely comfortable about slavery. The great if temporary emphasis on natural rights during the war could not easily be confined only to whites. Perhaps 5,000 blacks fought on the patriot side. Slavery was dying in the North anyway, so many states were inspired to abolish it. Pennsylvania led the way in 1780 by deciding that all slave children born after a certain date would be free on coming of age. This formula was widely copied. Southern states did not end slavery, but it was mitigated in many places. The requirements for manumission were changed so as to make freeing one's slave easier. When the first national antislavery convention met in Philadelphia in 1794, the delegates had reason to be optimistic, even though horse trading at the Constitutional Convention earlier had done the cause little good. Both slavery and the slave trade were protected. The South was allowed to count in three-fifths of its slave population in determining the number of representatives it sent to Congress. All the same, the tide of public sentiment seemed to be running against slavery everywhere.

Events soon disposed of the cheerful theory that slavery might come to an end. Humanitarianism was indeed on the rise. Laws were passed in some parts of the South making it a crime to murder a slave. There appeared to be a distinct improvement in the living conditions of slaves. This tended to undermine the argument against slavery. Slaves being better off, there was less reason to free them. The victorious struggle to end the slave trade had the same effect. The importing of slaves was constitutionally protected for only twenty years. When that time was up, Congress, prodded by President Jefferson, outlawed the slave trade. It was thought the worst part of slavery, and with its termination the pressure against slavery eased. At the same time there were positive reasons to retain slavery. Eli Whitney's cotton gin, as everyone knows, increased the demand for labor. The post-Revolutionary era was a time when property rights were viewed with a special enthusiasm, including, inevitably, the rights of slave owners. Slave uprisings made Southerners all the more eager to repress blacks. In 1800 an attempted rising was prevented in Virginia and some thirty to forty conspirators were hanged.

Later conspiracies were also frustrated, but they destroyed the Southern antislavery movement nonetheless. And they inspired the garrison-state psychology that would soon turn the region into a closed society. In 1806 Virginia sharply restricted the right of owners to manumit their slaves. This was, perhaps, the crucial event in the key Southern state as far as reversing the postwar libertarian trend went. Thereafter it was all downhill, in the North too. Freedom did not of itself solve the problems slavery had created. There was the matter of fitting ex-slaves for life as freemen. And there was the racism that went along with slavery. The North handled these matters to its satisfaction by imposing segregation. Such facilities as blacks would enjoy thereafter would be separate from white society's. Within broad limits it did not matter what blacks did as long as they did it by themselves.

Thus at the very beginning the basic patterns were laid down that would govern the nation's whole racial history: slavery in the South and—in the North at first but everywhere later—segregation. The treatment of black people was then and would continue to be the worst part of the American experience. The crimes committed against blacks were as terrible as those against Indians, and even

more consequential. They would lead to civil war and then to generations of racial strife that would belie the claims of national moral excellence and threaten the quality of American life for millions of whites as well as blacks. Jefferson spoke more truly than he knew when he said of slavery: "I tremble for my country when I reflect that God is just." Slavery and segregation seemed cheap and easy solutions at the time, but they proved costly in the end. A bill was run up then that subsequent generations would have to pay again and again and again.

Selected references

Jackson T. Main, *The Social Structure of Revolutionary America* (1965), is a careful and penetrating analysis. A spendid collection of essays showing how current scholars view the revolution together with a brilliant synthetic introduction by the editor is Jack P. Greene (ed.), *The Reinterpretation of the American Revolution, 1763–1789* (1968). It includes a thoughtful essay by Edmund S. Morgan entitled "The Puritan Ethic and the Coming of the American Revolution." On the redistribution of power locally in the Revolutionary period, see Bruce G. Merritt, "Loyalism and Social Conflict in Revolutionary Deerfield, Massachusetts," *Journal of American History* (September 1970). On the period between the Revolution and the writing of the Constitution see Merrill Jensen, *The New Nation* (1950). The Constitution has been the subject of intense debate, most of it provoked by the seminal Charles A. Beard, *An Economic Interpretation of the Constitution of the United States* (1913). For the opposite point of view see Forrest McDonald, *We the People: The Economic Origins of the Constitution* (1958).

FIVE

What It Takes to Form a More Perfect Union

Period covered: 1783–1800

Emphases: Diplomacy and politics

Major events: Ordinance of 1784

Shays' Rebellion, 1786

Ordinance of 1787

Constitutional Convention in Philadelphia, 1787

Inauguration of George Washington, 1789

French Revolution, 1789

Neutrality Proclamation, 1793

Whisky Rebellion, 1794

Jay Treaty, 1794

Alien and Sedition Acts, 1798

Virginia and Kentucky Resolutions, 1799

Convention of 1800 with France

Election of Thomas Jefferson, 1800

James Madison's notes on the proceedings of the 1787 Constitutional Convention contain the following famous passage:

Whilst the last members were signing, Dr. Franklin, looking toward the President's chair at the back of which a rising sun happened to be painted, observed to a few members near him that painters had found it difficult to distinguish in their art a rising from a setting sun. "I have," said he, "often and often in the course of the Session, and the vicissitudes of my hopes and fears as to its issue, looked at that behind the president without being able to tell whether it was rising or setting. But now at length I have the happiness to know that it is a rising and not a setting sun.

Franklin's great sigh of relief in discovering a rising sun on the back of George Washington's chair at the signing did not ease the fears of many present in that room. Of the forty-odd delegates to the Philadelphia convention which drafted the proposed Constitution of the United States, some were convinced that they had failed. Others believed that they would fail when the document was presented to the states for approval and ratification. The first group thought the Constitution unworkable as written; the second had doubts it would ever be accepted.

Outside the hall where the delegates had debated each provision and clause of the document, the people were almost evenly divided on the merits of the Constitution and its acceptability. The very process by which the document had been produced, a small closed caucus, raised fears of a new conspiracy to deprive Americans of their battle-won liberty. These fears had produced some strange notions inside the hall, too. The seemingly harmless provision for congres-sional control over the 10-mile-square area to be used for the national capital, for instance, led one opponent to charge that a huge fortress was being readied from which fifty or a hundred thousand men could sally forth to enslave the populace. George Mason of Virginia did not go quite so far, but he was concerned enough to ask for an amendment limiting Congress's power over the capital area.

The Anti-Federalists (a historical misnomer for opponents to the proposed Constitution) could not agree, however, on the best way to attack the plan or its proponents. Some wanted to take a stand against any change in the Articles of Confederation; others said they would be satisfied if certain amendments protecting individual liberties were added before ratification. With varying degrees of intensity the Anti-Federalists did believe that their cause was nothing less than a continuation of the fight they had already waged against Great Britain to free the colonies. That did not mean all Anti-Federalists were democrats or men of the people and all Federalists aristocrats and elitists at heart.

A prominent South Carolina conservative, who had fought for independence in the recent war, and who probably would have preferred an even stronger document wrote a friend that he planned to have his family seal traced back in England: "for as our steps toward monarchy are very obvious, I would wish my Children to have all the Rights to rank, & distinction, which is to be claimed from Ancestry. . . . We are getting back fast to the system we destroyed some years ago."

But which system did he mean? Reunion with the British Empire and crown, or the establishment of a similar form of government in the United States? His neighbor down the road might hold conservative views, too, but oppose the Constitution in order to protect local rule. There were even men who voted for ratification, and then prepared for the worst should the Constitution be accepted.

Common Sense revisited

The first shock had come even before the ink was dry on the Treaty of Paris ending the Revolutionary War. In the flush of victory the Americans had hoped to convert the world to republicanism by example. They were brought up short when European capitals made it plain that the American republic was not welcome in the family of civilized nations. Later revolutionaries in France and Russia would also feel themselves agents of an all-powerful destiny which would sweep aside whatever obstacles lay before them in building the new world. There were always practical men around, however, who convince their comrades to abandon ideology and prophecy to save essentials. But even practical men in the American Revolution had counted on one thing: that Europeans would see the wisdom, and the benefit for themselves, of opening their ports to American commerce. Paine's *Common Sense* was filled with ideology and prophecy, but his analysis of European wants and needs had seemed logical enough. And indeed Adam Smith's famous treatise on political economy, *The Wealth of Nations*, published in the same year as *Common Sense*, confirmed the eventual demise of mercantilism for much the same reason. But it did not confirm the timing or that the benefits automatically assumed in Paine's argument would result from such a change. In December 1783, Paine himself took a second look at the situation and concluded, "while we have no national system of commerce, the British will govern our trade by their own laws and proclamations as they

please." Liberty at home under the Articles of Confederation had depended, in the original formulation, on securing liberty abroad. Obviously some rethinking was needed.

One example of British ability to govern American trade was the decision to enforce the Navigation Acts strictly in the West Indies, thus denying a vital prewar trade to Americans except under conditions which effectively channeled it through English ports. The Continental Congress lacked the power to retaliate against European restrictions because, under the Articles of Confederation, each state regulated its own commerce. Some had adopted free trade; others were busy building local mercantilist systems. It is a mistake, therefore, to say that those who spoke out against the excesses of "liberty" permitted under the Articles were simply concerned with the behavior of individuals or the "democratic" mob which threatened property rights. They also deplored, perhaps even more, the excessive liberty allowed each state under the Articles. Of course these questions were not always separate matters, but it gave conservatives like John Adams little comfort to know that a state like Connecticut had avoided the worst evils of democracy. If the aristocracy of Connecticut ruled their state without regard to the fate of the nation, ultimately neither states nor individuals could be secure, let alone prosper.

Rufus King, Massachusetts's powerful conservative spokesman, took a somewhat different view. He foresaw a division of the country along sectional lines resulting from the Continental Congress's inability to enact or enforce national measures. Perhaps that would not be so bad. If the Southern states wanted none of a commercial country, he declared, then so be it. The Northern states had it in their power to become a great commercial nation on their own. They could retaliate against British regulations—and they could build ships for a merchant fleet and navy.

Revolutionary idealism was not enough, Thomas Jefferson soon discovered. Or perhaps it was that his idealism had deep roots in Virginia's tobacco plantation soil. Either way the result was the same. Jefferson had counted on a full commercial accord with France after the war to provide a much-needed outlet for the crop which sustained the Old Dominion's social system—as improved by Jefferson's Declaration of Independence. Denied such a market, the Virginia planters would inevitably fall under British domination once again. Sent to France as Franklin's successor in 1784, Jefferson set out to negotiate an advantageous commercial treaty. He was thwarted in part by the private efforts of individual American entrepreneurs, who arranged things for their own benefit with the French government. Although he won a few concessions, there was no reason for the French to deal with the representative of the United States when they could get better terms by playing off the representatives of the thirteen states against one another.

Finally, and with great disappointment, Jefferson admitted to his colleague John Adams, Ambassador to England, that his motive had changed. Now he wanted to get a treaty so as to bring "all our commerce under the jurisdiction of Congress. . . ." Adams needed no convincing. His mission to the Court of St. James's had been a most unhappy experience. George III had told him that of course England would let bygones be bygones—if America gave British commerce special preference. He could wait until doomsday, wrote the infuriated Adams to Jefferson. More than Jefferson, Adams was prepared intellectually and practically to go all the way: to tariffs, navigation acts, tonnage

acts, ship subsidies—to whatever was needed to enable the United States to "stand upon high ground." They both realized, however, that nothing approximating what was required could be achieved under the Articles of Confederation. Historian Jackson Turner Main has generalized this concern felt by Adams and Jefferson to "all parts of the country." "The commercial interest with its ramifications, including those who depended primarily and directly upon commerce, were Federal, and the 'non-navigating folk' were Antifederal." Yet there were certainly other forces at work within Adams and Jefferson and throughout the nation.

The western impetus

Jefferson received many communications from two fellow Virginians, James Madison and James Monroe, while he was Ambassador to France. Virginia had formally ceded her ancient claims to western lands to the Continental Congress in 1781. So had the other states. But Virginia maintained a vital interest in the development of the area up to and bordering on the Mississippi River. When the British proved slow to evacuate their forts still located within American territory, Virginians in the Continental Congress grew worried that their fellow delegates from other states might mishandle the independent-minded Westerners or even subvert their interests to those of Northern commerce. Tidewater Virginians no longer claimed formal territorial rights over the backwoods, but they felt that their interests were inextricably linked to the men who inhabited those areas.

Before leaving for Paris, Jefferson had authored the Ordinance of 1784, which provided for the admission, on very liberal terms, of new states carved out of Western lands. He had designed a balanced ordinance, assuring that Congress would retain broad powers "necessary for the preservation of peace & good order among the settlers" until the territories qualified by population and development for admission into the Confederation yet not so restrictive as to alienate the sensitive Westerners and drive them toward allegiance with other powers still located on the continent.

In 1786 a "rebellion" in western Massachusetts took place which cast doubt on the ability of state governments to control their own populations, let alone feel safe about the unorganized territories. Named for its leader Daniel Shays, a former captain in the Revolutionary army promoted for exceptional bravery at Bunker Hill, the rebellion was apparently sparked by the refusal of the state's legislature to respond to petitions demanding paper money, abolition of prison sentences for debt, tax relief, greater representation for Western towns, and sundry other grievances. An underlying cause, however, was the depression in the distilling industry brought on by the new British restrictions on rum imports into the West Indies.

Led by Captain Shays, the farmers took things into their own hands, forcibly preventing the courts from carrying out any more mortgage foreclosures and other judgments against debtors. The outraged Governor and his legislature recruited a cavalry regiment —largely from Harvard College—and sent it forth to carry out the law and arrest that brigand Daniel Shays. The revolt collapsed, but the episode, if not quite on the same order as the "Shot heard round the world," still sent a shiver through men in the thirteen states who had only recently fought for liberty—but liberty with order—from the British.

Madison and Monroe kept Jefferson fully up to date on these events—and on another matter that troubled Southerners even more. John Jay, the Secretary for Foreign Affairs, was attempting to negotiate a commercial agreement with Spain which would involve surrendering United States claims to navigate the lower Mississippi for some years to come. On January 30, 1787, Jefferson replied to both items. He was not much worried about what had taken place in western Massachusetts. "The tree of liberty," said the author of the Declaration of Independence, "must be refreshed from time to time with the blood of patriots & tyrants. It is its natural manure." Things looked different closer to the scene. As George Washington wrote to Madison, "We are fast verging on anarchy and confusion!"

But if Jefferson was benevolent toward Daniel Shays, he was a good deal less so about John Jay's negotiations. Such a treaty would, he complained, alienate our "subjects" in the lands bordering on the great river. It was essential to retain those people until their governments became settled and wise, and then "they will remain with us always, and be a precious part of our strength and our virtue." Southern opposition blocked Jay's treaty with Spain, but like Shays' Rebellion, the episode gave a powerful impetus to the movement for stronger control of the West—and a stronger central government in the original states. The next time a crisis arose threatening American control over the West, it might come as the result of Spanish or British maneuverings to win the favor and allegiance of disgruntled westerners.

Monroe, a bitter opponent of the abortive treaty and a firebrand for liberty, became the principal author of the Ordinance of 1787, which took as its model the British system of colonial administration and applied it to the Western territories. "It seemed necessary," wrote Richard Henry Lee, yet another Virginian, "for the security of property among uninformed and perhaps licentious people, as the greater part of those who go there are, that a strong toned government should exist, and the rights of property be clearly defined." Under the new ordinance the entire Northwest Territory was to be administered by a single governor, three judges, and a secretary. These and other officials including every officer above the rank of major in the local militias were to be appointed by Congress. When there were 60,000 inhabitants in any part of the territory designated as a provisional "state," it could petition Congress for full statehood in the Union. The Ordinance forbade slavery and guaranteed the inhabitants personal and religious freedom. The provision forbidding slavery was an advance for personal freedom, in one sense, but it certainly limited Westerners in another way by denying them the same advantages as Southerners. Stranger things were to come concerning that issue in the Constitution.

Both the Ordinance of 1784 and its successor measure of 1787 required a reconciliation of republicanism with imperialism. The first is sometimes called the "settlers' ordinance," the second the "speculator's ordinance." Quite clearly one motive behind the Ordinance of 1787 was to limit the West's ability to restrict Eastern money and men by local legislation. The authors of both these measures promised equality and statehood within the American system at the end of the apprenticeship period, but until then they were to enjoy fewer privileges of self-government than Britain had granted her colonies. The irony is doubled when one remembers that these measures were the handiwork not of Adams, King, or Hamilton but of Jefferson, Madison, and Monroe.

Jefferson's fear that the Jay negotiations would alienate the men of the Western waters and make them susceptible to the connivings and schemes of foreign powers was fully justified. There was a real danger of separation, as the following letter from a "gentleman at the falls of the Ohio, to his friend in New England" indicates:

In case we are not countenanced and succoured by the United States (if we need it) our allegiance will be thrown off, and some other power applied to. Great Britain stands ready with open arms to receive and support us. They have already offered to open their resources for our supplies. When once reunited to them, 'farewell, a long farewell to all your boasted greatness.' The province of Canada and the inhabitants of these waters, of themselves, in time, will be able to conquer you. You are as ignorant of this country as Great Britain was of America.

The letter, which was printed in the *Secret Journal of the Continental Congress*, confirmed everyone's fears about what might happen. The Ordinance of 1787 was not enough, not nearly enough to deal with the myriad problems emanating from the West. National unity and strength required a central government capable of resolving sectional tensions, state rivalries, and factional disputes.

The great compromises

Virginia's delegation arrived in Philadelphia in May 1787 with a proposal for an entirely new government. It was no use now, Madison insisted, to try to amend the Articles of Confederation. That would only make things worse. Virginia had taken the lead the previous fall by inviting the states to send delegates to Annapolis, Maryland, to consider "the trade of the United States." Representatives from only five states showed up in Annapolis, but it was enough to convince Congress to call a general convention to consider what must be done.

The essential features of Madison's plan were (1) a national legislature composed of a lower and an upper house (the latter elected by the former), both apportioned according to population; (2) a national executive and judiciary appointed by the legislature; and (3) binding oaths by the state governments to support the new Constitution. Whatever regulatory legislation was passed by the national government under its new powers would, therefore, become the law of the land.

The most famous compromise of the convention came when Virginia and the other big states agreed that the upper house, instead of being apportioned by population, would consist of two representatives elected by each state legislature. Madison accepted the change because he perceived that "the real difference of interests lay, not between the large and small, but between the northern and southern states." Madison's simple truth explains many other things about the Constitution and its seemingly paradoxical nature. After the first compromise, everything else fell into place. The North got through the convention a provision that navigation acts might be adopted by a simple majority of states; the South was guaranteed the right to continue the slave trade until 1808. The small states in the North received equal representation in the upper house; the large states of the South were allotted additional representatives in the lower house by a provision which counted three-fifths of the slaves for the purpose of apportioning legislators.

And so the first great revolution of the modern world ended with a Constitution for the new nation which not only sanctioned slavery but assured its continued power in the new government by increasing the representation of the slaveholders in Congress. What irony! For all their boasting about liberty and the rights of man, the Americans wrote a document which chained them to the past and the rule of man over man. Another irony: the Americans had put their cause before the opinions of mankind, their claim to freedom from the tyranny of the British Empire. Yet it was the British Empire which abolished the slave trade and slavery within its domains first, in 1833, and which did so without a war.

The Constitution thus denied 700,000 slaves liberty or any rights at all. By 1861 that number had grown to 4,000,000. But the native Indian population, which had resisted enslavement, fared even worse at Philadelphia. Slavery had given many delegates some difficult moments. They saw, if they did not act upon, the contradiction.

Men from all sections of the country struggled with their consciences over slavery, but when they went into the arena of the Constitutional Convention other forces were at work. Delegates from the upper South were ready to end the slave trade, but not slavery. The lower South demanded twenty years to catch up with Virginia, and claimed that their friends from neighboring states thought only of the price rise for home-bred slaves. The Indians were a different matter. The only thought given to the Indians at Philadelphia was how to find the most effective way to deal with them. Men from all sections of the country struggled with their consciences over slavery, yet gave hardly any concern to the Indians. And when they did, it was in terms of disposing of them as expeditiously as possible. George Washington, the presiding officer of the Philadelphia convention, had already given his views on the Indian question: "if a weak state with the Indians on its back and the Spaniards on its flank does not see the necessity of a General Government there must I think be wickedness or insanity in the way."

Neither were in the way at Philadelphia. Even with all the compromises, however, the delegates still feared that competing interest groups would tear the country apart, leaving each region to fend for itself in a world of European empires. They also feared class conflicts. Madison spoke to these points on several occasions during the debates, and again later in *Federalist No. 10*, the most famous in a series of papers authored by Hamilton, Jay, and Madison in defense of the Constitution.

The simple answer, argued Madison, was to enlarge the political sphere. Where had trouble occurred, he asked? In Rhode Island, the smallest of the states. There one class rode roughshod over every other. There a debtor-controlled legislature issued paper money and ruled that creditors and merchants must accept the stuff in payment for honest obligations. And there riots were even now occurring. At the mention of these dismal events in Rhode Island, the delegates would shudder and think: old Dan Shays' spirit was loose again, only this time his followers actually controlled a legislature.

"All civilized societies," continued Madison, were "divided into different sects, fashions, and interests, as they happened to consist of rich and poor, debtors and creditors, the landed, the manufacturing, the commercial interests, the inhabitants of this district or that district. . . . The only remedy is to enlarge the sphere, and thereby divide the community into so great a number of interests and parties, that a majority will not be likely to

have a common interest separate from that of the whole or of the minority."

Madison had set out to counter the Anti-Federalist argument for lodging most powers in the state governments. But if it was logical to enlarge the sphere by vesting powers in a central government, was it not just as logical to argue that the only protection from an overweening central authority lay in enlarging the sphere outward—beyond the original thirteen states—to ensure a continuing balance of federal interests and local rights? Madison apparently thought so, as did a succession of Presidents under the new Constitution.

Celebrations of this serious young Virginian's political genius reverberate throughout American history and its writing. Most recently Samuel Eliot Morison, the dean of American historians, has summed up the debates at the Constitutional Convention this way:

Enlarge the sphere, and balance the interests: has not American history proved Madison's wisdom? And has not the completely contrary communist theory, of recognizing no interests except those of the "workers" and the state, brought an end to personal liberty wherever put into effect? [1]

Is it enough to condemn the "communist theory"? Such judgments ought to be balanced by giving some thought to those on the other side of the enlarging sphere. How did things appear to the American Indians, who were pushed back ahead of the moving frontier, or to those who were dragged along in slavery until the Civil War? And one might want to ask, after considering these groups

[1] *The Oxford History of the American People,* Oxford University Press, New York, 1965, p. 307.

that were left out of the great compromise and consensus, how essential to the formation of a more perfect Union in 1787 was Madison's hypothesis? How essential would it be in ten years, or fifty, or one hundred?

Federalists and Republicans

Washington's election to the presidency may have been foreordained, but it was nevertheless regarded as essential by the Federalists. It would reassure the citizenry, especially those who might have been persuaded by the arguments of the Anti-Federalists, that the Constitution would establish a tyrannical power over the states. Above sectional interests and factional disputes, the Revolutionary War commander stood alone, the symbol of a united nation. In the future, after great upheavals and Constitutional crises, party leaders would seek out new war heroes to occupy the presidential chair while they established their rule. Following the Mexican War and the ensuing debate over the expansion of slave territory, the Whigs nominated generals. After the Civil War, the Republicans turned to Ulysses S. Grant. After World War II and Korea, it would be Dwight D. Eisenhower.

In the first experience with this technique, however, the problem of the succession was an immense one. Groups would form around the leadership of an individual or against the influence of a suspected enemy. So it was with Jefferson and Hamilton. Ironically, James Madison had urged Hamilton's appointment as Secretary of the Treasury. At the time, of course, their differences were concealed under the rubric of Federalist unity. Moreover, Alexander Hamilton's influence on President Washington was far less noticeable at the outset than that of either Madison or Jefferson.

Things began to change with Hamilton's report on the public credit. His proposal for converting the nation's debts into assets was classic in its simplicity and set an example for future new nations. Hamilton asked that government bonds be issued for all official obligations, domestic and foreign, national as well as state, and that these be exchanged at par value for certificates of indebtedness, in whatever form these might appear (no one was sure of the total), from fancily printed bonds of the Continental Congress to hastily scratched IOUs handed out by General Washington's quartermasters when requisitioning supplies.

At one stroke, Hamilton believed, America's creditors would be transformed into financial supporters of the new government. He was aware, even before Madison protested it in the House of Representatives, that the original holders of the debt had sold out to speculators, often for less than 10 cents on the dollar. All the better for his and—he still supposed—every Federalists purpose. By rewarding the speculators for their business acumen, Hamilton's plan would put large sums of capital into the hands of the very men best able to put it to good use. Every underdeveloped country confronts a serious problem of capital formation: how to pool small sums of money into holdings large enough to accomplish socially and economically worthwhile projects. Madison's counterproposal for funding the debt—partial payments to the speculators with the remainder going to the original holders—would defeat the very object Hamilton had had in mind in presenting the report on public credit.

Hamilton's plan was straight out of mercantilist theory, but Madison wondered if in this instance private vice was not being put too far ahead of public virtue. (The mercantilist theorem "Private vice converted into public virtue" suggested that selfish motives, properly harnassed, could be made to serve the public good.) It is worth noting, however, that variations on Hamilton's plan have been tried by later revolutionary governments, even by Cuba's Fidel Castro who, in 1959, unsuccessfully attempted to persuade American businessmen to accept Cuban government bonds in payment for expropriated properties. The circumstances in this latest instance were very different and the theory originated in a different conception of political economy, but the method was strikingly similar. The point is, of course, that undeveloped countries, capitalist or socialist, have many of the same problems.

And it is also true that differences over methods occur within a consensus of men who share essentially the same view of man and society. Thus Madison's opposition to Hamilton was not rooted in agrarianism or provincialism or, as the newest fad would have it, the "politics of paranoia," but in other concerns. Madison was the acknowledged leader of the Federalist bloc in the new House of Representatives. It was Madison who introduced tariff measures into the first session, and pressed for a tonnage act. And it was Madison who chastised his Southern colleagues for taking the short view on measures designed to improve America's economic bargaining power vis-a-vis other empires.

But the Hamilton credit plan seemed to him to have serious long-range consequences. In effect, it would open a double drain on Southern capital—first, because Virginia would be taxed to pay for state obligations of Northern states who had been lax in attending to their debts and, second, because money which might have gone to hard-pressed planters and yeomen was now earmarked for Northern speculators. Didn't

the South deserve better from a government it had invested its monies in during the late war? And didn't the South need the capital if it was to escape a permanent state of underdevelopment within the nation? Instead of strengthening national bonds, therefore, the Secretary of the Treasury's plan would reopen old disputes: poor against rich, land against city, North against South. This was not ranting, emotional agrarianism, but politics at the highest level.

Jefferson finally agreed to help obtain Southern votes for the plan in exchange for Hamilton's pledge to support the plan for placing the permanent national capital in a district between Virginia and Maryland. Jefferson regretted his bargain ever afterward. A few months later Hamilton submitted a second report on public credit; this time he asked for the creation of a nationally chartered bank. Madison and Jefferson argued against the bank as going beyond Constitutional limits on federal power. Hamilton replied simply that a government would be helpless if denied implied powers. Washington agreed and signed the bill. The President drew the line, however, when his Treasury Secretary proposed in his third report a system of federal subsidies and bounties to encourage the growth of manufactures. Congress took no action on this report so Washington was spared the necessity of vetoing the measures, though he had informed Hamilton of his position.

To pay for the debt funding, Hamilton proposed adding to the tariff various excise taxes. The most famous was the whisky tax, at 9 to 25 cents per gallon. The tax most affected those farmers who had learned to convert their bulky grain crops into highly concentrated liquid for easy shipment across the mountains. Another drain on agrarian interest groups to the benefit of the merchants and capitalists? When would it stop? "Now!" declared the farmers of western Pennsylvania, and they refused to pay the tax. The "Whisky Rebellion" of 1792–1794 came at a time when Washington felt the new government endangered from several directions. Hamilton favored using force at the first sign of resistance to the excise tax; he saw a show of arms as a positive good, the counterpart to his reports on public credit and finance. Moreover, he was convinced that Madison and Jefferson were, by opposing his plans, at least morally culpable for the situation and the spirit of subversion that he thought surrounded the new government, looking for any opening to destroy it.

The President resisted Hamilton's advice in 1792. If he called out the Army, said Washington, "there would be the cry at once, 'The cat is let out; We now see for what purpose an Army was raised.'" Force could only be the last resort. Washington had seen something in the situation which escaped the Secretary of the Treasury: What would happen if the Governor of Pennsylvania, an old political opponent, refused to respond to a call to mobilize his militia? It was essential to try peaceful means of negotiation before embarking on a military course. If there was to be a test of national against state power, let it come under the best of circumstances for the administration.

By midsummer of 1794 the rebellion had grown worse. Washington opened an executive conference on the crisis by stating that events around Pittsburgh struck "at the root of all law & order." Hamilton eagerly seconded the President, declaring that it was nothing less than a crisis over "whether the Government can maintain itself." Pennsylvania officials present at the meeting demurred; one contended that the use of military force would be worse than anything done so far by the

Figure 5-1 Republican theorist James Madison contested with Alexander Hamilton for intellectual leadership of the new nation. Their clash was politics on the highest level. (*Culver Pictures*)

Figure 5-2 The Whisky Rebellion provided the first real test of power for the new government. Washington approached the problem with great caution, acting only after he had assured himself of state support and only after it appeared the rebels might seek aid from foreign nations. (*New York Public Library*)

rioters. The conference ended without a final resolution, but Washington had agreed to try negotiations at least one more time.

Letters from his emissaries indicated that negotiations would bring no results and would only give the rebels the time they needed to tamper with the situation in Kentucky. Rumors also abounded in Philadelphia that the rebels were seeking an alliance with the English crown—as incredible as that might seem. The decision to mount a military expedition was made within twenty-four hours. Washington also decided, at Hamilton's urging, that he personally should lead the column, which, at 15,000, turned out to be a larger army than he had commanded in the war for independence.

The rebellion collapsed at the first sight of Washington's force as it came across the Allegheny Mountains, but the President could say with a good conscience that he had pursued a moderate course as long as possible. Overwhelming force had been necessary in this instance, he informed state governors, because "we had given no testimony to the world of being able or willing to support our government and laws."

Republicans against Federalists

Why was such testimony needed? The Whisky Rebellion, to begin with, was set against a background of turmoil in the Revolutionary

War and the sometimes boisterous political fight over ratification. During Shays' Rebellion, secondly, there had been concern over the lack of federal-state cooperation. Third, however incredible, evidence of a rebel desire to associate with the British was a real consideration, raising as it did that persistent specter of disunion and separation. But the President had something else on his mind; he was sure that the Whisky Rebellion constituted the "first formidable fruit of the Democratic Societies," those political "clubs" which had sprung up in the wake of Citizen Edmond Genet's famous 1793 tour of America in search of sympathy and support for revolutionary France.

Washington devoted the largest part of his Sixth Annual Address to Congress to a report on the campaign against the insurrection stirred up by these "self-created societies" which had reached out for "an ascendency over the will of others by the guidance of their passions. . . ." Fear that the wave of terror which had swept across France in the summer of 1793—the burning and pillage and looting, yes, and murder, too—was now coming to America, though the Democratic-Republican societies thrived on reports of the trouble in the Pennsylvania backwoods. The notion that these societies had descended from the old Sons of Liberty did not reassure Washington.

The French Revolution began in 1789. It was a major issue in American politics from the start. Jefferson, every schoolboy knows, rejoiced at the news—not because he was romantically pro-French (a particularly unfortunate piece of historical mythology perpetuated by people who should know better) but because he had always believed that the success of the American Revolution depended upon the expansion of republicanism. At least the success of the Revolution as he conceived of it in the Declaration of Independence, and Tom Paine imagined in *Common Sense*, depended on it. Something else was happening in America now, something that was not quite right. In the 1780s he had been persuaded, with great reluctance, to the position that a new Constitution and an American mercantilist system were probably necessary in a world of empires.

But with France in revolt against monarchy (and mercantilism?), the spirit of the American Revolution could be reclaimed from Alexander Hamilton and his dark minions who had persuaded the once virtuous Washington to go along with their plans. There was good reason to help that the future would permit the *original* American Revolution to succeed. Madison did not share all of these views or draw the same conclusions for the future of the American political economy. But they were close enough on who the enemy and what must be done.

Paine meanwhile had relocated himself in France, apparently hoping to repeat his American achievement in a new pamphlet, *The Age of Reason*. But in America the Age of Reason had seemingly become the Age of Obsession. Things reached a low point when England and France went to war in 1793. Despite Secretary of State Jefferson's objections, Washington immediately issued a neutrality proclamation on April 22, 1793. Jefferson had felt that by delaying such a proclamation, one side or the other or perhaps both might be forced into concessions to American points of view. Ever alert to the possibility of securing political liberties through economic expansion, the Secretary of State simply refused to give up. His persistence matched Hamilton's.

Washington resisted Jefferson's advice for the same reason he had refused to accept Hamilton's counsel of immediate force against the Whisky rebels. Jefferson's policy would have risked war abroad and political disaster at home. As it was, and was expected, both sides carried out attacks against American shipping. In a last effort to change the course of American foreign and domestic policy, Jefferson, just before he retired to Monticello, sent Congress his *Report on the Privileges and Restrictions on the Commerce of the United States in Foreign Countries.* In brief, the report called for discriminatory duties against British ships and merchandise— the British being the more guilty of the warring parties. It envisioned the creation of an American mercantilist system oriented, for the time being at least, toward France.

Madison, perhaps even more than Jefferson, had become obsessed with the belief that the only way to establish American independence was to break the "unnatural" monopoly held by Great Britain over the nation's foreign trade. Almost everything that he thought had gone wrong since 1787 could be attributed to that one cause—and, of course, Hamilton's unswerving diligence in perfecting an economic system which put the nation in the hands of pro-British merchants and financial speculators. With this concern foremost in his mind, Madison introduced a series of resolutions designed to put the report into effect on the floor of the House of Representatives early in 1794.

The ensuing debate, like those on Hamilton's fiscal reports, would be repeated in twentieth-century revolutionary societies. Madison argued for restrictions on economic relations with Great Britain even though, as he admitted, the short-run cost of going it alone would be high, especially for the South, until Northern manufacturers could provide a satisfactory outlet for the region's raw materials. Hamilton's friends replied that Great Britain was the only source of capital to develop the new country. Yes, but if we relied on foreign capital, countered an ally of Madison's, would not that turn over all the choices to the nation supplying the money? It could, and undoubtedly would, select industries and areas to invest in regardless of what actual needs the United States felt were most pressing. It would not be easy, either way, for the United States or for later undeveloped countries.

Jefferson's report received support from those disaffected by the Treasury's excise taxes and from other Westerners who were angered by the continuing presence of 6,000 British soldiers in what was supposed to be American territory. Washington was upset, too, by the redcoats in the wilderness. So long as they remained, the nation's sovereignty was yet to be finally achieved. The possession of the forts occupied by these troops gave the British control of the fur trade, encouraged Indian tribes to resist the authority of the United States, and even (if things developed differently) encouraged dissidents to seek aid from a foreign country. All in all, a bad situation.

A bill providing for nonintercourse with Great Britain actually passed the House of Representatives in April 1794 and was defeated in the Senate only by the tie-breaking vote of Vice President John Adams. Party lines had been drawn. Those who followed the Federalist lead set by Hamilton opposed those who rallied to a Republican standard raised by Madison. Washington forestalled a showdown by appointing John Jay Minister Plenipotentiary to Great Britain with instructions to negotiate a comprehensive treaty.

The damnation of John Jay

It was not an enviable assignment under the best of circumstances, especially not for a man suspected in the South and the West of being willing to sell out their interests in negotiations with Spain. Whatever leverage Jay might have had in London, moreover, was reduced by Hamilton's private assurances to the British Ambassador that President Washington would never join European neutrals in a policy of arming merchant vessels to resist British high-handedness on the open seas.

Jay returned with a treaty, nevertheless, which only set off a new round of Republican outbursts. Damn John Jay, went the refrain. Damn him most of all for coming home with a treaty good enough to win acceptance in the Federalist-controlled Senate and bad enough to humiliate patriotic Americans. Washington deliberated for some time before sending the treaty to the Senate for ratification. The Senators struck out one article dealing with commercial access to the West Indies considered by everyone as simply too insulting, then ratified the pact by a vote of 20 to 10, the exact two-thirds total required. Madison made a last effort to force the issue back into the more friendly House of Representatives by insisting that the economic provisions could not be carried out without the lower house's approval. The strategy failed and the treaty came into force.

The choice, President Washington had finally concluded, lay between the treaty and war. Indeed, the damnation of John Jay and anti-British riots in Boston made him all the more sure of his proper course. On many points the Jay Treaty was vague; others were left to be settled sometime in the future by a joint commission. Yet some provisions marked significant progress for the new nation in its diplomatic encounters with the outside world. The British did agree, for example, to evacuate Northwest posts by 1796. The Jay Treaty also provided early evidence that the new Constitution at least made it possible to deal with foreign policy problems in a reasonably orderly manner. Finally, the treaty with England was made more palatable by the successful negotiation of a second treaty, the Pinckney Treaty with Spain, which provided that the United States might freely navigate the Mississippi and enjoy the right of deposit in warehouses located in New Orleans.

Trial by succession

John Adams, elected President in 1796 knew what was in store for him; he also knew that he lacked the temperament to bear up under the strain like Washington, who had kept the lid on by the force of his personality. Lacking the first President's prestige, Adams faced four years of unremitting criticism, much of it from disappointed Federalists who felt he was not tough enough on the disloyal Republicans. The latter, of course, accused Adams of harboring a secret desire for war with France.

During the first sessions of the Senate in 1789, Adams had sought to give the presidential office an honorific title, such as "His Elective Majesty" or something equally suitable to buttress the new government in the eyes of the people. For his efforts in this debate, opponents awarded Adams, then Vice President, the title "His Rotundity." Their amusement at Adams' infatuation with titles and symbols was replaced by whispers of suspicion once he occupied the President's chair.

Relations with France had grown steadily worse since the Jay Treaty, and Adams inherited a situation almost equal in every way to that Washington had confronted a few years earlier in Anglo-American relations. Incensed by the Jay Treaty, the new French government insisted that America had forsaken its obligations under the old 1778 treaty with Louis XVI.

Figure 5-3 John Adams, successor to George Washington, lacked the first President's prestige. Yet he managed to steer the nation through four stormy years without a war—or an internal revolt. Hated by both high Federalists and Republicans, Adams proved that the government could survive the ordeal by succession. (*Courtesy of the Harvard University Portrait Collection*)

With characteristic concern for the finer points, Hamilton had dismissed such a charge by pointing out that Louis XVI no longer had his head and the French Revolutionary government no longer had its wits if it assumed that obligations owed to the former government still held.

That didn't help Adams, who set out to repair his diplomatic fences with France by sending a three-man commission to Paris. They were met by three go-betweens who said they represented the Foreign Minister. If the Americans really wanted to reestablish good relations with France, said the mysterious threesome known only as X, Y, and Z, it would cost $240,000 cold cash and the promise of a large loan. Hence the name of this strange encounter: the XYZ Affair.

It may have been intended as a lesson in manners: one did not play around with solemn obligations. But Adams called it bribery and put the country on a war footing. His practical wife, Abagail, stocked the Presidential mansion with sufficient supplies of staples to last through any seige period. In Congress, Federalist Senators and Representatives responded to the President's requests by authorizing the purchase or construction of twenty-four warships. Without waiting for Adams, the legislators also ordered the immediate enlistment of a 10,000-man Army and set long range goals for a 50,000-man force. Who would command this huge army? There was no one the nation trusted, it seemed, except Washington. The old general agreed to serve, but only if Alexander Hamilton was named second-in-command.

Naval engagements were fought on the high seas, but neither side wanted to call it a war. Rumors of a suspected French invasion soon disappeared. The Republicans asserted that the war threat had been trumped up to cover far more sinister purposes. Hamilton's appointment confirmed their suspicions: the real reason for creating a standing army was to suppress domestic opposition. They were, in fact, partly right. In accepting Adams' commission to command the army, Washington had written the Secretary of the Army in capital letters: "THERE CAN BE NO DOUBT OF THEIR ARMING OUR NEGROES AGAINST US. "THEIR" referred to the French, but also to supposed sympathizers in America. Thus Benjamin Stoddert, another Virginian and Secretary of the Navy, wrote: "I believe a small army to be kept together to awe the Jacobins and to keep up appearances to France a very proper thing." *Jacobins* had become a general term, used like *Communists* in the 1950s, to describe anyone suspected of heretical views.

With the army bills, moreover, came a spate of emergency legislation affecting civil liberties. The Naturalization Act of 1798 increased from five to fourteen years the time required before an emigrant could apply for citizenship. This was followed by the Alien Act, which authorized the President to expel any foreigner suspected of "treasonable or secret" intentions toward the government. Most encompassing of all was the Sedition Act of July 1798, which made it a high misdemeanor for anyone, citizen or alien, to oppose the execution of laws or to plot an "insurrection, riot, unlawful assembly, or combination." But that was not all. The act also provided for the punishment of anyone convicted of publishing "any false, scandalous and malicious writing" discrediting the President, Congress, or the federal government.

The Republicans usually gave as good as they took, though of course they lacked the backing of federal power. And if the Federalists were preoccupied with running to ground the Jacobins in their midst, some Republicans, at least, did seem willing to accept French aid in a second war for independence against the Federalist tyranny. Jefferson's friend Henry St. George Tucker was heard to declare that if the French ever landed an invasion force it would be joined at once by 100,000 Americans. He might be among them, he told his startled listeners. Would you fight with the French against your own country, he was asked? No, but he would join the French to fight *for* his country, replied Tucker.

The Virginia and Kentucky Resolutions

Believing the crisis of the new republic imminent, Jefferson and Madison rushed to the ideological barricades with the Virginia and Kentucky Resolutions. Madison wrote in the first, introduced in his native state's assembly on December 24, 1798:

A spirit has in sundry instances been manifested by the Federal Government to enlarge its powers by forced constructions of the constitutional charter which defines them; and to . . . consolidate the states, by degrees, into one sovereignty, the obvious tendency and inevitable consequence of which would be to transform the present republican system of the United States into an absolute, or, at best, a mixed monarchy.

The Kentucky Resolution of February 22, 1799, declared that nullification "of all unauthorized acts" was the "rightful remedy" for state government desiring to halt the spread of despotism.

Things cooled off when Adams, despite the protests of a group of Federalists more loyal to Hamilton (and his conception of Federalism) than to the President, sent a new mission to France. He had received hints from a variety of sources that the governing Directory in Paris desired better relations with the United States. This proved to be the case, and the Convention of 1800 brought to an end the quasi-war. It also replaced the Alliance of 1778 with a generalized statement which, in effect, canceled America's first political commitment to a European power. There were to be no others for 150 years.

Adams' decision to deal with France was prompted by something besides hints from Paris. He, too, feared what Hamilton might do with a standing army. Enlistments for the 50,000-man force never reached more than a third of the total authorized; nevertheless, Hamilton's influence (even within his own cabinet) was something to be reckoned with, all the more because it could not always be pinpointed. If the potential was there, that was enough. At the height of the crisis with France, several Federalists suggested to Adams that the United States seek a formal military alliance with Great Britain. The President put them on the defensive with the reply that the revolutionary fever might spread to England, in which case "a wild democracy will probably prevail for as long a time as it did in France." Would not the danger of that "delirium" infecting America "be increased in proportion to the intimacy of our connections with that nation?"

The President sensed Hamilton's influence also in the reports that came to him of intrigues for allying the army with a British plan to "liberate" Spain's colonies in America. Deceitful and untrustworthy as they were, the French might be easier to deal with than this pernicious influence within his own party.

Opposed by the so-called "high" Federalists and the Republicans, Adams was defeated for reelection in 1800. The mantle fell to the sage of Monticello: but the "Revolution of 1800," as Jefferson's supporters liked to think of it, proved instead that the succession problem could be handled not only from Washington to Adams but from Federalist to Republican.

In a private letter, Jefferson wrote: The late chapter of our history furnishes a lesson to man perfectly new.

It furnishes a new proof of the falsehood of Montesquieu's doctrine, that a republic can be preserved only in a small territory. The reverse is the truth. Had our territory been even a third only of what it is, we were gone. But while frenzy and delusion like an epidemic, gained certain parts, the residue remained sound and untouched, and held on till their brethren could recover from the temporary delusion; and that circumstance has given me great comfort.

Sooner than he expected, Jefferson would have to deal with these assumptions and their implications in his own Presidency.

Selected references

The great controversy over the making of the Constitution goes on among historians. Charles A. Beard started it with his *An Economic Interpretation of the Constitution* (1913), which won him eternal condemnation in some quarters. His critics have taken apart his methodology, piece by piece, but have not themselves established a successful anti-economic interpretation. Beard's second book on the era, *Economic Origins of Jeffersonian Democracy* (1915), is in some ways even more suggestive than his flawed work on the history of the Constitution. The anti-Beardians include R. E. Brown, *Charles A. Beard and the Constitution* (1956), and Forrest MacDonald, *We the People* (1958). The Anti-Federalists have received their due in Jackson Turner Main, *The Antifederalists* (1961), a book used extensively in this chapter. Samuel Flagg Bemis has written the most comprehensive account, *Jay's Treaty: A Study in Commerce and Diplomacy*, and Arthur P. Whitaker's *The Mississippi Question, 1795–1803* (1934) remains indispensable.

Long neglected for more glamorous subjects, the Ordinances of 1784 and 1787 are explored by Jack Ericson Eblen in *The First and Second United States Empires* (1968). Joseph Charles, *The Origins of the American Party System* (1956), was one of the first efforts to integrate closely the conduct of foreign affairs into the origins of the political parties. Also important to this chapter was Felix Gilbert, *The Beginnings of American Foreign Policy* (1961). John C. Miller's *Alexander Hamilton: Portrait in Paradox* (1959) and Nathan Schachner's *Thomas Jefferson* (1951) have always repaid my repeated visits to their pages. Richard Kohn's article, "The Washington Administration's Decision to Crush the Whiskey Rebellion," in the December 1972, *Journal of American History,* was a key source and inspiration.

SIX

The First Republican Era

Period covered:	1800–1828
Emphases:	Diplomacy and politics
Major events:	Louisiana Purchase, 1803
	Chesapeake-Leopard Incident, 1807
	The Embargo Act of 1807
	Nonintercourse Act, 1809
	Macon's Bill No. 2, 1810
	Declaration of War of 1812
	Peace of Ghent, 1814
	Transcontinental Treaty with Spain, 1819
	Panic of 1819
	Missouri debate, 1819–1821
	Monroe Doctrine, 1823

Figure 6-1 The sage of Monticello. Jefferson was the first President to occupy the White House. From that perspective it was no longer so easy to tell where Republicanism ended and disloyalty began. The "Burr Affair" was a perfect example. (*Independence National Historical Park Collection, Philadelphia, Pa.*)

Jefferson's new-found peace of mind was short lived. Rumors that Spain had sold Louisiana to France reached the new national capital within weeks of Jefferson's inauguration. He was still trying to fathom Napoleon's intentions when news came of the Spanish governor's decision to withdraw transit and storage privileges granted to American exporters who used the port of New Orleans. Without the opportunity to store produce in New Orleans at the mouth of the Mississippi River, the value of the 1795 treaty with Spain guaranteeing equal navigation rights diminished to almost nothing.

If Spain and France thus cooperated to close off the West's principal outlet to the world, the bright dawn of Republican rule would become a very long and very dismal season of discontent. Only this time the Republicans, not the Federalists; would find themselves blamed for the situation: and not Adams but Jefferson would be cast in the role of oppressor. The President was extremely sensitive to all these concerns and had been ever since his days in Paris. He was almost claustrophobic about any threat to American expansion, aside from practical problems connected with Western support for the Republican party. Madison had reasoned out the case for expansion in *Federalist No. 10* but Jefferson felt the need from his innermost being. In September 1793, Jefferson, then Secretary of State, had sent a long protest to the British Foreign Minister condemning interference with neutral trade, but the thoughts that went into that note reflected a lifetime concern:

We see then a practice begun, to which no time, no circumstances, prescribe any limits; and which strikes at the root of our agriculture—that branch of industry which gives food, clothing, and comfort to the great mass of the inhabitants of these States. If any nation whatever has a right to shut up to our produce all the ports of the earth, except her own, and those of her friends, she may shut up these also, and so confine us within our own limits. No nation can subscribe to such preten- sions—no nation can agree, at the mere will or interest of another, to have its peaceable industry suspended, and its citizens reduced to idleness and want. The loss of our produce, if destined for foreign markets, or that loss which would result from an arbitrary restraint of our markets, is a tax too serious for us to acquiesce in.

Eight years later, in 1801, Jefferson faced an equally ominous situation. Although the Federalists were badly divided, that split did not threaten the nation's unity. If the Republi- cans could not hold together and eventually absorb discontented factions, the future of the nation was bleak indeed.

A noble bargain

Spain's ability to promote disaffection among the Westerners was presumed to be, over the long run, virtually nonexistent. But a Span- ish Governor's order shutting down New Or- leans warehouses to Americans—followed by French occupation of Louisiana—that was quite a different matter. "What can we do to prevent it?" Jefferson asked the Cabinet. There were not many suggestions, so the President answered the question himself. We could offer to purchase New Orleans and Florida. But if the French refused to sell the city? The day that Napoleon took possession of New Orleans, Jefferson declared, from that very moment, "we must marry ourselves to the British fleet and nation." Then, at the sound of the first cannon in Europe, the United States would fall upon Louisiana, "tearing up any

settlement she [France] may have made. . . ."

What a turnabout! The dimensions of this first crisis in the Republican era can be measured by the President's willingness to consider a military alliance with Great Britain against France. Adams had never gone so far—except in Jefferson's imagination. The first thing to do, however, was to see if France would sell New Orleans. If Napoleon was not himself dreaming of a new French empire in North America, he should be willing to listen to a reasonable offer.

Secretary of State James Madison asked himself why, if empire were not the reason, had France sought to regain Louisiana? And he answered:

1st, A jealousy of the Atlantic States as lean- ing to a coalition with Great Britain, not con- sistent with neutrality and amity towards France, and a belief that, by holding the key to the commerce of the Mississippi, she will be able to command the interests and attach- ments of the Western portion of the United States; and thereby either control the Atlantic portion also; or, if that cannot be done, to seduce the former into a separate Govern- ment, and a close alliance with herself.

The first possibility was easily dealt with: the United States could simply reassure the French that it had no desire to ally itself to Great Britain. The second possibility gave the Republicans somewhat more concern. Madi- son was determined to deal with it in his own way; that is, he would convince the French by sheer logic of the folly of expecting support for their imperial schemes from the back- woodsmen. "Our western fellow-citizens," he instructed the negotiators sent to purchase New Orleans, were "bound to the Union, not only by the ties of kindred and affection" but through self-interest. They realized, even if the French did not, that a separate nation in the American hinterland would have to pay double for essential imports which could only reach them through the Atlantic states. At present, moreover, the West shared in all revenues collected by the Treasury. The Westerners would forfeit those benefits, and pay a second tariff to boot, as an independent nation.

Suppose, on the other hand, this new "nation" aligned itself politically with France, continued Madison. "A connection of the Western people as a separate State with France implies a connection between the Atlantic States and Great Britain. It is found," Madison wound up the argument,

from long experience, that France and Great Britain are nearly half the time at war. The case would be the same with their allies. During nearly one half the time, therefore, the trade of the Western country from the Mississippi, would have no protection but that of France, and would suffer all the interruptions which nations having command of the sea, could inflict on it.

Madison's long soliloquy on the dynamics of centrifugal and centripetal force on the North American continent established again that he was the most profound thinker among the Founding Fathers. He was also the most sophisticated in employing what might be called wish-fulfillment logic. It is interesting to speculate on what might have happened had France persisted in refusing American offers for New Orleans. Luck, not Madison's logic, changed the French position. Napoleon had indeed been dreaming of a North American empire. His vision was not really different from Jefferson's. He imagined an empire fed from the rich granary west of the

Mississippi and centered on New Orleans. This all came to naught when his expeditionary army failed to suppress an independence movement and slave revolt in Haiti. The French army not only failed to defeat the blacks led by Toussaint L'Overture but was nearly destroyed by an epidemic of yellow fever.

Needing money for a new war with Great Britain, Napoleon offered to sell the whole territory of Louisiana for $15 million. The American negotiators were stunned, but they quickly recovered their composure and completed the transaction. On May 20, 1803, the purchasers called on the French Foreign Minister to straighten out a few last details—among them the boundaries of Louisiana. Talleyrand replied, "I can give you no direction; you have made a noble bargain for yourselves, and I suppose you will make the most of it."

Great expectations

A land without boundaries. Well, perhaps not quite. Yet it almost seemed so to men who had lived through those tense months. Jefferson was exhilarated. Republican prospects had literally doubled overnight. A few Federalist cynics pointed out that the President's ideas on the Constitution had undergone a remarkable transformation since the days of the great debate over Hamilton's reports on finance and commerce. Where did the Constitution say that the President could buy an empire just because the price was right? What Hamilton had proposed was small by comparison. Jefferson had stretched the Constitution to reach across the Mississippi. Had he also changed the nature of the American government?

It was not an idle question. Republican

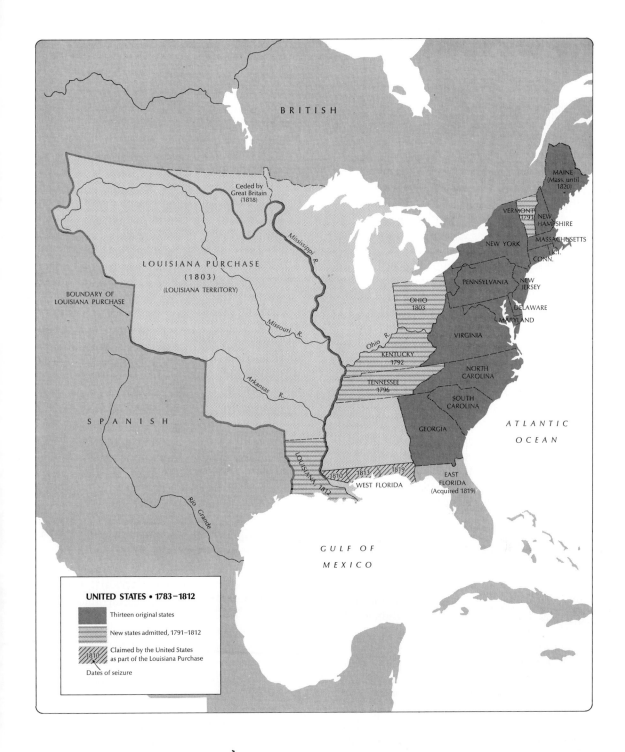

BRITISH

Ceded by
Great Britain
(1818)

Mississippi R.

LOUISIANA PURCHASE
(1803)
(LOUISIANA TERRITORY)

BOUNDARY OF
LOUISIANA PURCHASE

Missouri R.

Arkansas R.

Ohio R.

OHIO
1803

KENTUCKY
1792

TENNESSEE
1796

MAINE
(Mass. until
1820)

VERMONT
(1791)

NEW
HAMPSHIRE

NEW YORK

MASSACHUSETTS
R.I.
CONN.

PENNSYLVANIA

NEW
JERSEY

DELAWARE

MARYLAND

VIRGINIA

NORTH
CAROLINA

SOUTH
CAROLINA

GEORGIA

ATLANTIC
OCEAN

SPANISH

Rio Grande

LOUISIANA 1812

1810
WEST FLORIDA

1813

1819

EAST
FLORIDA
(Acquired 1819)

GULF OF
MEXICO

UNITED STATES · 1783–1812

Thirteen original states

New states admitted, 1791–1812

1810
Claimed by the United States
as part of the Louisiana Purchase

Dates of seizure

(*From* A History of the American People *by* Graebner, Fite, *and* White. Copyright ©
1970 *by* McGraw-Hill, Inc. *Used with permission of* McGraw-Hill Book Company)

purists felt uneasy about the President's determination to direct the civil, judicial, and military government of the territory himself until Congress had made specific provisions for its governance. Such scruples were brushed aside in the final debate on the treaty. Jefferson received broad authority to act on his own to ensure the inhabitants of Louisiana "full enjoyment of their liberty, property, and religion."

But Louisiana was not granted immediate statehood. Jefferson wanted to bring the territory into the Union in good time. "But above that," he went on in a private communication,

the best use we can make of the country for some time, will be to give establishments in it to the Indians on the east side of the Mississippi, in exchange for their present country, and open land-offices in the last, and thus make this acquisition the means of filling up the eastern side, instead of drawing off its population. When we shall be full on this side, we may lay off a range of States on the western bank from the head to the mouth, and so, range after range, advancing compactly as we multiply.

The Indians, of all people, would thus provide the control mechanism needed to make *Federalist No. 10* work properly, eliminating these periodic Western crises. They could be moved about at the whim of the Republicans, filling a gap here or holding the line there until the Americans were ready to lay off the next range of states. The Louisiana Purchase thus encouraged Jefferson's successors to follow his lead and resolve political and social questions by the simple process of laying off yet another range of states. It also provided the basis for the myth that both America and American power were limitless. These were essential ingredients in

what would come to be called Manifest Destiny in the 1840s and 1850s.

One could, and Jefferson did, look forward to the time when Cuba would "add itself to our confederation." Possibly Mexico would too. America's boundaries even extended into the ocean. "We begin to broach the idea that we consider the whole gulph [sic] stream as our waters," he wrote to his Secretary of the Navy, "in which hostilities and cruising are to be frowned on for the present, and prohibited so soon as either consent or force will permit us." If he were to revise his famous *Notes on Virginia,* published during the American Revolution, Jefferson commented in 1805, he would amend the sections on the dangers that cities posed to the safety of the country. "I had under my eye, when writing, the manufacturers [Jefferson means laborers engaged in manufacturing here] of the great cities in the old countries." In the America of 1805, doubled by the acquisition of Louisiana, "our manufacturers are as much at their ease, as independent and moral as our agricultural inhabitants, and they will continue so as long as there are vacant lands for them to resort to; because whenever it shall be attempted by the other classes to reduce them to the minimum of substance, they will quit their trades and go to laboring the earth."

Jefferson also moderated his position against Hamiltonian proposals for aiding commercial enterprise. In his second inaugural address, the President asked Congress to amend the Constitution to permit using the surplus revenue for "rivers, canals, roads, arts, manufactures, education and other great objects within each state." His Secretary of the Treasury, Albert Gallatin, once suspected as a Whisky Rebellion leader, proposed what some historians have called an American Five-Year Plan to accomplish a national system of internal improvements. A New York Republican, Robert Livingston, sponsored and encouraged Robert Fulton to develop the steamboat for American rivers, which did so much to spread the market economy through the West.

Jefferson and his fellow Republicans pinned many hopes on an orderly development of the West, yet, like the Federalists, they remained, deep down, ambiguous about the frontier. When historian Frederick Jackson Turner wrote his famous treatise entitled *The Significance of the Frontier in American History* in the 1890s, he posited a "safety valve" theory of the frontier. Turner's critics argued that the theory never worked that way, that people went to the cities, not the frontier, in times of economic distress. No one, however, has successfully disputed his contention that American leaders from Franklin and Jefferson on *thought* the theory valid, and *acted* upon that premise. There is an additional question, however, about the "safety valve" theory: both Federalists and Republicans were determined (as were their successors later in the century) not to lose control. They would decide when to turn it on and when to turn it off. Not always successful in this endeavor, Eastern political leaders succeeded often enough to draw a steady fire from Western settlers, which, in turn, only reenforced their determination to keep a firm grip on the "safety valve," lest it explode the price structure through skyrocketing wages or destroy the two-party political container of American democracy.

It was an especially delicate task for the Republicans, the first opposition party, because they numbered as supporters men who had opposed the Constitution and were leery of all central government. An astute Federalist newspaper observed:

There are among the leaders of the democrats [Republicans], many men who have sense enough to know that the principles they advance, in opposition to federalism, tend to the subversion of order and the destruction of society. They sin against light, knowingly and willfully.—But as there is no other way of putting down federalism and putting themselves up, they ostensibly unite with the real jacobins, and make with them a common cause. When they succeed, they well know that adherence to their declared opinions would ruin society and whelm themselves in the general destruction. Hence they are disposed to attempt some restraint, upon the very vice and passions they have cherished. They begin to adopt many of the salutary maxims of the federalists, but the floodgates they have opened are not easily shut. They find their pupils in violence and insubordination unmaneable, and are in turn denounced by them as tyrants, aristocrats and oppressors.

The article was concerned with the rise of third-partyism in states which had gone Republican in recent elections, but it might well have been describing the "Burr Conspiracy," which occupied so much of Jefferson's attention at the outset of his second term.

A serious farce

On the face of it, the Burr conspiracy was preposterous. But then, so was so much else that went on in the Western woods, which, at times, must have seemed peopled only by conspirators lurking behind every tree. One had to know what plots to take seriously. It was part of the education of every American President. The Burr conspiracy was Jefferson's Whisky Rebellion. Both ended satisfactorily from the point of view of the central government, but not without some tense moments in each instance.

Figure 6-2 A Republican outcast, Aaron Burr went West to build a new Empire of Liberty, with himself at its center. He failed, but in doing so, gave the President some bad moments. (*Courtesy of the New-York Historical Society, New York City*)

The Republicans had indeed moderated their positions since the debate on Hamilton's programs and the Virginia and Kentucky Resolutions. They even split over what kind of reception to give Tom Paine, who returned to his adopted homeland in 1804. Radical Republicans wanted to give him a hero's welcome. Jefferson preferred to let the homecoming pass without much notice and even sent word to Paine through Sam Adams that he should stop writing controversial newspaper articles on controversial subjects.

Aaron Burr was several cuts above the average conspirator, both in intelligence and—more important—in the wherewithal with which to implement his schemes. A popular figure in New York Republican politics, Burr received the same number of electoral votes as Jefferson in the election of 1800, thus throwing the decision into the House of Representatives. This odd situation, the first of many in the Burr affair, was caused by the fact that electors cast two votes for the Presidency prior to the adoption of the Twelfth Amendment in 1804. The highest total vote gave a man the President's chair, but the next highest received the Vice President's seat in the Senate. That situation permitted political opponents to hold office at the same time. When political parties emerged, the system became obsolete and dangerous. Hence the Twelfth Amendment.

When the election went to the House, Hamilton used his considerable influence to ensure that the lesser evil, Jefferson, was elected. Burr became Vice President but was treated almost as badly by his own party. He had carried New York for Jefferson, but he was ignored in the distribution of political patronage for that state and was told to read the newspapers if he wanted to find out what was going on in the administration. The Republicans dropped him from the ticket in

1804, whereupon he challenged their regular candidate for the governorship of New York. Defeated in that campaign too, Burr turned his wrath upon the still powerful Alexander Hamilton, challenging him to a duel over a slur the latter had made on his character in the newspapers. For once in a position to strike back at his foes, Burr aimed, fired, and killed Hamilton.

With no place left to go in the party system, Burr looked westward, like many another desperate man before him and yet to come. After all, that was the way the safety valve was supposed to work, wasn't it? Before leaving Washington, however, he contacted the British Ambassador with a strange proposal. If Great Britain put up a half million dollars and promised to have a fleet ready to support him, he would detach Louisiana from the United States.

Shunned by respectable Easterners, Burr's popularity rose in the West, where he was acclaimed for his feat in felling the hated Hamilton, author of the excise taxes. Andrew Jackson welcomed him to Tennessee and even promised to make Burr a United States Senator should he decide to settle down there. But Burr had bigger things in mind. Arriving In New Orleans, he was feted by the best citizens; in return, he sympathized with their complaint that Jefferson had sent a territorial governor to rule them. To some of these dissatisfied new Americans who had expected immediate statehood, Burr confided a plan to liberate Mexico from Spanish rule and then to join it to Louisiana in an independent republic. Why should the Atlantic states be the only ones allowed an imperial vision? To others he implied that he carried a secret commission from President Jefferson authorizing him to recruit and launch an expedition against Mexico. It was all hush-hush stuff that the President could not be held accountable for lest it damage the nation's diplomatic relations. Given the topsy-turvy situation prevailing throughout the early Republican era, either plan could be made to seem credible.

Encouraged by their responses and his own imagination, Burr set up headquarters near Lexington, Kentucky, to begin active recruiting for his expedition. The latest version called for an uprising in Louisiana, followed by an urgent summons to Burr to accept the presidency of the new government, and finally an invasion of Mexico. The British had long since disavowed his madcap schemes, but various men with various degrees of loyalty to the United States listened to Burr. Some merely wanted to learn so as to report to Jefferson; others hedged their bets to keep options open.

Jefferson learned enough through these reports and newspaper accounts of Burr's activities to realize that he should prepare for any eventuality. He himself had given more than passing thought to Mexico. Under different circumstances, he might have encouraged a plan by Louisianans to liberate the colony. Three decades later Andrew Jackson sent Sam Houston to Texas on a similar mission. But Burr was too independent to be trusted on such an assignment; and the West was too unstable to understand that there must be only one empire in North America. "A few days will let us see whether the Western states suppress themselves this insurrectionary enterprize," Jefferson advised a correspondent, "or we shall be obliged to make a great national armament for it." Meanwhile, Jefferson himself drafted a bill "authorizing the employment of the land or naval forces of the U.S. in cases of insurrection" and another bill permitting the arrest of any person on the "suspicion" that he intended to commit a misdemeanor against the United States. He sent these to a friend in Congress, asking him to copy the drafts and burn the originals, as Jefferson did not want to "meddle personally" in legislative proceedings.

That was an interesting distinction for a man who had openly spoken of disunion over the Alien and Sedition Acts. For all the hullabaloo Burr raised, in the end his expedition came down to a few flatboats, fifty-five men and boys, and a few women, children, and servants. The armaments this desperate band carried were the usual muskets and rifles found on any trip into unknown territory. But General James Wilkinson, one of Burr's former coconspirators and commander of the U.S. Army in the West, fell on New Orleans, seized several of Burr's alleged followers, and instituted martial law.

Burr's arrest brought the first phase of the affair to an end. But Jefferson wanted to make an example of the conspirator and instituted a treason trial against him. The trial proved to be a landmark case because, much to the President's displeasure, the presiding Chief Justice John Marshall insisted upon strict adherence to the Constitution's definition of treason: an overt act sworn to by two witnesses. Since the collapse of the expedition and Burr's arrest had taken place before the commission of any overt act of war against the United States, treason could not be proved.

The Burr conspiracy demonstrated that the central government's authority over men and boundaries was still shaky. The President's willingness to go to the edge of political suppression to prevent secession, the continuing problem of a satisfactory definition of loyalty, and the Republicans' own expansionist proclivities against their neighbors on the North American continent all suggested that unresolved tensions would rise to the surface again—not as farce but as tragedy. And what of Burr? He later returned to live out his days in the United States accompanied by a new wife whose principal distinction was her claim to have been the only woman to have slept with both Napoleon and George Washington.

Coercion and commerce

The war Napoleon had been expecting when he sold Louisiana to the Americans began within a few weeks of the sale, and he declared it. American shippers, who had expected to reap big profits from the situation, did so for a time, especially in the sugar trade from the French West Indies. Sugar was brought from those islands to the United States, where a duty on it was collected. It was then reshipped to Europe as neutral cargo. Damned clever, those Yankee traders.

Aroused by complaints about this practice from British sugar planters and merchants and disgusted that their blockade around France was being nullified, the Royal Navy enforced the so-called Rule of 1756 against American shippers. This "rule" stipulated that trade not open to the world in peacetime could not be opened in wartime. Only a nation which dominated the seas, as Britain did, could impose its will in such arrogant fashion. At the same time the Royal Navy also resumed a policy of impressing sailors from American ships on the open seas. Undeniably, the higher wages paid by American owners induced many British subjects to desert to the merchant fleets of the new nation. Printers in seacoast towns were kept busy supplying false citizenship papers for these valuable young expatriates, who contributed their considerable talents to a rapidly growing American industry.

As the controversies grew more serious, Jefferson inquired of his cabinet officers about the possibility of curtailing this last practice so that the only British-born sailors found on American ships would be genuine naturalized citizens. He was told that such an agreement would materially hurt American shipping and commerce. So much for that plan. In June 1807 the impressment controversy produced a crisis which almost led to war. A British warship, the H.M.S. *Leopard*, intercepted the U.S.S. *Chesapeake* within the very portals of Chesapeake Bay. When the American naval vessel refused to heave to and be searched for deserters, the *Leopard* fired three broadsides into the *Chesapeake*'s hull. Then the *Leopard*'s captain came aboard the *Chesapeake* and took off a British deserter, an American Negro, an Indian, and a native of Maryland.

Not much of a haul for the man-o-war, but a war cry went up in America. Congress was not in session at the time and President Jefferson did not want to summon the legislators to declare war. The President and James Madison, his successor, both insisted that they could employ American commerce to achieve the same end. The acquisition of Louisiana and New Orleans buttressed their convictions in several ways. Most important, the United States now controlled the Midwestern grain trade from New Orleans, a trade that Napoleon himself had once considered vital to the feeding of his army. Secondly, possession of New Orleans would enable the United States to put great pressure on Spain to cede West Florida. This, in turn, would assure greater control of the Gulf of Mexico and increasing trade with the newly independent states of South America. The opportunity presented by that inter-American trade would also presumably hasten the development of North American manufactures.

It is harder to understand how these considerations led Jefferson to conclude that his best strategy was to press Congress for an Embargo Act, which was passed in December 1807. Apparently he expected quick results. For fourteen months American merchant ships were forbidden to sail—not only to Great Britain but anywhere. Nothing happened. Nothing, that is, except a near catastrophe for American commercial interests. Jefferson tried his best to put a good face on things, claiming that if the embargo was dropped at once his own state would import only half what it had in earlier years—so much had domestic manufactures grown. Northern Republicans were ready to bolt the party when Jefferson at last signed a repeal bill on March 1, 1809, three days before he retired for the last time to Monticello.

Madison asked Congress to give him instead a nonintercourse bill which would forbid trade only with England and France. He also wanted the power to restore commercial relations with either if and when it repealed its decrees affecting American commerce. A treaty between England and the United States was actually drafted—providing for an end to British attacks on American shipping in exchange for a pledge to continue nonintercourse against France. London, however, repudiated the proposed pact. Perhaps Madison had found the right tactics to use with Jefferson's strategy. A slight variation might be all that was necessary now. On May 1, 1810, Congress passed Macon's Bill No. 2, which reversed the procedure employed in the nonintercourse act. This law provided that commerce would be restored immediately with both belligerents, but should either one recognize its error and stop denying neutrals their full rights to trade with either side, the United States would reimpose a full embargo on trade with the other, unrepentant nation.

Figure 6-3 The embargo. What led Jefferson to believe that he could use American economic power in a negative fashion? For fourteen months American merchant ships were forbidden to sail—not only to Great Britain but anywhere. Nothing happened. Nothing, that is, except near catastrophe for American commercial interests. (*American History Division, The New York Public Library, Astor, Lenox and Tilden Foundations*)

SEVENTEEN YEARS

HISTORY,

OF THE

LIFE AND SUFFERINGS

OF

JAMES M'LEAN.

AN IMPRESSED

AMERICAN CITIZEN & SEAMAN.

EMBRACING BUT A SUMMARY

OF WHAT HE ENDURED,

WHILE DETAINED

In the British Service,

DURING THAT

LONG AND PAINFUL PERIOD.

WRITTEN

BY HIMSELF.

HARTFORD:

PRINTED FOR THE AUTHOR,

BY B. & J. RUSSELL.

1814.

Napoleon, who obviously had the least to lose as a land power, took Madison up on this offer. Madison then solemnly declared that all trade with England would come to an end on March 2, 1811. On June 16, 1812, the British finally suspended their obnoxious Orders in Council pertaining to neutral trade. The Jefferson-Madison plan had worked, but not in time. The President had already asked for a declaration of war on June 1, 1812, and Congress had given it to him on June 18, long before word of what had happened in London could reach Washington. A terrible case of faulty timing and careful planning gone awry? Probably not. President Madison had sought something like Macon's Bill No. 2 knowing the risks involved. He had been prepared to take such risks since 1794, when he pressed for strong actions against Great Britain not simply to sustain American honor but to establish a truly independent American mercantilist system. Madison seldom went into anything without calculating the political situation down to the finest detail. For Madison (as for political leaders in other new countries) the revolution would not be complete until economic independence was also established. If the Revolutionary generation did not complete its task, who would? As Madison knew only too well, the political unity of the nation depended upon strong economic ties between the regions and interests. He had always agreed with Hamilton on that point. The problem was to cement those interests and regions without doing injustices to any, injustices which would be stored up in resentments and finally come out in destructive ways.

Madison's war message tried to establish the basis for a strong national unity. The British blockades and attacks on American commerce had occurred, he said, not because this country's trade threatened the successful prosecution of the war against Napoleon, but because it endangered "the monopoly which [Great Britain] covets for her own commerce and navigation." This was the real reason why "our commerce has been plundered in every sea, the great staples of our country have been cut off from their legitimate markets, and a destructive blow aimed at our agricultural and maritime interests." The "War Hawk" Congress, which brought men like Henry Clay and John C. Calhoun to Washington in 1811, had many grudges—both real and fancied—against Great Britain. All, however, echoed Madison's call for war on the broadest basis possible.

Andrew Jackson, only lately involved with Aaron Burr, declared:

We are going to fight for the establishment of our national character, misunderstood and vilified at home and abroad, for the protection of our maritime citizens, impressed on board British ships of war and compelled to fight the battles of our enemies against ourselves; to vindicate our right to a free trade, and open a market for the production of our soil, now perishing on our lands because the mistress of the ocean has forbid us to carry them to any foreign nation. . . .

If the Burr conspiracy had demonstrated that the country did indeed need to establish a "national character," Jackson was the very

Figure 6-4 A British view of Jefferson's economic diplomacy. It hurt enough to force a repeal of the Orders in Council, but too late to prevent war. (*The Grolier Club; American History Division, The New York Public Library, Astor, Lenox and Tilden Foundations*)

Figure 6-5 Determined to complete the job of forging American independence, Madison went to war in 1812. He almost lost the war, but found a new nationalist spirit in the West where he hoped it would be. (*Culver Pictures*)

sort of person Madison needed to recruit in such an endeavor, a Westerner with a popular following. The President's talents as a war leader, however, never matched his political organizing abilities. Indeed, he almost bungled the whole thing. Part of the blame rested with Jefferson, who had allowed the nation to believe that it could engage in economic power politics without a military or naval force to fall back on should that option fail. Madison continued this policy even as he threw down the gauntlet. When the war began the United States did not even have an army capable of defending the nation's frontiers.

War and politics

That did not prevent Madison from ordering an invasion of Canada. After all, the colonies had not maintained a standing army, and yet they whipped the British regulars to a fare thee well, didn't they? But not this time. The first land campaign of the war was doomed to failure. Poorly officered, the American force of a few thousand rough-hewn militiamen invaded western Canada in mid-July, proclaiming their intention to free the Canadians from the colonial yoke. For some perverse reason, the Canadians did not see it that way, and they sent the American force packing in a humiliating defeat.

The Canadian campaign was an accurate barometer of worse defeats yet to come. President Madison walked through the War Department with a red, white, and blue cockade in his hat in an effort to boost morale, but these personal appearance tours had little noticeable effect on the course of the war. The military reverses gave New England Federalists a new lease on life. That section of the country had opposed the war from the beginning; now it raised the threat of secession.

With Napoleon's defeat accomplished, Great Britain made ready to deal out a crushing blow to those pesky Americans. Its navy had already achieved complete dominance on the sea. From the summer of 1813 the waters around the United States were controlled by enemy frigates which preyed upon merchant shipping. And the whole coastline was open to attack whenever the British decided.

They decided in August 1814, landing in Maryland for an assault on Washington. The President and his aides evacuated the government into the surrounding countryside, from which unhappy vantage point they could watch the burning of the capital city. Meanwhile, New England Federalists gathered at Hartford to denounce "Mr. Madison's War." Condemning the foolish Republicans for their "ruinous perseverance" in attempting to coerce great powers through commercial means to the detriment of the American economy, the Federalists also blamed them for admitting "new states into the Union formed at pleasure in the western region." The original balance of power among the thirteen states had been destroyed.

On this point the Hartford Convention scored a hit. Madison had always hoped to strengthen bonds between the South and West, and had used the war to achieve his purpose. Like other Virginians, Madison suspected New England's commitment to economic nationalism or to fair dealing for the South. Had the war lasted much longer, the Republicans might not have survived as the dominant party, if at all. Forced to give up a demand that the British renounce impressment, Madison now hoped only to prevent an actual loss of territory. A peace treaty was signed at Ghent on Christmas Eve 1814. Nothing was said about the issues America had gone to war to settle, but the treaty saved

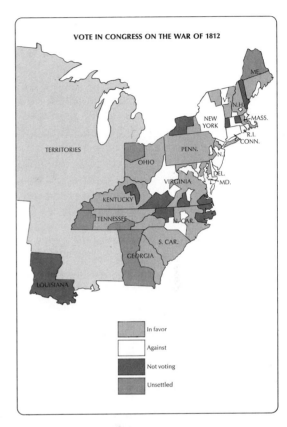

VOTE IN CONGRESS ON THE WAR OF 1812

In favor
Against
Not voting
Unsettled

(*From* A History of the American People *by Graebner, Fite, and White. Copyright © 1970 by McGraw-Hill, Inc. Used with permission of McGraw-Hill Book Company*)

both sides from continuing on a struggle which had become pointless.

And the nation forgave the Republicans their follies when word reached the capital of a battle fought at New Orleans on January 8, 1815. Tennessee's Andrew Jackson had given the British invaders a sound thrashing—three weeks after the peace treaty had been signed. Never mind such details. All's well that ends well: The nation had a war hero and future President whose feats would nurture the growing myth of American invincibility and whose Western origins symbolized a new national unity. Madison was elated and set himself the task of developing a nationalist economic program which would include a high tariff and a new charter for the Bank of the United States. The former "War Hawks" eagerly joined in this campaign, which continued into the adminstration of James Monroe, elected President in 1816.

An alliance restored

After consulting the Republican patriarch in Monticello, Monroe invited John Quincy Adams to become his Secretary of State, thus restoring the old Virginia-Massachusetts alliance of the Revolutionary era. As the leading figure in a cabinet filled with ambitious men, Adams set out to obtain world recognition for the idea that "our proper dominion [shall] be the continent of North America." By committing himself to territorial expansion, the new Secretary of State turned his back on Federalism as recently practiced by his fellow New Englanders. For his part, President Monroe, once a Southern sectionalist unable to see beyond Virginia's needs, picked up on Jefferson's original theme by encouraging Congress to pass an amendment to the Con-

stitution authorizing the government to carry on a program of internal improvements.

The difficulties the nation would face once this postwar spirit passed would center, Monroe believed, in disagreements over federal power and states' rights. If he could remove doubts about the national government's authority to build canals and roads, he would eliminate a potentially disastrous division within the party and between the sections. Ironically, given what would happen later, much of the opposition to internal improvements came from Northern states which had gone ahead on their own with major projects. In his message asking for such an amendment, Monroe acknowledged, "The only danger to which our system is exposed arises from its expansion over a vast territory." On the other hand, "it is believed that the greater the expansion within practicable limits—and it is not easy to say what are not so—the greater the advantage which the states individually will derive from it." Extent of territory, he went on, marks the extent of a nation's resources, its population, its physical force. "It marks, in short, the difference between a great and a small power."

Until natural economic and political ties developed between states spread over such a vast territory, it was essential to supply the bonds between them in the form of internal improvements. John Quincy Adams had the easier task: everyone favored extending the territorial boundaries of the United States. The trouble with that was, as both Adams and Monroe had come to understand, the American system needed both external expansion and internal improvements. Yet the more territory Adams added, the less Monroe himself seemed able to understand the necessary role of internal improvements as a unifying factor. Expansion, in fact, was the only unify-

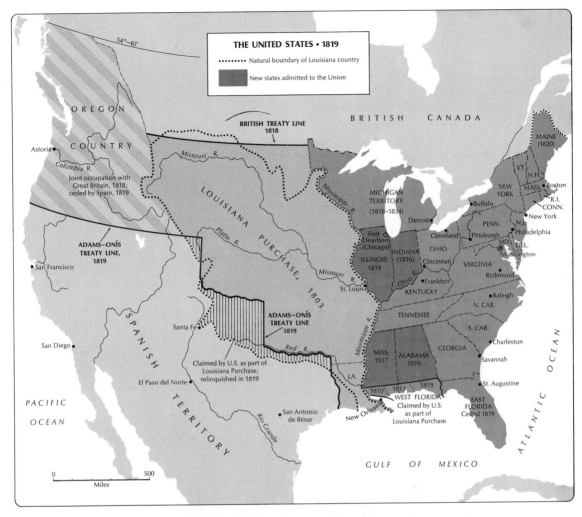

THE UNITED STATES • 1819

········· Natural boundary of Louisiana country

New states admitted to the Union

54°–40'

OREGON COUNTRY

BRITISH TREATY LINE 1818

BRITISH CANADA

Astoria

Columbia R.

Joint occupation with Great Britain, 1818; ceded by Spain, 1819

Missouri R.

MAINE (1820)

VT.

N.H.

NEW YORK

MASS. Boston

R.I.

CONN.

Buffalo

New York

MICHIGAN TERRITORY (1818–1834)

Detroit

PENN.

N.J.

Philadelphia

ADAMS–ONÍS TREATY LINE, 1819

LOUISIANA PURCHASE, 1803

Platte R.

Cleveland

Pittsburgh

MD.

DEL.

Washington

San Francisco

Fort Dearborn (Chicago)

ILLINOIS 1819

INDIANA (1816)

OHIO

Cincinnati

VIRGINIA

Richmond

Missouri R.

Ohio R.

Frankfort

St. Louis

KENTUCKY

Raleigh

N. CAR.

San Diego

SPANISH

Santa Fe

Red R.

TENNESSEE

S. CAR.

Charleston

ATLANTIC OCEAN

Claimed by U.S. as part of Louisiana Purchase; relinquished in 1819

ADAMS–ONÍS TREATY LINE 1819

MISS. 1817

ALABAMA 1819

GEORGIA

Savannah

El Paso del Norte

TERRITORY

Mississippi R.

LA.

PACIFIC OCEAN

San Antonio de Béxar

Rio Grande

1810 1813 1819

New Orleans

WEST FLORIDA Claimed by U.S. as part of Louisiana Purchase

St. Augustine

EAST FLORIDA Ceded 1819

GULF OF MEXICO

0 500

Miles

(*From A History of the American People by Graebner, Fite, and White. Copyright* © *1970 by McGraw-Hill, Inc. Used with permission of McGraw-Hill Book Company*)

ing goal Americans shared by the end of the Republican era.

The Transcontinental Treaty

Americans had coveted Florida for a long time. Spain's control over that peninsula had weakened with each passing year, as had its grip on Latin America. Americans saw Great Britain (who else?) as their main rival in both areas. Whatever British meddling had occurred in stirring up the Seminole Indians against white settlements in Georgia had been magnified into one of the causes of the War of 1812. The war's end brought no peace on the Georgia-Florida frontier; hostilities actually grew worse. The Seminoles resented the American Army's claim that it had a right to hunt for fugitive slaves on the Spanish side of the boundary; Georgians resented Indian scalping parties which operated on the American side. Monroe ordered Andrew Jackson to put a halt to the latter. The hero of New Orleans and his Tennessee militia found this job very much to their liking; so much so that they seized several Spanish forts, expelled the colonial governor, and, for good measure, hanged two British citizens accused of instigating Indian raids.

Madrid demanded an apology and a repudiation of Jackson's raid. Everyone in the Monroe Cabinet agreed that was the best way to avoid a war with Spain—and possibly Great Britain. Everyone, that is, except Secretary Adams, who argued that this was a golden opportunity to demonstrate Spanish ineffectiveness in Florida. There was only a small chance Spain would go to war and even less chance that Britain could be persuaded to fight alongside the Spaniards in such a dubious cause. Besides, Great Britain was primarily interested in the trade of Latin America, not in adding Florida to its overseas political responsibilities.

Monroe stood firm, as Adams hoped he would, and the incident speeded up negotiations for the purchase of Florida. The 1819 Transcontinental Treaty removed Spain from Florida at a cost of 5 million dollars. But Adams had higher stakes in mind. He wanted and got a Spanish cession of all claims to the Oregon country. Spain's claims to Oregon hardly amounted to anything, but in ceding them to the United States, Madrid gave this country its first legal claim to territory on the Pacific Coast. Spain wanted more than 5 million dollars, too; it wanted Adam's pledge that the United States would not recognize the revolutionary governments in Latin America. The Secretary had gone along with this cave-

at during the preliminary negotiations, but at the last minute he refused to make such a promise. Left high and dry, the Spanish Ambassador agreed to his terms anyway.

It was an outstanding achievement for American diplomacy and for Adams personally. The Secretary had wanted to try for Texas as well, but on this point Monroe's Cabinet held back, fearing a divisive debate over the extension of slavery. Adams, ironically, received the brunt of the criticism leveled at the administration for abandoning American claims to Texas as the western boundary of the Louisiana Purchase. The slaveholders in the Cabinet were sensitive to the slave question just at that time because of the Missouri question, which had come before Congress in the midst of a financial panic and depression.

The Adams prophecy

The panic of 1819 ushered in the worst depression in the young nation's history. Once again, as in the years before the War of 1812, Western farmers were the hardest hit. Cotton prices fell from 32.5 cents a pound in 1818 to 14.3 cents at the outset of the panic. The reasons for the downturn, like those to come later in the century, can be traced to speculation and overexpansion, both at home and in Europe. In Virginia, Jefferson wrote, "lands cannot now be sold for a year's rent." It was also the first depression to produce major unemployment problems in the cities, from the Eastern states into the new Western centers, in Pittsburgh, Cincinnati, and Lexington.

Unlike the prewar economic situation, however, the victims of the panic of 1819 had a domestic scapegoat for their difficulties: the Bank of the United States. The retrenchment policy of the bank and its branches throughout the country was blamed by Westerners who lost mortgaged lands and businesses in the depression. Old sectional issues arose again to plague the Republicans. The riddle of how to preserve a balance of power in a federal system was proving more difficult than Jefferson and Madison had ever imagined. It was not to be solved simply by laying off a new range of states. Monroe's solution, a Constitutional amendment permitting internal improvements, failed to gain support among groups who feared it was only another excuse to impose Eastern power and Eastern institutions, like the Bank of the United States, on the rest of the country.

Chief Justice John Marshall's famous decision in *McCulloch v. Maryland,* placing the bank above any state power to tax or limit its operations, reenforced such fears. Marshall even contended in delivering his opinion that the Constitution permitted the federal government to withdraw "any subject" if it so chose from the power of local state taxation. A program of internal improvements could not have had much appeal in areas which felt, correctly or not, that they were already oppressed by the power of national institutions.

In this charged atmosphere, the ensuing debate over Missouri's admission to the Union as a slave state became also a debate over the federal government's ability to shape the internal institutions of each state. The political crisis began when a lame-duck Representative from New York, James Tallmedge, Jr., attached a proviso to the enabling bill admitting Missouri to the Union. This proviso said that no additional slaves could be introduced into the state and that all children of slaves already there were to be emancipated at age twenty-five. Tallmedge thus emerged from obscurity to strike at the most vulnerable spot in the Republican compact, the gentleman's agreement over slave expansion. He

Figure 6-6 The greatest Secretary of State, one of the worst Presidents? Or was it that Adams simply got caught in the middle when the Union began to pull apart? Adams believed that there was danger in spreading the Union too thin, but he had no success in convincing others to adopt his proposed remedy. (*North Carolina Museum of Art*)

knew what he was doing and had acted out of revenge for being dropped by the Albany Regency which controlled New York Republicanism. Once again the fragile bonds of Union were to be tested by an outcast, another in a list which would include Shays, the Whisky rebels, Aaron Burr, and, in the next generation, John Brown.

Tallmedge had tangled things so well that it took more than two years to get the issues separated into manageable form again. At stake was the balance between slave and free states in the Senate and the House of Representatives. Closely related to that problem was the exercise of federal power over and within the states, especially if John Marshall's views in *McCulloch v. Maryland* held up. The successful cultivation of cotton depended upon the political weather and decisions in support of a slave economy on such issues as the tariff and easy acquisition of public lands. Whichever section held the balance in Congress would be able to legislate its will on such matters unless the powers of the federal government were restricted to certain agreed-upon essentials.

The Missouri question remained unsettled until 1821, when Kentucky's Henry Clay pushed through a solution. The essentials were simple enough: Missouri would come into the Union as a slave state and Maine as a free state. As anyone could see, that plan would work only as long as new territory could be found to deal out on a one for you, one for me basis, and only as long as everyone agreed on the boundary between slave and free states. Celebrators of the Missouri Compromise, and Clay's political genius, pass over other points. The Missouri Compromise did not simply legalize slavery in one state; it resulted in second-class citizenship for free blacks in other states. Antiblack legislation in various Northern states now received a stimulus from Congressional approval of a compromise that would prohibit free blacks from traveling in Missouri, for where slavery was, free blacks were not welcome. Slave prices, depressed in this time of economic distress, rose with the prospect of new buyers in Missouri and still more Missouris to come south of the Compromise line.

Cotton cultivation was spreading rapidly into Alabama, Mississippi, and Louisiana. It had doubled within five years of the Peace of Ghent and redoubled itself in the next five. Virginia's tobacco plantations, home of the tidewater elite of Revolutionary years, were now in a depressed state. As Jefferson put it: "We must either attend to recruiting our lands or abandon them & run away to Alibama [sic] as so many of our countrymen are doing." Those who ran away wanted their chance, and they did not intend to allow Easterners, North or South, to deny them. The Missouri Compromise, moreover, offered Virginians another alternative to recoup something of their lost status: slave breeding for the new states.

Finally, the Missouri Compromise gave an added impetus to the so-called proslavery argument fashioned from biblical writings and "scientific evidences" of the black man's innate inferiority. Jefferson, Madison, and Monroe had all believed the answer to sectional divisions over slavery would be diffusion; now every issue had become one of boundaries. And the need for westward expansion became greater than that of *orderly* westward expansion. The Missouri question, said Jefferson from Monticello, had wakened him like a "fire bell in the night" and would become the death knell of the Union.

John Quincy Adams publicly accepted the Compromise, but he knew how dangerous it would be for the country to go on as if nothing serious had happened. His foreign policy was premised on the assumption that colonialism was outdated, especially in the Western Hemisphere. Slavery was an extreme form of colonialism and must soon perish. Yet the dismal marriage between Southern cotton and the textile mills of England might perpetuate slavery in the United States beyond its normal lifetime and thus sustain a backward-looking "colonial" influence in American politics.

At the height of the Missouri crisis, Adams and Secretary of War John C. Calhoun talked of these matters late one afternoon following a Cabinet meeting. Calhoun, a "War Hawk" nationalist before the panic of 1819, had done a complete turnabout and was already well on the way to becoming the leading spokesman for Southern sectionalism. This discussion began with Calhoun volunteering the information that if the slavery issue divided the Union, the South would seek a military alliance with England. Adams replied that the South's relationship with England could not end there; the South would have to return to colonial status. If that happened, said Calhoun, it would be because the North forced the situation on the Southern states. Did Calhoun believe that the North would allow itself to be cut off from the sea, Adams then asked? Or that it would allow the South to become a British military outpost? If the Union did split over the slavery issue, the Secretary of State ended the discussion, one thing would become certain—the emancipation of the slaves.

The Monroe Doctrine

As the Missouri crisis passed over the United States like a dark cloud across the sun, diplomatic questions with England and Spain's former colonies in Latin America again came to the Monroe administration's attention. In London, Foreign Minister George Canning had proposed to the American Ambassador that the United States and Great Britain join in a common policy to prevent an expected Franco-Spanish attempt to recolonize the new republics of Latin America.

Again it was Secretary Adams who stood against the majority of the Cabinet. Why should the United States "come in as a cockboat in the wake of the British man-of-war," he asked, when it could avow its own principles in the full knowledge that Great Britain would support its declaration? The British interest was a commercial interest, like America's, but over the long run the United States had two advantages: its anticolonial and revolutionary origins and the steady development of its manufactures. Nothing should be done to compromise those advantages.

Adams also felt he could put forward another claim to the Pacific Northwest in the context of a general anticolonial statement directed against not only France and Spain but also Great Britain and Russia. Russia's recent declarations concerning Alaska's boundaries worried the Secretary as the possible forerunners of a claim to part of Oregon. Monroe supported Adams on this occasion as well, and he used his annual message of December 2, 1823 to set forth what became known as the "Monroe Doctrine." This stated that the American continents were henceforth not to be considered as subjects for colonization by any European power and would feel threatened by any such attempt. For its part, the United States had not and would not in the future take part in Europe's wars. Adams's contribution to the message ended there, but Monroe had something more to say. "It is manifest that by enlarging the basis of our system and increasing the number of States the system itself has been greatly strengthened in both its branches. Consolidation and disunion have thereby been rendered equally impracticable." Monroe, if pressed, would probably have admitted to some doubts; but if the nation saw no need for a federal program of internal improvements, then so be it. One could hope for the best.

End of an era

Andrew Jackson won the popular vote in 1824, but he lacked a majority in the electoral college. In the House of Representatives, Henry Clay's supporters threw their votes to John Quincy Adams, giving him the Presidency. When Adams then named Clay Secretary of State, the embittered Jacksonians cried out in rage against the corrupt deal which denied their man his rightful office. Here was evidence, if any more was needed, that the Eastern "establishment" would go to any lengths to keep control of the government. The same forces which had profited from the economic distress of the Panic of 1819 were now plotting to keep the government to themselves.

Events had come full circle on the Republicans. As they had once done, the Jacksonian Democrats now filled the role of protestors against the power elite. Adams's Presidency never had a chance: The Jacksonians were absorbed in their own rhetoric and preparations for 1828. Calhoun's followers were equally distracted in the development of a sectional outlook and policy. Adams was thus left with only a third of the old Republican constituency. Dropping Monroe's suggestion for a Constitutional amendment, the last of the original Republican Presidents renewed the appeal for a program of internal improvements. Thinking that perhaps he could shame Congress into acting, he said: "While foreign nations less blessed with that freedom which is power than ourselves are advancing with gigantic strides in the career of public improvement, were we to slumber in indolence or fold up our arms and proclaim to the world that we are palsied by the will of our constituents, would it not be to cast away the bounties of Providence and doom ourselves to perpetual inferiority?"

Neither indolent nor palsied, as Adams well knew, the powerful men and forces of an emerging new order waited impatiently for Adams's term in office to end. Capitalists in the North and planters in the South were anxious to get on with the business at hand: the removal of whatever federal restraints remained on individual enterprise. Within both sections, moreover, the same conflicts between old wealth and new wealth, tidelands and backwater, original states and new states further reduced the ability of the President to make claims upon the nation or to call it to task for allowing "foreign nations" to outdistance it in fulfilling the purposes of the Creator.

Congress even refused to support the President's policy toward the 1826 Pan-American Conference, where, Adams had hoped, the United States might take a leading role in forming a strong Western Hemisphere alliance and, not incidentally, initiate a commercial reciprocity policy with the leading states of South America. Instead, Congress bickered back and forth with the President over the appropriation of funds, a mere $40,000, required to send the American delegates to Panama. The legislators even contested his assertion that advantageous commercial treaties could be signed with those nations attending the conference. If they wanted American commerce, said the congressional committees which responded to the request for an appropriation, then treaties could be negotiated through normal processes in due time. If not, nothing was to be gained by sending a delegation to Panama.

Adams had also argued that the conference offered the United States its best chance to advance the cause of religious freedom throughout the Americas. Congress reacted to this claim with skepticism, underlining the prevalent mood of the new order. It was a mood which found Presidential leadership in prescribing moral standards in domestic or foreign policy both presumptuous and dangerous: presumptuous in assuming that the nationalistic morality of an outdated era was still relevant, and dangerous in that it ran counter to the spirit of compromise and adjustment that would be needed if capitalism and slavery were to coexist on the North American continent.

Adams blamed the slave interests for preventing him from carrying through on the Monroe Doctrine and for his defeat in 1828, but the forces allied against him were not limited to one interest or one region. John Taylor of Caroline, Virginia, the man who had moved the 1798 resolution in that state's legislature against Federalist "tyranny," had written a new attack on the dangers of centralized power in the government in 1820. His editor wrote in the introduction: "The period is indeed by no means an agreeable one. It borrows new gloom from the apathy which seems to run over so many of our sister states. The very sound of State Rights is scarcely ever heard among them; and by many of their eminent politicians is only heard to be mocked at."

The sound of states' rights would be heard above all others for the next three decades, punctuated by cries for Texas, and Oregon, and California.

110

Selected references

The first Republican era has stimulated many fine histories, old and new. Among these Frederick Jackson Turner's *Rise of the New West* (1906), George Dangerfield's *The Awakening of American Nationalism* (1965), and Richard Ellis's *The Jeffersonian Crisis: Courts and Politics in the Young Republic* (1971) were especially useful for this chapter. On special topics, Thomas Perkins Abernathy, *The Burr Conspiracy* (1954), Julius Pratt, *The Expansionists of 1812* (1949), Bradford Perkins, *Prologue to War* (1961), Reginald Horsman, *The Causes of the War of 1812* (1962), and Glover Moore, *The Missouri Controversy, 1819–1821* (1953) help the reader grasp the more intricate points of the era.

On diplomacy, see A. P. Whitaker, *The United States and the Independence of Latin America, 1800–1830* (1941), and Samuel Flagg Bemis's classic *John Quincy Adams and the Foundations of American Foreign Policy* (1949). Two volumes of unusual importance for understanding long-range economic developments are D. C. North, *The Economic Growth of the United States, 1790–1860* (1961), and Stuart Bruchey's *Roots of American Economic Growth* (1965). I also want to mention a poet, William Carlos Williams, whose *In the American Grain* (1933) gave the outcast a voice in American history only now being heard by historians, and a good friend and colleague, Rudy Bell, who showed me the connections.

SEVEN

The Expanding Nation

Period covered: 1800–1860
Emphases: Evangelical religion.
The frontier.
Jacksonian democracy.
The Old South.
Major events: The Great Revival, 1800
Election of Andrew Jackson, 1828
The Compromise of 1850
Election of Abraham Lincoln, 1860

Settling the West

Independence opened up the West for settlement, but at first little happened. Kentucky, Tennessee, and Vermont were populous enough to become states in the 1790s. Ohio was admitted in 1803. There was no immediate rush to take advantage of the Louisiana Purchase. Then about 1812 the great migration began. Louisiana became a state that year. After the War of 1812 many more states were added to the Union: Indiana in 1816, Mississippi in 1817, Illinois in 1818, Alabama in 1819, Maine in 1820, and Missouri in 1821. The census figures explain why seven states in nine years were admitted while it had taken twenty-three years to create the first four new states. In 1810 one American in seven lived west of the Alleghenies; in 1820, one in four. This great migration was partly a function of better roads and partly a response to the Indian exodus (after 1815 a series of treaties forced the tribes to become farmers or migrate west of the Mississippi). For whatever reasons, the West became a reality rather than a concept. Thereafter what Westerners thought and did mattered. They helped bring on the War of 1812, and in the 1820s and 1830s they created the modern system of mass electoral politics. The Revolution somewhat—and the rise of Jefferson's party even more—democratized politics. But it was not until the West became important that popular democracy emerged. The West also made imperialism popular. It contributed greatly to the dominion of evangelical Christianity that was established after 1800.

Religious diversity

There were many revivals before the Great Revival of 1800. Few had much permanent effect. The Great Awakening had faded rapidly, while the back-country revivals of the colonial era had mostly local effects. American Protestantism, though freshened by these emotional outbursts, remained formalistic as a whole. It met the challenge of Deism and skepticism in the late eighteenth century by becoming, if anything, more rationalistic. Inevitably, some ministers called for an infusion of the spirit and looked to revivalism to strengthen the church against secularism and infidelity. There were revivals in the East, but the West was more fertile ground. Local revivals began in 1797, and by 1800 they were attracting thousands. In August 1801, between ten and twenty thousand people gathered at Cain Ridge, Kentucky, where the Great Revival achieved its zenith. Preached to at all hours of the day and night by batteries of ministers, the people had fits, spoke in tongues, and performed peculiar exercises such as the "jerks," in which they would twitch convulsively. Some fell to the ground and crawled on all fours. When they gathered about a tree to bark madly at it, the exercise was known as "treeing the devil."

As always, the enthusiasm for religion produced new sects and divided old ones. But while sectarianism flourished, so did orthodoxy, especially among Baptists and Methodists: Baptists because their doctrinal net was so broad, Methodists because of the circuit-riding preachers who bound scattered bands together in one fellowship. Baptists did especially well in the South, and soon the genteel Anglicanism of colonial days was pushed aside in favor of an austere religious code emphasizing sin and guilt. Methodism was better suited to the North apparently, and, as Methodism emphasized social justice more than most religions, it paved the way for the later revivals that did so much to promote reform. Though in cities the extremes of behavior associated with Western revivals were less noticeable, evangelical Christianity took firm root there, especially among the middle classes. By midcentury, American Protestants were typically evangelical. Evangelism, being aggressive and expansive, was, in a sense, the religious equivalent of imperialism. It sought not only to convert others but to regulate the conduct of everyone, whether saved or not. On the one hand it encouraged moral arrogance, inquisitiveness, and a sense of mission that justified infringing on the public's liberty (to drink or gamble any time or to play on Sunday, for example). On the other, it also frequently widened the social consciousness of believers and made them take seriously the injunction to be their brother's keeper. All these traits were to become fixed in the national character.

Since 1893 when Frederick Jackson Turner wrote his great paper *The Influence of the Frontier in American History,* Americans have seen the frontier as the source of national virtue. Turner fixed the popular image of the frontiersman in one great sentence. "That coarseness and strength combined with acuteness and inquisitiveness; that practical, inventive turn of mind, quick to find expedients; that masterful grasp of material things, lacking in the artistic but powerful to effect great ends; that restless nervous energy; that dominant individualism, working for good and for evil, and withal that buoyancy and exuberance which comes with freedom." That is how we have long thought of ourselves, though there is more poetry than truth in it. For Turner the frontier was not so much a place as a mystic process, a "crucible" in which the tag ends of half the world were fused into something wholly new—the American. The further West settlers went, the more American they became—that is to say, more freedomloving, individualistic, and democratic. Because Turner described so powerfully the American as he wished to see

himself, the "Turner thesis" became the most influential ever put forward by an American historian.

While we honor Turner for his poetry, imagination, and generous sympathies, it is wrong to think that the ideal frontier he spoke of ever existed. For one thing, there were many frontiers, and few of these displayed the characteristics Turner thought important. Settlement did not proceed along a line but according to geography. Some frontiers, especially in what became the Midwest, were democratic and run by independent yeomen. Others, especially in the South, were dominated by handfuls of great landholders and speculators. Turner largely ignored these last, though they had a far more important effect on subsequent developments than the scouts and mountain men of legend. Even where small holders survived as in east Tennessee, they were often given to mob action and a demagoguery. Open land did not make for democracy of itself, hence the self-perpetuating oligarchy that ruled Mormon Utah. The frontier was not a crucible, for there, as in the cities, ethnic groups tended to persist rather than assimilate. Clusters of Germans, Scandinavians, and others retained their distinct identities for generations.

Nor was the frontier a "safety valve" for urban discontent, as Turner thought. Careful studies have shown that only a handful of urban workers ever settled in the West. Mostly the frontier was peopled by farmers and the children of farmers who moved West, sometimes more than once, when the good land in their neighborhood was taken up. Nor did the frontier do much for American institutions. Education, law, and the family were not improved. Indeed, they often deteriorated. In 1820 James Fenimore Cooper estimated that there were only 8,000 living college graduates, nearly all of them in the East where the colleges were. Education later improved in the West, but not until long after the frontier was gone. Most of the great nineteenth-century reforms had Eastern, even urban origins.

The frontier did contribute mightily to American life, but its legacy was a mixed blessing. The first stage of frontier life, as most people agreed, was distasteful. In the absence of law, violence and license prevailed. Modern readers brought up on Western movies and TV programs do not need to be told about the violence. Here is a description from the journal of a French fur trader of what happened at Fort Clark, in the spring of 1842, when his boat landed and the Indians swarmed down on it.

The great end which these poor ignorant and licentious wretches had in view in flocking so eagerly to the boat, appeared to me, not so much to cohabit with the whites for the pleasure of the thing, as the remuneration they expected after the rutting business was over. . . . Fathers and Mothers led their daughters and husbands their wives, to the obscene and abominable shrine of Venus . . . . Never perhaps since the days of Adam, or since public markets were first instituted did any species of animals or goods prove more marketable, or meet with more general demand and ready sale, than the hind-quarters of these ignoble and prostitute females.

Conditions were not this bad everywhere, and they got better when white women arrived on the scene, but domestic morals and manners improved slowly. People lived for years in lean-tos and rude shacks, deprived of the meanest instruments of civilization. They were, as was said, "half wild and wholly free."

What the frontier gave to America was exactly what might have been expected. Violence and the absence of law created counterviolence—Judge Lynch and vigilantism. The right to bear arms became sacred and persisted long after the need for it, hence the shamefully lax gun laws of today. As there were few schools except of the most basic and practical sort, the frontier stimulated that antiintellectualism which has remained ever since a salient national trait. Because schoolteachers were generally women, culture was regarded as "women's work," hence not to be taken seriously.

Individualism in the back county was defined as freedom from legal constraint, not as the right to be different. Deviance was possible on the frontier only as long as there were few settlers. Once community life developed, the normal conformity of small-town and rural America prevailed. This was especially true in the South, which was settled almost entirely by white Anglo-Saxon Protestants. Social freedom existed for the most part only in cities, where anonymity gave rise to liberty. Being so large and diverse, cities cannot identify deviants and impose social sanctions on them as effectively as rural areas. And the frontier was a stronghold of all those disagreeable traits—insularity, isolationism, nativism, racial prejudice—which, while hardly unique to rural areas, tend always to flourish there.

The frontier also strengthened the myth of the garden, as Henry Nash Smith calls it, the agrarian ideal already so prominent in Jefferson's day. The richness of the Mississippi Valley made it possible to envision an empire of free yeomen there. It would be the garden of the world. Though based on a certain reality—the many free homesteaders in the great valley—it was a poor vision for the country at large. The myth envisioned an unchanging community of subsistence farmers, yet early on the valley was a great surplus-producing agricultural factory that soon possessed banks and cities, like the East. America was destined to be chiefly an urban, industrial society. Yet during much of the crucial period when this transition took place, Americans still thought of themselves as sturdy yeomen. This made coherent planning for the future difficult, as did the size of the "garden" and the variety of local conditions within it.

Jacksonian democracy

The rise of Andrew Jackson both symbolized the frontier's new importance and promoted it, so John W. Ward tells us. Jackson stood for the triumph of natural values, as found in the West, over the corruptions of upper-class urban life. He was thought a natural man not only because he was simple and straightforward but more importantly because he was sustained by nature. He grew, wrote the Massachusetts historian and politician George Bancroft, "as the forest trees grow." Jackson and his men prevailed at the battle of New Orleans because they were natural men and hence superior to the English soldiers, who were only the degenerate products of a decaying civilization. This characterization was heightened by Romanticism, a great current of sentiment which swept across America in Jackson's day. Unlike the Enlightenment, Romanticism glorified the mystic power of nature and saw intuition, not cognition, as the avenue to truth. Eastern intellectuals were victims of mental overdevelopment. Jackson surpassed them because, as *The New York Times* put it, "his mind seems to be clogged by no forms, but goes with the lightnings' flash and illuminates its own pathways." Romanticism, Jeffersonian agrarianism, and the myth of the garden all combined to make the Jackson image a great political force. He

would not, probably, have become President without them. And once he was in office, they helped him define the national purpose in these same terms.

Two great—and opposing—visions of the future then dominated men's minds. The best Whigs—John Quincy Adams, Henry Clay, and others—hoped for a federally sponsored program of national development. In his first annual message Adams called for "Laws promoting the improvement of agriculture, commerce, and manufactures, the cultivation and encouragement of the mechanic[al] and of the elegant arts." He called for roads and canals, a national university, scientific exploration and research, and other measures. In his four years (1825–1829) the government spent almost as much on internal improvements as in the previous twenty-four years. The Bank of the United States followed a parallel policy. Under the direction of Nicholas Biddle, this government-sanctioned but autonomous financial agency moved to become a true central bank. It tried to stabilize an expanding economy by credit manipulations that would discourage overextension in flush times and encourage investment in lean ones. It established a national system of credit balancing that was advantageous to both West and East. It had some success in saving the shaky Western banks from their own greed and inexperience, then the causes of so many bank failures. This outraged speculators, wildcat bankers, and others who, as William Appleman Williams has said, wanted "help without responsibility. In their minds, at any rate, that was the working definition of democratic freedom."

By defining liberty in terms of unimpeded commercial opportunity and expansion, Jackson was able to preside over an odd but powerful coalition of landlords, entrepreneurs, Western farmers, and urban workingmen. The Bank of the United States was made to represent the money power, aristocracy, and privilege. Its destruction by Presidential veto in 1832 symbolized the triumph of opportunity over privilege and in a real sense assisted the spread of laissez faire, now seen as the best economic policy for a free people. This meant there would be a few effective means of controlling industrialism and no real way of making it responsive to the public interest. Indeed, the very sense that there was a public interest apart from the needs of individuals was fatally weakened. John Quincy Adams had cast the role of government in a positive mold. "The great object of civil government is the improvement of the condition of those who are party to the social compact." After him government was increasingly seen as having a negative function. Its prime duty was to remove the barriers to individual enterprise.

The greatest effect of the West's opening, then, was an unrestrained commercial exploitation that was to do the farmer who supported it both harm and good. The next greatest was to make imperialism the keystone of American national policy. Americans had spoken of empire even before the Revolution. It was fought in part, as Tories rightly observed, to create an American empire. It took time, however, to determine what that empire would be like. Americans saw expansion as the solution to most national problems, but they did not agree on how expansion should be managed. Eastern merchants saw foreign trade as the area in which expand, while Westerners were committed to the annexation of fresh land. Trade did increase, but in the 1830s and 1840s it was decided that America's future lay chiefly in the West. This was not simply because the land was there to be taken but also because agriculture was still seen as more virtuous than trade. Foreign commerce was not moral-

ly elevating. It did not improve the character, as living close to nature did. While there was a clear divine mandate for annexation, there was none for trade. The Jacksonian victory was, therefore, in effect a national decision for empire in the West. True, it was to be a benevolent empire created for the sake of freedom-loving yeomen in harmony with nature, a popular, even a democratic, empire in the sense that most American citizens would support it. But it would be an empire all the same, built, like the existing United States, by theft and conquest.

Imperialism justified

The decision to make a continental empire having been made, it was necessary to justify it. There were already many explanations as to why it was moral to seize good land. As God had assigned the country a special mission, He clearly intended the United States to have whatever was necessary to execute it. In 1787 John Adams remarked that the United States was destined to occupy all the northern part of this quarter of the globe and that, when accomplished, this would be "a great point gained in favor of the rights of mankind." American expansion was thus not based on greed but altruism, and it was sanctioned by natural law. One enthusiast in the 1850s carried this so far as to claim that since Americans were a chosen people, they had "a natural right. . .to possess the earth." Americans also had a special claim by virtue of the superior use to which they put the earth. It was proper to take land from the Indians because land was destined to be farmed, not hunted. Agriculture, as later mining and manufacturing, had a higher moral claim than hunting. In the case of the war with Mexico, this was amended to include more efficient as well as higher uses. Mexicans practiced agriculture for the most part, but badly. Thus God and Nature meant them to give way to better farmers. Collectively, these rationalizations became known as the theory of "Manifest Destiny."

A few Americans had no need of such labored defenses. Sam Houston said that as Americans had always cheated Indians and Mexicans were no better than Indians, "I see no reason why we should not go on the same course now and take their land." Most people could not face the facts so squarely, hence the need for apologetics. Some even went to the extreme of arguing that imperialism helped its victims. The Indians gained from the civilizing, Christian influence of white society. When the question of annexing Mexico came up, it was argued that the Mexicans were a decadent people who would be regenerated by contact with American virtue. The most powerful defense always, though, was probably the idea that American expansion increased the area of freedom.

Once people had worried that if the country got too large, freedom would decline. But having filled up the land east of the Mississippi and acquired the Louisiana Purchase with, it was thought, no ill effect, these fears diminished. People worried instead that if, for example, Texas was not annexed, it might become a tool of reactionary foreign despotisms. Thus failing to expand would endanger freedom. The extension of freedom was understood by Southerners to mean that by adding more states, their power in relation to the central government would increase. In effect, as abolitionists charged, "we were to extend the area of freedom by enlarging the boundaries of slavery." Individualism was an important part of this concept. As pioneer farmers were the best examples of individual liberty, expansion was necessary to increase their number, even at the expense of others. By virtue of their democracy, Americans were

entitled to deprive inferior peoples of their inferior rights. This notion of American superiority inspired one newspaper in the 1840s to suggest that America repudiate its debts on the ground that Europe had been sufficiently compensated by having helped spread American civilization.

The frontier thus created a demand for fresh lands, and it then provided the excuse for taking them. This became the distinctive feature of American imperialism. All peoples are given to self-deception. Americans were neither the first nor the last to try to make theft and murder seem altruistic. But the magnitude of American pretensions has been extraordinary, by world standards, since the second quarter of the nineteenth century. Americans had good reason to admire themselves in the Revolutionary era. A remote, underpopulated cluster of provincial societies managed to create a prosperous, self-governing nation with probably the best system of representative government in the world. This was a great feat and widely hailed as such. But the westward movement created, as we have seen, an empire riddled with contradictions. In economics the common good was to be secured through individual rapacity. American rights would be ensured by denying Indians, Mexicans, women, and others theirs. The area of freedom would be enlarged by the expansion of slavery. That national schizophrenia, so often remarked on by foreigners in modern times, dates essentially from this period.

The most immediate effect of the westward movement was the Civil War. As long as slavery was confined east of the Mississippi River and south of the Ohio, it seemed no great problem to Northerners. But it was made a problem by the fresh lands beyond the Mississippi, lands which it was America's manifest destiny to absorb. The difficulty was that destiny did not clearly manifest which labor system was to prevail there. The admission of Missouri showed that there were two different visions of what the American empire should be: the North wanted a commonwealth of independent farmers and the South wanted an extended manorial system. The Missouri crisis did not agitate the country so much as it did Congress, but it was a harbinger of the greater crises to come, "a fire bell in the night," as Jefferson said.

Throughout, the crisis was more political than moral. Federalists hoped to revive their failing fortunes by uniting the North behind them in a campaign for sectional dominance. Democrats, being strongest in the South, aimed to extend their influence by extending slavery. The morality of slavery and the interests of slaves were not at issue, either then or later. The split was papered over for a time by the Missouri Compromise, which banned slavery in the Louisiana Purchase above latitude 36° 30'N. But thoughtful men knew that the issue would arise again. Jefferson said: "A geographical line, coinciding with a marked principle, moral and political, once conceived and held up to the angry passions of men, will never be obliterated; and every new irritation will mark it deeper and deeper." This is precisely what happened, especially after the Mexican war opened up vast new territories for exploitation. Northern farmers saw the future of their empire as dependent on access to these lands. They believed that if slavery were not banned from them, slave labor would destroy free labor and the plantation would displace the family farm, as in the South. Southerners believed with equal fervor that the expansion of slavery was essential to its preservation. New lands were needed to replace the old ones worn out by cotton growing—as practiced then, a form of agriculture so wasteful that it has been called "soil mining." New slave states were needed to maintain the sectional balance in Congress

that alone, it was thought, would stave off abolition. Lincoln's election in 1860 marked the triumph of the Northern vision of empire over the Southern. It made secession inevitable. The North accepted war not to free the slaves but to secure the yeoman's interests. Slavery was the cause only in the sense that it introduced into the westward movement an irreconcilable conflict between planters and free farmers.

Slavery and the South

Though the expansion of slavery was the proximate cause of war in 1861, a deeper reason was that slavery as an institution had made the South in some respects a different country. The colonial South had many distinctive attributes—a plantation economy, different manners and customs and such—but its political and cultural values were enough like those of the North to make union possible. Washington and Jefferson had the same basic frame of reference as Adams and Franklin. This was still true in the early stages of the westward movement. The Kentucky frontier had much in common with the Ohio frontier. But by the 1830s Southerners had come to resemble one another much more than they did Northerners or even Westerners. They had their own culture and with it what can best be called a national sense. Because of this the Civil War was, as Southerners rightly saw it, a fight for independence.

One of the most curious features of slavery was that so few people gained tangibly from it. The typical white Southerner was a small farmer with a few acres planted in some cash crop, cotton or tobacco mainly. In some areas—South Carolina and Mississippi especially, where half the white population owned slaves—slave holding was widespread, but in most places only a minority had any slaves at all. One-quarter of the white families had slaves in Virginia and only one in thriteen owned slaves in Delaware. In 1860, 88 percent of all owners had less than 20 slaves. Almost 50 percent had less than 5. The slave-owning aristocracy consisted of about 10,000 planters with holdings of more than 50 slaves.

The plantation system in its mature form, as practiced on these large estates, was far more complex than the organization of free farm laborers. For one thing, as slaves had few incentives, they needed constant supervision—field hands especially. Planters thus became dependent on overseers, men of low status and modest abilities, and the overseers depended, in turn, on slave assistants called drivers. Despite intense surveillance, discipline on the plantation was a constant problem. Slaves wanted to be free and nearly always accepted manumission, even when it meant being transported to Africa by colonization societies. (Africa was as alien to most slaves as it was to whites.) Others escaped or ran away when they could and soldiered on the job when they could not. Poor work, even covert sabotage such as breaking tools and burning barns, was commonplace. Theft was usual; it was not seen by slaves as a crime but rather as compensation for the labor stolen from them by their masters. These were the most widespread forms of slave resistance, though murder and rebellion were not unknown. They were, however, infrequent because rebellion of any sort was nearly always unsuccessful and followed by savage reprisals. White fear of rebellion was nevertheless intense and expressed itself in widespread panics that periodically swept the South. These led to night patrols in plantation areas, upgraded militia training, and other military responses.

The most horrid and obvious evils associated with slavery included being sold down the river, whippings and torture, and the general tendency to overwork and underfeed slave laborers. Given the large capital investment planters had in slaves, they might have been expected to be solicitous of their wellbeing. But on the whole slaves seem often to have been treated worse than domestic animals. Medical care was minimal to nonexistent. Beatings, short rations, and long hours of work gave slaves a life expectancy perhaps only half that of free men.

But the worst aspect of slavery was probably not simple brutality. Since people are not animals, even when viewed as such, more subtle mechanisms are required to ensure obedience. Slave owners evolved a code of etiquette that tended to destroy the slave's identity and make him dependent on the master class and its values. Slaves were treated as children, beaten when they misbehaved, and rewarded with small trifles and privileges when they did well. Few were educated. Slaves were called "boy" or "girl" even when fully grown. The only religion tolerated on most plantations was the type that encouraged passivity, obedience, and other worldliness. The slave would be rewarded in the next life for his sufferings in this one.

Personality destruction and infantilism would have resulted had the system worked perfectly. It was not designed in advance, like the Nazi concentration camps, but developed slowly over time. Stanley M. Elkins has compared the plantation with the concentration camp all the same. Both were founded on terror and both were destructive of personality. Most concentration camp inmates did become infantile. Few escaped the sad fate of identifying with the system that oppressed them. Far from hating their guards, most came to see them as father figures. Some, the *Kapos* (camp equivalents of the slave drivers), outdid the SS guards in sheer brutality.

All these features of concentration camp life were found on plantations also, though not to the same degree. The plantation, since organized to turn a profit, was never so efficient as the camp. The chief evidence of this is the speed with which blacks adjusted to freedom. If their personalities had been destroyed, so many could not have escaped or resisted. Nor could they have become upright, self-supporting citizens, as most did on gaining their freedom.

But though it was inefficient as a destroyer of persons, the slave system left deep scars all the same. One of the ironies of slavery was that it worked not, as Americans thought, because blacks were so primitive but because they were not. Most black Africans came from sophisticated tribal cultures based on agriculture. They adjusted to slavery, despite the fearful trauma that enslavement and transportation inflicted on them, because they were accustomed to social order and discipline and were habituated to the rhythms and mandates of agricultural life. Indians could not be enslaved because most were too primitive to make the transition from nomadic food gathering to settled good growing as a way of life. But while blacks survived on the plantation, their original culture did not. The rich heritage they were born to was taken from them, like their labor and frequently their lives. This contributed to the difficulties free blacks encountered later. No constitutional amendment could heal wounds that had been centuries in the making.

Perhaps the most terrible single aspect of slavery was what it did to the black family. Whatever the situation today, in the past civilization has been closely linked to family life. Slave families had no legal existence. Normally children stayed with their mothers, but this was a matter of custom, not right. Fathers did not have even that much security. They might be sold down the river at any time.

There could be no marriage under these conditions, especially as slave women had little control over their bodies. They could not easily prevent members of the master class from having sexual intercourse with them. As they were rewarded for having children, there was a positive incentive to change mates when sterility was suspected. Promiscuity was thus built into the system. Slave women were sexually exploited. Slave men were denied all the normal attributes of manhood. They had no authority over mates and offspring and not even any assurance of continued proximity to them. They could neither provide for their children nor protect their women.

American slavery was, however, a more complex system than this suggests. Slaves did have a culture of their own. It would later produce jazz, a unique kind of folk religion, and other institutions. Family life, even though extralegal, was maintained. Drivers were not just assistants to the overseers but natural leaders, as the prominent role they played in Reconstruction shows. To a degree, they represented the slave's interest to the master and shared in the decision-making process by which plantation policies were arrived at. Though in theory the master was omnipotent, in practice the slave system required its victims' consent to be profitable. The planter held the high cards, but not the whole deck. He could not unilaterally determine the conditions of labor beyond a certain point without encountering resistance and declining output. The actual balance between his minimum demands and the slaves', which though smaller were no less real, was apparently determined through a mixture of trial and error and collective bargaining in which the drivers played a key role. Thus, while black slavery in America was a monstrous institution, it was not wholly destructive, nor were its victims entirely without resources of their own. The proof of this came during Reconstruction when ex-slaves, who might be supposed utterly lacking in the attributes of free men, became self-supporting and self-governing almost overnight—which fact attested both to slavery's weakness and to the black's strength.

Most people know, and knew even then, that slavery was a great wrong. Southerners had a bad conscience about slavery in the eighteenth century and only came to applaud it out of necessity in the nineteenth. Southern apologists never developed much conviction. It was hard to say that owning human beings was a good thing, especially as libertarian and humanitarian sentiments were rising everywhere in the Western world. Part of the hysteria with which Southern whites justified slavery in the 1840s and 1850s was surely a consequence of repressed guilt. People called on to defend the indefensible can hardly do so rationally. So Southerners made the wildest claims for their own virtue and cast the vilest aspersions on their critics. What else could they do?

The South was not without strengths; few viable societies are. Southern men regardless of station were famous for their politeness and hospitality. This helped disguise the class system, since a poor white could normally expect affability and respect from a planter even when they were not related—as in newer parts of the South they often were. The South was also easy on failures. No white, however impoverished, could occupy the bottom of the status ladder, which was reserved for blacks. And it was hard to starve, as the soil was so rich and the climate so mild that a few acres would support life. Poor whites had some reason to care for the South, as they would demonstrate in the Civil War. They fought fiercely and sacrificed much for a society which was harmful to them in many ways but which they loved all the same.

Perhaps this is only to say that nationalism can never be understood by foreigners. No one from the North can comprehend why Southerners of all stations loved the South, why a Robert E. Lee, who hated slavery and secession alike, would give everything to their defense. In some ways it is easier to see why people love the South today. Its worst features—segregation and the abuse of blacks—have been greatly modified. Its best features—courtesy, warmth, simple dignity—remain. No one coming from New York to New Orleans can fail to notice how much gentler ordinary human transactions are. There is no better place to ask for help, which complete strangers give cheerfully. Now the South shares its defects with the whole country, while its virtues are still its own.

Among the most striking features of the Old South was precisely that poor whites, though economically exploited by the system, were loyal to it. Slavery degraded white labor. Even when slaves did not compete directly with free workingmen, and they frequently did as skilled workers hired out by their owners or as factory hands rented by mill owners and the like, they made physical labor a mark of inferiority. Everyone aspired to be a planter or at least to live like one. Successful merchants and professional people bought slaves and cultivated the plantation style. Poor farmers, scratching out a mean living on what little good land escaped the planters, did not so much resent as envy their betters. If they could not live like planters, they could and frequently did follow the planters' lead. They repeatedly voted for politicians who served the planters' interests, not their own. And they imitated the planter by growing the cash crops he did, thus helping keep the region dependent on outsiders.

The whole South was victimized by its colonial economy. It exported raw materials and imported finished goods to the benefit of outsiders. The South lived on New York credit. Cotton was frequently shipped to New York before it went abroad. Many planters believed that New York creditors and middlemen took 40 cents out of every dollar of Southern profit. Though New Orleans exported half the volume of commodities that New York did, it imported only a tenth of the goods. Southerners complained bitterly of their economic subservience to the North, yet even *DeBow's Review,* the great organ of Southern commercial nationalism, was printed in New York.

The planters were often rich, but the South was poor. It sold its resources in the world market at unprotected prices and bought its finished goods dearly, thanks to tariffs that kept the price of manufactured products up. Planters were not interested in paying taxes for much of anything, so there were few public schools in the South. According to the census of 1850, the white illiteracy rate in the South was 20.3 percent, in the middle states 3 percent, and in New England 0.42 percent. These figures were probably low in each case, but the proportions seem about right. Planters did provide for higher education, since it benefited them directly. There were more colleges per capita in the South than the North, though their quality was poorer. They preached the planter line and, as so many were military academies, readied the planters' sons for martial leadership.

Even when poor whites were literate, they had nothing to read that could make a difference. Newspapers were censored throughout the South from the 1830s on. Laws were passed against printing or distributing abolitionist literature. More important, a paper could not survive without ruling class approval. To take the wrong line would cost the editor not only subscriptions and advertising but sometimes even his life. Some were murdered and more were challenged to duels. As

the laws against dueling were rarely enforced, the chief requirements for editorial independence were good marksmanship and physical courage. One Richmond editor fought eight duels in two years. His was an exceptional case. The threat of a duel was enough to bring most editors into line, other forms of pressure having failed. Southerners did not read many books other than the novels of Walter Scott. When sectional tensions got really high, Northern newspapers and magazines were effectively embargoed, often by postmasters. Southern churches were devoted to slavery and were another means of encouraging uniformity of thought and expression. They stiffened the public opinion that was the principal instrument of social control in the South as elsewhere.

When law and public sentiment did not ensure conformity, violence rarely failed to. As John Hope Franklin points out, the South was the most violent region of the country as measured by the incidence of murders, lynchings, and military enlistments. Though a minority of the white population, Southerners produced two-thirds of the soldiers who fought in the Mexican war. Militia units were more common and enjoyed higher status than elsewhere. When war broke out, there were 700,000 Southern militiamen, often well armed and frequently well led by graduates of the numerous military academies. Individual violence was usual, partly because much of the South remained underdeveloped and frontier conditions hung on longer there. The village bully was a regional institution. The upper classes dueled. Vigilantism was more important in the South than anywhere else, perhaps for the same reason. Vigilantes fought Indians—on whom it was always open season—and chased runaway blacks and criminals. In 1859 in Louisiana, 3,000 vigilantes ran down 150 outlaws, executing many and exiling the rest. This was typical of what

Figure 7-1 Former slave quarters on a model plantation, Oak Lawn, in Louisiana. 1864. (*Culver Pictures*)

passed for law and order. Even the more conventional processes of justice were tainted. Southerners did not like to house prisoners (except debtors, a practice which lasted until the 1840s in some areas), so corporal punishment in lieu of imprisonment continued right up to the war. Flogging, branding, mutilation, and castration (for rape) were cheap and, it was thought, effective deterrents. They were therefore hard to stop. Penal reform in the South was confined pretty much to the building of penitentiaries, a sign of moral progress that had not yet appeared as late as 1860 in four states. Since it was so widespread and so widely condoned, violence was a mighty influence sustaining Southern uniformity. When the sectional crisis worsened, it was easy to erect a kind of police state in the South that kept unpersuaded elements—Whigs, merchants sometimes, and independent farmers in certain areas— silent.

Nowhere else in the country did misery flourish on such a scale. Whites exploited blacks, planters exploited everyone else. Poor whites were kept down by being kept ignorant. They were manipulated into supporting a system that degraded their labor, destroyed their future, and led them finally into a rebellion from which they had nothing

to gain and everything to lose. Even upper-class white women suffered. Though idealized for their presumed purity and virtue, their condition depended on pretending that their sons and husbands were not having sexual relations with slaves. There were few large planter families that did not have enslaved relatives who, though unacknowledged, were not unknown. There were planter children who were served by their own half brothers and sisters. These facts made a mockery of Southern domestic ideals. Southerners proclaimed the sanctity of their homes and the purity of their women. Yet they violated black women, and the issue thus produced gave the lie to both. Their homes were profaned. The honor of white women was only ignorance or, what was worse, the appearance of it. Women who knew better had to pretend that they did not. The moral and psychic harm done by such contradictions is impossible to calculate.

The discrepancy between what Southerners said and did was very great but while they were quick to point out Northern contradictions, they were blind to their own. Poor white farmers were persuaded that they had a great stake in the institutions—slavery and the plantation—that were ruining them. White women preached domestic pieties that anyone with eyes to see knew were widely disregarded by their men. A class of *nouveau riche*, uncultivated planters, many of them living barely a step removed from the frontier, characterized themselves as a race of noblemen and spoke perpetually of honor and chivalry while practicing or condoning barbarities. These illusions were so extravagant and so widespread that they could not be sustained except in isolation. The South became a closed society, not just in self-defense against a North that was expanding more vigorously but also to preserve those fragile deceptions on which the integrity of Southern civilization depended.

In the 1840s and 1850s the South became in fact another country with a distinctive culture (in the anthropological sense) of its own. Distinguished by poverty at the bottom, arrogance at the top, and ignorance all the way through; nurturing the most pervasively brutalizing folkways of its era; wholly cut off from the artistic, intellectual, and humanitarian achievements of the age; the South yet claimed to be a land of honor, courtesy, cultivation, and elegance. In the end it preferred war and ruin to exposure. For though the war was fought to extend the area of slavery, it was rightly perceived by most Southerners as the only way of maintaining the region's delicate internal balance. Lincoln's election did not mean that the slaves would be freed. It did signify that the locus of power was moving north. The South could no longer stay in the Union and still keep the nineteenth century at bay. Northern dominance meant inevitably the future triumph of Northern values. Southern culture could not forever withstand this pressure. Neither, probably, could slavery. Having lost the struggle to build an empire in the West, having failed to attract immigrants to offset the North's population growth, without an

ideology to capture the popular imagination —like the Northern cry of free soil, free labor, and free men—and handicapped by an underdeveloped colonial economy, the South had to secede to survive. This long process, that saw the South corrupted by its "peculiar institution" and then destroyed by the effort to preserve it, is the most tragic sequence in American history. It produced some of the most frightful crimes against humanity ever committed by Americans and led to the most destructive war ever fought by them. Its consequences are with us yet.

Selected references

A good survey is John C. Miller, *The Federalist Era, 1789–1801* (1957). Two books by Noble E. Cunningham, Jr., are useful: *The Jeffersonian Republican . . . 1789–1801* (1957) and *The Jeffersonian Republicans in Power . . . 1801–1809* (1963). George Dangerfield, *The Era of Good Feelings* (1952) and *The Awakening of American Nationalism, 1815–1828* (1965), are finely written accounts. Glyndon G. Van Deusen, *The Jacksonian Era, 1828–1848* (1959), carries the story forward. A comprehensive social history is Alice F. Tyler, *Freedom's Ferment: Phases of American Social History to 1860* (1944). Vernon L. Parrington, *The Romantic Revolution in America, 1800–1860* (1927), is dated but matchless. There is an enormous literature on Turner and his theory. A good place to begin learning it is the American Historical Association pamphlet by Ray Allen Billington, *The American Frontier* (1958). One of the most influential works of modern scholarship is Henry Nash Smith, *Virgin Land: The American West as Symbol and Myth* (1950). An interesting study is John W. Ward, *Andrew Jackson: Symbol for an Age* (1955). On Jackson's war with the bank, see Bray Hammond,

Banks and Politics in America: From the Revolution to the Civil War (1957). The standard work on the ideology of expansion is Albert K. Weinberg, *Manifest Destiny* (1935). William A. Williams, *The Contours of American History* (1961), is an outstanding critique of expansionism from colonial times to the present.

Allan Nevins, *Ordeal of the Union* (1947), in two volumes, is good on the politics leading to war. Avery O. Craven, *The Growth of Southern Nationalism,* 1848–1861 (1953), shows how the South acquired a national consciousness. Clement Eaton, *The Growth of Southern Civilization* (1961), deals with the region's peculiar culture. The most subtle, anguished, caring analysis remains W. J. Cash, *The Mind of the South* (1941). There are many books on slavery, the most impressive of which is Kenneth M. Stampp, *The Peculiar Institution* (1956). The comparison between slavery and concentration camps is developed in Stanley M. Elkins, *Slavery* (1959). The standard history of American Negroes is John Hope Franklin, *From Slavery to Freedom* (1967). See also his *The Militant South* (1956).

EIGHT

The Antebellum Crisis

Period covered:	1800–1860
Emphases:	Economic growth.
	Urban violence.
	Utopian communities.
	Reform movements.
	Abolition.
	Literature.
Events:	Revival of 1830
	Publication of Emerson's *Nature*, 1836
	Oneida Community, 1847
	First women's rights convention, 1848
	Publication of Thoreau's *Walden,* 1854
	Burn's rescue, 1854
	John Brown's raid, 1859

Economic growth

Though in the end politics would dominate the era, most of the time people were concerned with the problems of everyday life. By the 1820s the basic character of the nineteenth century was already established. The population grew rapidly and moved frequently, from east to west and from rural areas to urban ones. The combination of a high birth rate and a high immigration rate doubled the population every twenty-five years or so. In 1820 there were about 10 million people in the United States, 13 million in 1830, 17 milion in 1840, 23 million in 1850, and 31 million in 1860. By then there were more people in America than in the United Kingdom and nearly as many as in France. Most people were still farmers in the 1820s and 1830s, but improved transportation stimulated commerce once the panic of 1819 subsided. Rivers were exploited by the new steamboats, of which several hundred plied Western waters by 1830.

The Great Lakes had a thriving seaborne commerce carried by steamships as well as sailing vessels. To the natural waterways ingenious Americans added artificial ones that gave the Northeast and Great Lakes area a good long-haul freight system. This was chiefly because of the 350-mile-long Erie Canal, the greatest construction effort yet attempted in America, which opened the back country to New York City and gave it a permanent lead over rival ports. Other seaboard states tried to equal the Erie Canal system but none succeeded. Together with feeder canals that tied the major rivers of Indiana and Ohio to Lake Erie, this great canal made possible the rapid development of the upper Mississippi Valley that followed. Farmers now could send their surplus either down river to New Orleans or cross country to New York. Railroads later made this long-haul system even more efficient, but the waterways played a crucial role in developing the country for generations. The U.S. Merchant Marine, led by the great clipper ships, flourished too for a while, until in the late 1850s British steamships powered by government subsidies became dominant.

As America was an underdeveloped country, individual entrepreneurs needed plenty of help, which they got from the state and national governments and from abroad. Washington provided a protective tariff, land grants, internal improvements, and certain commercial and banking services. The states and some municipalities accumulated a bonded indebtedness of some $200 million in the antebellum period for bridges, canals, railroads, and other internal improvements without which economic growth could hardly have been sustained. They were greatly assisted by foreign investors, Englishmen especially, who put another $200 million into the economy, mostly by purchasing state and municipal securities which were wrongly thought to be more reliable than private issues. After the panic of 1837, local governments often simply defaulted, some permanently. All the same, this great surge of investment had done its work. It was the contemporary equivalent of foreign aid and enabled the United States to reach what W. W. Rostow calls the takeoff point, the stage in economic development at which growth becomes self-sustaining. Thereafter foreign capital, though useful, was not essential.

The transportation revolution, as it has been called, was a prelude to the industrial and urban revolutions of the antebellum period. There were less than 10,000 miles of railroad track in 1850. By 1860, thanks partly to federal land grants, there were over 30,000 miles of track. Increasingly, local short lines with various widths of tracks were consolidated into trunk lines with standard gauge tracks. The magnetic telegraph helped the railroads operate more efficiently and bound the sprawling transcontinental empire into a single communications network. By 1860 there were 50,000 miles of telegraph wire laid. A year later the Pacific telegraph, 3,595 miles of wire, linked New York with San Francisco. The telegraph and the rotary steam press made a national news gathering and distributing network possible. In 1846 the Associated Press was organized to collect news by wire. Newspapers no longer had to depend on exchanges with other papers for their news. By 1860 there were 3,000 newspapers led by the great metropolitan dailies of New York, like Horace Greeley's *Tribune* and James Gordon Bennett's *Herald.* They had large circulations and some national influence. But journalism remained personal nonetheless, as the publisher was usually his own editor-in-chief.

Magazines went national also. There had been hundreds, perhaps thousands, of short-lived magazines before the 1850s. But with *Harper's Monthly* (170,000 subscribers), the *Atlantic Monthly, Putnam's,* and *Harper's Weekly*, the country acquired durable organs of middle-class culture. These advances in transportation and communication were essential to the development of a national spirit, which was most intense in the most developed regions. All the newspapers in the South had a smaller daily circulation than the New York *Herald* and the *Tribune* combined. And many Southern papers were so heavily censored by public opinion that they could only promote regionalism anyway. Elsewhere in the 1840s and 1850s, however, a true national identity was created that made secession, when it came, a far more odious act than it would have been a generation earlier.

Patriotism was as much a consequence of the printing press as of the empire.

The factory system grew apace too. Better transportation and communication systems, water and steam power, and various technical changes made machines more important than men. Craftsmanship declined. Mass production increased. Eli Whitney had shown that even something as complicated as the firearm could be mass produced thanks to the principle of interchangeable parts. Invention followed invention thereafter. In 1830, there were 544 inventions patented; in 1860, 4,778. These included the Howe-Singer sewing machine, in 1846, which made possible ready-to-wear shoes and garments. A process for vulcanizing rubber was discovered by Charles Goodyear in 1839. Agricultural implements multiplied, including the mechanical thresher and especially John McCormick's reaper, which was patented in 1834 and manufactured at the rate of 3,000 a year by 1850. In that year, for the first time, manufactured products were roughly equal in value to agricultural products.

Textiles were the most highly organized branch of industry in the antebellum period. The first complete cotton factory had been built in Waltham, Massachusetts. By 1819 it employed 300 workers, mostly women. The great age of textile expansion began soon after when Lowell, Massachusetts, the first important factory town, was founded. In 1839 the Lowell mills employed about 8,500 workers; in 1848, 13,000, about two-thirds of them women. The Northeast had the most developed industrial economy of any region, and it hinged on textile production, coarse cotton, woolens, and silks for the most part. In 1860 the Northeast alone had over half the capital invested in manufacturing and two-thirds of the manufacturing output by value.

The factory system created an industrial

proletariat. In 1860 there were 1,311,000 workers employed in industry, half of them women and children. In many places workers lived in company dormitories, where their private lives could be monitored as efficiently as their working lives. Others lived in tenements and such. An investigator in Lowell in 1847 found a house containing a store and 120 people, more than half of them adults. One room was occupied by two families, one of which consisted of two parents, eight children (four of them over fifteen years of age), and four adult boarders. Pay was low, hence the overcowding; and hours were very long in most factories. Federal workers obtained the ten-hour day by executive order in 1840, but few others did. Some states passed ten-hour laws that were rarely enforced. In Massachusetts it took over thirty years of agitation to get the 1874 ten-hour law. In most places workers put in an eleven- or twelve-hour day, which was only slightly shorter than the average work day of the eighteenth century and far more onerous, since it was conducted under industrial conditions where discipline was close and dirt, noise, and danger were the worker's constant companions.

Naturally, workers made many attempts to organize and many strikes were conducted, but to little effect. Unions organized in flush times collapsed during depressions, when workers took what they could get. In the depression that followed the panic of 1837, one-third of the working population of New York City was unemployed. In New England, from 1839 to 1843, wages fell from 30 to 50 percent. The making of this exploited, degraded, and frequently despised proletariat was an early and durable consequence of the industrial revolution. The worst abuses lasted for a century and some are with us yet.

The special feature of America's proletariat was its racial, ethnic, and religious diversity.

Disraeli spoke of "the two nations" to describe the gulf between rich and poor in England. America was not two but a dozen—a score of nations. The rich differed from the poor, and the poor differed from one another. These distinctions were to make every social problem more severe, every solution more difficult to find. Before 1830 American diversity posed few problems. Many immigrants were English and adjusted easily. The Dutch in New York and the Germans in Pennsylvania had been here a long time and their neighbors were used to them. Mostly farmers, they created no social problems to speak of. Then the rate of immigration began to pick up and the immigrant population began to change. In the 1830s, some 500,000 immigrants arrived, many of them Irish. In the 1840s, 1½ million Europeans arrived; in the 1850s, 2½ million. By 1860 there were 1½ million Irishmen and a million new Germans. Most of these were working people who, unlike earlier migrants, remained in the cities.

The cities grew and changed astonishingly in consequence. New York expanded from 312,000 persons in 1840 to 805,000 in 1860. In the same period Philadelphia went from 220,000 to 565,000 people. The new Western cities grew even more remarkably. From a city of 10,000 in the 1830s, St. Louis had become home to 160,000 people by 1860. During these same years Chicago's population rose from 250 to 109,000. Not all this fabulous expansion was the result of foreign immigration. The movement from country to city was well underway. Rural areas in New England were already declining in population. All this made for an extraordinarily mobile society. The westward movement, immigration, rural depopulation, urban growth, and internal mobility (Peter Knights's study of Boston indicates that 30 to 40 percent of the population changed residences every year during the 1840s) combined to make for a population flux as great as any that came later. We talk of physical mobility today as if Americans had all stayed put until automobiles were invented. But in fact everything has been in motion for a long time.

Enormous changes produce enormous effects. The most striking of these was the rapid increase of violence after 1830. There was already a great deal of what might be called background violence. Slavery generated a continuous stream of violence in the form of corporal punishment, slave uprisings, and the fear of them—which produced repression even when there were no slave conspiracies. In the South and on the frontier, lynch law and vigilante actions were commonplace. Aggression against the Indians was more or less continuous. In a literal sense the American empire was built in these years on the bodies of Indians and Mexicans. After 1830 three new causes of violence were added to the standard list just drawn.

Urban violence

The swelling cities made urban crime an important national phenomenon for the first time. There are no reliable ways of measuring the increase, but even if crime grew only as rapidly as the urban population did, it would have been important. Most likely it grew even faster. For one thing, with the city came the slum, whose lumpenproletarians are the most common breeders of crime and its usual victims. Slums developed in New York City as early as the 1830s and in other booming cities soon after. As few cities had the will or resources to cope with their staggering growth, there was nothing to restrain the slums and little in the way of services for their deprived inhabitants. Often there were no

sewers, and water supplies quickly became contaminated—hence the great cholera and typhoid epidemics of the period. So many people dwelt in cellars in New York that one-twentieth of the population was said to live underground. One dwelling, an old brewery called the Den of Forty Thieves, was home to a thousand inmates, mostly Irish and Negro, and averaged a murder at night. New York's infant mortality rate showed the effects of this appalling congestion. From a base of between 120 to 145 deaths per thousand live births, it rose to 180 in 1850, 220 in 1860, and 240 in 1870.

There was no one to keep the peace among these desperately overcrowded and destitute populations. Police normally entered the Five Points district of New York and similar places only as paid guides. Street gangs exploited the poor and fought one another as they pleased. Prostitution, gambling, and every sort of crime and vice flourished as never before, even along such major thoroughfares as Broadway in New York. Later in the century political machines, expanded police forces, and other developments restored some order to the cities. Thus it is probably fair to say that lawlessness was most pronounced in the mid-nineteenth-century city. The old mechanisms for keeping order had broken down, and new ones had not yet been devised.

The second novel source of violence in this period was antislavery. Abolitionists committed some violent acts, as when freeing recaptured slaves in the North. Much more was committed against them by proslavery or unionist mobs. This type of violence probably reached its peak in the 1830s.

Immigrants contributed heavily both to urban crime and proslavery mob action, but they were also victimized by nativist mobs. The American dream was always a white

Anglo-Saxon Protestant dream. Blacks threatened it as slavery tried to expand in the 1840s and 1850s, and so did the Irish. When they began entering America, the Protestant response was swift and brutal—especially in the cities where Irishmen tended to settle and where revivalism was important. Acts of violence were committed against immigrants, fired by the anti-Catholicism which was an inherited prejudice in England's colonies. Revivalism gave it a new energy, for while not all evangelical Christians were anti-Catholic, many were. Elijah Lovejoy, though an abolitionist martyr, was a raving bigot. Lyman Beecher's book *A Plea for the West* (1835) urged that the country be saved from a conspiracy of European despots to destroy republicanism by peopling the West with Catholic immigrants.

The Irish replied in kind. In 1833 a band of drunken Irishmen beat a Protestant to death in Boston, and an anti-Catholic mob burned down homes in retaliation. The next year Lyman Beecher gave three anti-Catholic sermons in Boston, after which a well-organized mob burned down the Ursuline convent school in nearby Charlestown. The secular press and establishment leaders, including Beecher, condemned this act. But attempts to convict the conspirators failed. In the meantime, the Irish were still organizing mobs of their own. In 1834 a speaker for the nativist Protestant Association was attacked while addressing a group of Baltimore Baptists. The next year another gang broke up Broadway Hall in New York, where a debate on popery was being held. These acts brought considerable support to the Protestant Association, which organized more such debates in the next several years.

The Irish, even when not defending their faith, were quick to fight. In 1834 an Irish mob in New York put the mayor, sheriff, and a posse to flight and terrorized the city. In 1844

the effort of New York City to ban swine from the streets provoked a riot by Irish pig owners. Immigrant workmen on the railroads and canals were especially unruly. In 1839 a riot between Irish and German workmen on the Chesapeake and Ohio Canal ended only after the militia had killed ten of them. As this suggests, the Irish did not have a monopoly on mob violence. In Cincinnati in 1842 a parade of German military companies ended in rioting after some of their officers stabbed a boy who had annoyed them.

All this stimulated nativist political action which reached an early peak in Philadelphia in the summer of 1844. Nativist candiates aroused the Irish, and in May and July there were days of violence that claimed thirteen lives. Several churches were burned down. No-popery candidates were widely blamed for the rioting; therefore nativism, having been discredited, subsided for a while, unless one counts the Astor Place riot of 1849 as a nativist event, which it was in a way. The mob that lost twenty lives attacking a New York opera house did so because they were inflamed by nativists against a noted English actor playing there. The arrival of Monsignor Gaetano Bedini, a papal nuncio, in 1853 renewed the struggle in earnest. Violence was continuous thereafter. Several Catholic churches were burned in the mid-1850s, often after local mobs had been aroused by itinerant anti-Catholic revivalists.

Though frequently ignited by specific events, bigotry was fed by a stream of poisonous literature throughout the period. This included the pornographic *Awful Disclosures* of Maria Monk, which purported to tell of orgies and atrocities in a Montreal convent and sold 300,000 copies between 1836 and 1860. Equally important were the more conventional publications of established evangelical bodies like the American Bible Society, the American Tract Society, and the

American Home Missionary Society. These children of the evangelical movement became solidly anti-Catholic in the 1850s and made nativism respectable. Several decades of this kind of propaganda and agitation produced one of the oddest movements in American history—the short-lived Native American party.

In 1850 a number of nativist secret societies combined to form the Supreme Order of the Star-spangled Banner. Members were pledged to secrecy and obliged to answer questions with "I know nothing," hence the term Know-Nothings. In 1854 the order created a political arm which immediately won stunning victories. In the fall Know-Nothings, alone or in concert with Whigs, carried five states and sent seventy-five men to Congress. In Massachusetts, the Governor, every state officer, the entire senate, and all but two of the 378 house members were Know-Nothings. In 1856 their Presidential candidate, the immortal Millard Fillmore, got 25 percent of the popular vote. After that the party collapsed.

Like the Whigs, Know-Nothings succumbed to sectionalism. Then too, they were unable to make good on their promises to restrict immigrant political rights and make naturalization more difficult. Even in Massachusetts they could not translate local dominance into anti-Catholic legislation. The Native American party could not have risen so rapidly had the national party system not been in such disarray. Still, its astonishing if brief success at the polls was evidence of the deep fears and hatred that immigration provoked.

Utopian communities

If the antebellum period was a time of conservative nationalism and sometimes hysteria, it was also an age of reform. Another paradox was that during it individualism and socialism flourished together. While Jacksonians, entrepreneurs, Romantics, and revivalists were going one way, Shakers, communists, perfectionists, and the like were going another. There had been Christian communists in America since the seventeenth century. In the Ephrata Monastery and other communities they held all material things in common and lived as they imagined early Christians did. The Shakers were the most important of these millennial communists. The Shakers' leader, Ann Lee, claimed to be the feminine equivalent of Christ. She came to America from England in 1774, and by 1800 there were a dozen small Shaker communities, chiefly in the West.

They were millennialists: that is, they believed that the end of the world was at hand. But they were not proselytizers, since they expected their great mission to occur in the next life, when they would help mankind achieve perfection. Being unconcerned with numbers, they practiced strict celibacy and sexual equality. After 1800 they increased all the same, partly because they offered certainty and security in a time of bewildering change and partly because the Great Revival stirred currents of belief that made people want to live Christlike lives—something that was clearly easier in the monastic circumstances of a Shaker community than elsewhere. New Light Baptists proved to be especially responsive. By the 1840s there were perhaps 6,000 Shakers in dozens of Northern and Western communities.

It was a peculiarity of the age that whereas their unorthodox religious beliefs generated much hostility against them at first, their unusual social and economic practices arroused little controversy. The Shakers were industrious farmers and artisans. Their furniture and manufactured products were both functional and beautiful—in fact, beautiful because functional—and in great demand at the time for being sturdy and practical. Now they are eagerly sought after for aesthetic reasons. The Shakers were in many ways the most successful nineteenth-century utopians. Their internal structure was carefully designed to ensure justice and tranquility. Their prosperity enabled the sect to continue for generations while most other communist experiments quickly perished. Some Shaker communities survived into the twentieth century. As John Humphrey Noyes put it: "Their success has been the solid capital that has upheld all the paper theories."

The most interesting utopian experiment was Noyes's great Oneida Community. He was the son of a prosperous merchant who was converted when the Finney revival swept into Vermont. He enrolled in the Andover Seminary, but, finding it too arid and formalistic, moved to New Haven. There he encountered Dr. Nathaniel W. Taylor of Yale, who taught that perfection was possible in this life. Already a millennialist, Noyes became a perfectionist too. This was sufficiently irregular to cost him his license to preach in New Haven. But Noyes was even more heretical for believing that the millennium had arrived and that the Kingdom of God was already begun. His ideas resembled those of the Shakers, but he disagreed with their view that sex distinctions did not persist after death. Hence, though personally attracted to celibacy, he turned instead to the question of what kind of sexual arrangements were consistent with the divine order. He early decided that marriage could not be among them. In the late 1830s he wrote:

When the will of God is done on earth, as it is in heaven, there will be no marriage. The marriage supper of the Lamb is a feast at which every dish is free to every guest. Exclu-

siveness, jealousy, quarreling, have no place there, for the same reason as that which forbids the guests at a thanksgiving dinner to claim each his separate dish, and quarrel with the rest for his rights. In a holy community there is no more reason why sexual intercourse should be restrained by law, than why eating and drinking should be—and there is as little occasion for shame in the one case as in the other.

After failing to unite the scattered groups of New England perfectionists, Noyes settled down to build a community of his own in Putney, Vermont. He married, and his wife promptly had four miscarriages. Like other men in the same situation, he resolved not to expose his wife to such hazards again. Unlike them, he looked for a way to continue having sexual relations. As there was no reliable contraceptive available then, he decided on intercourse without orgasm which had the added value of calling for male self-restraint—a useful discipline in its own right. It also encouraged foreplay, thus making for a mutually enjoyable experience. Under these conditions sex became what Noyes thought it should be, a sacrament that expressed love of one another and of God. Male self-restraint became the physical foundation on which complex marriage was built.

By 1843 there were twenty-eight adults and nine children in the Putney Community. Gradually they moved toward communal ownership of property, absorbed Noyes's teachings, and worked out the practical details of communal life. While Americans ate many hot meals a day, four being not unusual, the Putney group had only one. This alone freed women from endless drudgery. In 1846 they began practicing complex marriage, which to outsiders seemed like nothing so much as free love. They were driven out of

Putney and ended up in Oneida, New York, where a tiny perfectionist group had established a sawmill. There, in the heart of the Burned-Over District where religious enthusiasm was high, they felt free to refine their basic institutions—Bible communism, complex marriage, and mutual criticism.

Bible communism was the fully shared life as predicted by the Bible and practiced in heaven. Complex marriage was the extension of Christian virtue into family life. Whereas ordinary marriage divided mankind into tiny, isolated groups and stimulated jealousy, possessiveness, and other vices, complex marriage united humanity into one loving fellowship. In order for man to reconcile himself with God in this most intimate area, he needed to understand that love and propagation were quite different matters. The union of two people was higher than and different from the fruit of that union. Masculine self-control made it possible to implement in practice this theoretical distinction. Sex was vital not to reproduce the species but because human nature required it. Celibacy and promiscuity alike were perversions of the divine order, as was the rush to orgasm, which Noyes compared with gluttony.

In order to prepare people for the sacrament of complex marriage, an elaborate training program was devised at Oneida. This included not only formal instruction but lab work in the discipline essential to complex marriage. On coming of age, young men were introduced to the practice of self-restraint by older women who were past menopause and hence in no danger of pregnancy when the inevitable mistakes occurred. Only after they were adept at giving pleasure and preventing conception were they free to establish relations with women their own age. Nor were these arrangements left to chance. The same women who provided sex education also served as intermediaries between the young people, making sure that both parties were agreeable to the relationship and that it conformed to the customs of the sect. Thus young people were prepared for successful unions and spared personal rejection when the other party was not agreeable—both great improvements on the dating game practiced by young Americans then and with greater energy if not better results today. Complex marriage, which seemed to outsiders so licentious, was a carefully structured alternative to monogamy that offered variety without promiscuity while protecting the rights and assuring the pleasure of women in ways that conventional society has rarely approached.

Noyes was against laws and government in theory since he believed heaven did without them. Yet Oneida had to be governed in some way. Noyes's own personal authority provided much of it, and mutual criticism took care of the rest. This was a practice by which members of the community had their faults publicly examined at regular intervals. Everyone was free to speak at these times, feeling limited only by loving fellowship and the knowledge that they too would be examined in their turn. Mutual criticism did work, as evidenced by the small number of people who had to be expelled from the community. It was further evidence to believers that they had achieved perfection, though Noyes's skill in guiding these sessions probably had much to do with their effectiveness in molding character and conduct.

Oneida was one of the most prosperous utopian communities ever, partly through luck but mainly because it was work-oriented and well managed. Samuel Newhouse, a legendary trapper, was converted, and thereafter Oneida manufactured a superior animal trap of his design with great success. Later it added tableware and other products to its line. High sales enabled the community to hire hundreds of workmen from the neighborhood. These workmen were well paid and became defenders of what to others seemed a bizarre institution. As a mainstay of the local economy, Oneida had the support of that public opinion which counted most in its struggles with higher authority.

In the end, Oneida was a victim both of history and its own success. As time went on, Victorian prudery worsened. The Comstock Act was passed, denying the use of the mails to "obscene" material. This made it impossible for Noyes to publicize complex marriage and the ideas behind it. The hostile climate of opinion also prevented the community from gaining new recruits and transformed it from an advance guard of the new religion into a holding action. Prosperity enabled the community to have its young men educated at the best colleges. Noyes was not afraid of such new ideas as Darwinism. He thought science and religion were entirely compatible and was himself a practical social scientist. Oneida was the only community to become a laboratory for eugenics (Noyes called it stirpiculture), the science of breeding human beings advocated by Francis Galton and others. Fifty-eight children were conceived along these lines. Two-thirds of them lived far beyond the normal life expectancy of their time. But the result of sending Oneida men to secular colleges was that they became secularized. Most, on returning home, brought with them the conventions and beliefs of Victorian America. The faith Oneida was built on waned. As Noyes grew older, his powers failed, and with them his authority. The great weakness of Oneida, though also responsible for its early vigor, was its dictatorial structure. As a young man Noyes had broken his mother's claim on him and bent her to his will. When one of his own sons

rebelled, Noyes had him put in an insane asylum. By denying the young their share in Oneida's governance, Noyes forced them to choose between submission and revolution. Having been raised too well for the former, they naturally chose the latter. Noyes, like so many other autocrats, was his own worst enemy and the architect of his own destruction. After he was overthrown, the community voted to dissolve and transformed itself into a corporation which, as Oneida Community Silver, prospers even today. It was an appropriately ironic conclusion to the most brilliant of all nineteenth-century communal experiments.

There were a great many religious communities in early America and a good many secular experiments too. But the secular groups never prospered as the Shakers, and other religious bodies did. The most spectacular failure, because it was the best financed and most publicized secular community, was New Harmony, Indiana. It was founded by Robert Owen, a pioneer English industrial who attempted to make New Lanark, where his mills were, a model working-class town. Unlike most of the cotton lords, Owen did not think his wealth a function of personal genius and virtue. He understood that it came from the new technology which had so greatly increased productivity, and he thought that, as wealth was a social product, its benefits should extend to the whole society that had created it. He tried to make Parliament think so too. That failing, he resolved to secure radical changes beyond the modest reforms of New Lanark by creating ideal communities from scratch. Their brilliant example would transform society by osmosis. It would be a nonviolent revolution. Labor-saving machinery would reduce work and enhance profits; communal dining and marketing arrangements would secure further economies. In time, Owen came to favor the classless society and the abolition of private property. He then saw private capital as both the cause and consequence of individual greed, and likened business competition to a civil war in which the few prosper by stealing from the many.

Unlike most radical theorists, Owen had both the wealth and the will to implement his views. In 1824 the Rappites of Harmony, Indiana, a German pietist community, put their property on the market, having decided to return to Pennsylvania (where, at Old Economy in what is now metropolitan Pittsburgh, they thrived for many years). For $135,000 Owen acquired from them a ready-built community of 20,000 acres with 180 structures and housing for 700 people. This was a great bargain but a fatal one. Once news of it got out, people began drifting out to Harmony—now called New Harmony, thus depriving Owen of the chance to select members. This was bad enough, but even worse was Owen's failure to work out in detail the practical arrangements needed to translate his theories into reality. This was what enabled squatters to distort his plan at the outset. Owen was one of those men whose grasp of affairs was limited to business. Confronted with a situation beyond his experience, he was quite unable to display those practical gifts that made him rich in the first place. Owen arrived in the United States to considerable acclaim, much of it generated by himself as he spoke widely and successfully on behalf of his ideas. He met a host of great Americans and addressed a joint session of Congress, proof again of the contemporary tolerance for secular radicalism. The only real attacks on New Harmony were directed against its presumed aetheism.

Owen's energy and eloquence were, however, less effective in New Harmony than in Washington. He attracted a distinguished group of colonists (in addition to the frontier farmers already on hand) who proved more interested in cultural and intellectual pursuits than in agriculture or industry. New Harmony enjoyed a brilliant round of lectures, debates, and discussions. Six different constitutions were adopted during one eight-month period. The community had many parties and frolics along with the usual fire and militia drills. Freedom of religion naturally obtained, and New Harmony's pulpit was frequently occupied by visiting preachers who indicted the community for being godless. In the meantime, the Rappites's small factories were allowed to languish. There were not enough reliable farmers, and the rate of turnover was high. In the end, New Harmony lived mostly off Owen's capital. Factionalism inevitably developed and secessions took place. In 1827 Owen gave up and returned to England, having spent most of his fortune (though his sons inherited New Harmony, which as a real estate investment prospered in the long run). This sad experience discredited Owenism, as did the failure of numerous small imitations of New Harmony. Secular utopianism did not revive until the 1840s, when dozens of short-lived "phalanxes" were established in accordance with the ideas of Charles Fourier as interpreted by his chief American disciple Albert Brisbane. Most did not last two years. Only one, Ceresco in Wisconsin, was in the black when it was dissolved (after five years).

Little came of this outpouring of collectivist energy. The American environment was sympathetic to the creation of utopian ventures, but there was something deeply prejudicial to their success here. It was easy to start a commune but very hard to make one work. Thousands were established in the nineteenth and twentieth centuries. Few lasted long and none had any marked effect on national customs and values. Bad management and undercapitalization were the most common weaknesses. But even when these problems were solved, as at Oneida, all failed in the end or else embraced what they had once opposed. Oneida (and the Amana communities in Iowa) turned from Bible communism to capitalism. The Mormons, polygamous and communal at first, became monogamous, capitalistic, and ultraconservative later. They are the most durable product of the communitarian movement of the 1830s and 1840s and in some ways its exact opposite.

Reform movements

If utopianism represented the left wing of early-nineteenth-century social change, it was numerically less important than the more conventional reforms which multiplied then. All had their origins in earlier movements, but the great stimulus to most of them was the Finneyite revival of 1830. Charles G. Finney, who began his great work in 1824, took the social responsibility element of revivalism to its logical conclusion. Rejecting orthodox Calvinism with its emphasis on infant damnation and the like, Finney concentrated on the function of salvation. Calvinism made salvation the end of life, but for Finney it was the beginning. He also wanted to see the fruits of salvation, the good works redemption led to. His converts felt this even more strongly. Where Finney and his followers went, social reforms tended to follow. Noyes was converted, as we saw, as were many others who would struggle to reform great areas of American life. Revivalism prepared the ground for antislavery and temperance, and generated interest in prison reform and the care of deaf, blind, and insane persons. It helped build

what historians call the benevolent empire, a network of charitable and reform societies that attacked poverty and sin in antebellum America.

Though revivalism was the most vital force for purposeful social change, it was not uniformly felt. The movement for women's rights, for example, owed little to it—though Finney did give women a higher place than most religious leaders. The spread of democratic and humanitarian ideas in general affected women as it did others, and it made their legal and practical disabilities seem more disagreeable than before. More specifically, the dominant set of values about women, the cult of pure womanhood, had an unintended effect. Society compensated women for their exclusion from public affairs by elevating their moral station. Women were said to be more pure and refined than men, hence especially suited to ethical and domestic activities. The result was, as William R. Taylor and Christopher Lasch have argued, that women became the only fit companions for one another, men being so morally inferior. But associating together helped women discover their own special interests. This led first to church societies, women's clubs, and other bodies concerned with such feminine concerns as motherhood, child welfare, and the like. These activities heightened their consciousness further and involved them obliquely in public affairs.

Then too, women responded to the same moral impulse as men, but they met obstacles peculiar to themselves. The first American women to speak regularly in public were the Grimké sisters of South Carolina, who had become abolitionists in reaction to slavery as they saw it practiced. Their addresses were resisted by men, like the Congregational ministers of Massachusetts who attacked them in 1837 for unladylike behavior. They became feminists because they needed their rights as women in order to campaign for the rights of slaves. Susan B. Anthony later had the same experience with temperance workers. Temperance brought her into public life, but the opposition to women playing an active part in the movement was so great that she came to see women's rights as a prerequisite to the other reforms women hoped to advance. Antebellum feminism did not amount to much. There were some scattered women's rights conventions, like the Seneca Falls (New York) meeting organized by Elizabeth Cady Stanton in 1848, the first of its kind. There were some notable publications including Sarah Grimké's *The Equality of the Sexes and the Condition of Women* (1838) and Margaret Fuller's *Woman in the Nineteenth Century* (1844). Still, women organized more effectively for other causes than for their own. This was to remain a constant theme in the history of women. Having been persuaded that it was their duty to serve others, women never felt easy about serving themselves.

Religion affected education also. Ministers were commonly the organizers and directors of school systems. The conflict between Catholics and Protestants over religious instruction was influenced by them. More important, probably, was the effort to establish free public education in the North. Public high schools were rare before the 1870s, but Horace Mann and others did inspire educational reforms. Some free schools were founded, and efforts were made to improve teacher training. The first normal school was founded in Lexington, Massachusetts, in 1839 for this purpose. Women were now entering the profession in large numbers, it having been decided that teaching was a respectable occupation for gentlewomen—in fact, almost the only one. As always, when women took

over an occupation it declined in status and perhaps also in pay. Mann tried all the same to raise the standards of teacher education and to reform teaching methods. He wanted less emphasis on punishment, especially when physical, and more incentives. And he thought it was better to arouse student interest than to train memories.

These admirable ideas did not produce very impressive results at first. Being taxed to support free schools for other people's children was a novel and not an especially welcome concept to many. In time, though, it prevailed. Generation after generation of reformers would complain about public schools. People were constantly discovering that teachers favored obedience over originality, that a good memory helped students more than an inquiring mind, that order was valued above excitement. Like most other institutions, the public school was never as good as it might have been. All the same, Americans were the first to try to educate at public expense the entire juvenile population. Whatever their weaknesses, these schools were impressive—not so much because the people showed generosity in allowing themselves to be taxed for free schools but because they demonstrated that equal opportunity was more than just a slogan. Schools were instruments of social control. They aimed to imbue the poor and the alien, while they were being made literate, with middle-class values. Yet middle-class Americans believed these values to as important as knowing how to read, write, and figure, and they were correct. In a bourgeois society it was wise to think as the bourgeoisie did. Thrift, diligence, propriety, and looking to the future were all useful traits. Textbooks, then as now, often gave a false picture of society. But they were not wrong to encourage those virtues which society de-

Figure 8-1 Fashions in dress. (*American History Division, The New York Public Library, Astor, Lenox and Tilden Foundations*)

Figure 8-3 The Bloomer costume, sensible but seventy-five years ahead of its time. (*The Bettmann Archive*)

Figure 8-2 Caricature of a women's rights meeting in New York. To feminists probably the most insulting feature of this cartoon was the young lady in the lower left-hand corner, for no respectable woman of the day would show her stockinged legs publicly. (*Library of Congress*)

Figure 8-4 School days in the early nineteenth century. (*The Bettmann Archive*)

did not were the first coeducational inter-racial college (Oberlin), and the first women's college (Mount Holyoke Female Seminary, though it was not chartered as a college until 1888). Adult education was introduced by the lyceum movement, which provided lectures for workingmen and others beginning in 1826. Public libraries, a logical extension of adult education, lagged behind. The first important public library did not open in Boston until 1851.

Abolition

Of all the great antebellum reforms, none was so consequential as abolition, and it was plainly a child of evangelical Christianity. Slavery had its critics earlier, but it was not until the 1830s, when revivalism had done its work, that antislavery became important. Not all abolitionists were Finneyites, yet most were intensely pious, moved chiefly by moral and religious sentiments, and practitioners of an active Christianity that took good works to be the result of salvation. The first important steps toward organization were, however, a consequence of Finney's great revival. Finney converted Theodore Weld, who also became a charismatic preacher. He attacked slavery in his own revivals and attracted a cadre of dedicated young men who aimed to save souls and destroy slavery with him. The most important of these was James G. Birney, himself a slaveowner, who later became an antislavery candidate for President on the Liberty party ticket.

Weld's group needed a spiritual home and thought they had found it in Lane Seminary. Located in Cincinnati, Lane received financial help from the Tappan brothers of New York, the main financial backers of evangeli-

pended upon and which most individuals needed if they were to do well in life. Middle-class Americans exaggerated the degree to which opportunity was really equal. They neglected those who, through no fault of their own, were unable to compete. Nonetheless, the public school remains an impressive monument to their faith that, given the tools, all who could succeed would succeed.

Colleges were not ignored in the antebellum period, though it was not until later that the system of higher education we know came into being. Antebellum colleges were small and narrow. Unless one wanted to be a minister or a lawyer, there was little reason to attend one—and not much more even if one did. Yet the number of colleges grew. Of 182 colleges in operation when the Civil War broke out, 133 had been established since 1829. Many later failed, but among those that cal reform. Being theologically more conservative than the Finneyites, Arthur Tappan halped make Lyman Beecher president of Lane. Beecher was a famous minister and parent, the father of more brains than any man in America, it was said. He believed in colonization (the transportation of free blacks to Africa), though in ten years fewer blacks had been sent to Liberia than were born slaves in a single month. This ensured trouble, for Weld was dedicated to immediate abolition. Lane had an exceptionally distinguished and mature studentry; nine were over thirty years of age and thirty were over twenty-six. They were soon busily offending the community by, among other things, running a school for free blacks.

Matters quickly came to a head. Though Weld had the numbers, having converted the student body to immediacy, Beecher had the power. Few at Lane believed in colonization; Beecher insisted on it all the same. Early in 1834, forty students led by Weld resigned. Some remained in Cincinnati to teach blacks in a school provided by Salmon P. Chase, a young lawyer of whom more was to be heard later. Weld and some other Lane rebels were attracted to the infant Oberlin College, then on the verge of collapse. Oberlin needed students, and it needed the financial support of Arthur Tappan even more. To get both, it agreed to admit black students and made Finney himself professor of theology. Thereafter Oberlin was the West Point of antislavery. From Oberlin the Lane rebels moved into the field, using revival techniques to spread the gospel of abolition. Weld himself went from town to town, speaking as long as five hours at a time and as often as twenty-five times in a given area until it was saturated. He was abused and physically attacked, but he often ended by converting his enemies. His

prize catch was Joshua Giddings, who would become leader of the congressional abolitionists. These great sweeps in 1835 and 1836 created a solid body of antislavery opinion in Ohio, Vermont, western Pennsylvania, and New York.

Organization proceeded elsewhere. By 1838 the American Antislavery Society (A.A.S.), though only four years old, had perhaps 1,350 local chapters and 250,000 members. There were thought to be 145 societies led by William Lloyd Garrison in Massachusetts alone; 274 societies in New York State, where the Tappan brothers were most influential; and 213 in Ohio. This growth was proof that opinion was beginning to turn against slavery. It was also testimony to the propaganda of Garrison and others and to the effectiveness of Weld's techniques. The A.A.S. appointed him to create a body of antislavery evangelists who became known as the Seventy. Weld had burned his voice out on the stump, but the Seventy carried on his work. When the petition fight began in Congress, the A.A.S. was ready. This struggle began almost by accident. John Quincy Adams, ex-President and now a member of Congress, had not wanted at first to see slavery become an issue in the House. He voted with the South to block discussions of it. But Southerners went too far when they passed so-called gag rules that tabled petitions on the subject without discussion. Adams cared much for the Union and very little for slavery, but for free speech above all. The gag rule launched him on a campaign that lasted the rest of his life.

Adams was a tremendous fighter—persistent, ingenious, and totally self-assured. While Minister to Russia, he was bitterly characterized by the English representatives as a bulldog among spaniels.

Age—he was nearly seventy when the struggle began—had not made him less formidable. He alone in Congress had both the prestige to take on the South alone and the will to do so. In January 1837 he began trying to introduce petitions despite the gag. Gilbert H. Barnes described Adams at work this way:

Enjoined by the rule from reading the petitions themselves, he "wantonly tortured the feelings of [the Southern members] by the minuteness with which he . . . dwelt upon the contents of offensive petitions and the names and character of those who signed them. . . . Possessed of few of what were deemed in his time the necessary elements of oratory, Adams's stinging tongue was master of every tone of passion. No man however placid could sit unmoved under the lash of his vituperation, and none of his antagonists had the skill or the hardihood to balk him in his course against the gags. Whether rated as only "a mischievous bad old man," as Calhoun called him, or "fierce as ten furies, terrible as hell," as he seemed to Andrew Johnson, Adams was the nemesis of the Southern conspiracy of silence, the bane of the slavery cause.

The A.A.S. collected hundreds of thousands of signatures for the petitions Adams needed. A small band of antislavery Whigs gathered behind Adams, though he continued to work alone for the most part. They brought Weld to Washington as their chief of staff and lived in the same boarding house. All were "professors of religion": five were Presbyterian elders, and several were revival men. Three had been converted by Weld himself. Whig leaders tried in 1840 to censure first Adams and then Giddings, who resigned his seat and was reelected by his district in the Western Reserve of Ohio, now solidly

antislavery. Thereafter party leaders had to concede the right of antislavery Whigs to speak on the floor as the price of their party regularity. The petition issue receded thereafter and antislavery moved into the mainstream of national politics. Abolitionists no longer needed antislavery societies, and they faded away.

This makes the early work of abolitionists seem easier than it was. The first effect of abolition was to raise passions to the boiling point. Garrison was mobbed and had to be put into protective custody. Weld and Birney were attacked more than once. Lewis Tappan's home was burned. Prudence Crandall's school for black girls in New Haven, Connecticut, was forced to close. Elijah Lovejoy, an antislavery editor, was murdered defending his press in Alton, Illinois, in 1837. Hundreds of less famous people suffered too. Abolition was the riskiest profession a man could practice in those days. Much of the danger has been blamed on Garrison, the most inflammatory and abusive of the great abolitionists and the man who more than any other drove the South into paranoia. But Garrison had little influence in the West, where some of the worst violence occurred. Proslavery mobs fell on Garrisonians and moderates like Tappan with equal fury. Slavery was so fundamental an issue that it could not be attacked then without bringing out the mob. Many people were simply antiblack. Many more loved the Union more than they hated slavery and knew that abolition might destroy it.

Garrison's actual effect is difficult to measure. In the first issue of his *Liberator* he decried moderation and said "I am in earnest—I will not equivocate—I will not excuse—I will not retreat a single inch—*and I will be heard.*" He made good on all those promises. At first he was sustained by only a few hundred subscribers, mostly free blacks.

But Southern attacks on his paper brought him to national prominence quickly. He made enemies more easily than any man in reform history. Though pious, he loved strong language. He called the editors of one newspaper "rum drinkers, lechers, pimps, and knaves." Another editor was "an irresponsible libeller, a shameless bastard, and a miserable craven." This was strong stuff, even by the robust editorial standards of the day—Victorian delicacy having not yet emasculated journalism. Garrison offended other abolitionists by being dogmatic and unscrupulous. He refused to compromise with fellow reformers and took what was left of the American Antislavery Society away from Lewis Tappan in 1840. And he upheld so many radical causes that it was very hard for others to work with him, since that was to risk being associated with perfectionism, women's rights, pacifism, and other unpopular causes dear to his heart. His solution to the slavery problem was nonviolent secession of New England from the Union, if nothing else. He burned a copy of the Constitution in public to show his contempt for a government that protected slavery.

Some historians have argued that Garrison did the cause more harm than good. He soon helped drive the South into a singleminded defense of slavery. He divided abolitionists while making the label so odious that reasonable people shrank from it. Garrison and his followers created the no-compromise atmosphere that made peaceful solutions impossible. The Garrisonians did add fuel to the fire, yet it would surely have burned without them. The division between North and South was so great and the political system so little able to repair it that at most radical abolitionists only brought the war on sooner. Other publicists, like Harriet Beecher Stowe, were important too. So were the Tappans, Welds, and more moderate leaders. Most of all, of course, the slave owners themselves made war inevitable by their actions in Congress which offended millions and created the spectre of a conquering slaveocracy bent on destroying liberty.

By insisting on the Fugitive Slave Act in 1850, they implicated Northerners in the system while giving them an opportunity to see how it functioned close up. Slave hunters appeared in many Northern communities and often met violent resistance. Sometimes their prey was taken from them. In 1854 an escaped slave was captured in Boston, after which abolitionists tried to storm the courthouse and set him free. The state militia had to be called out before he could be sent South at a cost of perhaps $100,000. "We rejoice at the capture of Burns," said the *Richmond Enquirer*, "but a few more such victories and the South is undone." Burns was the last escaped slave taken in Massachusetts. It and a number of other states passed what were called personal liberty laws that nullified the Fugitive Slave Act. Though unconstitutional, they showed what Northerners felt about legislation that made them accomplices of slavery. The struggle over Kansas, provoked by the Kansas-Nebraska bill of 1854, had a similar effect, for here too the slaveocracy seemed to be trying to impose itself on free men. The South was its own worst enemy and by its own acts created a hostile public opinion far in excess of anything the Garrisonians had provoked.

Moreover, the radical abolitionists did not justify themselves solely in terms of results. When told that his extreme positions retarded rather than advanced emancipation, Wendell Phillips said "honesty and trust are more important than even freeing the slaves." The Burns case made Thoreau an abolitionist, and—significantly—his first public address on the subject was called "Slavery in Massachusetts." The extreme abolitionists were moved as much, in many cases more, by the damage slavery did the commonwealth as by what it did to slaves. It was not an abstract moral question to them but a living force corrupting public life everywhere. Phillips repeatedly made this point. More than any of the great abolitionists, he explicitly defined their social role in this larger sense.

Phillips was unique in several respects. One of the few abolitionist intellectuals, he was also one of the few to come from a distinguished family. Abolition drew heavily on the middle and professional classes and rarely attracted aristocrats such as Phillips. He was first converted to Christianity by Lyman Beecher and then to antislavery by Garrison—whom Phillips first saw with a rope around his neck being led through the streets by a mob in 1835. This was the martyr era of antislavery, and the prospect of defying the ignorant herd was irresistibly appealing to Phillips. He brought the cause three assets: a great name, eloquence, and a developed theory of agitation. He would sometimes dispose of critics by remarking that they were men of no family. But when he took them seriously it was even worse, for he was as abusive as Garrison and a far better speaker. He called Daniel Webster "a great mass of dough" and Edward Everett, famous for his oratory, "a whining spaniel." He once said of New England churches that they manufactured hypocrisy just as Lowell manufactured cotton. The Know-Nothing Governor of Massachusetts was "a consummate hypocrite, a man who if he did not have some dozen and distinct reasons for telling the truth would naturally tell a lie." A Boston critic described one of his addresses as "a dish of tripe and onions served on silver, or black-strap presented in a goblet of Bohemian glass . . . Mr.

Phillips thinks like a Billingsgate fishwoman, or a low pothouse bully, but he speaks like Cicero." Attacks so stimulated him that at public meetings his admirers would sometimes hiss to provoke his best efforts. He was indeed, as a Southern editor put it, an "infernal machine set to music."

Phillips believed that free people always needed agitators like himself and Garrison because democratic institutions were always in the process of decaying. Public office was inherently corrupting. "Every Secretary of State is by the very necessity of his position an apostate." A society that trusted to constitutions and political mechanisms to secure its liberties would never have any. What corrupted especially was the tyranny of popular opinion. "In a country like ours, of absolute democratic equality, public opinion is not only omnipotent, it is omnipresent. There is no refuge from its tyranny. . . . And the consequence is that instead of being a mass of individuals, each one fearlessly blurting out his own convictions, as a nation, compared with other nations, we are a mass of cowards. More than any other people we are afraid of each other." This was an aristocratic conception of democracy, though not quite a hostile one. He shared many ideas with foreigners like De Tocqueville, but he never doubted that democracy would succeed—if only there were enough agitators to make it work. "Our institutions floating unanchored on a shifting surface of popular opinion, cannot afford to hold back or to draw forward a hated question, and compel a reluctant public to look at it and to consider it." That was work only an agitator could do.

By breaking through individual defenses, the agitator forced each man to confront his own conscience. Once this was accomplished, Phillips thought, decent men could be relied on to make decent judgments. But as most feared public opinion and trusted feeble institutions, the agitator's job was a difficult one. It could not be done by temporizing or compromising but only by speaking the whole truth, however painful or destructive. This meant agitators would always be thought intemperate and unreasonable. "Call us fanatics, revile us for our personality, say that we attack reputations—what of that? We did not come into the world to keep ourselves clean. It is not our first and only duty to see that you love us. Popularity is not the great end of creation."

Phillips was not a typical abolitionist—if there were such. Few accepted his definition of the agitator's role or pursued it so faithfully. Once slavery was destroyed, Phillips put his talents to the service of freedmen and organized labor. He tried to get land for blacks and unions for workers. If more had followed him, the consequences of emancipation might not have been so dismal or the human costs of industrialization so great. But many did accept his thesis that slavery was first of all a threat to freedom in the North, and this was in fact the case. There was no great slave-power conspiracy to enslave workingmen, as some supposed; yet slavery could only be preserved by being enlarged, and this could only take place at the expense of free farmers in the West and civil liberties everywhere. It was not abolition that made compromise impossible but the remorseless demands of the slave system itself.

The chief weakness of antislavery had little to do with extravagance or intemperance—how was it possible to be excessive in condemning something as wicked as human slavery?—but rather the opposite. Most who supported antislavery took a narrow view of the question. Garrison, Phillips, Elizabeth Cady Stanton, and others who fought slavery as part of a larger effort to secure a more just

society were not representative of public opinion, and few Northerners cared for black people as such. This was true even of some abolitionists, who discriminated against blacks in the movement. Black leaders like Frederick Douglass, an escaped slave who founded his own newspaper to advance black freedom, were convinced that they would have to look after their own interests. As Douglass put it: "Our elevation as a race is almost wholly dependent upon our own exertions." Though mostly poor, segregated, and discriminated against, blacks fought for equality. They held national conventions—especially in the 1840s and 1850s. And though Jim Crow was spreading in the North, they made some gains. In 1843 segregated railroad coaches were abolished in Massachusetts. In the 1850s Douglass led a successful fight to desegregate the schools in Rochester, New York. Massachusetts outlawed school segregation in 1855.

Like whites, blacks were divided on the question of colonization. The colonization movement was inherently antiblack in that it proposed to solve the racial problem by exporting all blacks to Africa, where the state of Liberia was established to receive them. A good many blacks, perhaps most leaders, reacted to this by attacking the American Colonization Society, which had been organized by Southerners in 1817. Some, however, like Paul Cuffe—a black Quaker shipowner and merchant—sympathized with the idea. Cuffe petitioned Congress in 1818 to help transport blacks to Africa, though not so much to reduce American racial tensions as to uplift and Christianize black Africans. Some blacks, however, did feel that justice would never done them in America and saw colonization as an answer to their own problem. This was especially true in the 1850s, when leaders such as Martin R. Delany, a physician and editor, strenuously promoted emigration.

On the whole, though, while nationalism was not unknown, antebellum black leaders were inclined to favor integration and assimilation. And many felt that whatever the ultimate solution, the freeing of the slaves had to be the first concern of black people. Many were active in the abolition movement; Garrison's *Liberator* would soon have expired without black subscribers. Among the blacks who campaigned against slavery were many women. These included the famous Sojourner Truth, an ex-slave who spoke to great effect at feminist as well as abolition meetings, and Frances Ellen Watkins Harper, a poet and lecturer for the Maine Antislavery Society. A legendary handful of blacks helped run the underground railway, that chain of conspirators who assisted runaway slaves in getting to Canada. The most famous of these was Harriet Tubman, who escaped from slavery when nearly thirty years old and then, over a ten-year period made nineteen journeys into the slave states to bring back more than 300 men, women, and children. Slave owners put the unheard-of price of $40,000 on her head, but she was never caught.

Abolitionists, white and black alike, did noble work. Their problem was that the South would not give up slavery unless made to and the North did not think slavery important enough to risk disunion over. It was only when the South seceded that emancipation became possible because, the worst having already happened, Northerners felt there was nothing more to lose. The abolitionists cannot be said to have failed, since by making slavery an explosive issue they helped bring on the crisis that ended it. But they cannot be said to have changed many minds about black people either. Thus, when slavery was ended, the position of blacks in both North and South still left nearly everything to be desired. And this despite very strenuous efforts in the postwar period to remove the disabilities from which blacks suffered.

Literature

The great age of reform was also a golden age of literature. Before about 1820 the best American minds, except for Washington Irving, were preoccupied with religion and politics. Then came James Fenimore Cooper, Herman Melville, Walt Whitman, Edgar Allan Poe, Ralph Waldo Emerson, Henry David Thoreau, and Nathaniel Hawthorne. All made distinguished contributions to world literature and together constituted an array of talent worthy of a mature civilization—much less a raw, emerging nation like the United States. Most of these writers had little in common, but several belonged to the Concord circle that produced in Emerson the most influential writer of the period and in Thoreau one of the most durable.

Emerson was ordained a Unitarian minister but soon rebelled against what he saw as Unitarianism's intellectual sterility, complacency, and formalism. Its secular counterparts, Lockean liberalism and rationalism, were on the wane; its opposite, Romanticism, was on the rise. Emerson went to Europe in 1832 and was influenced somewhat by such German philosophical idealists as Kant (*idealism* here referring to the concept of an ultimate reality beyond the sensible, material universe—as against the word's modern use to describe people with innocently high moral aspirations) and by the English Romantics—Coleridge, Carlyle, and Wordsworth—even more. He left the Unitarian church and, in his essay "Nature" (1836), advocated transcendentalism, a doctrine he later described as "idealism made modern." The purpose of transcendentalism was to find "the whole in which all things are beautiful; the proper relationship with nature that would enable man to merge with the Universal Spirit." Standing on the bare ground, he said, "the currents of the Universal Being circulate through me: I am part or parcel of God." In his Harvard Divinity School address two years later he said that when a man was faithful to his inner vision he became God. This was a kind of perfectionist heresy that led in Emerson's case to a lifelong interest in inspirational and mystical religion. Transcendentalists, and Emerson particularly, had something in common with the counterculture of the 1960s. Both groups believed in intuition, nature, and individual will as sources of truth and both distrusted science, reason, and the cognitive faculties generally. Both found inspiration in sacred Eastern writings. One crucial difference is that the transcendentalists were not isolated from the everyday world. Their whole society was charged with romantic and perfectionist ideas. Transcendentalists took these further than most, but not so far as to seem especially queer or freaky. Hence, though often intensely critical of society, they were not alienated from it in the modern way. Our postindustrial or technetronic culture is far more hostile to the spirit than was Emerson's Romantic age.

Emerson's ideas were sometimes difficult, even contradictory. He came to them painfully, after extensive readings not only in Western literature but also in Oriental religious sources. But the tendency of this thought was towards an easy optimism that belied the facts of his own life. Of his five brothers one was mentally defective and two died young of tuberculosis, as did his first wife. He and his second wife were both afflicted with the disease. Emerson met the problem of evil, so dramatically illustrated by his own experience, with the old doctrine of compensated evil—that it contained the seeds of a larger good and was a stage of good becoming itself. Since the good that evil produces is not always evident, however, this doctrine rests on faith alone and was not so much a solution to the problem of evil as a way of disregarding it, an evasive habit of mind especially congenial to Americans—and all the more so in an age of physical expansion and material progress.

Emerson did not believe in material progress himself, but he became increasingly nationalistic all the same. In his later years when he had become the country's official moral philosopher, he preached that America had a mission to turn good ideas into reality. The United States was to become the leading guide and lawgiver to the world. He was no imperialist, the Mexican war shocked him as much as Thoreau, but the effect of his arguments was to justify American power in terms of the nation's moral greatness. In this he and Walt Whitman, in many respects so different, were much alike. Both saw Lincoln as the personification of the masses' virtue. Both disliked much about American democracy in the present but looked to posterity to fulfill its promise. This undergirded the double standard of national morality that was already well developed. European evil was the natural product of a corrupt civilization. American evil only proved that the national movement toward moral perfection was as yet incomplete. Still, too much can be made of Emerson's optimism and nationalism. We admire him, as David Grimsted remarks, because Emerson admitted life was not easy but believed in man's capacity to surmount hardship. "Emerson stresses democratically that all men can be great; Thoreau insists, more cynically and realistically, that most men won't."

Henry David Thoreau, whose family gained a poor living making pencils, went to Harvard College during one of its dullest periods. He graduated in 1837 when Emerson was thirty-four and at the height of his powers. Thoreau's real education was gained in Concord, where—besides Emerson—Dr. Ripley, Hawthorne, and Bronson Alcott lived. He thought first to be a teacher, but his career in the public schools lasted only two weeks. Corporal punishment was employed at the school, but Thoreau agreed with Alcott (an educational reformer who punished himself rather than his students for their misdeeds) on its futility. Ordered to flog his students, he (gently, one imagines) flogged six chosen at random to show the irrelevance of such discipline and resigned. With a brother he operated his own school until ill health forced his brother to drop out in 1841. After that Thoreau gave up trying to improve society and concentrated on improving himself. Others in Concord were interested in educational reform, women's rights, antislavery, and the like. They produced in Brook Farm the best-known utopian community in American history. Most of this passed Thoreau by.

Inspired by Emerson's "Nature" and the *Baghavad-Gita*, a sacred Hindu text, he believed that to study nature is to know God. This became the driving passion of a life devoted to self-understanding and development. For a while Thoreau drifted from job to job, trying to find some way of supporting himself that was not marked with the blighting hand of industrial civilization. Like Emerson he was appalled by how economic advances were made. Both felt, as Thoreau put it, that "we don't ride on the railroad; it rides upon us." Thoreau found the answer to his personal dilemma in the *Gita*, which advises that "the wise man seeketh for that which is homogeneous in his own nature." This led him to

Walden Pond where, on land purchased by Emerson, he built a cabin and lived for several years. This was both an intelligent solution to his personal needs and a statement on materialism. There, he could support himself for a year on six weeks' work, living more fully than before. At Walden Pond he was closer both to nature and to himself.

In 1847 he left Walden Pond to manage Emerson's household while the sage was in Europe. He finished *Walden* in 1849 but delayed publication until 1854. (In the meantime he published *A Week on the Concord and Merrimac Rivers*, which did so poorly that after four years most copies remained unsold. Thoreau had to buy them, which led to his famous quip that he had a library of nearly 900 volumes, over 700 of which he had written himself.) *Walden* has two great themes. The first is that "a man is rich in proportion to the number of things he can afford to leave alone." His experience showed that living richly is not a function of possessions. The second great theme is his attack on social organization. "The mass of men lead lives of quiet desperation," he observed. Noting the obsession of farmers with work, he wrote, "the better part of the man is soon ploughed into the soil for compost." *Walden* is a handbook for spiritual survival. It is also a text on sociology and economics more penetrating than any monograph.

Thoreau had little interest in politics, but the Mexican War and slavery politicized him in certain ways. He did not speak publicly against slavery until 1854, when the Burns case moved him to write his lecture "Slavery in Massachusetts." "I have lived for the last month—and I think every man in Massachusetts capable of the sentiment of patriotism must have had a similar experience—with the sense of having suffered a vast and indefinite loss. I did not know at first what ailed me. At last it occurred to me that what I had lost was a country." Thoreau's conclusion was that "we have used up all our inherited freedom. If we would save our lives, we must fight for them." Thoreau was not speaking rhetorically here. Five years later he wrote "A Plea for Captain John Brown," showing himself to be as good as his word. Most people in the North thought Brown had gone too far in attacking Harper's Ferry, that he was indeed some kind of lunatic. Thoreau disagreed on both counts, making him out to be a sensible New England farmer and one who took the only way open to a man of honor. Thoreau was certainly wrong in part. Brown was, if not insane, all the more monstrous for having massacred unarmed proslavery settlers in Kansas. The Harper's Ferry raid was a mad act that had no chance of success and could only worsen an already desperate political situation. Yet if that was what was wanted— Thoreau himself welcomed disunion—then Brown's folly made sense. Brown was a dangerous fanatic, but his raid drove another nail in slavery's coffin all the same. If bloody war was the only way of ending slavery, as they believed, then they were right to back John Brown. Thoreau was widely condemned at the time for taking such an irresponsible line. Posterity, more opposed to slavery than his contemporaries, has thought better of him. His defense of Brown remains the most morally ambiguous act of Thoreau's life because it meant that he welcomed having other men die for his principles—the very thing he had deplored in the government's declaration of war on Mexico.

"Civil Disobedience," the essay he wrote after the Mexican war, remains the most valuable of his political writings because the means advocated in it are consistent with the ends sought. It grew out of his refusal to pay the poll tax (though he actually had not paid it for years) on the ground that he would not let his dollar buy "a man or a musket to shoot one with." (Someone else paid his tax, so he only had to spend one night in jail. Later, his point having been made, he began paying the tax again.) "Civil Disobedience" argues that "that government is best which governs not at all." Thoreau was an instinctive anarchist and thought all men would be the same once they were prepared to live peacefully without a state. In the meantime, they suffered from a government that needed to be peacefully resisted. "The proper place today, the only place which Massachusetts has provided for her freer and less desponding spirits, is her prison. . . . It is there that the fugitive slave, and the Mexican prisoner on parole, and the Indian come to plead the wrongs of his race should find them; on that separate, but more free and honorable ground, which the State places those who are not with her, but against her,—the only house in a slave State in which a free man can abide with honor."

Thoreau was a man of small consequence in his lifetime. Few outside Massachusetts knew of him. His books sold poorly. He lived in obscurity, supporting himself after 1848 by working one month a year as a surveyor. He and Emerson both thought that things were in the saddle and rode mankind. But Emerson's optimism and nationalism tended to cloud the picture, making his strictures against materialism seem the kind of pious exhortation to higher things that Americans are used to ignoring. Thoreau was not so easily watered down. One cannot imagine him giving a lecture that would not stick in the public's craw. Yet history has been kinder to Thoreau than Emerson, and for just that reason.

No one today cares much about their religious and philosophical convictions, but many share their distaste for industrial capitalism, especially as its consequences are so much more apparent now than they were then. Thoreau especially spoke against it with a force and clarity that few have equalled and none surpassed. His words are fresher and more pertinent today than when first written. "Civil Disobedience" inspired generations of peaceful revolutionaries—Gandhi and Martin Luther King in particular. *Walden* has more admirers now than at any time before. Thoreau neither changed the world nor ever meant to. He wanted instead to change men's minds, and while those who built the society he condemned are long since forgotten, his words live still.

Like Thoreau, Herman Melville had few admirers in his time. And also like Thoreau he was subsequently discovered to be one of the great adornments of American thought and culture. He would have appreciated the irony, for he was no transcendentalist but a man who saw the worst in life and expected nothing better. His deep pessimism, want of confidence in America, and suspicion of the future assured the failure of his books when first published. They are, together with his genius, precisely why Melville is read today. Expansive, ambitious, patriotic ages do not care to be told that evil is real and history unforgiving. It was only after the limits of American greatness were sensed that Melville could be fully appreciated.

The son of a business failure, Melville went to sea as a youth and traveled the South Pacific. His first novels were set there and seemed enough like conventional romances to get by. *Typee*, published in 1846 when he was only twenty-seven, was about what happened when civilization invaded an earthly paradise. It was full of enthusiasm for spontaneity, sensuousness, and other primitive virtues. Though romantic and hence almost conventional by then, *Typee* was suspect, its popularity notwithstanding. Horace Greeley, the most famous journalist of his day, said it

"was unmistakably defective, if not positively diseased in moral tone." Other novels followed with diminishing success until in 1851 he published *Moby Dick*, his most dense and complex work and some think his greatest. Few American novels have been studied so closely. Whether the white whale is a symbol or not, and if so of what, has been grist to the critical mills for generations.

But whatever else *Moby Dick* may be, it is a repudiation of transcendentalism. Ishmael falls into transcendental reveries while on lookout—reveries which prevent him from seeing real whales and threaten his life by loosening his grip on the rigging. When a character falls into the fragrant head of a sperm whale, Melville wonders how many men "had like-wise fallen into Plato's honey head and sweetly perished there." The crew is destroyed, Loren Baritz argues, because most are susceptible to abstract passions and see the world in terms of one metaphor or another. Starbuck, the first mate, is a Christian; Captain Ahab an anti-Christian. The men succumb to a collective mania in which the whale is seen to embody some great principle. Only the three harpooners and Ishmael reject the Captain's mad vision, the harpooners because of their primitive simplicity and Ishmael because of his knowledge. He sees nature for what it is, an existential fact. The others see nature as metaphor, hence Ahab's ability to compel them through the superior force of his illusions. *Moby Dick* sets the reality of evil and the material world against the idealization of nature and man by Emerson, "this Plato who talks through his nose" according to Melville. It was a great failure, being too difficult for a popular audience and too unattractive for a critical one. Hawthorne liked it, but then he would, since he too repudiated transcendentalism and had a tragic view of life.

Billy Budd, Melville's last novel, is a clear-

Figure 8-5 A scene from the movie *Billy Budd*. Captain Vere faces angry sailors. In the background, Claggart and Billy look on. (*Culver Pictures*)

er statement of his philosophy. Budd, a sailor on a British warship, personifies innocent virtue. Claggart, the master-at-arms, is pure evil. He provokes Billy who, in a moment of justifiable rage, accidentally kills him. Captain Vere cries out when he learns of this that Claggert has been "struck dead by an angel of God. Yet the angel must hang." Vere is the finest product of civilized life as Budd is of the natural order. But because he is civilized—that is, part of a complex social structure—Vere must hang Billy Budd while knowing him to be virtuous. The other officers want to save Billy for justice's sake. Vere responds by grasping his coat and asking "do these buttons that we wear attest that our allegiance is to Nature? No, to the King." This is Melville's last word on the subject. Nature is neutral. It is only man's need to be the center of creation that makes him think otherwise. There is no point to man's life on earth. The effort to find one only leads men to build struc-

tures that add fresh wrongs to existing evils.

Melville did not rely on inference to say what he thought of patriotism. If mankind as a whole has no destiny, obviously neither does America. He puts this plainly in his long narrative poem *Clarel* (1878), which tells of a student's search for truth. Among other things, *Clarel* indicts the factory system. "How many Hughs of Lincoln, say, / Does Mammon, in his mills, to-day, / Crook, if he does not crucify?" He disposes of the national sense of mission as easily. "Our New World bold / Had fain improved upon the Old; / But the hemispheres are counter-parts." The New World is no better than the old. Columbus did not give mankind new hope, quite the contrary. "Columbus ended earth's romance. / No New World to mankind remains." As there was no other place for man to go thinking to build a better society, he would at last have to stand and face himself if he would know the truth.

Humanity could not live in a universe that was not designed to serve human ends. Americans could not live in a country that was like other countries. The superpartiotism and nationalism of his age, as ours, depended on superstition. If America was not meant to serve grand and noble purposes, what excuse was there for the evils committed, the mediocrities endured, for greatness's sake? None said Melville, an answer hardly more acceptable now than then. Melville's vision was, perhaps, too bleak. Yet an optimistic, self-satisfied nation has need of him, if only to mitigate the flow of nationalistic platitudes behind which Americans hide, especially from themselves. There have never been enough Melvilles—all the more reason for being glad that there was even one.

For all its accomplishments, antebellum civilization was not quite equal to the challenges it faced. Mostly this was because the country grew so much, physically and economically. Expansion was what made America rich and, soon, great. It created jobs and enlarged the gross national product, among other good things. It was probably inevitable and in any case the preferred solution to national problems. But it exacted a great price. Physical expansion set the imperial ambitions of North and South against each other and led to war. Economic expansion worsened the boom and bust cycle. As America became more urban and industrial, the human costs of economic growth became greater. A country made up largely of subsistence farmers was little bothered by economic contractions that had desperate consequences for wage earners. Unrestrained urban growth produced crime, congestion, and disease. Economic and geographic expansion created an unlimited appetite for cheap labor, so immigration too was unchecked. Immigrants kept down wages and

made unionization even harder. They stayed mainly in cities, peopling the slums, enlarging the crime rate, and straining such charitable agencies as existed. Both as victims and aggressors, they added enormously to what was even without them an unbearably large amount of violence.

These great forces broke down the institutions of Federalist America. The Federalist and Whig parties, which stood for a kind of national planning and orderly growth, were destroyed. So was the Bank of the United States. Cities acquired the basic attributes of industrial civilization—the railroad, the factory, the slum. Local governments struggled to cope with them. Professional police and fire companies were formed, waterworks constructed, and new hospitals, schools, orphan asylums, and prisons established. But though much was done, demand seemed always to outstrip supply. America was growing at such a rate that even with the best will it was hard to keep up. And the will was not always there. Businessmen and politicians were coming to view the public good as something best advanced by private greed. Enterprise was becoming more free, hence more careless of human needs. In an expansive, individualistic age it was difficult to persuade people that the disadvantaged had a claim on their purses and still more difficult to gain support for the view that government should undertake vast programs for the benefit of others.

The country suffered in two ways, therefore: first from the effects of great social and economic forces that would have been troublesome under the best of circumstances and second from a national ethic that made it impossible to deal with these forces. The result was a crisis so profound that it could only end in war. This solved the sectional problem and determined what kind of empire would be built in the West. The war also discredited the more sentimental and perfectionist aspects of reform thought, but it did nothing to solve the urban, industrial, and ethnic problems that were vital parts of the crisis. These all continued and some grew worse. The antebellum crisis of American civilization was never resolved, only abated. Slavery and sectionalism, its most irreconcilable elements, were destroyed. Everything else was handed on to posterity.

Selected references

George R. Taylor, *The Transportation Revolution, 1815–1860* (1951), is the standard work. W. W. Rostow's theories, as explained in his modestly titled *The Stages of Economic Growth: A Non-Communist Manifesto* (1960), are controversial and stimulating. On labor see Norman Ware, *The Industrial Worker* (1924). Peter R. Knights, *The Plain People of Boston, 1830–1860* (1971), is good on mobility. Antebellum nativism is discussed at great length in Ray Allen Billington, *The Protestant Crusade, 1800–1860* (1938). Alice F. Tyler, *Freedom's Ferment* (1944), discusses some utopian movements. On the religious communities see Stow Persons, "Christian Communitarianism in America," in Donald Drew Egbert and Stow Persons (eds.), *Socialism and American Life* (1952), in two volumes. On other communitarians, see T. C. Seymour Bassett, "The Secular Utopian Socialists," in the same work. R. A. Parker, *A Yankee Saint* (1935), is a sympathetic biography of John Humphrey Noyes. On the Owenites, see Arthur E. Bestor, Jr., *Backwoods Utopias* (1950).

Whitney R. Cross, *The Burned-over District* (1950), has a great deal of material on Finneyism. On the condition of women, see Eleanor Flexner, *Centuries of Struggle* (1959); William L. O'Neill, *Everyone Was Brave* (1969); Barbara Welter, "The Cult of True Womanhood; 1820–1860," in the *American Quarterly* (Summer 1966); William R. Taylor and Christopher Lasch, "Two Kindred Spirits: Sorority and Family in New England, 1839–1846," in the *New England Quarterly* (March 1963); and Gerda Lerner, *The Grimke Sisters from South Carolina* (1967). Timothy L. Smith, *Revivalism and Social Reform* (1957), is very instructive. Of the many books on abolition, two basic works are Gilbert H. Barnes, *The Anti-slavery Impulse, 1830–1844* (1933); and Louis Filler, *The Crusade against Slavery, 1830–1860* (1960). See also the marvelous essay on Phillips in Richard Hofstadter, *The American Political Tradition* (1948). On the writers, see F. O. Mattheissen, *American Renaissance* (1941), and Lewis Mumford, *The Golden Day* (1926). Loren Baritz, *City on a Hill* (1964), contains intriguing essays on Emerson and Melville.

NINE

The Jackson Legacy

Period covered: 1828–1856
Emphases: Diplomacy and politics
Major events: South Carolina Exposition and Protest, 1828
                 Commercial treaty with England, 1830
                 Nullification controversy, 1832
                 Jackson's veto of the bank bill, 1832
                 Indian removal bills and policy, 1830–1838
                 Texas revolution, 1836
                 Panic of 1837
                 Annexation of Texas, 1845
                 Oregon settlement, 1846
                 War with Mexico, 1846
                 Free-Soil party, 1848
                 Compromise of 1850
                 Ostend Manifesto, 1854
                 Kansas-Nebraska Act, 1854

The Jacksonians had little in common. A good number voted for "Old Hickory" in 1824 and 1828 for the sheer pleasure derived from defying their "betters" in the local community or perhaps because they somehow *felt* the general understood their needs and was for them. Others, perhaps an equal number, simply voted their interests. Andrew Jackson's once-delayed entrance into the White House symbolized the triumph of a powerful if unlikely coalition of rising and falling classes momentarily united in opposition to the status quo. On one side men boosted the general up into the Presidential saddle with the expectation that he would lead the charge against vested interests and privilege. On the other side he was aided by men who simply wanted him to sit there, an equestrian statue, while they went about the business of improving their fortunes unrestrained by the government.

From tidelands to frontier and back again, aspirants to wealth and power joined cause with farmers and artisans in the Jacksonian Democratic party. A Tennessee-New York alliance soon replaced the Massachusetts-Virginia compact which, up until this time, had supplied the nation with its Presidents and its political dialogue. Self-made, one-generation aristocrats displaced the first families of Boston and Charleston as social leaders in Washington. Laissez faire rhetoric resounded in the halls of Congress, driving out the echoes of solemn mercantilism. At the center of it all sat Jackson, symbol of an age. But what did he symbolize?

Jackson triumphant

Martin Van Buren, Jackson's successor, once said that the secret of Jackson's strength was his deep natural understanding of the people.

"They were his blood relations—the only blood relations he had." Andrew Jackson consciously felt himself and the movement he symbolized to be antimonopoly and antiprivilege. Whatever the issue—tariff and commerce, Indian removal, the Bank of the United States, the Specie Circular, or the acquisition of Texas, Oregon, and California—the Jacksonians always used the same metaphor: they were opening up opportunities and lands. Whatever obstacles stood in the way had to be pushed aside. A self-made man who had risen in life and legend to political preeminence, Jackson's early experiences with the Eastern establishment of the day had embittered him forever against bankers. To destroy them he would, as President, pursue policies directly contradictory, and succeed, ultimately in fastening tighter the grip of capitalism on both the workers and the planters, the reverse of what he apparently wanted to achieve.

In Tennessee, however, as a member of the slaveholding aristocracy, he had consistently opposed economic reform movements. The answer to this seeming paradox is really fairly simple: Jackson believed it to be the federal government's primary duty, and its only legitimate duty under the Constitution, to keep the marketplace open to all. It was the duty of state and local governments to protect the successful against both the speculator and the propertyless who would strip them of their gains. He could (and would) deny any role for the federal government in promoting and participating in internal improvements; he could (and did) threaten any state which raised the possibility of nullification and separation. He summed up the philosophy and policy of laissez faire in one sentence of his 1830 Annual Message to Congress: "If the interest of the Government in private companies is subordinate to that of individuals, the management and control of a portion of the public funds is delegated to an authority unknown to the Constitution and beyond the supervision of our constituents; if superior, its officers and agents will be constantly exposed to imputations of favoritism and oppression." Hence there could be no government role in the economy except as guardian of the marketplace and protector of those who profited from its exchanges. Anything more than that disrupted rather than helped.

But even more fundamental to laissez faire than the question of whether federal intervention disrupted or helped the economy was the conviction that such interference was actually a violation of the compact among citizens formalized in the Constitution. Later reform leaders in the Presidential office would also insist that the Constitution meant, when it began "We the people," that the union of the people was more important than the union of the states. In the Age of Jackson, political leaders of that persuasion argued that such an interpretation compelled them to prevent special interests from receiving favors. As long as the nation was expanding both territorially and economically, such a position made sense for laborers and capitalists alike, dirt farmers and planters, East and West.

The loyal opposition: An overview

Jackson's opponents also had little in common. They numbered among them violent antislave voices and the defenders of the South's "peculiar institution," conservative establishment figures and men who felt better about national internal improvements than they did about state or private efforts, tidewater aristocrats bemoaning their lost power and Midwestern go-getters looking for more power. About all they could agree on was a common dislike for "King Andrew's" use of the Presidential power. They called themselves Whigs for that reason; it was a label they had taken over from traditional English opponents of royal prerogative.

Henry Clay's efforts to retrieve postwar economic nationalism, which he gave a patriotic twist by calling his program of high tariffs and internal improvements the "American System," brought him less than 43 percent of the popular vote in 1832. Against Martin Van Buren four years later, the Whigs even failed to agree upon a national candidate, so they ran three—one for each section! In the two decades of its short lifespan, the Whig party managed, by trading on Old Hickory's image, to elect two Presidents: General William Henry "Tippecanoe" Harrison, an Indian fighter of note in 1840, and General Zachary "Old Rough and Ready" Taylor, a Mexican War hero in 1848. They nominated Winfield "Old Fuss and Feathers" Scott, a third general, in 1852, but he lost to the Democrats' "Young Hickory of the Granite Hills," Franklin Pierce.

An interesting sidelight on the nominations of Taylor and Scott was that the majority of Whigs probably opposed the Mexican War yet were willing to take its heros for Presidential candidates. An explanation of this behavior begins with the dilemma of the growing antislave forces in the party—and outside the party. Given the party system of government, dissenters had to choose to vote their beliefs by supporting a third-party candidate who could never win, thus helping to elect proslavery candidates, or to be expedient by voting for the lesser of two evils. The dilemma was certainly not restricted to the Jackson period or to the slavery question.

The plethora of third parties in the Jackson era, like the nomination of war heroes on so many occasions, suggested an unsettled state of affairs and men searching for a reconcilation of ideas and reality. These parties seldom did more than prick the thick-skinned Democratic majority. They did serious hurt to the Whigs, however, particularly in the 1844 election when the Liberty party, dominated by antislave forces, deprived Henry Clay of New York State; thus throwing the election to Tennessee's James K. Polk. These splinter organizations represented former pieces of the Democratic coalition which had broken away once it became clear that Jacksonian egalitarianism meant only that a slave state was equal to a free state, a planter to a capitalist, and Oregon to California in the race to the Pacific.

Both Whig Presidents died in office, leaving the fortunes of the party, such as they were, in the hands of men less able to develop a program in opposition to the Democrats, less interested in doing so, and without any semblance of a national following. Clay's influence stamped itself on the East-West coalition led by Abraham Lincoln and William Henry Seward in the 1850s, the alliance which finally gave birth to the Republican party. The Republicans, however, began with the premise that there was no national constituency for an opposition party. The slave issue had grown so big that it enveloped every other issue and reached beyond the Constitution to some higher law.

What had brought Eastern capitalists and their allies together with Midwestern farmers to form a new party in that decade, however, was a worldly concern: a straight bargain between men who knew precisely what they wanted and were prepared, come what may, to do whatever seemed necessary to get results. Slavery was a moral issue; its expansion was a political issue, which also interfered with the well-being and beliefs of the free states. The slave issue ran ahead of

Jackson's heirs in the race to the Pacific. It was always there to bedevil and confound the best of his successors as they tried to avoid a crisis. By the time Stephen A. Douglas began his attempt to bring these forces under control, it was much too late. From "Bleeding Kansas" east and west, the Democrats had no more answers. The Republicans, having severed Southern interests from their ranks, would have their opportunity.

The dangerous tariff issue

From hindsight it is easy to see that one of the earliest issues in the Jackson era, the tariff question, clearly foreshadowed what was to undo the bonds of national loyalty. But the Democrats realized at the time that it posed a real difficulty for laissez faire theory: did a high tariff fall into the prohibited category of a special subsidy to manufacturers (and since the country was dividing sectionally into commerce and agriculture, a special subsidy to the North), or did this revenue measure belong in the permitted category of legitimate measures to protect Americans in the enjoyment of their marketplace? Jackson and his managers, wary of rushing into a premature decision on the question, made a cautious commitment to a high tariff in 1827. The candidate needed Northern votes and was sensitive to that area's demands that higher duties be placed on British woolens, the major threat to a rapidly growing American industry. The situation was complicated, however, by divergencies from the Northern norm among manufacturers, some of whom desired cheap raw materials and were prepared to risk a lower tariff to get them.

The South opposed any tariff increase. To defeat the bill, Southern Congressmen adopted a strange strategy, voting with both Northern factions for a series of obnoxious amendments. The hope, apparently, was that the bill would become so repulsive in its final form that no one could support it. But the ploy backfired. By a close vote, Congress passed what immediately became known as the 1828 "Tariff of Abominations."

Now South Carolina's John C. Calhoun stepped forward to undo the damage to his section's interests and pride. His "South Carolina Exposition and Protest" marked the final conversion of Madison's old ally. What that President had first put together, Calhoun, using different logic, took apart piece by piece. The treatise began with a formal challenge to the constitutionality of the tariff, but it passed on quickly from legalism to a lengthy consideration of the tariff's gross inequity. He calculated, to begin with, that the South paid all or at least most of the tax on imports, which he estimated at $23 million annually. He reached this conclusion by asserting that Northerners were compensated for the tariffs they paid by higher profits in the home market. But the South lived by exporting to the world market a total of $37 million each year, or two-thirds of the national total of exports. "We export to import," declared Calhoun. "The government is supported almost exclusively by a tax on this exchange." It followed, therefore, that the Southern states, composing but one-third of the Union, were being forced to pay two-thirds of the national government's expenses—directly by duties on foreign goods and indirectly through higher prices to protected Northern manufacturers. It was difficult to fault Calhoun's premises or his reasoning. But there was more.

"We are mere consumers," he continued with increasing passion, "the serfs of the system—out of whose labor is raised, not only the money paid into the Treasury, but the funds out of which are drawn the rich rewards

of the manufacturer and his associates in interest." So far everything he had said was consistent with Jacksonian theory (if uncomfortable), but Calhoun could not stop there. He proposed a remedy that recalled the Virginia and Kentucky Resolutions of the 1790s. States, said Calhoun, should have power to declare a questionable law null and void within their borders, until the national government had submitted the dispute to arbitration, by asking for a specific constitutional amendment to that end. There was ample precedent here, including Monroe's desire to secure such authority for internal improvements. Approval would require a three-fourth's majority. "And thus in either case," ended the Exposition and Protest, "the controversy will be peaceably determined."

A Henry Clay-engineered tariff bill put Jackson on the spot in 1832. As soon as the President signed it into law, South Carolina's representatives in Congress called for a state convention. As expected, it passed a nullification ordinance which declared that the tariff gave "bounties to classes and individuals . . . at the expense and to the injury and oppression of other classes and individuals." It was all right out of Jackson's handbook on laissez faire political economy, or so the South Carolinians argued; but the President had no intention of being trapped by that damned Calhoun. Speaking to those he knew would convey the message, Jackson declared he was ready to "hang every leader . . . of that infatuated people, sir, by martial law, irrespective of his name or political or social position."

He spoke a good deal more carefully in public, seeking to engage the disgruntled Southerners in a discussion of the Union's origins and advantages yet promising to carry out the law. He made military preparations, asked Congress to give him specific powers to enforce federal laws, and called for a lower tariff. Congress responded with a compromise tariff, which lowered duties to the 1816 level (20 percent) over a ten-year period ending in 1842, and passed the Force Act, which specifically empowered the Executive to uphold federal supremacy by whatever means necessary. South Carolina then repealed its nullification ordinance but solemnly declared the Force Act null and void. It was a standoff, for the time being.

Another way out

Tariffs, and tariff history, usually bore everyone, including academics. There is nothing of the stuff of *Gone With the Wind* in its pages. Jackson wanted to keep it that way. The less exciting the tariff was, the better off everyone would be, especially the Democrats. Although his predecessors had spent much time trying to perfect a state trading system according to mercantilist tenets, Jackson outdid them all in efforts to expand American foreign trade. He succeeded in 1830 in negotiating an agreement with Great Britain reopening the West Indian trade. As he noted in his Annual Message for that year, this was "a question that has for years afforded matter for contention and almost uninterrupted discussion, and has been the subject of no less than six negotiations. . . ." Exports to England and the colonies doubled in his term of office from $26 million annually to $52 million by 1837. To a certain extent, of course, Jackson was lucky in this agreement: he happened to be in office when the British decided to dismantle their mercantilist trade restrictions as outdated and harmful to the expansion of their overseas commerce.

Nonetheless, the energy of the Jacksonians in reaching out for foreign markets has received far too little attention. In addition to the agreement with England, Jackson signed pacts with Austria, "opening to us an important trade with the hereditary dominions of the Emperor"; Prussia, in order to "open that vast country to the enterprising spirit of our merchants on the north"; Turkey, "we now enjoy the trade and navigation of the Black Sea and of all the ports belonging to the Turkish Empire and Asia"; Central America, "a commerce of the greatest importance if the magnificent project of a ship canal through the dominions of that State from the Atlantic to the Pacific Ocean, now in serious contemplation, shall be executed"; and even the Sultan of Muscat and the King of Siam, "It having been represented to me by persons whose statements and opinions were thought worthy of confidence that the trade of the United states might be extended and rendered more lucrative by commercial arrangements with the countries bordering on the Indian Ocean. . . ."

"Every effort in my power will be continued to strengthen and extend [commercial relations] by treaties found on principles of the most perfect reciprocity of interest, neither asking nor conceding any exclusive advantage," Jackson told Congress, "but liberating as far as it lies in my power the activity and industry of our fellow-citizens from the shackles which foreign restrictions may impose." Foreign trade increased rapidly, especially in the last three years of his administration, when exports went up from $90 million to $129 million annually. But imports climbed even faster, from $108 million to $190 million, resulting in an unfavorable balance of trade, which raised other problems.

An enlarged marketplace was the best way to avoid arguments over sectional inequities; and to liberate Americans from the shackles of foreign restrictions was a favorite way out not only in Jackson's day but ever afterward. Sometimes it worked better, sometimes worse. Sometimes it did not work at all, but because it was supposed to work, Presidents always tried it. In Jackson's case, the unfavorable balance of trade probably reduced the benefits of increased exports and was a contributing cause of the panic of 1837.

And another

Indian removal appealed to Jackson as yet another way out of domestic difficulties. Here again, the solution was not unique with Jackson. Thomas Jefferson had first proposed, at the time of the Louisiana Purchase, something like what Old Hickory wanted to do. Jefferson had in mind putting the Indians into settlements along the east bank of the Mississippi River, where they would serve the dual purpose of providing a buffer between the United States and Spanish America and of regulating what he feared (rightly enough) would be a tendency toward too rapid expansion, far-flung settlements, and political irresponsibility—perhaps even separation. The Indians would hold the line, so to speak, while the United States adjusted its boundaries westward in an orderly fashion.

Since Jefferson's day, however, things had not quite developed in that fashion. Georgia

Figure 9-1 Some of his best friends were Indians, but laissez faire had no place for the red man—at least not as an organized "nation" within the Union. (*Culver Pictures*)

had ceded its public lands to the federal government in 1802, with the stipulation that the United States would remove the Creek and Cherokee Indians as soon as possible. The independence of the Cherokee "nation," on the other hand, had been guaranteed by the United States in a treaty of 1791. Monroe had begun a policy of removing certain tribes from the old Northwest and lower South, but this did not affect these two tribes, which inhabited portions of Georgia, Mississippi, and Alabama. On its own, Georgia had been carrying out removal using a combination of persuasion and coercion. Frustrated at the slow progress and incensed at the spectacle of its citizens abandoning Georgia for richer lands in the West, the state finally demanded that John Quincy Adams carry out the 1802 agreement.

Led by a chief named George Gist or Sequoyah, as his Indian name was anglicized, the Cherokees had developed a written language; built roads, houses, and churches; adopted a constitution; and elected a legislature. The Creek nation had also attempted to emulate its white neighbors' "civilization." Some even held black slaves. By the treaty of Indian Springs in 1825, the Georgia Creeks obligingly ceded all their lands to the state. But the principal chief who had signed this treaty was put to death by the Creeks for violating the rule of the tribe and the decision to sell no more lands. Georgia authorities prepared to survey the lands anyway in anticipation of taking them over.

At this point President Adams called upon the state to cease all such activities until a new treaty could be negotiated When this was accomplished, over the strong objections of Georgia's Governor Troup, the Creeks re-

Figure 9-2 Civilized Indians. But to the Jacksonians, the only good Indian was a *transported* Indian—outside the Union. (*McKenney and Hall,* History of the Indians of North America; *American History Division, The New York Public Library, Astor, Lenox and Tilden Foundations*)

tained a narrow strip of land on the state's western border. The size of the remaining Creek Indian holdings soon became less important than the issue of federal versus state sovereignty; and, of course, there were still the Cherokees to be dealt with. Governor Troup advised Congress that any attempt to keep his surveyors out of the lands ceded originally in the treaty of Indian Springs would be met by force: "From the first decisive act of hostility," he also wrote the Secretary of War, "you will be considered and treated as a public enemy."

After Jackson's inauguration, Alabama and Mississippi joined Georgia in asserting state jurisdiction over all Indian reservations, regardless of existing treaties, and began setting up county governments to replace tribal rule. And Congress passed an Indian Removal Act in 1830, allocating half a million dollars for the resettlement of the tribes on the west side of the Mississippi River. Jackson then promised the Indians he would pursue a "just and liberal policy" with humane and "considerate attention to their rights and wants" consistent with the "feelings of our people." His first step in this just and liberal policy was to inform the Indians that "their attempt to establish an independent government would not be countenanced by the Executive of the United States," and to advise them "to emigrate beyond the Mississippi. . . ." In other words, the old treaties were no longer valid.

When criticisms arose in the North, Jackson, in his messages to Congress, reminded those who "wept over the fate of the aborigines" that they had not objected to whatever means were used to remove the tribes from their midst. Many once-powerful tribes had disappeared from the earth, just as one generation had to be extinguished to make room

for the next. The monuments of an unknown people spread over the regions of the West demonstrated that powerful tribes had once roamed over the very areas Congress now designated for the Creeks and Cherokees. Was this to be regretted? And,

What good man would prefer a country covered with forests and ranged by a few thousand savages to our extensive Republic, studded with cities, towns, and prosperous farms, embellished with all the improvements which art can devise or industry execute, occupied by more than 12,000,000 happy people, and filled with all the blessings of liberty, civilization, and religion?

Jackson always allowed the Indians the option of remaining as individuals—subject to all laws made by those states—within the states where they had lived for generations. It was not much of an option, because what the states would not take by persuasion they could get by enacting laws disenfranchising the Indians. When Chief Justice John Marshall decided in a test case that the laws of Georgia did not apply to Cherokee lands, Jackson snapped: "John Marshall has made his decision. Now let him enforce it." So much for constitutional checks and balances.

That episode ended one phase of the nation's Indian policy and began another, which would continue until the last remaining tribes were confined to reservations on lands nobody else wanted. Georgia led off with a lottery to dispose of the Indian lands it had acquired. In 1838, a last appeal to President Van Buren having been ignored, the Indians were rounded up by federal troops and started on the "Trail of Tears" to the lands set aside for them beyond the Mississippi. About 4,000 perished along the way out of nearly

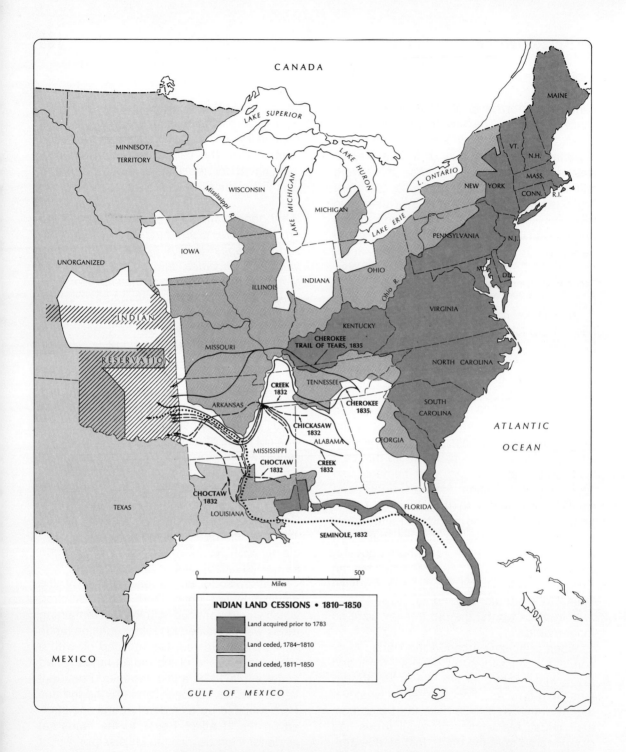

CANADA

LAKE SUPERIOR

MINNESOTA
TERRITORY

WISCONSIN

LAKE HURON

LAKE MICHIGAN

MICHIGAN

L. ONTARIO

LAKE ERIE

MAINE

VT.
N.H.
MASS.
NEW YORK
CONN.
R.I.

PENNSYLVANIA

N.J.

IOWA

UNORGANIZED

MISSISSIPPI R.

ILLINOIS

INDIANA

OHIO

MD.
DEL.

Ohio R.

INDIAN

MISSOURI

KENTUCKY

CHEROKEE
TRAIL OF TEARS, 1835

VIRGINIA

NORTH CAROLINA

RESERVATION

TENNESSEE

CREEK
1832

ARKANSAS

CHEROKEE
1835

SOUTH
CAROLINA

CHICKASAW
1832
ALABAMA

GEORGIA

ATLANTIC

OCEAN

MISSISSIPPI

CHOCTAW
1832

CREEK
1832

TEXAS

CHOCTAW
1832

LOUISIANA

FLORIDA

SEMINOLE, 1832

0   500
Miles

INDIAN LAND CESSIONS • 1810–1850

Land acquired prior to 1783

Land ceded, 1784–1810

Land ceded, 1811–1850

MEXICO

GULF OF MEXICO

*(From A History of the American People by Graebner, Fite, and White. Copyright ©
1970 by McGraw-Hill, Inc. Used with permission of McGraw-Hill Book Company)*

16,000. In the infamous Bataan Death March of World War II, 60,000 American soldiers were marched to Philippine prison camps by the Japanese invaders. Of these, 10,000 died, and America decried the deaths as a war crime and an atrocity.

It should be noted that the South Carolina nullification controversy was reaching its critical stages at the very time Jackson was "advising" the Indians to emigrate from Georgia, Alabama, and Mississippi. None of these states supported South Carolina. Whether or not there was a direct connection, Jackson used his Indian policy as an example of federal restraint and of the advantages of maintaining the Union to ensure the broadest possible opportunity for the individual and the state. The passage in his message to Congress of December 6, 1830, concerning the states and the Indian question, was a masterpiece of the age:

Toward the aborigines of the country no one can indulge a more friendly feeling than myself, or would go further in attempting to reclaim them from their wandering habits and make them a happy, prosperous people. I have endeavored to impress upon them my own solemn convictions of the duties and powers of the General Government in relation to the State authorities. For the justice of the laws passed by the States within the scope of their reserved powers they are not responsible to this Government. As individuals we may entertain and express our opinions of their acts, but as a Government we have as little right to control them as we have to prescribe laws for other nations.

It was every bit as reasonable as Calhoun on the tariff question and a good deal more acceptable to Jackson's Northern constituency.

St. Andrew and the hydra of corruption

Jackson could hardly wait to launch his attack on the Second Bank of the United States. In his very first Annual Message to Congress, the new President reminded the legislators that the bank's charter would expire in 1836, and, since its stockholders would no doubt apply "for a renewal of their privileges," it was none too soon for them to begin deliberations on the subject.

What Jackson really thought about the bank was unprintable, if not unspeakable, but the President was demonstrating admirable restraint and choosing his words with great care. Like other Westerners who had suffered in the panic of 1819, Jackson had blamed the bank for most of his troubles. Even without the panic, however, he had already stored up resentments aplenty against the financial power of the Eastern establishment. There were a large number of younger entrepreneurs located within that very geographical area, however, who had their own complaints about the credit policies of the Greek temple on Chestnut Street, as they called the bank.

These men favored more banks, especially on Wall Street. Jackson's friend from New York, Martin Van Buren, had advanced the state's economic interests at every opportunity. As Governor of that state, he had sponsored legislation authorizing a system of state banks. New York's rapid growth as the nation's primary seaport, the program of state enterprises including the Erie Canal, and its economic power through connections with the "rising empire of the West" were making the city and state the capitalist center of the nation. Already in 1835 the value of exports from New York was three times that of Boston, and greater than Philadelphia's. The destruction of the Bank of the United States meant an orgy of bank expansion in the state. Van

Buren was even warned that the state's legislature had become a matter of "bargain and sale" for speculators, so much so that New York Democrats split into two factions—the Regulars and the Locofocos—on the banking question.

All Democrats used agrarian rhetoric against the Bank of the United States. Some meant it. The bank was charged with discouraging new enterprise by restrictive credit policies; but it was also blamed, on the other hand, for encouraging inflation by farmers and mechanics who complained that wages and crop prices could not keep up with increases on items they required to eke out a living. "As the currency expands," complained these groups, "the loaf contracts." In crude terms, New York and Tennessee thus combined against old wealth and old power.

These charges were both exaggerated and contradictory, but the bank's president, Nicholas Biddle, actively encouraged notions of its great strength, if only to assure stockholders and customers of the bank's ability to contribute to the rational development of the national economy. That did little to reassure the bank's enemies of its benevolence. Taking the President at his word, Clay guided a bill through Congress calling for a renewal of the bank's charter. Jackson returned it with a veto message on July 10, 1832. This message was a real labor of love; he cherished every sentence of it from beginning to end.

He began by pointing out that the bank enjoyed a monopoly of national government favor and support. These favors, bestowed gratuitously by the government and therefore by the American people, increased the value of the bank's stock far above its par value and operated as a special benefit for the stockholders to the tune of "many millions." Many stockholders, he noted, were foreigners. By passing the act to recharter the bank, Jackson asserted, Congress "proposes virtually to make them a present of some millions of dollars"—a present which must inevitably come out of the American people's earnings.

But this gift to dukes and princes was only one aspect of the bank's wrongdoing. The nine Western and Southwestern states held only $140,200 of the bank's stock, yet about $1,640,000 of its profits accrued from that area. In other words, the bank was steadily drawing the wealth out of the West to the benefit of Eastern stockholders and the shadowy European creatures who stood behind them. Several pages later, Jackson concluded his veto message with an almost audible sign of relief: "I have now done my duty to my country. If sustained by my fellow citizens, I shall be grateful and happy; if not, I shall find in the motives which impel me ample grounds for contentment and peace."

Quite aside from the tensions between the mercantilist world view and the President's laissez faire outlook discussed in this chapter, the passion of his veto message reminds one of Madison's vehement attacks on the British influence in the 1790s and his insistence that to rely on England for development capital meant turning over the economic future of the country to the whim and the desires of foreign capitalists. There were to be later echoes of this protest, especially in the 1890s, when William Jennings Bryan became the West's champion against the East.

Meanwhile, Jackson's economic policies after the veto message stimulated an inflationary spiral and a boom-town psychology throughout the West. Land prices soared. Canal building became almost as commonplace as the digging of irrigation ditches—or so it seemed. Freed from Biddle's stern glances and the formal restraints of the Bank of the United States, state banks issued paper money enough to fill cash drawers and

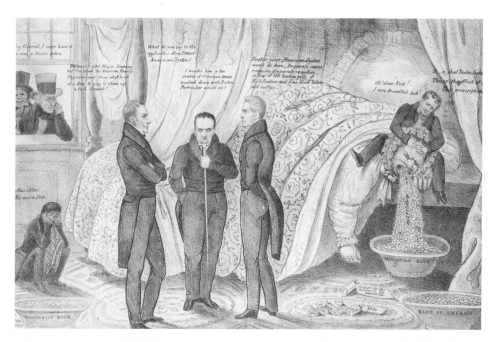

Figure 9-3   King Andrew destroys the temple of the infidel on Chestnut Street. Since 1819 Jackson had hated Eastern bankers; now he had the opportunity to do something about it. (*The Library of the American Antiquarian Society*)

locked strongboxes of merchants and prosperous farmers—and more. Jackson had taken the government's cash surplus and placed it in "pet banks" around the country, giving an added fillip to this already galloping paper credit speculation.

In response to the Locofoco wing of the party, Jackson issued the "specie circular" on July 11, 1836, which required that purchasers pay hard cash for public lands. Its stated purpose was to curb the speculators who were buying up the good land by using their bank credits and paper currency. The results were the opposite because the speculator, not the poor settler, had greater access to specie, and, second, because only the speculator profited from the withholding of public lands for specie. He could buy or sell

as the market suited him. The settler could only buy. The "specie circular" was not the only, or even the primary, cause of the panic of 1837, but the blame fell on President Van Buren, Jackson's hand-picked successor.

Crop failures and a fall in cotton prices produced a crisis atmosphere in the United States. Van Buren's inability to get out of the way of the careening economic bandwagon as it reversed its path gave the Whigs a chance to elect "Tippecanoe" Harrison in the Log Cabin campaign of 1840. John Tyler of Virginia had been added to the ticket for sectional balance—and to provide an alliterative slogan: "Tippecanoe and Tyler Too!" Harrison caught cold on inauguration day and died of pneumonia exactly one month later.

Henry Clay had been waiting for a Whig President and Congress to get through most if not all of his so-called American system. Tyler, an aristocratic slaveholder, held Jacksonian principles on banks and internal improvements. Clay's program was doomed again, except for an upward revision of the tariff. Tyler wanted to be reelected on his own, however, and hoped to achieve this feat by bringing Texas into the Union.

The eyes of Texas

Adams and Clay had once attempted to persuade Mexico to sell Texas. Secretary Clay had instructed the American Ambassador to explain to Mexican authorities that Texas was already part of the U.S. frontier (more than 10,000 settlers had gone there in the early 1820s); that this country was better able to deal with the Indians located there (whatever that meant); and, finally, that by selling Texas, Mexico City would become the geographical center of the Spanish-speaking country. The Mexicans had taken precautions against losing Texas by importing Americans to settle the area under the aegis of their authority and the leadership of Stephen Austin, who actually became a Mexican citizen.

Jackson took up the issue where Clay had left it, only instead of offering to relieve the Mexican government of an Indian problem, the new President suggested that the rapid influx of slaveholders into Texas confronted the Mexicans with an even more serious problem, since their constitution forbade slavery. He would solve their problem by graciously agreeing to take Texas into the Union. Moreover, he would pay $5 million for the territory. Rather than leave a foreign power in possession of "heads of our leading branches of the great Mississippi on its west," he told Secretary of State Van Buren he would willingly pay such a sum. It had always appeared to him, he added, "that the whole of the western branches of the Mississippi was necessary to the security of the great emporium of the west, New Orleans, and that the god of the Universe had intended its great valley to belong to one nation."

Lest anyone still dispute his legal authority to make the purchase, Jackson also explained, there was no longer any constitutional doubt about federal power in the area of territorial expansion. Jefferson had settled all that with the Louisiana Purchase. Besides, he went on, he had even more justification than Jefferson. The United States would soon have to support the Texans (and their institutions) against Mexico—even, he should have added, if he had to create the revolution himself. Whatever else it accomplished, Jackson's openly aggressive Texas policy pushed the Mexicans into taking measures which irritated American settlers and undermined Austin's authority. When the long-anticipated revolution actually came, it was led by Sam Houston, an old Tennessee friend of the President and his former campaign manager. Jackson had sent Houston to Texas with words of encouragement, and Houston repaid the confidence in full.

The Texas revolution demonstrated again that a laissez faire President did not mean a passive President. Quite the opposite. Jackson wielded more power than any of his predecessors in expanding the marketplace, removing the Indians, and exporting revolution to Texas. Reform Presidents have always been strong Presidents. By that definition Jackson was indeed a reformer. He became very circumspect, however, in dealing with the touchy political issue of formal annexation. Recognition of Texan independence—let alone statehood—had already become an issue, with antislave forces insisting it was intended as a prelude to an attempt to make not one but several slave states. The great size of the area suggested that, as in the case of Louisiana, the executive might well appoint several territorial governors and initiate a process that Congress would find difficult to reverse. If so, the balance of power would be tipped in favor of slavery. Led by former President John Quincy Adams, the antislave groups had originally taken a different position: that diplomatic recognition of an independent Texas Republic would check slave expansion, at least inside the United States. Their suspicions of Jackson's motives had caused them to reverse positions. The debate forced the President to lay aside plans for annexation, but he did grant formal recognition in 1837, just before his second term came to an end.

Plagued by economic difficulties, Van Buren was even more circumspect. He left Texas strictly alone. Already read out of the Whig party, John Tyler—who became President in 1841, on the death of Harrison—had nothing to lose by going ahead with the business of annexation. Perhaps he could make it a national issue and reenter the White House through the Texas gate. The only way he could get the votes from Congress for an annexation treaty would be to devise an appeal to moderates. He gave the assignment to Mississippi Senator Robert J. Walker, who produced a piece of political tomfoolery that was just absurd enough to swing the needed votes. The Northern-born Southern Democrat turned out an appeal, published early in 1844, entitled simply, "Letter of Mr. Walker, Relative to the Annexation of Texas."

It began with the required twist of the British lion's tail: if Texas remained independent, it would become a British satellite, leaving New Orleans unprotected in the face of a potential enemy. Then came a standard argument directed at Northern manufacturers: Texas would afford a huge new outlet for their products.

Finally, there was his clincher: annexation would not expand slavery but contract it! At least six states, Walker calculated, would eventually become free territory if Texas came into the Union. Why? Because slaveholders would move to the new state for simple economic reasons, taking their slaves with them; and, as Texas lands wore out, the slaveholders would push on to Mexico and Central America or set the slaves free, being careful to point them in that direction. If Texas were not annexed, horrible thought, the slaves would roam northward as freedmen, and everyone (especially husbands and fathers) knew what that would mean.

Tyler's new Secretary of State, the venerable Calhoun, called into the Cabinet for bipartisan purposes, negotiated an annexation treaty; but he refused to engage in Walker's elaborately conceived ruse. Instead, he put forward an annexation proposal for the Senate's approval clearly labeled salvation for the South. He stressed the argument that Britain was determined to bring Texas within her sphere of influence but claimed that her real reason for this was a desire to destroy slavery in Texas. According to this view, London wanted to see slavery brought to an end throughout the United States, since slave labor enabled American products to undersell those of the British Empire. Southern planters had indeed become afraid of a close relationship between an independent Texas and Great Britain, a relationship which could endanger their chief market for cotton. They also heard rumors that England was ready to offer Texas a large loan if it would adopt free trade principles, so as to become both a source of supply for English factories and a market for English goods.

Calhoun placed these arguments before Northern legislators and businessmen, urging them to put aside differences over slavery and join with the cotton South to prevent British success and to expand American export markets. The argument had more appeal to a group of Southern leaders in the New Orleans area who hoped, frankly, to use Texas in similar fashion and as an entering wedge to the commerce of Latin America. If the North had grown prosperous by imitating Great Britain, the South could find markets for its own young industries (if the slaveholders would go along) in Texas and Latin America. The urgency for such planning took on added weight within the South as the debate grew more bitter. "Texas must be a slave country," Stephen F. Austin wrote to his sister. "The interest of Louisiana requires that it should be; a population of fanactical abolitionists in Texas would have a very pernicious and dangerous influence on the overgrown population of the state."

British abolitionism and free tradeism thus posed a dual threat to the slaveholder's interests. Calhoun's treaty became part of a campaign to insulate the South from its domestic and foreign enemies by building an area from the Mason-Dixon line which would eventually include the Caribbean and Mexico—all the way down to the nearest slave nation in Latin America, Brazil. By the 1850s serious men were absorbed in such fantasies.

But Calhoun was too frank with his old Senate colleagues. The annexation treaty received but sixteen yes votes, against thirty-five nos.

Polk the pragmatic

Behind the scenes of the Texas debate, two former Presidents glowered at one another.

Adams saw his nemesis Jackson lurking behind Tyler and Calhoun: only Old Hickory could be capable of such double-dealing. And Jackson fulminated at that "arch fiend" Adams, the leader of all those who would yield Texas to Great Britain and thus allow that nation to fasten "an Iron Hoop around the United States, with her West India islands that would cost oceans of blood, and millions of money to Burst asunder." Democratic leaders since Jefferson's day had been fond of the metaphor. Stephen A. Douglas would use the same image to denounce the Republicans in the next decade, and Woodrow Wilson during his campaign for the Presidency and expanded exports, constantly talked about a nation smothering in a straitjacket.

More about that, and the reasons, later. The 1844 election was fought in an atmosphere of tension and confusion. Before the party nominations were awarded, Van Buren, the likely Democratic candidate, and Clay, the inevitable Whig standard bearer, made a pact not to argue about Texas. Jackson was outraged. So were Southern Democrats who wanted a candidate who stood four-square for annexation. They found him in yet another Tennessee politician, James K. Polk.

Clay's refusal to stand four-square against annexation, on the other hand, brought on the defection of the so-called Liberty party in New York State, which would cost him the national election. Polk was a far shrewder man than either Clay or Tyler. He campaigned on the slogan: "The Re-Annexation of Texas, and the Re-Occupation of Oregon." If Northern Democrats worried about new states being carved out of Texas, he would give them the chance to gain the same advantage by getting hold of the Oregon territory. It had always worked before, why not now?

Northern Democrats had come to the convention demanding "fifty-four forty or fight!" A

Figure 9-4 The last of the great Jacksonian Presidents. James K. Polk went out fighting. He defeated the Mexicans, but lost the war in the Democratic party. (*American History Division, New York Public Library, Astor, Lenox and Tilden Foundations*)

boundary line drawn at that point would have given the United States half of British Columbia and the certainty of war with England. Nevertheless, Polk encouraged the plan during the campaign. Not surprisingly with such a clear-cut position, Polk won the election. Tyler actually fulfilled the Texas half of his campaign promise for him by securing approval for a joint congressional resolution annexing the independent republic to the United States. Such a resolution required only a majority vote, but it was clear that many had shifted their stand since the vote on the annexation treaty. Polk's Oregon promise had eased fears of a shift in power to the slave states.

But now he had to come through with the goods. The new occupant of the White House continued to strike a defiant pose whenever anybody wanted to talk about Oregon. He nearly scared his conservative Secretary of State, James Buchanan, out of his wits with these tactics. But then when some sober second thoughts finally spread through the caucus rooms of Congress, he brought forward a secretly negotiated compromise treaty setting the boundary between Oregon and Canada at the 49th parallel. He asked the Senate to tell him what to do: sign it or prepare for war? It was a brilliant gambit. The Oregon issue was thus settled.

Northern Democrats, who had been storing up resentments against the Southern-dominated leadership of their party, gave Polk his due, but many began to depart for the Free-Soil party—and political territory beyond. There were other frontiers to be explored and other means to obtain their ends. The old Jacksonian cry against internal improvements no longer had a pleasing sound in Polk's time. The President solemnly denounced internal improvements as nothing but "schemes" contrived to transfer money "from the pockets of the people to the favored classes." But what about Texas and Oregon? came the disgruntled response of those leaving the party. When the slaveholders wanted Texas, the Democratic leadership had responded with one voice; but when it came time to secure Oregon for free institutions, Polk betrayed his supporters. Such doubts became outright disbelief: internal improvements were *not* bounties to the rich and favored classes, Midwesterners began to say, but essential to economic growth and prosperity.

Determined to see it through his way, Polk repeated the litany: "Our system may be safely extended to the utmost bounds of our territorial limits, and that as it shall be extended the bounds of our Union, so far from being weakened, will become stronger."

The war for the Democratic party

"Fifty-four forty or fight," the eminent historian William B. Heseltine used to insist, really meant "Fifty-four forty or fight the Democratic leadership." When Polk asked Congress to declare war on Mexico in 1846, he precipitated an open conflict within his own party. Rumblings of discontent and statements of disbelief became declarations of conscience and denunciations of all who would not choose a side.

Polk had one last trick up his sleeve: California. Interest in California was not confined to party or section. Democrats and Whigs had long and longingly looked at the Mexican province on the West Coast and especially at San Francisco, a perfect jumping-off place for the China trade. Tyler, the Whig President with Democratic principles, had done his bit by negotiating the first commercial treaty with China in 1844. Polk would work things out on this side of the Pacific.

Polk moved on several fronts at once. He offered to buy California at the same time he was sending agents into the province with instructions to stir up demands for annexation to the United States, a la Jackson in Texas. When these ploys fell through, he maneuvered the Mexicans into firing the first shot. The Mexican War had its immediate origins in President Polk's hard-line stand on the boundary between Texas and Mexico. The Texans claimed the Rio Grande as their southern border, but Mexico City insisted that the Nueces River was the proper line. In addition, American citizens felt they had claims against Mexico amounting to $2 million.

Polk's emissary had originally offered a package settlement: if Mexico would agree to sell California for $25 million, everything else could be arranged. Regarding the offer as a gross insult, the Mexican government refused even to accept the American Ambassador. Polk responded by moving General Zachary Taylor's forces across the Nueces River and down to the Rio Grande.

Faced with a choice of war or humiliation, the Mexicans chose the former. Secretary of State Buchanan almost spoiled everything at the last minute. He sent to the White House a note he had planned to use to inform American officials abroad on the reasons why the administration had gone to war. He included a paragraph which stated that the United States would not annex any territory as a result of the war. Polk replied gently that the last paragraph was unnecessary, as the first part of the note explained our position perfectly. Moreover, while the nation had not gone to war for California, that would be the only way Mexico would be able to indemnify this country.

Buchanan protested that the British Ambassador had already questioned him on the point. If some disclaimer was not made, England and France might intervene. Polk hit

Figure 9-5 A British view of the American "land of liberty." (*Punch Magazine*)

the ceiling. "I told him," he wrote in his diary, "that before I would make the pledge which he proposed, I would meet the war which either England or France or all the Powers of Christendom might wage, and that I would stand and fight until the last man among us fell in the conflict."

It might have been better for the Democratic party if England and France had intervened. Polk asked Congress to declare war on the ground that American blood had been shed upon American soil. With that statement he had a fight on his hands with the legislators. An unknown Whig representative from Illinois named Abraham Lincoln introduced a series of "Spot Resolutions" calling upon the president to identify the spot on American soil on which American blood had been shed.

Outside Congress protests spread across the nation from New England intellectual centers and abolitionist strongholds in the Middle West. Henry David Thoreau went to jail rather than pay taxes for the war, thus providing an inspiration for all later war protestors and India's great nationalist leader, Mahatma Gandhi. Passive resistance became a favorite tactic of Thoreau's emulators.

Then, too, the war went badly. Polk had ordered the enlistment of Spanish-speaking chaplains in the Army, instructing them that they were to assure the Mexicans that America would guarantee them the right to practice their religion—as citizens of the United States? There is much evidence that Polk wanted to try for Mexico, but for almost a year American forces were stalled in an area of northern Mexico. Polk blamed "Old Rough and Ready Taylor" for the debacle, claiming he was a clever Whig schemer; but another Whig, "Old Fuss and Feathers" Winfield Scott got things moving at last with a successful march on Mexico City from Vera Cruz in the spring and summer of 1847. There followed another long delay, occasioned this time by the search for a suitable peace treaty. One was not signed until February of 1848. Known as the Treaty of Guadalupe Hidalgo, it gave the United States the Rio Grande boundary desired for Texas, the New Mexico territory (including Arizona), and California. Mexico received a $15 million payment.

Polk had saved the country $10 million under his original offer. Some people are never satisfied, such as Democrat David Wilmot, another obscure representative from Pennsylvania, who sought a congressional prohibition on slavery in any of the territories acquired from Mexico. This Wilmot Proviso was finally defeated by Polk's supporters and antislave expansionists. Politics makes strange bedfellows the saying goes, but not lasting love affairs. Polk had lost the affection of Northern Democrats for good.

A last warning

Calhoun had voted against war with Mexico. It was one of those strange occurrences, an act which at first sight seems totally inconsistent with everything one knows about a man or a situation. When the explanation finally appears near the end of a good novel, the act proves not inconsistent at all. So it was with the South Carolinian's vote. He cast his vote against war while uttering a prediction that the acquisition of any more territory would reopen the debate on slavery in such a way that it could never be closed off again. Enthusiastic about the war, other Southern leaders had encouraged Polk's sudden ambition to annex all of Mexico. Why *not* Mexico, with its seemingly inexhaustible mines, which might be developed by slave labor to produce new riches? Why not Mexico, with the

Figure 9-6   (Left) Henry Clay and (right) John C. Calhoun. The Compromise of 1850 brought these two together for a final round of congressional problem solving. For thirty years cracks in the Union had been patched over this way. Now Congress was running out of cement-makers. (*Photo of Henry Clay courtesy of the Chicago Historical Society; photo of John C. Calhoun courtesy of the National Portrait Gallery, Smithsonian Institution, Washington, D.C.*)

possibility for a new outlet for the interregional slave trade?

The idea was certainly not new; it had been around since Jefferson's time. Was it any less respectable than the desire to annex Canada? After all, several military campaigns had already been fought to take Canada, and here was Mexico for the taking. Polk's imagination had been fired by reports that white settlers in Yucatan were willing to see the province annexed to the United States rather than risk losing it in a long struggle with local Indian tribes. His ardor had cooled somewhat

as a result of the debate on the Wilmot Proviso when a voice from the Old South spoke a dire warning: If Mexico were acquired, the imperial powers necessary to control such a far-off land, a land with no democratic experience and mixed racial society, would centralize power in the federal government to such a degree that the Constitution would surely be destroyed—and with it the only protection for American institutions, including, of course, slavery. "Mexico is for us the forbidden fruit; the penalty of eating it would be to subject our institutions to political death."

Revolutionary intimations

Revolutionary disturbances spread across Europe in 1848. Nothing quite so dramatic happened in the United States, but a close observer of the American political scene would have noted one harbinger of the coming realignment of forces in this country. The event was the nomination of Martin Van Buren, the Jackson loyalist and former President, by a new political group calling itself the Free-Soil party. A fusion of "Free Democrats" and "Conscience Whigs," the party adopted the slogan "Free Soil, Free Speech, Free Labor, and Free Men." Van Buren's willingness to accept this nomination signaled the destruction of the New York-Tennessee alliance, which had dominated politics since Jackson's time.

Joshua Leavitt, an old abolitionist who had never found any reason to praise Van Buren for anything, rose at the party's nominating convention to ask that the choice be made unanimous. Choked with emotion, Leavitt declared: "Mr. Chairman, this is the most solemn experience of my life. I feel as if in the immediate presence of the Divine Spirit." Of such stuff revolutions are made.

If the antislave forces had found a way to defeat the Democrats, they still had not found a way to get across their own program. In 1844 they had helped to end Clay's hopes for the Presidency; in 1848 they defeated Lewis Cass, the Democrat from Michigan, but got Zachary Taylor, a Whig slaveholder, into the White House. But "Old Rough and Ready" surprised both his friends and enemies by declaring that he was opposed to the extension of slavery anywhere.

Sides had been drawn, after the Wilmot Proviso had been defeated, over the admission of California and New Mexico. Henry Clay had enough breath left for one more compromise: California was to come into the Union as a free state; nothing would be said about New Mexico; the slave trade in Washington, D.C., would be ended; and a new fugitive slave law would be passed to guarantee the South its property by forcing the North to recognize its legitimacy. Massachusetts's Dan Webster supported Clay, but Calhoun, a dying man whose speeches had to be read for him, opposed any more compromises: the South had compromised enough. Webster's willingness to incur the wrath of his constituents rested on his conviction that the nation at large still did not have an abolitionist conscience.

The two most powerful voices against compromise were removed from the scene by death. Calhoun's had been expected; Taylor's was a surprise—the result, his doctors said, of eating too many iced cherries and milk after participating in Fourth of July ceremonies on a very hot day. With these men gone, the Compromise of 1850 was achieved in September, after nine months of harsh debate.

The Whig interlude

Neither Taylor nor his successor, Millard Fillmore, could devise an effective alternative to cope with the burgeoning slave issue. Like the Democrats, but with even less possibilities, the Whigs still hoped to resolve the problem from the outside in—not territorially of course, but by expanding the marketplace commercially. Taylor's conversion to adamant opposition to territorial expansion, for example, is usually ascribed to New York's William Henry Seward, an advocate of transcontinental railroads and overseas economic expansion. Perhaps Taylor was simply afraid of the issue, like Calhoun, but Seward's advice filled a need for some new direction and method.

Taylor and Fillmore actively opposed all so-called "filibustering" expeditions launched from the United States against Cuba and Central American. The ultimate goal of the filibusterers was usually annexation or protectorate status for the "revolutionary" governments they had established. These movements, which appeared in the wake of the Mexican War, proclaimed an American "Manifest Destiny" and called upon "Young America" to remake the world in its image. Even more than the Constitution itself, however, the "Young America" movement was contradictory on slavery, proclaiming at once its allegiance to revolution and human bondage.

The Whig administration repudiated filibusters and undertook economic negotiations with Great Britain. These produced the Clayton-Bulwer Treaty of 1851 for joint construction of a canal through Central America. Secretary of State Daniel Webster took a like interest in Hawaii, warning European nations not to undertake any imperial projects there. He also initiated the mission which opened Japan to American commerce and led to the signing of a formal treaty. The Whigs had now pioneered commercial pacts with both China and Japan. Jackson's legacy seemed equally divided between Democrats and Whigs. He had tried to expand the marketplace both ways; but that was no longer possible for one party, nor could they share the legacy peacefully.

Commodore Matthew Perry, the commander of the small fleet which "gently coerced" Japan into its new friendship with the United States, warned his countrymen against Great Britain's determination to capture Asian commerce. "Fortunately the Japanese and many other islands of the Pacific are still left untouched by this unconscionable government; and some of them lie in a route of great commerce which is destined to become of great importance to the United States. No time should be lost adopting active measures to secure a sufficient number of ports of refuge."

Taking his own advice, Perry seized the Bonin Islands, but he was advised by the Democratic administration which came to power in 1853 that the President could not take possession of distant territory without congressional approval. Undaunted by this rebuke, Dr. Peter Parker, another enterprising American, a medical missionary transferred to an official post in China, advised annexation of Formosa. He even ordered a naval officer to keep the American flag flying over the island until he could hear from Washington. Once again the Democrats said no. Angered by what he charged was a government dominated only by slaveholders, Senator William H. Seward, now a Republican, denounced the Democrats for ignoring Parker's great accomplishment. The Whigs were willing to go after strong points safely located thousands of miles away, but they wanted no more slave states.

Once more with feeling

"My administration will not be controlled by any timid forebodings of evil from expansion." So spoke New Hampshire's Franklin Pierce on inaugural day, 1853. The Democrats had run out of space on the North American continent; it was time to go after Cuba. Throughout Pierce's term and that of his Democratic successor James Buchanan, the Cuban question arose almost daily. The Democrats kept after Cuba to divert attention from Whig and Republican proposals and from their own internal problems. But the Southerners played a large role as the campaign for an insulated Western Hemisphere slave bloc reached its height in the 1850s.

Historian Eugene Genovese explains the complex of slaveholder motivations:

They desired Cuba in order to secure political control of the Caribbean, as well as for economic reasons. . . . The need to push forward in order to ward off concentrations of hostile power arose from the anachronistic nature of the slave regime. By 1850, if not much earlier, world opinion could no longer tolerate chattel slavery, and British opposition in particular was both formidable and implacable. The transformation of the Caribbean into a slaveholders' lake and an alliance or understanding with Brazil held out the only hope of preventing a dangerous and tightening containment.

If the Whigs had Commodore Perry to speak for commercial expansion, the Democrats had another naval officer, Lieutenant Matthew F. Maury, to speak for them:

I cannot be blind to what I see going on here. It is becoming a matter of faith—*I use a strong word—yes a matter of faith among leading Southern men, that the time is coming, nay that it is rapidly approaching when in order to prevent this war of the races and all its horrors, they will in self-defense be compelled to conquer parts of Mexico and Central America, and make slave territory of that— and that is now free.*[1]

Pierce's Secretary of State was ready to

---

[1] *The Political Economy of Slavery*, New York: Vintage Books, 1967, pp. 248–249.

offer $100 million or even more for Cuba, but, despite the President's promise that he would not be intimidated by any "timid forbodings," he did not move with Polk's boldness. Rebuffed by the Spanish, Secretary William L. Marcy ordered American diplomatic officials in Europe to confer on a plan for obtaining Cuba. They met in Ostend, Belgium, and produced the "Ostend Manifesto," which declared that the American Union could never enjoy repose or possess reliable security until Cuba was safely within its boundaries. The manifesto hinted at measures of "self-defense" should Spain still refuse to sell the island, but Marcy and Pierce found the Caribbean waters a little too cold for their liking, and refused to plunge into war. (Over the next century, and into the one after that, Cuba played a large role in American domestic politics: Grant and the Radical Republicans split over territorial expansion in the area; McKinley went to war to free Cuba and his administration from domestic pressure; John F. Kennedy risked war twice over Cuba, the first time because he had made Fidel Castro the key issue in 1960, the second because of a combination of external and domestic pressures in the missile crisis.)

The Ostend Manifesto provided a focal point for attacks by the newly organized Republican party. Ohio's Ben Wade summed up the accusation: The whole purpose of the Democratic party was to "go through the earth hunting for niggers," without whom it could no more run than a steam engine without fuel.

Buchanan, one of the authors of the Ostend Manifesto, was chosen by the Democrats to head the ticket in 1856. He won. But Jackson's heirs could not keep his legacy (and the nation) together. It was coming apart day by day. Buchanan only hoped the final blow would not fall during his term.

Selected references

Richard Hofstadter's justly famous *American Political Tradition* (1948) is especially strong for middle-period figures Jackson, Calhoun, and Lincoln. Marvin Meyer's *The Jacksonian Persuasion* (1960) is insightful, while Bray Hammond, *Banks and Politics in America from the Revolution to the Civil War* (1957), completes the demythologizing process. The most favorable account of Jacksonian democracy is Arthur M. Schlesinger, Jr., *The Age of Jackson* (1946). Sectional developments are traced in Frederick Jackson Turner, *The United States, 1830–1850* (1934), Robert R. Russel, *Economic Aspects of Southern Sectionalism, 1840–1861* (1924), and William B. Hesseltine and David Smiley, *The South in American History* (1060). Tyler and Texas, especially the role of Robert Walker, are treated in Frederick Merk, *Manifest Destiny and Mission* (1963). More general treatments of the era are Ray Allen Billington, *The Far Western Frontier, 1830–1860* (1956) and Albert Weinberg's still classic *Manifest Destiny* (1935). Norman Graebner's *Empire on the Pacific* (1955) is excellent on commercial motives for expansion, and John D. P. Fuller's *The Movement for the Acquisition of All Mexico, 1846–1848* (1938) remains standard. Whig policies in regard to the commerce of the Pacific area are detailed by Charles and Mary Beard in *The Rise of American Civilization* (1930). Putting it all together is Eugene Genovese's *The Political Economy of Slavery* (1967). Professor Genovese's "table talk" when he was a colleague at Rutgers University was, in some ways, even more valuable to anyone interested in these problems. We miss him.

TEN

Struggle for Supremacy: The Civil War and Reconstruction

Period covered: 1854–1877
Emphases: Politics and diplomacy
Major events: Kansas–Nebraska Act, 1854
Lincoln-Douglas debate, 1858
John Brown's raid on Harpers Ferry, 1859
Election of Lincoln, 1860
Civil War begins, 1861
Emancipation Proclamation, 1862
Grant's Virginia campaign, 1864–1865
Lincoln assassinated, 1865
Johnson vetoes Freedman's Bureau bill, 1886
Fourteenth Amendment, 1868
Grant elected President, 1868
"Liberal Republican party," 1872
Panic of 1873
Compromise of 1877

Nothing less than full equality in the territories could have satisfied the slaveholders. Perhaps not even that would have been enough. If the North's population continued to grow at the more rapid pace, the only alternative for the South was expansion outside the nation's boundaries. A proslave argument developed after the Missouri Compromise had pronounced slavery a positive good, at least as moral as the capitalist wage system, and therefore fully entitled to expand. The slaveholders had defended their system on moral grounds, but politics and morality grew together in the cotton fields of the South. To deny them the right to expand, insisted the slaveholders, was tantamount to an attack on slavery *within* the states where it had existed from the beginning.

How so, demanded serious Northern leaders? You Southerners are just too sensitive. Not at all, came the reply from Charleston and New Orleans. Once a moral distinction has been made and made to stick, other distinctions in law will follow until, at no far off date, the South would be reduced to colonial status. If the South lost equality in the Senate, its right to exist as an equal part of the Union would have to depend upon the proslave argument morally, and freedom politically, to enter the territories—whether or not a single slaveholder took a single slave into those areas. In the Southern argument, the whole was indeed greater than the sum of its parts.

The situation looked quite different to Eastern industrialists and Midwestern farmers. Their nascent alliance was born of a common opposition to demands that the settlement and development of each new territory must be open to the slaveholders. Slavery, they insisted, literally had no business outside the South. The effort to force it into the territories meant only political turmoil and unrest. Like Southerners they agreed that the issue did not

depend upon the actual entrance of slaveholders into a particular territory. The system itself was like a disease; its effects could be spread far and wide without the presence of the physical evidence in their midst. If the slaveholders succeeded with their argument, then the North and West would continue under the dominance of one section.

Ironically, the North and South still derived great economic benefits from the Union. The North pocketed a handsome profit from handling cotton exports, but both sections needed these sales to redress a continuing adverse balance of payments vis-à-vis Europe. In absolute terms, the Mississippi River actually carried more tons of Western produce to Southern outlets in the 1850s than it had in any previous decade.

The shift was taking place in the percentages. An increasingly higher proportion of Western produce moved East via the new canal system and railroads during this period. Grain receipts at Buffalo, the terminus of the Erie Canal, illustrated the change: in 1835 less than 3 million bushels had arrived there; by 1860 the volume from the West had increased tenfold, to over 30 million bushels.

The repeal of the British Corn Laws in the 1840s had given Western farmers a permanent incentive to produce for the European market. This trade was handled almost exclusively by Eastern brokers and shipped through Eastern ports. The future was across the ocean in Europe, not in the South, which, because of the dominance of the planters, would never attract a large population or build great cities. The outbreak of the Crimean War in 1854 sent wheat and corn prices soaring as the Europeans left their farms for the battlefield. When they came home, the boom ended. But American farmers had seen the potential and were not to be denied. Faced with a struggle for supremacy in European markets, the farmers joined with Eastern industrialists, who were also hard hit by the economic recession of 1857, to demand measures to alleviate domestic conditions that both groups felt worsened their situation. The Republican party embodied these complaints—and the aspirations that lay beneath them.

In 1861 the Union army marched off to war proclaiming an apocalyptic vision first uttered by John Brown. "John Brown's body lies a-mouldering in the grave," sang the soldiers in blue; "His spirit marches on." Few serious Northerners had ever expected to hear a battle hymn extolling that particular dead man's spirit. To Southerners—who out of necessity had developed the alternatives more carefully—it came as no surprise. It made little difference, they had always believed, whether the spirit of John Brown or that of someone like Abraham Lincoln were to prevail. Once the Republicans had political power and could force the South to capitulate, what difference did it really make who sat in the White House? War was a better risk, argued the secessionists, certainly better than political subservience and—if it came to that—a nobler end than slow strangulation.

Lincoln and the Republicans had declared they would not attack slavery in the states where it existed and had never said they would use military force to keep slavery out of the territories. But Lincoln and his party were, in Southern eyes, products of the same fanatical abolitionism which had produced John Brown and now eulogized his murderous deeds. After all, had not William H. Seward, the New York Republican leader, once asserted that there was a "higher law than the Constitution"? What did that mean if not exoneration for Brown and anyone else who applied the higher law by whatever means were at hand wherever they saw fit?

Unpopular sovereignty

If there was to be any way out of the morass of sectionalism, thought Stephen A. Douglas, Democratic Senator from Illinois, it would be found by laying the tracks of a transcontinental railroad or two. Seward and Lincoln had the same vision, though not the same means in mind. Quite naturally Douglas put Chicago at the nexus of any North-South or East-West transportation line. As early as 1843, he went on record against Jackson's Indian buffer zone west of the Mississippi, calling it instead a "savage barrier" against the white man. "It was under these circumstances, and with a direct view of arresting the further progress of this savage barrier to the extension of our institutions, and to authorize and encourage a continuous line of settlements to the Pacific Ocean," he recalled later, "that I introduced the first Bill to create the Territory of Nebraska. . . ."

In 1853 Douglas asserted: "No man can keep up with the spirit of this age who travels on anything slower than a locomotive. . . . We must therefore have Railroads [sic] and Telegraphs from the Atlantic to the Pacific, through our own territory." On January 23, 1854, the Illinois Democrat introduced a bill to divide the Nebraska territory into two parts, by creating a Kansas territory as well. To avoid a bitter discussion over slavery these two territories were to be organized on the principle of squatter, or popular sovereignty. President Pierce signed the Kansas-Nebraska bill on May 30, 1854. Douglas had sought to provide a ready-made compromise before there was an issue, but Pierce's action in signing the bill had repealed the 1820 Missouri Compromise. Once banished from the Louisiana Purchase above 36°30′N, the slaveholder was now seemingly permitted to take his property into Kansas and Nebraska.

Nearby farmers in Iowa and Illinois certainly did not object to pushing the Indians aside in the name of progress, even from lands Jackson had assigned them for a "permanent" settlement, but popular sovereignty became highly unpopular when it meant that the slaveholders would be given a chance to usurp "their" new frontier. A Missouri newspaper, on the other hand, reflecting the fears of slaveholders in the border states, thought Douglas had been mistaken to push the issue so soon after the Compromise of 1850. "Let us rather put off the evil hour, at least, till Cuba is annexed to the Union, (which day we opine is not far distant,) or until other States are admitted—carved out of Texas or New Mexico." Until then the South would be at too great a disadvantage.

But Douglas could not wait. His plans were endangered by rival proposals for a transcontinental railroad and his party was coming apart before his eyes. It was now or never. So be it, declared Seward, "We will engage in competition for the virgin soil of Kansas and God give victory to the side that is stronger in numbers, as it is in right." Senator David Atchison from Missouri picked up the challenge. The proslave forces will have 7,000 men in the territory on election day, he vowed. "We are playing for a mighty stake; if we win, we carry slavery to the Pacific Ocean."

A New England Emigrant Aid Society was quickly organized to supply antislave settlers with financial resources—and new breech-loading Sharps rifles—so that Kansas would become by votes or, if necessary, by violence a free state. Over the next months "bleeding Kansas" offered the nation a preview of Civil War scenes to come. The star (or villain) was John Brown, who, with his sons at his sides, became the scourge of proslave homesteaders. "I have no choice," declared Brown. "It has been ordained by the Almighty God . . . that I should make an example of these men." On a raid against proslave families living near Pottawatomie Creek, Brown and his sons used razor-sharp cutlasses to kill five people in cold blood. That was too much, at least for most sober men on the antislave side. So Brown and his sons, plus a few followers, went into exile in Canada. There they formed a Provisional Government of the United States of America and vowed to return to abolish slavery by the sword.

The Republican emergence

Violence spread from "bleeding Kansas" eastward to the floor of the United States Senate in 1856, when Preston Brooks, a Representative from South Carolina, attacked Massachusetts Senator Charles Sumner, beating him into unconsciousness with a heavy cane. Brooks said he had beaten Sumner because of a speech ("The Crime against Kansas") the latter had delivered which libeled a relative, Senator Andrew P. Butler. In this atmosphere the Republican Convention met at Philadelphia and nominated John C. Fremont, a Westerner, to run on a platform demanding congressional prohibition of those "twin relics of barbarism, polygamy and slavery" from the territories and calling upon the national government to subsidize a railroad to the Pacific Ocean.

The platform appealed to Northern Democrats as well because, no matter what Douglas wanted, the party was still dominated by minority slaveholding interests. As long as they ruled, said dissidents, the nation would stand still while the rest of the world moved ahead into the new industrial era. There would be no transcontinental railroad to supply the West with needed goods and to take its produce to the coasts for shipment to

Europe or Asia, no homestead bill to speed Western development, no tariff to protect new industries. None of these, nor any other measure required for the establishment of a modern political economy, could be expected from a Congress stopped dead in its tracks by the Southern bloc. "We cannot afford to have established on this continent the intolerable restrictions to commercial intercourse," said a spokesman for business, "which are fast dying out among the nations of Europe."

Republicans at the 1856 Convention were filled with a sense of mission, Democrats with apprehension. Republicans looked to tomorrow; while Democrats, looking at Republicans, feared disunion and destruction. Fremont carried eleven free states and polled an impressive 1,340,000 votes to Democrat James Buchanan's 1,838,000. The thirty-fifth Congress, elected in 1856, would have ninety-two Republicans in the House and twenty in the Senate. If he waited much longer, John Brown might be too late for the revolution.

Buchanan's last stand

Kansas was finally admitted as a free state during Buchanan's adminstration. A friendly governor of that territory had warned Buchanan that it was preposterous ever to have expected that slavery could secure a permanent base there. But, said the governor, Buchanan must move quickly to soothe the South: "Cuba! Cuba! (and Puerto Rico, if possible) should be the countersign of your administration, and it will close in a blaze of glory." Buchanan did use his Annual Message of 1858 to announce a plan for acquiring Cuba, but the nation's attention was focused elsewhere, on the senatorial contest in Illinois.

Stephen A. Douglas had been held re-sponsible for "bleeding Kansas" not only in the North but in the South as well, which meant that the Democrats would go into the next Presidential campaign bitterly divided no matter who the Republican candidate might be. Abraham Lincoln, from Douglas's own state of Illinois, thought it might be possible for him to win the Republican nomination by keeping the public's mind fixed on the Democratic Senator's responsibility for "popular sovereignty." Douglas had declared at the time of the Kansas-Nebraska Act that he could see enough territory in the area from the Mississippi to the Pacific "to form at least seventeen new free states." Lincoln set out to make the Senator responsible for the introduction of the slave controversy into every one of those new territories; "bleeding Kansas" was only the beginning.

Lincoln was aided, unwittingly of course, by the Democratic majority on the Supreme Court, which, hoping to dispose of the slave question in the territories itself, handed down the Dred Scott decision on March 6, 1857. According to Chief Justice Roger Taney and his four Southern associates on the Court, the slave Scott could not claim his freedom simply because his Southern master had once taken him to the Illinois territory, a free-soil area where slavery was forbidden by the Missouri Compromise. He could not claim his freedom, said the majority, because Congress had no right to deprive a citizen of his property without due process of law. If the decision stood, no territory or state could legally exclude slavery by any means.

Lincoln used the Court's decision to launch his 1858 campaign against Douglas for the latter's Senate seat, but both men knew the contest was for higher stakes—the Presidency itself. In his opening campaign speech, the former Whig turned Republican and long-time disciple of Henry Clay described the constantly increasing agitation caused by the slavery question. It would not cease, Lincoln insisted, "until a crisis shall have been reached, and passed."

A house divided against itself cannot stand.

I believe this government cannot endure, permanently half slave *and half* free.

I do not expect the Union to be dissolved—*I do not expect the house to* fall—*but I* do expect *it will cease to be divided.*

It will become all *one thing, or* all *the other.*

Either the opponents of slavery, will arrest the further spread of it, and place it where the public mind shall rest in the belief that it is in the course of ultimate extinction; or its advocates *will push it forward, till it shall become alike lawful in* all *the states,* old *as well as* new—North *as well as* South.

Throughout the campaign Lincoln elaborated on this basic idea, suggesting on one occasion that if the color of a man's skin determined whether the government would recognize him as a citizen or treat him as someone else's property, then each man must beware of all those lighter than himself. It was obvious hyperbole, but it made his point: If the states could not prohibit black slavery, either individually or collectively in Congress, the South's "peculiar institution" would cease to be peculiar to the South and would emerge in other forms throughout the country. The issue was not how many slaveholders came North or went West but whether, in a national environment suited to the needs of that class, free farmers would not be reduced to the condition of "poor whites" in the South, dependent upon a class of large landholders? Suppose not even a single slaveholder invaded Illinois, if federal policy discouraged the development of free agriculture in all

sections of the country, would not the result be the same as if hundreds came? And what could result, except white slavery?

Seeking to rationalize expansion and union, Douglas finally replied to Lincoln:

It is idle to tell me or you that we have territory enough. Our fathers supposed that we had enough when our territory extended to the Mississippi River, but a few years' growth and expansion satisfied them that we needed more, and the Louisiana territory, from the West branch of the Mississippi, to the British possessions, was acquired. Then we acquired Oregon, then California and New Mexico. We have enough for the present, but this is a young and a growing nation. It swarms as often as a hive of bees, and as new swarms are turned out each year, there must be hives in which they can gather and make their honey.

In less than fifteen years, if the same progress that has distinguished this country for the last fifteen years continues, every foot of vacant land between this and the Pacific Ocean, owned by the United States, will be occupied. Will you not continue to increase at the end of fifteen years as well as now? I tell you, increase, and multiply, and expand is the law of this nation's existence. You cannot limit this great republic by mere boundary lines, saying, "thus far shalt thou go, and no further." Any one of you gentlemen might as well say to a son twelve years old that he is big enough, and must not grow any larger, and in order to prevent his growth put a hoop around him to keep him to his present size. What would be the result? Either the hoop must burst and be rent asunder, or the child must die.

So it would be with this great nation. With our natural increase, growing with a rapidity unknown in any other part of the globe, with the

Figure 10-1 Lincoln vs. Douglas. It was altogether fitting that Lincoln and Douglas should debate the fate of the Union in a local contest for a Senate seat from Illinois. The issues divided men in nearly all states, and the contest for Illinois was in truth a contest for the future of the nation. (*Courtesy of the Illinois State Historical Library*)

tide of emigration that is fleeing from despotism in the old world to seek a refuge in our own, there is a constant torrent pouring into this country that requires more land, more territory upon which to settle, and just as fast as our interests and our destiny require additional territory in the north, in the south, or on the islands of the ocean, I am for it.

Douglas spoke from the heart. He believed every word of it.

Returning to more immediate questions—although it was difficult to separate basic philosophy from current issues in 1858—Douglas tried to reassure farmers in Illinois and neighboring states that a territory or state government could in fact keep the slaveholders out by simply refusing to enact police protection laws for that institution. Slavery was a timid institution; it would not venture

where an unfriendly climate existed. This so-called Freeport doctrine, named for the town where Douglas first announced it, brought him victory in the Illinois senatorial election, but it drove a deeper wedge between Northern and Southern Democrats. Just as we suspected, declared southern firebrands: Popular sovereignty was another Yankee trick! They agreed for once with Lincoln, who warned his fellow Midwesterners that popular sovereignty had about as much substance as chicken soup made by passing the shadow of a scrawny chicken across a pot of boiling water.

The return of John Brown

In June 1859 John Brown leased a farm near Harpers Ferry, Virginia. Throughout the summer he stocked it with arms for his coming expedition against the federal arsenal in the hill-encircled town. Finally, on October 16, the small army of his Provisional Government of the United States of America, eighteen men in all, fell on the sleeping town. The capture of the arsenal was designed to serve two purposes: first, it would provide more weapons and a base of operations; second, it would trigger a slave insurrection on nearby plantations. Actually there were no nearby plantations of any size, but Brown sent a special expedition to the home of Bushrod, George Washington's nephew, to secure the old general's Revolutionary War sword. It was needed for the new revolution.

The raid ended with Brown's capture and execution, but it sent a shock wave through the country. Southerners knew, or thought they knew, that Brown was financed by Northern abolitionists. Northerners were almost equally dismayed by the raid, even Republicans. Lincoln disavowed it, as did other leaders of the new party. But some intellectuals and literary figures raised their voices in support of Brown's purpose if not of his means. Henry David Thoreau compared Brown's execution to the crucifixion of Christ. Others followed with their praises. Throughout the South the raid raised tensions and spurred fears of Northern-supported slave uprisings elsewhere—where there were large plantations.

Lincoln's decisions

Coming in the midst of this most recent excitement, Lincoln's election had almost revolutionary implications, whether viewed from the North or from the South. Lincoln received 1,866,352 votes; Douglas, 1,375,-157; John C. Breckinridge (a Southern sec-tional candidate), 849,781; and John Bell (the candidate of a coalition of old Whigs and others), 589,581. If it is true that revolutions are always carried out by a minority, then the Republican candidate fully qualified as a revolutionary. Douglas and Bell, the two moderates, together polled over 100,000 more popular votes than Lincoln. But Lincoln was also a constitutional President, because in the electoral college he had well over the necessary majority—180 to Breckinridge's 72, Bell's 39, and Douglas's small total of 12. A paradox it was, and one not foreseen in the philosophy of the Founding Fathers. They had hoped by creating the electoral college to prevent the election of a dangerous man who had caught the public fancy, and to ensure the continuing significance of the states in a federal union.

Men seeking to avoid a Civil War appealed to the President-elect to reassure the South once again before the inauguration. It was even suggested that the Missouri Compromise line be extended to the Pacific. Lincoln refused, replying that if he agreed to such a scheme, the Southerners would be right back within a year clamoring for new slave territories outside the United States. The cry would go up again for Cuba and even Central America. After he took office, William H. Seward, now Secretary of State, came forward with an even more remarkable suggestion. Producing newspaper reports of Spanish designs on the Dominican Republic, Seward urged the President to demand explanations—not only from Spain but also from France, Great Britain, and Russia. If satisfactory replies were not forthcoming, Lincoln should ask Congress for a declaration of war, at least on Spain and France! Somehow Seward's "higher law" had gotten all turned around; he was now thinking of applying it to all Europe. Lincoln rejected that proposal too.

The President had promised the South that his administration would not "directly or indirectly interfere with their slaves or with them about their slaves." The South would "be in no more danger in this respect than it was in the days of Washington." It was not enough. Even if some moderates agreed that slavery did not have to expand to survive, their voices were not heard in the tumult demanding secession. With the firing on Fort Sumter in Charleston Harbor, the struggle for supremacy shifted from Congress and the White House to the cornfields of Virginia, Maryland, and Pennsylvania and to the mountains of Tennessee.

The legislative front

With the Southern Democrats absent from Congress after the secession, the Republicans had an easy time of it, enacting one piece of legislation after another. "Vote yourself a farm—vote yourself a tariff." That had been the rallying cry to voters in 1860. Now the Republicans did that—and much more besides. A Homestead Act opening new lands in the territories for easy settlement was passed in 1862. The tariff was raised to its highest point, and a national banking system was created. In 1864 a new Immigration Act was passed, authorizing contract labor arrangements which ensured a steady flow of cheap labor for manufacturers. Many new immigrants who came to America under this law would be employed in building not one but two transcontinental railroads that had been granted federal subsidies.

The war wrought long-range changes in the structure of the American governmental system—changes of even more importance than these measures. By 1865 Lincoln wielded political power such as no President had

Figure 10-2 A rendition of the dangers to the Union. (*American History Division, The New York Public Library, Astor, Lenox and Tilden Foundations*)

before or had dreamed of; and he commanded military and naval forces far beyond the imagination of his predecessors. To fight the war and complete its legislative program, the Republican majority spent nearly $3.5 billion, more than the total of all national expenditures since 1789. They left a national debt of $2.6 billion, forty times what it had been in 1860. Federal expenditures, an accurate gauge of government intervention in the economy, never again fell below an annual figure roughly four times what they had been in 1860. Lincoln began the war speaking of the "union" and its preservation; at his death, victory belonged to a "nation" which Republicans confidently assumed would surpass all the rest.

Lincoln continued to make every effort to keep the slave issue per se out of the war. Aside from the consideration that loyal border states still contained slaveholders, he was anxious not to do anything which might make it more difficult for pro-Union forces within all states to support his adminstration. The Democrats had charged the Republicans with favoring the black man over the white, an attack the latter responded to by pointing out that since they opposed slavery in the territories, they were "the only white man's party in the country." Republican racism was perhaps different in some respects from that practiced by Democrats, but it was almost as widespread in the ranks of the new party as among the Democrats.

The President needed the so-called "war Democrats" in the North to counter the poisonous and disloyal "Copperheads" who dominated the Democratic party in some states. The race issue was handiest for the Copperheads, and they made good use of it to oppose the war. A draft riot during July 1863 in New York City suggested that even strong Union states contained many young

men who had little desire to risk their lives to free the blacks. The revolt lasted three days, during which rioters seized blacks and hung or shot them according to what was available. In other cities and towns the draft met resistance, evasion, and desertion.

Several factors combined to force the President to abandon his original position. The first and most important was the strategic situation early in the war. Everyone knew that the Confederacy's only hope lay in securing European aid, especially from Great Britain. When early battles went against the Union, it became imperative to delay whatever plans European leaders might entertain for recognizing the independence of the Southern states and awarding them status under international law. So Lincoln was forced to make slavery a moral issue, just as the South had always insisted would happen. The preliminary Emancipation Proclamation of September 22, 1862, was a strategem to accomplish that end without weakening support for the Union in border areas. The Proclamation was so designed as to force *other* nations to consider the moral issue. It stated that on January 1, 1863, all persons held as slaves within a state "or designated part of a State" then in rebellion against the United States "shall be then, thenceforward, and forever free." The message seemed plain enough: those who defected to the Confederacy stood to lose their slaves without compensation; but those who remained loyal could look forward to pecuniary aid from the federal government when and if their states voluntarily adopted emancipation laws. By establishing January 1, 1863, as the effective date for emancipation, the President had also given the rebellious states one last chance to reconsider and thereby retain their slave property.

Some months later, in his annual message of December 1, 1862, Lincoln took up the emancipation question in greater detail. The time had come, he said, to stop wasting the Union's strength "in struggles among ourselves" over the issue. Then he proposed a constitutional amendment granting the states up to 37 years to abolish slavery. Those that complied would receive compensation from the national treasury. It was best to settle the matter once and for all in this fashion, because the North had been no less responsible for the introduction of the slaves into America than the South. He was extremely blunt on that point: "we all use cotton and sugar and share the profits of dealing in them. . . ."

Lincoln's American system

The President's desire to substitute a national solution to the slave question in place of the sectional antagonism which had led to war was all the more remarkable for its open invitation to the Southern states to join in the process of amending the Constitution. Throughout his 1862 message, Lincoln sustained a mood of intense nationalism. There was no line, he declared, "straight or crooked, suitable for a national boundary upon which to divide." Aside from the obvious practical difficulties of trying to draw an exact boundary between free and slave country, either north-south or east-west, there existed a fundamental reason why separation was impossible. The "great interior region" of the country, already a "most important" producer of grains and provisions for the world, had no seacoast. As part of one nation, its people could find "their way to Europe by New York, to South America and Africa by New Orleans, and to Asia by San Francisco." But if the country were separated into two nations, "as designed by the present rebellion, . . . every man of this great interior region, is thereby cut

Figure 10-3 U. S. Grant, architect of the Union victory in the first great war of the industrial age. Heroes and gallantry are for losers; victory goes to the mechanized army in blue which marched through the wilderness to the heart of the Confederacy. (*The Bettmann Archive*)

off from some one or more of these outlets, not perhaps by a physical barrier, but by embarrassing and onerous trade regulations."

These outlets, east, west, and south, are indispensable to the well-being of the people inhabiting and to inhabit this vast interior region. Which of the three may be the best is no proper question. All are better than either, and all of right belong to that people and to their successors forever. True to themselves, they will not ask where a line of separation shall be, but will vow rather that there shall be no such line. Nor are the marginal regions less interested in these communications to and through them to the great outside world. They, too, and each of them, must have access to this Egypt of the West without paying toll at the crossing of any national boundary.

If there existed no way to separate the country, there also existed no way to separate political and economic issues from the slave question. Lincoln recognized this in the final sentences of his message. "In *giving* freedom to the *slave* we *assure* freedom to the *free*—honorable alike in what we give and what we preserve."

The military front

Whatever plans Lincoln had for assuring "freedom to the free" depended, of course, on the outcome of the war. By any quantitative index, the North started at an advantage: it had more men, better logistics, and an industrial base. The South had chivalry and a conviction that one soldier from Dixie was worth ten Yankees whatever the situation. At the very top, the equation seemed to be true; General Robert E. Lee appeared to be more than a match for any ten Union generals. From the first campaign against Richmond in 1862 until the battle of Gettysburg more than a year later, Lee's generalship was the outstanding military fact of the war.

Union strategy aimed at capturing Richmond, the Confederate captial, blockading Southern ports, and seizing control of the Mississippi and Tennessee Rivers. Stymied in the 1861–1862 peninsular campaign against Richmond, Union forces had their major successes in the first years of the war in the west. New Orleans fell before a naval assault in April 1862, depriving the Confederate government of its most important seaport. The high tide of the Confederacy came in July 1863 at Gettysburg, Pennsylvania, when General Lee sent his forces head-on against the Army of the Potomac. Marching with drill-ground precision, the men of Pickett's charge were methodically cut down by Union riflemen as they attempted an assault on Cemetery Ridge. Gallantry had at last proved no match for efficiency plus mass.

Lee retreated with the remnants of his army into Virginia; that same day, July 4, 1863, Vicksburg fell to General Ulysses S. Grant. With the Mississippi River now completely under Union control, the Confederacy was effectively cut in two, with Arkansas, Louisiana, and Texas severed from the main body. Promoted to Lieutenant-General and named to command all Union forces, U. S. Grant assembled a 100,000-man army and began moving against Lee's men in May 1864. His advance became known as the Wilderness campaign; from it thousands would never return. In the first encounter, Grant lost 18,000 men; a few days later another 12,000 fell at Spotsylvania; then 12,000 more in a single day at Cold Harbor. At the end of one month the Union Army had lost more men than were enlisted in Lee's entire army.

The difference was that Grant could afford

such losses while relentlessly pursuing his adversary deeper into the heart of the Confederacy. Meanwhile, another Union Army commanded by General William Tecumseh Sherman had marched all the way from Chattanooga across Georgia to Savannah. Then turned northward and swept through South Carolina on its way to Raleigh, North Carolina. The devastation wrought by Union Armies left the Confederacy in a shambles. In September 1864, Grant ordered General Philip H. Sheridan to invade the Shenandoah Valley, Richmond's granary. At the end of the campaign the once-rich and fertile area was said to be so completely burned out that "a crow flying over the country would need to carry his rations."

Union ranks were increased by the addition of freed blacks after the Emancipation Proclamation. These men may not have played a decisive role militarily, but without the more than 200,000 blacks who served in the Union Army, for a long time at half pay, the war would have gone on even longer. They fought and died with soldiers who often despised them almost as much as did the men in grey. Slavery was coming to an end, but the race question was really only beginning. Inevitably, some Northerners resented the blacks as the cause of the war and the death of sons and husbands. Service on the Union side had given the blacks a moral claim, not only to their own freedom but to decent treatment. How the Republicans would respond to that challenge was soon to be not a military but a political question.

On April 7, 1865, General Lee asked for terms. Grant agreed to meet him at Appomattox Court House, a village in Virginia, on April 9, 1865. The war was over. Casualties in the Civil War were greater, proportionally, than those suffered by the British and French in World War I. Union deaths totaled 364,500;

140,000 in battle, 225,000 from other causes. Confederate battle deaths totaled nearly 90,000; another 160,000 died from other causes. Including the wounded, battlefield casualties on both sides exceeded one million. The American Civil War was, in sum, the first of the industrial age's "total wars," even though it was limited geographically to one country. Grant's unheroic victories, accomplished by human-wave tactics, set the standard for modern warfare. Heroes belong to the losers under such conditions.

The President and Congress

The political cost of modern warfare raised obstacles to Lincoln's plan to reconstruct the Union just as soon as possible. His opponents, the so-called "radical" Republicans in Congress, used the public's grief and desire for revenge to build support for a *Southern* Reconstruction policy, which, to all intents and purposes, was a colonial policy. Some radicals were obviously motivated by the highest of moral purposes; others were political gut fighters who asked no quarter and gave none. Historians have spent a great deal of time, probably too much, sorting out the radicals into subcategories of these two groups—to the neglect of more interesting and important questions.

Just as soon as federal troops gained footholds in Tennessee, North Carolina, Arkansas, and Louisiana, President Lincoln appointed military governors and assigned them the task of organizing loyal citizens so that elections might be held. Two congressional representatives were promptly chosen in districts of Louisiana under Union control and sent to Washington. On December 8, 1863, Lincoln announced an executive amnesty policy which provided that when 10 percent of a seceded state's voters had taken a loyalty oath, it might be restored to all its former political rights and privileges within the Union.

No less nationalistic than Lincoln, congressional radicals saw the issues from a different perspective. The "revolution" (meaning the total Republican program regardless of individual motivations) would never be secure as long as slavery existed anywhere; under the President's announced proposals, that could be another four decades. To readmit the seceded states without their having abolished slavery meant endangering the hard-won gains of both political and military struggles; it meant allowing the Democrats a chance to dominate Congress; it might even mean the undoing of what had cost so much to achieve. The radical leader in the House of Representatives, Thaddeus Stevens, wrote to his law partner that what the country needed was someone in power, "with sufficient grasp of mind, and sufficient moral courage, to treat this as a radical revolution, and remodel our institutions. . . . It would involve the desolation of the South as well as emancipation, and a repeopling of half the Continent. . . ."

Not all radicals went so far as Stevens, but they all did eventually come to the position that since the freedman needed protection against his former master and the Republican party needed protection against the Southern Democrats, it was logical that Reconstruction would have to include immediate suffrage rights for the former slaves. That was an issue which would bring the radicals into conflict with the President. The struggle for supremacy, which had now shifted from the battlefield to a contest between Congress and the Executive, began with the Wade-Davis Bill in 1863, a response to Lincoln's Amnesty Proclamation. Declaring the President's action to

be a "studied outrage on the legislative authority of the people," the supporters of the bill demanded that no state be reconstructed and admitted into the Union until 50 percent of the white male citizens had taken the loyalty oath. That alone would take a good deal of time. Only then could the military governor order an election for a convention to amend the state's constitution to abolish slavery, repudiate the Confederate debt, and disenfranchise all civil and military officials above a certain level who had served the Confederacy.

The Presidential counterattack

The Wade-Davis bill passed so late in the congressional session, that Lincoln could avoid an immediate clash simply by failing to sign it into law. But the battle lines were drawn. For a brief moment in 1864, the radicals hoped to rid themselves of Lincoln by replacing him on the national ticket with Salmon P. Chase, a man more congenial to their way of thinking. The President had already counterattacked, however, making such a coup impossible and jeopardizing the radicals' position within the party. For some time he had been thinking of reorganizing the Republican party into a National Union party by including the war Democrats. He had encouraged such a development in Illinois, Pennsylvania, and Ohio for local elections in 1863. The move proved successful, enough so that he could go ahead with the next step and select Andrew Johnson, a war Democrat who had served as provisional governor in Tennessee, for his running mate.

After the election, Congress passed the Thirteenth Amendment, abolishing slavery without any provision for compensation. It was sent to the states for ratification on January 31, 1865. A few days later, the President met secretly with a delegation of Confederate leaders at Hampton Roads, Virginia, and assured them of his desire to treat the seceded states with "liberality" once they had acknowledged the "national authority" and accepted the new amendment. The conference produced no agreement, but Lincoln went ahead on his own with Louisiana, which he considered the best of the "10 percent" governments. To a crowd which had gathered outside the White House on the evening of April 11 to celebrate Lee's surrender to Grant at Appomattox, Lincoln delivered not a victory oration but a sophisticated defense of his action in recognizing the new state government in Louisiana. Candidly admitting that "we, the loyal people, differ among ourselves as to the mode, manner, and measure of reconstruction," the President explained in detail what had taken place under his directions in that particular situation. He noted that the franchise had not been given to the freedman under Louisiana's new constitution. He would have preferred otherwise, but the question was not simply whether the new state government as it stood was quite all that was desirable. "The question is, will it be wiser to take it as it is and help to improve it, or to reject and disperse?"

If we reject Louisiana, Lincoln concluded, the country would lose one vote in the ratification of the Thirteenth Amendment. At first hearing or reading one misses the point—as Lincoln may have intended; after it sinks in one can understand why the radicals were so alarmed. Lincoln was saying that Reconstruction only involved restoring states still legally within the Union—states that could vote on constitutional amendments like all other states—to their proper relationship within the nation. The radicals insisted on something quite different. Their position was that the

seceded states had ceased to exist, or had committed suicide, when they joined the Confederacy. Therefore, only Congress could deal with the situation, which resembled the case of territories in the process of qualifying for admission.

Lincoln's assassination three nights later left his successor, a Southern Democrat and former slaveholder, without a clear idea of strategy or tactics to implement executive Reconstruction. Lincoln had banked on his personal ability and prestige as war leader in the coming struggle with Congress. He could, if necessary, appeal to the people for support. Little was known about Andrew Johnson, except that he was said to hate the planter aristocracy. Johnson sprung from the Southern poor white class, but he had landed in the not-quite-accepted class of self-made men who were to people the novels of postbellum writiers. Like them, he was envious of the upper class and filled with hatred and fear of those who might push him downward once again into anonymity and poverty.

The ordeal of Andrew Johnson

The differences between the dead leader and his successor were great. Whereas Lincoln was arriving at a new place in society, Johnson was fleeing from an old place. Yet there were important similarities, too, which help to explain certain aspects of the Reconstruction period and its continuing aftereffects in the nineteenth and twentieth centuries. Both men started out in states which had been populated from an original "border" state, Kentucky, and both regarded slavery as an impediment to the progress and prosperity of their class and area. Illinois men feared the slave power in Congress; Tennesseans lived under the dominance of the planters. But

Figure 10-4 Lincoln was arriving at a new place in society; Johnson was fleeing from an old place. Yet both men regarded slavery in the border states where they started out as an impediment to progress and prosperity. It was Johnson who faced the dilemma of Reconstruction and reunion. He failed, but so did the radical Republicans. (*Ewing Falloway*)

where the farmers of Illinois were made free by the Republican victory in 1860, the men of Johnson's class had to live with the fear that the black man would once again be used to dominate them by some new power remoter than the slaveholders, who at least had offered the "poor white" a minimum opportunity to rise above his origins.

Lincoln's occasional references to the possibility of resettling the freed slaves in Liberia suggested that he had perhaps considered this dilemma but given less consideration to it than a plan for reconstructing the states. When a delegation of Quakers came to the White House to appeal to the new President to support Negro suffrage, Johnson assured them that he was well acquainted with the problem, and wanted to help. But then he went on: "You tell me, friends, of the liberation of the colored people of the South. But have you thought of the millions of Southern white people who have also been liberated by the war?"

Johnson went ahead with what he thought to be Lincoln's Reconstruction "plan" by extending recognition to new governments in Virginia, Arkansas, and Tennessee. Encouraged by Secretary of State William H. Seward, he also issued an amnesty proclamation to the citizens of the Southern states —excluding those who had once taken an oath of allegiance to the United States, such as military officers, those who had held civil or military office in the Confederacy, and those who possessed $20,000 or more in property. These excluded groups were required to apply for special Presidential pardons. Seward wanted the leaders of the rebellion to reaffirm their loyalty to the United States on an individual basis; Johnson wanted to prevent the resurgence of the planters.

All these steps were taken while Congress was not in session in the summer of 1865. The radicals returned in the fall determined to carry out their own Reconstruction plan based on black suffrage and military rule of the South. They had supposed, wrongly, that Johnson was sympathetic to their goals. In the days following Lincoln's death, the new President had vowed that traitors must be punished, but the radicals mistook his meaning. Senator Benjamin Wade exclaimed, "Johnson, we have faith in you. By the gods, there will be no trouble now in running the government."

Reconstruction alliances

The rapid deterioration of Johnson's relations with the radicals hastened the development of new alliances. Where Lincoln may have hoped to reunite the old Southern Whigs with a reconstituted National Union party in 1864, Johnson apparently turned that plan around in hopes of building a bridge between his own class and the Democratic planter aristocracy, but with the former on top. Seward had advised Johnson to adopt a soft Reconstruction policy in general but also to require special oaths of allegiance from specified former Confederate officials. As he saw it, the United States faced an increasingly hostile world environment, filled with competitors eager to take advantage of any divisions within the country to their own benefit. Seward's dream of American domination in the marketplaces of the world could not be fulfilled by a cripple continually plagued by old wounds that refused to heal.

Johnson, on the other hand, seemed to enjoy his new role as royal pardoner of the planter elite. Very soon he had reason to look upon the amnesty declarations in a different light: perhaps he could use this policy to build a political alliance between the old antagonists of his own section and link it to antiradical groups in the North. As far as he

could see, the radical Republicans had little to offer the other freedmen of the South, the poor whites. Without the black man between them, as slaves or as tools of the radicals, the whites could work together for common goals.

The President's behavior alienated him not only from the radicals but from moderate Republicans as well, thus forging an alliance between those groups which gave the radicals their real power. Meanwhile, the newly freed blacks, totaling nearly 4 million in a Southern population of 9 million, waited for Washington to decide if they were citizens—or what. The most persistent rumor throughout the South was that every freedman would receive "forty acres and a mule." Land redistribution on that scale would have meant more than the destruction of the planter elite as a dominant class, it would have entailed a complete social reordering of the South and enforced economic changes which could have triggered demands in other sections of the country. The ghost of John C. Calhoun walked the halls of Congress late at night as the Republicans considered their policies. Maybe some heard him saying again, as he had said in 1838, that the South was

the balance of the system; the great conservative power, which prevents other portions, less fortunately constituted, from rushing into conflict. In this tendency to conflict in the North, between labor and capital, which is constantly on the increase, the weight of the South has been and ever will be found on the conservative side; against the aggression of one or the other side, whichever may tend to disturb the equilibrium of our political system.

Whether they heard Calhoun whispering in their ears or not, the radicals faced a very tricky situation perfectly exemplified by the

Figure 10-5a The attitude toward freedmen depicted here led first to the black codes and later to the end of black Reconstruction. (*Harvard College Library*)

Figure 10-5b Klansmen of the 1870s. (*The Rutherford B. Hayes Library*)

Figure 10-5c The South Carolina legislature, which alone of the reconstructed assemblies had a black majority. (*The Bettmann Archive*)

"forty acres and a mule" rumor. How would they reconstruct the South without going too far in the direction of undermining respect for property rights in all sections of the country, or, conversely, without turning the job back over to the planters? In the end, the radicals would opt for the second alternative, but not before they assured themselves that the political changes wrought since 1861 were permanent and accepted as such even by the so-called Southern redeemers.

But that did not mean the radicals were insincere, mere rhetoricians without principle. Much of what they tried to do was embodied in one measure, the March 1865 bill creating the Bureau of Freedmen, Refugees, and Abandoned Lands. Administered by the War Department, the Freedman's Bureau was assigned the task of preparing the ex-slaves for social and economic independence. In its first year of operations, the bureau concentrated on providing rations on an emergency basis to anyone needing them, black or white. It provided a total of over 13,400,000 meals in those dread-filled months while the South still lay in desolation.

Once functioning on a normal basis, the bureau moved ahead swiftly, setting up schools, banks, and employment offices. Both public and private funds were channeled through its offices. Nor did it limit its activities to helping the black man. "Schools for refugee white children are also established," reported its director, "and their formation is everywhere encouraged by the bureau." There was little doubt but that the Freedman's Bureau constituted a potentially revolutionary instrument for social change. Recognizing it as such, and concerned about reestablishing their control over the blacks, Southern state governments passed so-called "black codes" to solve the social and economic problem on a basis somewhere between slavery and complete equality.

With the most dedicated radicals now directing congressional affairs through the Joint Committee on Reconstruction, a bill was passed extending the life of the bureau and enlarging its functions to give it the power to act as a court to secure equal justice for the former slaves. An agent of the bureau was to be sent into each county to see that equal justice did indeed prevail and that confiscated property might be allotted or sold to the freedman as the bureau saw fit.

Forced to choose between the radicals and the new governments of Southern states, between his fear of the old aristocracy and the danger posed by the "do gooders" who wanted to make the black man a ward of the nation (or the Republican party), Johnson came down on the side of states' rights and white supremacy. His veto message called the Freedmen's Bureau bill "class legislation, . . . well calculated to keep the public mind in a state of uncertain expectation, disquiet and restlessness. . . ." It would encourage "interested hopes and fears" that the national government would continue to furnish to certain "classes of citizens" means of support and maintenance whether they chose "to pursue a life of indolence or of labor." In another veto message, Johnson protested that the former slave was not "so exposed as may at first be imagined."

He is in a portion of the country where his labor can not well be spared. Competition for his services from planters, from those who are constructing or repairing railroads, and from capitalists in his vincinage or from other States will enable him to command almost his own terms.

Running through his speeches and messages was one overriding theme: "Slavery was essentially a monopoly of labor, and as such locked the States where it prevailed against the incoming of free industry." Its removal meant that "free labor" would now have a chance to develop the "immeasurable resources" of the South. He certainly had not imagined that the national government would interfere with this natural process as it now threatened to do.

The radicals responded by passing a second Freedmen's Bureau bill over the President's veto and then a Civil Rights bill assuring the black man's franchise and a new constitutional amendment giving him national citizenship. The Fourteenth Amendment was an omnibus measure, forbidding the states from interfering with the privileges or immunities of "citizens of the United States" or from depriving "any person of life, liberty or property without due process of law." It also provided for a reduction in the representation of any state in the House of Representatives in proportion to the number of male citizens not permitted to vote. Finally adopted in 1868, the Fourteenth Amendment capped the radicals' program.

Where they came out

The frequency with which corporation lawyers invoked the Fourteenth Amendment to defend their clients against state regulation and taxation in the Gilded Age suggests once again the basic paradox of the radical position and the reason for its ultimate abandonment. The Civil War had deprived the planters of more than $1 billion in slave property. To replace the political economy of slavery, the radicals offered an entrepreneurial capitalism. Traveling through the south immediately after the guns fell silent, William D. "Pig Iron" Kelley, a Republican representative from Pennsylvania, lectured the Southerners on their past mistakes: What had states rights brought

them? he challenged. What the South needed was federal support for rivers and harbors bills and a factory system producing goods for domestic and foreign consumption. The radicals, some of them at least, wanted to establish the black man as a participating element and sustaining force of their political "revolution." To do that required interference in the basic institutions of private property: the black man could not be protected against the loss of his property, after all, until he had first achieved ownership—on his own or from some other class. On that problem, the Republican coalition and consensus finally came apart.

Johnson's resistance to the radical program led to a temporary impasse in the national government, which the radicals tried to remove by impeaching the President and convicting him of high crimes and misdemeanors. They failed by one vote in the Senate; but they failed in a much larger sense by not coming up with an effective answer to the challenge he had put before them in his veto messages. They could not find a way to give the blacks equality and yet carry out the capitalist revolution in the South. Faced with the rise of violent opposition led by the Ku Klux Klan and other "nightriders" as well as with simple noncompliance on the part of local governments, the radicals paused and then backed off. If they had gone ahead, as some of their extreme leaders wanted, the only paths led toward permanent military rule or thoroughgoing economic transformation, perhaps even to redistribution of property. The first amounted to "imperialism" in its worst form and would not really guarantee stability for any class or property rights for any individual. The second raised the spectre of "socialism," not alone for the defeated agrarian society but for the whole nation.

And so it became a question of time: How

long would it take for emotions to cool off enough to allow a bargain to be struck, turning over the black "problem" to the redeemers of the new South? The radicals passed laws to curb the violence and secured yet another amendment, the Fifteenth, to guarantee the former slaves the vote. But the lack of agreement within the Republican party was perfectly illustrated by their choice of Ulysses Grant to run for the presidency in 1868. A war hero could hold the party together and pursue domestic policies on a more pragmatic basis. To the remaining radicals, Grant represented a last hope that Reconstruction would be carried out to its logical end, no matter where that led; but to the rising leadership in the Republican party, the general offered the best way out of a deadlocked situation. He satisfied neither group, and the scandals associated with his adminstration added new troubles to the list of Republican woes.

By 1872 the party was in crisis. An alliance of civil service reformers, low tariff advocates, and states' rights supporters launched the "Liberal Republican party" on a national scale. Its Presidential nominee, Horace Greeley, ran on the promise of ending Reconstruction, which he blamed for the nation's ills. The country was sick to death of it. His correspondents had reported to him that the Northern-inspired "carpetbag" governments of Southern states were ruining the South with their taxes and corruption. And the only way to get rid of the Ku Klux Klan was to throw them all out. "Had it not been for carpetbag mismanagement," Greeley proclaimed, the South "today would be filled with millions of Northern or foreign yeomanry carving out farms, or working in . . . iron, copper, coal, and marble."

Thus was born the myth of the ruinous carpetbag state governments, dominated by Northern fortune seekers and their ignorant black allies. The truth was that many of these state governments, and many black state legislators, provided their populations with a considerable body of social and economic legislation and perhaps came closer to resolving the dilemma of securing equality for all without destroying the economic system than the national government. Was it mismanagement or social change that Northerners feared most by 1872?

There was widespread corruption in the South during Reconstruction, but hardly more than that revealed in the highest levels of the national government during Grant's tenure. The worst of these scandals centered in the lavish handouts awarded railroad builders which had begun before Grant's time; they had begun, in fact, with the Republican triumph. Crédit Mobilier of America, a construction company organized to protect the interests of Union Pacific stockholders, had given blocks of stock in the company to key Republicans in the Senate and House. The object in bestowing these awards to friendly legislators was to secure favorable treatment in laws pertaining to the repayment of federal loans to the railroads. Enough other scandals were revealed in Grant's administration that the Crédit Mobilier affair could conveniently be included in a list of that President's sins and not laid at the doorstep of the "system" itself. Thus the corruption charge could be used successfully against truly radical change in the South, and, at the same time, to explain away the first betrayal of the public trust by the new capitalist order. It was possible, apparently, for the nation's leaders to have their cake in the North, and eat it too in the South.

If the Republicans had been truly worried about mismanagement and corruption by the "carpetbag" governments or worried enough about a Reconstruction policy that would not leave the black man at the mercy of the Bourbon redeemers, perhaps other alternatives would have suggested themselves. But by 1872, the splits within the party ruled out such choices. Grant withstood the challenge of the so-called "Liberals" and returned to the White House for another four years, but the voters turned their backs on the party in 1874 congressional elections. Democrat Samuel J. Tilden of New York won the popular vote for President in 1876, but the Republicans kept possession of the White House by trading off Reconstruction (or what was left of it) for the necessary Southern support in the electoral college. President Rutherford B. Hayes withdrew the last federal troops from the South, and with their withdrawal came a return of full economic relations between the masters of capital and their former enemies.

Through the years

Reconstruction's end came none too soon for economic leaders in all sections of the country. The panic of 1873 and the severe depression which followed strained the original Republican coalition almost to the breaking point: Western farmers joined the Granger movement, formed the Greenback party, and demanded control of the railroads; radical laborers joined unions and demanded a voice in establishing wages and working conditions. New alliances were formed by men of wealth and power across the old Civil War battle lines. The two political parties no longer represented the cutting edge of contending political economies but a vague consensus flexible enough to contain discontent and rechannel it into nonrevolutionary alternatives for improving the system.

It was a consensus built without the freedmen and their counterparts, the "poor whites." It was built, in fact, largely at their expense. For almost a century the party system worked almost to perfection: blacks voted Republican (where they could) and poor whites in all sections voted Democrat. Racial antagonisms which were not overcome, let alone healed in Reconstruction, effectively prevented a coalition between the two groups which both needed to achieve their goals. Southern reform leaders themselves fell into a monotonous pattern of racism: Tom Watson, Ben Tillman, Huey Long, Lester Maddox, and, finally, George Wallace. Some, like Watson and Long, began as genuine reformers; others, like Maddox and Wallace, sometimes talked like reformers. But they were all Andrew Johnson's heirs and the products of a "revolution" which had failed to go beyond John Locke and John Brown. Andrew Johnson's bitter complaint that the radicals would set race against race became George Wallace's accusations that the "limousine liberals" had bought the blacks for their slaves by using welfare and busing. And what of the blacks? For a century they remained where Reconstruction had left them, suspended between slavery and citizenry.

Looking back on Reconstruction in 1901, Woodrow Wilson offered the sophisticated readers of the *Atlantic Monthly* an interpretation of the era as the triumph of a new national consciousness. "All policy thenceforth wore a different aspect," he wrote. "We realize it now, in the presence of novel enterprises, at the threshold of an unlooked-for future. It is evident that empire is an affair of strong government, and not of the nice and somewhat artificial poise or of the delicate compromises of structure and authority characteristic of a mere federal partnership." The empire, of course, was America's new thrust outward, not alone, not primarily for territory, but for Seward's vision of commercial expansion. As Wilson put it: "Undoubtedly, the impulse of expansion is the natural and wholesome impulse which comes with a consciousness of matured strength; but it is also a direct result of that national spirit which the war between the states cried so wide awake, and to which the processes of reconstruction gave the subtle assurance of practically unimpeded sway and a free choice of means." There were dilemmas in Wilson's time, too, which had to be overcome before the new empire could be rationalized into the national spirit—dilemmas which arose in part from the experiences of governing a conquered territory during Reconstruction. These issues began to be debated almost at once. Reconstruction, in fact, had not come to an end before the Senate was debating proposals to purchase Alaska and to annex Santo Domingo to the United States.

Selected references

Politics in the 1850s, and especially the demise of the Democracy, is the subject of Roy F. Nichols's *The Disruption of American Democracy* (1948), an invaluable book. James C. Malin's *The Nebraska Question, 1852–1854* (1953), and Frederic Bancroft's still useful *Life of William H. Seward* (1899) were my guides on the territorial issue and party politics. Benjamin P. Thomas, *Abraham Lincoln: A Biography* (1952), has written the best single volume on the Republican President. Avery Craven and David Potter have given the student much to think about in *The Coming of the Civil War* (1957) and *Lincoln and His Party in the Secession Crisis* (1942), which carry the story down to the firing on Fort Sumter and the response.

An overview, from the perspective of other revolutions, is provided in Barrington Moore's *Social Origins of Dictatorship and Democracy* (1966), while an inner look at the Republicans in victory is given by Robert Sharkey in *Money, Class and Party* (1959). Tactical questions are reviewed by W. R. Brock, *An American Crisis: Congress and Reconstruction, 1865–1867* (1963). Andrew Johnson's reputation bounces up and down (mostly down recently), but start with Howard K. Beale, *The Critical Year* (1930), before going to LaWanda and J. H. Cox, *Politics, Principle, and Prejudice, 1865–1866* (1963). John Brown is even more controversial, but Malin's *John Brown and the Legend of Fifty-six* (1942) locates him within a concrete situation. Edmund Wilson's *Patriotic Gore* (1962) is supposed to be a study of literary figures, but Wilson's mind is never confined by his titles. It is a must. Another colleague, Tilden Edelstein helped me understand John Brown, Lincoln, and Andrew Johnson.

ELEVEN

The Gilded Age

Period covered: 1860–1877
Emphases: Economic growth. Social thought.
Major events: Panic of 1873
Railroad strike, 1877

The Civil War

The war was the most tragic, wasteful, and scarring event in American history, an experience so immense and awful that it marked not only those who fought the war but also those born afterward. It dominated the politics, and the imaginative life even more, of two generations. To the South it gave a romantic myth that impeded change for nearly a century; to the North a heroic myth that excused, even justified, the shortcomings of an era. No living American can fully understand the consequences of this great drama, for no upheavel in modern times has cut so deeply. The First World War and the cold war were repudiated by the next generation. Children born during the Great Depression but raised in affluence sometimes dismissed their parents' experience out of hand. It was not so in the late nineteenth century. Children growing up then hardly dared measure themselves against their parents. Even in the progressive period reformers still lived in the shadow of ancestors who had destroyed slavery and preserved the Union. Knowing they could not equal their legendary fathers and grandfathers, progressives hoped only to be worthy of them.

Given its monumental nature, who can be surprised that no scholar or artist has yet done justice to the war? Splendid efforts have been made. Still, the subject somehow eludes us. We know it was great and terrible, full of contradictions while it lasted and productive of even more afterward. Its moral resonance echoes down the generations. But we cannot come to terms with it yet. Perhaps the first difficulty is that it was a fratricidal war, fought by people who had much in common. Everyone is familiar with Lincoln's Gettysburg Address, the noblest expression of Northern goals. Few know Jefferson Davis's first speech to the Confederate Congress, which, though rhetorically inferior, had equal dignity.

We feel that our cause is just and holy; we protest solemnly in the face of mankind that we desire peace at any sacrifice save that of honor and independence; we seek no conquest, no aggrandizement, no concession of any kind from the States with which we were lately confederated; all we ask is to be let alone; that those who never held power over us shall not now attempt our subjugation by force of arms.

A more fundamental problem is that Americans generally believe with Emerson that evil is a stage in the unfolding of good. But except to profiteers and to patriots for whom saving the Union was justification was enough, the war brought little good. The slaves were freed in name, though in fact most became sharecroppers—that is to say, serfs. Serfdom was better than slavery. Who could be sure whether this was improvement enough to justify the 600,000 dead? Western farmers no longer had to fear the competition of slave labor, but they were soon locked in a deadly struggle with railroads, monopolies, creditors, and other elements which were as threatening and even more formidable. Some, in the old upper class especially, thought the war had a good effect on character. Oliver Wendell Holmes, Jr., who was badly wounded, later wrote, "In our youth our hearts were touched with fire. It was given us to learn at the outset that life is a profound and passionate thing. While we are permitted to scorn nothing but indifference, and do not undervalue the worldly rewards of ambition, we have seen with our own eyes, above and beyond the gold fields, the snowy heights of honor, and it is for us to bear the report to those who come after us." Perhaps the most poetic response was Walt Whitman's "Reconciliation."

Word over all, beautiful as the sky,
Beautiful that war and all its deeds of carnage must
    in time be utterly lost,
That the hands of the sisters Death and Night incessantly
    softly wash again and ever again, this soil'd world;
For my enemy is dead, a man divine as myself is dead,
I look where he lies white-faced and still in the coffin—
    I draw near,
Bend down and touch lightly with my lips the white face
    in the coffin.

The war was thought by some to have moral benefits. Haughty slaveowners were brought low. Pleasure-loving, mobocratic Northerners were exposed to suffering and discipline. Yet the slaveowners' fall was short-lived. They were soon back in power and black people, as sharecroppers and tenants, were nearly as oppressed as before. Southern politicians did not always recover their old positions, but in alliance with conservative Northern politicians they became strong enough to protect upper-class Southern interests and prejudices for a century. Many citizens suffered from the war, but to little visible effect. Southerners in consequence did not give up their old values. Northerners did not become more ruly and docile. The greatest riot in American history took place as a direct result of the war. In 1863 a new draft law set off a surge of violence among the Irish of New York that

claimed hundreds, perhaps thousands of lives and ended only when federal troops retook the city. The war did little to sustain the old upper class. This was because it greatly advanced those socioeconomic forces that were making the old elite irrelevant. Modest wealth and a famous name counted for little in an age when a man could say, "where Vanderbilt sits, there is the head of the table. I teach my son to be rich."

George M. Frederickson has shown how the traditional elite found ways to maintain some influence after the war. Philanthropy proved useful here, as the United States Sanitary Commission (U.S.C.C.) discovered. The commission was the principal mechanism for dispensing relief during the war, and it was run by a handful of aristocrats including Frederick Law Olmstead, the great landscape architect, who was its executive secretary. The commission declared that "its ultimate end is neither humanity nor charity. It is to economize for the National service the life and strength of the National soldier." Commission propaganda stressed the practical advantages of restoring wounded veterans to combat over drafting raw recruits. The outburst of wartime benevolence struck the commission as a grave problem. "How," it asked, "shall this rising tide of popular sympathy, expressed in the form of sanitary supplies, and offers of personal service and advice, be rendered least hurtful to the army system?" One method was for the U.S.S.C. to become the sole agency dispensing relief. Another was to rely on paid agents instead of volunteers—"Good Samaritans," as they were contemptuously called. The commissioners defended their agents on the grounds that relief work was "altogether too full of toil, drudgery, and repulsive reality, to be upheld by any mere sentimental pity or sympathy for the poor soldier." Walt Whitman, who regularly visited wounded soldiers, called the agents "hirelings" and said the wounded hated them.

Posterity would ignore the harsh philosophy of the Sanitary Commission and remember only that it did administer relief. The next quarter-century seemed to contemporaries a great age of benevolence. By 1880 charitable directories needed as much as a hundred pages to list all the organizations doing good works. But philanthropy was still marked by the war. It continued to be led by a conservative elite who saw charity as a means of disciplining people and providing an important social role for displaced aristocrats. These included, besides men, women like Louisa Lee Schuyler, who founded the New York State Charities Aid Association after the war, and her disciple Josephine Shaw Lowell, who started the New York Charity Organization Society (C.O.S.).

The charity organization movement had begun in London, but it was especially popular in America for embodying the austere conclusions of wartime benevolence. Scientific philanthropy, as this ethic was called, taught that casual relief was morally enervating. The purpose of charity was to distinguish between the deserving and the undeserving poor. The undeserving poor were to be scrapped. The deserving, however, were to be raised up by modest amounts of relief efficiently dispensed and even more by elevating contacts with their superiors. The C.O.S. itself did not administer relief but rather harmonized the work of existing agencies. These, in turn, relied on "friendly visiting," in which upper-class volunteers under the direction of paid agents gave advice and assistance to the poor. Poverty was thought to be a function of character rather than economics. Charitable workers, therefore, had to promote

moral betterment. They rarely gave direct aid.

The consequences of these ideas were entirely satisfactory to philanthropists. Poverty increased, but so did opportunities for the self-righteous moralism at which charity workers excelled. Few took the one as reflecting invidiously on the other, a notable exception being Mrs. Lowell. In 1889, having decided that want was caused chiefly by the degradation of labor, she resigned from the New York State Board of Charities and Corrections. Believing that it was better to prevent poverty than relieve it, she devoted the rest of her public life to improving the condition of labor.

The robber barons

Philanthropy and other mechanisms provided consoling work for aristocrats but could not conceal the fact that power had passed from them. In the postwar world, the robber barons, not the brahmins, ruled, and the scale of their achievement was staggering. The war did not make them supreme, but it gave them, especially the worst of them, added momentum. It did not stimulate manufacturing to any great extent. In fact, some economic historians think the war actually retarded industrial growth by diverting capital from productive enterprises. What the war did was stimulate certain key areas—railroads particularly—while creating enormous opportunities for profiteering. As during the Revolution, government largesse, inflated paper money, and the military's enormous need raised up a whole new class of speculators and crooked suppliers—the "shoddy aristocracy," as they were called—business operators who made great fortunes from the war. The poor who could not pay $300 for a substitute were drafted. The flower of the old elite volunteered, frequently to die. Those who did not join, like Henry Adams and William James, however good their excuses, felt something missing in their lives ever after. They had failed to share in their generation's supreme experience. All through the North people sang that noblest of our patriotic anthems, "The Battle Hymn of the Republic," with its great exhortation "as He died to make men holy let us live to make men free."

But Jim Fisk, Andrew Carnegie, young J. Pierpont Morgan, and their kind were too busy making money to make men free or even to sing about it. They stayed home and got rich or, if rich already, richer. Morgan speculated profitably in gold, which grew more valuable with every Union defeat. Commodore Vanderbilt enlarged his fortune during the war by chartering rotten sailing hulks for the government at a handsome profit. Congress gratefully awarded him a medal for service afterward. By then he was using his swollen capital to consolidate the New York Central Railroad. When the war began, he was worth $11 million; at his death in 1877, nearly $100 million. He is best known for having said, when told something he meant to do was illegal, "Law! What do I care about the law? Hain't I got the power?" His son and heir William, though not the man his father was, had the same spirit. On being advised that people would not tolerate one of his ventures, he said, "The public be damned."

These great business leaders were notable for taking what they could by any means at hand. The Erie Railroad war was a classic example of their contempt for law and custom. The Erie was the principle competitor of Vanderbilt's New York Central. In 1866, Vanderbilt began trying to buy control of it away from Jim Fisk, Jay Gould, and Daniel Drew. All three were speculators and had bought into the Erie to milk it. Vanderbilt had pion-

eered the technique of issuing watered stock (stock shares in excess of assets). Henry Adams estimated once that there was $50,000 of water for every mile of Central track. But the Commodore at least ran a good railroad, while the Erie gang were looters pure and simple. When Vanderbilt started buying, they merely printed more stock. Since Vanderbilt could not himself support the watered stock's price, Erie shares collapsed, costing him millions.

This was only the first round. Next the Commodore persuaded a judge to issue an arrest warrant for the three, secured a court injunction against the further issuance of Erie stock, and started buying again. As he controlled New York City, Gould and Fisk moved to New Jersey with their printing press. After buying up the local officials, they fortified their hotel with armed guards and three cannons and went on printing worthless Erie shares. The stalemate was finally broken when Jay Gould went to Albany with a suitcase full of money and bought the state legislature for, it was said, $1 million. It legalized the newly printed stock and assured the Erie gang of control. An investigation later exposed these dubious practices, but to no avail. Jay Gould summed up his feat thus: "In a Republican district, I was a Republican; in a Democratic district I was a Democrat; in a doubtful district I was doubtful; but I was always for Erie!"

The Erie war was not unique. Another time the Erie was struggling with J. P. Morgan for possession of a branch line, of which each side controlled a terminal. Morgan sent a train full of thugs up the line to capture it, but Jim Fisk armed a train of his own and rolled down to meet them. The two trains collided, and after a pitched battle Fisk was worsted. He then beat a hasty retreat, tearing up track and burning bridges behind him. When he

Figure 11-1 J. Pierpont Morgan in battle dress. (*Edward Steichen, collection of the Museum of Modern Art*)

got back to his terminal, he called out the militia, of which he was an officer. In the end, after the customary legal maneuvering and corruptions, Morgan got the line, prompting Fisk's famous boast that "nothing is lost save honor." Fisk had unusual panache even for a robber baron, and it ruined him. In 1872 his ex-mistress's lover shot the "prince of Erie" dead.

Jay Gould was more conventional. He did not spend his money on fast women and horses, like Fisk. He did not command a militia regiment. He was only the greatest business pirate of his day. In 1869 he nearly cornered the gold market, and though he failed, he still made millions by selling short. This touched off a market panic, but Gould escaped scot-free when the subsequent investigation was called off. (This was done after it was learned that someone in Grant's administration had made the plot possible.) Gould squeezed the Erie dry. When a stockholders' uprising forced him out in 1872, the line was bankrupt. He later did the same thing on a larger scale to the Union Pacific and other great corporations. At his death in 1891, his income alone amounted to $10 million a year.

Though few possessed Gould's daring and ruthlessness, many railroad men were cut from the same cloth. Railroads were the pivot on which the postwar economy turned. They were the largest consumers of iron and steel and, with their construction companies, the biggest employers. They occupied something like the position that auto companies do today. As the railroads went, so went the economy. The 30,000 miles of track in 1860 became 52,000 in 1870, 93,000 in 1880, 163,0000 in 1890, and so on up to 252,000 in 1920. This was the greatest rail network in the world, and the most costly. It took so long for earnings to pay off the capital investment needed to build a railroad that few major lines anywhere in the world were created without public assistance. In most industrial countries this meant that the railways were owned as well as subsidized by governments. But in America the roads, though publicly subsidized, were privately owned.

This was an early form of what later would be called "socialism for the rich." The public takes the risk and businessmen the rewards. Such a policy makes very little sense, especially where railroads and telegraph lines are concerned. They are "natural monopolies" in that the cost of construction is so great that competition is either unlikely or socially undesirable. But then, even more than now, it was an article of faith that private enterprise is always superior, if only morally, to public enterprise. So when it was decided to have railroads which the public must help build, there was never any question of the public also owning them.

If subsidized, railroads were fantastically profitable to build. The first transcontinental line, consisting of the Union Pacific and Central Pacific roads, was awarded 20 square miles of land for each mile of track laid and a generous thirty-year loan. The government also accepted a second mortgage on this loan, allowing the companies to issue first-mortgage bonds up to the limit of their official debt. Thus fortunes were made before a wheel ever turned. This fully justified the Big Four (Collis Huntington, Leland Stanford, Mark Hopkins, and Charles Crocker), who spent all their money lobbying for the contract on the sound theory that once they got it, there would be plenty more forthcoming. Their Central Pacific got loans and grants from local authorities in California—whose communities would otherwise be bypassed—to begin work. It was laid out not so much according to geography as according to the ability of towns to pay for the privilege of having rail service.

The Union Pacific and Central Pacific directors also owned the construction companies that built their lines, and they hired the services of these companies at generous rates. The Crédit Mobilier, which built the Union Pacific, charged $73 million for work that cost it $50 million to do. Together the two railroads got 20 million acres of land and $60 million in government loans. When the orgy of transcontinental construction was over, counties and municipalities had provided the builders with $300 million. State governments put up about $228 million, subscribed to stock, and donated 50 million acres of land. Washington granted over 130 million acres plus more than $60 million in loans. At the century's end there were five transcontinental lines, four of which had been awarded land grants which together were equal in size to the state of Texas. Only one, Jim Hill's Great Northern, was built with private funds.

In many cases it paid more to build a railroad than to operate it. Subsidies created the temptation to overbuild so as to enlarge construction profits. Between 1865 and 1873, railroad trackage doubled. This was an expansion far in excess of need. When it ended, railroad shares tumbled, contributing greatly to the panic and subsequent depression of 1873. This crisis was triggered by the collapse of Jay Cooke, a great banker who ruined himself trying to finance the Northern Pacific. Excessive construction went on after recovery, however, bringing with it intensive competition between parallel lines. Looting, bad management, overbuilding, and rate wars led to the bankruptcy of 450 roads during the 1870s. The panic and depression of 1893 drove 318 companies into receivership.

These periodic collapses were themselves

Figure 11-2 The railroad as robber baron. (*Courtesy of The New-York Historical Society, New York City*)

partly responsible for the decline of free enterprise. In the antebellum period, business life was not very competitive. The small towns and rural areas where most Americans lived had few commercial enterprises. There was no real national market economy as yet. After 1865, railroad expansion, the capital inflation brought on by war, and new industrial techniques greatly expanded the scope of business enterprise and created a true national market economy. But the new opportunities these developments brought were not equally distributed. Every crash ruined thousands of businesses, which either perished or were bought up cheaply by competitors. Men with cash reserves profited during depressions. After the panic of 1873, Thomas Scott's railroad empire was bought up by Gould and Huntington. When Carnegie's partner Andrew Kloman, whose technical skill was the rock on

which their fortunes were built, needed money, Carnegie bought him out cheaply. The Vanderbilts added new roads in the Midwest to their New York Central, which was at last able to enter Chicago on its own tracks. J. P. Morgan replaced the bankrupt Jay Cooke as master banker to the new industrialists.

Thus, even before the great monopolists began trying as a matter of rational policy to end competition, free enterprise proved to be self-destructive. It never was terribly free, as railroad subsidies showed. Unregulated competition led to depressions, which ruined some companies and forced others to sell out. The natural tendency of enterprise to destroy itself was augmented by the desire of businessmen for order and security. Few enjoyed competition for its own sake. Fewer still liked the looting and wrecking that Gould and his fellows practiced with such gusto. These schemes invariably meant short-term profits at the expense of long-term growth. By the 1890s the advantages of order and control were so apparent that industry after industry tried to secure it by deliberate means.

The triumph of laissez faire

There were many reasons why businessmen were free to do pretty much as they pleased in this era. The new plutocrats rose so quickly and their scale of operations was so great that the opposition had little time to respond and less room for maneuver. The old mercantile elite in its best days never enjoyed such power as the robber barons had. As they were unprecedented, there was no body of experience to draw on in coping with them. Labor was too weak to influence the trusts, and consumers, though exploited, were no better organized than they are today. Farm groups repeatedly failed to translate their numbers into effective power. Only politicians could face business on something like equal terms, and they were less interested in restraining the new capitalism than in profiting from it. Local chieftans such as Boss Tweed of New York and state bosses such as Pennsylvania's Don Cameron and Ohio's Benjamin Wade fattened on the plunder they extorted from business interests. Capital preyed on the public, and corrupt politicians preyed on both. This created a sentiment for political reform among businessmen, some of whom later became progressives in part because graft was so costly and inefficient. Some politicians got rich. Some rich men became politicians. Thus, while there was always tension between capitalists and officeholders, they had a community of interest too. By 1900 there were at least twenty-five millionaires in the Senate.

Still, the robber baron era was a consequence of ideology too. Americans have never been thought to be ideological. And this is true if ideology is narrowly defined as a fixed body of doctrine like Marxism or Christianity. But if ideology is taken to mean the basic assumptions on which a population operates, then Americans, like other peoples, have always been ideological. In the early national period the public philosophy of Americans was what William Appleman Williams has called mercantilism. Mercantilists viewed the public interest as more than the sum of individual interests, holding that it was government's duty to so order national affairs that no one sector prospered at the expense of another. Like all great goals, this one was imperfectly realized. Yet mercantilists did manage to involve government in a broad range of activities. As Federalists and later Whigs, they founded a national bank, raised the protective tariff, funded internal improvements, regulated trade, provided subsidies for steamships and bounties for fishermen, donated land for schools and universities, ran hospitals for seamen, and so on. State governments were sometimes even more active, especially in assisting the transportation revolution.

Even so, the mercantile tradition was not as strong here as elsewhere. Individualism sapped it. American conditions made it hard to exercise the sort of control a well-regulated economy demands. The growth of classical economics was, accordingly, faster here, and its triumph was more complete. Liberal economists such as Smith, Ricardo, and Bentham compared the economy with the natural universe. They insisted it too was governed by natural laws that were tampered with at great risk. Chief among these natural laws was the principle of free competition—which was the great regulator, the "invisible hand" it was called, that determined wages, prices, and profits. Government interference with this great regulator could only do harm. This doctrine was extremely attractive to men on the make, Jacksonians especially. Individualism was now applied to popular economics as well as sociology and morality. The sense of community declined, along with the fact of it. By the 1860s, many intellectual restraints on capital had already crumbled.

Classical economics gained an ally in social Darwinism, which became important about this time. Men were already used to explaining social process with metaphors drawn from science. Newtonian physics had led to the Enlightenment view of society as governed by mechanical laws, and now Darwin inspired men to think in biological terms. Herbert Spencer, an English social scientist who was more widely read in American than anywhere else, argued that two biological principles were especially important—the law of equal freedom and the law of conduct and consequence. The first law decreed that everyone should have complete freedom short of the right to harm others. This position could easily have led to anarchism. As with most doctrines, however, few people took it literally. Those who did included an English group called Individualists. They took Spencer at his word and opposed nearly all taxes and many laws, especially those relating to moral conduct. Individualists believed that free divorce, even free love, were private matters except where children were concerned.

Spencer's second law, which was usually known as "the survival of the fittest," held that progress came when each person felt the entire force of his own acts. In business this meant that the weak must be destroyed, not protected from their weaknesses or mistakes by tariffs, subsidies, fair practices bills, and

the like. Spencer was against most legislation on the ground that politicians did not understand the interrelatedness of society and hence were unable to predict the long-term consequences of what they enacted. He also opposed public education, charity, and all else that aided the unfit. Since the poor were by definition inferior, helping them only perpetuated weakness at the race's expense.

Laissez faire (meaning noninterference), as this combination of classical economics and social Darwinism was called, dominated the thought of an entire generation and retains some currency even today. Academicians and lay publicists spread the good word. Mugwump Republicans and conservative Democrats were equally convinced of its truth. From the 1860s to the 1880s, all organs of authority —government, the law, universities, churches—were bent to its service. Religion might have been thought a barrier to such a severe and un-Christian ideology. To a degree it was, since the Protestant churches continued to think charity a good thing, and charity was a form of interference. But the generosity of evangelical Christianity was compromised by scientific philanthropy, with its distinction between the deserving and undeserving poor. Social Darwinism and scientific philanthropy combined to make churchmen harsh judges of moral worth. Henry Ward Beecher, the greatest of his day, said that "God has intended the great to be great and the little to be little." And he believed that "no man suffers from poverty unless it be more than his fault—unless it be his sin." Russell H. Conwell, a Baptist minister, wrote an address called "Acres of Diamonds" that was so popular it made him enough money to found Temple University. In it he said "the richest people are generally those of the best character. It is wrong to be poor." Another minister declared that a policy which relieved people of worry or "the fear of want only degrades, pauperizes and brutalizes them."

Economists believed that labor unions were monopolies in restraint of trade. Edward Atkinson thought that all an honest worker needed was a better oven (the Aladdin Oven that he had devised for this purpose) which, by saving five cents a day on food and fuel, would ensure success. Businessmen and preachers had similar views. The Reverend Lyman Atwater of Princeton called unions "conspiracies against the laws of God, the rights of man, and the welfare of society." Henry Clews, a financier and candid autobiographer, described the Knights of Labor program as "utterly revolutionary of the inalienable rights of the citizen" and "completely subversive of social order."

The law was helpful too. Courts and legislatures developed useful concepts that sanctioned business activities once thought dubious. An important doctrine the courts employed was called the principle of implied limitations. It held that certain things were forbidden the government even though not prohibited by the Constitution. In practice these implied limits mainly concerned property rights. From this principle it was deduced that taxation was valid only when it was designed to serve a specific official purpose—to pay the army, for example—but invalid when meant to regulate wealth or support publicly owned enterprises. An even bolder stroke was deciding that the due process clause in the Fourteenth Amendment, written originally to protect freedmen, applied to corporations as well. Thus a corporation had, besides those peculiar to itself, all the rights enjoyed by citizens.

Judges who went against the conventional wisdom found themselves in trouble. A classic example was Chief Justice Waite's ruling, in *Munn v. Illinois* (1877), that businesses affected with a public interest were subject to state regulation and the rates set subject to judicial review. It was called the worst decision in court history, a return to the Middle Ages, and a threat to business and private property everywhere. An alarmed court gradually retreated and capitalism was saved. Generally, though, the courts did not need to be told their duty. When the Sherman Antitrust Act was passed in 1890, the courts immediately found labor unions guilty of conspiring to restrain trade. Corporate monopolies, being the products of natural law, were rarely dissolved.

Of course, no popular ideology is ever wholly consistent. Some people, workers especially, never accepted laissez faire. Others, the majority perhaps, did so selectively. Businessmen defied it where doing so paid. They opposed monopoly except when they themselves were monopolists, the tariff except when their product needed protection, and subsidies except when they wanted them for themselves. Some even gave to charity, though in an efficient free-market economy the poor would perish. As one industrialist told Congress: "The poor and the weak have to go to the wall to some extent of course. That is one of the natural laws that we cannot get over except by providing for them by charity." A few, notably Andrew Carnegie, elevated this contradiction to the level of philosophy. He preached the "gospel of wealth," which held that men must be allowed to make lots of money so as to use their fortunes for the general good. He compared millionaires to bees that made the most honey, then donated it to the hive after having gorged themselves. Public benefactions were, in fact, a decree of nature. The millionaire "cannot evade the law which . . . compels him to use his millions for the good of the people." Carnegie led all the rest in practicing what he preached, though most of his fortune went to universities, libraries, and other middle-class institutions. Little of it trickled down to the workers from whose sweated bodies his money was wrung. For men like Carnegie, these years were gilded indeed. Little wonder that in 1886 he remarked: "If asked what important law I should change I must perforce say none; the laws are perfect."

There were, however, malcontents. Not all academicians were quite as happy as businessmen. William G. Sumner, the most prominent economist to argue for laissez faire, was appalled not only by reformers but by plutocrats as well. Though in favor of wealth as such—since without capital there could be no progress—he was alive to its abuses. But he blamed these mainly on the state which, by mischievously interfering with the economy, invited capital to defend itself by fair means or foul. Sumner most admired the industrious middle classes whose probity and thrift made the system work. Sumner called his ideal citizen "the forgotten man" and condemned government for neglecting him. The state assisted only plutocrats and the indigent, both enemies of the forgotten man.

Sumner had probably the best mind of anyone in the laissez faire camp, but he was never a popular figure. While he praised the middle classes, they could not in that optimistic time warm to so pessimistic a figure. He believed that an apocalyptic struggle between labor and capital was coming and that it would be disastrous, regardless of who won. Reformers could hardly like someone who thought all programs of social amelioration dangerous and unnecessary. He frequently remarked that any honest worker could maintain himself and his family, "misfortune apart, in a condition of substantial comfort." On the other hand, big business

disliked him for opposing the tariff and plutocratic methods generally. He always insisted that capital could not have it both ways. Laissez faire would never work as long as individual businessmen demanded free enterprise for others and protection for themselves. He was against socialism for the rich as well as for the poor. Even among academic spokesmen for laissez faire, who tended to be more consistent than businessmen, Sumner was unusually rigorous.

Feminism

During the war, feminists were preoccupied with relief work, though Elizabeth Cady Stanton organized the National Woman's Loyal League to support abolition and women's rights. Its circulated petitions to this effect accumulated 400,000 signatures. When peace came, radical feminists assumed that the hour had struck for women as well as blacks. They could not believe that black men would be given the vote and white women denied it. Even the Kansas elections of 1867, which defeated both black and woman suffrage referendums, had little effect on their views. But it was crucial to the thinking of conservative feminists and most male friends of the movement. They concluded that tying votes for women to the black franchise would only doom both. Since the black's need was clearly greatest and more likely to be realized, it was common sense to get black suffrage first and worry about women's rights later. This reasoning had no effect on Elizabeth Cady Stanton, Susan B. Anthony, and their followers. They refused to cooperate, and the movement divided into a more conservative Boston-based wing called the American Woman Suffrage Association and the radical National Woman Suffrage Association headquartered in New York.

Though the Fifteenth Amendment to the Constitution was the proximate cause of this division, ideology mattered too. The Boston group took a more cautious and limited view of social questions than New York. It was closer to Mugwumpery than not, while the New Yorkers were still perfectionists. They supported a great range of causes from free divorce to, in some cases, socialism. They were slow to accept the new moral climate of America. But New York's defiance was short-lived. Mrs. Stanton associated with Victoria Woodhull, a flamboyant eccentric who besides being a feminist was a spiritualist and an advocate of countless movements and enthusiasms. When she declared herself to be a practicing free lover and met the inevitable hostile response by saying that Henry Ward Beecher was one too, she assured the women's movement of a conservative future. It is hard to say which of her follies was the more dangerous. To speak for free love in the most sexually repressed era in American history was surely madness; and to throw dirt on the most popular preacher in New York, perhaps the country, was equally risky—even if her charge was true. Victoria Woodhull and her sister were ruined and forced into exile. The woman suffrage movement was morally tarnished for a generation.

Thereafter nearly all feminists were scrupulously respectable, and by 1890 there was so little difference between the two wings of the suffrage movement that they reunited. Most likely the women's movement would have become more cautious and genteel even without Mrs. Woodhull. She traumatized it by being so extreme, but the springs at which her spirit was nourished were running dry in any case. Both she in her mad way and Mrs. Stanton far more rationally were products of a waning impulse in the national life. The women's movement recovered after-

wards. Women's organizations of all sorts multiplied in the late nineteenth century, making possible victory in the twentieth. But the broad, generous, hopeful, even passionate spirit of the antebellum era was gone for good.

The workers

Workingmen tried to organize also, but with little success. There were many reasons for this. Traditionally unions grew during booms and collapsed in depressions. There were two great depressions after 1865 that took up most of the 1870s and 1890s and there were several recessions as well. More important probably was the enormous physical mobility of Americans, especially working people. Several recent studies show how great this movement was. In Poughkeepsie, New York, for example, during the years 1850-1880, only one of fourteen trades had as many as half its workers remaining in town from one census to the next. And this underestimates mobility, because many craftsmen arrived in town after one census and left before the next, thus failing to be recorded. Turnover among journeymen, apprentices, and young workers generally was even greater. Only one-fifth of the families in Newburyport, Massachusetts in 1880 had been there thirty years before. Obviously it was difficult to build unions on such unstable foundations. Stability was related to property ownership, and only a minority of Poughkeepsie workers achieved that status. This seems to have been the common experience of unskilled working people and helps to explain why so few were organized.

A further reason was the great diversity of the American proletariat. In Europe unions were based on ethnic and usually religious uniformity. Class consciousness was more easily inspired among people who spoke the same language and went to the same church. American workers in the early Gilded Age included a high proportion of Europeans—Germans and Irishmen especially. Native workers felt little in common with immigrants, against whom they were often deeply prejudiced—particularly against Catholics, which meant most of the Irish and a great many Germans. By the end of the century, just when immigrants were becoming assimilated, a new wave of even more alien immigrants from eastern and southern Europe arrived. No great independent trade union movement in the world ever had to contend with such diversity. This fact alone would account for the feebleness of unions in the Gilded Age and after. Other countries (Argentina, Canada) had more immigrants as a proportion of the total population, but none had so many different immigrants. During the period of 1820 to 1945 the United States received 12 percent of its immigrants from Italy, 13 percent from Austria-Hungary and its successor states, 16 percent from Germany, 10 percent from Russia and Poland, 6 percent from Scandinavia, and a third from the British Isles. Most of these (62 percent) lived in the cities, whereas only 26 percent of native born whites with native parents did. Trade unions, socialist parties, and the other means of proletarian advance are creatures of the city. But American cities were too fragmented ethnically for them to take root. Diversity weakened class consciousness where it did not stimulate bigotry. Even when good will was present, language difficulties and cultural barriers made organizing hard. Shrewd employers capitalized on this by mixing their work forces. Steel companies, for example, would list job openings not only by title but also by nationality.

American workers suffered also because their employers were unusually powerful. American capitalists were not held back by the ancient institutions of Europe—the church and the aristocracy—with their inherited rights and privileges and, sometimes, tradition of noblesse oblige. These constrained European capital to a degree unknown in America. Here business had a free hand with labor. When threatened with violence, the last resort of desperate men, capital could respond with overwhelming forces up to and including federal troops. It had an effective monopoly on physical force. Given this power and aided further by the popular hatred of foreigners (which waxed and waned but never died out entirely in the Gilded Age), it was hardly surprising that labor disputes caused appalling amounts of violence.

In 1877, near the end of a long depression, wages were cut on certain railroads. The workers responded not only by striking but by seizing railroad property and sometimes destroying it. The Pennsylvania station in Pittsburg was burned by a mob against which even the militia could not prevail. It took federal troops to break the strike, during which perhaps a hundred people were killed. This was the first American uprising that had elements of real class warfare in it. The middle class was alarmed, even terrified in some instances, and took steps to ensure its future. These involved strengthening the instruments of repression. Militia units, which had proved to be ineffectual in Pennsylvania and elsewhere, were reorganized. Sometimes state police forces were upgraded. The use of private detectives, especially from the famous Pinkerton agency, as labor spies and plant guards became more common. These tactics worked to the extent that workers never seized the instruments of production on such a scale again until the 1930s. They failed in the sense that violence or the threat of it was a central feature of labor-management relations until World War II. There was only one real solution to the "labor question"—fair wages and decent treatment. The middle classes would be a long time learning that, which was hard for them but harder still for the workers.

Selected references

A book which captures something of the Civil War's emotional resonance is Edmund Wilson, *Patriotic Gore* (1962). George M. Fredrickson, *The Inner Civil War: Northern Intellectuals and the Crisis of the Union* (1965), is very good. On private benevolence, see Robert H. Bremner, *American Philanthropy* (1960). The classic study of the new rich is Matthew Josephson, *The Robber Barons* (1934). Also entertaining is Stewart H. Holbrook, *The Age of the Moguls* (1953). An elegant series of contemporary essays on the railroad scandal is Henry and Charles Francis Adams, *Chapters of Erie* (1871). Popular ideologies are discussed in E. C. Kirkland, *Dream and Thought in the Business Community* (1956); Richard Hofstadter, *Social Darwinism in American Thought* (1944); and Sidney Fine, *Laissez Faire and the General Welfare State* (1956). On feminism, see Eleanor Flexner, *Century of Struggle* (1959), and William L. O'Neill, *Everyone Was Brave* (1969). Norman J. Ware, *The Labor Movement in the United States, 1860–1895* (1929), is useful.

TWELVE

Victorian Life

Period covered:	1878–1900
Emphases:	Social thought. Urbanization.
Major events:	*Progress and Poverty*, 1878
	Haymarket bombing, 1886
	Looking Backward, 1888
	Panic of 1893

Business concentration

Many businessmen tired quickly of individualism and competition. However desirable in theory, free enterprise made for uncertainty, cut throat practices, and waste. A sizable number of big businessmen, even while singing the praises of competition, moved to restrict it through consolidation. J. P. Morgan, though not the only great figure in this process, stood above the rest. Once he too had been a speculator and competitor, but now he dreamed of rationalizing the entire economy.

The Morgan group either had full control or was allied with the management of the following railroads: the Northern Pacific, Great Northern, Baltimore & Ohio, Southern Railway, Erie, New York Central, and Pennsylvania among others. The only important roads not associated with Morgan were the Harriman and Gould lines (Central Pacific, Union Pacific, and Southern Pacific), financed by Kuhn, Loeb and Company and Rockefeller's National City Bank. Together, these two great combinations controlled over half the railroad mileage in America. For a time they fought each other, but their struggle to get the Chicago, Burlington and Quincy (C. B. & Q.) convinced them that cooperation was best, especially as their competition produced a stock market panic. In 1901 they formed the Northern Securities Company, consisting of the Great Northern, Northern Pacific, and C.B. & Q. The government later forced them to dissolve Northern Securities as an illegal monopoly, but the agreement it signified proved durable anyway. There were no more great rail wars.

In a general way this was the history of some key industries in the antebellum era. They grew rapidly, experienced periods of savage competition, and eventually looked for ways to stabilize business conditions. Businessmen spoke in praise of competition even as they tried to end it, and they used three devices to this end. First—in terms of time—was the pool. This was merely an agreement among corporations in the same industry to follow certain practices. As they depended on the good faith of competitors, pools never worked very well, so they were replaced by the trust—the second device designed to undermine competition. The first big trust was the Standard Oil Company of Ohio, organized by John D. Rockefeller. In 1882 the stockholders of seventy-nine oil companies transferred their shares to nine Standard trustees, receiving from them trust certificates entitling the owners to collect dividends on their securities. The trustees thus acquired operating control of 90 percent of the nation's refined oil and soon Rockefeller, immensely rich to begin with, had over $800 million—the greatest industrial fortune in the world. In a time of stable prices and low taxes, this was incomparably more valuable than a like sum would be today. Probably no one will ever again own as much real wealth as John D. Rockefeller did.

Where there were only a few important companies in an industry, a trust was not always needed. James B. Duke created a near monopoly in the tobacco industry in 1890 by merging five large firms into the American Tobacco Company. J. P. Morgan created United States Steel by buying out Andrew Carnegie, the largest steelmaker in the country, and adding a group of smaller companies to form the United States Steel Company (always known as the steel trust, though it was not quite). It controlled only about three-fifths of the country's steel production.

The trust's chief drawback was that it

frightened people. Having been told that competition was vital to the American way, Americans naturally were alarmed at the prospect of losing it. And, more sensibly, they feared these great concentrations of unregulated power. At the very least, monopolies might mean higher prices. The protective tariff was a form of subsidy that most industries enjoyed and most consumers paid for. The tariff kept steel at $65 a ton while Carnegie was making it for $35. Monopolies, protected from foreign competition in this way, had complete price control and could charge all the traffic would bear. As concentration advanced, public resistance built up. The Sherman Antitrust Act of 1890 was a response to popular anxiety, and—while in practice it did little good—it showed how the wind was blowing. Trusts were vulnerable to legal action, so increasingly business turned to its third expedient—the holding company. The first important trust to become a holding company was the American Sugar Refining Company (1891). The board of directors actually *owned* in the company's name, rather than merely holding them in trust, the securities of member concerns. This permitted greater centralization and perhaps efficiency. In 1899 Standard Oil obtained a New Jersey charter as a holding company and bought up the securities of member companies once held in trust. Other holding companies formed in this period included Amalgamated Copper, United States Rubber, International Harvester, and, of course, U. S. Steel, the first billion-dollar "trust"—a word now used by the public to mean any great firm, however organized. Most industries remained competitive, since trusts were the exception, not the rule. But people feared them all the same, attributing to business combinations even more power than they actually possessed.

Critics and reformers

Laissez faire never lacked critics, and before long these became so numerous that it was no longer a viable ideology. It dominated middle-class thought for about a generation, but by the 1890s it was clearly on the defensive and in the Progressive era failed entirely, though it has a small following still. Perhaps the most serious blows to laissez faire came from popular writers like Henry George, Edward Bellamy, and Henry Demarest Lloyd. George who came from a middle-class family that fell on hard times, left school at the age of thirteen and drifted aimlessly thereafter. He arrived at San Francisco in 1858 and became a journalist. In 1878, when he was thirty-eight, he finished his great book *Progress and Poverty.* It was based partially on his experience in San Francisco, the growth of which, from a cluster of shacks to a major city, convinced him that institutions were changeable. George disagreed with the conventional wisdom which held that poverty was a consequence of bad character. He saw it instead as a function of progress in a society dominated by plutocrats who were able to reserve the benefits of economic growth for themselves. George thought that society itself was the source of wealth, yet wealth did not return to those who created it. He proposed to remedy this defect in the existing order by taxing land.

The single tax idea had both the advantages and disadvantages of simplicity. It was appealing because many Americans believed that land was the chief material base of wealth and that a confiscatory tax on its abuse would set things right. In a sense, George proposed to nationalize land that was underdeveloped or held for speculative purposes. This would eliminate speculators and profiteers while producing revenues sufficient to deal with poverty and other social problems. The drawback to his scheme was that it would not have worked, but George was probably right in saying that landlords were the most important recipients of unearned increment. Their advantage stemmed from the fact that as the population went up, so did productivity, and land then became more valuable even where the owners did nothing to improve it. This was, no doubt, unjust, but it was not the whole reason for poverty. The single tax would not have benefited the millions of wage earners who were poor though fully employed. George was a shrewd critic of classical economics, but, perhaps because he lived in the West, where land counted for more than industry and capital, he never appreciated the complexity of an industrial economy.

Yet George was important all the same and converted thousands of people to reform. Some, like George Bernard Shaw, went on to socialism or other kinds of radical activity; others formed single tax clubs. But every convert, regardless of his politics, became a force for change. Single taxers were never very numerous, but they were extremely important in the Progressive era as politicians (Mayor Tom Johnson of Cleveland), philanthropists (Joseph Fells), and reformers (Frederic Howe). They were a strategically placed elite who counted for much more than their numbers might suggest. And, if few people became single taxers, many who rejected George's solution accepted his analysis of the problem.

Edward Bellamy was perhaps even more influential than George. He too was a journalist, but he lived in a small town near Springfield, Massachusetts, and admired those village traits of neighborliness, community, and mutual support that were becoming steadily more irrelevant. As an heir of the prewar communitarian and associationist movements that had such influence in New England, it was not surprising that Bellamy saw a kind of socialism as the answer to what ailed America. He detailed his solution in *Looking Backward*, a utopian novel that appeared in 1888. It concerns a young man, Julien West, who is accidentally rendered unconscious and then preserved to awaken in the year 2000, after a collectivist world order has been established. His guide in this new era is Dr. Leete, who explains that it came about peacefully. Instead of the violent revolution which radicals anticipated and conservatives dreaded in Bellamy's day, capitalism was merely subverted. First, the public demanded municipally owned utilities, and eventually these were nationalized. Then federally owned stores and factories were established causing the decline of private enterprise, which could not compete with them. Thereafter everyone was drafted into the "industrial army" for a twenty-five-year term. People could choose, within reason, the work most congenial to them. Unpleasant jobs were shortened so as to make them equal, in practice, to more agreeable ones, and everyone shared alike in the wealth thus produced. In this just order there was no aggression, no acquisitiveness, no want.

Later generations who had seen "utopianism" at work in Nazi Germany and Soviet Russia would think the notion of an industrial army rather sinister. But Bellamy had no way of knowing what such power in the wrong hands would mean. He was himself a transcendentalist and the last person to repress individuals for some larger goal. Bellamy thought individual well-being was the highest purpose and assumed his scheme would ensure it, but with the benefit of hindsight we can see how wrong he was. Capital was already too deeply entrenched to be out-maneuvered in the bloodless way he envisioned, and the cooperative virtues he admired were already too attenuated to be of much use. It would take a real revolution to get what he wanted, and there has never been any substantial enthusiasm for that in America.

But again, even more than George, Bellamy planted seeds that another generation of reformers would harvest. Bellamy clubs sprang up around the country and Bellamy socialists, who usually called themselves Nationalists, multiplied. He founded a magazine, *The New Nation*, to coordinate their efforts. In addition to columns of advice, essays, news items, and such, it put art in the service of reform. One exposé was called "The Political Economist and the Tramp." It described how an economist refused to give a tramp alms and explained how, being indigent, the latter was unfit to survive.

My words impressed his dormant thought, "How wise," he said, "is nature's plan! Henceforth I'll practice what you've taught, and be a scientific man.

We are alone—no others near, or even within hailing distance; I've a good club, and now right here we'll struggle for existence.

The weak must die, the strong survive—let's see who'll prove the harder hittist, so, if you wish to keep alive, prepare to prove yourself the fittist."

At which, seeing the point, the political economist handed over his money. Some Bellamy-ites joined the socialist movement. More later became Progressives. The 600,000 copies of *Looking Backward* that were sold within a few years of publication were important contributors to the reform sentiment that followed,

and the book inspired at least nineteen similar efforts, most notably William Dean Howells's *Traveler from Altruria* (1894).

The chief defect of Bellamy's thought, a weakness common to most middle-class reformers of the day, was that it diverted attention from the most plausible alternative to capitalism—Marxist socialism. Great changes have come about only where socialist movements were strong enough either to impose them or to force conservatives to do so in self-defense. Capitalism has not been destroyed in any advanced industrial country, but reforms and sweeping welfare benefits have been secured in those where socialism was important. The United States has changed less than most—chiefly, it would seem, because socialism remained so weak here. One reason for this was that Bellamy and his kind provided timid middle-class people with a halfway house between radicalism and reform. This met their emotional need to promote radical change, though in fact obstructing the change itself. Few middle-class radicals were able to accept the force of events that made Marxism, or some variant of it, the most effective instrument for a nonviolent social revolution. One who did was Henry Demarest Lloyd, which makes him especially noteworthy.

Though not the most influential critic of laissez faire, Henry Demarest Lloyd wrote perhaps the best attack on nineteenth-century business practices. Lloyd, an Easterner, attended Columbia College and entered the New York bar in 1869. He worked for a time with Mugwump reformers of both parties in such organizations as the Young Men's Municipal Reform Association and the American Free Trade League. But he tired of law and business and, in 1872, accepted a position on the *Chicago Tribune*. Reporting suited him well, and he was freer than most journalists because he married the daughter of one of the *Tribune's* owners. Her small block of shares gave them enough to live on so that, when he needed time for study or reflection, he could take it. In 1881, he began writing exposés, a technique that would later be called muckraking. In 1885 his health led him to resign from the *Tribune*, though he continued investigating. He was a warm partisan of the anarchists who were unjustly convicted of inciting murder after the Haymarket bombing in 1886, and also of striking coal miners. Failure in both cases persuaded him that mere exposure was not enough. It changed no capitalist's mind and left conditions as they were.

He resolved, therefore, to work up a specific case against the capitalist system that would establish in detail both its immoral and retrograde character. Lloyd was unusual among reformers in thinking the system anachronistic and impractical as well as socially destructive. He had read Darwin but, unlike social Darwinists, discerned that cooperation was as much a law of nature as competition. Moreover, he noted, survival and progress were not the same thing. In industry, not the fittest but the "fightinist" survived. Businessmen prospered not on account of virtue or intelligence but because they were cunning and unscrupulous. These were not traits he believed in deeding to posterity. The idea for *Wealth against Commonwealth* (1894) occurred to him even before the Standard Oil Company was formed. He had been watching it when it was still the South Improvement Company, and as it grew into the greatest corporation in the world, it became the perfect subject for his researches. By showing in detail how the Standard was built, he could expose laissez faire as a shabby bundle of apologetics.

There never was such a book as *Wealth against Commonwealth.* No reformer ever delved so extensively into the history of a single corporation, and few wrote as well. The book owed much of its impact to exhaustive research, but the brilliance with which Lloyd employed his research accounts for a considerable measure of the power *Wealth against Commonwealth* still has. Emerson was Lloyd's literary master, and he had the same gift for epigrams and cogent similes. Of political corruption, he wrote, "the Standard has done everything with the Pennsylvania legislature except to refine it." Mergers and monopolies inspired him to remark that "corporations have no souls, but they can love each other." One of his most powerful chapters, "The Smokeless Rebate," compared the Standard's way of getting lower freight rates than its competitors to smokeless gunpowder.

That entirely modern social arrangement—the private ownership of public highways—has introduced a new weapon into business warfare which means universal dominion to him who will use it with an iron hand. This weapon is the rebate, smokeless, noiseless, invisible, of extraordinary range, and the deadliest gun known to commercial war. It is not a lawful weapon. Like the explosive bullet, it is not recognized by the laws of war. . . . The gentlemen who employ it give no evidence of being otherwise engaged than in their ordinary pursuits. They go about sedate and smiling, with seemingly friendly hands empty of all tools of death. But all about them as they will, as if it were only by wish of theirs which attendant spirits hastened to execute, rivals are blown out of the highways, busy mills and refineries turn to dust, hearts break, and strong men go mad or commit suicide or surrender their persons and their property to the skillful artillerists.

The Standard survived Lloyd's attack as it has all others, but laissez faire, his real target, did not. If Lloyd is viewed only as a muck-raker, as he sometimes is, he was incomparably the greatest of them all. His research was complete and his poise and thrust as a writer unequalled. He was one of the first to realize that a reformer must be an expert if he is to undo what other experts have done. But Lloyd did not limit himself to criticism, as most muckrakers did. He understood that the corporate economy itself was the chief barrier to effective change. Most reformers believed that the system was fundamentally sound, that only its abuses needed correcting. Lloyd knew better, and he accepted—slowly and painfully at times—the implications of this fact. It meant that he had to support labor unions which, he admitted, were often wrong, "but theirs is always the right side." He finally came to accept socialism as the best way of managing industrial problems, but he did not do so unthinkingly. He disagreed with many socialists who approved of trusts, thinking that industrial concentration would make the nationalization of industry simpler. Lloyd feared that "we may find too late that the process of preparation has annihilated us." So the trusts had to be fought at every step lest they grow so great as to be unconquerable. He was among the finest products of his age—a true heir of Thoreau and Wendell Phillips and one of those who kept their great tradition alive in hard times.

Another element that nourished intellectual resistance to laissez faire was the social gospel. Though many Protestant ministers had gone over to social Darwinism, many did not. The old evangelical tradition of good works retained adherents, but others became convinced that blaming the poor for their problems was no way to get them into church—especially since urban churches were losing ground and this harsh doctrine seemed one reason why. The concept of evolution made headway among progressive clergymen, and the secularized theology this inspired opened the way to social reforms. Even among ministers, theology seemed less important and sociology (defined then as the study of social problems) more so. Some defenders of the social gospel hoped to forestall socialism by making timely reforms, and a few became Christian socialists, notably the influential theologian Walter Rauschenbusch. More often they were single taxers or Bellamy Nationalists. They all preferred cooperation to competition, responsibility to individualism, and were, accordingly, stout critics of classical economics and social Darwinism. Their argument that a Christian must also be a reformer prevailed in many Protestant churches.

They were greatly assisted in this work by the emergence of academic philosophers and social scientists who undermined the theoretical foundations of laissez faire. The academicians who had made it respectable were not, as a rule, trained men in the modern sense (William Graham Sumner, for example had done his graduate work in theology) and many had no graduate training at all. This was chiefly because there were no real universities in America to offer it. Higher education consisted of some hundred of colleges—mostly small, denominational schools. Advanced study of a sort was available only in law, medicine, and theology. But after the war true universities on the German model were established. Cornell was founded in 1868 by Andrew D. White. The next year Charles William Eliot became president of Harvard and led it to greatness. Johns Hopkins was established in 1876 to offer nothing but graduate instruction. First Michigan and then other public universities followed suit.

Three things made it possible in the 1880s and 1890s especially to create the university as we know it. The first was that a sufficient number of Americans had studied in Europe, mainly in Germany, to build graduate faculties using scientific methods and the seminar system. The second was that capitalists gave enormous sums to higher education. The largest cash gift ever received by Columbia before 1860 was $20,000, but between 1878 and 1898 American colleges and universities received private donations amounting to at least $140 million. This enabled something as expensive as graduate education to be provided on a large scale. Governments supported public secondary and higher education more lavishly also. The number of public high schools rose from about 1,000 in 1870 to 6,000 in 1900, and in 1898 there were five times as many pupils in secondary schools as there had been twenty years before. During the same period, the number of college students increased 2½ times as rapidly as the population.

Thanks to these changes, universities grew larger, but better still they became more autonomous. Private philanthropy broke the clerical hold over private education, and philanthropists were usually less ideologically demanding than ministers, more concerned with practical results. They wanted schools that would teach science, engineering, and business rather than theology. Their wants were backed by Darwinism and the new academic disciplines, which weakened theology's intellectual claims. So the modern university—secular, relatively autonomous, scientific—was born, with its graduate schools, laboratories, research seminars, and great libraries.

The new academicians, so much more rigorous than the self-taught authorities who preceded them, challenged the assumptions and methods of laissez faire at almost every point, biting, as it were the hand that fed them. Among philosophers William James and John Dewey were especially important. James was one of the first to benefit from higher standards of graduate instruction. Though he received an M.D., he was trained at Harvard's Lawrence Scientific School and soon was publishing devastating attacks on the psychology and philosophy of social Darwinism. His own approach to knowledge, called pragmatism, saw theories as experimental instruments rather than finished answers. He said truth "happens to an idea" and looked for ways of proving out ideas by their consequences. He used the unfortunate phrase "cash value" of an idea to mean not commercial worth but practical utility. To James knowledge, and the knower, were dynamic and evolutionary. James had only a casual interest in social questions, but his approach could be applied to them.

This was done most notably by John Dewey, who was led by James to think of intelligence as a tool that could move the world. Instrumentalism, as Dewey preached it, held that one must participate in social questions to understand them and understand them so as to change them. Both James and Dewey were too complex to be summarized briefly, and no doubt few people really grasped their theories. But the effect of pragmatism and instrumentalism was to liberate men from the paralyzing hold of laissez faire. To read them was to know that change could be willed.

The social sciences were similarly affected. In economics men like Richard T. Ely and Simon Patten, armed with German graduate educations, attacked classical economics for dogmatism, simplicity, and exaggerating self-interest as a guide to human conduct. Ely led, in 1885, in forming the American Economic Association, whose statement of principles endorsed the state as an agency of progress and said "while we appreciate the work of former economists, we look not so much to speculation as to the historical and statistical study of actual conditions of economic life for the satisfactory accomplishment of that development." To aid their efforts to anchor economics in the real world, Thorstein Veblen contributed a biting attack on the notions that productivity was a function of acquisitiveness and wealth an index of character. *The Theory of the Leisure Class* (1899) argued that natural selection in the business world operated to magnify fraud, cunning, and avarice. In sociology, which Spencer had hoped would be a means of teaching people to leave things alone, laissez faire also declined. Led by Lester Ward and such disciples as E. A. Ross and Albion Small, sociology moved away from biological analogies and toward psychology. Like economics, it became interested less in justifying the status quo and more in understanding and reforming it.

Urban growth and Mugwumpery

Mugwump, said to be an Indian name for "chief," was applied at first only to certain independent Republicans. Yet the position they took was so representative of the best middle-class opinion in the Gilded Age that it deserves a wider use. Most reformers then were not single taxers or Bellamy Nationalists but Mugwumps. They believed in honesty, cheap and efficient government, competition, and personal virtue. These were generally thought adequate to the public's need. But as they were not, the public's need increased. Machine politicians, though responsive to personal suffering on the local level, were neither concerned nor equipped to deal with large urban, not to say national, problems. Neither were Mugwumps. When they prevailed, which was seldom, the civil service was reformed and not much else. They had little sense of what cities needed to be worth living in and less appetite for the taxes this required.

Yet urban growth remained the most conspicuous feature of American social change throughout the century. From 1850 to 1890 the number of cities with populations of more than 100,000 grew from 6 to 28, the number with populations between 20,000 and 100,000 went from 24 to 137. In 1880 the assessed value of rural property was about equal to that of urban property, but ten years later urban property had twice the value of rural property. In the Midwest one person in five lived in towns of over 4,000 in 1880; in 1890 this concentration had increased to one in three. Chicago alone doubled in size during the 1880s, reaching a million in 1890.

The prevailing ethic did not keep these exploding metropolitan areas from developing some public facilities. Waterworks and sewage systems multiplied. Streets were illuminated by gas and in the 1880s with arc lights. Sometimes they were even paved, though as late as 1890 only 629 of Chicago's 2,048 miles of streets had paving of any sort, and half of this consisted of wood-block covering. Telephones, of which there were 800,000 in the country by 1900, laid the basis for an adequate communications network. But in general public services always lagged behind need, and a look at one case in particular shows why.

Chicago was lucky, by modern standards, in having only a few companies engaged in public transportation. Other cities in the Gilded Age counted theirs by the dozen. But this was not seen by prominent Chicagoans as an asset. They were interested in promoting competition, and having few transit companies raised not the possibility of an integrated regional transportation system but the spectre of monopoly. Reformers often were not concerned with good service or low fares because few of them relied on public transportation. They were mainly upper-middle- and upper-class businessmen and professionals who lived in expensive residential areas near their places of work. What bothered them most about transit companies was the fact that they were engaged in shady dealings with politicians.

The effect of Mugwump reformers in Chicago, according to David Weber, was to keep the transit companies from consolidating their lines and often from extending them. Consolidation meant monopoly, they feared. Extension threatened the interests of property owners along the right of way. Reformers also kept the transit companies from getting long leases. This was meant to restrain corruption, but it encouraged owners to view public transportation as a short-term, high-risk proposition. The result, again, was poor service and high fares. For the sake of property owners and from a false view of what municipal corruption consisted of, Chicago was kept throughout the nineteenth century from getting a public transit system equal to its needs. Reformers could see that the street railway companies enjoyed corrupt relations with the city council, but they failed to see that their efforts made these practices inevitable. Short-term franchises meant that the companies were always having to buy off councilmen, as that was the only way to get or renew a franchise. Competition enabled anyone to create companies of their own that were ostensibly competitive with existing lines but that were really aimed at forcing the operators to buy them out—a form of blackmail at which councilmen were especially

adept. Mugwump crusades against "traction magnates" and dishonest councilmen aimed only at the symptoms, not the causes, of this pathology. Even when successful, Mugwump reformers did little for the riding public, since better service was not their main objective.

The experience of Charles Yerkes, the most notorious traction magnate of his day, was a case in point. Yerkes bought into Chicago transit lines in the 1890s and soon discovered how inefficient the overlapping system was and how costly expansion could become, since property owners under existing practices asked almost prohibitive compensation for the use of streets they fronted on. The council forced him into politics by demanding bribes and even more by refusing to stay bribed. He wanted to rationalize the Chicago transit system, but this involved getting a state law making long-term franchises possible. Without them he could not attract investment capital to extend and modernize existing lines. He got the bill, but it was then vetoed by Governor John Peter Altgeld, who was no Mugwump but a Chicago property owner who shared the general prejudice of his class against traction companies. Balked at every turn, vilified by an extraordinarily hostile press and critics who openly threatened him with lynching, Yerkes ended by staging a gigantic stock swindle and pulling out of Chicago entirely. His flight was hailed as vindicating the sound principles of his critics, but in fact it demonstrated their futility. Decades later Chicago's inefficient, over-capitalized lines were consolidated (under public ownership), as Yerkes knew they had to be. Fortunes were lost and half a century of inconvenience was suffered by Chicagoans in order to get what they could have had at the beginning and for less cost under Yerkes.

This is not to excuse Yerkes, who even more than his fellow traction magnates was a bad character. The fact remains, though, that he and the other businessmen who bought into municipal transit in the 1890s and tried to rationalize local systems were right and their Mugwump critics wrong. The cities needed good transportation, and it could be had at a price. Since public transportation was a natural monopoly, part of the price was an end to competition. But Mugwumps believed in competition above all and would not give it up. Where they prevailed, there was competition and, sometimes, honest government; but there was also poor service—and not only in transportation. The problem in the late nineteenth century, then, was not the inability of reformers to seize power from the bosses and plutocrats but the fact that they had no real answer to what ailed the cities. In many respects Mugwumpery was worse than its alternatives. Mugwump reformers lacked the farsightedness of the shrewder capitalists, like Yerkes, and the compassion and humanity of some political bosses. The Mugwump answer to personal distress was self-help and scientific philanthropy. The boss offered bread, coal, and frequently a job. In some places 20 percent of the work force owed their employment to the district leader. Unlike nearly all reformers, the boss lived among his people; in most cases he was one of them. No wonder Lincoln Steffens, the great muckraker, liked the bosses more than reformers; though in the end he rejected both in favor of revolutionaries. Little wonder too that bosses were more popular and more readily electable than reformers. It was not their corruption but their humanity that kept them in office; it was their want of it that kept reformers out.

Mugwumpery on the national level was equally shortsighted. Civil service reform, free trade, and antimonopolism were the Mugwump formula for good government and a successful economy, but these were all largely irrelevant to what ailed the country. What the government needed was not more honest officials but a broader and more vigorous sense of the public interest. Grover Cleveland ran the most honest administration of any in this period, but that counted for little when the panic of 1893 struck. His government was not only helpless but absolutely unwilling to relieve distress or make any provision against future catastrophes. Competition did not always work, as we saw, yet reformers still made a fetish of it, even where it was inappropriate and a natural monopoly was the obvious solution.

Broadly speaking, there were only two ways of solving the problems of an urban industrial society. One was socialism, as it would be practiced in northern and western Europe later, and the other was the combination of labor unions, social welfare benefits, and government regulations that the United States employs today. Neither approach is perfect, but they both have the effect of smoothing out economic movements to prevent the terrible boom-and-bust cycle of unrestricted capitalist development and both offer some security to working people and make some effort to ensure fair play in the marketplace. None of these things was possible in the Gilded Age. Marxist socialism was pretty much confined to a handful of German immigrants in the nineteenth century, since it was repellent to all important sectors of the population, even to workers who elsewhere were most responsive to socialist appeals. American workers generally asked only for a larger share of the pie. The middle classes were opposed to social welfare and, though interested in restraining monopoly, were unable to do so. Even if they had, it would not have made much difference, since monopolies were not at the heart of most national problems. Douglass C. North estimates that if all monopolies had been abolished in the Gilded Age, per capita income would have gone up by $5 a year. Organized farmers took a broader view of things, but all attempts to translate their vision into political power failed. Neither the Greenback, Granger, nor Populist movements accomplished much.

Labor

In 1886, during a strike at McCormick Harvester in Chicago, police killed four strikers. The next day a mass protest meeting led by anarchists was held at Haymarket Square. The police ordered it dispersed, and then someone threw a bomb—killing seven policemen and injuring sixty-seven others. The police responded by firing blindly into the crowd and killing four more people. Honors were about even, but the bourgeois community—which, as usual in this period, blamed everything on anarchist provocateurs—demanded revenge. Eight local anarchist leaders were arrested and, though no evidence at all linked them with the crime, were swiftly convicted of murder on the grounds they had incited the nameless bomber. One committed suicide, four were executed, and three sentenced to prison. (Governor Altgeld later pardoned them and ruined his political career.) In 1893 Henry Clay Frick broke the steelworkers' union for Andrew Carnegie at a cost of seven strikers and three strikebreakers killed. His armed Pinkertons were beaten in a pitched battle with the strikers, and it took the state militia to recapture his plant at Homestead, Pennsylvania. Federal troops had to be called out that same year in Idaho's Coeur d'Alene district to end the fighting between silver miners and strikebreakers, and federal troops were used again in 1894 to break the American

Railway Union strike against the Pullman Company.

Encounters with immigrant workers were even more sanguinary. In 1891, for example, 14,000 coke workers, mostly Slavs and Magyars, struck Frick's Pennsylvania works. Militiamen broke the strike after killing 10 and wounding 50. And in 1897, during an anthracite strike, an unarmed band of 160 Slavic miners encountered sheriff's deputies who killed 21 and wounded 40 more. Italian workers were peculiarly subject to lynch law. In 1895 during a Colorado coal strike, 6 were massacred by a lynch mob. In Louisiana 11 Italians were lynched in 1891 after a jury refused to convict them. Five years later in the same state, 3 more were taken from jail and hanged by a mob. This showed that while there was little class consciousness among working people, there still was a class war going on.

There was also a race war. In 1892, 241 lynchings occurred, 160 of the victims being black. They were often for trivial offenses, and all but 4 took place in the South. One man, for instance, was lynched for beating his wife. In Louisiana in 1892, two men were lynched on suspicion of hog stealing. A striking case occurred in Roanoke, Virginia, in 1893. When a black man was arrested for having allegedly raped a white woman, a mob gathered and the mayor called the militia out. When the jail was assaulted, the militia killed 9 rioters and wounded 40. The next day a larger mob gathered, forcing the mayor, who had been wounded earlier, to leave the city. It then lynched the black suspect. More men by far were lynched in these years than died in labor struggles, though the latter got far more attention.

Despite everything, workers did manage to organize, but the form of organization that prevailed was dictated by adversity as much as by ideology. The two different union concepts in this period were embodied in the Knights of Labor and the American Federation of Labor, respectively. (There were also a few radical unions of little consequence.) The Knights began as a semisecret lodge, a common form of trade union organization in the 1860s. But as they grew, the Knights became more open and inclusive. Gradually they moved toward industrial unionism, the idea that all workers in a given industry, and later all workers in all industries, should belong to one big union. They overrode craft barriers, and—to a degree—ethnic and racial lines also. In 1884 they struck the Gould railroads and won a partial victory when Gould agreed not to discriminate against Knights of Labor men and to rehire those he had fired. Little as it was, this gave the Knights a great boost, and by 1886 they had 700,000 members. But soon they lost another strike on the Gould lines and were hit by the Haymarket backlash. Though not involved in the Haymarket affair, the Knights were blamed for it and accused of being led by anarchists and socialists. These two events had a fatal effect on the Knights, who declined rapidly thereafter. Though industrial unionism was the wave of the future, that future was so distant that the Knights gained nothing for their foresight. The large, generous conception of trade unionism that they advanced faded with them.

The AFL survived because it was the exact opposite of the Knights of Labor. Where the Knights had reservations about the wage system, the AFL accepted it. Where the Knights meant to abolish craft distinctions, the AFL exploited them. It was an association of independent craft unions who were obliged to cooperate with the federation only so long as they agreed with its principles. These were so narrow—having to do only with wages, hours, and working conditions—that few craft unions had trouble complying. The AFL marked the triumph of what is usually called "business unionism." Nonpartisan and unideological (except for being procapitalist), the AFL was the proletarian counterpart of industrial capitalism. But whereas capitalism grew rapidly and consolidated industry after industry, the federation grew more slowly and was not remotely equal in power to the combinations it dealt with.

Under Samuel Gompers, its president for more than a generation, the federation resisted all attempts to change it. The most important of these probably came during the great depression of the 1890s. In 1893, partly because of the depression and partly through admiration for the British Independent Labor party, a motion calling for the collective ownership by the people of the means of production was submitted by the AFL convention to its affiliates. The next year it was defeated at the convention only through Gompers' parliamentary manuevering. Resentment was so great on account of this that Gompers was not reelected president for the only time in his thirty-four years with the AFL. All the same, his was a decisive stroke. At a time when European workers were moving toward socialism, the principal American union organization moved away from it. 1894 was the high-water mark of AFL radicalism and perhaps the only time when there was a serious chance of altering its character. Thereafter the federation was unflaggingly loyal to the principles of craft organization and business unionism. In consequence, craft unions enjoyed a modest prosperity at the expense of the great mass of unskilled workers ineligible for membership in the AFL and too weak, for the most part, to create unions of their own. This was a further example of the power of bourgeois ideas in the Gilded Age, and a permanent one. Today the AFL-CIO remains the only great independent union movement in the world that is solidly procapitalist in principle, even though some others are in practice.

Urban life

Given the power of capital and the weakness of labor, no one need be surprised that worker earnings were low, unemployment common, and poverty great. This was especially true in the cities, where population growth was most rapid. When Jacob Riis made his classic study entitled *How the Other Half Lives* in 1890, not half but two-thirds of the 1½ million people in New York City lived in tenements housing twenty-one persons or more—that is to say, in slums. These grew progressively worse, if infant mortality rates are a fair measure. Whereas the infant death rate had risen to 180 per 1,000 live births in 1850, it reached 240 in 1870. In certain areas—factory towns especially—where most adults worked in unhealthy atmospheres, the adult death rate was nearly as high. In the mill town of Lawrence, Massachusetts, a third of the spinners died within ten years of going to work. Half of these died before their twenty-fifth year. Pneumonia, tuberculosis, and other respiratory diseases killed 70 percent of the operatives, compared with 4 percent of farmers in the area. Operatives lived to an average age of forty, while farmers typically lived to reach sixty. The mean age of death in Lawrence dropped from twenty in 1870 to fifteen in 1900. In the 1870s, Lawrence workers made an average of $400 a year (compared with a statewide average of $476); but this dropped until, in 1893, they averaged less than $300 a year. Unions were particularly weak, as they were bound to be in a place where there were immigrants from fifty-one countries speaking forty-five different languages.

Despite the ghastly conditions of life and work in mill towns, mining camps, and big cities, the condition of working people improved during the Gilded Age. Nationally, the infant mortality rate fell from forty-three per 1,000 live births in 1850 to thirty in 1900, though the life expectancy of the average man at age twenty did not change much. Prices declined from 1865 to 1900, while wages in manufacturing increased. This made it possible for a growing percentage of the work force to buy their own homes. Upward mobility from the working class was slight, but what Stephan Thernstrom calls property mobility was a fact. His study of Newburyport, Massachusetts, shows that while few manual laborers became white-collar workers, a substantial fraction did become homeowners. That conditions did actually improve for workers, however slowly, was probably another reason why workingmen did not rebel on a larger scale and, no doubt, why three out of four immigrants, even though frequently disappointed by what they found here, stayed in America.

Immigration remained fairly constant. From 1860 to 1900 about 14 million newcomers arrived in this country, a much larger number than the 5 million who came over during the antebellum period, but, since the whole population rose from 31 to 76 million, the rate of immigration was about the same. In 1880 the ethnic composition of American society was much as it had been fifty years before. Until 1896, the number of old immigrants from Northern and western Europe exceeded the new immigrants from southern and eastern Europe. At that time eighty percent of the foreign-born came from Germany, the United Kingdom, Scandinavia, France, Switzerland, and the Low Countries. America was used to them by this time, and so immigration was not so troubling as before the war. The arrival of new immigrants stimulated xenophobia once

Figure 12-1 Street corner on the lower East Side of New York when it was one of the most congested residential quarters in the world. (*Culver Pictures*)

more, but the second great nativist upsurge was an essentially twentieth-century experience, like the new immigration that provoked it.

Agriculture

The farm situation is harder to summarize. As in industry, production went up strikingly. The number of farm families increased also. But prices fell drastically on account of rising outputs. In the 1860s wheat sold for $1.60 a bushel; in the 1890s, for 49 cents. In the same period corn fell from 75 cents a bushel to 28 cents and cotton from 30 to 6 cents a pound. The farmer felt he was doing more and more

for less and less. The cost of operating a farm either increased, because of the need for more equipment, or held steady because suppliers' prices were protected by tariffs and monopolies. The farmer's prices were set by the world market, so he operated in an open system while his supplier benefited from a closed one. Cheap land and low initial costs had once made agriculture attractive, but as land and equipment became more expensive, the capital costs of farming increased—hence, also the number of farm mortgages in many areas, and the government's light money policy made capital more dear. Farming was beginning to change from a way of life to a business. Although agriculture was never as profitable as industry, the farmer got other compensations from it—but increasingly these were no longer sufficient to offset the economic facts of life. Farmers smart enough or prosperous enough to operate a high investment-low profit enterprise in a rapidly fluctuating market survived. Those that could not perished. In the Gilded Age, farmers tried to cope with their changing circumstances by political action, but these efforts mainly failed. Later they would reorganize as a pressure group and succeed, but that day was a long time coming.

Middle-class life and culture

The middle classes gained most during this period, although they had their discontents. The old business leaders and many professionals resented being pushed aside by the new tycoons. They feared monopolies, foreigners, and anarchists. As progress meant downward as well as upward mobility, some worried about bankruptcy or umemployment. One of the most powerful metaphors in *Looking Backward* was Bellamy's comparison of society to a great coach drawn by the toiling masses, atop which the happy few rode in comfort. The drawback was that bumps in the road sometimes threw people off, who then had to join those pulling the coach on which they had formerly ridden. But for native-born Americans, the odds against falling off the coach were high. In Boston after 1890, five out of ten natives began their careers in white-collar jobs, and they were twice as likely to rise in them as to fall. For immigrants, it was just the opposite. Only two out of ten first- and second-generation immigrants began in white-collar jobs, and their chances of falling were twice as great as of rising. Income distinctions between white- and blue-collar jobs were far greater then than now. In Chicago in 1890, white-collar workers made twice as much—on the average—as skilled workers and three times as much as unskilled workers.

Although middle-class people have a higher income today than the working classes, the gap is not nearly so great as in the Gilded Age, and in those days money bought a great deal more. There were as many domestic servants in 1890 as in 1950 (about 1½ million), though the middle class grew enormously in between. When Woodrow Wilson took his first position as an assistant professor at Bryn Mawr College, he supported a family, two cooks, and a maid entirely on his salary. No academician without private means lives in such comfort today, nor do many other proprietors, managers, or professional people. Nearly everyone is better off now in absolute terms, but the middle classes are relatively deprived. Their increased incomes will not buy them a fraction of what their counterparts in the Gilded Age enjoyed. What they took for granted—like servants and spacious townhouses—is now reserved for the wealthy.

For the middle and upper classes (who, all being bourgeois, differed chiefly in that the latter had more money), this was an age of confidence and ostentation. The triumphs of science, industry, and, it was thought, morality created a certainty about life—amounting often to smug purposefulness—that no generation coming of age after 1914 would know. Victorian Americans, like their English models, believed firmly in progress and their own rectitude. Later generations would mock their self-assurance. Exposing their shortcomings and hypocrisies never became so great an industry here as in England, but it flourished all the same. Every rebellious generation has condemned what is always (though wrongly) called their Puritanism. This meant a genteel and uplifting culture based on an attenuated evangelical religion and distinguished by sexual repression.

The most grotesque expression of this last was Anthony Comstock who, as secretary of the New York Society for the Prevention of Vice, was the country's most noted censor. He crusaded not only against pornography but eroticism of every sort, birth control, and nude art. He liked to quantify his accomplishments and would boast of having driven so many to commit suicide and destroyed so many freight-car loads of smut. Great numbers of people, women especially, campaigned successfully against the licensing of prostitution. This did nothing to reduce the number of prostitutes but was nevertheless thought a great stroke for morality. The instances of plays censored, scandals exposed, and sin-

ners hounded were too numerous to mention. Women were becoming the chief patrons of culture and hence also the arbitors of taste. In deference to his customers, Richard Watson Gilder of the *Century* magazine turned down a story in 1896 for including this line: "the bullet had left a little blue mark over the brown [male] nipple." He also edited the indelicacies out of *Huckleberry Finn* before serializing it.

Standards of chastity and discretion were so high, however, that they were unenforceable. Prostitutes could be arrested and harrassed, but this did not keep men from patronizing them. The poor had their humble red light districts, the rich their sumptuous bordellos. Beneath the repressed surface of urban life there was a lively underground, which was all the harder to cope with for

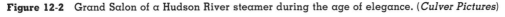

Figure 12-2 Grand Salon of a Hudson River steamer during the age of elegance. (*Culver Pictures*)

being denied so often. The great number of single immigrant men made prostitution a virtual necessity, as did the fact that single middle-class men were denied sexual access to women of their own class and married men were frequently kept from their wives. Thus, the Victorians ensured what they meant to prevent. Sexuality could be channeled to a degree but never destroyed. Denying it in one place meant that it would break out in another. This was the great contradiction in the Victorian sexual ethic that subsequent generations have been so quick to condemn. Yet Victorians paid a high price for their customs. Prostitution, venereal disease, illegal abortions, and such were all commonplace and rarely subject to control.

Among the middle classes, where control was most effective, a psychic toll was exacted that was no less real for being so secret. Middle-class women were raised to think sex existed only for procreation. They knew little about it—prudery being an effective barrier to sex education—and what they did know they disliked, even feared, and with reason. Victorian men could not have been very good lovers. Worse still, childbirth remained dangerous and painful. There were no effective birth control devices generally available, and even if access to them had been easier, contraception, like masturbation, was thought to be both physically and morally dangerous. Ignorance and principle alike made abstinence the usual form of family planning, and it was widely employed. Urban families were smaller on the average than rural families. Middle-class people succeeded in having small families partly by starting late (men commonly married in their thirties, women in their late twenties) and partly by spacing children out. Victorians believed that three-year intervals between children were ideal. Richard Sennett, who studied a middle-class neighborhood in Chicago, concluded that the typical family could have had intercourse during only one period every three years. For women sex must have been rare and unpleasant, especially as it was usually followed by the trauma of childbirth. Men, consequently, also had few outlets save for masturbation and prostitution, both of which involved guilt and the fear of disease.

Posterity was certainly right to mock Victorians for their prudery. It was silly to keep pregnant women out of sight, to call legs "limbs," and to tell children the stork had brought them, and it was vicious to hound Mormons, unwed mothers, and others who broke the narrow rules of good sexual conduct. All the same, those who championed these attitudes suffered as much as their victims. Lives marked by such intense repression and denial and by so much guilt and fear, cannot have been, however pleasant otherwise, entirely agreeable. Moreover, this stringent ethic was not born of sheer perversity. Though ideology had something to do with it, the fact remained that city people, including much of the urban middle class, could not afford large families. And since abstinence was the best-known contraceptive, Victorians could not allow temptation to sap their will. They knew that repression could not be perfectly effective, and frequently tolerated the sexual underground as long as it stayed out of sight. That way they at least kept their own environment clean. All that can be said for this strategy is that it worked, if badly. Later generations can afford to be scornful of the way in which the Victorians handled a problem that, thanks to effective birth control techniques, no longer exists. We can enjoy levels of sexual stimulation that in the Gilded Age would have had fatal effects on middle-class living standards. Such repression as exists now seems merely anachronistic. But it would be wrong to look at Victorian habits with the same attitude. What today appears comic at best and vicious at worst was in part, at least, the product of necessity, and that is never very amusing.

Victorians offset their marital tensions by idealizing family life, and no period is richer in sentimental evocations of domestic bliss. Though the divorce rate went up steadily after 1860, middle-class life was not much affected. In the Chicago neighborhood cited earlier, of 8,000 adults in 1880, only 44 were divorced. Even today many see the Victorian family as the ideal towards which all domestic units should strive. Paternal authority seems to have been maintained, and few married women worked, whatever the family income. This produced tensions also, since expanding opportunities for women caused some resentment, especially among the educated. Some responded to their heavy domestic obligations by becoming nags; others went in for club work, philanthropy, and the various fields of volunteer enterprise then being created.

The most obvious compensation for the strains—social, sexual, and economic—felt by middle-class people was the sumptuous quality of bourgeois life, since, during the Gilded Age, ostentation and display were not a monopoly of the rich. Houses became more ornate, thanks to the scroll saw and other technical advances. In the cities this was an age of brownstone fronts and stamped leather walls. In the suburbs and small towns, Gothic and Queen Anne cottages with intricately cut scrollwork patterns multiplied. Furniture and decorations were rich and abundant. There were Oriental rugs, overstuffed chairs and couches, wall-to-wall pictures, tables, lamps, and ornaments without end. Public buildings also were noteworthy for detailed ornament and romantic extravagances—factories that resembled fortresses, colleges that looked like chateaux, hotels that were in fact palaces with acres of lush carpeting and tons of

Figure 12-3 Brooklyn Bridge, the glory of its age. (*Wide World Photos*)

Figure 12-4 The Columbian Exposition of 1893, which brought together everything Victorians thought most noble about their civilization. (*The Bettmann Archive*)

marble, and Pullman cars of astonishing luxury. Subsequent generations thought this display ugly and vulgar. Where Victorians had been lavish, they would be chaste and severe—hence the glass boxes, steel cages, and uniform tract housing of today. In the 1960s, people began envying Victorians for the visual richness and variety that earlier seemed in such poor taste—but too late. Middle-class incomes no longer permitted such opulence. Mass production no longer allowed for the detail and craftsmanship that were still possible in the nineteenth century.

The Gilded Age was not remarkable for its fine art, but it had a varied cultural life all the same. Though architecture was mainly derivative, this did not keep the Chicago school from giving birth to the skyscraper. Louis Sullivan did his best work then and Frank Lloyd Wright got his start, while Frederick Law Olmsted made landscape design a high art. Despite the genteel tradition, Henry James, Mark Twain, William Dean Howells, Walt Whitman, and Emily Dickinson wrote brilliantly. Serious magazines including the weekly *Nation* and such weighty monthlies as *Scribner's,* the *Century, Harper's,* and the *Atlantic* maintained high intellectual standards. Indeed, the quality of their language has probably never been equalled since. In the Progressive era, even the best magazines started trading elegance for timeliness, punch, and wit. This sometimes produced a more interesting magazine at the expense of literary quality. The late nineteenth century remains a golden age of cultivated journalism.

The popular culture of the day flourished. Dime novels, music halls, vaudeville, and burlesque proliferated. But the interimmediate level of culture blossomed even more remarkably. The Chautauqua movement enabled millions to hear distinguished speakers, and lecture bureaus operated on an even wider scale. Touring music and dramatic companies multiplied. Robert Roberts says that "it may well be that one opera house in a middle-sized American town in the 1880s offered more of the classic tradition in music and drama in one year than the combined television networks of the U.S. do in the same period of time in our own age." Cheap editions made the best literature available on a scale not matched until the paperback revolution of recent years. Good-quality reproductions did the same for pictures and prints. As art producers, Americans may not have equalled the French, but as consumers they were already second to none.

It was an age of extremes, of great poverty and great luxury. Labor-management and race relations were conducted with extreme brutality, and middle-class culture was excessively genteel and sentimental. People were both supremely confident of the national destiny as a great capitalist power and terrified of organized labor and radicalism. Confidence and uncertainty, vulgarity and delicacy, walked hand-in-hand. Differences between social classes and geographical regions, between town and country, were very

marked though narrowing. In the twentieth century, American life would become more homogeneous. Wealth would not be flaunted so nakedly and poverty would diminish. These were all important gains as, no doubt, were the moral and social benefits that attended them. Few would wish the clock turned back to the Gilded Age. Still, there remains something solid and attractive about the Victorians with their superb if unwarranted self-confidence and control, splendid architecture, and magnificently varied physical environment. The country we live in now, for better or worse, owes much to them. They still have a hold on us, though it is weakening fast.

Selected references

Reformers are discussed in Morton G. White, *Social Thought in America* (1949), and Daniel Aaron, *Men of Good Hope* (1951). On religion, see Henry F. May, *Protestant Churches and Industrial America* (1949), and Charles H. Hopkins, *The Rise of the Social Gospel in American Protestantism, 1865–1915* (1940). A masterful study of higher education is Laurence Veysey, *The Emergence of the American University* (1965). On feminism, see again Flexner and O'Neill. Urban growth is covered in Blake McKelvey, *The Urbanization of America, 1860–1915* (1963). The struggle for street railways in Chicago is dealt with in David Weber, *Rationalizers and Reformers: Chicago Local Transportation in the Nineteenth Century* (unpublished Ph.D. dissertation, University of Wisconsin, 1971). A fine, brisk economic history of the country is Douglass C. North, *Growth and Welfare in the American Past* (1966). Still useful is Norman J. Ware, *The Labor Movement in the United States,* 1860–1895 (1929). An important work is Stephen Thernstrom, *Poverty and Progress: Social Mobility in a Nineteenth Century City* (1964). A good collection of articles representing the new urban history, with its emphasis on demography and quantitative data, is Stephen Thernstrom and Richard Sennett (eds.), *Nineteenth Century Cities* (1969). Sennett's own *Families against the City* (1970) is thought by some critics to have serious methodological shortcomings. All the same, it is a provocative analysis of family life in a Chicago neighborhood during the 1870s and 1880s. An entertaining biography is Heywood Broun and Margaret Leech, *Anthony Comstock, Roundsman of the Lord* (1927). A useful collection of essays on the period is H. Wayne Morgan (ed.), *The Gilded Age* (1970), which includes Robert R. Roberts, "Popular Culture and Popular Taste." On literature see Larzer Ziff, *The American 1890s* (1966), and the early part of Alfred Kazin's classic study, *On Native Grounds* (1942). Lewis Mumford, *The Brown Decades: A Study of the Arts in America, 1865–1895* (1931), is valuable, as is the lively Russell Lynes, *The Taste-makers* (1955).

THIRTEEN

Beyond Imperialism: The American Way

Period covered: 1877–1900
Emphases: Politics and diplomacy
Major events: Railroad strikes of 1877
   Berlin Congo Conference, 1884
   Pan American Conference, 1889
   Panic of 1893
   Venezuelan boundary dispute, 1895
   Free Silver campaign, 1896
   Outbreak of Cuban revolution, 1895–1896
   War with Spain, 1898
   Annexation of Hawaii, 1898
   Annexation of Philippines, 1898
   McKinley reelected
    in referendum on foreign policy, 1900

The Civil War proved yet again, Americans believed, that they were building something new on the North American continent. Colonial empires belonged to Europe and to European ways of thinking. The future belonged to what Americans sometimes called the "Empire of Liberty," by which they meant the expansion of liberal-democratic institutions. No American ever let an opportunity go by for impressing this point on foreigners or for drawing favorable comparisions between his young, vital society and the worn-out civilizations left behind in Europe.

Post-Civil War attitudes toward Canada among American policymakers reflected this zeal. Having purged their country of slavery, the worst form of colonialism imposed by the Europeans on the New World, some Americans felt that their northern neighbors would now, of their own free will, seek to become a part of the United States. Radical Republicans like Sumner and Stevens went further; they believed that Great Britain should be made to pay for its transgressions during the recent war—the aid it gave the Confederacy—by turning Canada over to the United States. One radical Republican, Ben Butler, put it this way: America should expand "so far north that wandering Esquimaux will mistake the flashings of the midnight sun reflected from our glorious flag for the scintillations of an *aurora borealis*."

Many Canadians, as well, believed that political union with the United States was only a matter of time, however they regarded the prospect. Everything seemed to point in that direction—the similarities of population and traditions; the mutual experience of the Westward movement; and, most important, the growing desire for close economic relations. When such a union was actually consummated, and that was likely to be sooner rather than later, the Empire of Liberty would encompass the entire continent except for Mexico, and European colonialism would have lost its last servants in North America.

A new reality

Somehow, things went wrong—or at least went in a different direction. Great Britain met the American threat by granting Canada self-governing status within the empire, something not dreamed of in radical Republican philosophy. More remarkable, perhaps, was the continuing strength and expansion of the Old World empires. In the last thirty years of the nineteenth century, Great Britain added $4^3/_4$ million square miles of territory to its imperial domain, an area considerably larger than the whole of the United States. France added $3^1/_2$ million square miles; Germany, a latecomer to the race, acquired 1 million square miles. Only Spain of all the colonial powers seemed to be entering into a final decline, leaving the fate of its possessions for others to decide.

Spain's troubles were not necessarily advantageous to the United States. What if Cuba should fall into the hands of England, France, or Germany? American investments in Cuba had increased rapidly in the post-Civil War era, as had the volume of Cuban-American trade. What happened to Cuba was of considerable economic importance to the United States and its wealthier citizens, but Cuba loomed as a much bigger question throughout the entire era. It had been assumed since Jefferson's day that the island would someday fall into an American-controlled Caribbean like a ripe apple into an orchard.

But in the context of late-nineteenth-century realities, Cuba's fate became tied to a contest between the Old World empires and the American Empire of Liberty. Mankind's future hung in the balance, or so it seemed to popular commentators of the day. In England, *The Spectator* asserted that American attacks on European civilization by the writer Mark Twain had as their objective the substitution of "the very inferior ideal of the sentimental, broad-bottomed, ranting, dollar-hunting Yankee with all his blater about liberty and progress."

Oratorical excesses like this were common on both sides of the Atlantic; they reflected, on the American side, deep concern about the partition of Africa and the subjugation of Southeast Asia. The next obvious target for the European land grabbers would be Latin America. In the immediate postwar period, the United States had supplied arms and materials to the Mexicans in a successful effort to aid them in the struggle to rid their country of French colonialists. But who could say what would happen in Cuba? And after that, what?

Cuba became an obsession for several reasons. It was the closest colony to American shores of any significant size; it was in a state of almost perpetual revolution; it might tip the balance against America in the world. With their new possessions in the rest of the world, Europeans could already apply tremendous leverage in the New World. American labor leader Samuel Gompers summed up this view in 1896: "The independence of the Cubans is essential." Essential first to Cuba's economic reorganization, said Gompers, but also essential to Americans, because "Liberty, truth, and freedom was the basis of the make-up of the world. . . ." Other reformers spoke the same sentiments about Cuba. As we shall see, however, this put them in a bit of a bind when they got what they wanted: the chance to "liberate" the island from European rule.

Meanwhile, another aspect of the post-Civil War American reality confronted policymakers with hard decisions. A boom-bust cycle had begun to repeat itself with distressing regularity and deepening intensity as the century came to a close. Of the quarter-century which began with the panic of 1873, half were years of depression: 1873–1878, 1882–1885, and 1893–1897. Looked at from the sod huts on the prairie or from city slums, the land of equal opportunity was fast becoming the land of special privilege. Things looked bad from the top, too, where nagging fears of overproduction spilled over into business journals. "A foreign market becomes more and more necessary," said *Bradstreet's* in August 1883.

The expansion of European colonialism threatened to shut off world marketplaces just at the most critical time. If that happened, domestic problems could only increase. The railroad strikes of 1877 provided a perfect example of the growing relationship between domestic and international problems. These strikes were the first nationwide encounters between capital and labor and the bloodiest thus far. Federal troops were brought in to suppress the strikers, establishing a precedent for similar action in later years. Of more significance over the long run, perhaps, was the dawning realization that the railroads were literally a bridge between agricultural expansion and industrial expansion, both at home and abroad. The trains delayed by the striking workmen in 1877 were carrying agricultural surpluses to East Coast ports for shipment to overseas markets. The American economy depended to a large degree on those markets, especially for wheat and cotton in the 1870s and 1880s and for pork and beef in the 1890s.

The determined "Granger" campaigns for railroad regulation in the 1870s and 1880s should be viewed in this light. The Master of

Figure 13-1 The use of federal troops in the railroad strikes of 1877 raised the unhappy possibility that America's future would see the nation occupied by its own army. (*Culver Pictures*)

the Iowa Grange, Albert B. Smedly, understood that the railroad problem was "not only *national* but *international*," and that even state regulation would not solve the basic problem, which he defined as "reaching the markets of the world as seems to be demanded in the present and must become a necessity at no distant day." Industrialists also used the railroads to carry farm implements to Eastern ports for sale in foreign countries. The internal demand for farm implements had generated a huge industry in the United States after the Civil War—an industry, which, in times of depression, sought out foreign buyers. Even railroad locomotive manufacturers themselves hoped to exploit foreign sales to balance out their ledger sheets in slack times.

It was no coincidence that the railroads were at the center of these various concerns. Closely associated with the opening and development of the West, those connected with

railroads were among the first to look overseas for new places to put down the tracks of progress. Back at home, meantime, users were demanding national regulation of the railroads to assure access for all to the marketplace. It was an ongoing process. But where exactly was it going? Toward imperialism?

Faced with these circumstances, American leaders could opt to emulate the Europeans in the scramble for new colonies; they could graft dependencies on the Empire of Liberty. There were a few outright advocates of that course, but never enough to shape the key decisions. Too many things were against it: the danger that such a graft would destroy the republic (by corrupting its institutions), the recent bitter experience of governing a conquered people during Reconstruction, and the simple fact that by the time the nation was ready to enter the colonial race the best prizes were already gone. Unlike European nations, moreover, the United States had within its territory most of the minerals and raw materials being sought by European imperialists.

At the other extreme, the United States could have adopted the proposals of radical reformers and socialists who argued that a change in property relationships and the mode of production would eliminate the periodic crises now suffered by the republic. Once again there were too many objections: America's strong heritage of protecting the individual's property rights, the failure of Reconstruction to change the basic institutions of the defeated South or to transcend the limits of radical Republicanism, and the simple fact that the men who led the nation and a majority of the citizenry had no intention of abandoning capitalism. Presidents from Grant to McKinley wrestled with the alternatives, struggled with Spain for Cuba, and contested the rest of Europe for supremacy in the Pacific.

Grantism

Secretary of State William H. Seward had pushed through the purchase of Alaska from Russia in 1867. Some Senators may have regarded the purchase as foolish, but none compared it with the South's pre-Civil War interest in extracontinental expansion for new slave states. Alaska was a back door to the British Northwest, said Seward and his supporters and, with its Aleutian Island chain, little more than a hop, skip, and jump from northeast Asia. He went after Hawaii for the same reason and failed there, but he did pick up Midway Island—a potentially useful way station for American ships in the Pacific. President Grant continued along this line by negotiating a commercial reciprocity treaty with Hawaii. This brought that island

kingdom under American economic influence and, eventually, internal domination by American sugar planters. But Grant's sudden eagerness to annex Santo Domingo offended radical Republicans and others for two reasons: first, it resembled the pre-Civil War filibustering expeditions and was ideologically unacceptable; second, it endangered efforts to assure Latin Americans that the United States was not just another nation seeking colonial adventure and was therefore commercially unacceptable. Grant's response to these charges was a curious mixture of Democratic Manifest Destiny oratory and Republican optimism:

I do not share in the apprehension held by many as to the danger of governments becoming weakened and destroyed by reason of their extension of territory. Commerce, education, and rapid transit of thought and matter by telegraph and steam have changed all this. Rather do I believe that our Great Maker is preparing the world, in His own good time, to become one nation, speaking one language, and when armies and navies will be no longer required.

Surveying his Presidency in his last annual message to Congress, Grant came back to the Senate's refusal to ratify his treaty annexing Santo Domingo: "If my views had been concurred in the country would be in a more prosperous condition to-day, both politically and financially." He could not refrain from boasting of what would have followed. "Hundreds of American vessels would now be advantageously used in transporting the valuable woods and other products of the soil of the island to a market and in carrying supplies and emigrants to it." But that was only the beginning. "The island is but sparsely settled, while it has an area sufficient for the profitable employment of several millions of people. The soil would have soon fallen into the hands of United States capitalists." Annexation would have gone far toward solving the problem of the "emancipated race of the South," many of whom could find a congenial home on Santo Domingo "where their civil rights would not be disputed."

Finally, annexation of Santo Domingo would even have helped to resolve the Cuban question, already a major issue in the 1870s. The President devoted six pages of his 1875 message to Cuba and Spain's efforts to suppress a revolt by those demanding independence for the island. It had become a "ruinous conflict," said the President, and should Madrid prove incapable of resolving the matter, the United States would be compelled to consider "the only remaining measures possible—mediation and intervention." By annexing Santo Domingo, he now argued, we would have forced Spain to reconsider its colonial policies and to abolish slavery in Cuba, a key source of Cuban-Spanish disagreement.

Grant's opponents on Santo Domingo did not object to "annexation" of more Indian lands. Hostilities in the Black Hills area, Grant told Congress, had "grown out of the avarice of the white man, who has violated our treaty stipulations in his search for gold." The question might be asked, he went on, why the administration had not enforced the treaty. The answer was simple: gold had been found in such quantities that if troops were sent in to disperse the miners, the bulk of them would have deserted. It was easier to remove the Indians.

Grant would never have tolerated such behavior as commander of the Union Army. But that was war; this was peace and Republican laissez faire. There was a lot of Jacksonian Democracy in it, right down to the Indian removal policy. But neither annexation of Santo Domingo nor Indian removal offered very much of a solution to long-range problems or even the immediate questions posed by the depression of 1873–1877. Santo Domingo, after all was said and done, was still only one small island, and there simply were not enough Indians to remove.

The search goes on

Farmers led the way out of the depression of the 1870s by taking advantage of an export bonanza. Sales of foodstuffs jumped from $216 million in 1875 to $488 million in 1880; raw cotton went up more slowly, from $191 million to $212 million in those same years. If anything was clear, it was that cotton was no longer king. "There is . . . a touch of joyous and characteristic humor in the way in which the American Republic celebrates its attaining 50,000,000 of population," proclaimed the *Nation* magazine on January 6, 1881, "by 'breaking' the European wheat, cheese and pork market." There was, however, a serious side to this achievement. "This mode of exciting hatred and envy has been hitherto unknown, and marks more vividly than anything else the beginning of a political revolution."

The 1880s saw Congress and the executive branch endeavor to stake out the elements of a comprehensive program to meet this challenge and to take advantage of every opportunity. A long-run commitment to export solutions meant, for example, increasing participation in the political affairs of other nations, if only to assure American freedom of action. The American government soon found itself involved, as the *Nation* had predicted, in an agricultural war with Germany, France, Austro-Hungary, and Great Britain over restrictions on American agricultural exports.

The solution depended upon vigorous diplomacy but also upon increasing domestic regulation of agriculture by the federal government to ensure that quality standards were maintained in accordance with European regulations.

The Garfield-Arthur administration, 1881–1884, also took a big step into world affairs by participating in an international conference on the fate of the Congo basin in Central Africa. It marked the first time ever that Americans had agreed to take part in a discussion of "colonial" issues with European nations. Rival claims to the Congo basin had given German Chancellor Otto von Bismarck a chance to secure an "open door" opportunity for his capitalists in Central Africa. Persuaded that it would be to America's advantage to second the German position, President Chester A. Arthur sent a delegate to the 1884 Berlin Congo Conference. "We gain everything which we could gain by owning the country," reported that delegate through the pages of the *North American Review,* "except the expense of governing it."

Closer to home, Arthur's Secretary of State, Frederick Frelinghuysen, tried to negotiate commercial treaties with Cuba, Mexico, Santo Domingo, El Salvador, and Colombia. A treaty with Spain over Cuba, Frelinghuysen explained to the House Committee on Foreign Affairs, would bring the island within the American commercial orbit and would confer "upon us . . . all the benefits which would result from annexation were that possible."

Grover Cleveland, elected President in 1884, did not agree with the American delegate to the Congo Conference or with former Secretary of State Frelinghuysen. Perhaps it was that, as the first post-Civil War Democrat to occupy the White House, he wanted to dramatize differences with previous occupants. However that may be, he refused to submit the Congo Convention for Senate ratification and allowed those commercial treaties which had not already failed in Congress to gather dust in his office.

On the other hand, Cleveland supported renewal of the reciprocity pact with Hawaii because, as he put it in 1886, "those islands, on the highway of Oriental and Australasian traffic, are virtually an outpost of American commerce and a stepping-stone to the growing trade of the Pacific." In another context, he asserted that the watchful care and interest of this government followed its citizens whenever they went into a foreign country. Especially concerned about a Mexican statute which he thought limited the rights previously enjoyed by Americans in that country, Cleveland said in his 1886 message to Congress: "The overflow of capital and enterprise from the United States is a potent factor in assisting the development of the resources of Mexico and in building up the prosperity of both countries."

To assist this good work, therefore, and to remove all grounds of apprehension for the security of person and property, such laws should be modified in "the interests of good neighborhood." Cleveland expanded this nascent doctrine in 1895, when the United States warned European powers that its desires in Latin America took precedence over all other considerations.

The Republicans launched a new navy in the 1880s with major ship construction bills in 1883 and 1890. In a Senate debate over additional steel cruisers, California's John F. Miller asserted that Latin America was "our India," capable of providing the United States with new markets to keep the nation's businesses running full time. America needed ships to protect "this great prize of commerce" from jealous rivals and to extricate ourselves from "complications" pursuant to commercial expansion. The fullest statement of an American naval philosophy for the modern industrial age, however, came from Benjamin Tracy, Secretary of the Navy in the Harrison administration from 1889 to 1893. "While we built railroads," Tracy explained simply, "other nations built navies." Just as railroads had once been essential to the rapid development of the interior, a navy was now essential to foreign expansion. "The sea will be the future seat of empire," said Tracy. "And we shall rule it as certainly as the sun doth rise." By the end of his term, the United States had moved up from seventeenth to seventh in over all naval strength—and was climbing rapidly.

Some Blaine thinking on critical issues

The man who came closest to providing a *modus operandi* for American policy in the 1880s was James G. Blaine, Republican senator from Maine, twice Secretary of State in those ten years, and his party's Presidential nominee in 1884. He said in his letter accepting that nomination,

We seek the conquests of peace. We desire to extend our commerce, and in an especial degree with our friends and neighbors on this continent. . . . While the great powers of Europe are steadily enlarging their colonial domination in Asia and Africa, it is the especial province of this country to improve and expand its trade with the nations of America. . . . Our foreign policy should be an American policy in its broadest and most comprehensive sense,—a policy of peace, of friendship, of commerical enlargement.

Blaine had no real chance to implement his plans until 1889 when, as Benjamin Harrison's Secretary of State, he presided over the first Pan-American Conference since

1826. Blaine hoped he could complete what Monroe and Adams had started by advancing a plan for a Western Hemisphere customs union or free trade area. Fearful of North American domination, both economic and political, the delegates from the Latin American countries would agree only to consider bilateral trade treaties. A few were negotiated and one or two had significant commercial results, but Blaine had oversold the treaties as a remedy for agrarian distress in the United States. Yet his vision was not limited to the interests of manufacturers, as some critics charged, nor to Latin America in isolation. Blaine's thoughts on the development of the West Coast and that area's growing dependence upon an expanding Asian outlet accurately forecast William McKinley's policy a decade later.

Back in 1881, Blaine had drafted Commodore Robert Shufeldt's original instructions on the opening of Korea to American commerce. Two years later, in 1883, a Korean-American commercial treaty was signed in Seoul, and representatives of the King were sent to Washington to repeat the ceremony. "You are our neighbors," President Arthur told the Koreans. "The United States from their geographical position, are, of all others, the nation with which the Orientals should cultivate friendship and a commerce which will prove to them and to us alike beneficial and profitable, and which must constantly increase."

Fully aware of the deepening East-West tension within the Republican party and the agricultural-metropolitan split which closely paralleled geographical lines, Blaine consistently pursued what he thought was the obvious remedy. The faster the West Coast developed, he reasoned, the sooner these tensions would abate and the greater credit that would go to the Republicans for perfecting the Empire of Liberty. It all seemed to depend upon successful integration of "our Pacific possessions," in which he included Alaska and Hawaii (an economic dependency since the 1875 reciprocity treaty) in key roles, along with an American-owned "Isthmian channel." Blaine once explained:

Taking San Francisco as the commercial center on the western slope, a line drawn northwestwardly to the Aleutian group, marks our Pacific border almost to the confines of Asia. A corresponding line drawn southwestwardly from San Francisco to Honolulu marks the natural of the ocean belt within which our trade with the oriental countries must flow. . . . Within this belt lies the commercial domain of our western coast.

Once an Isthmian canal linked the two coasts—"a purely American waterway to be treated as part of our own coast line"—the "extension of commercial empire westward" would be assured.

When we survey the stupendous progress made by the western coast during the thirty years of its national life as a part of our dominion, its enormous increase of population, its vast resources of agriculture and mines, and its boundless enterprise, it is not easy to set a limit to its commercial activity or foresee a check to its maritime supremacy in the waters of the Orient, so long as those waters afford, as now a free and neutral scope for our peaceful trade.

That was the full vision. It presumed that the West Coast (and the interior) would develop through Asian markets, just as the East Coast had prospered from its trade with Europe. Admittedly, it *was* a vision, but the riches of the Orient had enticed navigators and

Figure 13-2 "You are our neighbors." Arthur made it clear that America regarded all Asians as neighbors and potential good customers. (*New York Public Library*)

nations since the time of Columbus. Now, with transcontinental railroads no longer a dream and an Isthmian canal only a question of time, Americans were about to complete Columbus's original voyage. Less romantically, they were about to take the next obvious steps to expand their marketplace.

To ensure that these steps could be taken, or, as Blaine put it, to ensure that the Pacific waters afforded in the future "as now a free and neutral scope for our peaceful trade," the Harrison administration moved vigorously to check any adverse developments along the path to Asia: First at Samoa, where both Germany and Great Britain also had interests they were willing to pursue vigorously; then in Korea, where Japan was a major competitor;

and, finally, back in Hawaii, where Harrison himself pushed for annexation to preempt outside interference in a revolutionary situation. In instructions to the American delegation to the 1889 Berlin Conference, which worked out a tripartite Samoan protectorate, Secretary Blaine cited the steady growth of American commerce in the Far East, and the "certainty" of an "early opening" of Isthmian transit to prove that "in any question in the Pacific the United States can't be even temporarily subordinate. . . ."

In addition to an active Secretary of the Navy, Benjamin Tracy, and a far-seeing Blaine, the Harrison administration also boasted a vigorous Agriculture Secretary, Jeremiah Rusk, who sent special agents to Europe in search of new outlets for farm products. The single most important achievement of his tenure, however, was his determined (and ultimately successful) effort to open European markets to the American hog. "Two years ago," he wrote in 1893, "our pork products were interdicted in practically every country of Continental Europe. To-day the gates are open to the American hog, and he may march triumphantly and without hindrance from one end of Europe to the other."

Harrison left his successor everything he needed except time and good fortune.

The Cleveland rerun

Grover Cleveland had no sooner finished rearranging the furniture in the White House following his reelection in 1892 than disaster struck. On Black Friday, May 5, 1893, a financial panic began which could quickly deepen into the nation's worst depression yet and would last nearly five years. "Never before," reported the *Commercial and Financial Chronicle* in August 1893, "has there been such a sudden and striking cessation of industrial activity. . . . Mills, factories, furnaces, mines nearly everywhere shut down in large numbers . . . and hundreds of thousands of men thrown out of employment." The total of unemployed reached 4 million in 1894, the year of Coxey's Army and the bitter Pullman strike in Chicago. The Pullman strike was brought to an end only when Cleveland sent in federal troops. A few years later the leader of those strikers, Eugene Debs, became the socialist candidate for President.

"Capital has disappeared," wrote an English observer, "like a snowflake on the river." Dissidents within his party, along with a great number of Westerners from both parties, blamed Cleveland for holding onto the gold standard in an effort to save himself and his supporters while the rest of the country went swirling along in the economic torrent. Ever since the Civil War, groups of inflationists had challenged the orthodox belief that a sound economy depended upon a gold-backed currency. The continuing shortage of gold, it was argued, prevented a needed expansion of the currency. The Greenback movement of the 1870s and 1880s had been replaced in the 1890s by the Peoples party or Populist movement, which demanded free coinage of silver and advocated government ownership of railroads, telephones and telegraphs, a graduated income tax, an end to land grants to railroads, and restriction of immigration. Free silver became the rallying cry of a diverse collection of economic "thinkers" and "doers" who claimed that by adopting a bimetallic monetary standard the United States would liberate itself from dependence upon European creditors and be able to launch an expansionist policy at home *and* abroad.

Left-wing Populists might have opted for socialism outright if given a chance, but in

1896 the party rallied behind William Jennings Bryan, the Democratic nominee. Bryan's speech to the Democratic Convention summed up the silver argument so well that the delegates demanded his nomination as the party's standard bearer. "The money question is paramount to all others," Bryan had told the Democrats. "Gold monometallism is a British policy, and its adoption . . . [has] brought other nations into financial servitude to London. It is not only un-American but anti-American." Across the continent in Boston, a quieter meeting of bimetallists reached a similar if less emotional conclusion: if the United States did adopt silver as well as gold, might it not gain significant trade advantages in silver-standard countries like Mexico and China? It was worth some thought.

Cleveland's remedies for the depression fluctuated, asserted opponents, between timidity and sporadic hyperactivity leading nowhere. He refused to annex Hawaii when a revolutionary junta of American sugar planters overthrew the monarchy and petitioned Texas-style for American intervention, but he intervened in a Brazilian revolution with American naval power and risked war with Great Britain over a boundary dispute between Venezuela and British Guiana. Secretary of State Richard Olney—who as Attorney General had ordered troops into the Pullman strike—served notice on Great Britain in 1895 that America's "fiat is law upon the subjects to which it confines its interposition"—at least in the Western Hemisphere.

The Venezuelan boundary dispute policy found support in the ranks of anti-British free-Silver Democrats, but it was not popular with some of his Eastern backers. Segments of the business community opposed the President; others agreed with his policy. But whatever reactions his policy stirred, Americans

agreed generally that England's threat to "Africanize" Latin America had to be countered. It was the duty of the United States, the President asserted in a special message to Congress on December 17, 1895, "to resist by every means in its power, *as a willful aggression upon its rights and interests*, the appropriation by Great Britain of any lands or the exercise of governmental jurisdiction over any territory which after investigation we have determined of right belongs to Venezuela"—in other words, the Monroe Doctrine at work. British military control of the Orinoco River, Republican Senator Henry Cabot Lodge agreed in a speech on December 30, would make the Caribbean a "British lake" and surrender control of the commercial traffic flowing into and out of northern South American to Queen Victoria's servants.

The point is that many who most bitterly opposed the President, for this or that particular reason, felt the world constricting around them. Britain's designs on Venezuela were only the beginning. What they disliked about Cleveland was his unwillingness to see that an alternative policy had to go beyond challenging Great Britain in Latin America; the United States must be able to go out into the world, it must go on the offensive. The President's efforts to restore the frontier at home by reclaiming lands originally granted to the railroads as subsidies was laughed at in the West. The frontier had run out, and neither Indian removals nor what was left of the railroad lands would bring it back.

Eastern conservatives, on the other hands, professed themselves unable to understand what excited their fellow countrymen West of the Mississippi, particularly that emotional young man Bryan. There was one Westerner among them, Professor Frederick Jackson Turner (who had recently joined the faculty of Harvard University), who might be of some help. Turner's fame had spread far and wide since 1893 when he had read his scholarly paper entitled "The Significance of the Frontier in American History" at the World's Congress of Historians meeting in Chicago. No better explanation of what Americans meant by an Empire of Liberty had ever been given. The young professor from Wisconsin began his remarks on that occasion by referring to an 1890 census report which affirmed what others knew from first-hand experience: there was no longer any line within the nation's boundaries between established settlements and new territories. There was no frontier anymore. The implications of this simple discovery were tremendous.

"American social development," continued Turner, "has been continually beginning over again on the frontier. This perennial rebirth, this fluidity of American life, this expansion westward with its new opportunities, its continuous touch with the simplicity of primitive society, furnish the forces dominating the American character." But now, in 1893, "four centuries from the discovery of America, at the end of a hundred years of life under the Constitution, the frontier has gone, and with its going has closed the first period of American history." Among Turner's more interested readers were two other historians—Theodore Roosevelt and Woodrow Wilson; with him they pondered what the next period of American history would bring. By 1896, they knew, or feared they knew, the answer. As Turner had suggested on another occasion: "The age of machinery, of the factory system, is also the age of socialistic inquiry."

Writing on "The Problem of the West" in the *Atlantic Monthly* in 1896, Turner offered another possibility. "The West, at bottom, is a form of society, rather than an area." There

Figure 13-3 The nation finally ran out of frontiers and Indians. What direction now? (*Culver Pictures*)

had been a series of American "Wests," in fact, and contemporary American society was a product of that layering process. Therefore, "The Western problem is no longer a sectional problem: it is a social problem on a national scale." Indeed, if there was a sectional problem, it was Eastern. If the "Old West" were now to unite with the "New South" politically, the likely result would be "a drastic assertion of national government and imperial expansion under a popular hero." In other words, there would be social reform *and* expansion—the very ingredients of the Progressive coalition.

Enter William McKinley

Turner thus predicated that imperialism and reform might come together, but William McKinley was an unlikely model for the "heroic" figure to lead the movement. Yet he won the election of 1896 against the "Populist" hero, William Jennings Bryan, and he would have to make the choices. McKinley has been underestimated, especially by historians. He was no stand-patter as Governor of Ohio, nor was he unsympathetic to the "West," either as an area or as a form of society. He agreed with the men who launched the National Association of Manufacturers (NAM) in 1895: the social problem was directly related to an expansion of foreign trade. "We want our own markets for our manufactures and agricultural products," McKinley told the first NAM convention in Cincinnati, "we want a tariff for our surplus products which will not surrender our markets and will not degrade our labor to hold our markets. We want a reciprocity which will give us foreign markets for our surplus products and in turn that will open our markets to foreigners for those products which they produce and which we do not."

It was really Blaine's old strategy, given a face-lift by the former Secretary of State's most important convert; but McKinley faced an entirely different set of circumstances, at once more perilous and more favorable to any program for expanding the marketplace. Even as McKinley stood up to take the oath of office, events outside the nation had fused with the domestic crisis to produce a highly volatile situation. Beginning in 1895, a new insurrection had spread throughout Cuba. It soon became obvious that Madrid would be unable to put down the revolt, but as Grover Cleveland observed in his last annual message, the Spanish seemed bent on pursuing this objective until the island was utterly ruined and made worthless.

Cleveland had also observed that the insurgents had gained sympathy among the American people, especially "the more adventurous and restless elements of our population." Cleveland used his last annual message to warn the Spanish that Americans had both material and moral interests in the outcome and could not be expected to remain passive as these were swept up in the conflagration. The clamor for intervention arose first not in the business community but with the Populists and other groups who felt themselves oppressed by Eastern capitalists and who identified with the insurgents as fellow rebels against the colonial system. The Populist party declared in its 1896 platform that the government "should recognize that Cuba is, and of right ought to be, a free and independent state." The American Federation of Labor, behind Samuel Gompers's driving leadership, resolved that Cuba's freedom was essential to the workingmen of America.

Historians and other writers on the Spanish-American War have, throughout the years, paid a great deal of attention to the "yellow press" campaign for war. Journalists William Randolph Hearst and Joseph Pulitzer outdid one another in reporting (and making up) atrocity stories concerning Spanish rule in Cuba. What is sometimes missed about the "yellow press" factor, whatever its direct influence on policy makers might have been, is that Hearst and Pulitzer took advantage of assumptions Americans held about *their own* revolution, and concerns they felt about the current denial of those rights, and transferred them to the Cuban cause. Put another way, they pictured the struggle as everyman's struggle against the rule of the few. Mark Hanna, McKinley's political adviser, was surprised at the vehemence of Protestant clergymen who demanded that Cuba be set free from the tyranny of medieval Spain—and more astonished to find himself blamed by these same gentlemen for counseling against war in the name of capitalist interest groups who supposedly feared war as a possible threat to economic recovery.

There can be little doubt that McKinley would have liked to settle things with Spain without war, but he came into office determined to use the national government to promote prosperity. His ends would determine the means, in both foreign and domestic policy.

Where Cuba was concerned, McKinley was ready to do whatever he felt was necessary without prompting from the yellow press. His first instructions to the American Ambassador to Madrid served notice that this nation's material interests demanded an immediate cessation of hostilities. Nor were these interests limited to investments and trade. The "chronic condition of trouble and violent derangement" in Cuba provides "a continuous irritation within our borders, injuriously affects the normal functions of business, and tends to delay the condition of prosperity to which this country is entitled." McKinley also acted quickly to remove a

potential danger to future prosperity in the mid-Pacific, submitting a Hawaiian annexation treaty to the Senate in June 1897, nearly a year before the war with Spain. For the new President, annexation had emerged as the only solution to what was essentially a commercial problem. He had pushed for the acquisition of Pearl Harbor since 1891, and his views accorded with those of his colleagues on the Senate Foreign Relations Committee, who had concluded in 1892 that in "the absence of a policy to establish a colonial system and of any disposition for territorial aggrandizement," United States policy should be to encourage a "free and independent" government in the islands. If for any reason, however, that should prove impossible, then Hawaii should be encouraged "in its tendency to gravitate toward political union with this country."

McKinley felt the Cleveland administration had not encouraged that tendency, as indeed it had not, and he was disposed to correct the mistake. Moreover, McKinley believed Japan posed a serious threat to American interests in the islands. "We need Hawaii just as much and a good deal more than we did California," he told his secretary. "It is manifest destiny." Not everyone agreed with the President; indeed many of the same groups desiring intervention in Cuba opposed the Hawaiian annexation treaty. A key issue thus emerged which persisted throughout the debate on Hawaii, then on Cuba and the Philippines at the conclusion of the war with Spain, and even the Presidential campaign of 1900.

On one side were those who saw the Cuban question and the annexation of Hawaii and the Philippines as very different, in fact opposite, problems. Intervention to end Spanish repression and a colonial economic system in Cuba was, as they saw it, part of the responsibility mandated upon the United

States when it first proclaimed its new Empire of Liberty. It went back to Thomas Paine's *Common Sense*. To annex Hawaii or the Philippines, on the other hand, would be to violate that very same obligation and to reduce America to the level of a second-rate European colonial power. It made no sense, economically or morally, this group contended, to imitate discredited European policies.

Aside from this purely ideological consideration, colonialism stirred deep fears in the trans-Mississippi West for another reason. The adoption of such policies would alter the internal character of the nation. Colonies meant a standing army, which might easily be used against dissent at home; indeed the army already had been used against strikes. Imperialism meant the strengthening of special interests who would, in turn, use their power and wealth to dominate domestic politics. These fears brought together a diverse collection of volunteers under the banner of anti-imperialism, including not only William Jennings Bryan and the Populist hordes from the wild West but also such conservatives as former Secretary of State Richard Olney and industrialist Andrew Carnegie.

On the other side were a small band of genuine imperialists or colonialists, jingos who, like the giant at the top of the beanstalk, smelled the blood of Englishmen—and Frenchmen, and Germans, and anybody else who stood in the way. McKinley was not a jingo, however. Neither he nor his close advisers ever saw "colonial" acquisitions as an end in themselves. Never that. These small islands were but stepping stones to the Asian marketplace and thus to power and prosperity. Of course there were other routes to those ends, but one played the cards as dealt. The stakes in this game were far too high to permit emotion to dictate policy or to throw away

good chances in search of better cards which might or might not turn up in the next deal. Mark Hanna's biographer, Thomas Beer, recounted an episode which conveyed the serious, no-nonsense mood in the White House. At a Washington social gathering in the winter of 1897–1898, young Theodore Roosevelt, Assistant Secretary of the Navy, was going on at impassioned length about his hope that the Spanish and British flags would be gone from the map of North America before he reached the age of sixty. "You're crazy, Roosevelt!" Hanna interrupted: "What's wrong with Canada?" Later the disconcerted White House adviser said to his wife that it was a good thing McKinley had not put Roosevelt in the State Department, "or we'd be fighting half the world."

The winter of 1897–1898 was a good season of jingos, but the men who made the decisions in the McKinley administration were not among them. Full-blown imperialists often cited economic advantages as a reason for taking on new territorial obligations; McKinley's advisers reversed the proposition, territorial acquisitions were a necessary but limited means to a larger end.

Remember the Maine—and California

As Hanna suggested, nothing was wrong with the Canadian situation. Things were fine up there with American trade and capital prospering, but down in Cuba a good deal was wrong—and it was getting worse. War with Spain could not be avoided unless Madrid soon found a way to put an end to the conflict. On January 24, 1898, McKinley ordered the armored cruiser *Maine* to Havana. Spanish authorities reacted to this move by requesting the United States to do something to show the Cuban rebels that they should give up the struggle and accept Spain's offer of autono-my. That was as far as Madrid would go. "Our American idea," replied the American Ambassador, "is that Governments derive their just authority from the consent of the governed." It was not for the United States to interfere in order "to keep a people under monarchical rule, who are seeking to establish a republic." Although this exchange was only one in a long series, the direction it pointed was not just to war but beyond that to American responsibility for Cuba's future.

Then came the revelation, carefully managed by agents of the exiled Cuban revolutionary junta in New York, that Depuy de Lôme, the Spanish Minister, had written a latter describing McKinley as a weak and vacillating politician. Demands for de Lôme's recall went beyond anger and press headlines; de Lôme came to represent a deep-seated feeling that the Europeans, all of them, were still trifling with America and preventing it from achieving its rightful place. A week later an explosion on the *Maine* sent it to the bottom of Havana harbor with the loss of more than 250 seamen. McKinley's handling of this final turn in the Cuban crisis proved de Lôme had been wrong. The *Maine* went down on February 15, 1898, but McKinley did not ask for war for five more weeks. He used the time to mobilize his resources because, as he told the chairman of the House Committee on Appropriations, "Who knows where this war will lead us; it may be more than war with Spain." He wanted to be sure of each step along the way, and especially of the sentiments of the business community, many of whom had opposed the idea of war.

Satisfied on all counts, the President finally asked for war on April 11, 1898. Ironically, perhaps, the change in the business community from opposition to consent (if not enthusiasm) was based on a feeling that war probably would not delay a full return to prosperity so much as would continued indecision. A new export boom in 1897 had given many businessmen a greater sense of commitment to foreign expansion as the ultimate solution to the boom-bust cycle; and the public shout "Remember the Maine!" pointed the direction in which the whole nation wanted to go.

So war came, without the "colonial" issue having been finally decided. Annexation of Hawaii was voted on July 6, 1898, the determining argument being that the primary alternative, a protectorate over the islands, would not in fact protect America's interests adequately. But the antiannexationists were better prepared to make a stand against the Philippines, when the time came, than they had been to oppose Hawaii's annexation when this was rushed through almost as a war measure. Anti-imperialist William Graham Sumner had even conceded that Cuba might also be an exception without doing irreparable damage to the nation. His reasoning is of some interest, however, because the administration used similar logic to conclude that the Philippines had to be annexed. "If we could go to the island [Cuba]," Sumner had written in 1896, "and trade with the same freedom with which we can go to Louisiana, we could make all the gains, by investment and commerce, which the island offers to industry and enterprise, provided that either Spain or a local government would give the necessary security, and we should have no share in political struggles there." What a nice solution that would have been for both Cuba and the Philippines, but it was not realistic with America's leading rivals, Great Britain and Germany, already making their own plans for the Philippines should the Americans prove fainthearted.

William Jennings Bryan made almost the same proposal during the campaign of 1900. After establishing a stable government in the

Philippine Islands, he said, the United States should protect them from outside interference "while they work out their destiny, just as we have protected the republics of Central and South America, and are, by the Monroe Doctrine, pledged to protect Cuba." Bryan shared a common concern with the administration, despite his role as the Democratic Presidential candidate. Both he and McKinley were alert to rising American interest in the China trade and to the possible usefulness of a Philippine entrepôt in gaining full access to that potentially vast market.

Appointment in the Pacific

Possession of the Philippines had been of little concern to the men who originally agitated for a stronger China policy in the mid-1890s. They had prodded the Cleveland administration for aid in securing a railroad concession in China proper and issued warnings about the activities of the other powers interested in China. But if the islands were to be separated from Spain by military action, their strategic position offered the United States some leverage in the coming contest over China, as they did for rivals if left unattached.

Japan had defeated China in a short war in 1894–1895, exposing the "Celestial Kingdom's" appalling weaknesses and vulnerability to partition. The European powers then joined together to force Japan to disgorge the fruits of war; but not out of sympathy for China. Rather, they acted as they did to secure time to reconsider their own policies in this new light.

Russia made up its mind quickly. Seeking to protect the proposed Trans-Siberian Railroad and to ensure its commercial success as the main route through the Far East, St. Petersburg demanded special concessions

in Manchuria. Imperial Germany was close behind, forcing Peking to grant it a ninety-nine-year lease over the Shantung Peninsula. The British, who exercised an informal sphere of influence in the Yangtze Valley, began to worry; they inquired on March 8, 1898, whether the United States would be prepared to join in opposing preferential treatment to foreign leasees or the leases themselves. American policy since 1895 had been to give informal support to private efforts to obtain railroad and other concessions, but not to mix in China's relations with other powers. McKinley reaffirmed this stance, but there was growing business pressure for a stronger policy. Denouncing the German moves in China, *The New York Times* reminded its readers that "We need no more territory," but "we must have more markets, or suffer a terrible check to our growth and prosperity."

Still, there seemed no compelling reason to act with Great Britain, especially at a time when the nation's energies were absorbed in preparations for war with Spain. The war itself lasted only four months. Admiral Dewey's victory over the Spanish fleet in Manila Harbor brought the Philippine question to center stage. McKinley quickly resolved to retain a base in the islands, an "American Hong Kong," as it were, for commercial penetration of Asian markets. Possession of such a strong point might even make it unnecessary to join in an alliance, then or later, in order to protect America's growing interests in Asia. At first, therefore, McKinley had followed Sumner and Bryan in thinking that this might be possible by keeping Manila and leaving the islands as a whole to Spain.

This option was ruled out by the Philippine insurgents, who opposed a return of the Spanish (and would oppose American rule). Left to themselves as an independent country—the second option—the Philippines might collapse into anarchy or be "rescued"

Figure 13-4 For decades observers had been predicting a Russian-American meeting in Asia. Now here it was. (*New York Public Library*)

I confess I did not know what to do with them. I sought counsel from all sides—Democrats as well as Republicans—but got little help. I thought first we would take only Manila; then Luzon; then other islands perhaps also. I walked the floor of the White House night after night until midnight; and I am not ashamed to tell you, gentlemen, that I went down on my knees and prayed Almighty God for light and guidance more than one night. And one night it came to me this way—I don't know how it was, but it came: (1) That we could not give them back to Spain—that would be cowardly and dishonorable; (2) that we could not turn them over to France or Germany—our commercial rivals in the Orient—that would be bad business and discreditable; (3) that we could not leave them to themselves—they were unfit for self-government—and they would soon have anarchy and misrule over there worse than Spain's was; and (4) that there was nothing left for us to do but to take them all, and to educate the Filipinos, and uplift and civilize and Christianize them, and by God's grace do the very best we could by them, as our fellow-men for whom Christ also died. And then I went to bed, and went to sleep, and slept soundly, and the next morning I sent for the chief engineer of the War Department (our mapmaker), and I told him to put the Philippines on the map of the United States [pointing to a large map on the wall of his office] and there they are, and there they will stay while I am President!

by Germany or some other rival with a "civilizing" mission. Finally, at a White House meeting with his peace commissioners who were to do the actual negotiating with Spain, McKinley explained his reasons for retaining the islands; aside from certain negative considerations, it was his conviction that United States's tenure of the Philippines offered the opportunity to maintain the American policy in China, a policy he then defined as "no advantages in the Orient which are not common to all."

The President reviewed the evolution of his Philippine policy in a more famous meeting with the General Missionary Committee of the Methodist Episcopal Church in the White House on November 21, 1899. "When . . . I realized that the Philippines had dropped into our laps," he told the assembled churchmen,

McKinley's prayers had been answered, but, working on the sound theological principle of the times that the Lord helped those who helped themselves, he made very sure that the treaty ceding the islands had smooth sailing in the Senate. He did not want a repetition of the amendment the Senate had passed concerning Cuba at the time war was

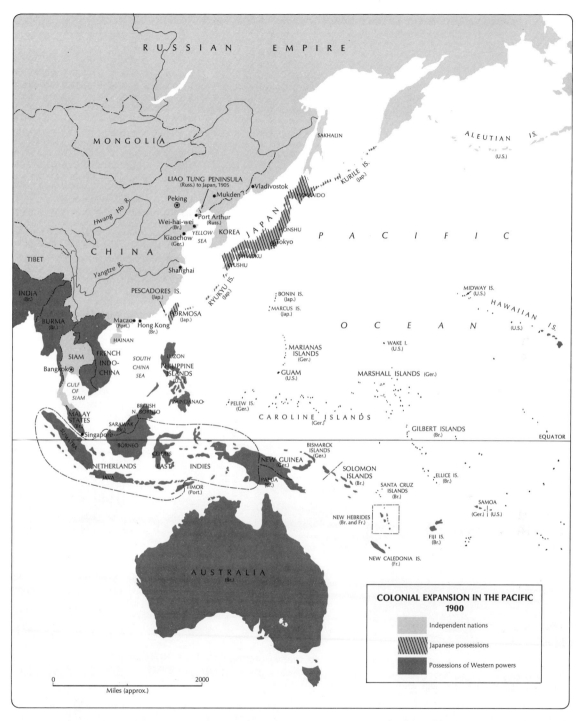

RUSSIAN EMPIRE

MONGOLIA

ALEUTIAN IS.
(U.S.)

SAKHALIN

LIAO TUNG PENINSULA
(Russ.) to Japan, 1905

Peking ⊛

Vladivostok

KURILE IS.
(Jap.)

HOKKAIDO

Mukden

Port Arthur
(Russ.)

Wei-hai-wei
(Br.)

HONSHU

KOREA

J A P A N

Kiaochow
(Ger.)

YELLOW
SEA

Tokyo

P A C I F I C

CHINA

SHIKOKU

Hwang Ho R.

KYUSHU

Shanghai

Yangtze R.

TIBET

PESCADORES IS.
(Jap.)

BONIN IS.
(Jap.)

MIDWAY IS.
(U.S.)

INDIA
(Br.)

RYUKYU IS.
(Jap.)

MARCUS IS.
(Jap.)

H A W A I I A N   IS.
(U.S.)

BURMA
(Br.)

FORMOSA
(Jap.)

Macao
(Port.)

Hong Kong
(Br.)

O C E A N

HAINAN

MARIANAS
ISLANDS
(Ger.)

WAKE I.
(U.S.)

SIAM

FRENCH
INDO-
CHINA

SOUTH
CHINA
SEA

LUZON

PHILIPPINE
ISLANDS
(U.S.)

GUAM
(U.S.)

MARSHALL ISLANDS (Ger.)

Bangkok ⊛

GULF
OF
SIAM

MINDANAO

PELEW IS.
(Ger.)

MALAY
STATES
(Br.)

SUMATRA

BRITISH
N. BORNEO

SARAWAK
(Br.)

C A R O L I N E   I S L A N D S
(Ger.)

GILBERT ISLANDS
(Br.)

EQUATOR

Singapore

BORNEO

CELEBES

NETHERLANDS

EAST

INDIES

JAVA

NEW GUINEA
(Ger.)

BISMARCK
ISLANDS
(Ger.)

PAPUA
(Br.)

SOLOMON
ISLANDS
(Br.)

SANTA CRUZ
ISLANDS
(Br.)

ELLICE IS.
(Br.)

TIMOR
(Port.)

SAMOA
(Ger.) | (U.S.)

NEW HEBRIDES
(Br. and Fr.)

FIJI IS.
(Br.)

AUSTRALIA
(Br.)

NEW CALEDONIA IS.
(Fr.)

**COLONIAL EXPANSION IN THE PACIFIC
1900**

Independent nations

Japanese possessions

Possessions of Western powers

0   2000

Miles (approx.)

(From A History of the American People by Graebner, Fite, and White. Copyright © 1970 by McGraw-Hill, Inc.
Used with permission of McGraw-Hill Book Company)

declared, the famous "self-denying ordinance" introduced by Colorado's Henry M. Teller which prohibited annexation.

Finale and prophecy

It was very important to Americans, as the Teller Amendment demonstrated, that they continually reassure themselves that they were not adopting an imperial policy but expanding the Empire of Liberty, not repeating European mistakes but forging ahead along a new path. McKinley was not off on a colonial binge, but he had to assure the success of his policies in Cuba with the Platt Amendment to the peace treaty. This treaty fulfilled the letter of the Teller restrictions yet gave the United States effective control of the island through various expedients, including the right to maintain a large naval base on the island and explicit restrictions over Cuban economic policies. By the Platt Amendment, the United States also gained the right to intervene politically should it be necessary to restore and maintain internal order.

Figure 13-5 McKinley got down on his knees to pray about the Philippines. American soldiers made sure his prayers were answered. (*Culver Pictures*)

American expansion McKinley believed, "depends less on large territorial posses-sions than upon an adequate commercial basis and upon broad and equal privileges." The Philippines gave the United States the desired strong point in the Pacific. They pro-vided a foundation for the announcement of Secretary of State John Hay's Open Door policy toward China in September 1899. Secretary Hay's first diplomatic note to the powers on China asked for assurances of equal commercial treatment within their spheres of influence in that country. He had not received final answers to that message before the outbreak of the Boxer Rebellion, an antiforeign uprising, in early 1900. It soon looked as if the powers would try to use the situation to complete the partition of China.

Washington suspected that the troops Eur-opean capitals had sent to rescue their diplo-matic missions and to punish the Boxers for attacks on life and property would stay on for other purposes. McKinley ordered troops that had been assigned to "pacification" duties in the Philippines sent to China to participate in the suppression of the rebellion. But they were given strict instructions not to become part of any allied command or to take part in any action which might weaken the Chinese government. America was thus already deep-ly involved in China and China's relations with other nations when John Hay sent a second Open Door note in July 1900, calling upon the powers to guarantee China's politi-cal and territorial integrity.

The "Great China Market" never proved out. But the Spanish-American War had ended with America enjoying boom times— brought on by an extra boost from new export surpluses—and exuberant about the future. In this mood, the nation had little time for warn-ings that the way they had chosen could be just as dangerous as old world "colonialism."

They wanted to listen to other things. "The Baldwin Locomotive Works," McKinley de-clared before the Union League Club in Phil-adelphia on April 27, 1899, "does not always follow the flag, but often precedes it, [laugh-ter] and I am told that its products are every-where. [Laughter] Indeed, the city of Phil-adelphia is getting everywhere [Laughter] It is doing as the army and navy have been doing in the last twelve months. [applause] I am told you are about to span the Nile with a bridge built in the city of Philadelphia. [applause]"

John Hay once called the Spanish-American War "A splendid little war!" There is no way to quantify such a statement, but McKinley's speech to the Union League Club (and its reception) suggested a new con-fidence in the nation: confidence that Cuba had been kept out of European clutches and that therefore the final decline of European imperialism had begun; confidence that the United States could define its interests and secure them in war and diplomacy; con-fidence that American economic interests could go abroad enjoying the protection of a major power which had proved its right to share in the world marketplace. No one want-ed any more territory; that was for reaction-aries.

A little more than two years later McKinley went to Buffalo, New York, to speak at the Pan American Exposition. He had decided to talk about the tariff—more especially on the prob-lem of initiating a comprehensive reciprocity policy. He scarcely mentioned America's new territorial possessions but called for an end to the rigid divisions between Democrats and Republicans over the tariff rate and ac-ceptance of a modern, flexible policy which would assure the country of expanding for-eign markets. Along with this trade policy, the nation needed subsidies for a new merchant marine and diplomacy to secure an Isthmian canal. "This exposition would have touched the heart of that American statesman whose mind was ever alert and thought ever constant for a larger commerce and a truer fraternity of the republics of the new world. His broad American spirit is felt and manifested here. He needs no identification to an assemblage of Americans anywhere, for the name of Blaine is inseparably associated with the Pan-American movement. . . ."

The next day McKinley was shot by an assassin, a grim reminder that not all dilemmas had yet been resolved. But the Empire of Liberty was alive and well—and expanding.

Selected references

The literature on late-nineteenth-century politics and expansion is as varied as it is voluminous. My source on Grantism was William B. Hesseltine, *Ulysses S. Grant: Politician* (1935). Another biography, Margaret Leech, *In the Days of McKinley* (1959), restores somewhat that President's reputation but is by no means the whole of the story. For that, broader surveys are needed, including Milton Plesur's *America's Outward Thrust: Approaches to Foreign Affairs, 1865–1900* (1971) and Walter LaFeber's *The New Empire: An Interpretation of American Expansion, 1860–1898* (1963). A more recent book on the agricultural-sectional disputes which shaped policymaking is William Appleman Williams, *The Roots of the Modern American Empire* (1969).

On the crucial debates over imperialism see Ernest R. May, *American Imperialism: A Speculative Essay* (1968), Marilyn Young, *The Rhetoric of Empire: American China Policy, 1895–1901* (1968), Charles S. Campbell, Jr., *Special Business Interests and the Open Door Policy* (1951), and Thomas McCormick, *China Market, America's Quest for Informal Empire, 1893–1901* (1967). The 1880s received their first serious treatment in David Pletcher, *The Awkward Years: American Foreign Relations under Garfield and Arthur* (1962), but much remains to be done on that decade. The Spanish-American War itself is the subject of Walter Millis's still useful study, *The Martial Spirit* (1931). An interesting interpretation of the late nineteenth century is Robert H. Wiebe, *The Search for Order, 1877–1920* (1967). A lovely little book I found in my grandfather's library, *If Not Silver What*, by John Bookwalter (1896), is still the best thing I have read on that issue's relationship to domestic and foreign trade. Grandfather was a Bryan man, a Democrat, and a silverite. After reading Bookwalter, I understood why, and why sectionalism plays such a large role in American history.

FOURTEEN

The Progressive Era

Period covered: 1890–1917
Emphases: Labor and radicalism.
Urban life. Reform. Popular culture.
Major events: Homestead strike, 1892
Panic of 1893
Pullman strike, 1894
Carrie Chapman Catt elected president
of Suffrage Association, 1915

Historians used to agree pretty much about the Progressive era. On the one hand it was marked by an uprising of the plain people against the interests, on the other by a quest for social justice. These were quite different though related impulses. The popular movement focused on antitrust legislation and corruption so as to keep the field clear for individual enterprise. The social justice movement was more humanitarian and philanthropic, being concerned with poverty and its consequences for the most part. The settlement house movement and the crusade against child labor were perhaps its best-known features. Later this simple portrait was modified by Richard Hofstadter's theory that Progressivism was led by middle-class professionals who resented having been pushed aside by robber barons.

In the last ten years, however, a new generation of historians has offered new explanations. No one doubts that resentment of the trusts was widespread. Yet it now seems that some Progressive politicians aimed not to restore business competition but to discourage it and to overthrow the boss not only because he was corrupt but because he was too representative of his immigrant constituency—hence poorly suited to the efficient, orderly, socioeconomic-political structure that big business and its allies wanted. This is not to say that there was no popular movement, or that the struggle for social justice was illusory. It does mean that the entire period was more complex, even at points contradictory, then used to be thought. The main thrust of organized middle-class people in this period was, as Robert H. Wiebe has put it, the search for order. But standing outside this thrust were artists and writers, who were conspicuously rebelling against old constraints. Many capitalists favored government regulation to maintain their ad-

vantages, while smaller and more competitive businessmen wanted fewer restrictions so as to increase their share of the action. There were conflicts of interest all along the line, and ideological clashes too.

The 1890s

A further element that makes understanding the Progressive era difficult was that it followed what was up to then the worst depression in American history. Unemployment was widespread and persistent from 1893 to 1898. Industrial strife was common also, especially at the beginning. Business consolidation moved at a faster pace, as always during depressions. Middle-class people were caught between their fear of trusts and their fear of labor. During the crisis, middle-class loyalties were exaggerated as the bourgeoisie rallied against challenges from below. Not until prosperity's return were people free again to complain of the trusts. This defensive psychology was first inspired by the Homestead and Pullman strikes especially and then maintained by the depression.

The Homestead strike was deliberately engineered by Andrew Carnegie. In 1892 his empire was reorganized into the Carnegie Steel Company, Ltd., capitalized at $25 million and employing 30,000 workers, 13,000 of them in iron and steel works. It was the most efficient firm in the industry, maybe even the world. Carnegie could make steel cheaply enough so that, had there been no tariffs, he could have undersold Birmingham Steel in England. Partly this was because Carnegie hired the best men and partly because the Amalgamated Association of Iron and Steel Workers of America was sympathetic to technological advances. It was a conservative, procapitalist union which was unusual in having contracts that paid skilled workers by tonnage rather than time. Even though it cooperated with management and included only skilled and some semiskilled workers, Carnegie felt it marred the perfection of his methods. He had often spoken kindly of labor, sometimes in print. But he was a business autocrat and, like all autocrats, wanted full control. He differed from his competitors chiefly in being more hypocritical.

In 1892 he went off to Scotland leaving his associate Henry Clay Frick to break the union. Frick announced that when the Amalgamated's contract expired there would be no new one and that wage cuts of up to 35 percent would take effect. He fortified the Homestead works and ordered 300 armed Pinkerton agents to man its defenses. A pitched battle followed. Total casualties were three Pinkertons and ten strikers killed, and thirty Pinkertons and an unknown number of strikers wounded. The strikers won the battle but lost the war. Frick called the state militia out and it broke the strike, though only after a long, arduous struggle lasting into the winter. At the end some strikers were rehired while others were permanently replaced by strikebreakers. The leadership was blacklisted and never worked in the iron and steel industry again. Carnegie and Frick then had a free hand to cut wages and institute the twelve-hour day and the seven-day week. Carnegie, Ltd., developed the most efficient system of labor exploitation in the country—one that became even more widespread in 1901 when Carnegie was merged with other firms to create U.S. Steel.

The most bizarre consequence of this momentous strike was an attempt on Frick's life by Alexander Berkman. Berkman and his associate Emma Goldman were young immigrants who saw in Homestead the opening

gun of the class war that would destroy capitalism. As anarchists they subscribed to the "propaganda of the deed" theory which held that a spectacular act, such as a bombing or an assassination, might be a catalyst that would politicize the masses and turn them toward revolution. Since Frick had become the leading class enemy by destorying the Amalgamated, killing him would be a perfect propaganda of the deed. Accordingly, Berkman went to Pittsburgh where, lacking money to buy a gun, he wired Goldman for help. She had already given all she had to get Berkman in place and resolved, therefore, to make the ultimate revolutionary sacrifice by selling her body. Alas, though she walked the streets of New York all night, whenever a prospective client approached she hurried away. Goldman was in despair over her body's refusal to accept her brain's command when a kindly old gentlemen bought her breakfast, warned her against the easy life, and gave her $5 to start anew. She promptly sent the money to Berkman who bought a gun and attacked Frick.

Fortune was still against them. Berkman fired several times to little effect and then grappled with Frick, stabbing him several times. But Frick was only slightly injured and soon back at his desk. Berkman defended himself and was speedily convicted and sentenced to twenty years in prison. The worst irony of all, however, took place in jail while he was awaiting trial. A young Homestead striker was in prison with him on a charge of having thrown dynamite at Pinkerton agents. He was enthusiastic over Berkman's attempt on Frick as long as he thought it inspired by business rivalry; but was appalled to discover that Berkman's motives were entirely political. He explained that he and the other strikers were law-abiding men who fought the Pinkertons only in self-defense and welcomed the militia's arrival. They all opposed anarchism as hateful and un-American. This lack of class consciousness and identification with authority were, Berkman discovered, universal among native-born American workingmen.

Berkman and Goldman became convinced in time, thanks especially to the Frick affair, that most of what they believed about revolutionary action in 1892 was wrong. When Berkman was arrested, Johann Most, the leading anarchist in America, condemned him for attacking Frick, and Emma Goldman responded by whipping Most in public. In 1901, when President McKinley was murdered, Goldman came to the defense of McKinley's assassin, a deranged young anarchist. She told reporters, however, that as a nurse she would have gladly cared for the stricken President. This marked, as Berkman wrote her from prison, the distance they had both come in nine years. They now felt that assassinations were pointless in a country like America, where the conditions for revolt did not yet exist. McKinley was hardly a tyrant in the European sense. Killing him accomplished nothing. "The real despotism of republican institutions is far deeper, more insidious, because it rests on the popular delusion of self-government and independence. That is the subtle source of democratic tyranny, and as such, it cannot be reached with a bullet." And, as Goldman's remark on McKinley showed, they had both become much more alive to the need, among revolutionary thinkers, to distinguish between what was human and what institutional. As the symbol of capitalist government McKinley deserved no sympathy, but as a stricken man he did.

Middle-class Americans were, of course, horrified by Homestead, and the attack on Frick. Their fear was augmented when Eugene Debs's fledgling American Railway Union (ARU) struck in support of the Pullman workers. The Pullman Palace Car Company was much admired for having built a model community to house its workers. But that Pullman, as it was called, was still a company town gained little notice. In the winter of 1892–1893 wages were cut by an average of 25 percent on account of the depression but rents in company houses remained the same, though they were already higher than comparable quarters in the area. Pullman's workers were not organized, but they struck anyway and asked the ARU for help. It was a new union but already had some 150,000 railroad workers signed up, mainly the less skilled men ignored by the railroad brotherhoods. The ARU responded by declaring a boycott against Pullman cars, which were rented rather than owned by the roads. The Managers' Associations retaliated by firing switchmen who refused to handle Pullman cars, and when this happened the ARU struck. Soon roads in twenty-seven states were affected and nearly all traffic west of Chicago was stalled. Governor Altgeld of Illinois broke tradition by refusing to call out the militia when disorders followed. President Grover Cleveland sent federal troops instead, who protected strikebreakers and ended the strike. The ARU was destroyed and Debs and his leading colleagues given six months in jail for ignoring a federal court injunction. He emerged from the experience a socialist and became the most charismatic and effective enemy of capitalism in American history. The Pullman strike was one of those famous victories that a ruling class cannot afford many of.

These and other events had a demoralizing effect on labor, which failed to grow much until the decade's end, and on the bourgeoisie, though for different reasons. But as long as the depression lasted, neither could do much about what bothered them. Certain developments continued anyway. The trusts went on multiplying, and so did middle-class service and professional organizations of every sort.

Combination and competition

With the return of prosperity after 1898, these associations were able to implement their desire for rational, orderly, equitable policies, not only within their own interest groups but to some degree nationally as well. Much of Progressive politics reflected this. At the same time big businessmen were moving in the same direction. Some in the middle class hated trusts for reasons of status or ideology. But big business and many middle-class professionals also wanted to bring order and security out of the chaos made by unrestricted enterprise. Capitalists had first thought to do this on their own: Rockefeller, Morgan, and other empire builders hoped to stabilize industries by creating units large enough to dominate their respective markets. However this was, by and large, an unsuccessful strategy, as Gabriel Kolko has argued.

Trusts were formed, especially in the 1890s, but they failed to restrict competition. In the decade of 1899–1909 the number of manufacturing firms in the United States increased by 29.4 percent with most of the growth taking place after 1904. Of nine manufacturing industries with product value of over $\frac{1}{2}$ billion a year, only one had fewer than 1,000 separate firms. The merged industries proved to be less efficient than expected. A study of companies merged during the years 1888–1905 showed only 49 percent to have been successful in the sense that earnings compared favorably with others in the field; 40 percent failed altogether; and 11 percent

made below average profits. Nearly all merged companies failed to hold the share of the market they enjoyed when first established, and most were overcapitalized, as the profit in a merger came from issuing watered stock. Most proved to be less efficient than their individual components had been before the merger.

This led many large producers to seek federal regulations that would preserve their own advantages at the competition's expense. Large insurance companies wanted federal regulations that would keep independents from underselling them, and so did meat packers. Upton Sinclair wrote his famous muckraking novel *The Jungle* to show how the packers exploited labor. But meaning, as he said, to touch the country's heart, he reached its stomach instead. People were revolted to hear of the unsanitary conditions under which meats were prepared. They demanded federal inspection, and the big packers did too. Higher standards meant higher operating costs—which smaller companies were less able to bear—and higher standards would reassure Europeans that American meats were safe to eat, thus opening up overseas markets that the big producers were best able to exploit. Desirable as the law was in many ways, it did little for labor and still less for competition in the meat-packing industry.

Perhaps the classic example of how public outrage and the self-interest of big business combined to secure federal regulation was the Federal Reserve Act. In the 1870s and 1880s the largest banks were national banks which, because their operations were federally regulated, were forced to maintain large reserves and to take other precautions. This meant their rates had to be higher than those of competing nonnational banks, which multiplied greatly in consequence. In 1896 nonnational banks made up 61 percent of the total; in 1913, 71 percent. This new competition made the New York financial community less important than before, and it was weakened further by conservative investment practices that forced companies to finance their own expansion through profits. The increasing scale on which business was conducted also reduced the importance of financiers. In 1895 J. P. Morgan and a syndicate of New York bankers saved the gold standard by taking up a $65 million bond issue and restoring public confidence in the government's ability to maintain its gold reserve. But during the panic of 1907 these roles were reversed and, after Morgan had called on Washington for help, the government made large deposits in key New York banks on the edge of collapse, thus averting disaster.

The major bankers were now certain that federal regulation, properly arrived at, was their best hope for the future. It was secured in 1913 thanks partially to hearings by the Pujo committee of Congress, which seemed to demonstrate that Morgan's money trust dominated the economy. This was no longer true—if indeed it ever was—but popular outrage inspired Congress to pass the Federal Reserve Act. Though hailed as an attack on the money trust, it in fact halted the erosion of New York's position in the banking community. President Wilson filled three of five seats on the Federal Reserve Board with bankers, and the New York regional bank quickly became first among equals, performing a variety of crucial services for the other eleven regional banks. The Federal Reserve Act was a classic example of the way in which popular demands for reform were translated into laws that benefited those they were supposed to restrict. The Federal Reserve Board, like the Interstate Commerce Commission and the Federal Trade Commission, proved to be more of a lap dog than a bulldog where the interests of member industries were concerned. This was true also of the Sherman (1890) and Clayton (1913) Anti-Trust Acts. They were supposed to break up monopolies, but with few exceptions were used mostly to indict labor unions for conspiring to restrain trade.

The AFL

If business history for the Progressive era may be characterized as, in Kolko's words, the triumph of conservatism, labor's experience was more complex. The American Federation of Labor made a good recovery from the depression. From 400,000 members in 1897, it grew to four times that size by 1904, but after that things got tough again. Employer resistance stiffened, and The National Association of Manufacturers helped stubborn employers fight unions, as did the Supreme Court. In 1908 the court ruled that employers could discriminate against union members and require employees to sign "yellow dog" contracts which pledged the worker not to join a union. Later it ruled that a union boycott of a manufacturer could be prosecuted under the Anti-Trust Act and upheld an injunction stopping the AFL from putting a company's name on its list of unfair employers. The old custom of violent repression continued. In 1904, Colorado's Governor declared martial law and ordered the militia to destory the Western Federation of Miners (WFM). In 1908, the Governor of Nevada cooperated with mine owners in an effort to drive all union members out of the state, and President Roosevelt sent federal troops to help out. In 1914 the Ludlow Massacre, one of the more ghastly episodes in the history of industrial violence, took place. During a strike of Rock-efeller's Colorado Fuel and Iron Company, an encampment of miners' families was machine-gunned by the militia and the tents set afire, causing two women and eleven children to be burned to death. The Rockefellers responded to criticism by hiring a public relations man and increasing their philanthropies.

Many of the great strikes in this era were not made by AFL unions. The western miners were organized by the WFM and the Industrial Workers of the World (IWW). The IWW also led two of the most important textile strikes, first against the cotton mills of Lawrence, Massachusetts, in 1912 and then against the silk mills of Paterson, New Jersey, in 1913. Partly this was because the AFL did not like to strike and partly because the industries where strikes were most necessary were least attractive to the AFL, being made up chiefly of unskilled or semiskilled workers. The AFL's whole strategy was to organize workers who, because highly trained, were not easily replaced. Since immigration provided employers with unlimited drafts of unskilled labor, industries where they were worked were nearly impossible to organize and hardly worth the trouble from an AFL standpoint anyway. The textile mills of Lawrence, for example, had workers from thirty different nationalities. Where natural animosities and cultural and language barriers did not keep them from cooperating, employer manipulation of ethnic hostilities did. Owners also sometimes brought in black workers to break strikes, thus worsening race relations. And as John Golden of the United Textile Workers (AFL) once admitted publicly, even when organized, textile workers were not worth bothering with since a majority were women and children who could not pay full union dues.

The AFL's commitment to business unionism and organization by craft made it conservative to begin with and its experience during the Progressive era drove it even further to the right. The AFL's chief problems were, first, that the power of capital was not so much checked as enhanced by government and the courts and, second, that open immigration divided the work force, provided scabs when necessary, and aroused middle-class hostility against workers as a whole. Being procapitalist and nonpartisan, the AFL could not do much about its first set of problems. Besides, a direct confrontation with the establishment would require a working-class party like the British Labour party. Gompers and the AFL leadership generally were against such a party on ideological grounds and also because an ethnically fragmented work force whose native-born members had little class consciousness was poor material for such an effort. This meant that immigration restriction was the only practical way to improve organized labor's bargaining position. Though Gompers himself was a "new immigrant," most AFL members outside the garment and cigar makers' unions were either native-born or immigrants from northern and western Europe. The AFL favored Oriental exclusion almost from the start and in time supported national origins quotas that would stem the tide of new immigrants. If not so obviously, the AF' was also against women workers, despite the facts that women were a growing proportion of the work force and that the failure to organize them depressed wage scales in every industry where they were numerous.

Given its restrictive, elitist assumptions, the AFL moved inevitably towards racism and male chauvinism. Though individual unions and sometimes, as in Chicago, even citywide federations cooperated with liberals, Gompers himself managed to be both procapitalist and antibourgeois. Intensely suspicious of anyone who was not working class (and especially prolabor reformers), he yet became a director of the National Civic Federation (NCF) along with Mark Hanna, August Belmont, J. P. Morgan, and other tycoons. The NCF was designed to prevent class war and the splintering of American society along interest lines. These were the overriding concerns of farsighted business leaders at the time, but their value to labor was not so clear. Gompers was himself class conscious and spoke frequently on behalf of democracy, but in practice, like big businessmen, he cared most for order and security and believed manipulation from the top was the way to get them. He would demonstrate this again during World War I, when he worked to prevent strikes in exchange for promises of wage hikes and other benefits that often never materialized. Given the power of capital and the fact that only about 4 percent of the work force was unionized, this was an understandable strategy. But more frequently than not, it meant conceding defeat before giving battle. In effect the AFL said that what labor most needed—the organization of unskilled workers, especially in the mass production industries, and the acquisition of real political power—could not be gotten. This did not leave the federation with much of importance to do. It also meant that the fight for social justice on the national level had to take place largely outside the union movement, though locally union leaders were often allies of reform.

Broadly speaking, there were two kinds of people involved in this struggle, radicals and reformers. At the center it was often hard to tell them apart, since the difference between a conservative socialist like Victor Berger and a left-wing Progressive like Jane Addams

was negligible. But though frequently similar in practice and often allied, reformers and radicals did disagree in principle on whether capitalism should be saved. In the end, this was a crucial distinction.

Radicalism

The early part of the twentieth century was a golden age for American radicals. Not since the 1830s had the sap of change flowed so freely. Never before had there been so many engaged in radical action. Americans think radicalism strange, alien, and irrelevant, yet this attitude is itself peculiar since the United States and Canada are the only highly developed countries without strong socialist or labor parties. Nearly all underdeveloped countries outside Latin America that do not have military government (and some that do) claim to be socialist even when they clearly are not. Thus what needs explaining is not why other countries pay at least lip service to socialism but why the United States never has. The Progressive era is where we must look for answers to this question. It was the period in American history when organized radicalism was strongest and also the time when comparably developed countries, especially in Europe, acquired powerful socialist movements. The failure of America to do likewise is one of the great anomalies among industrial nations and one of the things that makes it unique.

Until after the Civil War, socialism in America was nearly always utopian. Communitarianism never died entirely, and there is a nearly unbroken chain of collectivist settlements running down to the present time. In the 1860s Marxist socialism arrived here, thanks mainly to German immigrants. This made Marxism seem even more alien than it might otherwise have done—the ghetto mentality of German socialists was equally discouraging. A classic example of their inability to deal with, much less recruit, outsiders was their treatment of Florence Kelley. She was the daughter of a famous protectionist Congressman known as "Pig Iron" Kelley. A graduate of Sage College of Cornell University, Miss Kelley pursued advanced studies in Zurich, where she was converted to Marxism and married a political refugee from eastern Europe. She translated Engels's *The Condition of the Working Class in England in 1844* into English before returning to America. In New York she automatically joined the Socialist Labor Party (SLP) but was expelled within a few years for, as she later put it, speaking English. She went on to become head of the National Consumers League and one of the great social reformers in modern history. A party that could not hold such a person deserved to fail.

Daniel DeLeon, who dominated the SLP, was educated in Europe before coming to the United States and enrolling in the Columbia University Law School. Upon graduating he secured a lectureship in international law. DeLeon became a Marxist by stages. First he worked in the mayoralty campaign of Henry George in 1886, then with the Bellamy Nationalists. Neither gave his powerful intellect much to digest, but Marxism did. He joined the SLP in 1889 and in 1891 became editor of the *People* and national lecturer of the party. His strength of mind, energy, and personal distinction made him the SLP's leader for the rest of his life and even afterward. Though he died in 1914, *People* still prints his editorials, which the faithful consider as relevant as ever. DeLeon did not view the SLP as a permanent institution. He meant it to be the political arm of a labor movement that would someday dominate all industry and enable

workers to seize the means of production and abolish the government. It would be replaced by a Congress representing industries rather than geographical areas. "Industrial Unionism," he said, "is the Socialist Republic in the making; and the goal once achieved, the Industrial Union is the Socialist Republic in operation."

But the very qualities that made DeLeon preeminent in the SLP kept him from making it a mass movement. He was the kind of intellectual to whom ideas are sacred. Once having made up his mind on a point, he tolerated no criticism, even from his own son—whom he expelled from the SLP for heresy. He was also a great polemicist, and his attacks on people he considered mistaken alienated those not already repelled by his autocratic manners. DeLeon tried successively to infiltrate the Knights of Labor and the AFL, but to no avail. In 1905 he helped found the IWW, which soon ousted him. He was no more successful at creating radical unions of his own. Though one of the most creative thinkers among American Marxists, DeLeon had fatal defects as a leader; but the SLP lives on, preaching his gospel still, a monument to his name and evidence of his failure.

The vital history of American socialism begins with the conversion of an entirely different type of man, Eugene Victor Debs. The son of an immigrant storekeeper in Terre Haute, Indiana, Debs went to work at the age of fourteen. The next year he became a railroad fireman but quit after three years to please his mother, who thought that the job was too dangerous. All the same, in 1875 at the age of nineteen, he became a charter member and secretary of the Terre Haute lodge of the Brotherhood of Locomotive Firemen. He helped organize other railroad men too and became, in time, a national officer of the brotherhood, paying most of his expenses out of his salary as elected city clerk of Terre Haute. He also served briefly in the Indiana legislature. This turned him against politics as, finally, his experience with the brotherhood did against craft unionism.

In the early 1890s he resigned from the brotherhood to form the American Railway Union (ARU) along industrial lines. It won a strike against James J. Hill's Great Northern in 1894, and membership rose within a year to 150,000. Then came the Pullman strike which sent Debs to jail and shattered the ARU. While a prisoner, Debs read Marx and talked with Victor Berger, who was building a strong socialist movement in Milwaukee. He tried to rebuild the ARU but was blocked at every point. This ended his career as union leader and turned him toward socialism. He first tried utopian socialism. His Brotherhood of the Co-operative Commonwealth meant to colonize a western state and eventually gain control of it at the polls. He soon rose above utopianism and organized what became—in 1901, after a fusion with a defecting SLP bloc led by Morris Hillquit of New York—the Socialist Party of America (SPA). Debs was the SPA's candidate for President in 1900, 1904, 1908. In 1908, he toured the country in a chartered train, the "Red Special," and won nearly 1/2 million votes. He ran again in 1912, and in that year got almost twice as many. His 6 percent of the popular vote that year was the biggest share any radical candidate for President would ever win.

Debs's popularity was partly due to his character and partly to his eloquence. He was a man of great compassion and humanity—a "Lincoln of the left," some called him. Debs gave his whole life to helping the poor and oppressed. While he appreciated his value to the party, he was anything but vain. When asked what he would do if elected President, Debs always answered that he would resign in favor of a better man. He was one of the great orators in an age—the last such—when public speaking counted heavily. He was not, like William Jennings Bryan, florid or grandiloquent, but a master of simple, clear, expressive phrases. When war broke out in 1914, he said, "I have no country to fight for; my country is the earth, and I am a citizen of the world." When America entered it, he did not change—even though speaking out meant going to prison. At his trial, where he offered no defense, he began his apologia with these words: "Your honor, years ago I recognized my kinship with all living beings, and I made up my mind that I was not one bit better than the meanest on earth. I said then, and I say now, that while there is a lower class, I am in it; while there is a criminal element, I am of it; while there is a soul in prison, I am not free."

Debs was indispensable to the SPA not only because he was far and away its most attractive figure but even more because he alone could hold its left and right wings together. Like many radical parties, the SPA was divided into a revolutionary left wing and a more cautious, reformist right wing. The left was smaller in numbers but militant, spirited, and creative. The right was more numerous. It included, except for Debs, most of the best-known leaders and officeholders and controlled the key party institutions—including the National Council, the Rand School of Social Science, and many publications. As the party grew, the tensions between left and right became more severe. By 1908 it had 46,000 dues-paying members. In 1910 it got 600,000 votes in local elections, and in 1911 it elected 1,000 people to political offices. At its peak it had hundreds of publications headed by the popular *Appeal to Reason*, a Western newspaper with perhaps 1/2 million subscribers, and the *New York Call*, a daily paper. It sent two men to Congress (both from ethnic districts—Victor Berger representing the Germans of Milwaukee and Meyer London the Jews of New York) and elected a number of mayors in such places as Schenectady, New York; Milwaukee, Wisconsin; and Berkeley, California. No radical party has ever come close to exercising the kind of influence that the SPA had in 1912.

Thereafter it declined, for reasons scholars still cannot agree on. Those who identify with the left wing think it was because the right became too conservative. In order to win office, socialists had to water down their platforms to the point where they became only the advance guard of Progressivism, and as such there was less reason to vote for them than for genuine Progressives who had better chances of being elected in most places. Other historians, identifying with the right wing, think the SPA was ruined by adventurous leftists who frightened voters with their revolutionary rhetoric and divisive enthusiasm for the IWW. The left did in fact disdain political action and supported the IWW—which was apolitical; a dual union (that is, one which competed with existing trade unions); and, worse still, an ineffective union in the sense that it could not consolidate gains. All these charges are true in their way. The left was often feckless and impractical while the right was sensible to a fault and tended to bargain away at the polls those things that they supposedly sought office to obtain. Debs was himself a leftist, often extravagantly so in terms of language, but he was loyal to the right and tried hard to keep both wings together. Nonetheless, in 1913 the National Council expelled Big Bill Haywood of the IWW, ostensibly for advocating violence, and the split this caused was never repaired. The SPA's strength declined thereafter, rose briefly when it attracted antiwar

Figure 14-1 "If that keeps on itching back there, I'll have to scratch." A socialist cartoon drawn by the great artist John Sloan for *The Masses* in 1913. (*The Masses*)

votes during World War I, and declined again in the 1920s. The war was also destructive in that most intellectuals ended up leaving the party when it resisted American entry, a stand which enabled the government to raid SPA offices and jail its principal leaders—including Debs, Berger, and Kate O'Hare (the foremost woman socialist) among others.

All these events contributed to the SPA's decline and fall. But the reasons for its collapse are probably not to be found through an internal study of the socialist movement and its leaders and factions or even the repression of 1917–1918. Most historians think that after 1912 the party was disintegrating, though these were the very years when in England socialism became a crucial element of party politics. The comparison is instructive even if not exact. The British Independent Labour party was founded in 1893, just when the SLP in America was making its bid to take over the AFL, an effort which failed, though in England organized labor was going socialist. American radicals and reformers knew what was happening in England and American efforts were frequently copies of English initiatives. Henry Demarest Lloyd in fact tried to organize a socialist-populist coalition in the 1890s directly modeled on the British ILP.

In 1900 there were two Labour Members of Parliament and perhaps 2 million trade unionists. The AFL, though smaller, grew rapidly in these years also, as did the Socialist party. But suddenly British radicalism became a real political force, while in America it grew slowly and then fell back. The two Labour MPs of 1900 became twenty-nine in the General Election of 1906. In America the election of two socialist congressmen was a singular event that was never repeated. The AFL, which was not socialist anyway, also failed to grow much after its spurt in the early 1900s. From 1912 on, labor and socialism in the two countries had practically nothing in common. American socialism perished, the trade union movement withered and then came back in the 1930s—but it never equaled the English union movement, which, through its Labour party, would share directly in governing the country.

Socialism failed entirely and labor partially in America, while in England they went together from victory to victory. The difference would seem to lie not so much in the peculiarities of the American socialist and trade union movements by comparison with their English counterparts as in the differences between the two countries. Both were chiefly urban and highly industrialized, though England was more so in each case. But English working people became class conscious in the early twentieth century while American workers did not. One reason for this surely was that, as class lines were more distinct in England, it was easier for workers to locate themselves. In America class lines were blurred by egalitarian dress and customs and even more by the widespread belief in individual mobility and self-help. But a second crucial factor, perhaps the most important, was that the English working class was not much divided by religion and nationality. Except in Wales, they all spoke English from infancy; and except for some Irish Catholics, they mostly worshipped in nonconforming chapels. English working-class radicals were not alien by birth or even sentiment—being, in most cases, intensely patriotic. English radicalism was thus solidly based on ethnic and religious unity.

American radicalism was enfeebled by religious and ethnic disunity, as was the labor movement; and, even more than labor, radicals had to fight against the taint of alienness. Native-born Americans who joined the party had to cope with their own prejudices sometimes and what others regarded as their questionable patriotism always. During the war, when xenophobia reached its peak, many socialist intellectuals felt they could show themselves to be patriotic only by leaving the party. Language barriers and ethnic hostilities made it hard for immigrants to organize and—once organized—to cooperate with others. The foreign-born had to be won over, since they made up such a large part of the work force. But once recruited, they made socialism offensive to native-born workers, who also needed organization. Ethnic locals were generally the most stable and effective, but the foreignness that united them kept socialism from growing. There was no way out of such an impasse. Without ethnic and religious uniformity there could be little class consciousness, and without class consciousness there could be no effective proletarian movement. So, while elsewhere in the developed countries democratic socialism flourished, in America it died.

This was one of the most important events in American history. It meant that those social problems—poverty, urban decay—that did not solve themselves would not be solved. While other countries, prodded if not led by social democratic parties, eliminated slums and real destitution and made good medical care available to all, the United States lagged farther and farther behind. There was no left, hence no way to make conservatives grant timely welfare concessions and no party with the strength to impose them. In America, designed social reform is carried out if at all by centrists and, being moderate, they are often satisfied with half measures. Democratic socialism has not, as its practitioners once hoped, meant the end of all exploitation, inequity, and want, still less the overthrow of capitalism. Revolutionaries have been quick to condemn it on this count. Yet it has led to a better utilization of natural resources everywhere it was strong, not only in compact little societies like Sweden but in great urbanized cultures such as those of France and Germany. And it has done so without the frightful human costs exacted by revolutionaries in Russia and elsewhere.

The significant fact about the Progressive era, then, is the change that did not take place. America had become more like Europe in the sense of being industrial and urban; it had lost, or would soon lose, several of the attributes that had once made it unique—notably free land and free immigration. But it did not make the same response to shared problems as Europe did. This produced the great American contradiction. On the one hand, it became the richest country in the world, and, on the other, one of the most mismanaged industrial societies with, in rela-

tion to assets, the worst social problems. Every subsequent generation would pay for this.

Two other forms of radicalism are worth noting here, though neither was as important as socialism. Anarchism enjoyed a mild vogue in the period, thanks especially to Emma Goldman and Alexander Berkman. In one sense it ought to have done well in America. There was an indigenous anarchist tradition that went back at least as far as 1827 when Josiah Warren founded his first Time Store, in which goods were sold for an exchange of labor rather than for cash. Even more important, however, was the Jeffersonian prejudice against government, which was so much a part of American culture. The frontier, where government was weak when it existed at all, played a part too. Americans commonly regarded the strong, central governments of Europe with distaste and congratulated themselves on having escaped them.

These feelings ought to have enabled anarchists to strike responsive chords here, but in practice they did not. This was probably because, in the 1880s and 1890s, anarchism became associated with foreigners and violence. For half a century, from the time when Johann Most arrived from Germany in 1883, the leading anarchists were nearly all foreigners. After Most, Berkman and Goldman were the best known of these. They were deported for opposing American entry into World War I. In the 1920s the Italian anarchists Sacco and Vanzetti, though never leaders of the movement, at least symbolized it, as did their execution. (They were executed nominally for murder and robbery but really for being foreigners and anarchists.) Carlo Tresca, another Italian, was the only anarchist of reputation left. He allied himself with the Trotskyists in their struggle against

Stalinism and was assassinated in 1943. Tresca was the last representative in America of the great European anarchist tradition.

The Industrial Workers of the World was a more significant phenomenon than anarchism, though in fact many anarchists belonged to it. In practice there were few differences between them and the syndicalists who led the IWW to death and glory. Both wanted an end to the state and despised parliamentary radicals who, they believed, would always be either defeated or coopted by the ruling class. In addition, syndicalists felt that the revolution should be brought about by trade and industrial unions. Afterward, the state would vanish to be replaced by local and national union federations. Syndicalism had European origins, but it spread rapidly among IWW leaders. Founded in 1905 by DeLeon, Debs, William Haywood of the Western Federation of Miners, and others, the IWW was first conceived of as a dual union, a rival of the AFL and, especially by DeLeon, as the industrial arm of socialism. But when the WFM pulled out, it moved to the left. "Wobblies," as IWW members were called, rejected not only business unionism and capitalism, but the political process as well. They thought to make a revolution by organizing workers to seize the instruments of production and destroy the state. In part their contempt for politics was the result of having seen law and government persistently used to advance ruling-class interests. This was especially true of miners like Haywood and others, who were veterans of the most violent class struggle in American history. Then too, as Wobblies were mainly immigrants and migrant workers who could not vote, political action was impossible anyhow.

The IWW fought a whole series of great strikes in both the East and West, but in the end it was destroyed. Like some socialists,

Wobblies had the disadvantage of being radical in a conservative society. They too found the want of class consciousness among American workers impossible to overcome, and they suffered from having so many immigrant members. They also opposed American entry into World War I and were repressed even more brutally than socialists. Finally, they were weakened by internal contradictions, between immigrants in the East and migrant workers in the West, from ideological divisions before 1917, and—after the Russian Revolution—from a power struggle between anarcho-syndicalists and communist sympathizers who wanted to bring the IWW into the Third International.

Most of all they could not harmonize the conflicting demands imposed on them by their dual status as unionists and revolutionaries. As revolutionaries they would not sign contracts because "The contract between an employer and a workman is no more binding than the title deed to a negro slave is just." They could not bargain for wages and hours like the AFL without ceasing to be revolutionaries. But if they did not bargain and sign contracts they could not build up stable locals. As Melvyn Dubofsky, their best historian, puts it, "In the end IWW leaders usually sub-ordinated reform opportunities to revolutionary necessities, while the rank and file, when it could, took the reforms and neglected the revolution." The IWW did win strikes, notably at Lawrence in 1912, but these victories rarely had lasting effects. The Wobblies have great claims on posterity's respect. They were brave, selfless, and unprejudiced proletarian leaders. They struggled on behalf of the worst-treated elements in the work force—those who needed organizing most and got the least attention from existing unions.

Yet it remains true that for the sake of what

they could not get the Wobblies sacrificed what they might have had. There would be no revolution in America, and the quixotic effort to start one was no less foolish for being so nobly made. There was, however, a chance of organizing industrial unions, as Lawrence demonstrated. It was one of the most important strikes in American history precisely because the workers included large numbers of women and children, and were divided into at least thirty different ethnic groups. This kind of work force was supposedly impossible to organize, yet the IWW did it. Wobbly leaders were arrested for murder and force was repeatedly used against them. The AFL tried to break the strike by organizing skilled workers and signing a separate contract. But the IWW won despite the fact that it had only modest help from outside. Afterward, employer resistance stiffened and the Socialist party cut the Wobblies off, so there was never another triumph like Lawrence. All the same, it proved that industrial unionism was possible. The failure of other radicals and liberals to admit that the IWW was doing vital work condemned unskilled labor to another generation of misery. Twenty years later the CIO would finish the job—better late than never—but too late for millions whose lives wore out because industrial unionism was so long delayed.

Urban life

Radicalism was largely a consequence of the maldistribution of wealth in the Progressive era, a problem made all the more obvious by rapid technological changes and increased productivity. By 1914 industry was producing 76 percent more goods than in 1899, but with only 36 percent more workers. The great profits thus generated were enjoyed by comparatively few. One percent of American families owned nearly seven-eights of the wealth. About one-fifth of all families lived in comfort or better. These were the people who had telephones (677,000 in use in 1900, 6 million by 1915), automobiles (4 in use in 1895, 5 million by 1917), and other innovations. The remaining four-fifths lived marginally or worse. At least one-eighth of the population, around 10 million people, lived in poverty, and this is a very conservative estimate. There were nearly 2 million child laborers. Workers were not only underpaid and overworked for the most part, but they frequently had dangerous jobs. In 1901, 1 railroad employee in 399 was killed and 1 in 26 injured. In 1907, 12 railway men a week died in accidents. Other industries were as bad or worse, and workers and their families were rarely compensated. Under the law, an employer was not liable for accidents caused by the negligence of employees. Even when blameless, the employee often had to go to court; and as few could afford this, they usually settled for what little they could get.

The conditions of working-class life can best be appreciated by looking at two representative cities, Pittsburgh and New York. We know more about Pittsburgh than any other iron-age community thanks to the Pittsburgh Survey, the first attempt to describe exactly the socioeconomic character of a great city. The survey's findings were published in six volumes between 1909 and 1914. They established how overworked nearly the whole labor force was, especially steel and railroad workers, who had a twelve-hour day and a seven-day week. Most workers did not make enough to support a family. Women workers often did not make enough to support themselves. The survey contrasted the wealth generated by Pittsburgh's industry with the poverty of working people and most public services, and declared: "Not by gifts of libraries, galleries, technical schools, and parks, but by the cessation of toil one day in seven and sixteen hours in the twenty-four, by the increase of wages, by the sparing of lives, by the prevention of accidents, and by raising the standards of domestic life should the surplus come back to the people of the community in which it is created."

Except in the brewery industry, which alone was fully unionized, wages and working conditions were uniformly poor. Worst of all was the steel industry where, since the union was broken in 1892, the oppression of labor had become a science. A majority of common laborers in the mills were "slavs," a generic term describing most immigrants from Eastern Europe. They earned 15 cents an hour for a twelve-hour day. Perhaps two-hundred men a year died in mill accidents. Many more died of work-related illnesses; their mortality rate for lung diseases alone was twice that of the general population. And a large proportion worked the dreaded "long turn," by which continuous production was maintained. Under this system a man worked twelve hours a day for twelve straight days and twenty-four hours on the thirteenth. After this long turn, which put him on the second shift, he got twenty-four hours off. Then the cycle was repeated. Men who worked like this

Figure 14-2 A Carolina textile mill. This is what the fight against child labor was all about. (*Library of Congress*)

spent nearly all their waking hours on the job or traveling to and from it. Probably never before had labor been exploited in so calculated a fashion. The Pittsburgh system, as developed in the Carnegie mills and further refined by United States Steel, was based on two principles—union busting and the speedup. Union organizing was prevented by a network of informers who enabled the companies to fire and blacklist union men. This tactic was so effective that when John Fitch (who wrote the Pittsburgh Survey volume on steel) met with workers, they would only speak with him at night, behind closed doors and drawn curtains, and even then with trepidation. Equally useful was the technique of mixing the work force by ethnic groups so as to maximize organizational difficulties. The companies also worked to reduce their dependence on skilled labor, which was most likely to organize. By 1908, about 60 percent of the workers were unskilled.

Given a helpless work force, the industry was free to increase productivity as it pleased. Fitch learned that the Homestead mills had doubled production since the early 1890s. A rolling mill in the industrial suburb of Duquesne that rolled 300 to 600 tons a shift in 1892 rolled 900 to 1,200 tons in 1908. Some of this was a result of technical improvements, but much of it came from driving the workers harder. Sheet mills were twice as productive as in the 1890s, though no technical improvements whatsoever had been made. The speedup depended first of all on paying workers according to the productivity of the gang to which they belonged. This was not only cheaper than paying men hourly wages or individual piece rates but had the further advantage of making workers assist in their own exploitation. Since the gang's pace was limited by its slowest members, the weaker were pressured by the stronger. When the gang's productivity went up, rates went

down. Thus men had to work harder and harder to stay in place. Unlike the men, foremen and supervisors got incentive pay and, when quotas were exceeded, supervisors earned bonuses. But quotas—once exceeded—were raised, so supervisors too were always having to press harder to stay in place. This system of gang rates, quotas, and bonuses was so effective that the Soviet Union later adopted it.

One of the most instructive features of the Pittsburgh Survey was its report on prostitution. This material was available because Pittsburgh was having a "reform" movement. In politics, as Samuel P. Hays has demonstrated, these reformers, mostly capitalists and their professional allies, were destroying the big ward-based city council dominated by ethnic and working-class elements and replacing it with a small council whose members were elected at large. This, done in the name of honesty and democracy, was in fact designed to replace a city government based on autonomous wards with a centralized one more responsive to business and professional interests. In education the drive was similarly to unite the local districts into a citywide school system directed by professional educators. One offshoot of this movement was a campaign against prostitution, which flourished chiefly in working-class wards. There were a few $5 to $15 houses of prostitution staffed by native-born girls, but most were $1 and $2 houses with Jewish, Pennsylvania Dutch, French-Canadian, Irish, and other low-status girls. (There was also a category of 50-cent houses for the lumpenproletariat staffed by east European Jewish and Italian girls and catering to men of the same ethnic background, and a handful of 25-cent houses for blacks.)

These existed chiefly because immigrant workingmen were frequently unmarried or separated from their families. The city elite did not accept this as a valid excuse and, in 1912, established a Morals Efficiency Commission to destroy prostitution. (The title reflected both the current passion for efficiency in all human affairs and a peculiarly domestic prejudice. Other countries have vice; Americans have inefficient morals.) The commission, according to its own reports, was able within eighteen months to reduce the number of houses from 247 to 71 and the number of prostitutes from 1,000 to 333. It closed all houses in which black prostitutes received white clients. Perhaps the most useful part of its work was a study of the economic history of prostitutes. While the sample represented a broad mixture of religious backgrounds (272 Protestant, 188 Roman Catholic, 67 Jewish), the individual cases had previous occupations in common. Nearly all had previously been domestic servants, factory workers, clerks, or waitresses making less than $10 per week. As prostitutes they made between $10 and $25 a week and enjoyed, so it seemed, shorter hours and better working conditions for the most part. This was proof of the radical contention that prostitution was a function of the economic system. Men were driven to prostitutes because they were too poor to marry or, if married, unable to bring their families from abroad. Women became prostitutes because they could not live on what working girls earned.

The Morals Efficiency Commission recognized the problem but had no answer for it, and in 1913 it closed all the houses on the North Side. By way of preparation, "Every house had been visited in February by members of the commission, and the girls had been spoken to individually. They were urged to save money and think of their future." The commission concluded by establishing a Morals Bureau with a salaried superintendent of morals to carry on the good work. It was

typical of the period that, in a city where men were literally worked to death, prostitution would seem the gravest moral problem. Also typical was an approach which destroyed the symptoms while leaving the disease untouched. Much that went by the name reform in these years was based on the principles that animated the Morals Efficiency Commission.

If Pittsburgh showed what concentrated heavy industry at its worst was like, New York, already a megalopolis, demonstrated what congestion meant. New York had slums as early as the 1830s. By the 1870s they were so bad that reformers sponsored a competition to design a model tenement. But as the model had to fit the standard New York lot, which was only 25 feet wide by 100 feet long, an efficient design could only make things worse. This was exactly what happened. The "dumbbell tenement," so-called because the apartments at either end of each floor were connected by narrow corridors, won the prize and soon thousands were built. Usually six stories high, the dumbbell tenement had four apartments with fourteen rooms and two shared water closets to a floor. They were arranged so that ten of the fourteen rooms depended on air shafts for light and ventilation. Supposedly, each three- or four-room flat was to house a single family, but families often took in boarders. Rather than walk down five or six flights of stairs, people used the airshafts as garbage bins. Waterclosets, being open, were available not only to the families (plus boarders) assigned them but to people off the streets. When, as was frequently the case, landlords did not keep them in repair, the toilets, like the airshafts, posed health and sanitation problems. New York passed housing codes against the worst abuses, but they were not enforced. By 1890 35,000 of the city's 81,000 dwellings were tenements in which more than 1 million of New York's 1½ million people lived.

This was the situation when Jacob Riis published, in 1890, his shocking exposé called *How the Other Half Lives.* Riis was a Danish immigrant who had become a successful journalist. A passionate assimilationist, he also defended immigrants at a time when nativism was rising, though it was not yet so intense as it would become. His argument was that the slums had to be abolished so as to create a suitable environment for assimilation. Riis was not without his own prejudices. He tended to rank-order immigrants by nationality, being most sympathetic to north Europeans and most hostile to the Chinese, of whom he wrote: "Ages of senseless idolatry, a mere grub-worship, have left him without the essential qualities for appreciating the gentle teachings of a faith whose motive and unselfish spirit are alike beyond his grasp." If Riis was something of a racist, he was not, at least, against blacks. He admired blacks more than he did most immigrants, chiefly, it seems, because they were already Americanized.

Riis's book made a great impression, especially because of the excellent photographs he took to illustrate it. The first result was an investigation in 1894 that discovered a group of 4,000 tenements with 33,000 units, only 51 of which had private toilets. It found that lower Manhattan was the most densely populated spot on earth with a population per acre of 986.4 (compared with the next-worst place, Bombay, India, which in 1881 had had 759.66 per acre). This investigation did not bear immediate fruit, partly because the experts still thought to reform the dumbbell tenement when what it needed was abolition. The first breakthrough came in 1900 when the Tenement House Commission, formed under Lawrence Veiller, accomplished that feat.

After 1901 dumbbell tenements could not be built and the existing ones became known as "old law" tenements. Veiller was a prototype of the expert reformers who became increasingly common in the twentieth century. He believed that to enact proper housing laws one must know everything about housing.

Yet he also had defects, as Roy Lubove has shown. For one thing, unlike Riis and the settlement house leaders who were interested in housing for what it contributed to community life, Veiller was interested in good housing for its own sake. Once everyone had a decent place to live in, he seemed to feel, the reformer's job was largely done. Worse still, Veiller made it impossible for low-cost private housing to be built, yet he resisted all efforts to secure public housing. He, and other reformers around the country, erected complex housing codes that raised standards until only middle- and upper-income families could afford the results. The poor were priced out of the new housing market by the very reforms that were supposed to aid them.

Veiller never admitted this. He went on calling public housing socialistic, though he had done as much as any man to make it essential. This is not to say that public housing is an ideal solution, only that if laws are passed which make it uneconomical for builders to construct low-rent housing, then the government responsible must obviously bear the consequences. Much later New York bowed to the inevitable and erected public housing, even if on too small a scale and with too little attention to community needs.

This was not a process confined only to housing or peculiar to New York City. There were urban reformers all over America attempting to cope with poverty and problems like housing and transportation. They won few great victories, but even when reform was not punitive, as in Pittsburgh, it was usually tied to market requirements. People still thought of essential public services as profit-making enterprises. Only when capitalism had clearly failed, as in low-cost housing and later in mass transit, did government accept responsibility—and then inadequately as a rule. Private enterprise was thought the best means of solving public problems, though it was almost always what had created them. Because cities had relied on business to house and transport and generally care for the immigrants and the farm boys it brought to town, slums grew and congestion increased. When cities did try to meet vital needs, they were still handicapped by old, restrictive charters imposed on them by rural legislators and by old attitudes. Business was said to be economical and efficient, so government was supposed to be too, and in the same way. This meant, as a rule, too little money and too much administration. What could be done cheaply was done sometimes and in a cumbersome way; what was expensive, however necessary or desirable, was not.

Given the size of their problems, and the meager results, urban reformers might well have been easily discouraged. But in fact, Progressivism was important chiefly because of the size and persistence of movements for local reform. During the Progressive era, for the first time, people worried most about cities. Still, different people worried about different things. The middle classes were especially concerned with machine politics, corrupt relations between government and business, and the immigrants. The poor worried about housing, employment, and mere suvrival. As they were weak and hard to organize, their anxieties did not have much effect except on politicians—machine politicians as a rule. But machine politicians favored short-term palliatives over fundamental changes. They might help the needy with a bag of coal or even a job, but rarely with broadened city welfare services. They might work for a lower carfare but seldom to improve or expand service unless there was profit to themselves in it. The poor found the middle-class reform politician's concern with honesty, efficiency, and the like irrelevant when not offensive. But immigrant ward healers and machine politicians, though better in the sense of meeting immediate needs and relating to them in human ways, were not a great improvement. They had neither the power nor the vision required to make a decent city.

The best reformers tried to meet both the bourgeois demand for honest, efficient government and the poor's desire for immediate relief and dignity. This was virtually impossible, though many spent a lifetime at it. Perhaps the settlement houses themselves illustrate the problem best. The first settlements tried to help the immigrant help himself in various ways. They also provided altruists with an outlet for their energies and educated, middle-class young women with ennobling social roles. When Jane Addams opened Hull House in 1889, there were only two other settlements in America, one of them a week old. By the Progressive era there were hundreds of settlements providing basic services, organizing for community and citywide action, publicizing problems, and trying to overcome both immigrant ignorance and native American prejudice.

Yet although the great settlements struggled for a generation to meet the urban crisis in this highly personal way, they could not accomplish much by themselves. They sometimes intervened in local politics usefully, and they got city services improved and desirable ordinances passed. But for all their energy, talent, and dedication and even though they attracted some of the brightest spirits of a generation, they were too few to have more than a moral effect. Even in their own neighborhoods they found it hard to get changes. They were best at offering social welfare assistance to women and children; few settlements attracted the men without whose support no great local enterprise could go forward.

Settlement leaders generally believed that good will was better than socialism. More than that, many were inspired to work in slums precisely because otherwise the poor might turn left. In practice this doubtlessly made little difference, as settlement workers rarely influenced immigrant opinion leaders one way or the other. But it is striking that the people who were closest to the urban problems of their day—most sympathetic to immigrants and most eager for the sweeping changes that alone would make great cities worth living in—could not admit that what they wanted could be had, if at all, only through something like the socialist movement. Their antisocialism was partly a matter of faith: the old belief that to change men's hearts is to change the world. If only immigrant and capitalist could be brought together all would, in the end, be well. But, more importantly, settlement leaders were appalled by the socialist doctrines of materialism and the class struggle. Even when they agreed with socialist programs, as frequently happened, they were against having them if class hatred was to be the price. They lived to bring men together, not drive them apart. And they would probably have preferred to go on in this fashion even if they knew, which few did, that in the end it was only by driving men apart, or at least accepting existing divisions as a fact, that great change could be accomplished. So the settlements continued, frequently to the present day, binding up wounds, salvaging lives, rendering vital ser-

vices. But the slums remained too. In northern and western Europe during the same years, the base was laid for that municipal socialism which has made most of their great cities safer and healthier than our own.

Yet things got better all the same. New York's slums may be as large as they were in 1900, but the city as a whole is larger still. Half to two-thirds of the population lived in substandard housing then; now perhaps only one-seventh or one-eighth do. Many other cities had a comparable experience. This was not because crucial urban problems were solved but rather because the increase in productivity translated into higher wages and living standards for most Americans. To the extent that the failure of planning in the Progressive era, as later during the New Deal, was redeemed, it was because of the economy's enormous strength. Its wealth gave America a margin for error that few other countries enjoyed. America had the greatest human and material resources of any country in the world. All were needed to make up for the failures of governments and reformers.

But though things got better, not everyone benefited equally. Some elements of the population did well, others poorly. Jewish, Chinese, and Japanese immigrants prospered, for example, while many other groups are still mainly in the working or lower-middle class. A look at the Jews, the only large ethnic group to make a rapid advance, may help to explain why the fruits of prosperity were so unequally divided. Since New York had the largest Jewish population of any city in the world, much can be learned from Moses Rischin's study of it. Until late in the nineteenth century, there were few Jews in America. New York City had a very small Jewish community which dated from the original Dutch settlement. They were too few to arouse much prejudice, and their talent and energy brought them rapidly to the top. For several centuries Jews were important members of the city's business and professional elite. In the middle of the nineteenth century a fair number of German Jews came to America. They too prospered, in commerce and banking especially.

Then, in the late nineteenth century, came the deluge. Catastrophies like the Polish famine of 1869 led many east European Jews to immigrate. The rise of anti-Semitism, in the Russian empire especially, moved others. Their condition was made worse by industrialization, which undermined the crafts and trades in which Jews had been prominent since the Middle Ages. Barred by law from many professions and occupations and frequently from universities too, ambitious Jews could not adjust to changing conditions or respond effectively to secular enthusiasms animating the young. Socialism, Zionism, and immigration were the natural consequences of all this. Whether out of frustrated ambition or despair, east European Jews came to America by the hundreds of thousands from the 1880s to 1914.

Here they were discriminated against more than most other immigrants, but they found opportunities anyway. No one could be kept out of the retail trades or the many small manufacturing establishments, sweatshops mostly, that New York abounded in. Making cigars, kitchenware, artificial flowers, and garments was no challenge to hard, dexterous workers, and doing so did not mean breaking any religious customs. This was especially true of the garment trades. In 1913 there were 16,500 clothing "factories" with 312,000 employees. The average was about five workers to a shop. In terms of hours, wages, and working conditions, the garment trade, like other sweated industries, was a scandal. Women and children worked sixty or seventy hours a week for a few dollars. But the subcontracting system on which the sweated industries were based drew a thin line between boss and worker. With very little capital one could buy or rent a few machines and start a shop at home. Many sweatshops were in fact cottage industries where the family slaved together. But by plowing their small earnings back into their businesses, they were able eventually to move their shops outside their homes and create real businesses.

This was an avenue that many Jews took. Others bought small stores or acquired rental property in the same painful way. A further road to advancement stemmed from the fact that most professions still did not require academic degrees, so it was possible for a young man willing to work hard to become certified as a lawyer or an accountant. The reform of medical education which reduced the number of schools and made ethnic quota systems more effective was just starting, so many Jews became physicians, often with help from their families. Between 1897 and 1907 the number of Jewish physicians on the lower East Side of Manhattan doubled and the rate of increase for pharmacists, dentists, and the like was even greater. Upward mobility was so rapid that, whereas in 1892, 75 percent of New York's Jews lived in the lower East Side ghetto, by 1916 only 23 percent did so. No other large racial or ethnic group ever bettered itself so rapidly.

The question then is why, since these opportunities were open to all, they were not exploited by all. The answer lies in the peculiar background of Jews as compared with other elements of the new immigration. Most other new immigrants came from peasant cultures. They were used to hard work but not to handling money, living in a city, changing status, moving physically, and all the other things that success in a capitalist system entails. They did create institutions of their own, but these were mainly inward-looking and conservative. The (usually Catholic) church and the lodge provided psychological support. These helped the immigrant to survive, but were not of much use in helping him to get ahead. Jews, however, had a different experience which prepared them for life under capitalism. Having been kept from owning land for many centuries, Jews had been forced into trade and commerce. They were merchants and money men in traditional agricultural societies. Thus they knew the great secret of capitalism, which is that money lives. Peasants typically cannot understand this. When they make a profit, it is hidden in the mattress or buried under the floor. The peasant works hard for little money, and what he makes is not invested except, if he owns his farm, in it. His aim is not to rise but to improve what he has. The businessman, on the other hand, knowing that money lives, makes it multiply. He thinks of money not as something to save for a rainy day but as capital which must be invested so as to make it grow.

Jews had other advantages also. Their long oppression made them experts in group survival. Peasants cannot think much beyond the family or at best the village, whereas Jews knew that they must help themselves collectively. Hence, in New York, they built a great infrastructure of trade unions, benevolent societies, political organizations, and the like for self-help and self-protection. Jews came from many different countries, and often the fact of being Jewish was all they had in common. But many did know Yiddish, which became the lingua franca of the lower East Side and enabled Jews of varied origins to live and work together. It was the medium for a rich cultural life that helped unify the community. Yiddish books and newspapers were printed and a lively Yiddish theatre blossomed. In fact, Yiddish culture flourished more richly in New York than anywhere in Europe.

Jews were helped also by their dietary laws. Ritual cleanliness meant that meats had to be inspected and foods carefully prepared. The great emphasis on purification and cleanliness made the lower East Side, though the most congested spot on earth, among the healthiest neighborhoods in Manhattan. It was pretty bad, however, and there were "lung blocks" in the ghetto as elsewhere that were notorious for the high death rate from tuberculosis. But cleanliness still gave Jews an edge.

Their political sophistication was important too. Other immigrants were led by politicians who provided services but little hope, vision, or prospect of change. But the Jews built one of the best political organizations in the country on a socialist base, sending Meyer London to Congress and electing many local officials too. The Socialist party of the lower East Side was not able to markedly improve the environment, yet it was another source of inspiration, morale, and solidarity for the ghetto. Except Milwaukee, no urban center was so thoroughly radicalized as the lower East Side. Nowhere else was an immigrant community so well organized on every level.

The ghetto was desperately poor, but while it lasted it had a vibrancy and a unique spirit and culture such as has never been seen before or since in America. This is not to make life there seem easy. The climb upward was desperate and painful; many perished along the way or wore out their lives to little profit. There were intense conflicts within the community, between the generations, and between the secular radicals—socialists and

Zionists especially—and the orthodox believers, who were as inward-looking as any religious group in the country. Still and all, the ghetto was an extraordinary place in its own right, and all the more so for the adversities overcome in building a community there. The irony is that success ruined it. The very qualities which enabled Jews to make the ghetto work were what helped them escape it. As their incomes rose, the Jews moved out. Only a minority were left by World War I, and later they vanished also. As the Jews dispersed, the community's cultural life withered. Younger generations did not know Yiddish, so less was written in it, and great ethnic publications like the *Jewish Daily Forward* declined or fell, as did secular publications such as the socialist *Daily Call* that depended on Jewish radicals.

Of this entire experience little remains. New York Jews are now like Jews in other cities, most having risen and so lost much of what once made them distinctive, the good and the bad alike. The Jews built a counterculture in New York more impressive than anything that went by that name later, but now they epitomize rather than confront the dominant culture. If no one regrets having lost the poverty and misery of the ghetto, the good that died with it is worth mourning still. Success has a price, and Jews paid more than most for it.

If the history of New York's Jewish ghetto illustrates the familiar American experience of prosperity undermining radical and spiritual values (for orthodoxy diminished too), it shows even more clearly why most new immigrants did poorly. American society was not, as people always called it, a great melting pot but a vessel in which the social elements remained suspended, each retaining its own traits. Even today Jews live near each other when possible and most intermar-

ry, as do other racial, religious, and ethnic groups. The national wealth is still unevenly distributed. The descendants of southern and eastern European peasants are closer to the bottom than the top. Thus, while the Jewish experience is instructive, that is mainly because it was so unusual. America for Jews was a promised land. For white, gentile ethnics and for racial minorities even more, it was something less.

The black experience

The great failure of Southern Reconstruction stemmed from the fact that although Congress had the power to compensate freedmen for their years of slavery, it lacked the will. Thus, while blacks were able to vote and hold office after the Civil War, very few acquired enough property to protect themselves when Bourbon rule was restored. Had Congress given every black family "40 acres and a mule" as was hoped, things might have been different. But without land or the money to buy it, most freedmen became tenant farmers or sharecroppers who survived on credit and were forever in debt, which became the bondage that replaced slavery. Public education was poor in the South for both black and white. Penniless families needed their children in the fields and could not afford to send them to school, even when there was one available. After Reconstruction, politicians often stirred up racist feelings for personal gain. The inability of Southern Populists to organize a poor black-poor white coalition that could beat the Bourbons led to even stricter segregation laws. Many blacks who had been allowed to vote until the 1890s were disenfranchised thereafter.

As blacks were so miserable and oppressed and so easily murdered if they stepped out of line, it was inevitable that black leaders would call on their people to accept these limits and do what they could within them. By far the best-known accommodationist leader was Booker T. Washington, who became the most famous black of his time. Washington was born in slavery, attended a black vocational institute in Virginia, taught school, and made a name for himself in black educational circles. When Alabama founded a normal school at Tuskegee in 1881, Washington became its first head. He made the Normal and Industrial School for Negroes a respected vocational school. His own reputation was assured by a speech at the Atlanta Exposition of 1895, where he said in effect that blacks would tolerate segregation and disenfranchisement in return for better treatment and more opportunities. Help my people educate themselves, he said, and "you will find that they will buy your surplus land, make bloom the waste places in your fields, and run your factories. While doing this you can be sure in the future, as in the past, that you will be surrounded by the most patient, law-abiding and unresentful people the world has ever seen."

Because of black powerlessness, Washington had little choice but to accept the status quo. Blacks were lynched by the score every year for trivial offenses against the white code of racial etiquette. Washington had a school to run that only whites could pay for. The trouble was that while accommodation was essential, it did not work. Washington was admired by whites for telling them what they wanted to hear, so Tuskegee was showered with money by Northern philanthropists—Andrew Carnegie alone gave it $600,000. But otherwise things got worse for blacks. From 1889 to 1899 there were an average of 187.5 lynchings a year, an increasing percentage of the victims being

Figure 14-3   Jack Johnson beating Jim Jeffries, one of many "white hopes" who failed in their duty to defend Caucasian honor by regaining the heavyweight championship of the world. (*The Bettmann Archive*)

blacks. Moreover, blacks were shut out of the very trades Tuskegee prepared them for. Washington encouraged blacks to become carpenters, printers, and bricklayers. Yet while black artisans had outnumbered Southern whites in 1865 by about five to one, they almost disappeared afterward. In New Orleans there were 3,460 black artisans in 1870 and only a tenth that number in 1904, though the black population had grown by 50 percent. Even if they could have gotten work as artisans, some black leaders would still have thought Washington's aim too low and that blacks needed intellectuals and professional men to lead them. And some believed Washington went further than he had to in currying favor with rich, conservative white men. Washington was fond of observing that the black did not strike and was not unionized, which made him a cheap and dependable worker. Unlike immigrants with their uncouth politics and radical philosophies, blacks were docile and safe, Washington pointed out. To other black leaders this was precisely the trouble.

His chief critic among blacks was W. E. B. DuBois, who was born in Massachusetts, educated at Fisk and Harvard, and who taught sociology at Atlanta University thereafter. DuBois wrote many monographs on the condition of blacks, and then in 1903 he produced *The Souls of Black Folks,* a collection of militant and sometimes poetic essays and reflections that made him preeminent among black intellectuals. Up to then he had not been very critical of Washington, but DuBois always wanted to concentrate black energies on training the brightest youngsters, the "talented tenth" he called them, instead of spending so much time and money on vocational education. Like Washington, DuBois believed in self-help and understood that, in the South especially, it was fatal to antagonize whites. But gradually DuBois came to

feel that Washington went too far in accommodating himself to white prejudices and that blacks had to defend their rights and dignity as best they could. And he resented Washington's stranglehold on white philanthropic donations to blacks. For about a dozen years, until around 1912, DuBois felt that the "Tuskegee Machine" had a veto power over nearly all financial contributions—which Washington used to discourage blacks with ideas contrary to his own.

DuBois attacked Washington in *The Souls of Black Folks,* and 1905 he organized the Niagara Movement of black intellectuals. It urged blacks to reject accommodationism, fight for their rights, and stop automatically voting Republican. DuBois wanted blacks to make both parties compete for their votes, but he was unsuccessful. Even in the Depression when blacks started voting Democratic, they moved over in a block rather than playing the two parties off against each other. In 1910 DuBois became Director of Research and Publications for the newly established National Association for the Advancment of Colored People, an offspring of the National Negro Committee formed in 1909 at the behest of Mary White Ovington.

Ovington was a white social worker who had lived in the black slums of New York City. Though small (only 60,000 blacks lived in New York then), these slums were terrible. She persuaded William English Walling, a socialist intellectual, Charles Edward Russell, a socialist journalist, and Oswald Garrison Villard, a famous publisher and reformer, among others, that a national civil rights organization was urgently needed. At first the NAACP could do nothing more than publicize the black condition and refute racial slurs. This meant that DuBois, though the only black in the organization at first, was also its most important member. *The Crisis,* its magazine, was the NAACP's principal weapon for a long time; and as DuBois was its editor, it reflected his views.

In the Progressive era civil rights work was extraordinarily difficult and unrewarding. Many books were written showing Caucasians to be the master race. Between 1900 and 1911 ten southern states elaborated their segregation laws. In 1913 a movement began in North Carolina to segregate farmlands. Wilson's election made things even worse. A Southerner himself, Wilson appointed many more Southerners to government jobs. Blacks were fired from the Treasury and the Post Office. Segregation was introduced in government offices "for safety's sake," Wilson explained. And there were periodic race riots—as in Atlanta in 1906, where one white man and twenty-six blacks were killed and hundreds more injured. All the same blacks were probably slightly better off than in the 1890s, chiefly because lynchings declined to somewhat more than a hundred a year.

Women's rights

Yet to concentrate solely on the failures and missed opportunities of the Progressive era is to miss what made the period exciting. Intellectually it was the most stimulating age since before the Civil War—a time for questioning and revising the assumptions of social Darwinism, classical economics, and laissez faire. The reform movements were real if limited. Both popular culture and the fine arts went through important changes. When in 1912 the Irish painter John Butler Yeats said that the fiddles were tuning up all over America, he reflected the confidence and enthusiasm felt by millions. If both were often misplaced, the sentiments themselves were genuine enough.

Perhaps no group had more vitality than feminists, for whom this was a golden age.

Feminism in general and woman suffrage particularly had made modest advances in the late nineteenth century. The two suffrage organizations of that period were reunited in 1890 as the National American Woman Suffrage Association (NAWSA). A few Western territories enfranchised women, and in 1890, when Wyoming entered the union, its women became the first to vote in national elections. Some effort was made to deny Wyoming admission until it abolished woman suffrage, but Wyoming instructed its delegation that the state would enter with its women or not at all. Two decades later most American women still lacked the vote. Their power grew all the same. For one thing, women organized during the Progressive era as never before, and in 1888 the National Council of Women was established. In 1890 the General Federation of Women's Clubs (GFWC) began bringing scattered clubs together, and by 1892 it had 20,000 members. By 1900 maybe 150,000 women belonged to the GFWC. A dozen years later the figure was closer to a million.

Though always subject to ridicule, women's clubs played a crucial role in the woman movement (as members most often called it at the time). They organized timid or conservative women who could not be reached in other ways, and they increasingly used their influence to effect civic reforms, especially where education, sanitation, child welfare, and related matters were concerned. After 1900 they also functioned as a national lobby and helped advance conservation, combat child labor, and the like. In 1914 the GFWC endorsed woman suffrage, thus openly admitting that it was a feminist organization (as its national officers had been for some time). It was not solely concerned with women's rights, like the NAWSA, but it was one of many social feminist groups—so called because of an interest in other issues besides the woman question.

Other large women's organizations with a social feminist element included the Women's Christian Temperance Union, the most powerful of all women's groups in the 1890s. Even the Daughters of the American Revolution (1890) had some interest in reform before World War I. In 1897 the National Congress of Parents and Teachers was founded to give shape to the growing PTA movement. In 1899 the National Consumers' League began organizing middle- and upper-class women against the abuse of working women and children. The majority of important women's organizations were created between 1890 and 1910. In one sense this paralleled the organization of men in service clubs, lodges, trade and professional associations, and such during the period. But it was also a response to the peculiar problems of women.

Some of these were a consequence of economic growth—more women were working. They made up a sixth of the work force in 1890. Also, more went to college—by 1920 a majority of undergraduates were women, and many of these became professional workers (about 35 to 40 percent of all professional workers were women at any given time after 1890). All working women, whether college teachers or clerks, had certain problems in common—unequal pay for equal work, job discrimination, and such. All were not equally able to help themselves, however. College graduates and professionals were most organized, women workers least. College women had the Association of Collegiate Alumnae (later the American Association of University Women) and, after World War I, the General Federation of Business and Professional Women's Clubs. They also frequently organized within the professions. Most unions were not interested in organizing working women, but middle-class women in the settlements and especially in the Women's

Trade Union League (1903) did try to help their working-class sisters. For the most part, however, feminism remained a movement of middle-class women even when it was concerned with working-class issues.

Social feminism was especially a product of affluence. This is not to say that most active women were rich but rather that it was the growing wealth of America that enabled so many to go to college and created such a large class of women with time to spare for volunteer work. Few became fulltime activists on the order of Jane Addams, Florence Kelley, and other heroic members of that brilliant generation which made American women envied around the world. Fewer still became fulltime feminists. But millions did participate in activities that reflected their social consciousness, if only as clubwomen. This was the constituency on which feminism was built.

Though social feminism was by far the largest part of women's public work in the Progressive era, the suffrage campaign was more glamorous and compelling. Yet the suffrage flower was late in blooming. In 1912, when great numbers of women were involved in socially worthwhile enterprises, only a handful belonged to the NAWSA. Theodore Roosevelt remarked comfortably at the time that he favored woman suffrage but did not think it an important issue or that many women wanted it. If they ever asked for the vote, he was certain they would be enfranchised. Yet only a few years later hundreds of thousands were demanding the vote, and less than decade later they got it.

Two things seem responsible for this sudden shift in feminine sentiment. One was the growing conviction among active women that they could not get the social reforms they wanted without the ballot, but this was in fact a spurious argument. Women had been voting in Colorado since 1893 with negligible results; and that state, though thinly settled (it had one major city and some industry), was more typical of the country as a whole than most Western states. Workingmen had been voting for a long time and no one felt their interests were much better served in consequence. But many were convinced all the same that women's votes would carry the social welfare movement to victory, and few social feminists wanted suffrage for what it would do for them. Perhaps no great reform since antislavery had been advanced for less selfish reasons.

Women also wanted the vote because withholding it insulted them. The rhetoric of antisuffragists not only said plainly that women were not fit to vote but it implied, as one male feminist remarked, that they were scarecely fit to live. This was offensive enough in itself. Contempt for women was even less palatable when expressed physically.

Alice Paul's main achievement was to provide this demonstration. A graduate of Swarthmore College, Miss Paul studied and did social work in England, where she was converted by the Pankhursts to militant feminism. Emmeline Pankhurst and her daughters, Christabel especially, began as orthodox feminists but, having concluded that men would never give them the vote, they resorted increasingly to violent demonstrations, sabotage, arson, and other crimes. When arrested, they went on hunger strikes. This presented the government with a choice between force-feeding them, which made them martyrs, or of releasing them to resume their old ways. Alice Paul meant to imitate them in America. On her return in 1912 she joined the NAWSA and went to Washington to revive the campaign for a constitutional amendment that would enfranchise women at one stroke. This

Figure 14-4 The ivory tower. College women in 1898. (*Culver Pictures*)

was not a new approach, but it had been neglected for years in favor of state-by-state campaigns. Few of these had succeeded, so the time was ripe for a national strategy.

She secured it by staging a demonstration to coincide with the inauguration of President Woodrow Wilson in 1913. Because the demonstrators were attacked by mobs of rowdies, Miss Paul and her handful of followers became celebrities and women everywhere were outraged by this display of male boorishness. Miss Paul had to leave the NAWSA for ignoring its policies and few joined her new organization, the Congressional Union (later the Woman's party). But increasingly women demanded the vote and saw a national strategy as the best way to get it. The militants' vigor contrasted sharply with the NAWSA's incompetence and led more conventional suffragists to demand new leadership. So Dr. Anna Howard Shaw, a formidable person and compelling orator but a poor manager, resigned in favor of Carrie Chapman Catt.

Mrs. Catt had served briefly as president of the NAWSA (succeeding Susan B. Anthony), and later became head of the International Woman Suffrage Alliance and the New York woman suffrage movement. She made New York the most dynamic and effective of the state organizations and nearly led it to victory in 1915. She became president of the NAWSA that year, but the momentum she had already given New York women enabled them to win the vote in 1917. In a few short years she expanded the NAWSA into the largest independent political movement in American history. Millions of women contributed to final victory in one way or another. During the war Congress was persuaded by a string of state victories to pass the Nineteenth Amendment and, after hard-fought ratification campaigns in many states, it became law in 1920. Thereafter the woman movement collapsed.

There were many reasons for this denouement. For one, it soon became clear that the vote had been oversold. Women were told that all sorts of reforms would follow in its wake, but none did. Not many women were elected to office and few of them worked for peace, social welfare, and the other causes which woman suffrage was supposed to advance. This retroactively discredited the movement. Secondly, enfranchisement had little effect on the lives of most women. It became clear that the vote as a symbol had been more important than the vote as a fact. While suffrage was an issue, the differences between women were obscured. Afterward, it became clear that women divided as men did, along racial and class lines, for example. Women were still nearly as discriminated against and disadvantaged as before and social needs were as great, but the high morale which had sustained suffragists and social feminists alike was gone. After 1929 liberalism came back, but women had to wait nearly half a century to see their movement revive again.

Culture

The cultural life of this age, both high and low, was notable for features that are with us yet; but more striking still are the things that make this a time long past. By the early 1920s American life was sufficiently "modern" so that we need make no great imaginative leap to understand it. But go back a few years and things seem a little out of focus or perhaps unformed. Most people move on rails instead of rubber tires. The language is subtly different. Colloquialism are rarely used in print, and then self-consciously. In his entire lifetime a man might never see a bare feminine leg. Art is as decorous as life except that, by custom, nude paintings and statues are allowed. Even so, artists sometimes run afoul of Anthony Comstock, the great censor, for works that posterity would find innocent enough. Sex is not talked about except when disguised or denounced. Architects still mostly copy classic or traditional styles.

But maybe the strangest thing of all is that adolescence does not yet exist. That long intermediate stage between childhood and maturity which has obsessed America for the past half-century is largely a post-World War I phenomenon. In the Progressive era most children had left school by the age of fourteen; no special provisions were made for them, and they grew quietly into adulthood. Few went to high school; fewer still to college. In 1900 only 4 percent of the college-age group was actually enrolled. Dropouts below the age of sixteen who worked were known as *child* laborers. But when they reached sixteen they lost this designation and simply became workers. High school and college students were, in effect, treated as children. No one thought of students as responsible individuals, and indeed many were not. But college students at least had a rich extracurricular life that compensated them for the strict system of rewards and penalties in force everywhere. Except for the handful who would go on to professional and graduate schools (and there were not even 6,000 graduate students in 1900), most students had no particular reason for being in college.

They were more like draftees than volun-

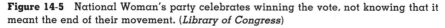

Figure 14-5 National Woman's party celebrates winning the vote, not knowing that it meant the end of their movement. (*Library of Congress*)

teers, and strict rules were needed to keep them in line. In the 1880s Harvard relaxed attendance requirements, only to tighten them again when students were found to be taking extended vacations in New York and, in at least one case, Havana. The universities had changed greatly by the turn of the century, but undergraduates were much the same as ever, though somewhat less rowdy. Their chief contributions to the new order were ever more elaborate customs and traditions, social organizations, and athletic contests—the whole being known as "college life." Still, students did not have much effect on the larger society. It was not until the 1920s that the leisure class of high school and college students would become large enough for adolescence to be recognized as a distinct stage of development. The youth culture was as yet unborn.

The popular culture was, however, well launched. In 1903 *The Great Train Robbery,* a twelve-minute epic, took moving pictures out of the novelty class. Within five years, 5-cent theaters, called nickelodeons, were in business. By 1914 Southern California alone had fifty-two movie companies waging a desperate struggle for this vast new market. Hollywood owed its rise to Thomas A. Edison, who in 1909 organized a trust called the Motion Pictures Patents Company. The trust enhanced its control of key patents by bullying independent producers, some of whom were unable to buy cameras or film while others had mysterious fires and accidents or lost shooting time when scenes broke into fistfights. In 1909 gunmen shot up an independent set, wounding five actors.

Independents went to Hollywood not only for the weather but to escape the trust. Then too, Mexico was only a hundred miles away should a foreign refuge be needed. The violence continued for a time anyway. When Cecil B. DeMille came to Hollywood in 1913

to direct his first movie, he was shot at twice by snipers and had the master copy of his film burned. Movies were worth the risk though. By 1916, twenty-five million people a day spent anywhere from a nickel to a quarter on the "flickers." The industry had produced its first superstars (Charlie Chaplin and Mary Pickford), its first geniuses (Charlie Chaplin and D. W. Griffith), its first comedians (Charlie Chaplin, Fatty Arbuckle, Ben Turpin, the Keystone Kops, etc., etc.), and its first sex symbol (Theda Bara). Griffith produced two great films, *Birth of a Nation* and *Intolerance,* before the World War. By then Chaplin was making more than $\$1/2$ million a year and producers were spending as much as \$2 million on a single film (*Intolerance*).

People reacted to movies then exactly as they have ever since. The poet Vachel Lindsay hailed Edison as a "new Gutenberg" and wrote a book glorifying the medium. Jane Addams commented extensively in her *The Spirit of Youth and the City Streets* (1909) on the bad effects of movies. She worried especially about the vulgarity and violence of these films and the warped vision of life they projected. After *Raffles the Amateur Cracksman* played in Chicago, she said thirteen youngsters were arrested with kits of burglar tools. Many thought the sensual films of Theda Bara ("the Vamp") and Gloria Swanson immoral, as indeed they were by Victorian standards. Perhaps nothing contributed more to the decline of Victorian sexual morals than movies. Films were the first truly mass media, harbingers of the world we live in now. Their greatest influence was still to come, but even before 1920 they had done much to undermine late Victorian culture.

By comparison, large-circulation magazines, popular music, and the like, though they reached millions, had a negligible influence. Magazines such as *Colliers, The Saturday Evening Post, Good Housekeeping,* and *The Ladies Home Journal* then, as in most cases now, did not form tastes and values, being too cautious and imitative. Popular songs like "Sweet Adeline," "In the Good Old Summertime," and "You're a Grand Old Flag" could not, by their nature, have much cultural resonance. It was not until the coming of jazz that popular music could be taken seriously. But the movies were doing their work all the same, as were automobiles, telephones, and the other artifacts of modern life. A real cultural revolution was brewing, though that would not be fully apparent for a while.

The revolution in mass culture was matched by equally striking changes in bourgeois culture. As perfected in the late nineteenth century, middle-class culture rested upon three pillars: the certainty and universality of moral values; the inevitability, especially in America, of progress; and the importance of literature. None of these had been easily arrived at or maintained without effort, but as late as 1912 they were still intact. The primacy of moral values was especially hard to protect against industrialization, the rise of robber barons, and Darwinism. But the thing was managed by incorporating evolution into Christianity so that evolution became not only compatible with God but, in a sense, God Himself. The god of the social gospel was evolutionary and scientific, like the new middle class that worshipped him. Several problems remained, however, even after this feat had been accomplished. The lower classes were untouched by these doctrines and worse still, they made religion dependent on history. While events seemed to be moving in a progressive direction, religion was safe. But a downward turn could ruin a faith which was now hostage to fortune.

Middle-class people, like Communists later, knew history was moving in their direction,

Figure 14-6 Hollywood's Theda Bara, who was called the Vamp because of her seductiveness. (*Culver Pictures*)

but, as did Leninists again, they believed in helping events along. At first evolution was thought to be automatic. By the Progressive era, however, people had come to believe that progress could be helped along. They were essentially satisfied with the status quo but—thanks to muckrakers and sometimes even radicals—they knew that certain abuses, the products mainly of individual wickedness, needed correction. As Henry F. May says, Progressives were people who wanted to make a number of sharp changes

because they were so confident of the rightness of things as they were.

The weakest of their values was traditional literature. By *literature* people meant English writings for the most part, especially obvious moralists like Tennyson and Mathew Arnold. History was still seen as the transmission of Protestant ideas and Anglo-Saxon culture. Roosevelt said "the greatest historian should also be a great moralist." Emerson and Whittier were the most admired American writers. Poe and Hawthorne were underrated and

Figure 14-7 A scene from D. W. Griffith's masterpiece *Intolerance,* his apology for having seemed to glorify bigotry in *The Birth of a Nation. (Culver Pictures)*

Melville ignored. These prejudices were buttressed by the colleges; such great publishing houses as Scribners, Harper's, and Putnam; and by solid weekly and monthly magazines like the *Nation,* the *North American Review,* and the *Century.*

Woodrow Wilson's election was the genteel tradition's finest moment. Wilson, the scholar in politics, embodied all that the bourgeois held most dear. His election seemed to show the strength and popularity of their principles. In fact, it was more a confirmation of Parkinson's law than anything else. Parkinson holds that institutions build their most splendid monuments after peaking out: for example, St. Peter's was erected by a declining papacy, not a rising one. Wilson was elected just when the genteel tradition had begun to fade. One fatal weakness was that it excluded too many groups—farmers, blacks, immigrants, and fundamentalists. Nor were the business classes much influenced by it. Sublimely confident as a group, businessmen worshipped efficiency most of all. The enthusiasm for scientific management as preached by Frederick W. Taylor expressed a deep faith that there was one right answer for every question, and that the most efficient. Universities, even many churches, joined the efficiency craze, sometimes at their peril. For if efficiency was the gauge of morality, then traditional morals had to be revised. The relativistic social sciences were dangerous too. Though dominated by men who believed both in morality and progress, the social sciences had a way of making progress the standard of morality.

Still more serious than these internal problems were the threats from outside. Even at its peak genteel culture remained suspect in the eyes of conservative pessimists like Henry Adams and, later, H. L. Mencken. Naturalist writers, especially Theodore Dreiser, were

outside the bourgeois consensus too; and foreign amoralists like Baudelaire and Oscar Wilde even more so. After 1910 domestic liberators and cultural rebels added a native force to alien ideas. The new science, especially Einstein's physics, undermined the Enlightenment view of the universe as unified, coherent, and understandable. Henri Bergson's vitalism, H. G. Wells's socialism, and finally—the strongest force of all—Freudianism were even more destructive. The young artists and intellectuals who rejected traditionalism were not themselves pessimistic or amoral, however much they admired Europeans who were. Henry F. May calls their movement "the innocent rebellion," because it was, among other things, cheerfully romantic. The rebels and liberators believed that life transcended thought and that life was open-ended and various. What they disliked most about traditional culture was precisely its ties to the past. Dogma was out, and the fear of change with it. Possibility was all.

In a few short years they had their way. The first rebellious painters were often called the Ashcan school for vividly depicting homely urban scenes. Then in 1913, the famous Armory show demonstrated to American artists how far ahead Europe was. Its expressionists, primitives, cubists, abstract sculptors, and so on had moved art light years beyond Victorian conventions—and this alone was liberating enough for some. Poetry changed radically too. In 1912 *Poetry* magazine was founded in Chicago to print what was too radical in form or content for established magazines. In 1915 it published T. S. Eliot's "The Love Song of J. Alfred Prufrock." In 1913 Ezra Pound and Amy Lowell launched the imagist movement, one of the first of many poetic schools that violated people's sense of what a poem was. New York was the chief port of entry for avant-garde art and soon

Figure 14-8 Marcel Duchamp's "Nude Descending a Staircase," part of the great Armory show of 1913, which introduced America to modern art. (*Culver Pictures*)

replaced Chicago as the headquarters of domestic cultural radicalism. The *Masses*—the most successful effort to unite art with revolutionary politics—was published there. The amateur Provincetown Players were the first in New York to perform Eugene O'Neill's rough plays. Young publishers such as Alfred A. Knopf brought out books traditional houses refused to touch. Intellectuals like Walter Lippmann began synthesizing those ideas that were submerging the old landmarks of thought and culture. Not since the 1830s had so much talent surfaced at once, and nearly all of it was hostile to the old, responsive to the new.

Even before the war custodians of traditional culture were fighting a losing battle. American entry finished them off. As May says, "The principles of moralism, progress, and culture, already linked disastrously to snobbery, racial pride, and prudery, were linked now to the Wilsonian version of the Allied cause. Inevitably, the country was to turn against both." Traditional culture was fatally wedded to the Allied effort partly because it was Anglophile to begin with but mainly because—for people like Robert Herrick, Ralph Barton Perry, and Barrett Wendell—the war was not so much in defense of the national interest as of those principles under assault at home. They were eager to divide everyone the world over into virtuous guardians and moral, sexual, and racial insurrectionists. American intervention was supported by WASPS but frequently resisted by those outside the dominant minority. The social gospellers endorsed it almost to a man. Fundamentalists saw it as yet another proof of the failure of liberal culture. Though some were pro-German and others pro-Allied, most young members of the cultural rebellion were simply dismayed. The war made a shambles of their cheerful optimism, just as it ruined the traditional faith in universal morality and progress.

But unlike traditionalists, who did not have much else to fall back on when their faith was mocked by events, the rebels had at least their culture. Both radicals and reactionaries lost their innocence in 1917 when the old bourgeois world came to an end, but they did not suffer equally. Avant-garde culture flowered more brilliantly after the war than ever. If it was also more bitter, aimless, and apolitical, this was not the worst price to pay for lost illusions. When the old culture was destroyed, Progressivism died entirely. It could not survive without progress and morality. Most of all, it was based on a sentimental idealism that had been wholly discredited.

Thus by 1917 or 1918 American life had changed for good. Largely this was a consequence of forces long in the making. Technology, urbanization, and increasing levels of productivity were transforming the physical, social, and economic environment and the mass culture that increasingly shaped people's private lives. Intellectual and artistic changes replaced the genteel tradition. Modern life was coming into being for these reasons, among others, and would have done so without the war. But it was decisive in many respects. It accelerated some changes and put an end to others. When it was over our world was substantially complete. To understand that world we must understand the war experience that was midwife to its birth.

Selected references

On the early years, George E. Mowry, *The Era of Theodore Roosevelt, 1900–1912* (1958), is standard. The greatest work of political history dealing with this period is Arthur S. Link's magisterial biography of Wilson, of which volume two, *Wilson: The New Freedom* (1956), is especially helpful. Many younger historians disagree with Link's traditional point of view, but his scholarship is of such a high order that the biography cannot be ignored. Richard Hofstadter, *The Age of Reform* (1955), interprets Progressivism in terms of status politics, a concept that younger historians also reject for the most part. All the same, it is a rich, speculative book that repays close reading. The following newer histories are especially important: Robert H. Wiebe, *Businessmen and Reform* (1962) and particularly *The Search for Order, 1877–1920* (1967); Gabriel Kolko, *The Triumph of Conservatism* (1963); Samuel P. Hays, *Conservation and the Gospel of Efficiency* (1959), a more significant book than its title suggests; and James Weinstein, *The Corporate Ideal in the Liberal State, 1900–1918* (1968). A provocative essay is Martin J. Sklar, "Woodrow Wilson and the Political Economy of Modern United States Liberalism," in Ronald Radosh and Murray N. Rothbard (eds.), *A New History of Leviathan* (1972).

A sympathetic biography of Emma Goldman is Richard Drinnon, *Rebel in Paradise* (1961). The standard work on the AFL is Philip Taft, *The A F of L in the Time of Gompers* (1957). Though prejudiced in favor of the right wing, Daniel Bell's book-length essay "The Background and Development of Marxian Socialism in the United States," in Egbert and Persons (eds.), *Socialism and American Life*, vol. 1 (1952), is important. A more neutral view is David A. Shannon, *The Socialist Party of America* (1955). James Weinstein, *The Decline of Socialism in America, 1912–1925* (1967), challenges the usual judgment that socialism began to fail before World War I. An excellent biography of Eugene V. Debs is Ray Giner, *The Bending Cross* (1949). Melvyn Dubofsky, *We Shall Be All: A History of the*

IWW (1969), is exemplary. Of the six volumes in the Pittsburgh Survey, John A. Fitch, *The Steel Workers* (1910), is particularly good.

The key essay on urban reformers in this period is Samuel P. Hays, "The Politics of Reform in Municipal Government," *Pacific Northwest Quarterly* (October 1964). Roy Lubove, *The Progressives and the Slums: Tenement House Reform in New York City, 1890–1917* (1962), is very useful. The best book on settlements is Allen F. Davis, *Spearheads for Reform* (1967). Also indispensable is the classic Jane Addams, *Twenty Years at Hull House* (1910). An outstanding ethnic history is Moses Rischin, *The Promised City: New York's Jews, 1870–1914* (1962). The standard history of black Americans is John Hope Franklin, *From Slavery to Freedom* (3d. ed., 1967). On feminism, see O'Neill, Flexner, and Aileen Kraditor, *The Ideas of the Woman Suffrage Movement, 1890–1920* (1965). See also Alan P. Grimes, *The Puritan Ethic and Woman Suffrage* (1967). A fascinating study is Garth S. Jowett, *Media Power and Social Control: The Motion Picture in America, 1894–1936* (unpublished Ph.D. dissertation, University of Pennsylvania, 1972). Henry F. May, *The End of American Innocence: A Study of the First Years of Our Own Time, 1912–1917* (1959), is brilliant intellectual history. On the efficiency movement, see Samuel Haber, *Efficiency and Uplift* (1964).

FIFTEEN

The World's Work: Progressive Era Foreign Policy

Period covered:	1900–1921
Emphases:	Diplomacy and politics
Major events:	Revolution in Panama, 1903
	Railroad regulation acts, 1903–1906
	Algeciras Conference, 1906
	Santo Domingo Customs Protectorate, 1906
	Mexican revolution, 1910
	Chinese revolution, 1911
	Occupation of Vera Cruz, 1914
	World War I, 1914
	America declares war, 1917
	Bolshevik Revolution, 1917
	Versailles Conference, 1919

In 1889 a young intellectual, Woodrow Wilson, delivered an address entitled "Make Haste Slowly." His theme was the coincidence of George Washington's inauguration under the new Constitution with the outbreak of the French Revolution. "One hundred years ago we gained, and Europe lost, self-command, self-possession." Twenty-five years later, Wilson, now President of the United States, watched Europe lose self-command and self-possession once again. On December 8, 1914, Wilson reviewed the first few months of the Great War and told Congress that European nations might soon "need our help and our manifold services as they have never needed them before . . . ," for "several of the countries of Europe will find it difficult to do for their people what they have hitherto been always easily able to do, many essential and fundamental things. . . . And we should be ready, more fit and ready than we have ever been."

It was typical of American leaders in the Progressive era to speak of their obligations to the world in the same breath as they spoke of commercial expansion. World War I dramatized both aspects of this world view, but they had always been there. It was also typical of American Progressives to link their reform program with self-command and self-possession and to contrast that program with revolutionary solutions adopted in Mexico, in China, or—most fully—in Russia. It was typical, finally, of these men that they recognized that domestic legislation could no longer be considered solely domestic, in cause or effect, and should be designed to take account of that fact. High on the Progressive agenda, for example, was banking reform. There had been no complete overhaul of the nation's banking system since the Civil War. When Woodrow Wilson called for passage of a Federal Reserve Act in 1913 to accomplish that objective, Secretary of State William Jennings Bryan singled out the provision in the act permitting American banks to establish foreign branches. The Federal Reserve Act, he declared, would "do more to promote trade in foreign lands than any other one thing that has been done in our history."

"The fortunate circumstance of America, my fellow countrymen," President Wilson once explained, "is that it desires nothing but a free field and no favor. Our security is the purity of our motives." That assumption and rationalization underlay much of American foreign policy in those years. All powerful nations and leaders throughout history have given themselves the benefit of the doubt; but none, perhaps, had so few doubts about the power of their own moral certainty, and what it could do to change the world, as did American leaders in the Progressive era. "There is nothing in which I am more interested," Wilson told delegates to a 1914 National Foreign Trade Conference, "than the fullest development of the trade of this country and its *righteous* conquest of foreign markets."

How does one determine America's share of the world's work in the Progressive era? A crude measure can be found in trade statistics, which demonstrate that Americans did indeed make "righteous conquest" of foreign markets a high-priority goal.

Raw statistics are, of course, the most misleading statistics of all, but these figures yield some interesting data. It took the United States a century, for example, to reach a point where it was exporting a billion dollars a year. That happened in 1892. By 1900 it was halfway to the next billion, which it reached in 1911. The big jump came with World War I, but more interesting than the export figure there is the leap in imports, which indicates not just a war boom for arms manufacturers or other special groups but the impact felt gen-

	in millions of dollars		
year	exports	imports	balance
1900	1,499	930	+570
1901	1,605	926	+680
1902	1,480	984	+496
1903	1,511	1,095	+417
1904	1,592	1,118	+474
1905	1,660	1,199	+461
1906	1,848	1,367	+481
1907	1,989	1,592	+397
1908	1,991	1,387	+604
1909	1,810	1,400	+410
1910	1,919	1,646	+273
1911	2,137	1,647	+490
1912	2,327	1,749	+577
1913	2,615	1,923	+692
1914	2,532	1,991	+541
1915	2,966	1,875	+1,091
1916	5,709	3,110	+2,599
1917	6,690	3,558	+3,131
1918	6,443	3,165	+3,278
1919	8,528	4,070	+4,457
1920	8,664	5,784	+2,880

(Source: *The Statistical History of the United States from Colonial Times to the Present*, New York, Horizon Press, 1965, p. 537.)

erally on the economy. Exports never again fell below $2 billion, even in the Great Depression. For better or worse, America was in the world to stay.

T. R. and the doctrine of righteous conquest

Theodore Roosevelt thrived on righteous conquest; he applied the doctrine to recalcitrant corporation presidents at home as well to those who interfered with American progress abroad. He once referred to the Presidency as a bully pulpit, and he loved using it to achieve desired ends. The world recognized T. R.'s achievements when he was awarded one of the first Nobel Peace Prizes for his successful mediation of the Russo-Japanese War. He turned over the prize money to the National Civic Federation, an organization consisting of conservative labor leaders and Progressive-minded capitalists, and dedicated to the promotion of "industrial peace" at home. Ever since the federal government had used troops to put down the railroad strikes of 1877 and sent them to Chicago to end the 1893 Pullman strike, thinking men had worried about the danger of such extreme remedies becoming permanent solutions. In the Reconstruction era, they had witnessed what happens to a nation's institutions when an army occupies a section of the country—even if it is your own army. Would the future struggle between capital and labor bring on a semipermanent reliance on force? Would the American Army occupy the United States?

The depression of the 1890s had stimulated the railroads and manufacturers to adopt various forms of cooperation and combination best summed up in the phrase "the trust movement." Labor unions were also moving toward national organization. In 1901, the age of corporate capitalism arrived with the formation of the United States Steel Corporation, the first billion-dollar business organization in America. Demands for regulation of the trusts, and for their destruction, had reached the halls of Congress. The alternative, said protestors, was industrial war.

Roosevelt warned against dismantling the giant corporations in his first Annual Message to the lawmakers, delivered only a few months after McKinley's assassination: "An additional reason for caution in dealing with corporations is to be found in the international commercial conditions of to-day. The same business conditions which have produced the great aggregations of corporate and individual wealth have made them very potent factors in international commercial competition." Nevertheless, the corporations could not be allowed to ride roughshod over the citizenry—or one another.

How T. R. intended to steer the country through these dangerous waters became apparent in the way he handled the 1902 anthracite coal strike in Pennsylvania. The issues supposedly centered in the miners' demand for higher wages, but beyond that question, as everyone including Roosevelt understood, was the principle of collective bargaining. The owners' position was absolutely clear: "There cannot be two masters in the management of business." As they saw it, recognition of the union meant two masters, each giving orders and each willing to see the other destroyed before yielding.

The strike began in May 1902; as it stretched into September, appeals were made to the President asking for his intervention. But instead of sending troops to quell the dispute, as the owners and their friends had hoped, Roosevelt invited both sides to come to Washington for a discussion of the issues. What did Roosevelt think he was doing? demanded the owners. What could be accomplished except the establishment of a dangerous precedent? T. R. told both sides that he hoped the issues could be settled by an arbitration commission. Union representatives were perfectly agreeable to such a procedure, but the operators denounced the plan and withdrew in a huff. Whereupon T. R. announced he would appoint a commission anyway and use the Army, if necessary, to get the coal out of the ground.

It never came to a showdown because the operators eventually agreed to the commission. Neither side got exactly what it wanted, but the strikers were back in the mines by early November, in time to avoid a nationwide fuel crisis. And T. R. had launched his Square Deal program. In succeeding years regulatory legislation was passed affecting several parts of the economy: New railroad laws were enacted requiring publication of freight rates, prohibiting rebates to favored customers, and authorizing the Interstate Commerce Commission to determine and prescribe maximum rates where complaints had been lodged against the railroads; a Pure Food and Drug Act was passed in 1906, providing for the inspection and federal licensing of meat packers and other producers; and conservation acts and executive orders removed millions of acres of forest and mineral lands from public sale and wasteful exploitation, and initiated a whole conservation movement across the nation. A close friend and adviser, Brooks Adams, wrote the President about railroad regulation in 1903: "I think all conservative men owe you . . . a great debt—for it is your policy or state ownership. There is no middle course. In a word, to live, this country must keep open the highways leading west; at equitable rates, and must command the terminus in Asia—if we fail in this we shall break down." Roosevelt responded: "As you so admirably put it, it is necessary for us to keep the road of trade to the east open. In order to insure our having terminals we must do our best to prevent the shutting to us of the Asian markets. In order to keep the roads to these terminals open we must see that they are managed primarily in the interest . . . of the commerce of the country."

Reform and expansion, he might have written, one and inseparable.

T. R. and the Monroe Doctrine

Another route to the Asian terminus, a sea passage through the Isthmus of Panama in Central America, had become a practical reality by 1900. American efforts to secure such a route by treaty from Colombia had been blocked by that country's legislators, who demanded more money for the right-of-way than the $10 million offered by President Roosevelt and Congress as an outright payment, plus $250,000 annual rental. T. R. later boasted that he had seized the Panama Canal route from those "cut-throats of Bogota," an essentially accurate statement of what happened if not of the character of Colombian legislators.

Officially the Republic of Panama was created by a group of Panamanian nationalists who revolted against Colombian rule; but the conspiracy was planned in the United States and could not have succeeded without American naval and diplomatic support. Along with the desired canal route, however, the United States had gained a protectorate in the Republic of Panama, which now joined Cuba as primary responsibilities of the United States in the Caribbean area. Roosevelt expanded these responsibilities even more in his Annual Messages of 1904 and 1905, which asserted for the United States the right to intervene between any "American Republic" and the rest of the world if and when it became necessary to prevent European seizure of customs houses within such republics, however temporary, to satisfy bad debts. By implication, moreover, he also asserted the right to see to it that Latin Americans behaved themselves in conducting their relations with the outside world. Quite a chunk of the world's work right there.

Santo Domingo, another Caribbean island

country, soon needed attention. "I have about the same desire to annex it," Roosevelt confided, "as a gorged boa constrictor might have to swallow a porcupine wrong-end to." But obligations were obligations, and the United States had assumed responsibility for keeping order in the Western Hemisphere. In this instance the solution was something less than annexation, a customs house receivership was enough, but a pattern of intervention had been established which would last long into the future.

Roosevelt the mediator

After the unpleasantness accompanying the 1895 Venezuelan boundary dispute wore off, Great Britain welcomed the United States into the world of imperial responsibility. Prime Minister Arthur Balfour told T. R.'s close friend Henry Cabot Lodge that Britain was most anxious to have the Panama Canal built, "for he feels that it will strengthen our position enormously and that with England at Suez and the U.S. at Panama we should hold the world in a pretty strong grip." And Colonial Secretary Joseph Chamberlain congratulated the President on the suppression of the Philippine insurgents on similar grounds: "This extension of American influence and dominion will work for the happiness of the native population . . . ," and the "experience in the problems of government under such circumstances will help the American people to understand our world-work, and I hope to sympathize with it."

Americans never completely reciprocated these expressions of good will or agreed that "our world-work" was precisely the same as that being done in London. The British Empire, while clearly a cut, maybe two, above the others, was still a European empire. American ambivalence toward the British Empire surfaced many times in the Progressive era, beginning with the Boer War episode in South Africa. There was tremendous sympathy in America for the underdog Dutch settlers, the Boers, as they fought for independence, but Roosevelt explained that despite his great respect and liking for the Boers, the American government had to support the British: "I think they [the Boers] are battling on the wrong side in the fight for civilization and will have to go under."

In the Far East, it was the Japanese who were leading the fight for civilization, especially against the Russians, for whom Roosevelt had no sympathy at all. The Czar's henchmen had consistently blocked the Open Door policy in Manchuria, thereby incurring the wrath of T. R. and the animosity of all Americans interested in the development of the China trade. Japan was willing to go to war to prevent Russian domination in Manchuria and Korea, and she did so with a surprise attack on the Russian fleet anchored at Port Arthur in February 1904. After Japan's attack on Pearl Harbor in 1941, Americans read back their anger and described both as unwarranted "sneak attacks" ordered by evil emperors against their peace-loving neighbors. At the time, however, Japan was admired for being willing to take on the bully down the street who was making things unpleasant for the entire neighborhood. American bankers even financed the Japanese war effort against Russia.

Exporters and railroad builders had eyed Manchuria—the Minnesota of the Far East—for more than decade. War, even a war against Russia, was disturbing to everyone's plans. Roosevelt offered his services as an honest broker to end the conflict, but not before he had received assurances from Tokyo that Japan would adhere fully to the policy of the Open Door for all nations once the war with Russia ended. St. Petersburg did not welcome American mediation but was in no position to argue the point very long. The war had gone badly, but the Czar had something else to worry about in his own capital: revolution. Even if the delegates from both countries came to Portsmouth, New Hampshire, to sit down with Roosevelt with fingers crossed behind their backs, the President thought he could direct them toward a peace settlement which would balance off Russian and Japanese interests in such a manner as to leave plenty of room for the United States to pursue its commercial goals in China.

For some time Roosevelt had been disturbed about another developing situation. Kaiser Wilhelm of Germany seemed to be going out of his way to provoke the British—by public expressions of sympathy for the Boers and by boasting about a German naval building program—without regard to the possible consequences. Next to Great Britain, most Progressives, including T. R., felt that Germany was the most enlightened of the industrial powers. When the Kaiser then set about disrupting an Anglo-French settlement covering Morocco in North Africa, T. R. became frankly worried about the possibility of war.

It came as a surprise, however, when the Kaiser asked him to mediate this potentially dangerous situation. Citing Roosevelt's peacemaking activities in the Russo-Japanese War and their mutual interests in broadening the application of the Open Door policy to countries other than China, the German ruler pressed for T. R.'s aid. At first the President wanted to decline the honor, fearing he would end up by alienating everyone for nothing. What interests did America have in that small North African territory worth risking his prestige? Several considerations led T. R. to reconsider this decision. First, he genuinely wanted to promote Anglo-German friendship, currently jeopardized by the Kaiser's naval program and a growing tangle of secret alliances. Second, German diplomats pressed the issue as "Open Door" diplomacy versus spheres of influence. Berlin, they said, was only defending the same right of equal access that John Hay had championed for China in his famous Open Door notes of 1899 and 1900. Third, it was already becoming apparent that the United States, if it intended to play a world role, could not always pick and choose among the issues, selecting only those which suited the president's temperament or special talents.

T. R.'s active policy in the Caribbean and Central America, his decision to build a Great White Fleet, and his mediation of the Russo-Japanese War were all more newsworthy. But they were all, in a sense, preliminary to the kind of role the President's representative played during the 1906 Algeciras Conference on Morocco—for the principle of the thing. "The critics in the senate of your policy in causing the U.S. to be represented at the Conference at all," a close friend, diplomat Henry White, congratulated him at its conclusion, "must now admit that it is possible for us to take an important part in a European assemblage . . . and to fully assert our right to equality of rights commercial and economical . . . and yet in nowise to take sides in any of the political questions."

Years later when Woodrow Wilson was contending with the warring powers of Europe for many of the same things, Walter Lippmann, the young editor of the Progressive weekly the *New Republic,* wrote: "Algeciras

grasped the problem of diplomacy—the conflict of empires in weak territory. Algeciras gallantly tried to control it. The men at Algeciras failed. If we cannot succeed where they failed, the outlook for the future is desperate."

They had failed, in Lippmann's view, because traditional balance-of-power diplomacy had not prevented World War I. France and Germany reached an agreement over Morocco, in other words, which only made war more likely over the long run. Maybe so, but T. R. had not failed personally. He had put the United States into the scene, at the forefront of the effort to work out permanent solutions to the colonial rivalries and national problems which threatened the peace.

Taft's nightmares

Roosevelt hand-picked his friend and Cabinet associate, William Howard Taft, to be his successor. Taft believed that he was only carrying out the logic of T. R.'s efforts at Portsmouth and Algeciras when he encouraged a powerful group of American bankers in 1909 to join with European financiers in a plan to secure railroad concessions in China. The bankers had a patriotic duty, Taft's Secretary of State Philander Chase Knox, himself a corporation lawyer, told the lords of Wall Street, to prepare the way for those who would come after, the builders and businessmen who were to make China America's new economic frontier.

Historians have never suspected Philander Knox of the slightest interest in social reform, but his November 1909 proposal to China and the interested powers suggested that the United States do for that country's railroads what T. R. and Congress had done for America's—and for the same reason. Knox suggested that the United States and the other powers loan China the money to buy back earlier concessions and modernize its rail system. "The most effective way," Knox advised the British,

to preserve the undisturbed enjoyment by China of all political rights in Manchuria and to promote the development of those Provinces under a practical application of the policy of the open door and equal commercial opportunity would be to bring the Manchurian highway, the railroads, under an economic, scientific, and impartial administration by some plan vesting in China the ownership of the railroads through funds furnished for that purpose by the interested powers willing to participate.

The rapid economic development of backward nations was bound to take place, wrote Herbert Croly, another *New Republic* editor. Liberal and socialist critics might oppose capitalist methods of doing it, but their opposition did not meet the difficulty. It could only bring about the retirement of the most scrupulous from the competition "and the abandonment of the victim to the unchecked lust of the less scrupulous of the capital-exporting nations." It was a very sophisticated argument indeed. If one accepted Croly's premise, reformers and socialists alike were virtually obliged to support the overseas expansion of American capitalism. Could any socialist do less if he really cared about the foundations of a decent world order? Reformers and socialists often get themselves trapped in this logic.

In this particular instance, it remained an academic argument (at least in these years) because of the overthrow of China's last rulers of the Manchu Dynasty in 1911. That ended Knox's Progressive dream of developing Chinese railroads according to scientific methods and sound banking principles. The turmoil inside China plagued Taft's final days in the White House and was still unresolved when Woodrow Wilson took up Far Eastern questions.

But Taft bequeathed the Wilson administration a far more explosive crisis nearer to home in Mexican-American relations. Long-time Mexican dictator Porfirio Diaz was overthrown in 1910 in a coup d'état led by moderate reformers who wanted only to give their country political democracy. There were several groups of agrarian radicals, however, led by men with more ambitious plans for Mexico's social reorganization. Taft had prayed that the old regime would manage to hold on, at least until he had departed from the White House. When Diaz fell Taft feared the worst. If Mexico started to come apart, the President confided to his wife, American investors would demand intervention. Francisco Madero was a weak leader, bad for Mexico, dangerous for America. A struggle for the soul of the Mexican revolution was soon underway. In early 1913 Madero succumbed to a counterrevolutionary force commanded by one of his own generals, Victoriano Huerta.

The American Ambassador, Henry Lane Wilson, had never had a very high opinion of Madero—a view shared by conservative Mexicans and Americans who lunched with Wilson in the Embassy or dined with him in outside society. Wilson's well-known attitude provided a powerful stimulant to anti-Madero forces on the right. It was not surprising, therefore, that Huerta and Felix Diaz, a nephew of the old dictator, met in the American Embassy after Madero's downfall to seal their alliance, a pact looking toward the restoration of the *ancien regime.* Nor was it surprising that they expected American support, morally and materially. Ambassador Wilson was long suspected of complicity in Madero's assassination, but his guilt or innocence of that charge is less important historically than the fact that the American Embassy had been deeply involved in the larger matter of determining or seeking to determine the shape of the Mexican revolution. By making known his opposition to Madero, Ambassador Wilson had given a green light to counterrevolutionaries. But he had, without meaning to, of course, set free radical forces as well. It was a lesson American policymakers had great difficulty learning over the next half-century, ending with President Ngo Dinh Diem's assassination in 1963.

All these events transpired just as President Taft was about to step across the doorsill out of the White House. Will had never been happy there. Republican insurgents had never given him a moment's rest, not from the beginning, when they attacked the high rates of the 1909 Payne-Aldrich Tariff as a sellout to the special interests. Things got worse after that, almost day by day. Much of the trouble was that T. R. was simply too restless to retire from public life and could be easily persuaded that his successor had abandoned the cause.

Fashioning the slogan "the New Nationalism," T. R. entered the race for the 1912 Republican nomination. Refused a place at the Chicago Convention—it was said that underneath the red, white, and blue bunting around the rostrum was barbed wire to prevent the insurgents from storming the platform—Roosevelt's supporters called their own convention to nominate Teddy by acclamation. Meanwhile the Democrats met and selected their standard bearer, New Jersey Governor Woodrow Wilson. The Socialist party picked Eugene Debs, who would poll nearly a million votes. Wilson ran his cam-

Figure 15-1 Taft was more than ready to turn over the Mexican situation to his successor. Already tangled, Mexico was to provide Wilson with his most persistent foreign policy problem. (*New York Public Library*)

paign against T. R., answering his New Nationalism with a call for "New Freedom" in America.

The crossroads of 1912

Both leading candidates liked to talk about America at the crossroads. As far as the average voter could tell, the New Nationalism promised regulation of the trusts for the general welfare while the New Freedom proposed a return to competition and small enterprise. Such distinctions existed mainly in the imaginations of the protagonists, who needed good targets to carry on the battle of the hustings. Wilson did enter office, however, with a long-standing suspicion of New York bankers and other special interest groups, groups which he believed derived their power from Republican policies, especially the high tariff. His first official act as President was to issue a summons for a special session of Congress to deal with tariff reform. He obtained what he wanted, the Underwood Tariff of 1913, which was the first downward revision of the tariff since the Civil War.

"We must abolish everything that bears even the semblance of privilege or of any kind of artificial advantage," the new President declared, "and put our business men and producers under the stimulation of a constant necessity to be efficient, economical, and enterprising, masters of competitive supremacy, better workers and merchants than any in the world." Wilson's understanding of the economic roots of imperialism followed from this position on the tariff. Imperialism was a choice which was forced on nations by special interests and one that could be avoided with enough will and strength of character. One could make depraved

choices, just as one could sin against God's law. It was up to the individual, and the individual nation.

Wilson and Secretary of State Bryan believed, for example, that Taft and the bankers had sinned in China by cooperating with European imperialists in an effort to take control of the country to exploit it. He promised to restore the "original" Open Door policy, which he said would enable Americans to get their fair share of the China trade and investments but would leave no room for any improper behavior.

His major task, Secretary Bryan informed a newsman after a few weeks in office, was to restore America's international reputation for fair dealing: "When the people of all other nations understand this, they will welcome American capital and American capitalists." Lest anyone miss the point, Bryan added this clincher: "The preceding administration attempted to till the fields of foreign investment with a penknife; President Wilson intends to cultivate it with a spade."

Wilson and Bryan agreed that General Huerta represented a backward step for the whole hemisphere. It would do little good to reform American institutions if right across the border the "imperialist interests" found a new home. Initial soundings of the Mexican situation strengthened their conviction that Huerta was nothing more than a tool of foreign investors, especially British oil concerns, who were willing to put up whatever money was necessary to see him established in power permanently. It was not right that Americans should suffer additional handicaps when they went into third countries. A difficult and complex proposition was this business of making the world safe for free competition. The deeper he became involved, the more Wilson realized just how difficult and complex it really could be.

Constitutional revolutionaries—
and others

For the next seven years Wilson did battle for the soul of the Mexican revolution. He would teach the Mexicans to elect good people, he vowed, and to write a decent Anglo-Saxon constitution. Then they would be protected and made ready to take their proper place in the modern world under America's tutelage. The President risked war in April 1914 to achieve these objectives by attacking and occupying Vera Cruz. Huerta's willingness to step down was the only thing which permitted Wilson to avoid the consequences of such a dangerous act, but he remained determined to do his duty, and sent special tutors to each of the dictator's possible successors. When one who felt betrayed by the President's decision to withdraw American support for his cause misbehaved by attacking several Texas border towns, the President dispatched General John J. Pershing halfway across Mexico in a futile punitive mission. After it was all over, the miscreant Pancho Villa was still running loose, the authorities in Mexico City were outraged, and relations between Washington and Mexico City were at an impasse.

Somehow, in the midst of all this turmoil, the Mexicans had written a new constitution. Instead of delight, it produced dismay in Washington. According to Article 27 of the 1917 Mexican Constitution, drafted under the leadership of a conservative nationalist Venustiano Carranza, ownership of all subsoil

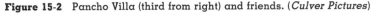

Figure 15-2 Pancho Villa (third from right) and friends. (*Culver Pictures*)

316

natural resources was to be vested in the central government. Aliens could own land or exploit mineral holdings only if they agreed in advance not to invoke the protection of their home governments in disputes with Mexican authorities about their property. These and other explicit checks on the operation of private enterprise went well beyond what Progressives imagined to be the limits of governmental intervention, either within the United States or in countries where United States citizens had invested their money.

Philip Dru: World administrator

The outer limits of the Progressive imagination were probably reached by Colonel Edward M. House, Wilson's very close friend and political adviser, in an anonymously published 1912 novel called *Philip Dru: Administrator.* Long used as a handy reference guide to the Progressive mind, the author's foreign policy views have gone largely unexplored, perhaps because of the persistent notion that domestic and foreign policy are two different things. House's fictional hero, Philip Dru, never looked at the world that way. The book is set in 1920, a year said to be filled with forebodings of danger for the nation. Special interests are in control of the United States Senate and, for all practical purposes, the rest of the country as well. It is also the year that Dru graduates from West Point.

Assigned to an isolated Western military post, Dru suffers an attack of blindness on the desert while trying to save the life of a very Victorian young lady and is forced to retire from the service. So he tries his hand at revolution. An odd vocation for a military officer and graduate engineer? Perhaps. But the Progressives often held that these types were the most disinterested of the nation's

citizens and could very well become America's future leaders should the politicians finally prove unworthy and incapable of the tasks before them. Besides, Dru's revolution turns out to be a nearly bloodless coup carried out against an enfeebled plutocracy which really wanted to be overthrown anyway. Dru then sets out to rewrite the American Constitution to bring it up to date. He will eliminate old-style politics and provide for government by scientific commission. Inefficiency and corruption are thus equated with special-interest rule, efficiency and honesty with a modern industrial nation.

But while he had been thus occupied, Great Britain, Japan, and Germany were secretly engaged in dividing up the world between them. Learning of these plans, Dru issues an appeal to the British people, whose instincts were always better than those of their policy makers, to demand a repudiation of the secret treaties. The appeal works, but Dru wants to do something positive as well and offers Germany and Japan an alliance, based on the Open Door policy, to develop the waste places of the earth—that is, the underdeveloped areas lacking strong central governments.

Having thus established a new order among the industrial nations, the administrator turns to a final task: "In spite of repeated warnings from the United States, Mexico and the Central American Republics had obstinately continued their old time habit of revolutions without just cause, with the result that they neither had stable governments within themselves, nor any hope of peace with each other." Dru himself leads the American Army in its final showdown battle against the Mexican force. Before the battle Dru makes a final appeal: "Our citizens and those of other countries have placed in your Republic vast sums for its development, trusting to your treaty guarantees, and they feel much concern over their inability to operate their properties, not only to the advantage of your people, but to those to whom they belong."

His words fall on deaf ears. The renegade dictator refuses to listen to Progressive reason, so the battle must be fought. When the smoke clears, Dru surveys the scene and predicts that in future years Mexicans will date their redemption and entrance into the modern era from this moment. In real life, it never quite worked out that way, but the story of House's secret missions to Europe in search of a negotiated peace settlement after the outbreak of the Great War reads like a chapter in his novel.

The labyrinth of neutrality

When war broke out in Europe in August 1914, those who had believed that the industrial powers could organize the world in an efficient and humane manner felt betrayed. Colonel House wrote in his diary about a conversation he had with the German Chancellor in early 1916: "I told him western civilization had broken down, and there was not a market-place or a mosque in the East where the West of to-day was not derided." Yet both House and Wilson yearned to show the warring nations the way out of their agony, back to self-command, self-possession. To do that required that the United States remain in the world but somehow not of the world—a task beyond the capacity of mere mortals, even Wilsonians.

The United States had two contradictory objectives in mind in August 1914 after the war began: The first was to find a way to assure that cotton and other so-called non-contraband goods could be shipped to belligerent ports on a business-as-usual basis;

the second was to assert its leadership of the neutral nations in the quest for a truly just peace and new world order. Germany's attack on little Belgium made Americans sympathetic to the Allied cause, as did the natural cultural affinity between the English-speaking powers. Economically the nation was still a debtor country, depending upon a steady market for its agricultural surpluses to balance current obligations and to reduce long-term indebtedness.

If the establishment of British sea power on the high seas would assure a continued outlet for the bulk of America's prewar output and a huge new market for war goods, neutrality demanded that the United States protest British blockade policies. The last time this had happened was in the Napoleonic Wars a century before, but would the result be the same? Like that French dictator, the Central Powers—Germany and Austria—had the most to gain from rules limiting surface blockades, and they agreed to abide by such limits. The Allies—Great Britain, France, and Russia—by virtue of British sea power, controlled the ocean surface and had the most to lose by allowing neutrals to trade with both sides. They therefore stalled the issue for as long as possible. Finally, Wilson asked the State Department to prepare a protest note to the Allies "with some teeth in it."

The proposed message came over to the White House on a September evening when Colonel House was dining with the President. Appalled by its language, the Colonel warned his friend that if it were sent Anglo-American relations might be damaged beyond repair. So, too, might be any chance of his successful mediation to end this frightful war. As House and Wilson defined mediation, moreover, a German victory (or even a stalemate) was ruled out. They had agreed, as House would put it, that if Germany triumphed, "we will have to abandon the path which you are blazing as a standard for future generations, with permanent peace as its goal, and a new international ethical code as its guiding star, and build up a military machine of vast proportions."

From this moment House became responsible for conducting the American peace effort; but Wilson was still responsible for maintaining American neutrality. To secure an American peace would eventually mean abandoning neutrality. Each step along the way made it more difficult to turn aside from the path ahead, no matter what happened. At first, Bryan and Wilson had ruled out loans to the belligerents as the worst kind of contraband and certainly the most likely to involve the United States on one side or another. Within a few weeks, however, the President had quietly modified this stand to exclude so-called short-term "credits," which he had been told were not the same as public loans.

The request for a change was premised on the legal grounds that loans were not unneutral, but it was motivated by the need to provide financing for regular exports and the anticipated sales of war materials to the Allies. In early 1915 the President further relaxed the ban to allow for long-term credits, and in August of that same year he completely abandoned efforts to block public loans. By the time America entered the war, the Allies had borrowed nearly $4 billion, the Central Powers less than $50 million. From the standpoint of consistency, it would have been better to have taken the position at the outset that loans were not unneutral. As it was, the Central Powers had a major grievance against American policy as biased in favor of their opponents and hypocritical by its own original standards.

Wilson had been told that not to make the

loans could be regarded as unneutral since international law did not prohibit them; he was also informed at the same time that not to make the loans would do severe damage to the American economy. "Our prosperity is dependent on our continued and enlarged foreign trade," Secretary of the Treasury William Gibbs MacAdoo said bluntly. "To preserve that we must do everything we can to assist our customers to buy." President Wilson could choose either rationale and end up back at the same place in this labyrinth called neutrality. And which choice could he make under such circumstances in order to avoid depravity? He was learning that special interests were not always distinct from general problems.

Colonel House in Europe

Colonel House felt confident that there was a way out and that he could find it, given enough time and enough authority by the President. After preliminary discussions with the German and British Ambassadors, House traveled to Europe on his first peace effort in early January 1915. His idea, as he explained it to Sir Edward Grey, the British Foreign Minister, was for Wilson to preside at a "second convention" at the time of the European peace conference. The peace conference would decide all the local issues; the second convention would occupy itself with the tasks of establishing rules for future warfare and neutral rights. He hastened to assure Sir Edward that the United States was not "pushing the question of peace," at least not until Berlin agreed to evacuate Belgium, pay indemnities, and negotiate a disarmament pact. If Germany would agree to these conditions, peace talks could get underway almost at once. From the outset of their discussions, Grey tried to make Wilson's emissary understand that the diplomatic issues could not be so easily resolved: France demanded Alsace-Lorraine, Russia expected the Dardanelles, and so on.

Nothing daunted by this response, House continued to develop his plan for a second convention while waiting for a favorable moment to travel on to Germany. As he thought about it, the "second convention" grew in his imagination. "It would be of far-reaching consequences," he wired the President, "more far reaching in fact than the peace conference itself." In Berlin he spread out the plan for a second convention before the Kaiser's chief advisers, but, he now confided to his diary, "in the back of my mind I have a hope that we can bring about . . . one [convention], and that the President will be invited to preside over it." He even talked as if it were already settled that America would take a leading role in the peace settlement under any circumstances. Taking the words out of Philip Dru's mouth, House even suggested that Germany might want to interest itself in the postwar economic development of South America. When Dru forced the British government to repeal its secret treaties with Germany and Japan, he had offered the other powers an alliance to develop the waste places of the world. Now House was suggesting to German authorities that if they agreed to meet his terms (or Wilson's terms), they might be compensated elsewhere. The Germans wisely did not take him seriously, because when House hinted at the idea in later conversations in the White House, Wilson reacted coolly to any notion of encouraging German penetration of Latin America.

He was on firmer ground with assurances to the Germans that the United States was just as concerned as they were about British high-handedness on the seas. Wilson was determined, House affirmed, to fight for "freedom of the seas" at the peace table.

The submarine crisis

Lurking beneath the surface of both the neutrality and peace effort questions was the new problem of submarine warfare. Berlin's early 1915 announcement that Germany had established a submarine counterblockade around the British Isles posed special difficulties for the Wilson administration. To be effective, a submarine campaign depended upon striking without warning, and it involved—on the high seas—a much greater loss of life than surface blockades. The Central Powers always contended, however, that the Allied economic blockade of the Continent struck directly at the civilian population.

Though Secretary of State Bryan urged a different policy, Wilson believed that he must uphold neutral rights for Americans to travel on commercial ships of the belligerents. A breach of this right, he argued, would open the way to the breakdown of the entire fabric of international law. Sooner or later, then, a confrontation with Berlin on the issue was inevitable. After some minor episodes, the crisis came with the sinking of the armed British passenger liner the *Lusitania* on May 7, 1915. More than a hundred Americans lost their lives when the ship went down. Wilson demanded an apology and warned that he would hold the German government to a strict accountability for future offenses.

Negotiations with Germany dragged on for months, and other ships were sunk in the meantime. "Shall we ever get out of the labyrinth made for us all by this German 'frightfulness'?" Wilson asked Colonel House on September 7, 1915, at the height of the crisis. Berlin finally agreed to halt the worst U-boat offenses in its reply to the *Lusitania* notes, but this provided only temporary relief from what was becoming a permanent agony of "neutrality." Symptoms associated with the condition included, besides submarine warfare, Allied blockade practices which grew steadily more obnoxious interfering with American trade throughout Europe; painful divisions within the country; and a rising fever of demands for military "preparedness." Economically, the war had brought prosperous times. Allied purchases swelled production of factory and farm, but it was not all healthy growth. The country, taken as a whole, was in a fretful condition. It looked to Washington for reassurance.

House was ready to try again. This time he proposed to offer the Allies a chance to invoke American aid to end the war—either by direct negotiations, or, if Germany refused the President's conditions, by coming into the war. Wilson would not allow him to go quite that far; he could say only that America would "probably" come into the conflict should Germany refuse peace terms. House took this message to Sir Edward Grey and his colleagues in January of 1916.

Sir Edward was, as usual, cordial, but he and his peers in the War Cabinet already had more than enough "understandings" without adding an overriding Wilsonian commitment at the top of the list. The Allies wanted American participation in the war, but not at the cost of pledging themselves to abide by the President's conditions. By June of 1916, it was fully clear to both House and Wilson that the Allies were not going to invoke American intervention to end the war—by any means. "An international situation can change as quickly as relationships between individuals, that is overnight," House wrote the President. "A situation may arise, if the Allies defeat Germany, where they may attempt to be dictatorial in Europe and elsewhere. I can foresee trouble with them," he ended.

Into the maelstrom

Over the next several months President Wilson delivered a series of speeches which carefully distinguished American war aims from those of the combatants. He ran as the "peace candidate" in 1916; but should it come to war, Wilson wanted to be ready. He accepted the need for "military preparedness" urged by his Republican opponents and submitted proposals to Congress for building an even larger Navy. If war came to the United States, so be it, and woe to those who sought to block the nation, militarily or diplomatically. In January 1917, Wilson called for "peace without victory," explaining to Congress that "so far as our participation in guarantees of future peace is concerned, it makes a great deal of difference in what way and upon what terms it is ended."

The German resumption of unrestricted submarine warfare a few weeks later forced Wilson to make good on his pledge to hold Berlin to a strict accountability. Seeing no other way to do this, the President asked for a declaration of war on April 2, 1917. "The world must be made safe for democracy," he declared in a statement that was aimed at all the belligerents, not just to the Central Powers. It made a great deal of difference also to Wilson that even as the nation went to war it be recognized as an "associated" power, not simply another "Allied" power. The United States would fight *with* the Allies on the battlefield; at the peace table it would fight *for* a separate set of war aims.

The best laid plans . . .

The "March 1917 Revolution" in Russia ended the Czars' rule and gave Russia a chance to develop a democratic government. This delighted American policy makers. First, it removed the blot of Czarism from the Allied cause, allowing Wilson to speak of a war to make the world safe for democracy; second, it removed one party to the "secret treaties" between the Allies, giving Wilson a chance to press for an end to entangling alliances. He looked forward to having the new Russian democracy on his side at the peace conference when it came to the final showdown over war and peace aims. American efforts to keep the provisional government in the war were thus dictated by more than military considerations; at least as important were these political concerns.

Despite American loans and other forms of aid, Alexander Kerensky, head of the provisional government, could not keep Russia in the war—or himself in power. The Bolshevik Revolution turned everything upside down. Now, instead of having a powerful ally at the peace conference, the President would be alone with the victorious Allies who would demand that Germany be made to pay for the war, and who, in the American view, wanted to do little more than parcel out the spoils. Moreover, they would use the Bolshevik threat to justify continuation of military policies in Central Europe as well as to play upon Wilson's genuine fear of Lenin's government. They shared his concern yet knew how effectively it could be turned to their advantage.

Wilson had outlined specific peace aims on January 8, 1918, in the "Fourteen Points" speech. Taken together, the points represented what Progressives regarded as a scientific and a humane new world order. They also provided the framework for an international constitution which Wilson believed would supply the foundation for a genuine League of Nations. The first five points were general in nature: an end to secret diplomacy, freedom of the seas, removal of economic barriers on international trade, reduction of armaments, and an adjustment of colonial claims in the interests of the populations concerned. The next eight concerned territorial adjustments within Europe. And point fourteen called for a charter and establishment of the League of Nations.

Germany offered to surrender in November 1918 on the basis of Wilson's Fourteen Points. To prove its good intentions, the German government deposed the Kaiser and proclaimed a republic. Wilson accepted on behalf of the Allies and set forth for the peace conference with high hopes.

Wilson's ordeal at Versailles began almost at once and lasted throughout the conference. Point five of the President's Fourteen Points had promised "a free, open-minded, and absolutely impartial adjustment of all colonial claims," with "strict observance of the principle that in determining all such questions . . . the interests of the populations concerned must have equal weight" as against claims put forward by those seeking title. The compromise finally worked out at the peace conference turned over Germany's African possessions and large sections of the old Ottoman Empire to a League of Nations mandate system. But for all practical purposes, the mandate system simply ratified previous inter-Allied understandings. The Allies would exercise the mandates and control the natural resources of the dependent areas.

To accept this "compromise" on the colonial question, President Wilson had to rationalize his situation by also accepting a key Allied argument: the "Huns" had ruthlessly exploited their colonies while the Allies had

Figure 15-3 Woodrow Wilson goes to Versailles to save the world for liberal democracy. (*The Bettmann Archive*)

administered theirs with due regard for the needs of the native peoples and were therefore entited to take over the management of areas formerly owned by the Central Powers. As further proof of his acceptance of this argument, Wilson apparently felt he must agree to participate in the League mandate system by asking Congress, as the Allies wanted, to accept responsibility for Armenia. "When you cease to be President," French Premier Georges Clemenceau joked, "we will make you Grand Turk."

It was not very funny to the American delegation, which had come to Paris convinced that the President would indeed see to it that the peace was written in accordance with the Fourteen Points. Compromise followed compromise (some said surrender followed surrender), each based on some variation of the Allied argument on the colonial question. The process was inexorable and

ended with Wilson's total acceptance of the "War Guilt" clause in the Versailles Treaty which made Germany, and Germany alone, morally responsible for unleashing the war that had nearly destroyed Europe and killed millions of its sons.

Wilson had pledged to come back with "an arrangement which will disentangle all the alliances in the world." He could not even disentangle the Versailles Treaty from the League of Nations and was forced to defend what he now acknowledged as wrongs with the only argument he had left: if the United States ratified the treaty, it could go into the League of Nations; and only if it went into the League of Nations could it correct whatever wrongs existed in the treaty. Many Democrats stood by their President and a majority of the Senate was willing to ratify the Versailles Treaty with certain reservations, but having compromised with European statesmen, the

President, sick and isolated in the White House, could not bring himself to deal with his enemies (or even his friends) at home. And even a healthy President would have had great difficulty in persuading the Senate to accept the logic of such a circular argument.

Wilson had counted on enlightened public opinion to sustain him over his foes at Versailles. The one time he tried to elicit support from the Italian people against their spokesmen at Versailles (over the annexation of Trieste) proved a disaster. He had lost the support and trust of the people at home as well.

At one point a few of the President's advisers proposed that he open up his options, narrowly circumscribed at Versailles by the Allied secret treaties, by establishing contacts with Lenin's government in Russia. On their own they authorized a special mission to Russia during the President's absence from Versailles, but Wilson refused to have anything to do with such a plan and refused to see the man who had met with Lenin's representatives. Wilson also refused to see revolutionary nationalists who came to the Hotel Crillon to plead their case against the colonial powers. Many of them had been inspired by the President's speeches and his vision of a new world order. Among these was a wispy young man who would one day attract world attention as Ho Chi Minh, the Marxist leader of the Vietnamese struggle for independence.

Wilson placed a diplomatic embargo on the Soviets which endured for fourteen years. It was the same "watchful waiting" posture he

Figure 15-4 Three's company, four's a crowd. At Versailles the Allies wanted as little to do with Wilson and his Fourteen Points as possible. (*Culver Pictures*)

had long since adopted toward the Mexican revolution but carried several steps further. For a long time Americans hoped that someone would turn up, a man who, with America's help, would lead Russia back to the Progressive path between reaction and revolution to join the world made safe for democracy. It was a time of bitter disappointment and angry recrimination—against the Treaty of Versailles, against the war, and even against Wilson.

The world's work would have to get done some other way.

Selected references

Howard K. Beale's highly readable *Theodore Roosevelt and the Rise of America to World Power* (1956) has been regarded as a classic almost from the date of publication. The two sources most frequently cited on Latin American policy in the era are Dana G. Munro, *Intervention and Dollar Diplomacy in the Caribbean, 1900–1921* (1964), and the older Scott Nearing and Joseph Freeman, *Dollar Diplomacy: A Study in American Imperialism* (1925). They often sound as if the authors were writing about two different worlds. To bridge the gap you may want to try Charles A. Beard, *The Idea of National Interest: An Analytical Study in American Foreign Policy* (1934).

Arthur Link's multivolume biography of Woodrow Wilson, of which five volumes have now been published, is definitive, but his shorter treatment, *Woodrow Wilson and the Progressive Era, 1910–1917* (1954), remains more than adequate for the needs of most students. Getting out of the rut of older studies is Peter Calvert's brillant *The Mexican Revolution, 1910–1914: The Diplomacy of Anglo-American Conflict* (1968). Yet another approach to American foreign policy under Wilson is N. Gordon Levin, *Woodrow Wilson and World Politics* (1968).

Two books on peacemaking and revolution are Arno Mayer, *Wilson vs. Lenin* (1963), and the same author's *Politics and Diplomacy of Peacemaking: Containment and Counterrevolution at Versailles, 1918–1919* (1967). If you have time to read just one memoir on the peacemaking period, let it be Herbert Hoover, *The Ordeal of Woodrow Wilson* (1958). It tells more about Hoover than Wilson, but also more about American policy than both.

SIXTEEN

The Great War at Home

Period covered: 1914–1920
Emphases: Reaction to war. Domestic war effort. Red scare.
Major events: World War I breaks out in Europe, 1914
America enters the war, 1917
Victory, 1918
Red scare, 1919–1920
Election of Warren G. Harding, 1920

Neutrality

When Europe went to war in 1914, most Americans were horrified. A general struggle fought with modern weapons of mass destruction seemed insane to them. America had no stake in the conflict and most people agreed with President Wilson that it was best to remain neutral in thought, word, and deed, but this proved impossible. Almost from the start, educated middle- and upper-class Americans identified with the Allies: to these Americans, Britain was the mother· country whose many virtues everyone learned in school, and, to aesthetes, France was beautiful and the fountainhead of modern art and culture. Germany, on the other hand, was thought of as brutal, efficient, and scientific—not very lovable traits. Probably a majority of Americans, therefore, were pro-Allied at heart even before the undersea war turned public opinion against Germany, but this did not mean they favored intervention. Their views were immaterial. Wilson had virtually committed the United States to war if the German submarine campaign was renewed. Whether or not the United States would intervene thus depended on German actions, not American decisions as everyone seemed to think.

People went on debating intervention, and most assumed that the choice between war or peace would be made democratically. If this seems foolish now, it is only because we are many wars the wiser. Then it appeared that, as no one was likely to attack the United States, intervention would be accepted or rejected on its merits, rationally, and with popular consent. Had that been so, America might never have fought. Although most political and business leaders appear to have favored intervention, many, perhaps a majority of Americans, did not. German-Americans,

the largest single ethnic group in the country, were opposed for obvious reasons, and the Irish did not want to fight for England, especially after it crushed the 1916 Easter rising in Dublin. Immigrants from the vast Austro-Hungarian Empire were in the same position as German-Americans, while many native-born WASPs still believed in the American tradition of avoiding Europe's wars. The struggle itself reinforced prejudices against the corrupt Old World while seeming to vindicate the new. Radicals thought it just another imperialist conflict from which everyone but the workers would profit.

Thus, despite their advantages, interventionists had difficulty persuading Americans to join the carnage abroad. Theodore Roosevelt, once an admirer of Kaiser Wilhelm but now pro-Allied, called endlessly for war to no effect. In 1916 he stumped the country for GOP Presidential candidate Charles Evans Hughes, accusing Wilson of "kissing the bloodstained hand that slapped his face." People shoved pictures of Wilson under his nose, even in Gallup, New Mexico where he had enlisted Rough Riders for the Spanish-American war and was very popular. Wilson had not wanted peace to be an issue in his campaign, ostensibly to keep his hands free, perhaps because he knew war was inevitable. His hopes, however, were quickly dashed. At the Democratic convention, keynote speaker Martin Glynn of New York had prepared a dull speech listing past provocations that had not led to war. As he droned through it the audience got more and more excited. He hesitated over a particularly outrageous incident in which American seamen had been hung by the British. "What did we do?" cried the people. "We didn't go to war," answered Glynn and the convention broke up screaming, cheering, and dancing. "He kept us out of war" became the Democratic slogan and turned Wilson's plurality of 1912 into a majority.

Sentiment for peace showed itself in other ways. In 1916, when Pancho Villa raided the United States hoping to provoke war between it and Mexico, the President sent troops after him and these clashed with the Mexican Army. Wilson almost asked for a declaration of war. But a pacifist organization, The American Union Against Militarism, took out newspaper ads with eyewitness reports showing that American troops had fired first. These provoked a flood of letters and telegrams that obliged Wilson to back down. The country was saved from an especially pointless conflict and Wilson from an embarrassing mistake that would have weakened his campaign in Europe later. Thus the peace movement enjoyed a rare moment of elation in its otherwise depressing history.

In the face of such sentiment, most interventionists dared not call for war. Instead, they advocated preparedness. Though the Navy was in good shape, the Army had only 80,000 men. Critics argued that preparedness was in effect to say "let us do as Europeans did so that what happened to them won't happen to us." Wilson accepted preparedness anyway, and in 1916 he got substantial military appropriations from a still reluctant Congress. Even so, much was left undone. Wilson had employed policies that would lead to war while insisting they would not, and to make that claim credible he had neglected to prepare either the Armed Forces or public sentiment for what was to come. Even after war was declared on April 6, 1917, many thought it would not be costly. More aid to the Allies and a naval campaign against German subs might do the trick.

In fact, the Allies were near defeat: Russia's Revolution had nearly taken her out of the war; the French Army was exhausted and mutinous; and Britain, which was losing 900,-000 tons of shipping a month, would be starved out if matters did not improve. Germany had gambled that by renewing the undersea war she would beat the Allies before America could mobilize effectively, and she nearly did. George Kennan would argue years later that either side would have been better off to accept the enemy's terms in 1917 rather than to fight on to the finish. Wilson himself, a few months before American entry, had called for peace without victory as the only peace likely to endure. But negotiations were out of the question, since neither side wanted them and both had sacrificed too much to settle now for what could have been gotten cheaply earlier. No government dared go to its people and say that millions had died in vain—only victory would justify such slaughter.

Intervention

By fighting a "war to end wars" and "making the world safe for democracy," Wilson proposed to turn tragedy into triumph. There were no especially compelling reasons to think this possible—only a terrible need to believe that what was done out of necessity would be turned to higher uses. Since few Americans were excited by the prospect of fighting merely for neutral rights or even to save the Allies, only the grandest war aims would do, however unlikely. Sometimes it seemed that the more implausible they were, the better. A few years earlier the great powers of Europe had appeared to be much the same morally. Now the Allies seemed righteous and Germany bestial, war having ennobled the one side and brutalized the other. Even France, once the epitome of vice and depravity to average Americans, had been "purified by the flames of war" it was said, as if nations had the same properties as water.

Moral absolutism was also necessary because of divisions at home. German- and Irish-Americans did not change their minds because a few ships were sunk; neither did Socialists, liberal pacifists, and others. They had to be suppressed and doubtful moderates had to be inspired. Washington used both the carrot and the stick to these ends.

The carrot consisted not only of extravagant promises about the future but also of concrete benefits at home. Many, relieved that the issue was at last decided, threw themselves into war work and found that a great range of activities were available. There were bandages to be rolled and bonds to be sold, both of which women did well, and they also helped write and deliver propaganda. As "four-minute women" they gave canned speeches in churches and theaters. They became motor car drivers, military typists, and the like, and hundreds of thousands replaced men in fields and factories. A Woman's Committee was added to the Council of National Defense. Women had been active pacifists before intervention, in their own Women's Peace party headed by Jane Addams as well as in older peace societies. Many now became just as active in war work. Even Jane Addams spoke for food conservation, the voluntary substitute for rationing organized by Herbert Hoover.

Reformers and social workers had figured largely in the peace movement, and Washington made it easy for them to join the war effort by the impetus it gave to long cherished reforms. The National War Labor Board, the War Labor Policies Board, the United States Employment Service, and other wartime agencies recognized collective bargaining, the minimum wage, and the eight-hour day; working conditions improved; women and children in industry got more protection; and the first public housing projects were set up to provide for war workers. The Commission on Training Camp Activities saw to it that camps were run efficiently, hygienically, and with due provision for constructive leisure activities. Prohibition, a favorite cause of social workers, was enacted as a war measure. People in the social justice movement had feared that war would destroy all they had worked for, but in fact the war effort was run along progressive lines and secured reforms they had despaired of getting in peacetime. The government offered tempting opportunities for service and few resisted them for long.

Other groups gained also. Labor got full employment and more protection on the job, while farmers got higher prices—as did business and industry. Academicians were needed in Washington in many new agencies and in the Committee on Public Information, the great propaganda apparatus (called the Creel Committee, after its leader, George Creel). Wilson, who had fudged the issue as long as he could, finally joined other world leaders in agreeing that women's contribution to victory showed them to be fit to vote. But American women would have gotten the vote anyway. In 1917 an equal suffrage referendum passed in New York State, showing that Easterners agreed with Westerners that it was an idea whose time had come. The war merely gave Wilson a pretext for doing gracefully what he could not have long resisted in any case.

President Wilson had as many sticks as carrots. A big one was the Creel Committee, whose job it was to whip up popular enthusiasm for war and hatred of the enemy while isolating and discrediting pacifists. Newspapers—running headlines like "Teuton Plan to Torture Captured Sammies" were already-ing printing rumors as fact, while U-boat

Figure 16-1 During wartime the popular prejudice against women as drivers and auto mechanics was suspended. (*The National Archives*)

captains were reported to have landed on the coast and moved inland, poisoning wells as they went. People suspected of being pacifists or pro-German were mobbed. The Creel Committee moved into the offices of the Carnegie Endowment for International Peace, whose president, Nicholas Murray Butler, had suspended its activities for the duration. Like many in the old peace movement, however, Butler was adaptable, favoring peace in peacetime and war in wartime. The Creel Committee was not a censor and it did not need to be, as the Espionage and Sedition acts empowered the government to do all that was necessary to suppress unwanted opinions. The Espionage Act of 1917 included not only spies and saboteurs but also those who should "willfully cause or attempt to cause insubordination, mutiny, or refusal of duty . . . or . . . willfully obstruct the recruiting or enlistment service." The Postmaster General was empowered to ban from the mails any publication he thought seditious, and the Sedition Act of 1918 gave authority even more leeway. It provided severe penalties for statements which were abusive of the form of government of the United States or any of its agencies or which might encourage contempt, scorn, contumely, or disrepute. Theodore Roosevelt and other Republicans who heaped abuse on the government were in practice exempt, no doubt because they were for the war.

The Creel Committee used newspapers, magazines, movies, posters, and teams of speakers to make its points. A typical ad in the *Saturday Evening Post,* headed "Spies and Lies," urged readers not to become a tool of the Hun by spreading rumors. Other injunctions followed, including this: "And do not wait until you catch someone putting a bomb under a factory. Report the man who spreads pessimistic stories, divulges—or seeks—confidential military information, cries for peace, or belittles our efforts to win the war. Send the names of such persons, even if they are in uniform to the Department of Justice . . . show the Hun that we can beat him at his own game. . . . The fact that you made the report will not become public."

Many were eager to surpass the Hun. Thousands of people were reported by business competitors or anonymously by disgruntled neighbors or unscrupulous people with scores to pay off. The Creel Committee's scholarship division alone put out 75 million pieces of propaganda. Movies like *The Prussian Cur, To Hell with the Kaiser,* and *The Kaiser, the Beast of Berlin* inspired Americans. Less successful was a picture called *The Spirit of '76,* which was suppressed for depicting a gallant ally unflatteringly. Its producer got three years in prison. Textbooks

were banned for ideological shortcomings; sometimes they were exposed by rival publishers.

Opinion was further inflamed by leading Americans like Theodore Roosevelt, who charged that pacifists were Socialists, Wobblies, and "a whole raft of sexless creatures." Virile patriots organized themselves in groups with names like the Anti-Yellow Dog League, the Boy Spies, the Sedition Slammers, and the American Protective League. This last was sponsored by the Justice Department, had 25,000 members, and boasted afterward that it had "brought to judgment" 3 million cases of disloyalty. Wilson himself sometimes asked the Justice Department to prosecute men whose seditious remarks caught his eye. The line between official prosecution and vigilante action was hard to draw. Both had much in common and they often went together.

The antiwar casualty list was too great to summarize properly. Radicals were nailed first. The anarchist leaders Emma Goldman and Alexander Berkman were sentenced to two years for supposedly engaging in a nationwide conspiracy against the government. Socialist leaders went to jail too, including Eugene Debs, Victor Berger, and Kate Richards O'Hare, a past National Secretary of the SPA. One hundred and fifty Wobblies and Socialists were given twenty-year sentences by Judge Kenesaw Mountain Landis, whom a grateful country later made Commissioner of Baseball. Socialist protest marchers were beaten by mobs and arrested by police. In Bisbee, Arizona, a Wobbly strike was broken by vigilantes who seized 1,200 men and dumped them in the desert. On September 5,

Figure 16-2 Showing the Hun we could beat him at his own game. (*Culver Pictures*)

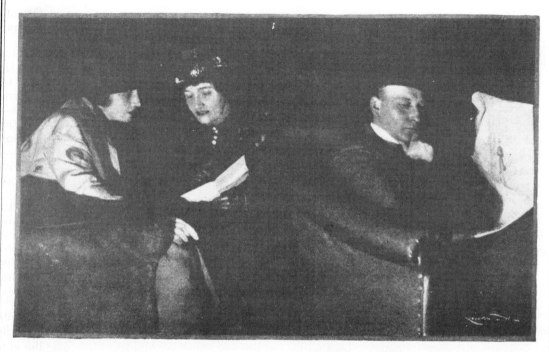

Spies and Lies

German agents are everywhere, eager to gather scraps of news about our men, our ships, our munitions. It is still possible to get such information through to Germany, where thousands of these fragments—often individually harmless—are patiently pieced together into a whole which spells death to American soldiers and danger to American homes.

But while the enemy is most industrious in trying to collect information, and his systems elaborate, he is *not* superhuman—indeed he is often very stupid, and would fail to get what he wants were it not deliberately handed to him by the carelessness of loyal Americans.

Do not discuss in public, or with strangers, any news of troop and transport movements, or bits of gossip as to our military preparations, which come into your possession.

Do not permit your friends in service to tell you—or write you—"inside" facts about where they are, what they are doing and seeing.

Do not become a tool of the Hun by passing on the malicious, disheartening rumors which he so eagerly sows. Remember he asks no better service than to have you spread his lies of disasters to our soldiers and sailors, gross scandals in the Red Cross, cruelties, neglect and wholesale executions in our camps, drunkenness and vice in the Expeditionary Force, and other tales certain to disturb American patriots and to bring anxiety and grief to American parents.

And do not wait until you catch someone putting a bomb under a factory. Report the man who spreads pessimistic stories, divulges—or seeks—confidential military information, cries for peace, or belittles our efforts to win the war.

Send the names of such persons, even if they are in uniform, to the Department of Justice, Washington. Give all the details you can, with names of witnesses if possible—show the Hun that we can beat him at his own game of collecting scattered information and putting it to work. The fact that you made the report will not become public.

You are in contact with the enemy *today*, just as truly as if you faced him across No Man's Land. In your hands are two powerful weapons with which to meet him—discretion and vigilance. *Use them.*

COMMITTEE ON PUBLIC INFORMATION

8 JACKSON PLACE, WASHINGTON, D. C.

George Creel, Chairman
The Secretary of State
The Secretary of War
The Secretary of the Navy

Contributed through Division of Advertising　　　　　　　　*United States Govt. Comm. on Public Information*

This space contributed for the Winning of the War by
THE PUBLISHER OF LESLIE'S WEEKLY

1917, the Justice Department raided 33 IWW headquarters, arresting 113 leaders.

Racial tensions increased also. Blacks, drafted into segregated units, were discriminated against in Army camps and even more on the outside. In Houston a group of black soldiers responded to police harassment by storming the city jail to free imprisoned comrades, and fifteen of them died in the fight. The Army held drumhead courts-martial that sent forty-one black soldiers to prison for life, while thirteen were hanged in an arroyo outside camp. Manpower shortages led many blacks to move North for the first time. Racial outbreaks followed, the worst of them in East St. Louis where forty blacks were killed by white mobs, hundreds more injured—often frightfully—and 300 homes burned.

Conscientious objectors suffered too. Draft boards assumed that nonreligious COs were fakers. But even members of the so-called "historic peace churches" were victimized. The Army was responsible for handling COs and did everything possible to make them accept some kind of military service. Beatings and solitary confinement were usual, and some 450 COs were court-martialed. Seventeen were sentenced to death, 142 to life imprisonment, and 345 got sentences averaging sixteen years. Some committed suicide. The most intransigent COs, including Mennonites and Dukhobors, were forcibly shaved and compelled to wear uniforms. Jane Addams reported one especially poignant case. A Dukhobor caught pneumonia and died after being hosed down in freezing weather for refusing to wear a uniform. When his widow claimed the body, it was dressed in the uniform he had given his life to escape. T. R. had no sympathy for men like these, thinking of them all as slackers who should be sent to the front. Thanks to the punishment

they took, about 16,000 of 20,000 COs ultimately did accept some form of military service.

These were only a few of the incidents that took place during the brief months of war. No one knows how many people were abused by vigilantes, forced to buy war bonds, or made to kiss the flag. Teachers were fired and ministers imprisoned; German was no longer taught in schools and performances of German music were banned; and sauerkraut became "liberty cabbage" while the frankfurter became the "hot dog." Only the seditious remarked that the government was destroying at home what it claimed to uphold abroad. John Reed—war correspondent, poet, and editor of a bubbly Socialist magazine called *The Masses*—wrote an article describing the outrages in Bisbee and East St. Louis, the trials of Goldman and Berkman, the mobbing of Socialists, etc., and called it "One Solid Month of Liberty." Soon *The Masses* was suppressed and Reed and six others were indicted under the sedition act. Oddly enough they were acquitted, among the very few to have this happy experience. This outcome was attributed by one juryman to the fact that they were all native-born.

The war remained unpopular in many quarters, as shown by the enormous number of draft evaders. The government resorted near the end to massive sweeps in which city blocks would be cordoned off and every male of draft age made to show his registration card. These so offended public opinion that they had to be stopped. There was, however, no effective way that pacifists could mobilize antiwar sentiments. The penalties for dissent were too severe for many to try it openly, and there was no center around which pacifists could rally. The Socialist party came closest, but its best leaders were in jail and the party was weakened by dissension. A majority of delegates had voted against supporting American entry at its 1917 convention. This made the Socialist Party of America the only one to stand by those ideals of proletarian internationalism which Socialists used to argue would prevent great wars. The workers of the world, it was said, would refuse to fight one another. When the war came, though, all the great European Socialist parties fell in line. So they survived the war intact while the SPA took heavy losses.

Many Socialists, among them some notable intellectuals, broke with the party. Algie M. Simons, for example, once a left-winger and editor of the *International Socialist Review,* became director of the Bureau of Literature of the Wisconsin Loyalty Legion (a 200 percent patriotic group) and charged Victor Berger with accepting subsidies from German agents. J. G. Phelps Stokes attacked his old friends too and asked Congress to investigate the treasonable activities of Senator LaFollette and other antiwar legislators. Charles Edward Russell, the Socialist candidate for Vice President in 1916, declared that antiwar Socialists were traitors who should be driven from the country. The antiwar Socialists never rejoined the party, while the prowar Socialists never forgave them.

Liberals divided too, of course. Most prominent intellectuals accepted the government line. John Dewey and the *New Republic* went to war, having found ingenious reasons to explain away their former doubts. Dewey, who had just written *Creative Intelligence,* was expected by many to oppose intervention as stupid and destructive. Instead, he supported it, on the curious ground that since further resistance was futile, pacifists should join the war effort so as to shape the right kind of peace afterward. What could not be prevented was now to be controlled.

Randolph Bourne, an ex-student of Dew-

Figure 16-3 "At last, a perfect soldier!" This was one of the most popular antiwar cartoons ever drawn. The artist, Robert Minor, a famous newspaper cartoonist, later became a full-time functionary of the Communist party. (*The Masses*)

ey's and a great believer in his philosophy of instrumentalism, was shocked. Dewey failed to see, he wrote:

War is just that absolute situation which is its own end and its own means, and which speedily outstrips the power of intelligent and creative control. As long as you are out of war, events remain to some degree malleable. This was the argument for "armed neutrality." But clamp down the psychic pattern of war on the nation, and you have precipitated an absolute where mastery becomes a mockery.

In a series of brilliant essays Bourne condemned Progressive intellectuals as a class for suspending judgment in wartime and collaborating with the very people who stood for what Bourne had supposed intellectuals were against. Instrumentalism itself was revealed as a philosophy that advanced technique at the expense of vision and confused motion with progress. Dewey proclaimed that war was just another instrument to be used by creative intelligence for beneficent purposes, but Bourne replied, in his best-known phrase, that "war is the health of the state" and only foolish idealists think to put it to their own uses. While the war lasted, Bourne was a prophet without honor. He died at the age of thirty-two in the great influenza epidemic of 1918, having seen his worst fears confirmed but before many others had come around to his point of view. They soon did, however. Having accepted the impossible, they rejected the inevitable.

Postwar reaction

When it became clear at Versailles that the Allies were not saintly after all and that Wilson's generous Fourteen Points were going to be compromised, intellectuals were stunned. They decided that Wilson had sold them out. Russian disclosure of the wartime "secret treaties" outlining each Allied nation's share of the spoils made them feel all the worse. Most liberals and intellectuals had taken the easy way out when war came by accepting the President's absurd claims for it at face value. Instead of standing on principle, they turned about, excusing themselves with rationalizations like John Dewey's slippery argument that further resistance would be morally futile while joining the war effort was "to connect conscience with the forces that are moving in another direction." Afterward, few were willing to take responsibility for their failures of nerve. It was easier to call the President deceitful than to admit they had deceived themselves. So, after supporting Wilson's war, many now refused to work for his League of Nations—the last chance, however remote, of salvaging something from the general ruin.

America did not join the League. Even had Progressives been less disillusioned and more helpful, Wilson had antagonized too many senators to get the Versailles Treaty approved. The national enthusiasm for foreign affairs was short-lived. People quickly reverted to worrying most about what was closest to them, and in 1919 there was a lot to worry about. With war controls removed, prices shot up. Organized labor responded with a wave of strikes involving some 4 million workers. These were resented by white-collar employees and others on fixed salaries whose income lagged behind. Farm prices rose too, but farmers were acutely aware of their higher costs. (In May 1920 when basic commodities lost their guarantees, farm prices fell, beginning an agricultural slump that lasted until the next war.) A series of novel strikes and radical outrages triggered a red scare that picked up where the wartime hysteria left off. The infant communist movement was too weak to cause much trouble. The Communist Labor party (CLP) founded by John Reed and others had perhaps 10,000 members, while the Communist party (CP) proper was larger, having drawn in some Wobblies and left-wing Socialists. Even so, it was small stuff compared to what the Socialist party had been before the war. Yet because Bolsheviks had made a revolution in Russia, American Communists were feared all out of proportion to their numbers and they were thought responsible when the great strikes began.

In August 1918 the AFL launched a drive to organize steelworkers led by William Z. Foster, an ex-Wobbly and future Communist party leader. Half of all steelworkers worked a twelve-hour day and half of these a seven-day week. Unskilled workers averaged less than the $1,500 a year that the Bureau of Labor estimated was the minimum subsistence level for a family of five. All the same, steel executives claimed the strike was a red plot and—when 400,000 men went out on strike in September—they broke it savagely. Strike leaders were sometimes kidnapped, while police and company gunmen broke up meetings and attacked picket lines. Along the Monogahela River in western Pennsylvania there were 25,000 men under arms in a 20-mile strip. At points there was a deputy sheriff for every striker. Mounted police rode down protesters—men, women, and children alike. In Gary, Indiana, black strikebreakers were used while state and federal troops prevented picketing. Eighteen strikers were killed there.

In January 1919, the shipyard workers of Seattle walked out and the Seattle Central Labor Council declared a general strike in sympathy. Although basic services were preserved and there was no violence, it was declared a communist outrage, since native-born Americans would never themselves take so radical a step. Mayor Ole Hansen, who threatened the use of federal troops and forced an end to the strike in February, became a national hero and resigned his job so as to lecture around the country on the dangers of Bolshevism. Tension increased when thirty-six identical bombs were mailed to public figures. Only one actually exploded, blowing off the hands of former U.S. Senator Hardwick's maid. Later, eight huge bombs went off around the country. The most effective one destroyed the front of Attorney General A. Mitchell Palmer's house. No one was hurt except the bombers, who left two mismatched legs in the debris. Palmer announced that a giant conspiracy was involved and laid plans for a massive response.

Most alarming of all, perhaps, was the Boston police strike of September 1919. Policemen were especially hard hit by inflation, and when the Mayor of Boston fired nineteen officers for organizing a police union, the force voted overwhelmingly to strike. When the 1,500 men walked out, there was no provision for their replacement. Several days of disorder followed before Governor Calvin Coolidge sent in National Guardsmen to restore order and break the strike. Only about $34,000 worth of property damage resulted, though three people lost their lives. The police offered to go back on duty pending arbitration, but the mayor decided to recruit a new force instead. This strike too was seen as a red plot, and all the worse for involving Roman Catholics. Coolidge became a national hero and the next Vice President.

These alarming events were exploited by businessmen eager to roll back the gains organized labor had made during the war. Led by organizations like the National Security League and the National Civic Federation, employers campaigned everywhere for the "American Plan," as they now called the open shop. The newly formed American Legion was a great help. Legionnaires beat up radicals and union organizers, and their first annual convention urged the deportation of all "who defamed the American way of life." The National Association of Manufacturers declared that "unionism is nothing less than Bolshevism," that it was, in fact, "the greatest crime left in the world." Samuel Gompers of the American Federation of Labor attacked communism too, but this did no good. The point of the anti-red campaign, after all, was to destroy unions. Labor could not save itself by joining in.

The witch hunt was very successful. Union membership fell drastically and labor was put on the defensive for years. Wobbly and other radical headquarters were raided or destroyed, while state and federal investigating committees purported to find evidence of a monstrous conspiracy. In November 1919 the Justice Department raided the headquarters of an organization called the Union of Russian Workers and arrested arrested 250 men. The New York State Lusk Committee raided 73 radical centers, arresting 500 people. Ultimately some 250 of these were judged deportable under a wartime alien control act and, on December 21, 1919, the *General Buford,* a former troopship, sailed for Finland with them. They were actually deported to Russia, but as the United States did not recognize the U.S.S.R., Finland was made her substitute. A memorable cartoon of the day showed the *Buford* outward bound, with smoke from her stack hiding the Statue of Liberty.

On January 2, 1920, the Justice Department staged the greatest raids of all. Its undercover agents in the CLP and the CP arranged for meetings to be held on that date,

and as many of these as possible were raided at once. Four thousand people in thirty-three cities were taken, often without warrants. Eight hundred were held for days in a corridor of the federal building in Detroit without food, water, or sanitary facilities. Eight hundred more were on Deer Island, Massachusetts, where conditions were so bad that one committed suicide, one went mad, and two died of pneumonia. The dragnet swept up some who were not radical at all, like the thirty-nine bakers of Lynn, Massachusetts, who were meeting to form a cooperative bakery. By 1921 a total of thirty-five states had some kind of syndicalist and/or sedition legislation to deal with radicals, and thirty-two prohibited showing the red flag. Perhaps 1,400 people were arrested under these laws and 300 sent to jail.

Finally, the tide began turning. The New York State legislature in 1920 refused to seat five Socialist assemblymen. Unlike Victor Berger, who was denied his seat in Congress for having been jailed during wartime, these assemblymen were guilty of nothing more than being Socialists. Charles Evans Hughes, former Governor of New York, former Republican candidate for President, and a future Chief Justice of the Supreme Court, upon offering to defend them, was attacked by assemblymen as pro-German and disloyal. This was both offensive and ridiculous and exposed the witch-hunting mentality to people who, though conservative, were not hysterical. A. Mitchell Palmer discredited himself by announcing that on 1920s May Day, a traditional radical holiday, there would be a red uprising. Precautions were taken in many cities, to the point of installing machine gun nests at crucial locations. When May Day came and went peacefully, Palmer was laughed at. Like all aggressive public men with Quaker backgrounds, he had been called the "Fighting Quaker." Now some said that the "Quaking Fighter," or "Faking Fighter," or perhaps "Quaking Quitter" would be more appropriate—and his Presidential hopes declined.

Assistant Secretary of Labor Louis Post took advantage of the changing climate to cancel deportation warrants and review all pending cases. Although Congress tried to impeach him for this, his defense was so acute and his revelations so startling that the attempt failed. Many Congressmen, in fact, had had no idea of the flimsy grounds on which people were deported, and newspaper editors were surprised too. Some of these turned against deportation after seeing Post's evidence.

Warren G. Harding's election in 1920 put an end to the postwar time of troubles. Confidence had begun to return. Harding himself was not, like Wilson, an unforgiving, even malicious man. Whatever his faults, and they were numerous, Harding meant well. His administration had little interest in persecuting dissenters, and he pardoned many political prisoners, including Eugene Debs. Historians have not been kind to Harding, which is a pity. He was himself a generous man and should be remembered for more than his mistresses and venal friends.

Though the red scare was over, its effects remained. The racial tensions that accompanied it cost many lives. Lynchings rose from thirty-four in 1917 to over seventy in 1919 and there were race riots that year in twenty-six towns and cities, most notably in Chicago, where twenty-three blacks and fifteen whites died. The Ku Klux Klan had perhaps 100,000 members by then, many in the North. Anti-immigrant hostility and the popular association of foreigners with radicalism enabled Congress to pass the Emergency Immigration Act of 1921. By establishing a quota based on

national origins, which became permanent in 1924, it was possible to exclude most applicants from southern and eastern Europe. Labor was weakened for years by lost strikes, by the open-shop campaign (which was highly successful), and by unfavorable court decisions. Unions lost a million members in 1919 and 1920. They were probably the most destructive two years of peace in American history—a fitting climax to the war itself.

The social reforms that reconciled humanitarians to the war effort proved temporary in most cases. After the armistice, many were cancelled and others, most notably the prohibition of child labor by Congress, were struck down by the courts. The best part of Progressivism, its concern for social justice and the plight of the cities and the agrarian Democrats' suspicion of big business, did not survive the war as effective forces. The worst aspects of Progressivism, bureaucratic decision making and a shortsighted view of what constituted success, prospered. This led to a decade of merrymaking, moneymaking, and self-satisfaction during which all the problems that had not been solved earlier were forgotten except by an impotent few. In this manner Progressivism gave way to what President Harding called "normalcy," a strange label for the years of novelty that followed.

Selected references

Historians have not written much on domestic affairs during the war except in passing. There is much useful material in the relevant volumes of Mark Sullivan, *Our Times* (1920–1935), in six volumes. Two great novels by John Dos Passos, *42nd Parallel* and *1919,* convey the flavor of life then. There is a chapter on feminists and the war in William L.

O'Neill, *Everyone Was Brave* (1969), and on social reformers and the war in Allen F. Davis, *Spearheads for Reform* (1967). A penetrating essay is Murray N. Rothbard, "War Collectivism in World War I," in Radosh and Rothbard (eds.), *A New History of Leviathan* (1972). The standard work on the government's repression of its critics is H. C. Peterson and G. C. Fite, *Opponents of War, 1917–1918* (1957).

Some of the best antiwar material published at the time is in William L. O'Neill (ed.), *Echoes of Revolt: The Masses, 1911–1917* (1966). Much of Bourne's finest writing, together with some important war essays by John Dewey and others are in Lillian Schlissel (ed.), *The World of Randolph Bourne* (1965). Robert K. Murray, *Red Scare* (1955), is excellent on the witch hunt.

SEVENTEEN

The New Era

Period covered: 1920–1929
Emphases: Social and cultural life
Major events: Election of President Harding, 1920
Coolidge becomes President, 1923
Scopes trial, 1925
Election of President Hoover, 1928
Stock market crash, 1929

Politics

Politics in the 1920s could hardly have been more boring. In 1920 the Democrats pledged to get America into the League of Nations. Their candidates, James M. Cox and young Franklin D. Roosevelt, were both Wilsonian Progressives. Warren G. Harding promised only to restore "normalcy"—he meant normality but mispronounced it, thus adding a new word to the language. Harding won 61 percent of the vote and carried every state outside the Deep South. Some voted for him out of hatred for Wilson, others because he looked to be a dull, indolent President, which, after eight years of "idealism," was what the country needed most. The GOP could probably have won with anybody but a convicted felon. It chose Harding because he was the most regular and pliable Republican senator, so much so that his father said it was a good thing he wasn't a woman, as he'd have been pregnant all the time.

Harding's friends were small-time, whiskey-drinking, card-playing bounders. He was better than they—as Alice Longworth Roosevelt remarked—not a bad man, just a slob. But he put some in high office, where they destroyed him. Certain appointments turned out well. Charles Evans Hughes, his Secretary of State, was brilliant, as was Herbert Hoover, the friend of small business he made Secretary of Commerce. The billionaire Andrew Mellon, so powerful that it was said three Presidents served under him, became Secretary of the Treasury. Men of their stature ran the government while Harding's friends looted it. In 1923 he began learning of their peculations, which may have amounted to as much as $250 million from the Veterans Bureau alone. To make things worse, his wife found out about his long-time mistress and had her sent away. Harding died of a heart attack soon afterward. Like the man, his heart was warm but weak. It gave out just in time to save him from disgrace.

Under Coolidge things worked better. He believed that the business of the country was business, and so he let Harding's business appointees go on running it while he slept as much as twelve hours a day. In his 1925 inaugural address he declared that the nation had achieved "a state of contentment seldom before seen." This happy condition he meant to sustain through creative inertia. Coolidge was famous for saying little, a habit attributed to his New England background, though in reality it was because he had nothing to say. When he opened his mouth a fly flew out, his biographer observed. Hoover and Mellon were the strong men of both administrations. Each represented a sector of business, Hoover the small and Mellon the large. Hoover believed in small government but quadrupled the Commerce Department in size. He also favored competition and helped small business organize trade associations to better compete. They were most effective, though, in setting uniform standards and prices which reduced competition. Hoover appears not to have noticed this.

Mellon fought mainly to reduce taxes on the rich. Apart from its being good business for him, he thought prosperity depended on large investors. The more they had to invest the more was produced. It was a familiar argument and may once even have been true, but in the twenties there were already too many unused industrial assets. In 1929, even before the crash, 19 percent of all plant capacity was idle. Congress resisted, but Mellon got his way finally. In 1926 income taxes were cut by two-thirds. Mellon saved $800,000 personally. Besides cutting taxes, he refunded as much as $3.5 billion in one way or another. This helps explain why from

1922 to 1929 corporate net profits went up 75 percent and dividends to stockholders up 108 percent. Given the excess plant capacity, these profits were too great to be entirely reinvested. A portion went to stock speculation, helping inflate securities far above their real worth and making a great crash inevitable.

People accepted business's favored position because it seemed to benefit everyone but farmers. Their income was lower in 1929 than in 1910. Most others gained, however. Industrial wages rose by 33 percent between 1922 and 1929, while salaries increased 42 percent. Prices remained fairly stable. Workingmen were hardly affluent yet. On the average they earned less than $1,800 a year the Bureau of Labor thought necessary for a minimum decent living standard. Even so, through installment buying, many acquired autos, refrigerators, radios, and the like. Few were willing to say that business domination was too high a price to pay for good times. The prestige and moral authority of business was so great that the best-seller in both 1925 and 1926 was a businessman's life of Christ. Bruce Barton's *The Man Nobody Knows* acclaimed Christ as history's greatest executive for taking twelve men from the bottom ranks of business and building a great organization with them. Not until *Jesus Christ, Superstar,* would any interest group identify its methods so closely with God's.

As the Republican party got credit for peace and prosperity, it had a head start over the Democrats in 1928. Its candidate was Herbert Hoover, who as Secretary of Commerce could claim to be one of the architects of prosperity. He had the further advantage of being dry and Protestant while Al Smith, the Democratic candidate, was wet and Catholic. This led to a campaign of slander directed against Smith's alleged drinking habits and religion. As expected, Hoover won easily, getting 21 million votes to Smith's 15. This margin was less impressive than it seemed. Smith, the candidate of urban immigrants, carried nearly every large city, doubling the Democratic vote of 1924 even in some agricultural areas. The GOP was strongest in the vanishing old America of farms and small towns, while the Democrats prevailed in urban areas where the immigrant populations were coming of age politically. Though acclaimed as the Great Engineer, the epitome of modern efficiency, Hoover, like his party, was obsolete. He represented the old WASP minority that remained dominant only because prosperity seemed to vindicate its leadership.

A new morality

If there was little excitement and less glamour in politics, there was plenty of both elsewhere. The many names given the period—the Jazz Age, the Era of Wonderful Nonsense, the Roaring Twenties—attest to that. They were unbuttoned days when manners and morals loosened as never before. It was the beginning of modern times. In the nineteenth century people were urged to work and save, pleasure was regulated, and sacrifices were made—voluntarily by the upwardly mobile, of necessity by the laboring masses. An underdeveloped country must generate capital if it is to become self-sufficient. Industrialization is always hard, and hardest of all for those least able to protect themselves. But in the twentieth century growth began to pay off. Problems of production were solved, income rose, and the work week shrank. The need to labor grew less compelling while pleasure became not just possible but essential if growth was to continue. By the 1920s consumer goods from automobiles to phono-

 342

Figure 17-1 Waiting for the college train. An undergraduate singalong in the Jazz Age. (*Charles Phelps Cushing*)

graphs had become crucial to prosperity. People were no longer urged to save but to spend. Installment buying enabled families with little cash to buy expensive products. Though incomes lagged behind profits and many were shut out of the new affluence altogether, America had in a halting, imperfect way entered the age of high mass consumption. Postindustrial society was born.

Technology played a vital role. Thanks to it the mass society had mass media, including national magazines but especially movies and radio. These promoted the new goods technology spawned as well as behavior appropriate to the age of high mass consumption. Movies did this especially well, showing millions how to act in speakeasies, roadhouses, and parked cars, how to dance the Charleston and Black Bottom. Even after movies began censoring themselves and nudity declined, they remained passionate. In *Our Modern Maidens* Joan Crawford was a married woman who flirted with another man, got divorced, and lived happily ever after. What films like this did for men, Rudolph Valentino's did for women. His bare-chested lovemaking raised expectations everywhere.

The sexual revolution was not just a matter of erotic films and novels (*Jurgen, The Sun Also Rises,* and the banned *Lady Chatterly's Lover*) but of changed conduct too. When the Kinsey group and others studied sexuality, they found that women born after 1900 were distinctly less chaste than women born earlier. Middle-class men frequently had pre- or extramarital relations with women peers, and prostitution declined. This was partly due to the pleasure principle, which rose as the work ethic fell, and partly to contraceptives. Condoms were now cheap, reliable, and ubiquitous, so sex became freer and less worrisome. Divorces did too. The divorce rate had been going up for generations despite efforts to combat it. In the 1920s, however, these efforts were largely abandoned. Though no state endorsed Judge Ben B. Lindsay's proposal for companionate marriage (which would have enabled childless couples to divorce at will following a trial period) and divorces continued to be messy, painful, and expensive for many, just about anyone who wanted a divorce could manage it. Still, a sexual millennium did not arrive in the 1920s. Then as now people got pregnant against their will, contracted venereal diseases, had their desires frustrated, and so on. Sexual ignorance remained enormous and

Figure 17-2 Doing the Charleston. (*Missouri Historical Society*)

fulfillment eluded many. One psychiatrist examined 200 married people and found that nearly half the women had never experienced orgasm.

All the same, never before was the pursuit of pleasure, including sexual pleasure, so frankly undertaken. The flapper and especially the liberated college girl were symbols of the new hedonism. College life fascinated the media. John Held, Jr., grew rich and famous caricaturing it in cartoons, comic strips, and illustrations for books such as F. Scott Fitzgerald's *Tales of the Jazz Age.* College women did indeed party and pet more. Also,

were more likely to get married and less inclined to have careers than their forerunners.

This dismayed feminists who had thought emancipation would free women to compete on equal terms with men. Instead, the proportion of college students who were women (though not the gross number) declined, as did the proportion getting advanced degrees and entering practicing professions. The sexual revolution distracted young women from the serious enterprises of earlier women activists, and it made marriage and domesticity more attractive. People rationalized this by

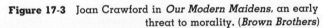

Figure 17-3 Joan Crawford in *Our Modern Maidens,* an early threat to morality. (*Brown Brothers*)

saying either that feminism had succeeded, hence there was no need to agitate for it, or that it had failed, making further effort pointless. The more sophisticated argued that psychoanalysis showed aggressive women to be neurotic sufferers from penis envy, castrating females, and worse. Like Victorians before them, though on different grounds, they insisted women's place was in the home —and in the bed, a more desirable place than formerly thanks to modern science and higher levels of sexual knowledge and expertise.

The pleasure principle found expression in other ways. Tabloid newspapers reached levels of sensationalism that made the yellow journals of an earlier day seem decorous. The New York *Daily Tabloid* ran a front-page photograph of convicted murderer Ruth Snyder at the moment of her electrocution. Crimes, especially of passion, were the tabloid's staple. The execution of Sacco and Vanzetti boosted the circulation of the New York *Daily News,* largest of the tabloids, by 185,000. Bernarr Macfadden, who extolled clean living, founded the *Evening Graphic,* a paper so salacious that it was called "The Pornographic." When pictures were not available, the *Graphic* faked them. Before one convict was executed, Macfadden told his managing editor to run a full-page picture of his face under a headline reading "Roasted Alive."

When the news was dull, tabloids made their own. The *Daily Mirror* resurrected a four-year-old murder, the Hall-Mills case, in 1926 and actually forced it to trial. The *Evening Graphic* made Edward "Daddy" Browning, a middle-aged millionaire who liked young girls, a national figure. His marriage to fifteen-year-old "Peaches" was played up heavily, and their divorce even more so. The *Graphic* printed each party's account of the marriage simultaneously. After its editors

were arrested on a complaint by the Society for the Suppression of Vice, the *Graphic* ran that story too. At one point libel suits totaling $12 million were filed against it. Rudolph Valentino's death was a triumph for both tabloids and the new art of publicity. Press agents hired twenty women to weep at the funeral, which was attended by 30,000 people. A picture showing Valentino meeting his compatriot Enrico Caruso in heaven raised the *Daily News*'s circulation by 100,000. The art of ballyhoo has hardly been improved on since. It was the first time when someone could become famous merely for being famous. Craze followed craze—flag-pole sitting, marathon dancing, crossword puzzles, Mah Jongg—all had their moment in the sun.

Sport flourished too. Jack Dempsey gave boxing its first million-dollar gates. Golf and tennis attracted millions of amateur players, while stars such as Bobby Jones and Bill Tilden made them commercially important spectator sports. For baseball it was an age of giants, led by Babe Ruth who, except possibly for the Prince of Wales, was the most photographed man of his time. In the 1920s college football went big time, led by Knute Rockne's Notre Dame squads which won 105 games while losing only 12 between 1919 and 1931. But greater even than Notre Dame's "Four Horsemen" was Red Grange of Illinois. When he turned professional in 1925, at a time when pro-football was still a minor sport, he made a million dollars in three years.

Prohibition

Of all the country's follies, none was so expensive as the prohibition of alcohol. A controversial issue earlier, it slid through easily—almost, as Frederick Lewis Allen says,

Figure 17-4 Chicago police arrest bathers for indecent exposure in 1922. Standards have since changed, but the struggle goes on. (*United Press International*)

absentmindedly—during the war. But the millions who drank before the Volstead Act went into effect in 1920 had no intention of changing their habits because politicians had decided booze was sinful. They constituted a vast market that lured businessmen into crime and criminals into business. The few thousand federal agents had little chance to arrest the army of smugglers and bootleggers that sprang up to meet this need. They earned little money and some were easily corrupted. Those who tried hard were embarassing, like Izzy Einstein and Moe Smith, masters of disguise who posed as almost anything, including football players, college students, and women. In their five years they were responsible for 20 percent of all the Prohibition cases that came to trial in New York and had to be fired for making other agents look so bad.

The traffic in liquor and especially beer led to fights between gangsters seeking to dominate the market. Al Capone became the greatest of these. His 700 employees literally destroyed the competition, most notably on St. Valentine's Day in 1929 when seven rivals were machine gunned to death in a garage. As in business, unrestricted competition proved self-defeating and gang leaders began to regulate trade. Thus was formed what later became known variously as the Mob, the Syndicate, the Cosa Nostra, or the Mafia. Profits from bootlegging went into prostitution, gambling, and sometimes even legitimate businesses, enabling the Mob to flourish even after repeal, though less colorfully.

Conservative reactions

Prohibition was one of the chief points of conflict between the old America and the new, though scarcely the only one. White, Protestant, native-born Americans, especially in rural areas and small towns, were slow to accept the facts of postindustrial life. Most welcomed Coolidge prosperity and the new technology that gave them telephones, motor cars, electric appliances, movies, and radio. But they resented the manners and morals of the age of high mass consumption. They could not keep their children from seeing movies, and though they forced filmmakers to censor themselves, films were still noteworthy for violence and license. Nor could they keep their children from wanting the family car and using it to neck and pet. It was impossible to keep girls from wearing shorter skirts and scantier undergarments. The young got harder to control, especially when they moved to cities.

What the old America could do was take political action to defend its beliefs or the symbols of them. Some joined the Ku Klux Klan, which besides being racist supported nineteenth-century moral standards. As Kenneth T. Jackson has shown, it had a great following among respectable, urban Northerners disturbed by social change. Laws were passed which forbade the teaching of evolution. Though long since adopted by natural science, it was denied by rural Christians in the South and Midwest especially, who preferred the Biblical account of creation. Tennessee passed such a law and in 1925 John Thomas Scopes, a young biology teacher in the small town of Dayton, agreed to test it. He was represented by three great attorneys including the legendary Clarence Darrow, a trial lawyer of eloquence and compassion who figured in more famous cases than anyone of his time. The prosecution was assisted by William Jennings Bryan, now almost a caricature of the man he had once been. The former Presidential candidate and Secretary of State had been reduced to selling real estate in Florida and defending the old-time religion in country towns. The press flocked to Dayton and wrote 2 million words of copy of the trial.

The defense hoped to use it to teach Americans something of what science had learned about nature, but the court denied permission for its expert witnesses to testify. Darrow was forced to discredit the prosecution by putting Bryan on the stand. Bryan foolishly agreed to testify as an expert witness on the Bible and assured Darrow that the earth was created in 4004 B.C., Jonah was indeed swallowed by a big fish, Eve was made from Adam's rib, etc. Scopes was duly convicted, but fundamentalism gained nothing in consequence. Reporters made fun of the proceedings and fundamental Christianity appeared both malign and ridiculous. Bryan died soon afterward, perhaps of chagrin. He had been generous, sometimes gallant in his time, and deserved a better end.

Lindbergh

As old heroes died or were discredited and old faiths ebbed, there was a desperate need to believe in something. The vulgarity and crassness of the ballyhoo years entertained but did not enrich. Business, though impressive, was also banal. That was probably why Charles A. Lindbergh became so admired. His feat, though notable, was not unprecedented. The Atlantic had been crossed by air before. But no one had flown it alone or over so long a route. When, after landing, Lindbergh proved to be modest and engaging, the country took him to its heart. He seemed to embody the threatened, perhaps obsolete individualism that was believed to have made the country great. President Coolidge dispatched a warship to bring him home. At his public welcome in New York, excited citizens dumped 1,800 tons of paper out their windows, as compared with 155 tons during the premature Armistice celebration of November 7, 1917. He was made a colonel and given the Congressional Medal of Honor, among other awards too numerous to mention. Lindbergh hardly relished his fame. Though he made the flight for a cash prize, he did not think it miraculous or himself especially lucky or heroic. It was a triumph of technology he insisted, and he gave his plane, *The Spirit of St. Louis,* equal billing in describing it.

Art

If this first phase in the development of post-industrial society was marked by self-indulgence, unrestrained commercialism and press agentry, cranky nostalgia for the past, and a crude, business-dominated public ethos, it also witnessed America's cultural coming of age. Few at the time appreciated this fact. Frederick Lewis Allen's classic account *Only Yesterday* hardly mentions the arts. The cultural phenomenon he noticed was the manner in which so many writers and intellectuals seemed alienated. "Here was a new generation . . . grown up to find all Gods dead, all wars fought, all faiths in man shaken," F. Scott Fitzgerald wrote. John Dos Passos' *Three Soldiers,* E. E. Cummings's *Enormous Room,* and Ernest Hemingway's *A Farewell to Arms* showed it to be disillusioned with the war, while Sinclair Lewis's *Main Street* and *Babbitt* reflected disillusion with American life. H. L. Mencken ridiculed nearly everyone and everything, not only Coolidge, prosperity, and the like but this "bilge of idealism." Religion, patriotism, and democracy all were scorned. He attacked his enemies, and they were legion, with stronger language than any writer of his time. They were mountebanks, charlatans, swindlers, witch-burners, homo boobiens. The farmers of Tennessee were "gaping primates" and "the anthropoid rabble." He was cynical, sensible, and immensely amusing.

Mencken was not wildly popular. At its highest point, around 1927, his *American Mercury* had only about 60,000 subscribers. But such vogue as he had demonstrated, as did that of Hemingway, Dos Passos, and others, that the alienation of certain intellectuals and artists was real. Disgusted with post-industrial society, some fled to Europe which, since it was less developed and more alien, seemed better suited to their talents and appetites. Thirty intellectuals contributed to a volume of essays called *Civilization in the United States,* which proclaimed that "the most amusing and pathetic fact in the social life of America today is its emotional and aesthetic starvation."

The paradox was that a country condemned so bitterly for its witch hunts, Scopes trials, KKK, censorship, materialism, and banality was never more culturally alive. Sinclair Lewis became the first American Nobel Prize winner for literature. Eugene O'Neill wrote upwards of twenty plays and received three Pulitzer Prizes. The older Theodore Dreiser wrote *An American Tragedy* and young F. Scott Fitzgerald three novels, including his memorable *The Great Gatsby*. William Faulkner gained recognition in 1929 for *The Sound and the Fury*. Then there were Sherwood Anderson, Willa Cather, Edna Ferber, Floyd Dell, and numerous others. Ezra Pound was near the height of his powers, and in 1922 T. S. Eliot wrote *The Wasteland,* perhaps the most influential poem of the century. Edna St. Vincent Millay became that rarity, a best-selling poet. Langston Hughes led black writers into the Harlem Renaissance. What Isadora Duncan had begun, Ted Shawn, Ruth St. Denis, and Martha Graham improved on to make America the world capital of modern dance, while George Gershwin, Aaron Copland, and Roy Harris became distinguished names among American composers. Jazz and Charlie Chaplin turned popular culture into art. Little theaters and new symphonies sprang up around the country, and art patronage increased. Universities tried to find new ways of teaching, such as the methods employed at Alexander Meikeljohn's Experimental College at the University of Wisconsin. All this in the land of Coolidge, Babbitt, and the booboisie.

Their success did not seem to lift the spirits of artists much. F. Scott Fitzgerald gained wealth and fame while sliding into alcoholism, and his was not an isolated experience. As early as 1926 he wrote that the parties were bigger, the pace faster, and morals looser than before. Young people were wearing out and drinking too much. Most of his friends did, and the more in tune with the times the more they drank. New York was "bloated, glutted, stupid with cake and circuses." Later, in "The Crack-up," he described how many people he knew broke down or disappeared "into the maw of violence," not during the market crash but in the boom itself.

The bull market and the Crash

The twenties ended with a bang, not a whimper, thanks to the market. The stock market was itself the most fabulous aspect of a fabulous age. It dominated the American consciousness after 1927 as nothing save war had ever done. Stocks rose through most of the decade, but the great bull market soared in its last years. The amount of money loaned to brokers to carry margin accounts swelled. (A buyer needed only to put down a fraction of the purchase price in cash, sometimes as little as 10 percent. His broker loaned him the rest, keeping the stock as security. These were called brokers loans or call loans as they were repayable on demand. Brokers, in turn, borrowed the money they lent clients.) In 1927 brokers loans increased from $2.8 billion to $3.6 billion. The week of December 3, 1927 saw more stocks change hands than any week in the New York Stock Exchange's history. Conservatives warned that this level of trading could not be sustained. Stocks were bound to decline. Instead, the market entered its most sensational phase.

On Monday, March 12, 1928, Radio opened at $120\frac{1}{2}$ and closed at $138\frac{1}{2}$. The next day it went to 160. Trading broke all records and the ticker fell six minutes behind. People speculated that 5 million shares might eventually change hands in a single day. The next week the ticker ran as much as thirty-three minutes late. The Federal Reserve Board raised the rediscount rate by half a point and then by a whole point, hoping to discourage member banks from borrowing money to lend speculators, but this had little effect as brokers loans were earning 8 or 9 percent. Money flowed into the call market from corporations with excess profits and even from overseas. The market rose and fell, but the general trend remained upward. By November, when Hoover was elected President, 5 million share days were commonplace. A seat on the New York exchange, which a few years earlier cost a few hundred thousand, now cost $580,000. Radio, thought overpriced a year before at 150, now was listed at 400. In March of 1929, stocks fell sharply; more than 8 million shares were traded in one day, and call money jumped to 20 percent. The New York Reserve Bank wanted to raise the rediscount rate again, but the Federal Reserve Board in Washington refused. The Bank tried to discourage brokers loans by selling securities and warning member banks that money would not be lent to them for reinvestment in the call market. National City Bank frustrated this plan by making $20 million available on call. The interest rate was fixed at 15 percent and buying resumed, while the aggregate of brokers' loans approached $6 billion. *The New York Times* warned that a crash was inevitable. Indeed, it twice announced that the crash had happened before it actually did. But, wanting the boom to go on forever, most authorities believed that it would, hope prevailing against common sense as so often in business. Professor Irving Fisher, a distinguished economist at Yale, argued that stock prices had reached a permanently high plateau.

Between March 1928 and September 3, 1929, the all-time market high, prices rose astoundingly. AT&T went from 179³/₄ to 335⁵/₈; GE from 128³/₄ to 396¹/₄; Montgomery Ward from 132³/₄ to 466¹/₂. Neither earnings nor assets had risen by much. These gains were solely due to the euphoria of investors willing to pay almost any price in the expectation of future rises. Early in September the market broke, and then it rallied somewhat. Charles E. Mitchell of National City Bank (who was using its money to support his own speculations) and others assured the public that stocks were fundamentally sound. On Tuesday, October 22, the market opened with a rally, then slumped again. The next day liquidation began in earnest. Over 6 million shares were traded and the ticker ran 104 minutes late. Leading stocks on the average lost eighteen points. On Thursday, October 24, 1929, securities went on sale in huge lots as brokers dumped hundreds of thousands of shares on the market. They belonged to traders whose margin was exhausted. There were few buyers, and as prices fell others began unloading. The gains of months vanished in minutes. Disaster was staved off in the afternoon when a bankers' pool led by the House of Morgan bought $20 to $30 million worth of stocks. Even so, losses were immense. Over 12 million shares changed hands.

Through the weekend conditions were fluid, but then on Tuesday, October 29, 1929, prices collapsed. Three million shares were sold the first half hour. At the day's end well over 16 million shares changed hands and the average price of fifty leading stocks had fallen nearly forty points. Prices did not reach bottom in 1929 until November 13, the averages for fifty leading stocks then being about half what they were in September. What no one guessed was that stock prices would go on slipping until 1933 and that a business depression had begun that would last over a decade. President Hoover insisted that the fundamental business of the country was sound. His encouragement did no good— quite the contrary. In 1930 the Chairman of the Republican National Committee announced that a conspiracy was afoot to discredit the administration, since every time it issued an optimistic statement the market dropped.

It was true that the country was very rich, which made the Depression hard to understand, but prosperity was unevenly distributed and often shakily based. The stock market itself was absurd. High interest rates made call money too plentiful, and margin requirements were ridiculously low. There was no effective regulation of stocks, so the line between fraud and overconfidence was hard to find. Holding companies proliferated. A holding company could gain control of an operating company frequently by buying a small share of its stock. It could then issue stock of its own, which might, in turn, be bought by other holding companies. Some operators built paper empires on this principle whereby a layer of operating companies would support a mountain of paper that in no way reflected real assets, only buyer enthusiasm. Investment trusts issued stocks to raise money to buy other stocks. By 1929 these trusts were worth $8 billion and had increased elevenfold in two years. As their assets frequently consisted largely of water, the collapse was ruinous to them. The great-

est investment trust, Goldman, Sachs, fell from a high of 236 to $1^3/_4$ after the crash.

This explains the market crash but not the resulting Depression. The primary cause was probably maldistributed income. A third of all personal income went to the top 5 percent of earners. The average worker did not make enough to continue purchasing at 1927 levels, so what was called overproduction resulted. Inventories built up. Factory production fell off in June 1929 while factory payrolls, freight-car loading, and retail sales declined in the fall. A recession preceded the boom and became a depression afterward when confidence declined and buying slowed down even more. Businesses failed, and banks too, as many were undercapitalized or overextended. American loans and investments abroad dried up, and as foreign countries depended on them to buy American goods, sales fell even more. Government, having failed to moderate inflation, was equally inept when deflation struck. The classical approach was to cut government spending, balance the budget, and sustain the gold standard. All these, being deflationary, made matters worse.

Selected references

A brisk, readable history of the times is William E. Leuchtenburg, *The Perils of Prosperity, 1914–1932* (1958). A marvelous contemporary account is the classic Frederick Lewis Allen, *Only Yesterday* (1931). On the Presidents, see Francis Russell, *The Shadow of Blooming Grove: Warren G. Harding in His Times* (1968), and William Allen White's amusing book on Coolidge, *A Puritan in Babylon* (1938). A splendid examination of small-city life in this period is the invaluable R. S. and H. M. Lynd, *Middletown* (1929). Two useful contemporary works on sexual behavior are the sensitive Gilbert Van Tassel Hamilton, *A Research in Marriage* (1929), and Katherine B. Davis, *Factors in the Sex Life of 2,200 Women* (1929). A good account is Andrew Sinclair, *Prohibition: The Era of Excess* (1962). Kenneth T. Jackson, *The Ku Klux Klan in the City, 1915–1930* (1967), is revealing. A fine history of the Scopes trial is Ray Ginger, *Six Days or Forever?* (1958). On the writers, Malcolm Cowley, *Exile's Return* (1951), is fascinating. Left-wing writers from 1914 to 1940 are covered in Daniel Aaron, *Writers on the Left* (1961). A fine biography of F. Scott Fitzgerald is Arthur Mizener, *The Far Side of Paradise* (1949). John Kenneth Galbraith, *The Great Crash* (1955), is very good.

EIGHTEEN

The Great Depression

Period covered: 1929–1939
Emphasis: Politics and social life
Major events: Election of Roosevelt, 1932
The hundred days, 1933
Second hundred days, 1935
Reelection of Roosevelt, 1936
The Roosevelt recession, 1937

National income fell from $87.4 billion in 1929 to $41.7 billion in 1932, while stocks declined in value by $74 billion. Perhaps 12 million people—one-fourth of the entire labor force—were out of work in 1932, and others were underemployed. The unemployment statistics are not entirely reliable, since they were fiddled with sometimes to make things seem better. Even when fairly recorded, they did not include people out of work for long periods who were termed unemployable and hence were no longer counted—real unemployment was probably always higher than figures showed. No one knows how many worked part-time, and nearly everyone who did work took pay cuts. Old abuses were revived. Pennsylvania sawmills paid 5 cents an hour, Connecticut sweatshops gave little girls 60 cents for a fifty-five-hour work week, a good cottonpicker could earn 60 cents for a 14-hour day. Many municipal employees went unpaid for months at a time. Foreclosures on mortgaged land were common. A quarter of the state of Mississippi was auctioned off in a single day.

The relief system, such as it was, collapsed entirely. In New York City relief families got an average of $2.39 a week, and three-fourths of the city's destitute received nothing at all. In other places conditions were worse. Even where relief was available, it usually extended only to food and fuel and was always given grudgingly. Some state constitutions denied the vote to people on welfare. Villages tried to keep the children of welfare recipients out of school, and many communities expelled welfare families from church. Being on relief was a terrible stigma even when there was no work, and people made heroic efforts to avoid it. Though unemployment was clearly no individual's fault, the old feeling that to be out of work showed moral weakness remained; and this feeling was frequently shared by the unemployed themselves. That this was nonsense was proved by the fact that when the war came and everyone who wanted to work could, unemployment disappeared completely. Yet people went on thinking that unemployment was somehow evidence of a weak character.

Businesses and families made desperate economies. Offices stopped their electric clocks to save current. Bethlehem Steel fired 6,000 of the 7,500 men it had brought to Lackawanna and then tried to evict them from company houses which were to be torn down to escape property taxes. Elsewhere, millions of telephones were taken out. The mails were lighter. Travel dwindled. Medical expenditures per capita fell by one-third between 1929 and 1933. In 1932, more people left the country than entered it, and 1933 was the only year during the twentieth century when farms gained population from the towns. No one starved, Herbert Hoover insisted, but this was untrue. Twenty-nine people died of starvation in New York City in 1933, and 110 more, mostly children, died of malnutrition. (Curiously enough, the death rate fell, starvation and the increased suicide rate notwithstanding. To a point, affluence seems more unhealthy than want.)

Hooverism

President Hoover fought back as hard as he could. He called meetings of business, farm, and labor leaders to secure voluntary stabilization of wages, prices, and output. These were caricatured as "no business" meetings since they produced nothing at first but press releases. Had the crisis been short, voluntary stabilization would have worked. Wages held fairly steady in 1930, and Henry Ford even raised his workers' pay and built a new plant.

But in 1931 America began to suffer from the European panic which followed the crash here. Most European countries went off the gold standard, in effect devaluing their currencies, and gold flowed out of America while Europeans dumped their American securities. Hoover tried to organize a voluntary $500 million emergency credit pool and asked insurance companies not to foreclose mortgages. When this failed, he asked Congress to establish a federal loan agency (which became the Reconstruction Finance Corporation) to provide additional farm credit, to reform banking laws to protect depositors, to reform bankruptcy laws to permit more speedy reorganizations, to lend $300 million to the states for direct relief, and to expand public works further. This was infinitely more than Presidents had done to combat earlier depressions. Congress was slow to act, perhaps because the program was so novel or maybe, as Hoover charged, for fear of making him look too good. But it did establish the Reconstruction Finance Corporation (RFC), authorize home loan banks, and grant other of his requests. The RFC loaned $1 1/2 billion to threatened businesses and remained a key agency through the New Deal and World War II.

The President had done all he could, but it was not enough. The congressmen who spoke of spending $40 billion over a five-year period had a better grasp than Hoover of the scale on which government needed to act. His tragedy was that Hoover was at least partially right too. Richard Hofstadter called him a utopian capitalist because of his great faith in nineteenth-century business axioms. As it turned out, his convictions were firmer than those of most economic leaders who, when the crisis came, lost their nerve. In 1931 the head of General Electric proposed what, under Roosevelt, would be the National Re-

covery Administration, giving the government power to regulate prices. Hoover rejected it, saying it was the "most gigantic proposal of monopoly ever made in history." Business might ignore the principles which had made America great, but Hoover would not.

He opposed federal relief for the unemployed, not because he was against helping the needy but because he thought it destructive of local initiative to do so. Relief was the job of states and even more of municipalities. "It is not the function of government," he said, "to relieve individuals of their responsibilities to the public." He opposed other forms of direct aid from Washington on similar grounds. "I want to live in a community that governs itself, that neither wishes its responsibilities onto a centralized bureaucracy nor allows a centralized bureaucracy to dictate to that local government." To extend the mastery of government over the daily lives of people was, he insisted, to make it the master of their souls and thoughts.

Hoover was not hard-hearted or self-interested. He had organized relief on a massive scale in Europe during the war and gave charitably from his own purse during the Depression. He held no special brief for big business, having looked out for the interests of small business while he was Secretary of Commerce. Years earlier he had welcomed labor unions as "proper antidotes for unlimited capitalist organization." He favored loans to corporations by the RFC because otherwise they would collapse, making conditions even worse. But he also supported loans to homeowners and small businessmen. Hoover could do no more because he believed that to save the country from Washington would be to ruin it morally. Cooperation and voluntary organization were what had made the country great and free. He had argued as early as 1921 that to do for people

356

Figure 18-1 They had left their old jobs for more lucrative positions as apple vendors.
(*Brown Brothers*)

what they refused to do themselves would, in the end, lead to fascism. This presented Hoover with an insoluble dilemma, since the Depression seemed to prove that voluntarism did not work. But abandoning it would forestall moral regeneration in the name of economic recovery, He did not think the economy that important, but nearly everyone else did. Thus Hoover lost the good opinion of voters and, perhaps, his place in history. Yet we know that he was right to fear centralized power, even though he was wrong not to help the needy. Hoover knew you could not have it both ways, so he sacrificed the poor to principle. That was immoral, perhaps, but so was the opposite.

Hoover had no political skill. He allowed Congress to maneuver him into signing a bill to aid livestock while vetoing another for direct relief to people. The appearance of apple stands manned by the unemployed inspired him to say that workers were giving up their old jobs for better-paying ones as fruit vendors. He called for a great poem to lift people's spirits when everyone else was thinking only of money. The Bonus Army showed him at his worst. In 1932 thousands of unemployed veterans gathered in Washington to lobby for early payment of a bonus scheduled for 1945, but Hoover refused to meet with them. When they would not disband, he ordered the Army to clear them out. There having been no war for years, Chief of Staff General Douglas MacArthur personally commanded his triumphant warriors as they burned the veterans' shacks and routed them with tear gas. It was a famous victory that did Hoover much harm.

The New Deal

All knew that whomever the Democrats nominated in 1932 would become President. Fortune, courage, and political genius combined to make that man Franklin D. Roosevelt. He was already an experienced politician when stricken with polio in 1921, having been State Senator in New York, Assistant Secretary of the Navy during World War I, and the Democratic candidate for Vice President in 1921. He had shown himself to be charming, affable, and politically astute, but he was thought by many a lightweight. After he was crippled, they felt he would give up politics. But Roosevelt turned out to have great bravery and stamina. With the help of his gallant and much-abused wife, Eleanor, he fought his way back to health—though he never really walked again—and reentered politics to succeed Al Smith as Governor of New York. Skillful preconvention maneuvering made him the favorite Presidential candidate in 1932. He almost lost his chance when the convention deadlocked, but John Nance Garner of Texas, Speaker of the House of Representatives, wanted no repetition of the 1924 Democratic fiasco when it had required 103 ballots to break a stalemate between rural and urban candidates. On the fourth ballot he switched to Roosevelt, giving him the nomination and the Presidency.

There was practically no way at the time to tell what sort of chief executive F. D. R. would be. Walter Lippmann thought him an amiable man with no important qualifications for the office beyond wanting it. His campaign speeches were carefully balanced to please all major interest groups. Among his few plain statements was a strong stand on behalf of public power and a promise to reduce federal expenses and balance the budget. He ac-

Figure 18-2 A little exercise between wars. General Douglas MacArthur and his aide, Major Eisenhower, watch the Bonus Army encampment burn in 1932. (*The National Archives*)

cused Hoover of being a spender and an enthusiast for big government, and Hoover retaliated with threats that Democratic victory would cause grass to grow in the streets and "destroy the very foundations of our American system." This seemed unlikely, if only because the Democratic program largely resembled Hoover's. In a touching display of blind faith, 57.4 percent of the electorate voted for Roosevelt anyway.

His critics were not wrong to call Roosevelt intellectually shallow. When asked to define himself, Roosevelt would say that he was a Democrat and a Christian. Beyond that, he was a Wilsonian and a gentleman. This about exhausted his ideology. What he was committed to was being well liked and getting ahead. He managed the one by being charming, the other by a great gift for picking people who could be useful to him. His "Brain Trust," a corps of intellectuals, supplied the ideas he lacked. He rummaged among them, seemingly at random but usually with a sense of what was politically viable and what was not. This trait is always called pragmatism rather than opportunism when displayed by major politicians. Roosevelt liked to keep people guessing and he hated to say no. So he had rival sets of aides and advisers and would play them off against each other. Whoever spoke to him went away thinking the President was on his side. But Roosevelt had only one side, his own. In the end, no one could really claim to have known him.

President Roosevelt had a great flair for publicity and for stunts that pleased without forcing him to concede much. When he took office, the banking structure was collapsing. Since 1930, 5,000 banks had failed; and as the rate increased, state after state declared bank holidays. By his inauguration banking was suspended or curtailed in all but one state. Hoover urged the President-elect to restore confidence by pledging to sustain Republican policies—the last thing Roosevelt wanted, or dared, to do. Yet he was far from ready for radical steps. Congress hoped for drastic measures, perhaps even for nationalization of the banks. Instead, Roosevelt declared a national bank holiday and then announced that only sound banks would be allowed to reopen. A bill was passed enabling the Federal Reserve System to issue notes against bank assets and the RFC to make loans to banks. This, together with a soothing "fireside chat" over the radio, restored confidence. There was no time to examine most banks. Three-quarters of them were reopened within ten days of the holiday anyhow. Yet as people believed them sound, they became so. Deposits flowed in again, and whereas over 2,300 banks failed during the crisis, practically none did in the years that followed. Roosevelt saved the banking system at almost no cost to bankers—an astounding slight-of-hand trick that showed how a President could be conservative and dexterous at the same time.

Roosevelt disappointed Congress by not hitting the bankers hard and again by making it pass an act cutting governmental expenditures. But he asked for more liberal bills soon, and they were passed almost without debate during what became known as the hundred days. Although these bills fell short of the "New Deal" promised Americans, they were important all the same. Among them were the Agricultural Adjustment Act to support farm prices, a bill establishing a Civilian Conservation Corps to put young men to work, direct grants to the states for relief through the Federal Emergency Relief Administration, and a bill creating the great Tennessee Valley Authority, which built dams and other improvements on a great scale. The keystone of his program was the National Industrial Recovery Act, which Congress passed in June 1933. It aimed to stabilize prices and production by industrywide codes which were to be drawn up by businessmen and enforced by the government. Antitrust actions were suspended, and labor was protected by clause 7a, which guaranteed its right to organize and bargain collectively. Purchasing power was to be maintained by a generous program of public works. This was in effect to abandon competitive enterprise and embrace the New Nationalism Theodore Roosevelt had advocated in 1912. Government would replace the "invisible hand" of the marketplace as the determining factor in economic affairs while looking out equally for the interests of business, labor, and the consumer. In one sense a radical act that brushed aside the old capitalist ethic, it was also conservative in that private property and the wage system were to remain untouched.

Whether radical or conservative, it was in practice unworkable. The National Recovery Administration (NRA) assumed that business could be trusted to comply voluntarily with the act's spirit. This was naive. In every industry where there were large producers that dominated the drafting councils and got codes that made their position stronger and weaker firms less competitive. The right of labor to organize was not respected. There were too many codes, they were too complex, and there was no way for government to enforce them. Worst of all, the NRA attacked recovery from the wrong direction. What was needed was not to raise prices or even to stabilize them, but to increase purchasing power. The NRA was no use here, and even the public works projects that were to put money into circulation did little good because Harold Ickes, the crusty ex-Progressive Interior Secretary, took years instead of months to spend the money. Well before the

Supreme Court declared the NRA unconstitutional, it had clearly failed.

During his first two years in office, Roosevelt seemed to think himself leader of all the people. He tried to mediate conflicts impartially, balancing off the interests of one group against those of others. This concept, which has been called the broker state (with the executive playing the honest broker), worked as long as there was agreement among most people, but it had two faults. The first was that in the nature of things Presidents get progressively weaker after elections, as they make decisions that alienate voters. Second, the strongest groups can, in practice, bring pressure on even the most honest broker. The NRA was most useful to big business, and the Agricultural Adjustment Act (AAA) benefited the largest agricultural producers. They could afford to restrict output and so become eligible for subsidies to make up the difference between actual prices and an agreed-upon price called parity. Small farmers could not cut back and so did not receive parity payments. Moreover, the large growers could use their subsidies to mechanize, thus throwing men out of work and widening their competitive edge.

In 1935 came the second hundred days. Angered by the Supreme Court's invalidation of the NRA and by attacks from the Chamber of Commerce which had earlier supported his New Deal, Roosevelt took stronger steps. The National Labor Relations Act, or Wagner Act, was passed, requiring employers to allow labor to organize and to bargain collectively. The Social Security Act went through, banking practices were further reformed, and TVA was expanded. the AAA was modified to avert another threatened veto by the Supreme Court. Roosevelt asked for an inheritance tax as well as an estate tax, gift taxes, higher income taxes for the rich, and a graduated corporate income tax. This has been called Roosevelt's shift to the left, and it came about partly by accident. When the NRA was declared unconstitutional, Roosevelt was able to save only Article 7a, which protected labor and which did not appear to violate constitutional prohibitions against monopoly. Thus, by accident, what was most liberal in the bill was also most salvageable. Another reason was that Congress had been regularly to the left of Roosevelt. Events now brought him off center and hence closer to a Congress still eager for change.

These events had chiefly to do with growing pressure from the right. By 1935 business was turning against F.D.R. As Ickes put it, there was a vast bitterness welling up from the "grass roots of every country club in America." He was considered prolabor, though 7a had been almost an afterthought and the Wagner Act passed without any help from F. D. R. until the last minute. His new taxes, though light, were vastly unpopular with the rich. As Roosevelt personified the new antibusiness era, he inevitably was blamed for the hatred directed against businessmen. They called him a traitor to his class since, being wealthy, he was expected to protect wealth. In fact, however, this is exactly what he did. Taking office during the greatest crisis in capitalist history, Roosevelt managed to save the system while imposing only modest restraints on it, and these restraints frequently worked in the long run to strengthen business. Banking regulations helped the strong banks and eliminated the weak while at the same time inspiring new confidence. The regulation of securities made people more willing to invest once conditions improved. AAA was a boon to big operators, agricultural businessmen, and the like. Direct relief enabled millions who would otherwise have been reduced to begging to buy goods and services.

The political scientist James McGregor Burns has argued that Roosevelt was really a conservative, though in the British sense. What has kept the Tories strong in modern times has been their willingness to change for the sake of staying in power. They concede what they must so as to protect what they have. Roosevelt did the same thing, and he managed to preserve capitalism despite itself. As businessmen were frequently unable to grasp this point, Roosevelt was forced, after 1935, to look elsewhere for support. He wanted to help the rich and poor alike, and when the rich rejected him, he could only turn to the poor. By helping them, however, he helped the rich too in the end. This was not so much ironic as typical in a country where the privileged sometimes have trouble seeing where their true interest lies.

Radicals

The Socialist party was unable to exploit the crisis, though its leader Norman Thomas got 900,000 votes for President in 1932. It could not hold the young, especially after 1935, for both the New Deal and the Communist party in their different ways seemed more attractive. Nor could the Socialist party heal the split between older right-wingers and younger radicals. In 1936 the old guard walked out, taking most of the party's physical assets with them. Then the rump Socialist party was infiltrated by Trotskyites who, when they failed to take it over, left with hundreds of members and much of the remaining youth. Thomas got only 186,000 votes in 1936. By 1938 membership was down to 7,000 and democratic socialism was finished as an organized movement in America.

The Communist party did better, though before 1935 there was little reason to suppose it would. During what is called the "third period," from the late 1920s to 1935, the communist movement was deliberately isolated and sectarian. Stalin insisted that its main enemy was democratic socialism, an error he repaired in 1935 when Hitler obliged him to admit that fascism was more threatening. He then ordered Communists to cooperate with antifascists, even if they were liberal. "Popular fronts" were established for this purpose and did rather well in America. Many Americans were antifascist and many more admired the Soviet Union's Five-Year Plan, which seemed to produce growth while Western economies were flagging. Russia proved that planning worked, and planning was what many liberals now thought America needed. Communist party members were admired for being tireless, dedicated, and helpful to blacks, the unemployed, and striking workers. The party exploited these feelings by holding rallies and organizing "front groups"—paper bodies for the most part that existed chiefly to generate propaganda and funds. Communism also enjoyed a brief cultural vogue during which middle-class sympathizers vied with one another in showing enthusiasm for all things proletarian.

The party's apparent strength was misleading, and the CP was still secretive, doctrinaire, and rigid. Turnover was always high, and even in its best years the party lost half its members annually, though new members made up these losses for some years. Worse still, the CP was not a true political movement but a creature of Moscow that existed mainly to support Soviet foreign policy. This became obvious in 1939, when the Stalin-Hitler pact was signed and American Communists, who for years had been promoting collective security, overnight became champions of neutrality. The CP's membership fell sharply thereafter, and except in some labor unions and briefly in Hollywood, it had little effect on American life. During its short time in the sun,

Figure 18-3 "Come along. We're going to the Trans-Lux to hiss Roosevelt." A ruling class hiss-in against President Roosevelt. (*Drawing by Peter Arno; copyright © 1936, 1964, The New Yorker Magazine, Inc.*)

American communism accomplished two things. By absorbing or outflanking other socialist movements, the CP destroyed the real left. And because hundreds of thousands had joined or brushed against the CP, many hostages had been given to fortune. In the McCarthy era they would be disgraced or humiliated, mostly for things which had been perfectly open and legal, if unpopular, at the time they were done. This was the most permanent legacy of what one feverish ex-Communist called the red decade.

The CP seems important now because of these after effects and because of its large if temporary influence on American culture. But at the time other left-wing movements were far more popular. There were millions of ordinary Americans who wanted the New Deal to go further and faster than it ever did. Marxism never attracted these people, who favored various home remedies instead. Senator Huey Long, a talented and dangerous demagogue from Louisiana, promised to "share the wealth" if elected President. In 1935 a survey indicated he might win 2 or 3 million votes on a third-party ticket—a threat that ended when Long was assassinated. Dr. Francis E. Townsend, an elderly physician, wanted every citizen over sixty years of age given $200 a month on the condition that all of each check would be spent. This would revive the economy besides providing for old folks. He was thought to have from 3 to 10 million followers. Father Charles E. Coughlin in a weekly radio broadcast, inveighed against bankers and evil men, calling for a "living annual wage" and the "nationalization of banking and currency and of national resources." Coughlin had a great audience, especially among Catholics, and considerable influence, though his anti-Semitism probably did him as much harm as good. Upton Sinclair, a long-time socialist, won the Democratic nomination for Governor in California by promising to end poverty.

None of these movements got very far. Huey Long's appeal was highly personal and did not survive his death. The Social Security Act of 1935 eroded Townsend's support, Coughlin was muzzled by his church, and Sinclair was beaten in California. When discontented people organized the Union party in 1936, it won only a million votes. There was no way to capitalize politically on the New Deal's failures. Though unemployment hardly ever fell below 8 million and in 1940 was still five times what it had been in 1929, Roosevelt was elected again and again. The New Deal brought hope even when it did not get results. F. D. R. had enormous charm, a great sense for public relations, and more of what would later be called charisma than any man of his time. This still does not explain why people would rather stick with Roosevelt than take a chance on Norman Thomas or Father Coughlin or whoever, if only on the grounds that things could harldy get worse. But no matter how bold they were in business or the arts, Americans proved themselves to be conservative politically. Well over a third of the electorate even voted Republican in 1936, though Alf Landon promised only to restore those policies which had brought America to the verge of ruin.

The CIO

Labor fared much better, though in the early 1930s there was little reason to expect it would. The American Federation of Labor, having been hit hard by the postwar reaction, was in no shape to launch organizing drives when the economy collapsed. It controlled only 5 percent of the work force and was too feeble to accomplish much even if it had tried. It remained wedded to the craft principle, which made organization of the mass-production industries with their hundreds of specialities all but impossible. And industry relied more on unskilled workers who, by definition, were ineligible for membership in craft unions. During the fifteen years ending in 1914 productivity had increased by a total of 10 percent. In the 1920s productivity went up by 7 percent a year thanks to mechanization, which enabled an unskilled man with a machine to do the work of many craftsmen. In 1926 the Ford Motor Company announced that 43 percent of its jobs could be learned in a day and 85 percent in two weeks or less. The obvious answer to this was industrial unionism whereby all the workers in a given industry would join one big union. But the AFL craft union leaders feared industrial unions would swamp them and allowed things to get worse and worse. By 1933, 70 percent of the working class was either unemployed or partially employed. With the period 1923–1925 as an index of 100, factory payrolls were down to 38.

Since workers did not wait for the AFL to move, wildcat strikes and spontaneous walkouts became common. Some workers developed their own leaders and methods and others were organized by radicals—not only Communists but also Socialists, Trotskyites, Musteites, and others who put their experience to good use. Most of these early efforts were defeated. Employers were quick to use force and employ strikebreakers, while many spent great sums hiring detective agencies to infiltrate labor organizations. At one time the Pinkerton agency alone had 100 operatives holding union offices, including one national vice president, 14 local presidents, and 34 local secretaries. Some firms stockpiled arms in anticipation of open warfare, but workingmen pressed ahead regardless. Min-

neapolis was famous as an open-shop town, but in 1934 truckers, many led by Trotskyites, struck twice. The first strike ended inconclusively but the second was bloody because an employer organization, called the Citizens' Alliance, used maximum force to keep the open shop. Police led an armed convoy through picket lines, and when they were resisted, the police fired on unarmed men. Sixty-seven were shot, two fatally. In the end, though, the truckers won and went on to make the teamsters' union great. That same year in San Francisco, Harry Bridges led longshoremen in a strike that, when supported by other unions, became a general strike. It was broken bloodily, yet the longshoremen won eventually too. Unlike the teamsters, who succumbed to racketeers when the Trotskyites left it to struggle elsewhere, the West Coast longshoremen stayed radical for decades.

By 1935 it was apparent to farsighted labor leaders that workers were going to have unions whatever the cost and that, if regular trade unionists did not become involved, many of these unions would be run by leftists. Moreover, as the New Deal was growing more interested in labor and a measure of recovery was leading to increased production, the time was right for a general assault on industry. No one felt this more strongly than John L. Lewis, patriarchal leader of the United Mine Workers (UMW), the AFL's only industrial union. In the early thirties it organized most coal mines in the East that were not directly owned by steel companies. These captive mines, as they were called, could only be organized if the steel industry was, giving Lewis yet another reason for favoring industrial unionism. In 1935 he tried to make the AFL accept the challenge. When it failed, he punched big Bill Hutcheson of the Carpenters, a conservative stalwart, in the jaw and formed the Committee on Industrial Organization with garment union leaders Sidney Hillman, David Dubinsky, and others. It was renamed the Congress of Industrial Organizations after being expelled from the AFL.

When Lewis moved he did so in the biggest possible way. The Steel Workers Organizing Committee (SWOC) led by Philip Murray was lavishly supported by CIO money, most of it supplied by the UMW, and sent 500 organizers into steel towns. They were joined in many cases by leaders of company unions, once tools of management but increasingly responsive to rank-and-file demands for genuine bargaining. Big steel gave in without a strike. On March 2, 1937, U.S. Steel, admitting that the handwriting was on the wall, recognized the union, and other large producers soon followed. This was surprising, as U.S.S. was the industry leader in labor exploitation as well as production. It had only abandoned the twelve-hour day and the seven-day work week a few years earlier under pressure from the Federal Council of Churches and President Harding. But U.S.S. had a new management that was not steeped in the Carnegie tradition, and it was competing for a large British armaments order that would be lost if U.S.S. was struck.

Even more surprisingly, some smaller steel companies who accounted for 40 percent of steel's output and who normally followed big steel's lead defected. When struck by SWOC, little steel fought back savagely. Company deputies at the Republic Steel plant in Massillion, Ohio, killed two strikers and wounded others. Worse was to come on Memorial Day in 1937. Strikers and their families had a picnic, then marched on the Republic Steel plant in South Chicago. Though unarmed, as newsreels of the event showed, they were attacked by police who kept firing when the strikers ran. A hundred people, including

women and children, were wounded and ten men were killed, while the police sustained no casualties. No one was ever convicted for this massacre. Little steel broke the strike, but in 1941 the National Labor Relations Board forced it to bargain collectively anyhow. The Memorial Day Massacre was the most futile atrocity in American labor history, and the last.

Though bloodily repulsed by little steel, the CIO did not lose momentum. Industry after industry was organized, frequently after sit-down strikes. This novel technique had been used infrequently before 1936, and no one knows why it suddenly became popular. Once begun, the strikes continued because they were successful, and they succeeded because, by occupying a plant, strikers make it hostage to the company's good behavior. Evicting them by force risked property damage on a large scale. It also threatened much bloodshed, and public officials were less willing to support violence against strikers than they used to be. The modest recovery of 1935, 1936, and part of 1937 made companies less willing to gamble than they had been in harder times when they had less to lose.

For whatever reasons, sit-down strikes were astonishingly effective. They toppled even the auto industry, which was, with steel, the field labor most wanted to organize. General Motors was first to go. The CIO struck seventeen GM plants in late 1936 and early 1937, most notably the big Fisher Body plant in Flint, Michigan. The sit-down strike there began in December 1936 and lasted forty-three days. GM tried to get Frank Murphy, the Democratic Governor of Michigan, to call out the National Guard, but he hesitated. Then, legend has it, after John L. Lewis threatened to expose himself to invading soldiers so as to be the first man shot, Murphy turned GM

Figure 18-4 The Memorial Day Massacre. The last slaughter of working people, and the most futile. (*Wide World Photos*)

down. This broke GM's spirit and it signed with the union, having wasted $1 million on detectives and spies in the two previous years. Other car makers fell grudgingly into line, though not immediately.

The 900 sit-down strikes of 1935–1937 organized all the large industries and many small ones too. They represented the most glamourous and successful technique in the history of American labor. Often they came spontaneously, and organizers had to work frantically to keep abreast of events. Myra Wolfgang of the CIO recalled later that she would get phone calls saying that workers had taken over a shop or soda fountain and wanted to know what they should do next. Once she walked into a department store to

organize the coffee shop, and when she gave the signal the whole store sat down. Another time Wolfgang was in a hotel signing a contract when she heard someone call out, "All chambermaids down to the eighteenth floor, all bellboys up to the twenty-fourth floor," and found herself in the middle of another sit-down.

When hotel workers struck the Statler in Detroit, 5,000 pickets swarmed in. Its manager, a member of the Intercollegiate Socialist Society, had known one of their leaders in college and, remembering the old vision of a triumphant proletariat, cried, "Tell me, Al, tell me, is this it?" Of course this was not *it*, the day of revolution, but it was a frightening day for middle-class Americans all the same. Had

Figure 18-5 Chrysler workers manning the barricade during an auto industry sit-in. (*The Archives of Labor History and Urban Affairs, Wayne State University*)

not Lenin called on workers to seize the instruments of production? And were they not doing so? Public opinion forced politicians to take a tougher line on sit-ins, and the courts ruled them illegal. This backlash came too late to save the mass-production industries, which were, in any case, now subject to the Wagner Act.

What the CIO began the National Labor Relations Board completed. By 1941 there were 9.5 million organized workers—5 million in the CIO; 4.5 million in the AFL which had been forced to compete despite itself; and a million in independent unions. Since the total work force numbered 56 million, this meant that most employed people were still not organized and probably never would be. Without unions they had no means of raising their often pitifully low wages. Forty percent of American families, for example, earned less than the $1,500 a year the WPA considered a "minimum health and decency" budget.

Big labor's emergence as a national force was, all the same, the decade's single most important feature. Big business now had to make room for big labor. (And big government too. The number of federal employees more than doubled between 1933 and 1941.) Yet this made far less difference than business had feared and radicals hoped. Because radicals were submerged in the CIO, where they controlled at their peak perhaps only a quarter of member unions, they could not make policy. Lewis used them skillfully while he needed experienced organizers, but he meant to keep radicals from changing the character of organized labor. Later, when Communists became a liability, the CIO ruthlessly weeded them out. The CIO used radical tactics for conventional ends. It did not challenge the right of business to make its own decisions except those relating to wages, hours, and working conditions, nor did it question the profit motive. Businessmen found that the CIO shared their frame of reference and differed only on how to share the pie. Unions turned out to have unforeseen advantages. By pushing up incomes, they enlarged the market for consumer goods. They insured management against wildcat strikes and disciplined the labor force, and most of the extra cost of having them was passed on to consumers anyway. But the trade union movement remained far weaker than business. Its success was dependent on a government which, through the Wagner Act, and other devices, made management cooperate. Union leaders knew that and afterward rarely broke the rules agreed on in the 1930s.

The Second New Deal

Improved business conditions and the second hundred days assured Roosevelt of re-election in 1936. He got 11 million more votes than Alf Landon, the GOP nominee, and carried forty-six states. The radical vote was negligible. This was the high point of Roosevelt's popularity and effectiveness. Thereafter he had no place to go but down, and he did. His first mistake was trying to pack the Supreme Court which had found such key New Deal measures as the NRA and the AAA unconstitutional. Without much warning he brought forward a bill allowing him to appoint an additional justice for every sitting justice who did not retire at age seventy. This would have allowed him to create six new justices at once.

In theory this was a clever move. The bill was moderate and required no constitutional changes. It was advanced in the name of efficiency rather than reform. Such cleverness was self-defeating. Had Roosevelt campaigned openly for a more liberal Court, he might have prevailed, since Democrats had a huge majority in Congress. But by preparing the bill in secret and arguing so disingenuously, he offended many who revered the Court and thought his approach demeaned it. Moreover, several justices turned about, producing a pro-New Deal majority for the Wagner Act and social security. This took the court effectively out of politics and led to a straight fight between Congress and President Roosevelt, who lost. This showed the limits of his charm and personal popularity and the fragility of his governing coalition. Though based on the urban vote, it depended on conservative Southerners too, and these reverted to type when the worst was over. Thereafter Congress was often hostile; all the more so after 1938, when his attempts to eliminate enemies by campaigning against them in local elections backfired. Most were returned and the Democratic majority shrank. Thereafter congressional investigations, previously held to support the administration, were frequently used against it.

The New Deal began declining as early as 1937, when the economy collapsed again. This was because Roosevelt feared inflation and wanted to balance the budget. Between January and August he cut the WPA in half, putting 1½ million workers on the street. This, together with an agricultural surplus that drove farm prices down, reduced consumption and hence production. In May 1937 the index of production was at 76, compared with a high of 117 the previous August. Four million people were out of work. Business blamed the New Deal for undermining confidence with its deficits and crazy reforms. Roosevelt thought business was at fault for keeping profits to itself and employing monopolistic tactics. He called a special session of Congress to increase public works and established the Temporary National Economic Committee to devise new antitrust measures. This response was absurd, and it became all the more so when he put Thruman Arnold in charge of the Justice Department's Antitrust Division. Arnold was a well-known opponent of antimonopoly legislation, having exposed its futility in a witty book entitled *The Folklore of Capitalism* (1937). Public works did make sense, however, and the $4 billion spent on them helped the economy, though not enough.

What makes Roosevelt's economic policies seem foolish is that John Maynard Keynes, a British economist, and others had already explained the relation between government spending and economic performance. Government spending was inflationary and saving deflationary. The correct strategy was to spend hugely and run up deficits when the economy faltered—and, when inflation threatened, to cut expenditures, raise interest rates, and the like. These were crude mechanisms that could not be applied readily to mild slumps and boomlets, but they were effective against serious economic movements. All Western countries now employ Keynesian mechanisms, and with considerable success. Roosevelt had Keynesian advisers, but he did not listen to them well enough. Partly this was because he did not understand economics, partly because he liked balanced budgets. Moreover, he instinctively favored compromise and Keynesianism demanded commitment—half a loaf was not enough. Roosevelt ended up with a program that was too liberal to please business and too conservative to work. This was typical of his Presidency.

Compared with earlier administrations, however, the New Deal was impressive. It put millions of people back to work, gave assistance to millions of others, and promoted some recovery. The Wagner Act aided organized labor enormously. The National Youth Administration helped 600,000 students through college and 1½ million more through high school. The Agricultural Adjustment Act of 1938 raised farm income by 1940 to its 1937 level. The Civilian Conservation Corps (CCC), Work Projects Administration (WPA), and similar projects gave men rewarding work and left the country a rich legacy of parks, dams, buildings, forests, and such. Tennessee Valley Authority (TVA) was a magnificent accomplishment that gave new life to a whole region. There were intangible strengths to the New Deal that must be allowed for too. Roosevelt inspired hope and confidence in despairing millions. He made Washington a lively place to work and government a more creative instrument than it had ever been before.

Yet in relation to need and to the opportunities it had, the New Deal was inadequate. There were still between 7 and 10 million unemployed in 1940. Production and income rose, sometimes to the levels of 1929, but the population was larger, so real prosperity did not return until the war made government embrace Keynes despite itself. Relief, though vital, was always too limited. At its peak, the WPA employed only a third of those out of work, paying them an average of $50 a month. In 1938 families on relief typically got $278 per year. Those with the least need—big business, big farmers, bankers—got the most help, while those whose need was greatest got the least. When Roosevelt took office and perhaps until 1937 or even 1938, he could get almost anything he wanted from Congress. The pity was that he wanted so little. He might have nationalized the banks, instituted comprehensive medical care, put all the unemployed to work, and much else, since the air was thick with radical proposals. But Roosevelt personally was conservative and—though always in motion—moved ahead slowly. There was no effective pressure from the left to make him do more. The loudest voices were on the right, and while they did not stop him from sometimes going against the grain of conventional thought, they reinforced his affection for the status quo.

The most lasting result of the New Deal era was its creation of what is now called the corporate state. Before 1933 business had a virtual monopoly of power regardless of which party was in office. Government was weak and therefore responsive to business, while labor was simply weak. This was not always so good for business as it seemed. Competition was expensive and, under free market conditions, it was hard to control. A complex, industrial society could not be managed solely by the push and pull of contending interests. This was the point made by New Nationalists earlier, though it was not grasped then. The Depression made it ines-

capably clear that national well-being could not be left to chance. The New Deal created both big government and big labor—not to deprive business of profit but to rationalize the system, build safeguards against the worst abuses of the past, and give it conscious direction.

New Dealers were not always clear in their minds about what was happening. Like Roosevelt, most took things a step at a time, shifting ground as new friends and enemies appeared. This was confusing, as was the opposition of business to measures like social security, regulating stock market and banking affairs more closely, and other steps which were really in its interest. It was hard to know what was going to come of all the political turbulence of those years. But what resulted—especially during World War II, which drove business, government, and labor even closer together—was a new order in which business made concessions to government and labor in return for certain benefits. The unions guaranteed a disciplined, predictable work force. Government smoothed out the economic cycle and assisted business in countless ways—sometimes with direct subsidies, often by regulating industries to their own advantage rather than the public's. Ordinary people accepted the favors shown business because they also gained from hundreds of federal programs ranging from loans to homeowners to cheap electricity for farmers. And government accepted in principle, if not always in practice, its obligation to provide for the needy.

The system was far from perfect. Millions of people—blacks, Chicanos, women—remained outside the benefit structure, and the fruits of prosperity were unevenly distributed. The proportion of Americans who have high incomes is about the same now as before the Crash. Rich people still pay proportionately lower taxes than the poor. While the struggle for advantage between interest groups goes on, it mostly remains within the limits established in the 1930s and early 1940s.

Selected references

A good short account of the thirties is William E. Leuchtenburg, *Franklin D. Roosevelt and the New Deal, 1932–1940* (1963). James McGregor Burns, *Roosevelt: The Lion and the Fox* (1956), is rich and original. A fine collection of documents and essays is Otis L. Graham, Jr. (ed.), *The New Deal* (1971). A thoughtful social history is Caroline Bird, *The Invisible Scar* (1966). A surprising portrait of Hoover is William A. Williams, *The Contours of American History* (1961). Richard Hof-

stadter's classic essay on Hoover is in his *The American Political Tradition* (1948). Communism's appeal to intellectuals is discussed in Murray Kempton, *Part of Our Time* (1955). Irving Bernstein, *Turbulent Years: A History of the American Worker, 1933–1941* (1970), is fair and comprehensive. Sidney Lens, *Left, Right, Center*, is an independent radical's view of labor in the thirties. R. S. and H. M. Lynd, *Middletown in Transition* (1937), shows how a small Midwestern city adapted to the Depression. There are many absorbing personal accounts in Studs Terkel, *Hard Times* (1970). Broadus Mitchell, *Depression Decade* (1947), is a readable economic history. A brilliant essay on the culture of the times is Warren Susman, "The Thirties," in Stanley Coben and Lorman Ratner (eds.), *The Development of an American Culture* (1970).

NINETEEN

From Versailles to Pearl Harbor

Period covered: 1921–1941
Emphasis: Diplomacy
Major events: Washington Naval Conference, 1921
Dawes Plan, 1924
World Depression begins, 1929
Japan goes into Manchuria, 1931
Hitler comes to power, 1933
Roosevelt and the New Deal, 1933
Neutrality·Act, 1935
Germany takes the Rhineland, 1936
Japan invades North China, 1937
Quarantine Speech, 1937
Munich, 1938
World War II begins, 1939
Lend Lease, 1941
Pearl Harbor, 1941

Woodrow Wilson's successors were serious, dedicated men. True, Warren Gamaliel Harding enjoyed his bourbon and poker; true also, he was careless about his choice of friends; but neither he nor his foreign policy advisers ever went on a binge like sending General Pershing chasing across Mexico after the elusive Pancho Villa. What had that fiasco gotten the United States? And, when one thought about it, what had all those other Wilsonian "crusades" produced except a general stalemate?

Perhaps that was an unfair description of what the Progressives had tried to do and where they had come out, but when the Republicans came to power in 1921, America was the only nation still formally at war. Charles Evans Hughes, the new Secretary of State, and Herbert Clark Hoover, his colleague in the Commerce Department, regarded themselves as realists. The country had rejected the League of Nations after a full debate—a debate which had, in fact, revealed some very real weaknesses in Wilson's peace-keeping organization, especially in connection with the Versailles Treaty. It was time to bury dead issues and get on with the business of living in the postwar world.

The Hoover world view

The overriding consideration for American leaders as the postwar era began was their belief that Europe could not send, or this country absorb, sufficient imports to provide capital for the reconstruction of a sound world economy. To attempt to do so would cause severe dislocations, perhaps even the collapse of the American economy. The severe recession which accompanied reconversion of the nation's industries and agriculture to peacetime use seemed proof enough of this thesis. America had become the greatest creditor nation the world had ever known, with a favorable balance of $12 billion. Future success would, thought Hoover and other policy makers, depend to a great extent on making effective use of that vast financial asset to keep the wheels of the world economy turning. "We are indeed at that changing point in our national economics," Hoover had told a conference of the nation's leading bankers in 1920,

that the British empire faced in 1860, when no longer could Britain take full value in commodities for the commodities which she exported, and that if she would continue to expand, continue to progress, she had to invest abroad, and by doing so they not only extended the capacity and the absorption of British goods, but they lifted the standard of living of the entire world.

Between 1922 and 1929, the United States exported capital at an average rate of $733 million per year. Just before the boom came to an end in 1929, the rate had reached $1 billion a year.

Hoover never believed that the process would sustain itself automatically or that all loans were equally good for the American economy or the world. He thought, for instance, that the federal government should act as a clearinghouse for loans to foreign countries. Just as British diplomats had once screened their bankers' proposals for any hidden political ramifications buried in the fine print, so now the Secretary of Commerce believed that it was his duty to make sure that American dollars did not go into wasteful nonproductive or counterproductive speculations—whether devised by Wall Street operators or by their foreign counterparts. He wanted to prohibit all loans to sustain uneconomical foreign "monopolies," a category which included state-supported industries in competition with private enterprise firms in the world market, loans to nations with unbalanced budgets, and loans which would enable countries to purchase armaments.

To be productive, foreign loans should increase American exports, but that was not enough. They should also encourage a free exchange of goods and services among *all* countries; they should reduce, whenever possible, the role of government in international and *intra*national business affairs; finally, they should discourage any incipient international arms race. Loans, in other words, should supply the adhesive for a rebuilt world order. As the Republican Presidential candidate in 1928, Hoover summed it all up: ". . . it is an essential part of the sound expansion of our foreign trade that we should interest ourselves in the development of backward or crippled countries by means of loans from our surplus capital."

Some early obstacles
and how they were overcome

Congress had a less complicated philosophy. Protection of domestic producers came first, last, and always, and the best way to provide this was by enacting high protective tariffs. The Emergency Tariff of 1920, which was the first step upward from the 1913 Underwood Tariff, was passed over Wilson's veto in a year when the United States had a trade surplus of nearly $4 billion. In the decade 1920–1929 the American trade surplus totaled nearly $16 billion. Yet the tariff kept rising with the 1922 Fordney-McCumber Act and then, as the Depression began, with the 1930 Smoot-Hawley Act. In fairness to the legislators of that era, it ought to be noted that American exports fell by half from 1920 to 1921 and remained far below war levels

throughout the decade. Imports also fell by half in the first year after the war, but they remained higher proportionally to exports throughout the 1920s. Thus, while imports were only 50 percent of exports in 1920, the percentage rose to 60 percent in 1921 and to 80 percent by 1925.

Still, it was hard to see how Europeans could possibly reestablish their economies and yet carry the burden of the war debts and the continuing trade deficits with the United States. Executive branch policy makers understood and sympathized with the desire to prevent European dumping in the United States. They also recognized that the history of American tariff legislation had been a story of congressional trade-offs which sometimes served the national interest and sometimes did not. The best thing to do was to go along with the legislators in the hope of securing provisions in the tariff laws which could be used to gain access to European markets, and those of Europe's colonial dependencies. Administration leaders also hoped to encourage multilateral trade by taking the lead against discriminatory tariffs and trade regulations. High but equal tariffs were the proper way to lead Europeans into a community of interests with one another while still satisfying Congress. Under the Fordney-McCumber law, for example, the President received power to raise tariffs against nations which discriminated against American trade. During World War I both the Allies and the Central Powers had set forth detailed plans for discriminatory blocs in the postwar era. American tariff policy in the 1920s was designed to prevent that from happening. As the major source of credits for reconstruction, the United States had good reason to believe it could lead the world back to multilateralism by proper policies.

Between 1921 and 1924, to take another example, the State Department used the tariff and other levers to open up colonial territories and League mandates to world trade. As one of Secretary Hughes's top aides explained in a policy memorandum, the United States wanted—and needed—an "open door" economically into the backward areas, including colonies. There were two ways to achieve this end: through trade treaties and through investments in "banks, shipping, railroads, and factories, and contracts for public works and government supplies."

Finally, America began lending money to Germany so that country could begin paying reparations to the Allies, money which then came back to the United States to pay for exports or to satisfy war debts obligations. Critics pointed out that the whole thing was a lot like a merry-go-round: what would happen when the music ran down? Government spokesmen replied that the money was not just traveling around from country to country in a locked strongbox. In each place it stopped, the money would (or should) stimulate production and economic activity. That was why it was so important to supervise foreign loans—to make sure that they did indeed perform this function. After all, England had managed the world economy in similar fashion during the hundred years from 1814 to 1914, hadn't it? That was what the *Pax Britanica* was all about; with far more capital at its disposal, the United States should be able to do it even better!

At Versailles, the American delegation had refused to accept the Allied proposition that war debts and reparations were linked. They had also, therefore, refused to talk about scaling down the war debts, partly because they did not trust the Allies to reduce reparations. During the war, English and French leaders had boasted to their peoples about squeezing the Germans until the "pips squeaked." That was one reason for America's "Uncle Shylock" approach at Versailles.

What Americans wanted was a reduction of reparations first; then there would be ample opportunity to talk about reducing Allied war debts to the United States.

They did hint at reductions if some action was taken to ease Germany's burden, and thus to restore the defeated nation to the European community politically and economically. The Allies, however, trusted the United States no more than Wilson's advisers trusted David Lloyd George or Georges Clemenceau. The result was a stalemate, with neither side willing to make the first move.

All too soon the war debts became an emotional issue. Those who felt that the United States should never have gone to war pointed to Allied debt attitudes as proof that Uncle Sam had been taken to the cleaners once again by John Bull. Europeans grew more and more irritated at American pretensions and their bill-collecting manner. Who had fought for three years to make the world safe for democracy while Wilson sat in his office writing notes and counting profits? For the Americans, it was said, World War I was a Hemingway adventure tale; for Europe it was sheer catastrophe.

Calvin Coolidge's oft-quoted reply to a question about forgiveness summed it all up: "They hired the money, didn't they?" Americans also had very little sympathy for their former Allies' determination to keep Germany from becoming a menace again. Aside from their belief that Anglo-French attitudes were mostly concerned with a selfish desire to check German competition for world markets, policy makers felt that a punitive reparations policy would burden the Germans with such a crushing debt that the Weimar government might collapse. Then what? challenged American diplomats. Would Paris and London rather deal with a "Bolshevik" Germany?

"French fear of German militarism is regarded with sympathy," Bainbridge Colby,

Wilson's last Secretary of State, explained in words that would set the tone for a decade of American diplomacy, but "restoration of law and order . . . is all-important for [the] peace and safety of the world."

German reparations obligations were finally set at the impossible figure of $35 billion by an Allied commission. When Germany defaulted in 1923, the French occupied the Ruhr area with a large military force to extract payment in kind. What folly! declared American observers. Even the French soon came to realize their error, if only because it was made plain to them that American bankers would not extend additional loans until there was some promise of European stability. The United States then proposed the so-called Dawes Plan for reducing Germany's annual payments to a reasonable level. Another feature of the plan was that authority should be given to an American reparations "czar" who would determine how much and when Germany could pay. Finally, the United States promised to participate in an international loan to Germany to enable that country to go back to work.

J. P. Morgan and Company was authorized to offer the American public a $100 million share of the Dawes loan, and the sum was oversubscribed within hours of its first advertisement on the stock market. Weimar Germany soon became the foreign equivalent of the 1920s Florida land boom. By the end of the decade, German banks, business houses, and government institutions owed foreign creditors a $3 billion private debt—most of it to American investors. Thus, when the worldwide depression began, German defaults were almost one-third of the total defaults by all countries.

Hoover's filters to screen out speculative loans had turned out to be sieves. They let everything through, good and bad alike. The theory that American loans could stimulate business abroad, making it possible for other nations to earn enough at home and in trade with third countries to more than balance their ledger sheets with America, would work only if each loan did its part. But once the flow of capital began, the government hesitated to discourage investors and bankers for fear it might be acting at just the wrong moment and might trigger a panic. The trouble was that any moment seemed wrong to someone, and so very little was ever done to bring speculation under control. The capital lacked sufficient outlets at home, and Hoover and Hughes could not impose strict rules on loans without endangering the steady flow of exports which America needed to sustain and expand prosperity. Therein was a dilemma— not an obstacle—and it could not be overcome.

The Washington Treaties

Weimar Germany was supposed to serve as a bulwark against the Bolshevik threat in Europe, and it was expected that Japan would serve as an important stabilizing influence in Asia. But first there had to be a better understanding between Washington and Tokyo. At the outset of World War I, Japan had seized the German leasehold on the Shantung Peninsula in China and there she stayed, citing obligations to England under the 1902 Anglo-Japanese Alliance for attacking the German position in Shantung. Later in the war Tokyo presented China with a list of twenty-one demands obviously intended to solidify her position not only in Shantung but throughout China and Manchuria. In 1917 Secretary of State Robert Lansing negotiated the so-called Lansing-Ishii Agreement, an agreement which State Department officials promptly released to the world as a mutual renunciation of special rights in China except those pertaining to Japan's geographical proximity. In Tokyo, Foreign Office spokesmen gave out a different interpretation of the document, claiming that it recognized Japan's paramount interests and special position.

Similar disagreements characterized Japanese-American relations as the war came to a close. Japan landed 50,000 troops in Siberia, ostensibly as their contribution to a joint Allied intervention against the Bolsheviks aimed in the first instance at keeping the Trans-Siberian Railroad out of Communist hands. But the Japanese settled down as if they meant to remain in control of Siberia long after the others had abandoned the project. So it went. At Versailles, Wilson had attempted without success to pry the Japanese out of Shantung. And the Japanese had tried, also without success, to get a racial equality clause in the charter of the League of Nations.

At war's end America and Japan were the only two Pacific powers left unscathed by the ravages of the European struggle, or revolution, or both. No one could tell what the next stage of the seemingly unending revolutionary turmoil in China would bring, but it seemed clear that if the prevailing trend in Japanese-American relations continued on its course toward collison, China might soon become the scene of a major confrontation.

Already the probability of a Japanese-American naval arms race was increasing with each passing day. England and Japan had long been allies in the Pacific, but like most "entangling alliances" (to use Wilson's favorite expression of disapproval), it was a marriage of convenience. The British were famous for putting practicality above principle, said American diplomats. But never mind, they went on, we can do better even on those grounds. If the Japanese were offered assurances that the United States did not intend to use the Chinese revolution as an excuse to deprive them of economic opportunities or plan to seek special arrangements with other powers to that end, then they should agree to the substitution of a multilateral security pact for the Anglo-Japanese alliance. Moreover, such a pact would make possible mutual reductions in spending for battleships and destroyers, a wasteful and inefficient use of scarce resources.

With these plans in mind, Secretary of State Hughes sent out special invitations to a naval conference to be held in Washington during the winter of 1921–1922. It was the diplomatic event of the decade. Hughes opened the meeting on Nov. 12, 1921, with a stunning proposal to scrap thirty American capital ships already under construction if the other powers would only agree to a ten-year shipbuilding holiday. Before the delegates had recovered from that shocker, the Secretary went on rapidly to outline a formal treaty establishing a 5:5:3 capital ship ratio for the United States, Great Britain, and Japan. It worked. Having reassured Britain and Japan that he wanted to deal *with them about China* and not *with China about them,* Hughes easily headed the lesser powers into the naval treaty and into two other agreements of equal importance.

The first of these other pacts was a four-power arrangement with Great Britain, France, and Japan which pledged the signers to consider together what should be done in any future Asian crisis. What special advantages did that treaty hold for the United States? It is easy to dismiss the Four Power Treaty as doomed to failure from the start, but given American options in the 1920s it was a shrewd move by Hughes and his associates. The United States could have joined the Anglo-Japanese alliance, making it a three-power pact, and also a three-power entagling alliance. But Hughes had not done that; instead, by adding just one other power, he had

Figure 19-1   The Washington Naval Conference. The treaties which were negotiated here were the centerpiece of collective security in the interwar period. (*Culver Pictures*)

converted the Anglo-Japanese alliance into a modern collective security arrangement. Allies cannot bring public pressure to bear upon one another nearly so well as can members of a collective security arrangement. The second pact was the Nine Power Treaty, a multilateral affirmation of the Open Door policy for China—the closest American diplomats ever came to transforming John Hay's turn-of-the-century initiative into international law. Speaking to a meeting of the members of the American Historical Association in 1922, Secretary Hughes announced that the Washington Treaties had not only made the Anglo-Japanese alliance unnecessary but that they had also eliminated the Lansing-Ishii Agreement—and with it the ambiguities of all such bilateral understandings.

The Washington Treaties thus became the centerpiece in the grand design of collective security in the 1920s. Only the Chinese delegates protested the treaties and China's exclusion from the decision-making process, but Hughes and his aides silenced the outcry with pointed assurances that it was all for the best. Besides, what could the Chinese do about it? They had been the objects of diplomacy for nearly a century, and the end was not in sight. It was all for the best as long as the powers observed restraint in their dealings with China—and with one another. And that would depend upon economic and political conditions beyond the control of the men who negotiated the Washington contracts.

Back to the hemisphere

Latin America, from Mexico to Tierra del Fuego, received a massive influx of dollars, more than $1.5 billion, in the postwar decade. Significant changes in the pattern of American investment occurred; geographically more money went into South America than before, and more went into extractive industries (oil, mining, and agriculture). Republican Secretaries of State in the 1920s developed something of a domino theory about Latin America: they assumed that what happened in Mexico would determine the pattern throughout the southern half of the Hemisphere. It behooved American diplomats, therefore, to resolve whatever remained of the old dispute over foreign property rights under the new Mexican constitution. They were aided by a new group of leaders in Mexico City who also wanted to resolve differences with Washington after nearly a decade of confrontation politics during the Wilson administrations. Finally, in 1928, "good-will" Ambassador Dwight Morrow, a former partner in J. P. Morgan and Company, sat down with Mexican President Plutarco Elias Calles and worked out an informal arrangement. Morrow got a Supreme Court decision favoring the investors, a new petroleum code, and a good dinner; Calles received assurances of more good will, a promise that America's newest hero—Charles Lindbergh—would put in a special guest appearance in Mexico, and a commission for Marxist artist Diego Rivera to paint some new murals extolling the virtues of the revolution. All in all, a good bargain.

Everything seemed to be working out just fine in hemisphere relations. Hoover and his Secretary of State Henry L. Stimson had purposely set out to eliminate the most overt instances of "Yankee imperialism" in the Caribbean and Central America by withdrawing troops from Haiti and Nicaragua and by renouncing the right to intervene in all but the most extreme circumstances. Then came the worldwide depression, and it came first to Latin America. Economic troubles became political revolutions. In 1930 and 1931 alone, eleven of the twenty Latin American republics changed governments, not in traditional *caudillo* fashion but as the result of popular unrest. As exporters of raw materials who depended upon steady world prices and high consumption, the Latin Americans were hard hit right away. American imports of raw materials, for example, fell from $4.4 billion in 1929 to $1.3 billion in 1933.

Japan's economy was given a thunderous shock by the depression. New York set the world price level for raw silk in the 1920s and when the bottom fell out in 1929, the Japanese received 50 percent less for their silk—not only in the United States but in other markets as well. With unemployment spreading across the land like the plague, Congress sought the remedy in an even higher tariff. That proved just about as effective as efforts by medieval town fathers to board up their cities against the disease, but in both instances the people felt some relief in knowing that their rulers were "doing something" about the situation.

Treaties and stovepipe hats

Japan's leaders tried something else; or perhaps a better way of putting it would be to say that Japan's leaders could not prevent the Army from trying to cure the situation. In September 1931 the Japanese Army launched a forward movement in Manchuria which the political leaders back in Tokyo could not or would not reverse.

It is still hard to determine, four decades later, whether Stimson and Hoover were more upset at Japan's threat to China's territorial integrity or at the prospect of not being able to trust Tokyo any longer. The great China market had never materialized, and Japan was still a good customer. But who could say where the Army would take Japan after Manchuria? If the United States said nothing, might not Japanese militarists—or those in other countries—be encouraged to risk new adventures? For all these reasons it was thought necessary to take a stand on behalf of the Washington Treaties. But how to go about it? After lengthy consideration, Secretary Stimson decided upon a nonrecognition doctrine. His idea was to deny diplomatic recognition to the puppet state Japan created out of Manchuria and, by expressing America's disapproval, to encourage Japanese "liberals" to stand up to their atavistic countrymen who still believed in military solutions.

"This fight has come on in the worst part of the world for peace treaties," Stimson admitted at a Cabinet meeting. The pacts "no more fit the three great races of Russia, Japan, and China, who are meeting in Manchuria, than . . . a stovepipe hat would fit an African savage. Nevertheless . . . the whole world looks on to see whether the treaties are good for anything or not. . . ." The "Stimson Doctrine" on Manchuria was accepted by President-elect Franklin Delano Roosevelt—somewhat to the surprise of the latter's advisers, who thought that the candidate's New Deal also meant a full repudiation of Republican foreign policy.

The New Deal and the rest of the world

When he refused to cooperate with Hoover's last-ditch efforts to find an internationalist solution to the depression, F. D. R. had, in fact, created the impression that he meant to repudiate Republican foreign policy in full. He then repudiated the World Economic Conference in the summer of 1933 with a "bomb-shell" message declaring that the restoration of prosperity within the United States was the first order of business—as it should be in other countries. This decision was applauded by conservatives and liberals alike—that is, those who believed that the Republicans had pursued what Roosevelt had labeled an "Alice in Wonderland" approach to international economic affairs. It was hard to find anyone to defend the Hoover view in 1933.

New Deal economic nationalism soon came under attack in foreign countries, however, where leaders argued that the United States now wanted to have it both ways more than ever: it wanted to enact high tariffs and import quotas and to pursue currency policies designed to subsidize exports on a purely self-interested basis. Meanwhile, they said, the United States was constantly preaching to others about political obligations, international morality, and respect for the opinions of mankind. In 1934, the New Deal took a slight turn toward economic internationalism with the enactment of the Reciprocal Trade Agreements Act, the first downward revision of the tariff since the end of the war. But critics remained skeptical, pointing out that the agreements negotiated by the United States under this act usually involved complementary products—machine tools for coffee, sewing machines for sugar, etc. These did little to encourage genuine multilateralism.

It was also apparent that most of these agreements were signed with Latin American countries, and the net effect of the plan, said foreign observers, was to reduce Western Hemisphere trade with the rest of the world. Was it fair, said the Japanese, for the United States to shut us out of Latin America and still demand an open door in Manchuria? Whether these complaints were fully justified or not, New Deal diplomacy was most active in Latin

America during Roosevelt's first term. His approach was called the "Good Neighbor Policy."

The Good Neighbor still had very sensitive feelings about Cuba, however, and moved in a heavyhanded way against those it regarded as unfriendly revolutionaries. A crisis in Cuban-American relations erupted in 1933 when a revolutionary government in Havana headed by Grau San Martin started talking about changing the fundamental pattern of the relationship. When "watchful waiting" proved unable to discourage Grau, Special Ambassador Sumner T. Welles encouraged Fulgencio Batista to establish a government with which the United States could do business. Batista took Welles's advice. Formal diplomatic recognition, a new trade treaty, and a series of economic subsidies (unofficial and official) sealed the bargain. Batista had real staying power. He ruled, sometimes through others, for twenty-five years. Then the clock ran out on American policy in Cuba. Fidel Castro came to power to complete a revolution which began—when? In 1933, or perhaps in 1895?

Meanwhile, Secretary of State Cordell Hull faced some embarrassing questions about Cuba at the 1933 Montevideo Conference of American States. He weathered them calmly and then renounced the old Theodore Roosevelt Corollary to the Monroe Doctrine, under which the United States had asserted a right to interpose between Latin America and the rest of the world. The next year, once Batista was firmly in power, Washington also renounced the right of intervention in Cuba under the Platt Amendment.

The Mexicans had critized Hull at Montevideo, a portent of more serious difficulties to come. All the old issues reappeared when President Lazaro Cárdenas began his own New Deal south of the border. F. D. R. had a good deal of sympathy for Cárdenas, but the State Department took a very dim view of his Mexican New Deal program. The economic royalists he attacked were foreign investors, and by "putting them in their places" Cárdenas meant expropriation of their property. First came large landholders and then the oilmen. On March 18, 1938, Mexico expropriated American oil companies and nationalized the industry.

Since 1917 the oil question had been a chronic irritant in Mexican-American relations; now, however, it became part of a world crisis. Secretary of State Cordell Hull called in the Mexican Ambassador to read him a lecture on the principles of the Good Neighbor Policy and the protection of private property; but besides boycotting Mexican oil in world markets there was very little else that could be done. What little could be done to bring pressure on Cárdenas was tried without effect. If Mexico was able to get away with this stunt, the oilmen warned Secretary Hull, the next crisis would come in Venezuela and the next someplace else. Soon *all* foreign investments in Latin America would be under attack.

But the oil companies had also assumed that without American operators, tank cars, and refineries, Cárdenas would be left high and dry. The oil would do him no good if it stayed in the ground. What they had not anticipated—and what troubled American officials—was that Mexico soon found a steady market for its oil in the fascist states of Europe—Germany and Italy. The policy makers wondered (reversing the argument advanced by the oilmen) what good the boycott would do if Mexico turned to those states for economic outlets and assistance. Other Latin American countries already seemed to be veering in the direction of fascism without shoving Mexico along that path, too.

"All right," Roosevelt replied to a question from an angry Senator on the Military Affairs

Committee during a discussion on Mexico. "All right, suppose we did not buy any Mexican silver. We are buying today, in small amounts, much less than we did. If we stopped buying Mexican silver, they would sell it to somebody else, possibly for a smaller sum." Why not curtail tourism? came the next question. "The President of Mexico would, I am inclined to think, sell more oil to Italy and Germany to make up for that amount. There isn't very much more you could do."

As the world crisis grew more serious in 1941, Hull told the oilmen that time had run out. A settlement was negotiated which left Mexico in full control of the oil fields and the oilmen unhappy. With the world torn apart by a struggle against fascism, Roosevelt was right: "There isn't very much more you could do."

The fascist challenge

At first, State Department officials had denounced the Mexican oil expropriation decree as just one more example of disregard for international obligations and private contracts like that shown by Communists and fascists. Mexico's decision to seek aid from the fascist states rather than yield to demands that expropriation be reversed put a new light on the problem, especially as the world fascist challenge grew more serious near the end of the 1930s. F. D. R.'s decision was a realistic one under those circumstances, but the fact that he had to make it worried American policy makers.

Hitler's triumph in Germany in 1933 had brought an end to Germany's first experiment in democracy and had established Nationalism Socialism in that country. Military-fascist forces now controlled three countries: Italy, Japan, and Germany. Each pursued aggressive foreign policies: Italy in North Africa, Japan in Manchuria, and Germany in Central Europe. They justified these policies on two grounds: first as preventive war against Bolshevism and second as the only way to protect themselves economically against the "have" nations among the capitalist powers. The United States and Great Britain had excluded them from world markets by tariffs and other economic means; hence they were entitled to take whatever measures they deemed necessary to protect their own well-being.

In 1936 these three powers signed an Anti-Comintern Pact supposedly aimed at containing the spread of communism, but the State Department thought that was just an excuse to cover their aggressive designs. Whenever the Japanese came up with the standard anti-Bolshevik argument to explain aggressive policies in China, American diplomats would respond cooly: "Ah, yes, we understand what you are saying. We are all concerned about Communism; but your policies will produce the very conditions necessary for a Communist takeover." Years later Premier Chou En-lai confirmed this prediction, remarking to visiting Japanese statesmen that the Chinese Communists owed their country a peculiar debt of gratitude for precisely that reason.

So long as the European Anti-Comintern partners limited themselves to "correcting" supposed injustices in the Versailles system, the democracies tolerated or "appeased" the fascists. Deeply worried about their own social malaise and the threat of left-right clashes as a danger to their internal stability, England and France refused to take a strong stand in 1935 when Italy invaded Ethiopia and in succeeding years when Nazi Germany went into the Rhineland and Japan into North China. American reactions to these events were at best ambiguous. Congress passed neutrality legislation in almost every year beginning in 1935, but the laws it fashioned were directed against a dead President's mistakes at the time of World War I and were almost totally irrelevant to the conditions of the 1930s. F. D. R. was able, for example, to maneuver the 1935 Neutrality Act so that he could use it against Italy's adventurism in Africa. But the President was himself ambivalent. In 1937 he proposed a quarantine against outbreaks of aggression. Since 90 percent of the world wanted peace, he said, some way had to be found to prevent the remaining 10 percent from plunging the world into chaos.

Dubbed the "Quarantine Speech" by newspaper reporters, F. D. R.'s remarks caused an immediate sensation. Newsmen pressed for more details. But all Roosevelt would say was: "It is an attitude, and it does not outline a program." He was, he implied, still looking for a program. If so, he never found it. Right up to the very eve of Pearl Harbor, Roosevelt was still hedging in public. Rearmament measures he proposed to Congress were always described to the lawmakers as necessary for keeping the United States out of foreign wars. The way in which America went to war was important—just as important, the President knew, as why it went to war.

The uproar caused by the "Quarantine Speech" convinced F. D. R. that while the nation looked to its Presidents for strong executive action, it did not want to be told the harsher truths about the world crisis. Congress had looked the other way when Roosevelt manipulated the neutrality laws in an effort to defeat Italy's aggression against Ethiopia. Moreover, the legislators had carefully designed the neutrality acts, or so they thought, to allow the nation's exporters to trade with the belligerents. The harsh truth they avoided in this instance was that if America wanted to stay out of a new war, it would have to give up neutral rights altogether.

Between 1935 and 1941 Americans managed to delude themselves, with the aid of the President and Congress, into believing that they could have their cake and eat it too, not once but over and over. In 1933 Roosevelt had asked Congress for emergency powers to combat the domestic crisis. Over the next five years the New Deal centralized the federal power in the executive branch to a greater degree than ever before, yet the President was stymied all the same on the legislative front. Business opposition, conservative senators and representatives, and the courts all had fought him to a standstill on one issue or another. None of his opponents had a better idea for overcoming the Depression, nor could they agree upon any remedy, better or worse.

The recession of 1937 and F. D. R.'s inability to purge his own party of chronic nay-sayers left the administration in an odd circumstance. Stalemated on the legislative front, the only way Roosevelt could move forward was by executive action. Meanwhile the dictatorships, unhindered by democratic restraints, were moving to solve their domestic problems in their own way. In 1936 Germany occupied the Rhineland militarily in a direct violation of the Versailles Treaty and the next summer Japan moved out of Manchuria into North China. Then in 1938 Hitler threatened war over the Sudentenland and was given a green light by England and France at Munich to take what he said belonged to Germany. The President's advisers began to say what they had been thinking for some time: it was no longer possible to talk about the domestic situation as if it were something separate from the world crisis, nor—and this was a crucial corollary—were the New Deal's opponents any better equipped to deal with the world situation than they were to provide a solution to the Depression. Roosevelt haters were Roosevelt haters, and no amount of persuasion could convince them that the President was concerned about anything except saving his own political skin when the New Deal finally collapsed.

Given these circumstances, it was easy for Roosevelt to convince himself that he must take whatever measures were necessary to preserve the American constitutional system, and everything within it, in this deadly confrontation with international outlaws. If necessary, he was ready to go outside the Constitution to save it. Surely the Founding Fathers had never intended that a President should risk endangering the nation's security because what he had to do was not expressly stipulated under the enumerated powers of the Chief Executive.

Jefferson had purchased Louisiana with only a nod in the direction of constitutional scruples. And there was Lincoln's decision to suspend the constitutional civil rights of individuals to preserve the Union in the Civil War. Precedent and circumstance both supported him, then, in doing what he felt he must do. Rather than going to the people with long explanations about this weakness in the American system, F. D. R. relied upon his instincts for sensing the public will. Later Presidents who emulated Roosevelt's behavior got stuck on the wrong side of the "credibility gap;" but, despite some Republican grousing, F. D. R. kept things under control—at home. He was fortunate, in this regard, in the nature and power of the enemy.

Complicated maneuvers

At first he took small steps, like allowing the French to purchase the newest American military aircraft without securing congressional approval. This was done in the aftermath of the Munich Conference and was intended to bolster French resistance to any new German demands. When the activities of the French purchasing mission came to light, Roosevelt put down the expected congressional outburst by pointing out that the Cabinet, in the light of the idleness of most American airplane factories and to stimulate production for our own Army Air Force, had found it desirable to obtain and fill the French orders as soon as possible.

The President actually came out of this skirmish with a strengthened hand. He had given a perfectly plausible explanation for allowing the sales, but it remained plausible only if one also assumed that he was right in offering the planes only to France and not to all powers. And that assumption—that France was a friendly nation—depended, in turn, upon a judgment about the world situation. To sustain Roosevelt's actions in making the sale meant sustaining his view of the correct attitude America should take about European affairs. But neither Roosevelt nor his congressional critics wanted to face a full-scale debate on foreign affairs. Few members of Congress wanted to go on record at this critical moment as being willing to do anything which might encourage Germany to more adventurism.

So the fuzzy area between congressional acceptance of responsibility and the executive's obligations to conduct a foreign policy in the nation's interest grew fuzzier—and bigger. It almost seemed, at times, that more than anything else Congress and the President wanted to avoid one another in that no man's land. For example, a month after the actual outbreak of war in Europe on September 1, 1939, the President met with a group of congressional leaders in the White House. He told them that he planned to go before a joint session of Congress to request repeal of the mandatory embargo provisions in the most recent Neutrality Act against cash sales of arms to belligerents. Repeal would hurt Hitler, he said, because "he can't get over here to get the arms and munitions and England and France can." Senator Warren Austin suggested that Roosevelt be just that frank in his message to the legislators. The President answered that he simply "couldn't," but would be "tickled to death" if Austin would say it during the debate.

It was all right, moreover, if word got out about what he had told certain congressmen privately; indeed he encouraged newsmen to "worm out from each one something of what happened" and add it all up in their stories. It might even deter the dictators if they knew what the President was really thinking. When he spoke on Capitol Hill, Roosevelt declared that repeal of the arms embargo would "keep us out of war." He said nothing about using munitions sales to bolster the allies.

Congress passed the arms embargo repeal. When France fell in the early summer of 1940, it also passed a series of national defense measures. The European war became a key issue in the Presidential campaign of that year. Republican candidate Wendell Willkie said he was "a frank proponent of aid to the Allies" as a way of keeping America out of the war! It was not a good year for candor or self-examination from either political party.

Willkie warned the public on alternate days, when he was not talking about aid to the Allies, that if Roosevelt were elected to a third term, dictatorship at home and war abroad would follow as night follows day. Roosevelt responded to these charges by assuring the "mothers of America" that "your boys are not going to be sent into any foreign wars." At this very moment, September 1940, the President and his leading advisers were considering a difficult problem: how to supply Great Britain with fifty overage destroyers to stave off defeat without risking a showdown foreign policy debate in Congress during an election year. Bulky legal briefs were produced to demonstrate that it was perfectly within the President's power to turn over the ships by executive agreement in exchange for ninety-year leases on bases in the British West Indies. Friends of the administration even induced General John J. Pershing, aged and in ill health, to broadcast a public appeal in support of the plan. "Today may be the last time when, by measures short of war, we can still prevent war."

Roosevelt called the destroyer-bases deal the most important acquisition of property since the Louisiana Purchase. There was loud protest from "isolationist" journals, but the deal went through without a hitch—and, despite his own fears, Roosevelt was reelected. Now came the biggest step of all. For some time it had been apparent that Britain would soon run out of "cash" with which to purchase war goods and possibly out of ships in which to "carry" the materials home. When that happened, there would be no way under the Neutrality Act for Great Britain to secure more war materials from the United States. (The law stipulated that only "cash and carry" purchases were legal. Meanwhile, Germany, Italy, and Japan had written a new pact: the Axis Tripartite Alliance. Henceforth every move by the Axis would be scrutinized as part of an overall plan to conquer the world. Roosevelt's solution to these new developments was the so-called Lend Lease bill, which, he insisted, was no more than offering to lend a neighbor your garden hose when his house was burning down. As anyone could see, that was the best way to keep the fire from spreading and burning your house down, too.

Montana Senator Burton K. Wheeler thought of a different analogy: "The lend-lease program is the New Deal's triple A

Figure 19-2 America becomes the arsenal of democracy and pulls itself up by its GI bootstraps. (*Right, The Anaconda Company; below, Wide World Photos*)

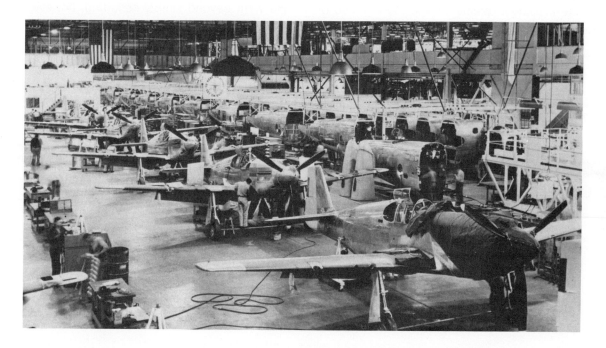

foreign policy; it will plow under every fourth American boy." The debate in Congress produced the showdown everyone had been expecting for many months. Administration strategy, as set by the President himself, was to present Lend Lease "as a step not toward war but away from war." If that was so, argued his opponents, then someone was running the projector backward, because the United States was getting closer to active participation all the time. Henry L. Stimson, the new Secretary of War, was far more candid when speaking to aides in the War Department. If anyone asked them if Congress's war-making power had been bypassed, the reply should be, "Congress has declared war to this extent at least."

After an acrimonious debate, H. R. 1776 or the Lend Lease Act passed both houses of Congress. The act gave the President authority to make or procure "any defense article for the government of any country whose defense the President deems vital to the defense of the United States." It was, simply put, the broadest authority to conduct foreign policy Congress had ever conferred upon the executive. As soon as the measure passed, Roosevelt sent the legislators an urgent request for an initial appropriation of $7 billion. Nothing in the domestic New Deal had approached this magnitude. It was bigger than the WPA, the PWA (Public Works Administration), and the TVA all rolled together.

The Lend Lease debate was the last serious discussion of the essentials of American foreign policy for twenty-five years, until the height of the Vietnam war. Henceforth the central issue in American politics would be foreign policy, and the President's expanded powers to conduct foreign affairs was the principal reason for the gravitation of power within the federal government to the White House. Henry L. Stimson, Roosevelt's Repub-

lican Secretary of War, was also quite frank in stating that since management of this vast new aid program would remain always in American hands, Lend Lease would make for a coordinated and effective war effort. And as the war came to an end, Lend Lease would become useful in holding the Allies together to achieve common war aims. American leaders sensed, then, that this time around, economic power would be managed from the outset in such a way as to guarantee victory on the battlefield and success at the peace table. There would be no second failure like Versailles.

The road to Pearl Harbor

Stimson was far less pleased with the President's undeclared war in the Atlantic. Roosevelt claimed that the power to convoy ships to England was implicit in the Lend-Lease Act. He went beyond simply escorting, however, and instructed the Navy to report German ship movements to the British fleet. Stimson worried about the political implications of this policy for American democracy: "I wanted him [the President] to be honest with himself. To me it seems a clearly hostile act to the Germans and I am prepared to take the responsibility of it." The President preferred to allow the public to become aware of his policy only after the fact. "It is not certain," Roosevelt cabled Prime Minister Winston Churchill at the time he initiated the policy, "that I would make a specific announcement. I may decide to issue the necessary naval operative orders and let time bring out the existence of the new patrol area."

Incidents occurred, as Secretary Stimson knew they would, involving clashes between American ships and German forces. The President used these to justify a "shoot on sight" declaration against German ships in the North Atlantic area out to Greenland. Hitler had plenty of excuses to declare war on the United States had he been looking for one, but he was not looking. Far more important to him was the new Russian campaign launched on June 22, 1941. It was there that the European phase of the war would be determined.

War came to America through the back door in the Pacific. Most Americans lumped Japan and Germany as "aggressors," but few really thought that when it came to a showdown, when it came to the moment of truth,

Figure 19-3   The first summit meeting of World War II. As America moved closer to active participation, F. D. R. wanted to set goals for the postwar world. This time around it would be different. (*Culver Pictures*)

Japan would attack. In the entire period of 1921 to 1941, U.S. policy toward that island country was premised upon an assumption that at some undetermined point Tokyo would back off. Japan's invasion of North China in July 1937 cast a few shadows on this certainty, and the 1940 Axis Tripartite Pact worried policy makers more than anything that had happened up to that time because it raised serious doubts about settling with Tokyo separately. With Germany as a military ally, Japan had more leverage. There was also the possibility, on the other hand, that Berlin might force an unwanted war on Japan.

Nevertheless, American policy makers continued to believe almost up to the last minute that economic pressure and moral condemnation would produce a change of heart in the land of the rising sun. Stimson reassured his new Cabinet colleagues in the Roosevelt administration that "in the autumn of 1919 President Wilson got his dander up and put on an embargo on all cotton going to Japan and a boycott on her silk, with the result that she crawled down within two months and brought all of her troops out from Siberia like whipped puppies." What worked then, it was felt, would work again.

The State Department had been practicing what Stimson recommended for some time—but to no avail. In 1939 Secretary Hull had served notice on Tokyo that the United States was allowing the 1911 commercial treaty between the two nations to lapse, thereby making it possible to change economic policies from one day to the next if it became necessary. Embargos on iron and oil products were enforced with gradually increasing degrees of severity.

All that these measures produced were new demands by Japan upon the Dutch East Indies and French Indochina for assured sources of raw materials. In July 1941, the Japanese occupied Indochina. The move forced Washington to drop the other shoe—the last one it had. A State Department press release stated that the occupation of Indochina raised vital issues connected with the national security. The United States could not tolerate the loss of such "essential materials . . . as tin and rubber which are necessary for the normal economy of this country and the consummation of our defense program." With that declaration came the shoe: The United States government was freezing Japan's assets in the United States. Short of breaking off diplomatic relations, this was it.

For some months Secretary Hull had been meeting with Japanese diplomats secretly in his personal suite in a Washington hotel in a last effort to avoid war. The American position remained constant from the day the talks began until the morning of the Pearl Harbor attack. There could be no serious discussion of specifics unless the Japanese first accepted the principles of the Washington treaties. Tokyo's representatives reversed the order: specifics first, abstractions later. They did appear to want a summit meeting between Roosevelt and the Japanese Prime Minister. But Hull opposed that suggestion, unless Tokyo first agreed to American principles and to evacuate her forces from China. In addition, Japan would also have to renounce whatever obligations it had, under the Axis Tripartite Pact, to come to Germany's aid should the United States become involved in Europe. That did not leave much to negotiate. Roosevelt put it another way to the Japanese Ambassador: "the United States was not in favor of the 'closed door' and it was Japan's turn to figure out ways and means of opening it."

The final Japanese answer came at Pearl Harbor early on the morning of December 7,

Figure 19-4 To Hull it all seemed obvious, but to the Japanese,
American policy appeared abstract in the extreme.
(*Wide World Photos*)

1941. It was a nightmare for those stationed
on the American fleet anchored there. But
Secretary of War Stimson confided to his
diary: ". . . my first feeling was of relief that
the indecision was over and that a crisis had
come in a way which would unite all our
people." Against a background of world depression, Nazi terror across Europe, and Japanese fanaticism in Asia, the United States
had suffered the torments of a nation uncertain of its future and suspended between
faith and disbelief in its fundamental institu-

tions. Terrible as it was, war came as something of a relief. Now there were concrete
objectives and goals. Now the federal government could put people back to work in
private industry and the factories could run
full time, even twenty-four hours a day, without producing a suffocating surplus; farms
could grow wheat, cotton, and corn without
fear of driving the market price down to below
subsistence levels. Now there would be no
paradox of poverty in the land of plenty.

The New Dealers were replaced by dollar-a-year executives from private corporations who signed authorizations for billions and billions of dollars. Men who had opposed spending money to keep men at work on government projects during the 1930s spent more in a day to keep war plants going than some New Deal agencies had spent in a year. Former Roosevelt haters filled the ranks of Assistant Secretaries in all departments of government, and, if they did not exactly forget old grudges, came to admit that the "old man" was not as bad as they thought. At least he had sense enough to put aside all that New Deal stuff to win the war.

"There is no need to fear," declared surviving New Deal adviser Adolf Berle. "Rather, we shall have an opportunity to create the most brillant economic epoch the U.S. has yet seen. It is entirely feasible to make the country at once more prosperous and more free than it has ever been." Perhaps the greatest danger posed by the Axis threat, because it was the most subtle, grew out of the temptation, implicit in Berle's remark, that all challenges had been reduced to one question and all failures caused by external enemies.

Selected references

The interwar years are surveyed in Selig Adler, *The Uncertain Giant, 1921–1941: American Foreign Policy between the Wars* (1965). Carl Parrini's *Heir to Empire: United States Economic Diplomacy, 1916–1922* (1969), handles a difficult subject, tariff diplomacy, with skill and insight. Two books on the 1920s which shed a good deal of light on the Hoover world view are Herbert Feis, *Diplomacy of the Dollar* (1950), and Joseph Brandes, *Herbert Hoover and Economic Diplomacy* (1962). William Appleman Williams, *The Tragedy of American Diplomacy* (1962), is also particularly strong on the 1920s. Akira Iriye's *After Imperialism* (1965) is a multidimensional, multiarchival study of the search for a new order in the 1920s. Not for beginners, it rewards advanced students with a fresh perspective on the key interwar problem.

Moods of the 1930s are captured in Robert Divine's *The Illusion of Neutrality* (1962); another survey is Lloyd C. Gardner, *Economic Aspects of New Deal Diplomacy* (1964). On the Good Neighbor Policy Bryce Wood, *The Making of the Good Neighbor Policy* (1961), stands out, as does Dorothy Borg's *The United States and the Far Eastern Crisis of 1933–1938* (1964) on that area of the world. Pearl Harbor itself is covered from a friendly point of view in Herbert Feis, *The Road to Pearl Harbor* (1950). There is still no better treatment of F. D. R. than Robert Sherwood's *Roosevelt and Hopkins: An Intimate History* (1948). And a thoughtful work on the dissenting side is William L. Neumann, *America Encounters Japan: From Perry to MacArthur* (1963).

TWENTY

Over Here:
The Last Really Great War

Period covered:	1940–1945
Emphasis:	Domestic mobilization
Major events:	The United States enters World War II, 1941
	Japanese-Americans interned, 1942
	Race and zoot-suit riots, 1943
	Liquor runs out, 1944
	Peace, 1945

Polls showed that although most Americans hoped not to enter World War II, they also thought American entry certain and preferable to a German victory in Europe. But Congress was more isolationist than the country at large, hence the long, unedifying struggle between it and President Roosevelt, who wanted rearmament on a large scale and intervention in Europe at the earliest possible moment but could not say so. The President announced during his campaign for a third term in 1940 that American boys were not going to fight in foreign wars; but in fact he was doing all he could to get the United States involved in the war. Lend Lease to Britain, which made America a de facto enemy of the Axis, was passed off by Roosevelt as pure neighborliness, like offering your garden hose to the man next door whose house is on fire. No one knows how much harm these deceptions did. Congress was not fooled by them; neither were the Axis powers. But to make them seem plausible, mobilization had to be advertised merely as a defense against invasion. This made effective planning difficult. When war came, the economy was unprepared, though the government had supposedly been reorganizing it for eighteen months. Business welcomed defense contracts—but not too many of them, for fear of being stuck with surplus productive capacity at the war's end. This slow start meant that as late as 1942 there were still 3.6 million unemployed workers.

Planning

When war came, the government thought to catch up by using big business. Two-thirds of the $240 billion in contracts let during the war went to the 100 largest contractors, though some 18,000 businesses were involved in defense work. Ten companies got nearly a third of the total spent, and half a million small businesses failed during that time. The government further subsidized big business by spending some $20 billion constructing war plants. This typified defense mobilization. Some liberals had hoped that the government would use its war powers to enhance the public's welfare, but this proved to be wishful thinking. What the government wanted was maximum output at a minimum political cost, which meant doing things as big business liked whenever possible. It also meant treating the war effort as a public relations problem. While experts handled mobilization as a purely technical exercise, the Office of War Information distributed propaganda showing how victory would automatically transform the human condition. In the event, this probably made little difference. Congress kept a sharp eye on the propaganda machine to make sure it did not covertly promote New Dealism; while the people, many of whom had lived through an earlier crusade, put little stock in the inflated claims of government. Most were satisfied that victory was worth having. Although they hoped the postwar world would be better than what had gone before, most people sensibly concentrated on the work at hand. Morale was never a serious problem on the home front despite shortages, rationing, and other annoyances.

Unlike World War I, when labor did as it was told, there were some strikes, and union leaders tried to make authority more representative. Labor distrusted the "dollar-a-year men" who gave their services free to government during the war while remaining on their company payrolls, and it disliked the assumption that a businessman appointed to public office put self-interest behind him while a labor leader did not. There were no dollar-a-year trade unionists. Walter Reuther of the United Auto Workers suggested that the car industry be managed by a council made up of labor and management representatives headed by a government official. CIO leaders hoped the same idea would apply to other industries. Bernard Baruch, who had run the economy during World War I, wanted mobilization handled by a government agency that would assign responsibility to industry councils. These councils would then be responsible for all decisions relating to production while being exempted from antitrust action.

It was finally decided that crucial decisions must be made by a government body, that industrial councils could be advisory only, and that important decisions must be approved by the Justice Department. This disposed not only of the Baruch plan but of the Reuther approach as well. Donald Nelson, head of the War Production Board (WPB), decided that too few executives would serve the government if they had to resign from their corporations, so the dollar-a-year men stayed on. A Smaller War Plants Corporation (SWPC) was set up to help little business get a share of the pie, but it was unable to overcome the military's enthusiasm for large business and the influence of dollar-ayear men in Washington. This meant not only that big business got most of the large contracts but also that it was protected against postwar competition. Research was one way to do this. Maury Maverick, head of the SWPC, disclosed afterward that of the roughly $1 billion spent by government for nonnuclear scientific research in private labs, two-fifths of the total went to ten firms and two-thirds to sixty-eight. Ninety percent of these contracts allowed the developer to patent discoveries made with public money.

The chief threat to big business came near

the war's end. War production reached a peak late in 1944; thereafter war orders declined, especially to small firms. Large companies pulled in work from subcontractors to keep their own plants going. Nelson and Maverick had a plan for reconversion that would enable small businesses without war contracts to go into peacetime production immediately. Big business wanted a plan for reconversion too, but not one that gave small business an advantage. The military, for odd reasons of its own, was against any planning. It feared that reconversion, even on a small scale, would weaken the people's dedication to victory. In fact, the military wanted a labor draft even though manpower needs were diminishing. When big business realized that it could not stop the Nelson program except by joining with the military to block all reconversion plans, it did so. Nelson was eased out as head of the WPB and big business's competitive advantages were sustained. As in the last war America was the arsenal of democracy, and, as before, sometimes more an arsenal than a democracy.

War prosperity

There were surprisingly few complaints about such favoritism. Ideologists concentrated on events abroad; ordinary people on the immediate problems of housing, transportation, and consumption. People were tranquilized by full employment and protests were mostly about specific instances of shortages or defective war materials—shortages more often caused by mismanagement than dishonesty. Prices and wages rose at about the same rate between 1939 and 1945, while civilian production dropped to about 80 percent of the 1939 level. The result was that personal savings rose from $6 billion in 1939 to $38.9

billion in 1944. When victory came, $140 billion worth of savings and war bonds were owned by individuals, and this despite greatly increased taxes. In 1942 the number of people required to pay income taxes had risen from 4 million in 1939 to 50 million. For the only time in modern history, the proportion of income gained by upper wealth holders declined. Thus war brought the abundance denied Americans in peacetime. Armaments were linked with wages and profits, an association that would have unhappy consequences in later years.

Treatment of minorities

Serious inequities remained. In 1945 half the work force earned less than $2,000 a year and owned less than 3 percent of the country's liquid assets. As always, blacks suffered most. In September 1941 a majority (51 percent) of all defense jobs were closed to them. Later, some were opened as a result of manpower shortages and tepid government efforts to force integration. But blacks only regained the ground they had lost since 1929, and in 1944 their average weekly income in industry was only $37.77 compared with $50 for white males. Women were discriminated against too. Industry was glad to have them, and about 4.4 million were added to the work force, most only for the duration. They averaged about 40 percent less pay than male production workers, but little attention was paid to such inequities. Women were considered patriotic volunteers, as in fact some were, working for love of country rather than gain. But most had joined the work force permanently. Blacks were, as usual, invisible—except to the workers they competed with for jobs and housing.

This competition between blacks and whites for jobs led to the most severe race riot in years. Few blacks moved North by comparison with the last war, only about 400,000. Yet in the industrial centers where they were concentrated, there were too many for the comfort of white workers. At the Packard plant in Detroit, 3,000 whites walked off the job in protest when 3 black workers were promoted. Blacks were seriously discriminated against in Detroit, where, though they made up 10 percent of the population, they held only 8.4 percent of the jobs. At 55 of 185 major war plants, they amounted to less than 1 percent of the labor force. Fifty percent of black dwellings in Detroit were substandard, compared with 14 percent of white dwellings. These conditions angered blacks, as did the segregation of black servicemen in the military and the segregation of black donations in Red Cross blood banks. Yet whites, not blacks, started the race riot in Detroit in June 1943 during which twenty-five blacks and nine whites were killed. Eight hundred of both races were injured. The riot was triggered by false rumors which inspired whites to invade the ghetto, and during it some 2 million manhours were thought to have been lost in area defense plants. Afterward, the city of Detroit issued a report blaming the violence on blacks, especially the black press and the National Association for the Advancement of Colored People. It contained the shocking disclosure that "A theme repeatedly emphasized by these [black] papers is that the struggle for Negro equality at home is an integral part of the present world wide struggle for democracy." There were other incidents too. In Mobile twelve black shipyard workers were badly beaten by whites for being promoted. In August 1943, Harlem flared up, leaving 6 dead and 543 wounded. Here the fight was waged almost entirely between blacks and policemen, a novelty

Figure 20-1 Women welders. (*Detroit Historical Society; Margaret Bourke-White*)

then though it would become common in the 1960s. Whites learned little from this experience, not so blacks. Membership in the NAACP rose from 100,000 to 500,000 in the course of the war.

Another ugly aspect of life on the home front was the growing prejudice against Mexican-American youths in Southern California. Known as *pachucos,* these young men wore a distinctive ensemble called the zoot suit, notable for its broad shoulders, narrow waist, long coat, and full trousers. They liked to jitterbug (a highly gymnastic dance style), and their cult was immortalized by the song "I Wanna Zoot Suit," which went:

I wanna zoot suit with a reat pleat.
With a drape shape and a stuff cuff
to look sharp enough to see my Sunday gal
I want a reave sleeve with a ripe stripe
And a dressed seat with a glad plaid. . . .

Pachucos had a low crime rate, but servicemen resented them all the same and there were frequent incidents. On the nights of June 3 through June 7, 1943, bands of servicemen beat zoot-suiters (and frequently more drably attired Mexican-Americans and Negroes too). Policemen helped by arresting zooters after they had been worked over. When it became clear they had no intention of halting the violence, Military Police and the Shore Patrol stepped in. A county supervisor praised the servicemen for having rioted. The District Attorney said that "zoot suits are an open indication of subversive character." The Los Angeles City Council made wearing one a misdemeanor.

People felt that conscientious objectors were better treated in this war than the last; for one thing, there was little physical abuse. The Selective Service Act of 1940 exempted men from military service who were against all wars by virtue of their religious training and belief. About 100,000 men claimed exemption, of whom some 25 to 50,000 served in uniform, either in noncombatant roles or because their claim was denied. Another 12,000 worked in Civilian Public Service Camps financed and directed by traditionally pacifist denominations called the Historic Peace Churches. These did useful work and, unlike the armed services, they were racially integrated. About 6,000 COs, three times as many as in the last war, were prosecuted for refusing to accept alternative service. Most of these were Jehovah's Witnesses and most went to prison, the Witnesses for an average of 42 months and other principled objectors for 34 months. By way of comparison, non-pacifist draft evaders received average sentences of 28 months; dope peddlers 20 months; and white slavers, 28 months.

The worst violation of civil rights was suffered by Japanese-Americans. When war broke out, there were 117,000 Japanese on the West Coast, mainly in California. White Californians had abused them for generations. Pearl Harbor enabled racists to call for a "final solution" to the problem, supposedly because Japanese-Americans were security risks but actually for racial and commercial reasons. The racism of American Legionnaires and the Native Sons and Daughters of the Golden West was only faintly marred by greed; not so the California Farm Bureau Federation and the Western Growers Protective Association. Japanese-Americans produced 40 percent of California's truck crops, and big growers coveted their land. Growers wanted armed Japanese-Americans shot and the rest permanently deported. The West Coast congressional delegations were not quite so blood thirsty, but they agreed almost unanimously that internment was necessary.

The delegations were furious that Washington took a less urgent view of the Japanese-American threat. Local politicians generally supported internment. Attorney General Earl Warren of California opposed evacuation at first, then changed his mind, noting that "we have had no fifth column activities and no sabotage reported." This inactivity supposedly proved that Japanese-Americans were planning villainous deeds in the future.

Other arguments were advanced to justify internment, most of them equally foolish. It was said that widespread sabotage in Hawaii showed the need for stern measures, yet both J. Edgar Hoover and Secretary of War Stimson pointed out that not a single act of espionage or sabotage by Japanese-Americans had been discovered there. None were ever found in California either. Before the evacuation, FBI agents staged hundreds of raids without uncovering a single piece of evidence that pointed to Japanese-American disloyalty. Another argument was that if not put in protective custody, the Japanese-Americans would be wiped out by vigilante action. There were some thirty-six instances of violent patriotism between December 8, 1941, and March 31, 1942, including seven murders, two rapes, and nineteen assaults with deadly weapons. Most of these took place before January 1, 1942. The total hardly seemed to warrant internment. In any case, the usual view is that people threatened with violence are to be protected rather than imprisoned. This seems not to have occurred to most Californians.

The actual decision to evacuate was made by Lt. General John L. DeWitt. The Justice Department had cooperated with him by arresting aliens involved in nationalist activities, staging raids and removing aliens from small districts DeWitt thought endangered.

Figure 20-2 Nisei child. (*Library of Congress*)

But it was against wholesale evacuations. Justice, however, was in Washington, shielded from the pressure on DeWitt by profit-minded growers and businessmen. Local papers demanded evacuation, and so, on February 12, 1942, did Walter Lippmann, the country's most respected journalist. On the thirteenth, a congressional delegation visited DeWitt. The next day he ordered all Japanese-Americans evacuated from the West Coast and interned. That this was done on racial grounds became clear when he testified before Congress and said "we must worry about the Japanese all the time until he is wiped off the map." He also subscribed to Earl Warren's theory that the absence of crime proves it will happen. "The very fact that no sabotage has taken place to date is a disturbing and confirming indication that such action will be taken."

Over 100,000 Americans were interned, losing—in many cases—their homes, lands, and businesses through forced sales, as well as years of their life which were wasted in barren prison camps. Congress passed a bill approving the deed, and the Supreme Court later ruled that imprisoning citizens without trial was constitutional. Where military requirements in time of war are concerned, it said, "it is not for any court to sit in review of the wisdom of their action or substitute its judgment for theirs." In other words, there are no rights in wartime that the government is obliged to respect. One curious feature was that Japanese-Americans, although supposedly all potential enemy agents, were allowed to join the armed services. They sustained enormous casualties in relation to their numbers, and fought in some of the most decorated and decimated American units. The moral seemed to be that they were fit to die for the country but not to live in it.

Figure 20-3 Rita Hayworth does her bit for the war effort. (*Photo Files*)

Life on the home front

The war changed America in many ways. Some aspects, like the military-industrial alliance, became permanent; others were temporary. Crime declined because the young, who commit most crimes, were in the service or at work. Prostitution increased, as did the number of V (for victory rather than venery) girls who hung around servicemen on a less professional basis. VD flourished in consequence. The marriage rate went up, and the birthrate soon afterward. The proportion of alcoholics who were women and got in trouble with the Chicago police rose from one in six in 1935 to one in two. Housing was inadequate. In Washington there were 280,-000 new federal jobs but little new housing. People doubled and tripled up and hotels allowed guests to stay only three days. Women had to do without stockings because all suitable textiles were declared critical. Hairdressers used toothpicks instead of bobby pins. Shoes came in six colors only, three of them shades of brown. Everything worth having was rationed, and in 1944 the whiskey ran out. Distillers had a five-year supply of liquor on hand when, at the outbreak of war, they shifted to producing industrial alcohol. But annual consumption went up from 140 million gallons in 1941 to 190 million in 1942. Substitutes made from potatoes and such were pressed into service, but while one could get drunk on them, it was not quite the same. Morale declined about as much as if a carrier task force had been lost. Sugar, shoes, coffee, gasoline on the East Coast, and other goods vanished at various times.

The greatest single shortage was rubber. At the onset of war there was only a year's supply on hand and no way of augmenting it, since most of the supply was in enemy hands.

Just enough synthetic rubber was produced to meet essential needs. There were no tires for civilian use. The only way to conserve rubber was to ration gasoline, but politicians shrank from doing so, knowing that it meant infringing upon the most cherished of all national rights. But eventually need drove President Roosevelt to order gas rationing. In consequence, the number of traffic deaths on Labor Day 1942 was only 169 compared to 423 the year before. Roads and highways were used at only about 20 percent of capacity. This was good for lungs and the environment but for little else, as mass transit was unable to take up all the slack. Railroads, with few additional cars, had to carry twice the volume of traffic as before. Traveling was hopelessly difficult, and so a new hunger for automobiles—that would devastate most American cities after the war—was created.

In the main, though, it was a good war for Americans, the best in this century. Some 300,000 American servicemen died in action, not many more than would have been killed or maimed in auto accidents had there been no gas rationing. By comparison, Russia lost 7,500,000 men; Germany, 3,500,000; and Japan, 1,220,000. Many young men got to see the world. There was no unemployment. The country was united as never before or since. Later there would be many complaints about how the war was fought, particularly the air war, and about diplomacy. There was not much criticism at the time except by partisan politicians, to whom little attention was paid. No one doubted the legitimacy of American war aims, which were minimal except for certain rhetorical flourishes. Few people took them seriously, judging by the lack of consternation when peace did not also bring universal freedom from fear, want, etc. Most Americans did believe that victory would make them more secure, and when it did not, many were outraged. But that was later. As of 1945, Americans were in excellent spirits, and rightly so. They had waged a long, trying struggle—that was as just as wars ever are—and without doing much more damage to the liberties of citizens than is customary in wartime.

Selected references

There are few good books on the home front. Richard R. Lingeman, *Don't You Know There's a War On* (1970), is agreeable social history. Bruce Catton, *The War Lords of Washington,* is an angry indictment of mobilization policies. On the internment question, see Morton Grodzins, *Americans Betrayed* (1949). Mulford Q. Sibley and P. E. Jacob, *Conscription of Conscience: The Conscientious Objector, 1940–1947* (1952), is useful.

TWENTY-ONE

The Cold War Complex

Period covered: 1945–1960
Emphasis: Diplomacy
Major Events: VE Day, 1945
Atomic bomb, 1945
VJ Day, 1945
Truman Doctrine, 1947
Marshall Plan, 1947
Berlin blockade and airlift, 1948
Formation of NATO, 1949
Chinese communist victory, 1949
Korean war, 1950
Dulles announces liberation, 1953
Intervention in Guatemala, 1954
Fall of Dien Bien Phu and Geneva Conference, 1954
Summit Conference, 1955
Middle East crisis, 1956
Sputnik, 1957
U-2 plane downed over the Soviet Union, 1960

Fear held the Big Three together through World War II. Once the defeat of the Axis powers was assured, the Grand Alliance came apart. By postponement, the Big Three—England, the United States, and the Soviet Union—had managed to avoid facing up to the contradictions of their alliance. Wartime disagreements provoked the first clashes in what would become the cold war, but the roots of the East-West conflict went back to an earlier time. The full complexity of the cold war is yet to be understood, but it is now possible to ask some of the questions historians will be trying to answer in the future. Questions such as who—or what—was the enemy?

Concern about a Soviet military attack on Western Europe was only one aspect of the early cold war years, and probably not the most important. Most Western statesmen and diplomats discounted the risks of a frontal assault, unless Stalin had already reduced the rest of Europe to internal chaos through some combination of subversion and bluster. Dean Acheson, Truman's Secretary of State, once confided to a colleague that he never once believed that the Soviets would deliberately instigate a war "unless they are absolutely out of their minds." Instead, they would seek their ends through political warfare, especially internal subversion, to destroy the will to resist. Such candor was infrequent in public rhetoric, however.

In public one always talked as if it was necessary to prepare for the attack that might never come—to build more atomic bombs and more long-range aircraft—because in the absence of preparedness the Soviets might push political warfare too far, might back the West into a corner where the only choice would be to fight or surrender. At a still more abstract level (one of many on which the cold war was waged), it was considered quite possible that the Western Europeans themselves might lack the will to resist Communism as the wave of the future. Military preparedness, it was argued, would supply some needed backbone.

There were many ways, then, that the enemy could operate to undermine what Americans called the free world. Limited to Europe from 1945 to 1949 (at least in the headlines), the cold war became incredibly more complex as it spread around the world. In 1957 John Foster Dulles, Eisenhower's Secretary of State, was asked to explain the term "international communism" and to relate it to the presumed military threat to American interests. The setting was a Senate hearing on legislation to give the President still more authority in foreign affairs, so Dulles had to choose his words carefully:

Secretary Dulles: *International communism . . . is a phrase which I assume has a meaning from the standpoint of the Congress because it uses it very frequently, and the phrase "countries controlled by international communism" is a phrase which we did not invent. We [the State Department] picked it out of the present Mutual Security Act. . . .*

Senator Jackson: *We want to know what it means in connection with this legislation.*

Secretary Dulles: *It means the same thing here, Senator, exactly as it meant and means in the Mutual Security Act.*

Senator Jackson: *What did it mean in the Mutual Security Act?*

Secretary Dulles: *Congress passed the act and I assume knows what it meant.*

After this ring-around-the-mulberry-bush routine ended, Dulles tried another approach, positing the existence of an international conspiracy composed of persons, "all of whose names I do not know, and many of whom I suppose are secret." That did not help much. Yet it was rare that congressional examinations of the issue came so close to facing up to the complexities of the cold war. Usually the legislators passed whatever legislation the President said was necessary in the fight against communism and devoted their energies to ferreting out wasteful expenditures and corruption in the federal bureaucracy. The English language suffered badly in the cold war; in fact, it became one of the principal casualties. Ersatz words and phrases such as "Comsymp," meaning someone who supported the Soviet position on a given issue or, often, someone who disagreed with you, were bad enough; but even worse were rubrics like "free world," which gave dictatorships like Spain, Greece, and Turkey equal moral status with governments like England and France in cold war rhetoric. The damage done to rational analysis by the cold war remains with us yet and probably will for a long time to come.

American objectives in waging the cold war also seem more complex than they once did. Resistance to communist expansion, a life-and-death struggle with Stalinist tyranny, protection of vital strategic interests, preserving the balance of power—these have all been used to describe American attitudes, but there was another theme running through American foreign policy. "If western Europe is overrun by communism," said Will Clayton, Assistant Secretary of State, in a typical expression of this concern, "I think the situation which we would face in this country would be a very grave one, even if we faced no great military danger—and we would. The economic consequences of such a disaster would be very, very great to us. We would have to reorder and readjust our whole economy in this country if we lost the whole European market." Such a reorganization would mean government regimentation, a super New Deal, and, eventually, the end of capitalism altogether.

The Vietnam debate forced Americans to reconsider their use of the mother tongue and the premises of the cold war as it had developed for more than two decades. The elusive enemy in Indochina had demonstrated an almost uncanny ability to confound diplomats and generals alike, and he defied explanation within the original premises of the cold war. Vietnam was the most complex problem of all, and the longest ever on the battlefield for Americans. To solve it required a fundamental rethinking, right down to ground level.

The origins of the cold war

The trouble, as everyone knew (but sometimes forgot), began with the 1917 Bolshevik Revolution. European Marxists had always felt that Germany was the most likely place for the communist revolution to begin. If not in Germany, they argued, then certainly in one of the other industrialized countries of Western Europe or in England, but never in backward, agrarian Russia. What had occurred must therefore be an aberration, a fluke produced by war conditions. The first successful socialist revolutionaries to overthrow a government, Lenin's supporters bore a heavy load of Marxist doctrine even as they gained power. What must be done? The answer was to send forth appeals to the working classes of the world. Unless these, or some other methods, produced revolutions elsewhere, unless the world revolution could be set in motion, the Bolshevik movement would collapse under the combined weight of dialectical materialism, outside pressure, and civil war in Russia.

An uprising did occur in Germany, and a communist regime actually took power in Hungary for a brief time in 1919; but the World War I Allies and the United States easily broke these first tentative links in the chain of world revolution and, by using economic relief supplies, successfully isolated the Bolsheviks, leaving them, as Wilson put it, to stew in their own juices. It is surprising how closely Lenin and Wilson agreed on this one point; both believed that the Bolshevik movement could not survive in Russia alone. This left Lenin with two choices: he could completely abandon the Russian Revolution, or he could proclaim a new doctrine. Lenin chose the latter, calling upon his comrades to establish socialism in one country. Meanwhile, however, the Western European countries and the United States had suffered through a "red scare," caused in part by uncertainty about Lenin's true aims and in part by concern that militant socialists and Communists within their own countries would in fact forsake allegiance to their governments even should Lenin fail and join an international movement to overthrow capitalism. Italian Fascists played upon these fears in the mid-1920s to establish Mussolini in power. The hysteria passed, but none of the capitalist powers escaped unscathed from this encounter, and none quite knew what to make of the Union of Soviet Socialist Republics.

Democratic socialists, and even some liberals in the outer world, were attracted to the Soviet "experiment" in the 1920s. A number of capitalist entrepreneurs ventured into the Soviet Union, as unsure of what they would find there as Marco Polo or Vasco da Gama had been when they set out to find new ways to riches. And, as in those instances, their governments watched these excursions into the unknown with a wary eye. Most capitalists stuck to the belief that a Marxist state was bad for business anywhere and especially bad for business-labor relations at home.

Capitalist antipathy made the building of the "brave new" Soviet society more difficult, but since the Soviet Union was a largely self-contained economy with all the raw materials necessary for industrialization, it was not a crucial problem for the Soviet leaders at this stage of the Revolution. Capitalist "encirclement" actually had some advantages for the Bolsheviks, who could excuse political repression on grounds of internal security and the threat of counterrevolutionary subversion. The "White scare" in the Soviet Union proved especially useful to Lenin's successor, Joseph Stalin, who carried socialism in one country to its logical end and personal dictatorship to a bloody extreme. Stalin's one attempt at Revolutionary diplomacy in China in the 1920s was a total fiasco. From it he gained a morbid suspicion of foreign communist leaders that remained almost as great as his fear of rivals within the Soviet Union. Yet he kept the Moscow headquarters of the international communist movement open in the 1930s. He could see what it was doing better that way; and he could (eventually) manipulate it to serve the Soviet Union's (and his own) ends.

In the mid-1930s the Kremlin decreed a Popular Front policy for all communist leaders. They were told to patch up their differences with the bourgeois parties in the West to form a common front against Hitler's Germany. The United States had extended diplomatic recognition to the Soviet Union in 1933, but Franklin D. Roosevelt wanted nothing to do with alliances against Germany—not yet anyway, and certainly not with the Soviet Union. The ruling parties in France and England also preferred not to deal with the

Communists on any front, political or military, and put their faith in "appeasement" policies. Even in the late 1930s many still felt Hitler was a strong bulwark against eventual Soviet domination. Others hoped the two totalitarian powers would exhaust themselves in mortal combat.

Strange bedfellows

In 1939 Hitler and Stalin surprised the world by signing a nonaggression pact. To the consternation of the democracies, the arch-enemies had agreed to divide Poland instead of going to war with one another. When Germany moved to absorb its half, England and France honored earlier commitments to Warsaw, and thus World War II began. Aside from claiming its share of Poland, the Soviet Union also attacked Finland and absorbed the Baltic states of Latvia, Estonia, and Lithuania per arrangements under the Nazi-Soviet pact. Though neither England nor France declared war on the Soviet Union, relations between it and the West virtually ceased to exist. F.D.R., for example, advised Joseph C. Grew, his Ambassador in Tokyo, that for the moment, at least, the American people were far more incensed by the Soviet attack on little Finland (the only nation to pay off its World War I debts to the United States) than they were by Japan's invasion of China. The Soviet Union was even expelled from the League of Nations—the only nation ever voted out, since the fascist countries had long since quit the organization of their own accord.

Attitudes changed overnight when Hitler turned on his erstwhile ally in June 1941. British Prime Minister Winston Churchill (who had recommended to the Allied leaders at Versailles that military measure be taken against Lenin) told the House of Commons on the day after Germany invaded the Soviet Union that if Hitler had invaded Hell, he (Churchill) would at least make a favorable passing reference to the Devil in his next speech on the floor. In fact, the British Prime Minister was already engaged in private dealings with the Devil in an effort to keep the Soviet Union in the war against Germany. To find out exactly what would be required, he had sent Foreign Minister Anthony Eden to Moscow.

Churchill had good reason for concern. England and France had not consulted Moscow about what they intended to do to appease Hitler at Munich, and their post-Munich overtures to the Soviet Union for a military agreement had been handled so clumsily and with so little enthusiasm that Stalin rightly suspected their hearts were not in it. On his side, the British Prime Minister had bad memories of the Soviet decision to leave the First World War and of what that had meant to the Allies on the western front. A separate Soviet-German settlement patterned on the Treaty of Brest-Litvosk could be disastrous for the British Empire.

Eden's hurried trip to Moscow aroused American curiosity. The odds were now, in midsummer of 1941, better than even that the United States would soon be in the war; but how soon and in what way was largely up to the Axis leaders. Roosevelt's greatest concern at this point was that he would lose the peace. He and his advisers remembered that Wilson had lost the battle for American war aims not at Versailles but in the neutrality period, when the Europeans arranged things among themselves in their "secret treaties." The Anglo-Soviet discussions were thus of no little interest to American diplomats. And from what they could learn by piecing together various sources of information, the diplomatic situation was not encouraging. If Stalin could deal with Hitler, he could obviously bargain with Churchill. Commissar or Czar, Russian or Communist, Old World diplomacy was America's nemesis at the peace table.

Roosevelt consequently pressed Churchill to give him public assurances that no postwar arrangements were being contemplated. The famous Atlantic Charter on Anglo-American War Aims signed at the first Roosevelt-Churchill meeting off the coast of Newfoundland in August 1941 was drafted with such a purpose in mind. Meanwhile, Stalin had made two demands of his new ally: (1) The same postwar borders as he had obtained from Hitler in the Nazi-Soviet Pact and (2) a second military front against Germany in Western Europe. Suspicious as ever, Stalin wanted to protect himself against a new *cordon sanitaire* (the name for post-World War I containment policies against Lenin) and a third invasion from Germany in the twentieth century. The British were now caught between American demands and Soviet threats. Without American support, the British Empire probably could not survive after the war; without continued Soviet participation in the war against Germany, the empire might not last through the war.

Seeking to extricate himself from this tight spot, Churchill appealed to F. D. R. in early 1942, asking that the Atlantic Charter, which promised self-determination after the war, not be interpreted to deny the Soviet Union its 1942 frontiers. Roosevelt refused, but he knew that he had to get Churchill off the hook—for both their sakes. What he could offer Stalin that the Prime Minister could not was the manpower and logistics needed to open a western front in Europe. That, in combination with large-scale Lend Lease aid and promises of postwar reconstruction credits, he felt, should be inducement enough to persuade the Soviets to drop their unreason-able territorial demands—unless, of course, they planned a postwar revolutionary offensive.

Diplomacy on the second front

When Soviet Foreign Minister V. M. Molotov accepted the President's invitation to come to Washington at the end of May 1942, both sides knew the essentials of the bargain. After consulting with General George C. Marshall, Roosevelt told Molotov that he could inform Premier Stalin that the government of the United States expected the "formation" of the second front in 1942. It was an audacious gamble, and when it failed to pay off, Roosevelt spent the rest of the war unsuccessfully trying to regain the diplomatic initiative.

It failed because Churchill insisted an invasion of the Continent was simply out of the question in 1942. And if he had his way, when such an attack did come, it would be launched against the "soft underbelly" of Europe in the Balkans—to cut off Soviet expansion into areas essential to the welfare of British interests. Roosevelt's anxiety to put American troops into action against the Germans somewhere in 1942 played into Churchill's hands. The President accepted a British proposal for a North African campaign, which delayed the second front in Europe for more than two years. By the time it was finally launched, on June 6, 1944, the question was no longer how to keep the Soviets from swallowing up portions of Eastern Europe but how far west the Red Army would get before Germany surrendered.

Loathe to gamble on preserving the empire's sphere of influence on the Mediterranean, so vital to imperial trade routes, Churchill sought Roosevelt's approval for a straightforward bargain with Stalin delineating spheres

THE COLD WAR COMPLEX

of influence in southeastern Europe. Now Roosevelt was caught in the kind of dilemma Churchill had faced in 1941. Increasingly aware of the need for Soviet assent to establish a stable postwar order (the war's destruction of the foundations of the old order was already apparent, and Stalin could do great harm to the effort to establish a new order simply by sending out messages to Western communist leaders), he doubted that a decent world order could be built on rival spheres of influence. Hence the President compromised, but he deceived himself in the process: he allowed Churchill to go ahead with Stalin but insisted it was to be only a military agreement, a temporary arrangement until the Big Three could meet and sort things out. Churchill and Stalin then went ahead to divide Yugoslavia and Hungary equally, to award Bulgaria and Rumania to the Soviet Union, and to give Greece to Great Britain.

The President's advisers were divided over how to undo this knot of Old World diplomacy. They prepared several proposals for the forthcoming Yalta Conference, to be held in February 1945; but when it came down to the actual give and take of Big Three discussion, none of these proved very useful. An agreement on the reorganization of the Soviet-sponsored Polish provisional government to include more non-Communists was negotiated, for example; but when the President's top military adviser saw it, he threw up his hands. "Mr. President," declared Admiral William D. Leahy, "this is so elastic that the Russians can stretch it all the way from Yalta to Washington without ever technically breaking it." "I know, Bill—I know it," F. D. R. answered. "But it's the best I can do for Poland at this time."

Roosevelt had very little time left. Arrangements for the United Nations' organization conference in San Francisco were nearing completion, the war in Europe was coming to a close, and the President's health was giving out. Even before the Yalta meeting, several advisers had suggested that economic aid was "the only concrete bargaining lever" America had to bring the Soviets into line. Secretary of the Treasury Henry Morgenthau believed that if Washington came forward with a really big offer, say $10 billion, "it would contribute a great deal towards ironing out many of the difficulties we have been having with respect to their problems and policies."

The majority of the President's advisers disagreed with that approach, however, arguing that it was precisely the wrong way to deal with the problem. Ambassador Averell Harriman cabled from Moscow on April 6, 1945, that a "generous and considerate attitude" was regarded by the Soviet leadership as a sign of weakness. The only hope for postwar cooperation from the Soviets was to select "one or two cases where their actions are intolerable and make them realize that they cannot continue their present attitude except at great cost to themselves."

F. D. R. had not made up his mind which course to pursue at the time of his death on April 12, 1945. He was plainly worried about the behavior of the Soviets in Central and Eastern Europe, but he was far from convinced that the "hard-liners" had all the answers. Fearing that the new President, Harry S. Truman, did not understand that each day's slippage reduced the chances of a successful peace settlement, Ambassador Harriman rushed home at Roosevelt's death to acquaint him with the realities of the situation: "that in effect what we were faced with was a 'barbarian invasion of Europe,' that Soviet control over any foreign country did not mean merely influence on their foreign relations but the extension of the Soviet system with secret police, extinction of freedom of speech, etc.,

Figure 21-1 The height of Allied unity. Yalta, the point of no return between triumph and tragedy. (*Wide World Photos*)

and that we had to decide what should be our attitude in the face of these unpleasant facts."

Truman takes over

Harriman was delighted to learn that Truman needed no convincing. They quickly agreed also that the President should make the inclusion of democratic elements in the Polish government such a test case and that the Soviets should be made to understand that postwar economic aid depended upon their

good faith in carrying out this American interpretation of the Yalta agreement. Truman did exactly that in his first meeting with Soviet Foreign Minister Molotov on April 23, 1945. Those present recalled that he talked to the Russian in Missouri mule-driver's language, an exaggeration not supported by the official minutes, but the message got through to Stalin.

Whether Truman's bluntness or the more conciliatory tones of his special emissary, Harry Hopkins, produced the change, the Soviet dictator suggested a compromise on

Poland that Harriman found satisfactory. If we continue to take a sympathetic interest in Polish affairs, the Ambassador advised Truman, "there is a fair chance that things will work out satisfactorily from our standpoint." By "satisfactorily" American leaders meant that Poland and the rest of Eastern Europe would be reopened to Western trade and ideas. Few policy makers thought that the markets of any individual country in Eastern Europe were essential to the survival of American capitalism; taken together they still accounted for only a tiny percentage of American exports or foreign investments.

Soviet occupation of Eastern Europe posed other dangers, however, which were thought to be far more consequential. The recovery and capitalist reconstruction of Western Europe would depend, to some extent at least, upon access to raw materials and trade outlets in Central and Eastern Europe. If Soviet-American tensions grew worse, Stalin's control of those resources would give him powerful influence in Western Europe's capitals. More difficult to gauge was the effect that a communist tier of states in Eastern Europe would have on the next tier, and so on. It was already apparent when Germany surrendered in May 1945 that the postwar governments of Western Europe would have to contend with strong leftist elements. In many cases—Italy and France for example—the opposition to the German occupation was led by left-wing "partisans." (A similar situation existed in the Far East, where the anti-Japanese guerrillas were led by men who had no intention of simply returning things to the prewar colonialist status quo. The fight against the Japanese invaders, it soon became apparent, was only the first stage in their revolutionary struggle against Western colonialism.) When these and other considerations were totted up, it seemed essential to do whatever was necessary and possible to force a rollback of Soviet power from Eastern Europe.

Truman's options at the Big Three Potsdam Conference in July and August 1945 were severely limited. The Red Army could not be dislodged without a war, and a war would hardly be possible at a time when most American military leaders still wanted Moscow's aid against Japan. Economic levers were supposedly still available as before, but policy makers remained unsure as to how they could be used to best advantage. And something new was on the horizon: the atomic bomb. Word of the first successful test of the powerful weapon reached Truman early in the conference. He was tremendously "pepped up" by the news, recalled one adviser, but that was still a long way from controlling atomic energy so that it could be channeled into diplomatic productivity.

The President thought he would "test" Soviet intentions with proposals for international control of key waterways which traversed the so-called spheres of influence. If Stalin really meant what he said, that all the Soviets desired was "friendly" states on their borders, there should be no objection to such a plan. If, on the other hand, he was planning "world conquest," Stalin would find some excuse to oppose the idea. The Soviet reply at Potsdam was more complicated, however, than a yes or no. Foreign Minister Molotov asked if such a regime was also being contemplated for the Suez Canal. This brought a rousing defense of British imperial interests from Churchill and another stand-off in the Big Three.

Potsdam became a series of such stalemates, and Truman came home resolved never to attend another summit conference unless it was to ratify agreements reached at a lower level. He was equally adamant about preventing Rumania, Bulgaria, and Hungary from becoming "spheres of influence of any one power." Increasingly, the members of the President's Cabinet and the President himself were coming to believe that the bulk of the world's troubles originated in Moscow.

Japan's surrender after the atomic bombing of Hiroshima and Nagasaki in early August only speeded up the deterioration of East-West relations. The Soviet Union's tardy entrance into the war, in time to occupy Manchuria, posed a threat to the pro-American government of Chiang Kai-shek and to the successful reconstruction of Japan along noncommunist lines. Truman vowed he would not give the Soviets a share in the military occupation of Japan. "We were not going to be disturbed by Russian tactics in the Pacific." Stalin's "election" speech in early 1946 announcing that a new Five-Year Plan had been made necessary by the likelihood of new conflicts within the capitalist world which might spread to the Soviet Union seemed ominous to some American policy makers. To liberal William O. Douglas, it sounded like a "declaration of World War III."

Former Prime Minister Winston S. Churchill came to America around this time to tell of the Iron Curtain which had descended across the Continent from Stettin in the Baltic to Trieste in the Adriatic. With Truman sitting behind him on the platform at Fulton, Missouri, Churchill then launched into an exaltation of American military power. "God has willed," he declared, that the United States should be the first nation to possess atomic bombs, not some "Communist or neo-Fascist state." As Churchill spoke these words, a new clash, the first outside Europe, was taking place in far-off Iran. During the war, the Soviet Union

and Great Britain had jointly occupied the Shah's ancient land, once called Persia, and a quarrel had developed over the timing of their withdrawals. The situation, like all cold war situations to come, was complicated by rival ambitions, not only between the Soviet Union and the West but among the Western powers themselves.

The Truman Doctrine

American interests had been steadily growing throughout the war in the Middle East, often at the expense of former British or French holdings. Iran, for instance, was the scene of some wartime scrambling for a preferred position near the throne when it came time for the awarding of oil concessions. The Shah had welcomed American interest in his land as a new counterweight to his traditional "protectors," the Russians and English. Things were just about settled between rival Anglo-American concerns for an oil concession when the "ham-handed" Soviets barged in with a request for similar rights to most of northern Iran. The stage was thus set for the "crisis" which lasted through the first half of 1946.

Several things were significant about its final resolution. First, the United States took the dispute to the United Nations, where it marshaled the votes of Latin American nations in a demonstration of majority rules "public diplomacy." Second, Washington mounted a demonstration of naval power in the Mediterranean which clarified for everyone the succession to preeminence at that "crossroads of Empire," not just around Iran but extending to Greece and Turkey as well. And third, far from demonstrating Soviet "adventurism" or implacability, the Iranian episode indicated that Stalin really could do very little about the extension of American power right up to his back doorstep.

Serious doubts about America's postwar foreign policy were raised in midsummer of 1946 by Secretary of Commerce Henry A. Wallace. Wallace, who had been dumped from the ticket in 1944 to please conservatives in the Democratic party, was considered by many liberals to be F. D. R.'s true and rightful heir. To them Truman was no more than an accident or—more bitterly—a usurper. Hence when the former Vice President spoke out against a get-tough policy at a September 1946 Madison Square Garden rally, the administration was embarrassed. Not only had Wallace cast doubts on the highly moralistic effort to get the Soviets out of Eastern Europe but he had also dared to suggest that the Monroe Doctrine amounted to an American sphere of interest in the Western Hemisphere. One was never supposed to say that. Wallace had a weakness, however; he insisted that political and economic questions were separate. That is, the Soviet Union should be allowed to exercise political hegemony over Eastern Europe but not to keep American trade out. Had not the prewar decade proved to everyone's satisfaction that political and economic questions could not be separated?

Truman wrote in a private memorandum:

I do not understand a "dreamer" like that. The German-American Bund under Fritz Kuhn was not half so dangerous. The Reds, phonies and the "parlor pinks" seem to be banded together and are becoming a national danger.

I am afraid that they are a sabotage front for Uncle Joe Stalin. They can see no wrong in Russia's four and one half million armed

forces, in Russia's loot of Poland, Austria, Hungary, Rumania, Manchuria. They can see no wrong in Russia's living off the occupied countries to support the military occupation.

Clearly, Wallace had to be banished from the Cabinet, but a wholesale liberal heresy was about to be uncovered. British behavior in Greece since 1944, when the Germans were driven out, had come under attack by these voices for being just as bad if not actually worse than what the Soviets were doing in Eastern Europe. Throughout the war Churchill and his aides had felt uneasy about the Greek situation—with good reason. His desire for an understanding with Stalin was based in large part on the need to protect his eastern flank while British soldiers reinstalled the exiled Greek King to his British-built throne in Athens.

Stalin dutifully stuck by his bargain, a stance the Prime Minister gratefully acknowledged in the House of Commons. But the British could not put the Greek monarch back on his throne, at least not without a fight from the partisan movements—led here as elsewhere by local Communists. While the Kremlin remained silent as British troops restored law and order, the American press let loose some terrific blasts at Old World imperialists. Later on, whenever Stalin wanted to counter Anglo-American criticism of his behavior in Eastern Europe, he or Foreign Minister Molotov would quote from the embarrassing press dispatches.

Gradually these criticisms subsided as the press began to see the "larger picture" in Europe. A strong residue remained, however, when the administration appealed to congressional leaders to support a request for funds for Greece and Turkey. The British had recently, in February 1947, declared themselves unable to pay for the civil war in Greece and quite without the resources to modernize the Turkish Army. Those legislators who heard this recounted at a White House briefing were skeptical at first: Was the United States going to have to pull British chestnuts out of the fire yet again? Were two world wars not enough?

Then Undersecretary of State Dean Acheson took the floor. Acheson was already an imposing figure; in Truman's second term, 1949–1953, he would institutionalize the cold war in American foreign policy and supply that policy with a rationale which, despite assaults from left and right, would endure for almost a quarter of a century. Acheson was a conservative in the tradition of Woodrow Wilson—or at least what he thought Wilson to have been. He never thought much of Franklin Delano Roosevelt, not from the beginning, when he found F. D. R.'s decision to go off the gold standard a departure from all the accepted values of Western civilization, monetary and spiritual. Revolutions, he firmly believed, never accomplished anything except to replace an orderly set of relationships with disorder and demagogues. He very much sympathized with the colonial offices in Paris and London which had to deal with those obstreperous half-literates who blindly demanded their independence without a thought to what could befall them outside the safe harbors of European guidance.

The situation in the Mediterranean, he began on that occasion, had nothing to do with British chestnuts; the only issue now was the protection of Western civilization. A communist victory in the Greek civil war would mean a victory for Moscow. Once in control of the eastern Mediterranean, the Soviets could penetrate into Asia and Africa almost at will. The psychological effect of the fall of Athens on Western European countries with their large communist minorities would be devastating and possibly conclusive.

When Acheson finished, the room fell silent. Finally Senator Arthur Vandenburg, a key Republican leader, declared: "Mr. President, if you will say that to the Congress and the country, I will support you and I believe most of its members will do the same." Truman lived up to Vandenburg's expectations and then some in his appearance before both Houses of Congress on March 12, 1947. "At the present moment in world history," he intoned, "nearly every nation must choose between alternative ways of life. The choice is too often not a free one."

Finally he reached the sentence later known as the Truman Doctrine: "I believe that it must be the policy of the United States to support free peoples who are resisting attempted subjugation by armed minorities or by outside pressures." Whether the President had really intended to mean "free peoples" anywhere or was just "scaring Hell out of the country," as Vandenburg had said he must, proved a difficult matter for administration spokesmen to discuss before congressional committees. Acheson reassured one group of doubters that each case would have to be judged on its merits and, despite all the rhetorical flourishes, by its relation to vital American interests.

For twenty-five years the secret Hearings Held in Executive Session on the Truman Doctrine remained unpublished in the files of the Senate Foreign Relations Committee. When they were released in January 1973, a new picture emerged of the legislative process which had brought the doctrine into being as national policy. Many Senators expressed doubts about the plan to aid Greece and Turkey, and more doubts about where such a stance might eventually lead. Finally, Senator Vandenburg responded that the committee members were not really "free agents," because they had "no power to initiate foreign policy. It is like, or almost like, a Presidential request for a declaration of war. When that reaches us there is precious little we can do except say 'Yes.'"

Once the President had taken the initiative, congressional failure to support the executive would be interpreted as a sign of weakness and could make the situation worse. "I think that if we failed within a reasonable time to support the attitude of the President of the United States, we would have lost any chance whatsoever to find a peaceful basis of settlement with the Soviet Union." How many times in the course of the cold war would Congress find itself in this trap? There seemed no way to curb the President's ability to initiate foreign policy without weakening national security, and no way to respond except to say "Yes."

Not everyone on the committee was convinced. Georgia's Walter George delivered an Old Testament prophecy which, after Vietnam, has an eerie sound to it:

I do not know that we will have to go anywhere else in this world, and I do not say that at the moment. I do not see how we are going to escape going into Manchuria, North China, and Korea and doing things in that area of the world. But at the same time that is another question, and we have got the right to exercise common sense. But I know that when we make a policy of this kind we are irrevocably committing ourselves to a course of action, and there is no way to get out of it next week or next year. You go down to the end of the road.

There were already voices calling for intervention in the Chinese civil war. "What about China?" demanded conservatives and pro-Chiang legislators. Surely it was clear to everyone except traitors (or New Dealers) that a communist victory there would mean far more to Moscow than what happened in little Greece. Chiang had fought the Japanese for four years before America came into the war, Roosevelt had made him an equal member of the Big Four, and now were we just going to shrug our shoulders and walk away from him? Something was wrong somewhere.

The containment world view

Something was wrong elsewhere in the Truman Doctrine as well. With its pronouncement the United States had said to the world that it would decide, unilaterally, when changes in the status quo violated the U.N. Charter, when revolutions were strictly internal affairs, and when they were the products of coercion, subterfuge, and infiltration. The publication of an anonymous article entitled "The Sources of Soviet Conduct" (*Foreign Affairs Quarterly*, July 1947) added to the impression that the United States was embarking on a "universalist" foreign policy and gave a one-word definition to the Truman Doctrine: containment. Mr. X was soon identified as Russian expert George Frost Kennan, who had toiled in obscurity in the corridors of power for two decades. He had come to the attention of administration leaders in 1946 as the author of a "long telegram" explaining Soviet postwar behavior in ideological terms.

Kennan's article was an elaboration which not only repeated his original interpretation in much greater detail and with more striking illustrations but which supplied a rationale for a successful response to Soviet policy. Kennan seemed to promise eventual victory in the cold war if his "containment" formula were adopted and followed to the letter. He wrote that by confronting the Soviets

with unalterable counter-force at every point where they show signs of encroaching upon the interests of a peaceful and stable world, [the United States would] increase enormously the strains under which Soviet policy must operate, . . . [forcing] upon the Kremlin a far greater degree of moderation and circumspection than it has had to observe in recent years, . . . [and thereby promoting] tendencies which must eventually find their outlet in either the breakup or the gradual mellowing of Soviet power. For no mystical, Messianic movement—and particularly not that of the Kremlin—can face frustration indefinitely without adjusting itself in one way or another to the logic of that state of affairs.

Ironically, Kennan had opposed military aid to Greece and Turkey in intragovernment debates, seeing in the Marshall Plan for large-scale economic aid to Western Europe a much better application of the containment policy. His colleagues were bewildered, then and later, at Kennan's ability to draw such fine distinctions. Kennan himself confessed in his memoirs that the language of the "X" article suggested military measures to meet a military threat, although he had been more concerned with political measures to meet a political threat.

No one understood (and feared) the ambiguities in this developing American policy better than Walter Lippmann, who wrote that it meant "unending intervention in all the countries that are supposed to 'contain' the Soviet Union." The pundit's dire prophecy seemed overdrawn in the next two years with the success of the Marshall Plan, the brilliant conversion of the Soviets' Berlin blockade into a psychological cold war triumph, and the formation of the North Atlantic Treaty

Organization (NATO) in 1949. The "Russkies" were on the run, exclaimed a delighted Senator Vandenburg. "They evidently know they have lost the cold war in Western Europe," he added, and were feeling pressure from their satellites to reopen East-West trade contacts. Containment was working as promised.

The perils of Asia

Containment seemed to be working at home too. Truman's strong stand against the Soviet Union proved politically sound in warding off threats from both the left and the right. Henry Wallace's forlorn attempt to build a new Progressive party from disaffected New Dealers to challenge the regular Democrats with a peace platform actually bolstered Truman in areas where he needed it and helped him to turn back the right wing of the party. The "isolationist" challenge from Senator Robert A. Taft and the Republican heartland also fell short. Taft's position was actually similar in one respect to that held by Wallace: both dissidents believed that the administration's initiation of the 1949 NATO military alliance, and the inclusion of West Germany in that pact, was provocative. Taft said that the Atlantic pact moved away from the purposes of the United Nations: "It necessarily divides the world into two armed camps. It may be said that the world is already so divided, but it cannot be said that by emphasizing that division we are carrying out the spirit of the United Nations."

Taft would have preferred a simple statement that if the Soviet Union attacked Western Europe, the United States would respond with atomic weapons. Truman's spokesman responded in two ways: first, that that was a more dangerous course than building up conventional strength and, second, that such a proposal would do nothing to overcome the political threat of internal subversion. The Senator's recommendation amounted to a statement of imperial isolation, arrogant and reckless in the extreme. That was not quite the case, but—if and when the Democrats faltered—the American right might have rallied around a less responsible leader than Taft who espoused such views. The Soviet Union's announcement of the formation of the Warsaw Pact in late 1949 as a counterpart for NATO in Eastern Europe further divided Europe, but it also brought a measure of stability and reliability to East-West relations in Europe. Military stand-offs made things easier for political leaders.

Two developments in the fall of 1949 clouded this picture. The first was unexpected—at least so soon; the second was expected but, paradoxically, much harder to accept. Truman's announcement that the Soviets had exploded an atomic device in September was followed only a few weeks later by the final victory of Mao Tse-tung's Chinese Peoples Army over the bedraggled remnants of Chiang's minions. The Soviet atomic bomb was a threat, but the very sort of technical challenge Americans usually welcomed; besides we had a bigger stockpile of bombs and a far more effective "delivery system" of long-range bombers. (That situation would change in later years, when missiles became the primary delivery system; but for the time being America still welcomed technological races.) The "loss" of China was something else. Perhaps not every American felt somehow diminished by the passing of our old friend "traditional" China, despite all the missionary energy expended there; but many did, and they made up in intensity of feeling for those who were unmoved. These emotions were in the background of political decisions in 1950, decisions that were to have a profound impact on the next generation of Americans.

Ever since the revelation of the secret Soviet-American Far Eastern agreement between Roosevelt and Stalin at Yalta, there had been charges of stupidity and even betrayal. For some, who knows how many, Yalta became a shorter word for treason. Throughout the war, F. D. R. had tried to find some way to save Chiang Kai-shek from his own folly (a role often played by American Presidents on behalf of traditional China, but never when the stakes were so high). At Yalta he had hoped to satisfy Soviet Far Eastern territorial desires in the following way: In exchange for leases on Port Arthur and Dairen, a few Japanese islands off the coast of Siberia, and a share in the management of Manchurian railroads, Stalin was supposed to come into the war against Japan (he would have anyway, but better for him to come into the war by arrangement than with a totally free hand) and support Chiang Kai-shek's government. This way, Roosevelt hoped, the Chinese Communists would be isolated.

After Roosevelt's death, Truman sent General Marshall to China with some further proposals. Now Chiang was asked to liberalize his government and take into the ruling coalition some leading Communists. For their part, the Communists were to agree to dismantle their Peoples Army and allow the units to be integrated into the Nationalist Army. No one expected the plan to work except Marshall, and even he gave it up early in 1947, returning home with the sounds of the fully resumed civil war booming in his ears.

Republicans seized upon the obviously unsuccessful China policy as a way to attack the Democrats. Out of power for nearly two decades, here was their opportunity. And they were prepared to use it when the right time came.

The first practical problem posed by the communist victory in China was what to do about the situation in Japan. Since the end of the Pacific war, General Douglas MacArthur had ruled Japan with almost viceregal powers. The results were mixed. Politically, much progress had been made toward establishing the foundations of a democratic government; economically, the Japanese were in trouble. The communist movement in Japan had flourished, and with the new regime in Peking providing it with added incentive, the outlook for a pro-Western Japan was not good. China had something to offer Japan's capitalist class, too: markets for its export surplus. Without alternative outlets, Japan would have to look to communist China for trade. Once in the communist orbit economically, it was only a matter of time before it went over politically—or so it seemed to pessimistic visitors to General MacArthur's headquarters in the spring and summer of 1950. The General himself was in a gloomy mood in those days, warning that America had at best five years to complete its self-appointed tasks in that country.

The only alternative outlets for Japan's exports existed in Southeast Asia, continued this litany of despair. And the situation there seemed to be going from bad to worse. The British were involved in a long-term guerrilla struggle in Malaya, while the French were locked in an even more desperate conflict with Ho Chi Minh's Vietminh forces throughout Indochina. Even in the Philippines, which had recently been given independence by the United States, there was a spreading insurgent movement which controlled the roads outside Manila after dark.

Hot war in Korea

How heavily each of these factors weighed on President Truman when he was told of the North Korean attack on South Korea late in the evening of June 25, 1950, is impossible to tell. His statement that the attack made it plain "beyond all doubt that communism has passed beyond the use of subversion to conquer independent nations and . . . [would] now use armed invasion and war," covered over a great many still unresolved questions about the Korean war. Later in that same statement he did say that the United States would send more aid to the French in Indochina and provide more support for the Philippine government, as well as interposing the Seventh Fleet in the Formosa Strait.

Korea was of little importance strategically to the United States, at least according to the Joint Chiefs of Staff, who had recommended on several occasions that the nation not get involved in a land war on that peninsula—regardless of how it got started. Secretary of State Acheson had formally placed Korea outside the American defense perimeter in a speech early in 1950, a point the Republicans would not forget when things really got bad in Korea. Acheson, they would say, had invited the attack.

"This is the Greece of the Far East," Truman said to members of the White House staff. "If we are tough enough now, there won't have to be any next step."

Korea, in other words, was to China (or China and the Soviet Union together), as Greece was to the Soviet Union: an ideological battleground on which the Communists had chosen to make a bid for world dominance. It fit into the Truman Doctrine and the containment overview, but not without some hauling and shoving. Truman did just that with a group of congressional leaders in the White House, telling them that the next likely move by the Soviets would be in the Middle East to secure more oil for war preparations. He did not ask Congress for a declaration of war nor for its approval in a less formal fashion.

Inside the Cabinet were those who wanted

to respond in Korea for another reason, to intervene in the Formosa Strait to protect Chiang Kai-shek, who was still on shaky grounds even in Taiwan. Communist China was much more concerned about Formosa than Korea in 1950 and had not launched the war in Korea. Nor do later accounts of Stalin's role suggest he was prepared to do anything more than approve a North Korean plan, certainly not to go on from Korea to some new adventure. He may have been testing American reactions for some purpose still known only in the Kremlin, but America was having enough difficulties fighting revolutionary movements in Asia without his interference. Yet another interpretation is that Russia wanted to protect its Far Eastern flank against Japan.

But because they were so preoccupied with containing revolution, on the other hand, American leaders sometimes ascribed to Moscow motives and actions to fit their own interpretation of events. Korea was a good example. Since 1945, when the Soviet Union and the United States had divided the country into occupation zones at the 38th parallel, friction between the two local governments had grown. Attacks back and forth across the parallel had become frequent, and both sides had asked for military aid to conquer the other. The Soviet Union gave North Korea tanks; but Washington was afraid to give its Korean ally, Syngman Rhee, offensive weapons because he had said publicly what he wanted to do with them.

The tanks gave the North Koreans a military advantage as the war began, but General MacArthur's brillant amphibious landing at Inchon on September 15, 1950, turned what had looked like sure disaster into the bright promise of victory. With Washington's approval, MacArthur carried the war to the North Koreans above the 38th parallel, promising to have the troops home by Christmas. Contain-

Figure 21-2 Modern wagon trains drawn up in a circle. A new chapter in the winning of the West, but the best Truman could get was a stalemate, and that was not good enough. (*Wide World Photos*)

ment became liberation, the Democrats rejoiced, and the Republicans lost a campaign issue.

The Republicans got it back sooner than they might have expected. As the combined U.N.-South Korean force moved toward the Manchurian border, the communist Chinese (who had been sending out warning signals through neutrals for some time) came pouring across the Yalu River. With human wave attacks, the quilt-uniformed Chinese drove the advancing armies back below the parallel. MacArthur cried out for permission to strike at the Chinese "sanctuaries," and when the administration failed to respond, he turned to the Republican leadership in Congress. The last straw was the General's effort to undermine diplomatic negotiations for a cease fire in April 1951. Truman had no choice but to grit his teeth and order MacArthur's recall. Not that he minded a political scrap, but the General was the only genuine hero in an unpopular war, and what was coming was more than a scrap.

Congress ordered hearings into the General's dismissal, but however much it now regretted allowing the President a free hand, it offered no alternative to continuing the "limited" war in Korea. It was a war which could not be won in any traditional sense but could be lost in a number of ways. Perhaps the only man who could avoid such a catastrophe made himself available to the Republicans as their 1952 standard bearer. General Dwight D. Eisenhower's hero's credentials were as least as good as MacArthur's, and his politics were well within the mainstream.

The perfect partnership

John Foster Dulles, the man Ike wanted for Secretary of State, had been developing a Republican alternative to containment which

he hoped would appeal to all wings of the party, East and Midwest, internationalist and isolationist. He called it "liberation," a prescription for freeing Soviet-held lands, and simultaneously releasing the United States from the evil spell the Democrats had cast with their containment potions. Dulles had been involved in foreign affairs since his childhood. John W. Foster, a grandfather, had been Secretary of State in the nineteenth century: Robert Lansing, a relative by marriage, had served Woodrow Wilson in the same capacity. Dulles had gone to Versailles, along with his brother Allen, as a minor aide to the American delegation. In the 1920s he joined a law firm which did much of its business for foreign clients and American corporations engaged in international business.

He was also a leading lay spokesmen on international affairs in the Presbyterian Church. During the Second World War he was widely recognized as Republican candidate Thomas E. Dewey's leading adviser on foreign affairs and the next likely Republican Secretary of State. His record and his writings had not placed him clearly within the internationalist wing of the party—an advantage in 1952, when the most likely Midwestern candidate, Robert A. Taft, would challenge the internationalists for control of the party. Dulles believed the French and British had appeased Nazi Germany in the 1930s because they were static powers, and he saw the postwar struggle with the Soviet Union shaping up in much the same way. The Soviet Union had now become a dynamic power, too dynamic to be contained by static methods.

To those who said that the attempt to "liberate" North Korea had failed, Dulles replied simply that it had not really been tried. Containment was an immoral, negative policy which condemned hundreds of millions to communist slavery—now and in the future.

But liberation was not a war policy, he said, far from it. If that sounded confusing, it was. Even Eisenhower was puzzled and upset when Dulles told a Buffalo audience that the United States should use all necessary means to liberate the captive nations of Eastern Europe. He called Dulles at once to remind him that they had agreed to preface remarks concerning liberation with the phrase, "by all peaceful means." "It's just a complete oversight," Dulles quickly explained.

Many were surprised, even his supporters, when Ike brought it off so quickly and easily: he got the United States out of Korea within six months on terms that would have led to demands for Truman's impeachment, and he increased his popularity tenfold in the process. Stalin's death in early 1953 had made things easier all around and encouraged Eisenhower to believe that the Korean truce might be the prelude to a general reduction of cold war tensions. His dour Secretary of State, the strong willed Mr. Dulles, held out few hopes that the old dictator's successors would see the error of Marxist-Leninist ways and travel a new road.

Dulles vowed that the United States *would* set out on a new path, however, and take the way to liberation. The Secretary's assessment of containment was not far off the mark, at least in one respect. It conveyed a static image: reaction to events, not their initiation; resistance, not impetus. He was also right in characterizing the era as dynamic: to stand still at such a time meant to be swept aside in the rush of historical forces as they raced toward the future. Dulles never stood still. He logged more miles than any Secretary of State before or since. A quip of the day had an exasperated Ike shouting to the disappearing Dulles: "Don't do something, Foster, just stand there!" The Secretary was often characterized as carrying the State Depart-

Figure 21-3 He brought it off. Ike got America out of war and into "peaceful coexistence." (*Wide World Photos*)

ment around with him under his black hom-
burg, a description which brought a wry smile
to the corners of his mouth along with the
usual disclaimers.

The third world

For Dulles the almost constant motion had
both symbolic and practical meaning. The
first trip he took after becoming Secretary of
State was to the Middle East, an area he felt
had been neglected in American diplomacy
(except for Greece, Turkey, and Israel) and
one where American policy was still overshadowed by the Old World attitudes of Great
Britain and France. If there was any place
where one could begin to align the United
States with the dynamic forces in the world
and vice versa, this was it. Arab nationalists
were fiercely anticolonial, but they were also
known to be anticommunist. The best opportunity for such a beginning was in Cairo,
where a revolution had brought to power
Colonel Gamal Abdel Nasser. Nasser's determination to force the British to pull their
military units out of the Suez Canal Zone area
was acknowledged and seconded in Washington where it was hoped that the Egyptian
leader would stand on his own two feet
against Soviet communism and would cooperate in the establishment of a regional defense pact.

Much to the Secretary's chagrin, Nasser
proved uninterested in playing such a role in
the cold war drama once the British had been
removed. He and two others—Yugoslavia's
Tito and India's Nehru—had their own act:
neutralism. Their performances baffled and
then infuriated Dulles, who was horrified at
such a display of playing off one side against
the other for fun and profit, especially profit.
The neutralists took the position that it was
more repugnant morally to spend billions of

dollars and rubles on military weapons (except when they needed them) when the world
lacked funds for economic development. The
Egyptian misadventure had further consequences, but it was only the first of several
disappointments to come.

Dulles had watched the situation deteriorate in Indochina since 1950, when President Truman commissioned him to negotiate
the Japanese peace treaty. Prior to that mission, his principal diplomatic experience had
been in Europe; but he came home from Asia
firmly convinced that the cold war would be
decided there. Soviet occupation of Eastern
Europe, he wrote in a magazine article, was
an unhappy consequence of the war. Communist expansion into Asia had come about
through a different process: revolution and
Western mistakes. Moreover, communist
China had a greater population mass than the
Soviet Union and possessed a cultural prestige throughout Asia that the Soviet Union
lacked even in Europe, where many countries
looked down on its Slavic origins.

Dulles was convinced, along with many
others, that the French were making a complete botch of things in the fight against Ho
Chi Minh. Associated with a century of colonial exploitation, even in 1954 they could not
bring themselves to understand that nothing
short of a complete renunciation of their ambitions to continue ruling the states of Indochina would win over the people. It was
probably too late even for that. The Secretary's plan was for France to grant Vietnam,
Laos, and Cambodia full independence and
then to join with other Asian powers (including the states of Indochina) and the United
States to form a Southeast Asian Treaty Organization (SEATO). The SEATO alliance
could then take over the war against the
Vietminh.

France welcomed American military aid,
but not on those terms. The upshot was that

Pierre Mendes-France, the new French Premier, promised to end the war in sixty days or resign. Whatever reservations he may have had about carrying out his pledge disappeared on the first day of the Geneva Conference, when news reached the assembled diplomats that the Dien Bien Phu fortress had fallen. For some weeks, American policy makers had been trying to put together some other ending to this fiasco, but nothing would stick. Eisenhower's own attitude perfectly summed up the problem. The possible consequences of the loss of Indochina, he told a news conference, were "just incalculable."

First, the President told a White House news conference on April 7, 1954, you have the loss of specific items needed by the free world, rubber, tin, and tungsten. These were very important. "But when we come to the possible sequence of events, the loss of Indochina, of Burma, of Thailand, of the Peninsula, and Indonesia following, now you begin to talk about areas that not only multiply the disadvantages that you would suffer through loss of materials, sources of materials, but now you are talking really about millions and millions of people." There was, he said, a falling domino principle. "You have a row of dominoes set up, you knock over the first one, and what will happen to the last one is the certainty that it will go over very quickly."

But one domino was bigger than all the rest. If you took Southeast Asia away from Japan, concluded the President, deprived it of those "millions of customers," that country would have only "one place in the world to go—that is, toward the Communist areas to live." At one point Eisenhower had attempted to obtain congressional clearance for a plan to aid the French militarily; but at a special White House conference with legislative leaders, Senator Lyndon B. Johnson objected that America's cold war allies had not been

consulted, nor were the Joint Chiefs of Staff in agreement on what steps ought to be taken. A decade later Johnson would ask for the very same power and get it in the Gulf of Tonkin Resolution. The only difference was that by then the French had long departed, and America was alone in Vietnam.

Congressional uneasiness had strengthened Ike's own resolve not to use land forces in Southeast Asia so soon after the Korean war. Air Force strategists had argued that tactical atomic weapons could do the job, but the President agreed with his old army colleagues that it would require foot soldiers—a great many of them—to change the outcome in Indochina.

The Geneva Conference of 1954 ended one war in Indochina by dividing Vietnam into temporary demobilization zones at the 18th parallel, but it laid the groundwork for a new struggle if all Vietnamese elections scheduled for 1956 failed to unify the country. American claims notwithstanding, the Conference did not create two nations. U.S. diplomats refused to sign the accord, but they did "promise" not to do anything to disrupt its operation. All in all, the settlement was probably better than the French could have expected and worse than American policy makers had hoped.

After Geneva, Dulles went in motion again, not stopping this time until he had his SEATO alliance. The only nonwhite powers in the alliance were Thailand and the Philippines. It was a little bit like locking the barn after the horse got away, but the Secretary had not given up all hope that somehow it could be found and brought back to the corral. The first thing to do was to get rid of the French to make way for a "genuine nationalist," Ngo Dinh Diem, who, with the aid of American advisers and Central Intelligence Agency friends, could transform South Vietnam into a nation like South Korea or West Germany. The time for the 1956 elections came and went, but the only polling that took place was in the South, where Diem rolled up an unrivaled majority for a "free world" leader. His victory margin even surpassed those of communist candidates in the Peoples Democracies of Eastern Europe. We might not find him and his ways to our liking, wrote one Diem enthusiast, but his one-man democracy perfectly suited the Vietnamese.

Tender loving care

Over the next four years American military and economic aid totaling $3 billion poured into South Vietnam, but even that sum was but a small down payment on an investment which would reach astronomical figures in another decade. The cost in human lives for keeping Saigon outside the "Bamboo Curtain" would run even higher. Both would go on long after Diem's 1963 assassination and his replacement by a succession of genuine nationalists.

"We are confronted with an unfortunate fact," Dulles admitted at the time of the French defeat in Indochina: "most of the countries of the world do not share our view that Communist control of any government anywhere is in itself a danger and a threat." Even the Latin Americans were not vigilant enough. That same year, 1954, the Secretary of State and his brother Allen, now Director of the Central Intelligence Agency, had to rig a counterrevolution against a leftist government which had surfaced in Guatemala. This was accomplished by first securing a roundabout authorization from the Organization of American States, a resolution which declared (by a 17 to 1 vote) that "International Communism" was incompatible with the concept of freedom in the Americas. The rest was easy. "There were a few old crates which flew around," Dulles later explained to aides, "and

dropped some firecrackers, but they were enough to turn the tide. In these countries, air cover has a tremendous significance."

But the "liberation" of Eastern Europe had to be postponed—indefinitely it became apparent, when the United States refused to send aid to the Hungarian "freedom fighters" who rose up against a repressive regime in 1956. The uprising in Budapest had come at a bad time for Washington, when everyone was distracted by fhe Anglo-French-Israeli invasion of Egypt following Nasser's nationalization of the Suez Canal. But even so, Dulles made it plain that any effort to intervene in Hungary would be sheer madness. "Does anyone in his right senses want us to start a nuclear war over Hungary?"

The Middle Eastern debacle was especially painful for Dulles. His original hopes for aligning the United States with Arab nationalism had all been frustrated. Nasser was tied instead to Eastern Europe by arms purchases and had extended a diplomatic hand to Red China. Moreover, Dulles had precipitated the crisis by bringing pressure on Nasser over funds for a key economic project, the proposed Aswan Dam. Let the Soviets finance it, if they can, said the Secretary when he cut off the negotiations. Unhappily, Moscow proved willing and able.

The trouble at Suez and in Budapest were elements in a reevaluation which began as the Secretary fell ill with cancer. His approaching death may have filled him with urgency to make another attempt to resolve European issues. The German question was the most difficult to settle, but both sides seemed ready to try again.

Divided since World War II, Germany was the principal cold war battleground in Europe. The Russian zone included the former capital, Berlin, but the city, too, had been divided into four occupation zones. Deep inside the Soviet-sponsored German Demo-

Figure 21-4 Face to face with the Kremlin boss. Secretary of State Dulles warned Ike about being too chummy with the Red leaders, lest the rest of the "free world" relax its guard. (*Wide World Photos*)

cratic Republic, West Berlin was a showplace for capitalism, a listening post for Western intelligence sources within the communist bloc, and an escape hatch for East Germans fleeing to the West. The first Berlin crisis in 1948 had proved that both sides still regarded the capital city as a political symbol of considerable importance. Stalin's successors wanted to "normalize" the situation in Berlin, by which the West insisted they actually meant recognition of the East German government. Shades of meaning were attached to the slightest change in the Berlin situation; thus the West regarded any attempt to turn over border checkpoints to East German guards as a fundamental effort to alter the balance in Europe.

From the Russian point of view the status quo was intolerable for themselves, and even more so for the East German government. In South Korea and South Vietnam, on the other hand, the United States and its allies had succeeded in gaining international status for the severed parts of countries now divided between Communist and capitalist. The Kremlin wanted the same for East Germany. As the 1950s came to an end, it seemed willing to risk forcing a new German crisis.

Dulles had always felt that the greatest danger for both sides was in a "neutral"

Germany which might try to shift its allegiance as self-interest dictated. Hence shortly before his death, the Secretary came up with an ingenious solution to the dilemma. Perhaps the East German guards could man the checkpoints as the "agents" for Russian authorities. The plan won him few friends in West Germany, and it is by no means sure that he would have ever been willing to advance the idea at a formal negotiating session.

Eisenhower may have had some similar solution in mind when he made one last effort to find an answer that would not leave West Germany unprotected or weaken the Western Allies' position in the divided city of Berlin. The President's hope for a solution went down with the American U-2 spy plane which the Soviet Union shot down over its territory on the very eve of a 1960 Paris summit conference. The new Soviet leaders had proclaimed an era of "peaceful coexistence with the West," but already Premier Nikita Khrushchev was having troubles of his own with recalcitrant hardliners, restless satellites, and the Chinese "comrades" who saw hints of a developing Moscow-Washington "understanding"—and did not like it. Both Eisenhower and Khrushchev were scored by critics at home for their ineptness in handling the U-2 incident and the abortive summit meeting. It was finally canceled by the Soviets when the President refused to apologize for the incident. Eisenhower's detractors in the Democratic party (and within his own) charged him with allowing the country to fall behind the Soviets in the development of missiles, citing as proof the 1957 Soviet "Sputnik" satellite, the first achieved by man in "conquering" outer space. They also accused him, and the late Secretary Dulles, with diplomatic rigidity in confronting complex cold war issues. And

they promised to get the country moving again—toward new frontiers.

Selected references

Cold war historiography is the fastest-growing field in the entire discipline. For background, consult Herbert Feis, *Churchill, Roosevelt, Stalin* (1957), and James McGregor Burns, *Roosevelt: Soldier of Freedom* (1970). A short yet somehow very thorough coverage of crucial events in early 1945 is Martin Herz, *Beginnings of the Cold War* (1966); continuing the story in this vein is Marshall Shulman, *Stalin's Foreign Policy Reappraised* (1963). Critics of the cold war receive their due in Thomas G. Paterson (ed.), *Cold War Critics, Alternatives to American Foreign Policy in the Truman Years* (1971).

Surveys of the entire period include Walter LaFeber, *America, Russia, and the Cold War, 1945–1971* (1971), and Paul Y. Hammond, *The Cold War Years: American Foreign Policy since 1945* (1969). Political and military aspects of the cold war are covered in Seyom Brown's excellent book, *The Faces of Power* (1967), the Far East in Tang Tsou, *America's Failure in China, 1941–1950* (1963), and the Korean War in David Rees, *Korea: The Limited War* (1964).

Spanning the Truman-Eisenhower period is Gabriel and Joyce Kolko's *The Limits of Power, 1945–1954* (1972), while Richard Goold-Adams, *The Time of Power: A Reappraisal of John Foster Dulles* (1962), is perhaps the most interesting study of that famous Secretary of State. A fascinating account by a true believer is Edward Geary Lansdale, *In the Midst of Wars: An American's Mission to Southeast Asia* (1972), which takes cold war policy back to Tom Paine.

TWENTY-TWO

Postwar Politics

Period covered: 1945–1960
Emphasis: Presidential politics
Major events: Republican Congress elected, 1946
President Truman reelected, 1948
Korean war begins, 1950
Eisenhower elected President, 1952
Kennedy elected President, 1960

The Truman administration

Politics after the war was nasty, brutish, and prolonged. The Democrats had overrrstayed their time in office and conservative Republicans were frantic to regain power—not only out of greed and ambition but for ideological reasons too, which was unusual. The party in power is often hated but seldom feared, but conservative Republicans were convinced that the New Deal was a social revolution that would become irreversible if not stopped soon, and these fears were not less violent for being silly. Unlike 1920, when postwar problems were faced by a new party that was technically not responsible for them, in 1945 the country's problems could be blamed on the administration. Most were not Harry Truman's fault, but he took the blame for them anyway. Truman was not greatly bothered by this. One of his two favorite mottos was "If you can't stand the heat stay out of the kitchen." (His other favorite was "The buck stops here.")

Foreign policy and the red scare made things worse. People had assumed that with peace interest in foreign affairs would diminish, as it had in the 1920s. Instead, it became more intense. Truman would later be much admired by liberal historians for getting America off to such a good start in the cold war, but at the time he received little credit for this. Point Four, the Truman Doctrine, the Marshall Plan, foreign aid—all the devices by which American power was extended around the world were hotly argued. Even when Truman prevailed, a legacy of bad feeling was left behind. Republican conservatives, who were strongest in the Congress, resented their position. They believed events had proved their prewar fears to be correct, thus entitling them to run the country. Yet they were still out of power. They hated communism like sin, with which they identified it. They

also hated foreign involvements. They demanded that communism be wiped out or rolled back and then voted to deny Truman the instruments an anticommunist foreign policy required. Frequently they seemed to think communism would go away if only America remained pure.

These were not viable positions, and in time Republicans accepted the fact that cold wars were expensive and entangling. They became as keen on new weapons as any liberal Democrat. All the same, they never forgave history for treating them badly or stopped blaming Democrats for the way things turned out. And many of them came to believe that the reason why socialism (that is to say, TVA, social security, and the like) flourished at home, as did communism abroad, was that the government was rotten with traitors. These feelings deepened after the fall of China in 1949 and after the revelations that some Americans were actually Soviet agents. Once they stopped being isolationists, anticommunism remained the conservatives only link with their prewar foreign policy and was all the more precious for that.

Conservative hostility on the part of both Democrats and Republicans made Truman's position nearly hopeless, though he kept trying to find popular issues (according to Samuel Lubell), zigging here and zagging there as events seemed to warrant. No plans had been made for reconstruction, so when the war ended people had plenty of money and little to buy with it. This led to inflation—though also to prosperity as manufacturers retooled madly to take advantage of the enormous demand for consumer goods. Having failed to plan when it had the power, government could hardly do so after the war when it did not. Truman wobbled this way and that, but in the end he allowed controls to lapse. Prices shot up and, as wages lagged behind, strikes multiplied. This led Truman to introduce a bill authorizing him to seize industries and draft strikers. It failed to pass, which meant that he had offended labor without satisfying the public. Republicans had little trouble gaining control of Congress in 1946.

But congressional Republicans had no plan either, only a boundless hatred for liberal Democrats. They could not respond to public demands for new social programs because they meant to destroy the New Deal, not extend it. Congress would not abolish the poll tax, pass an antilynching bill, establish a permanent Fair Employment Practices Commission, or furnish aid to education. It passed the Taft-Hartley Act, which prohibited using union dues for political purposes and allowed the President to temporarily enjoin strikes. Labor leaders called it a "slave labor bill," though it obviously was not, and rallied around Truman who was their only hope, however frail. Everyone still assumed that Truman would lose in 1948 and pollsters stopped sampling public opinion before election day because Thomas E. Dewey, the first Republican nominee for President since William Howard Taft to wear a mustache, was so far ahead.

Nonetheless Truman won, though only by accident. Henry Wallace, who had been Vice President during most of the war and a cabinet member until 1946, when Truman dumped him for being critical of American foreign policy, decided to run on a third-party ticket. He favored peace with the Soviet Union and more New Dealism. Then, when the Democratic convention endorsed a civil rights plank, Southern "Dixiecrats" walked out and formed a segregationist fourth party which nominated Strom Thurmond of South Carolina. These events were believed harmful to Truman, but they probably won the election for him. Wallace attracted left-wingers, freeing Truman's party of the communist taint. Dixiecrats aroused a larger than usual black Democratic vote and also offended white ethnics who associated states rights with nativism. Truman improved on his position by calling Congress back into session. The Republican platform promised all things to all men, as was customary. By recalling Congress, Truman proved that the conservative Republican majority would not enact what liberal Republicans had written into the platform. Republicans also talked of "flexible," meaning lower, price supports, thus bringing back the farmers who had sat out the 1946 election. Then too, since the Democrats had been in so long, voting for them was the safe thing to do—all the more so because Republicans were still blamed for the Depression.

These elements combined to give Truman a comfortable margin of victory in 1948, which was too bad. Having been, as they saw it, cheated of victory, Republicans cooperated with Dixiecrats and conservative Democrats to pay Truman back. Politics became more vicious than ever. Truman's efforts to get bills on civil rights, aid to education, and reformed agricultural subsidies were voted down, as was the best idea he ever had, a national health insurance program. The American Medical Association wrongly called it "socialized medicine" and spent $3 million to preserve "fee for service" and the "sacred doctor-patient relationship" or cash nexus, as laymen came to think of it. This enabled medical costs to shoot out of sight and made doctors richer than ever. More than ever they could say "your money or your life" and feel virtuous while doing so.

The loyalty issue

By far the worse feature of postwar politics was the loyalty struggle. Truman's anticommunist foreign policy did him surprisingly little good at home. Even after 1950, when the

Figure 22-1 Harry S. Truman on Election Day plus one, 1948. His finest hour.
(*United Press International*)

Korean war showed there were few lengths he was not prepared to go to in the fight against "communist aggression," his administration was always under attack for harboring traitors. Actually there were few Communists or fellow travelers (as communist sympathizers were called) in America after 1948, and none in important positions. Communism had been discredited first by the Stalin-Hitler Pact, then by subsequent outrages and revelations. There were only a handful of communist agents, and they transmitted little information of value for the most part. Even the nuclear research data which Julius and Ethel Rosenberg were supposed to have given the Soviets did not affect the balance of power.

Had the government steadfastly insisted, as Truman once said, that domestic communism was a "red herring," things might have gone better.

Instead, the government devised a vast security system. In 1947 Truman established a loyalty program broad enough, one might have thought, to satisfy the most ardent inquisitor. It ignored the distinction between espionage and subversion on the one hand and mere opinion on the other. It aimed to uncover not only those who were disloyal but anyone who might conceivably become so. Since the civil service was not clairvoyant, crude guidelines were established to chart the future of suspected persons. One criterion was membership in proscribed organizations, a list of which was compiled, subject to no checks whatsoever, by the Attorney General. His office thus gained the power to destroy organizations and ruin their members, since to be included on the list was fatal to all but the sturdiest. The program also established hearing boards to decide who should be fired from government jobs. These boards were authorized to use unnamed informers whom the accused could not see or cross-examine. Many people were discharged on the basis of anonymous accusations—which were valued more than the sworn testimony of the accused and his witnesses—and this occurred even when the board itself did not know who the informer was. In those instances it simply accepted the FBI's judgment that the informer was "reliable."

The FBI flourished under these conditions, hiring more agents and compiling dossiers on millions of people. Supposedly secret, these dossiers managed somehow to fall into the hands of friendly congressmen at crucial moments. As the only arm of government besides the Central Intelligence Agency whose budget was never questioned by Congress, the FBI was perfectly suited to this work. It spread a network of spies and informers across the country, fattening its files by every means possible. When criticized, its director J. Edgar Hoover had a ready answer. For example, when in 1949 the *Yale Law Review* printed an unfriendly article, he replied, "I find such opinions most frequently expressed on the pages of the *Daily Worker*," which, if anyone didn't know, he hastened to add, was "the publication of the Communist party."

This strategy did the administration little good. Witch hunters remained convinced that traitors were everywhere and that the loyalty program was only a device to mask them. And by instituting the program, government appeared to admit that disloyalty was a problem, though in fact it was not. Truman did not make things better by wavering. When Congress passed the McCarran Internal Security Act, an omnibus anticommunist bill, he vetoed it and then brought forward his own bill. Thus, instead of saying the McCarran bill was unnecessary and unconstitutional, as it proved to be, Truman suggested the need for something like it. While few real cases of disloyalty came to light, they aroused strong feeling. After being convicted of passing on nuclear secrets, the Rosenbergs were executed—something never before done in peacetime.

No case had more effects than the Hiss-Chambers affair, perhaps the most symbolic event of the witch-hunting era. It began in 1948 when Whittaker Chambers, an editor of *Time* magazine and formerly a communist agent, testified before the House Un-American Activities Committee (HUAC) that Alger Hiss had forwarded secret papers to the Soviet Union in the 1930s. Hiss, then president of the Carnegie Endowment for World Peace, had not been a policy maker in the State Department, but he had a responsible post and was the highest-ranking person ever accused of treason by a credible witness after the war. Hiss rushed to clear his name and denied ever having known Chambers. HUAC was impressed. Then, when Congressman Richard Nixon brought them together in a hotel room, Hiss admitted having known Chambers under another name during the 1930s. Chambers repeated his allegations over the radio without benefit of congressional immunity, obliging Hiss to sue him for slander, as Hiss claimed to want. Before the case came to trial, Chambers conveniently remembered incriminating documents he had hidden away long ago against just such an evil day. He secreted them again in a pumpkin, which for some reason was thought very funny later when he gave them to HUAC. Hiss was indicted for perjury, the statute of limitations on treason having run out, and convicted after a second trial—the first having ended in a hung jury. The "pumpkin papers," classified State Department documents which Hiss was supposed to have given to Chambers when he was still a Soviet agent, were probably decisive.

Much about the case remains unclear. It was never established why a well-educated man with a promising future would compromise it by passing documents on to Russia, and the defense insisted the documents were forgeries. Hiss's conviction depended on the testimony of a confessed former traitor, a man given, moreover, to the most extravagant fantasies. Chambers once said to a reporter that he was "a man who, reluctantly, grudgingly, step by step is destroying himself that this country and the faith by which it lives may continue to exist," as if convicting Hiss for an old and trivial crime (the documents were of little value) made any difference to the world. Chambers thought it would, not because what Hiss had done was so important but because by revealing it Chambers was exposing the entire liberal, or socialist, or communist (he used the terms interchangeably) conspiracy to hand America over to Moscow. This too was fantasy, but in those strange times many believed it. Hiss was a member in good standing of the Eastern liberal establishment. Dean Acheson had said, before turning his back on Hiss, that he would never turn his back on Hiss. The conviction for perjury proved that no one, however well placed, could be above suspicion. Liberals, whose self-confidence was already badly shaken by

events, now came to doubt themselves even more. Many vied with one another in repudiating their own political pasts. As witch hunters they were scarcely less vigorous though often more sophisticated than conservatives.

McCarthyism

On Feb. 9, 1950, Joseph McCarthy, an obscure Senator from Wisconsin, gave a speech in Wheeling, West Virginia, charging that there were numerous Communists (205, 81, 57, or a lot, depending on whose version of the speech is accepted) working in the State Department. He never identified these shadowy figures or produced serious evidence against them. All the same he became a great power in the country and raged unchecked for years. His attacks led Secretary of State Dean Acheson to testify before the Senate Foreign Relations Committee that not only did the United States never plan to recognize Communist China but that the idea was so odious it was never even discussed, which was absurd and untrue. Because of McCarthy and his fellow witch hunters, Truman could not get an armistice in Korea, since, whatever the terms, he would be accused of selling out to China.

McCarthy received a steady flow of information, some of it classified, from disgruntled federal employees; and when criticized for this he said publicly that he would "not abide by any secrecy directive of anyone." He terrorized the Department of the Army and humiliated career officers. He said to General Ralph Zwicker, a hero of the Battle of the Bulge, "You are a disgrace to the uniform. You're shielding Communist conspirators. You're not fit to be an officer. You're ignorant. You are going to be put on display next Tuesday." He personally negotiated with

Greek ship owners, whom he threatened to investigate unless they stopped taking cargo to the Soviet Union. Senators feared to discipline him because, in the elections of 1950 and 1952, McCarthy campaigned against his principal enemies in the Senate and all were defeated.

Most of the noise McCarthy made was based on slight, even silly evidence. He humiliated the Army because an allegedly "pink" dentist was promoted from captain to major. People were fired by the United States Information Agency (USIA) because two of his staff members found novels by supposed fellow travelers in USIA libraries overseas. One was let go because a lady employee claimed he made a pass at her—sexual irregularity being thought a peculiarly communist trait, the Kinsey report notwithstanding.

Except for cold war hysterics, it is hard to explain why someone could gain such power merely on the strength of bold lies. In fact, McCarthy only became a witch hunter by accident. In 1950 he began worrying about getting reelected in 1952, since he had not done anything to merit it. After conversations with friends and anticommunist authorities he decided to have a fling at witch hunting. To his surprise the press gave his wild charges in distant Wheeling a big play. After that there was no stopping him.

McCarthy was more skillful and unscrupulous than the usual witch hunter. Protected from libel suits by congressional immunity, he made so many charges that reporters were unable to keep track of them, much less check them out. Newsmen sometimes knew he was lying, but convention kept most from saying so. McCarthy pioneered the technique of holding a press conference to announce another press conference later in the day, thus making the papers twice even when, as

often happened, he had nothing to offer but more delays. Flimsy as these tactics seemed, they worked. The best proof of that was McCarthy's successful blackguarding of General Marshall, whose reputation for nonpartisan rectitude and patriotism was one of the Truman administration's greatest assets. McCarthy got away with saying that "Marshall would sell his grandmother for any advantage." After that no one was safe.

When the GOP took power in 1953, McCarthy failed to change his ways, which was his undoing. Senator Robert Taft, the Republican leader, had McCarthy assigned to the Committee on Government Operations, thinking it would limit his scope. But McCarthy used its subcommittee on investigations to carry on guerrilla warfare against what was now a friendly government. He investigated the Voice of America, though it had already been investigated to death, and got top officials discharged on the ground that they had broadcast material offensive to Papuan anticommunists. Then he went after the Army.

It appears he attacked the Army because his chief aide Roy Cohn was a friend of G. David Schine. When Schine was drafted, Cohn wanted him commissioned and assigned to antisubversive work. The Army refused, so Cohn got McCarthy to investigate it for having promoted a "fellow-traveling" dentist. The hearings went on for thirty-five days and were televised, McCarthy's second great mistake. (This error seems to have been a result of McCarthy's genuine inability to grasp the fact that people found his tactics offensive. He appeared to be honestly surprised when people he had smeared cut him socially.) Twenty million people saw McCarthy bullying witnesses. The Army's defense, brilliantly managed by a Boston lawyer named Joseph Welch, exposed the pressure brought on Schine's commanding officer,

Figure 22-2 Senator Joseph McCarthy (right) and attorney Joseph Welch during the Army-McCarthy hearings. Without his realizing it, McCarthy was being destroyed. (*Wide World Photos*)

who was made to give Schine weekly passes, permission to take or receive 250 long-distance phone calls, and other favors. Roy Cohn had to resign from the McCarthy committee.

This was McCarthy's first major defeat, and it nerved the Senate to finally take action against him. The hearings which resulted in a motion of censure were organized by conservative Senators who could not be red-baited. Afterward his power disappeared as suddenly as it had arrived. He was struck from the White House guest list, the Post Office would not appoint his nominees, and he died of drink and disappointment in 1957. McCarthy had been safe as long as he confined himself to Democrats and unpopular agencies like the State Department and the USIA. But by attacking a Republican administration he alienated his political allies, and by trying to smear the Army he offended moderate and conservative people whose

faith in the military was both touching and absolute. McCarthy's ruin was fatal to the witch-hunting movement, of which he had been the acknowledged champion. His exposure discredited the entire red scare, especially after Eisenhower became President.

General Eisenhower's prestige was such that only Democratic holdovers in the government could be red-baited, which left HUAC, the FBI, and other terrorists with few targets of general interest. They went on for years claiming to find reds in the schools and churches. But as the Communist party had dwindled to a handful of harmless senior citizens and FBI informers, people lost their fear of it. Virtually every Communist or fellow traveler of any eminence had confessed or been smeared. Even obscure ones were persecuted. The government ruled that Communist party members were ineligible to receive social security benefits, though some had paid into the trust fund for years. It also raided the headquarters of the New York CP for nonpayment of taxes. Thus the CP was a political organization for tax purposes and a foreign conspiracy for others.. Paying taxes was the only right a Communist enjoyed. Even when employed against admitted Communists, this kind of petty malice left a bad taste. A movement that was reduced to depriving pensioners of their retirement checks and completely disabled exsoldiers of their veterans benefits, as was done, could hardly expect to be widely admired or to convince people that national security was enhanced thereby. So the red scare faded away, leaving behind it a trail of ruined lives, and a fear of negotiating with communist governments that would inhibit Democratic administrations for years to come. Surprisingly enough, no major politician profited greatly from the witch hunt. Even McCarthy used it successfully for just four years. The exception was Richard Nixon, and then only because he knew when to quit.

The election of 1952

Few could have guessed in 1952 that calm was on the way. Unscrupulous partisanship reached a peak that year, but it was a peak, not a plateau as so many feared. The GOP was half crazed by the scent of victory but fiercely divided over who should be nominated for President. Conservatives wanted Senator Robert Taft. He was known as "Mr. Republican" for his integrity and partisanship. Taft was an isolationist—which conservatives still thought the only truly Republican approach to foreign affairs. Liberals wanted General Dwight D. Eisenhower, then head of the NATO command. His enormous personal popularity was the best assurance of Republican victory. He had no political record whatsoever,

hence no political enemies. He was able to seem all things to all men. Conservatives did not dislike Ike, as he was familiarly known. But they hated his backers, many of them liberal Eastern internationalists such as Thomas E. Dewey. Taft's campaign manager said that Dewey was a New Dealer in all but name, one of those who wanted "to take us down the road to socialism and dictatorship." At the GOP convention the loudest cheers were for Taft, ex-President Hoover, and Joe McCarthy, favorites of the party regulars, who, all the same, bought the idea that Taft could not win and grudgingly nominated Eisenhower.

The real Eisenhower is still hard to see. Democrats liked to make him seem amiable but inept while Republicans emphasized his boyish charm, but both these images seem beside the point. We know Eisenhower was skillful at managing men, which was why General Marshall jumped him over hundreds of senior officers to be supreme allied commander in Europe, a job that was as much political as military. Eisenhower assembled the most efficient military coalition ever constructed out of so many diverse elements and on such a grand scale. He took a liberal view of foreign affairs as it was defined then, and, ambition apart, ran for President so as to muzzle the GOP isolationists. In domestic affairs he felt that the country needed a Republican victory to preserve the two-party system. This was not quite right. The two-party system was hardly at issue. What the country needed was domestic peace after seven years of feverish controversy, and the only way to get it was for the Republicans to win an election. He also had vague prejudices against centralized authority and federal "paternalism," whatever that might be. In practice, what he cared for most was a strong dollar and a balanced budget.

Eisenhower ran, given the sordid atmosphere of 1952, a reasonably clean campaign. The dirt in it came from conservatives and from his running mate Richard M. Nixon, who was chosen because—being young, mean, and professional—he would offset Eisenhower's age, niceness, and political inexperience. He said the Democrats were corrupt and subversive, the party of "twenty years of treason." Since the GOP was making much of its virtue, Nixon had a bad moment when it was charged that he had raised money improperly for his personal expenses. All big politicians did the same, including the Democratic nominee Adlai Stevenson. Yet though it was a weak charge, it hurt him—the absurd being often more important than the real in politics, as the loyalty issue showed. Nixon beat off the attack theatrically. He went on television, bared his finances, said his wife owned but a humble cloth coat, and revealed that his children had been given a small dog named Checkers which he would never surrender. This was irrelevant but effective. Favorable telegrams poured in, Eisenhower said all was forgiven, and Nixon fell weeping into his arms.

The unenviable task of running against General Eisenhower in 1952 was assigned to Governor Adlai Stevenson of Illinois. He was an unusually attractive candidate, charming, mildly witty, and well educated. His grandfather had been a Vice President of the United States. He was literally drafted by the Democratic party despite an apparently genuine wish on his part to remain Governor. Though a lifelong Democrat, he, like Eisenhower, did not resemble the typical politician, which was an asset in 1952 when politicians were in disfavor. His hesitancy over running was attractive. He ran a respectable campaign and tried to defend Truman's record—as he had

to—without associating himself too closely with the administration.

Liberals were very fond of him, though he was not a notably liberal man. His running mate, Senator Sparkman of Alabama, was against civil rights legislation, which Stevenson nominally favored. (In 1956 Stevenson would oppose the use of federal troops in desegregation cases. He was against denying federal funds to segregated school districts.) Speaking to the American Legion, he poked fun at professional patriots. He also made the incredible remark that "Legionnaires are united by memories of war. Therefore, no group is more devoted to peace." After the election he praised the Nationalist Chinese dictator Chiang Kai-shek and in England said that he deplored Senator McCarthy's methods but that it was good to draw attention to the communist menace. He dutifully called communism the antichrist, and praised Truman for having "put the leaders of the Communist party in this country where they belong—behind bars." In 1952 he argued that the Democratic party was the real conservative party in America, which was probably true by then. Like many other Democrats, he wished chiefly to preserve what had been gained since 1933. This did not seem a very compelling reason for keeping Democrats in office, and Eisenhower was elected by a margin of more than 6 million votes.

The Eisenhower years

Eisenhower was the right man at the right time. Had a Democrat been elected, the Korean war would have dragged on—as would the red scare. During the campaign Eisenhower had promised to visit Korea personally and afterward did so, though it made little difference. He had apparently decided to accept a stalemate in Korea if the prisoner of war issue could be resolved. China was willing to deal, even after Syngman Rhee, the dictator of South Korea, tried to sabotage negotiations by freeing the North Korean POWs unilaterally. There was little cheering in America when the armistice was signed, since accepting the status quo was a tacit admission of defeat. Yet South Korea had been saved from communism, which—though it was the original point of the war—had been lost sight of. And Eisenhower knew that the blessings of peace would outweigh what was awkward about the settlement.

Eisenhower needed Democratic congressional votes, so he did not make partisan attacks as Truman did. Democrats, in turn, were reluctant to denigrate such a popular figure. Liberal Democrats and Eisenhower agreed generally on foreign policy and on some domestic issues. These elements combined to greatly moderate the fierce partisanship of earlier years. During Eisenhower's two administrations, the worst wounds inflicted by the loyalty struggle and the cold war healed. Soon critics began to complain of how frightfully boring politics was. Afterward, the Eisenhower era would seem uncommonly peaceful, the least alarming period in recent American history—no small accomplishment in an age of discord.

The fundamental political fact of the entire post-World War II era was that the GOP was too weak to take power and the Democratic coalition too unstable to use it effectively. Roosevelt's power had been based on the solid South, rural discontent, the GOP's inability to hang onto traditionally Republican black voters, and the rise to political maturity of the great urban ethnic groups who had not gained enough from Republican prosperity in the 1920s. After 1945, the movement of blacks into the Democratic party cost it Southern votes, farmers often voted Republican again, and the upward mobility of urban ethnics made them less reliable. The more middle class they became, the more likely they were to vote Republican. The association between Republicanism and hard times kept many in the Democratic party but did not prevent some from voting Republican at times. Thus, both parties were frustrated. The GOP had no issue that would win over marginal Democrats, and in fact the more Republican it was, the worse it did. The Democrats had no way of hanging onto their marginal elements except by avoiding controversy—hence innovation—whenever possible.

The one significant new issue in postwar politics was the race question, and neither party could use it to break the deadlock. Democrats, hesitantly under Truman and more vigorously under Johnson, won over black voters, but at the cost of Southern votes and with the continual risk of alienating urban ethnics who felt most threatened by rising black aspirations. The GOP could not exploit the racial crisis because to become the party of racial bigotry was dishonorable and dangerous. Republicans did make overtures to Southern Democrats and sometimes helped defeat civil rights bills in Congress, but no important Northern Republican catered to antiblack sentiments except in small ways. Blacks complained throughout the fifties and sixties that the major parties were not doing enough for them, which was true; but the Democrats could not go far and remain the majority party. The GOP had no reason to do much for blacks and some reason to exploit the backlash against them. To its credit, the GOP mostly resisted this temptation. The result was that on nearly all political questions, race included, the parties could take only marginally different stands. The distance between them was narrowed further because President Eisenhower needed Democratic votes in Congress most of the time.

Eisenhower's domestic policies were shaped more by necessity than conviction. Conservatives were disappointed when he failed to undo the New Deal, but Eisenhower had to accept the limited welfare state erected since 1933. He hoped to cut domestic spending, but in most areas he could not. He even offered modest bills of his own to promote health, education, and the like. Eisenhower also supported important public works proposals like the interstate highway system and the St. Lawrence Seaway. So the domestic budget continued to grow in the 1950s and, thanks to two small recessions and tax cuts, there were even federal deficits—though minor ones compared with those President Nixon would run up later. Liberals were frustrated by social needs that went unmet, conservatives even more by those that were. Though it was revived briefly in 1964, their hope that people had repudiated big government and the limited welfare state was dead.

Brown v. Board of Education, the Supreme Court's decision in 1954 that school segregation was inherently discriminatory and so violated constitutional rights, made the President unhappy. But he accepted it and, in 1957, when violence erupted over the integration of Central High School in Little Rock, Arkansas, he sent troops to enforce the Court's order. He also submitted weak civil rights bills to Congress in 1957 and 1960, where they were further weakened before passage. All the same, it was remarkable that anything called a civil rights bill got through Congress. That this was achieved was a measure of Lyndon B. Johnson's skill as Senate majority leader. Himself a Southerner, he managed in 1957, for the first time in history, to get a civil rights act through the Senate without splitting the Democratic party and without a filibuster. Eisenhower's civil rights record, though unimpressive, was important because it meant that the GOP was not going to exploit racial prejudice for political gain.

Eisenhower's only great domestic achievement was to keep military spending down. This was far more difficult than people knew, since big peacetime military budgets were still a novelty. Before the Korean war, defense had cost only about $13 billion a year. It shot up during the conflict, then declined, then crept up to $41 billion in 1960. The curious thing was that while these expenditures were large by earlier standards, Congress wanted them larger still, and there was very little pressure on Eisenhower to hold costs down. Business loved defense contracts, as did labor. The Democrats complained loudly that Russia was moving ahead in military research and development, especially after 1957 when Sputnik, the first artificial satellite, was successfully orbited. An alliance of businessmen, labor leaders, liberal and conservative Democrats, many Republicans, and the military worked to get ever costlier and more complex weapons systems authorized.

Eisenhower used several tactics against them. One was to concentrate on "massive deterrence," as the strategic weapons program was called. The theory was that you got "more bang for a buck" by investing in strategic weapons. Thus Eisenhower provided ample funds for nuclear research and development, long-range ballistic missiles, and the like at the expense of ground troops and limited war armaments. Another tactic was to set a ceiling on total military expenses and then let the services decide themselves as to how the money should be spent. This diverted their fire from him to each other. In practice the Navy and Air Force joined together against the Army, which declined in size during the late 1950s. (Eisenhower was surprisingly unsentimental about his own service. Twice he tried to abolish it, once by reducing it to a small guard force and once by merging it into a unified service.) Generals resigned in disgust and fired angry blasts at him to no effect.

This policy was attacked by liberals and conservatives of both parties. Nelson Rockefeller resigned from the government and financed private studies supervised by Henry Kissinger to show how Eisenhower's parsimony was hurting defense. President Eisenhower was unmoved. He believed in limiting military costs not only because they unbalanced the budget but even more because they were a threat to liberty. In his farewell address he warned against the "military-industrial complex." Earlier he had told Emmet John Hughes, a sometime speechwriter who broke with him over the issue, that "if we let defense spending run wild, you get inflation . . . then controls . . . then a garrison state."

Much remains ambiguous and contradictory about Eisenhower. His press conferences were famous for the garbled syntax he produced at them, yet in eight years he never said anything that hurt his interests. His speeches were notably dull, but his speechwriters agree that he was a meticulous and precise editor who struck out everything that was merely rhetorical. Some men achieve blandness accidentally, but he rose to it by design. Eisenhower was a powerful, complex, hot-tempered man who in public liked to appear simple, open, and mild. There is no way now of resolving this contradiction. All that can be said is that in his first term he

made peace in Korea, ended the frightful divisions at home, established that the limited welfare state was here to stay, eliminated isolationism as a political factor, and made Republican conservatives face reality. In his second administration he held down defense spending and stopped nuclear testing. He was the only President since Hoover to fight no wars. Even when set against his feeble domestic policies, these were not small achievements. Posterity is likely to value them more than the generation which knew him.

The election of 1960

The election of 1960 was a strange one. Nixon was the inevitable Republican choice; beloved by party regulars, he had Eisenhower's record of peace and plenty to run on. As Vice President, he had gotten tremendous public exposure. Yet he was not the strongest Republican candidate; Nelson Rockefeller, the Governor of New York, stood higher in the polls. But party regulars could not stand "Rocky" because he was thought too liberal and, being rich, had little need of the organization. Eisenhower was not enthusiastic about Nixon's candidacy. He did Nixon much harm at a press conference in which he was asked to name a big decision that Nixon had participated in. He replied that it would take him weeks to think of one. This was literally true, but Nixon was leaning hard on his claim to experience and the suggestion that this had been trivial hurt him badly. Though Eisenhower preferred other men to Nixon, he abominated Rockefeller for attacking his defense policies. As Rocky was the most likely alternative, Ike found himself tied again to Nixon.

Many Democrats wanted the nomination,

but only three—Senator John F. Kennedy, Senator Hubert Humphrey, and Adlai Stevenson—had much of a chance. Kennedy, though a Roman Catholic, was young, handsome, rich, and a hard campaigner who got enormous press coverage. So he was the front runner despite his religion. Humphrey was more liberal and had a better record, but no money or glamour. At primary time Kennedy beat him narrowly in Wisconsin, where he was well known, and swamped him in West Virginia where he was not. Since West Virginia was largely Protestant, this disposed of the argument that Protestants would not vote for a Catholic. At the convention the regulars were for Kennedy, who, unlike Stevenson, was a real politician. Kennedy won easily and chose Senator Lyndon Johnson as his running mate. People thought this odd because Johnson was square, Southern, unintellectual, and had wanted the nomination himself. In the event, it was a shrewd choice, for Johnson gained Southern votes that were crucial to their victory.

Nixon, who was much better known, ought to have had no trouble beating Kennedy whose religion cost the Democrats many votes. But events and his own mistakes combined to defeat Nixon. Years of Democratic propaganda convinced many that America had been falling behind the Soviet Union since Sputnik. Most believed there was a dangerous "missile gap." This was untrue, as Kennedy discovered once in office, but effective anyway. A major Eisenhower accomplishment—holding down defense spending while also keeping a strategic advantage over the Soviet Union—was thus turned into a Republican liability. (This was poetic justice, since the same thing had happened to the Democrats on account of their anticommunism earlier.) The U-2 affair, student rioting in Japan that prevented Eisenhower from visiting there, and Fidel Castro's turn to the left in Cuba all worked against Nixon, as did the mild depression in 1960 which bottomed out just before election day.

Nixon worked hard to make things worse. He tried to run everything himself, so he was frequently tired and made unnecessary mistakes. He failed to react strongly when Martin Luther King was jailed, but the Kennedys did, getting King out on bail and winning back black voters, like King's own father, who had earlier supported Nixon on religious grounds. Worst of all, Nixon agreed to debate Kennedy on television. Ever since the Checker's speech, Nixon had considered himself a TV star. The debates showed otherwise. Nixon was fatigued and poorly made up for the first and most decisive of the four shows. Kennedy was handsomer and won the beauty contest. Nixon did well on radio because he had a deeper voice and better delivery, and he recovered on subsequent telecasts which fewer people saw. But the advantages of his greater reputation and supposed knowledge-ability were lost, and with them the election.

Selected references

Samuel Lubell, *The Future of America Politics* (1952), is full of remarkable ideas that have stood up surprisingly well. The essays in Barton J. Bernstein (ed.), *Politics & Policies of the Truman Administration* (1970), are cogent and up to date. Alan Barth, *The Loyalty of Free Men* (1951), is a brilliant contemporary attack on Truman's loyalty program. Michael Rogin, *McCarthy and the Intellectuals* (1967), is a very important book showing, among other things, that McCarthyism was not the illegitimate child of Populism and Progressivism. Richard H. Rovere, *Senator Joe McCarthy* (1959), is good reading. Many books have been written about the Hiss case. Whittaker Chambers, *Witness* (1952), is an extraordinary mixture of brilliance, moral vanity, and paranoia. Alistair Cooke, *A Generation on Trial* (1950), though written before all the facts were in, is calm.

The only serious work by a professional historian on Eisenhower is Herbert S. Parmet, *Eisenhower and the American Crusades* (1972). The most revealing book by an aide is Arthur Larson, *Eisenhower: The President Nobody Knew* (1968). Emmet J. Hughes, *The Ordeal of Power,* is a typical liberal critique of Eisenhower.

TWENTY-THREE

Postwar Society

Period covered: 1945–1960
Emphasis: Social thought
Major events: None

Physical progress

The most striking aspect of life in America after 1945 was the amount of attention given subjective problems. Before then, Americans had mostly worried about concrete economic and political questions, and these did not fade away suddenly. People went on being anxious about the economy and their own stake in it, about who should govern and what policies should be adopted. But these practical matters were approached with considerable confidence, and, it was felt, success. People had feared that when the war ended millions of returning veterans would be unable to find work. There would almost certainly be a recession, as in 1919. This concern soon vanished when the pent up demand for consumer goods, together with the huge savings forced by war, proved that good times were here to stay.

The rising birthrate put great pressure on school systems. Most responded so vigorously that, by 1960, 81 percent of all sixteen- and seventeen-year-olds were in school and by 1970 nearly 90 percent (as compared with 43 percent in 1920). There was a great housing shortage which did not ease overnight. In 1950 total home mortgage indebtedness was only $34 billion, but ten years later it stood at $117 billion. Forty-two percent of all existing housing as of 1960 had been built in the previous decade. Similarly, when a flood of new cars led to congestion, a system of superhighways was begun that eventually would allow motorists to drive coast to coast without encountering a stop light.

What this prosperity meant for individuals is easily demonstrated. At the war's end 39 percent of American homes had no bathtub or shower; 35 percent lacked flush toilets; 45 percent used coal, wood, or oil stoves; and 21 percent had no electricity. By 1960, 88 per-

cent of all homes had a bathtub or shower; 90 percent had flush toilets; only 5 percent employed wood, coal, or oil stoves; and over 99 percent had electricity. In 1945, only 7 percent of American families earned more than $10,000 a year; in 1968, one in three did. Income was distributed unequally throughout, with the poorest fifth of the population earning only 5 percent of the national income. But as total income kept rising, even the poor were better off. Three-quarters of all families with incomes below $4,000 a year had washing machines; 60 percent owned automobiles; and 93 percent of all homes had television. While poverty remained and it was foolish to say that it had been conquered, as many did in the fifties, it was not so bad as formerly. If an income equal to $3,000 a year in current dollars is taken as the poverty line, three-fifths of families and individual wage earners were below it in 1913 but only one-third in 1945 and one-fifth in 1968.

Social anxieties

It might be supposed that such physical achievements would have inspired a sense of well-being. For many individuals they certainly did. But these prosperous years were also notable for the extent to which people worried about abstract questions—problems so vague, personal, and subjective that it is often difficult to find proof that they existed outside men's minds. The fear of domestic Communists is a case in point. The unease was real enough, but the cause of it was not. Relatively small to begin with, the Communist party got smaller by the hour. Yet people trembled at the thought of it for years. Intellectuals and journalists especially worried about even more remote problems, such as the presumed loss of identity and community.

To look at a representative book by Robert Nisbet, *The Quest for Community* (1953), is to discover that the entire intelligentsia believed alienation was rampant. Nisbet defined alienation as "the state of mind that can find a social order remote, incomprehensible, or fraudulent; beyond real hope or desire, inviting apathy, boredom, or even hostility." Young people who admired J. D. Salinger's picaresque novel *Catcher in the Rye* (1951) showed themselves to be alienated in this sense. So apparently did almost everyone else. Theologians complained that spiritual insecurity was rising. Social scientists discovered alienated people in factories and offices alike. Psychologists argued that alienation was the cause of neurosis.

David Riesman et al. wrote a very popular book, *The Lonely Crowd* (1949), showing that whereas people used to be morally self-sufficient because of internalized value systems, modern people were entirely dependent on the peer group for their moral values and sense of self. Instead of being "inner-directed," they were now "other-directed." In a powerful metaphor the Riesman group compared the old, internalized morality to a gyroscope and the new peer orientation to a radar set. Despite efforts at neutrality, the thrust of their argument made the inner-directed man seem nobler than his heirs. Most readers certainly thought so, and the book was a touchstone for many sermons on the breakdown of individualism and personal integrity. But this was not a necessary conclusion. As Allen Wheelis pointed out in *The Quest for Identity* (1958), it was just as easy to say that the new character type was no worse than the old, even though different. He agreed that character types had changed. The older generation had been work-oriented, independent, and strong-minded. But if the new generation was less dogmatic, it was also

more sensitive, quicker to see anxiety, disguised hostility, and to recognize masochism in itself and others. People understood their children better and coerced them less. His new perceptiveness meant that modern man "in losing the whole . . . has found some of the previously lost parts."

This view was not the common one. Anxiety about the present made postwar society as conservative and nostalgic socially as it was progressive physically. Objective reality—the need for homes, schools, roads—was met with confidence, but subjective reality—fears of change and of loss—was not so easily faced. Americans worked both sides of the street as usual. On the one hand, they proclaimed the universality and superiority of American practices and virtues to the world. On the other, they complained of moral laxness and called on people to restore the heroic days of old. Affluence was wonderful because it showed how good America was, terrible because it undermined the principles which had made the country great. Americans boasted frequently in the postwar years when they alone were rich and the world was poor, but this confidence was more apparent than real—as Sputnik demonstrated.

Excellence and the schools

When the Soviet Union orbited the first artificial satellite in 1957, prominent Americans carried on as if the whole of American civilization had been found wanting. A search for national goals followed that would have been amusing were it not so pathetic. *Life* magazine ran an interminable series of articles by national leaders to find out how lost greatness might be recovered. President Eisenhower, who found the whole thing bewildering, dutifully appointed a commission on national goals. People finally decided that America needed was "excellence." There had been too much fat living and moral sloth, it was now agreed. The time had come for hard work and high aspirations. John Kennedy claimed to embody this new spirit and made a good thing of it.

In theory excellence was something that all were now to labor for, as if in the past adult Americans had deliberately sought mediocrity. In practice demands for higher standards were made chiefly on the young. Adults were doing about as well as they could. In those areas where America lagged, and space was not one of them (as events soon demonstrated), it was because the thing wanted was believed to be not worth the cost. Individual mediocrity was, for the most part, achieved by accident rather than design, and there was no practical way to inspire adults to do better. This meant, by a process of elimination, that excellence was to be reached by browbeating youngsters. Not all the pressure was negative. Government began subsidizing young scholars with National Defense Education Act funds, and other incentives were also tried. But the largest part of the struggle for excellence consisted of blaming American shortcomings on "progressive education," a meaningless term that embraced whatever critics of education disliked. To secure measurably high performances, greater emphasis was placed on uniform testing and on the use of test scores to determine college admissions. This put even more pressure on middle-class youngsters—whose parents were neurotic on the subject anyway—and led to the outburst of youthful antiintellectualism which began in 1965. It is not clear that the drive for excellence had any other significant effects.

Attempts to change America by changing the schools were bound to fail. Parents were surely as important, if not more so, than schools. Few suggested that parents could be changed. The excellence campaign was very largely a matter of adults ordering children to shape up—hardly the way to bring about great innovations. Whatever prospect of serious gain might have been involved was lost because hardly anyone wanted to think seriously about education. An enormous amount of research had been done on the schools, but nearly all of this was ignored during the search for excellence. Doing so had certain advantages inasmuch as a good deal of educational research was worthless. But some work, notably the important study by James Coleman entitled *Adolescent Society* (1961), was valuable because it suggested that high schools could not be improved by concentrating on test scores.

The main reason why educational reforms had so little effect, Coleman made clear, was that while the schools tried to pull youngsters in one direction, adolescent culture pushed them in another. In almost every instance peer-group norms ran counter to the school's formal goals. And this was most true in the growing number of suburban high schools which prefigured the future. Thus, schools, especially after 1957, emphasized academic work while students valued popularity. Academic work was not ignored, but it took a distant second place in the student value system. Boys esteemed athletic success most because it translated into popularity, while girls wanted to be beautiful—for the same reason. The position of girls was particularly anomalous. They were more responsive to adult pressure for good grades than boys, and so they worked harder and did better as a rule. But they got fewer rewards for academic success than boys. A reputation based on scholarship handicapped girls socially. The result was that while girls earned better grades, they also received more uniform grades. Girls performed at about the same level in all courses while boys concentrated on their fields of interest. Thus, high grades for many girls did not signify dedication but only obedience, whereas a boy who earned high grades made a statement about himself and his future.

Nominally, girls were being prepared for later achievement, actually, they were being groomed for marriage. Girls were supposed to be attractive, pleasing to boys, and good students—though not so good as to be threatening. But at the same time as they were supposed to attract boys, girls were also supposed to repel them. At every school Coleman examined, sexual misconduct destroyed a girl's social position. Coleman observed that peer demands on girls conflicted with the school's formal demands on them. But in this respect peer norms reflected adult values. In the forties, fifties, and early sixties, women were urged to be feminine, that is, to focus on marriage and motherhood even when, as was increasingly the case, they also held down jobs. Peer pressure on girls was academically dysfunctional but appropriate to the roles they would play as adults.

Coleman found that elite students were more hostile to formal educational goals than nonelites, even when Jewish and thus presumably more ambitious. And elite students were more resistant to parental demands than nonelites, especially in the larger schools. Elite students at an upper-middle-class high school, the most affluent one studied by Coleman, were the most independent and least scholastic of all his subjects groups even though they also went on to college in larger proportions. Athletics were valued above academics because a good athlete reflected glory on his classmates while a good student

made them look bad. Athletics was unifying, scholarship divisive.

A final problem was that even when schools were successful, as measured by grades and test scores, they seemed to promote the wrong things. Other studies found that students with good grades tended to be persevering, sociable, and liked by teachers. Students who rated high in independence and creativity were often not very sociable, hence unpopular with teachers. High IQs and good grades were often inversely related, while conformity and good grades went together. The pressure on schools to produce excellence was thus self-defeating. When grades went up, there was little reason to suppose this meant anything as far as intellect and creativity were concerned. In the 1960s, when students rebelled against these pressures, they argued with some justice that high grades and real accomplishment were unrelated—and this was healthy up to a point. But many students refused to make qualitative judgments at all. Carelessness passed for freedom from arbitrary norms and self-expression, however banal, was deemed the highest good. Abolishing standards was no more productive than exaggerating them had been.

Students got it coming and going in the late fifties and early sixties. They were damned for not studying hard enough and letting the country down in its numerous competitions with the Soviet Union, and they were criticized for being too docile and conformist. Studies appeared to show that college students especially had no great ambitions but wished only to make a good living and raise happy families. This was considered spiritless of them by intellectuals who, having been radical when young, considered youthful excesses almost a prerequisite for citizenship. Students were in fact apolitical, which

Figure 23-1 Fashion's "new look" after World War II, a dark moment in the history of dress reform. (*Martha Holmes*)

should not have been surprising, as that was their normal condition. Only in the Depression were college students politicized, and then briefly. As adults they became less political or less radical or both. Student radicalism was only a memory in the 1950s, and a misleading one in that while a large minority of students were radicalized in the thirties, there had been no generation gap. Student radicalism mirrored adult radicalism and was controlled by adult leftists for the most part. Few who urged students to rebel in the 1950s gave much thought to what it might be like to

have radical students without adult counterparts.

Social criticism

There were good reasons for not rebelling in the 1950s. The old left was destroyed before the very eyes of young people, and poverty and social injustice seemed to have been largely abolished. Even the remaining noncommunist radical intellectuals appeared to think so. *Dissent* magazine, their best journal in the fifties, was preoccupied with American civilization, particularly the argument that America had become a mass society characterized by affluence and alienation. Intellectuals like Dwight Macdonald, who had once criticized the state, now criticized the culture. The corrupting effects of advertising and other affluent institutions were exposed. This strategy, while possibly useful, did not raise a flag around which militants could rally. As Daniel Bell pointed out, the attempt to take advanced cultural positions was undermined by society's new hospitality to avant-garde art. The young art critic Hilton Kramer said "bourgeois society has tightened its grip on all the arts by allowing them a freer rein." Bell also noted that the young were not given much to fighting against the generation of people (like Bell himself) who had been radical in the thirties. These thirties radicals had, as it were, led the counterrevolution against themselves by repudiating their pasts and celebrating the strengths of American society where once they had attacked its weaknesses. This created a political "lost generation" of youngsters that was denied its natural right to condemn the older generation.

Intellectuals, many of them ex-radicals, embraced a conservative political philosophy which Michael Rogin calls pluralism. Pluralists believed there were two kinds of politics, one of which was ideological, emotional, anti-industrial, anti-intellectual, and moralistic. Populism was one such example, McCarthyism another. The second, more desirable, and traditional kind of politics was conducted by the leaders of various interest groups who bargained and jockeyed for position within the system. Pluralist politics was rational, constitutional, and elitist—based on groups rather than on masses. In their radical days, intellectuals had seen self-interest as the curse of bourgeois civilization. In the

fifties they realized that it made the system workable, even perhaps admirable. Totalitarian movements abroad opened their eyes, as did McCarthyism at home.

Rogin shows that this analysis was based on faulty assumptions. McCarthy did not have a mass following and was not supported by neo-Populist agrarian radicals. People who voted for him in Wisconsin did not conform to the totalitarian personality profile drawn up by social scientists. Apart from the conservative small-town elites that were ideological, McCarthy's supporters were mostly attracted by his stature as an anti-Communist. But when he attacked institutions that moderates admired, like the Army and the Senate, his following melted away. Pluralists erred in thinking there was a direct link between early-twentieth-century Populism and McCarthyism, in exaggerating the mass character of both movements, in minimizing the importance of specific issues, and in assuming that only ideologists moralized when in fact moralism was a universal American political trait.

The important thing about pluralism is not so much that it was wrong as that it was necessary. Having decided that socialism did not work while capitalist democracy did—brilliantly in fact, ex-radicals had to find an explanation for McCarthyism and similar anomalies. Pluralism met this need and others besides. It showed that self-interest promoted the general good, as nineteenth-century liberals had believed, thus justifying the self-serving policies of business, labor, and the intelligentsia. Since pluralism was a theory of leadership, hence elitist, it relieved intellectuals of the need to feel guilty for being above the masses. The theory also made it easier to attack mass culture, which was difficult for radicals since what was popular, hence approved by the people, had also in some sense to be good. In the hands of men like Bell and Richard Hofstadter, the leading pluralist historian, it was not a narrow or mean-spiritied philosophy; quite the contrary. All the same, it was conservative, uninspiring, and rather closely tailored to the needs of ex-radical intellectuals in the 1950s. Little wonder that younger intellectuals soon rejected it.

Sex

Kinsey's reports would seem exceptions to the general rule that social life in the postwar era was conservative, defensive, and colorless. Both his reports were controversial, the first especially. Both showed that there was more sex out of wedlock than was usually assumed. Actually, *Sexual Behavior in the Human Male* (1948) and *Sexual Behavior in the Human Female* (1953) demonstrated that sex was becoming more common but also more commonplace. Traditional moralists were naturally outraged by Kinsey. One congressman tried to bar the report on women from the mails because it contributed to "the depravity of a whole generation, to the loss of faith in human dignity and human decency, to the spread of juvenile delinquency," and even, he remarked obscurely, "to the misunderstanding and confusion about sex." Most Catholic authorities rejected both reports for condoning pre- and extramarital sex. Margaret Mead criticized the report on women because, by showing how widespread premarital sex was, it would deprive young women of an important defense against it. Besides being roundly attacked, both reports were garishly publicized, not by the authors but by newsmen and entertainers who made them staples of the popular culture. The Rockefeller Foundation was so alarmed at this that it stopped supporting the Kinsey Institute.

All the same, neither report was censored, both were widely read, and most social scientists accepted Kinsey's main conclusions, though not always his assumptions. With Kinsey, sex research came of age, as did the national view of it, hysterical exceptions notwithstanding. Kinsey's method was to take exhaustive sexual case histories of as many people as possible. The report on men rested on 8,600 interviews, that on females on 7,800. Kinsey's reports are weakest on working-class habits, strongest on educated, middle-class people living in the Northeast, who, he believed, were the sexual trend-setters anyway. Most critics admitted that despite statistical errors, Kinsey was about as accurate as limited samples and the faulty memories of respondents allowed.

What most intelligent critics minded about the Kinsey reports was their reductionism. Victorians had seen sex as mysterious, terrifying, and dangerous—yet sometimes romantic. To Kinsey, who had been trained as a taxonomist and was a leading authority on the classification of gall wasps, sex, though subject to many variations, was a comparatively simple and straightforward form of behavior. He was astonished to find when he was asked to teach a course in sex education at the University of Indiana in the 1930s that hardly anything was known about it, so he set about repairing that defect. Kinsey had but one unit of measurement: the orgasm. To have one, by almost any means, was to know success. All orgasms save those involving harm to others were equal and honorable. This point of view angered moralists and psychiatrists alike. Reinhold Niebuhr, the great theologian, said that Kinsey's work was informed by an absurd hedonism, a limited view of nature, and a striking naïvete. "He is obviously ignorant of

Figure 23-2 Making out. (*Bruce Davidson from Magnum*)

the capacity of the person for self-deception and of the growth of that capacity with maturity and experience. The infinite complexities of the human spirit are in fact unknown to Kinsey, if they are above the level of refinements in erotic pleasure." A friendly psychiatrist regretted Kinsey's assumption that whatever was frequent was acceptable, as in the case of homosexuality and even bestiality. Kinsey said that people who had sexual relations with animals should be told not to worry because they were not alone. But Robert Knight pointed out that "guilt and shame do not spring from ignorance as to incidence of such behavior, but rest upon the unconscious aggressive and erotic significance of the animal contacts." The people involved needed therapy, not reassurance, he maintained.

Kinsey's flat, even banal approach to sex was precisely what made the reports so important culturally. Kinsey disregarded both the old view (that sex was terrible, dangerous, etc.) and the modern view (that it was complex, baffling, etc.). Kinsey's view might be called postmodern matter-of-factness. Sex to him was just something else to classify. He recognized that sex was emotionally highly charged but implied this was mainly due to that ignorance he meant to dispel. Matter-of-factness enabled Dr. William Masters to study human sexuality under laboratory conditions which would have been unthinkable before Kinsey. It allowed the President's Commission on Obscenity and Pornography to sponsor clinical tests and to announce in 1970 that pornography was harmless and perhaps even mildly beneficial. Matter-of-factness became the dominant sexual ideology among young people in the 1960s. Sex was no big deal, they would say, just something pleasant you did with friends. Many adults took almost the same position. "Swinging," as organized group sex was called, attracted hundreds of thousands in the sixties and seventies. It was characterized by an even greater disassociation between sexuality and emotion since it involved copulating with virtual strangers, something respectable people had never done before except with prostitutes.

Many Americans, perhaps most of them, remained frightened of sex despite Kinsey. Although antibiotics and the pill made it possible to love without fear, comparatively few did. Kinsey's studies, and others done later by his Institute for Sex Research, indicated that sexual behavior was pretty stable. Though it changed, the change was gradual, so that the sex life of average people in the sixties was not greatly different from what it had been in the twenties. The sexual revolution of the sixties, in fact, involved not so much deviant behavior as the sanctions against it. Swinging was new, at least on a large scale. That was about all. Much more striking was the inability of conventional people to punish deviations. Peer-group pressure, once such a powerful mechanism for keeping girls chaste, declined, and at colleges and universities some reversal took place. Virginity became more a mark of shame than a badge of honor. Sex continued, therefore, to be a source of anxiety even when traditional values were reversed.

Supreme Court decisions made literary pornography all but impossible to control. The Court wanted to protect lovely erotic works like D. H. Lawrence's *Lady Chatterly's Lover.* What was beautiful or had redeeming social significance was tolerable even if sexy, it ruled. This included *Fanny Hill,* a tasteful eighteenth-century classic. In practice it turned out that after these decisions no book, however lewd, could be proscribed. Soon it became hard to prohibit dirty pictures. In a moment of pique the Supreme Court sent Ralph Ginzburg to prison for filthy advertising, although *Eros,* the magazine he published, was not obscene by any judicial standard. But the advertisements for it were titillating and suffused, one justice said, with "the leer of the sensualist." "Leering sensuality" proved no more helpful as a guide than "redeeming social significance."

Nudity increased in films and plays. Parents complained about sex in movies (though seldom about violence, which increased also), and the industry responded with a classification system whereby erotic films were not proscribed, only x-rated. Youngsters were supposedly denied admission to them, and some newspapers refused to carry ads for x-rated pictures. These were only handicaps, not prohibitions. People soon grew so accustomed to sexy films that when hard-core pornography appeared in suburban theaters, few complained. In the 1950s an innocuous picture called *The Moon Is Blue* had aroused national controversy because in it forbidden words like "virgin" were spoken right out loud. In the early seventies, *Deep Throat,* a film largely devoted to oral sex, was barely noticed, except, strangely enough, in New York City. This was a significant victory for matter-of-factness if not for art.

Hardly anyone in the 1950s had supposed that sexual freedom would arrive so soon. His enemies had said that Kinsey would make sex freer, but that was mostly rhetoric. There is no proof even now that the studies influenced behavior, but there seems little doubt that they affected values in that matter-of-factness replaced Freudianism among sophisticated people. This was to the good insofar as the penalities for sexual errors or adventures lessened. Society, despite itself, became more tolerant of what was once considered wrongdoing. Homosexuals were persecuted less and abortions became easier to get even before the Supreme Court ruled in their favor. In this negative way the sum total of human happiness was probably enlarged.

It remains unclear whether matter-of-factness improved sexual relations. Young people may have had sex more often than formerly, but they did not seem particularly happier nor markedly pleased with the consequences apart from the fun they had shocking adults. Psychiatrists said feminine sexual aggressiveness was causing impotence among young men, while feminists complained that men were still lustful and exploitive. Even medical advances were mixed blessings. When the birth control pill became widely used and abortions easier to get, men stopped using condoms and venereal disease increased accordingly. In times past it was a joke that local laws allowed the sale of condoms only "for the prevention of disease," since everyone knew they were used to avoid conception. But they did protect against disease too, so the joke was now on the excustomer for not using them.

Figure 23-3 Marilyn Monroe, the greatest sex symbol of modern times and the victim of an American tragedy. (*Culver Pictures*)

The way of life

But this is to anticipate. In the fifties sexual freedom was only a glint in Kinsey's eye. People were still more interested in reproduction than intercourse, and family life was agreed to be the ultimate source of happiness. It was celebrated in novels like Sloan Wilson's popular *Man in the Grey Flannel Suit* (1955), which had its hero pass up an exciting job offer so as to spend more time at home. The birthrate, which had begun rising during the war, went up steadily until 1957. After 1946 the divorce rate declined, as did the age at which people married. No one had expected this golden age of domesticity. The experience of all industrial countries is that as real income goes up, the birthrate declines. The divorce rate had been rising in America for a century at least. This too was usual, and in the 1930s people assumed that the population had stabilized. That these historic trends should suddenly be reversed in the 1940s was startling. At first it was thought that people were making up for lost time, since the Depression and then the war had forced many to defer marriage and child rearing. But after 1945 there was no reason to wait any longer. In a few years, when the birthrate kept going up, other explanations were offered, none of them very convincing. For unknown reasons, a majority of young Americans had come to prize large families. There were 24.3 million children aged five to fourteen in 1950 and over 10 million more a decade later. To house them, thousands of new suburbs sprang up. There were 1.4 million new housing starts in 1950 and nearly as many in 1960. Family activities became more popular too. Only 1.5 million people camped in national forests in 1950, whereas ten years later there were 6.6 million campers. Church attendance, a favorite family activity, rose also. Never before had so large a part of the population been church members. Only about 10 percent of Americans were willing to deny any religious affiliations. The suburban house, the large, churchgoing family, and domestic recreations became national fet-

ishes. Critics charged that the new tract houses were poorly built and would soon decay. Instead, most development houses gained in value, often fabulously. Suburban living made car owning essential and multiple car ownership highly desirable, so public transportation was allowed to deteriorate. There were 277 million commuter railroad rides in 1950 and only 203 million a decade later. In the same period the number of people commuting to work in New York City by car rose from 640,000 to 866,000.

A carping minority aside, discontent in America as of 1960 was surprisingly limited and abstract. Few complained of pollution or the waste of resources, and those who criticized the suburbs did so as much for aesthetic reasons as any other. Tract houses were ugly, and suburbs were boring, it was said, because they were socially homogenous— but nearly everyone shrugged off these complaints. The culture boom—new symphony orchestras, rising museum attendance figures—showed American taste was good. Few mourned the decline of public transportation. Poverty was thought to have been overcome with—*Fortune* magazine observed in 1960—trifling exceptions. Discrimination against blacks was considered a Southern problem and not a very important one at that.

Judging by the media, what people worried most about were things like the missile gap, moral decay as evidenced by rigged TV quiz shows, the fact that "permissive" public schools produced less excellence than schools in the Soviet Union, "materialism," and the apparent shortage of national goals. These were peculiar anxieties for a country that was doing so well. There were real problems even so—poverty, racism, the deteriorating environment. Instead of facing them, however, people fretted about national prestige. Without knowing it, they were living in a fool's paradise, as events soon demonstrated.

Selected references

Beside those books mentioned in the text, Lawrence A. Cremin, *The Transformation of the School: Progressivism in American Education, 1876–1957* (1961), is excellent. A brilliant study of higher education is David Riesman and Christopher Jencks, *The Academic Revolution* (1968). On literature, see Ihab Hassan, *Radical Innocence: The Contemporary American Novel* (1961). The conventional wisdom is summed up in John W. Gardner, *Excellence* (1961). Daniel Bell (ed.), *The New American Right* (1955), is an important expression of pluralism. It and similar works are critically analyzed in Michael Rogin, *McCarthy and the Intellectuals* (1967). On the Kinsey reports, see Albert Deutsch (ed.), *Sex Habits of American Men: A Symposium on the Kinsey Report* (1948); Donald Porter Geddes (ed.), *An Analysis of the Kinsey Reports on Sexual Behavior in the Human Male and Female* (1954); and the essay on Kinsey in Lionel Trilling, *The Liberal Imagination* (1948).

TWENTY-FOUR

The Smash-up

Period covered: 1959–1968
Emphasis: Diplomacy
Major events: Castro achieves power in Cuba, 1959
Nixon-Kennedy debates, 1960
Bay of Pigs, 1961
Vienna summit, 1961
Berlin Wall, 1961
Cuban missile crisis, 1962
Partial test ban treaty, 1963
Overthrow of President Diem, 1963
Assassination of President Kennedy, 1963
Gulf of Tonkin incidents and Resolution, 1964
Beginning of bombing campaign, 1965
Intervention in Dominican Republic, 1965
Tet offensive, 1968
Johnson steps down, 1968

"The capital city, somnolent in the Eisenhower years, had suddenly come alive," wrote the chief chronicler of the New Frontier, Arthur M. Schlesinger, Jr. "The air had been stale and oppressive; now fresh winds were blowing. There was the excitement which comes from the injection of new men and new ideas, the release of energy which occurs when men of ideas have a chance to put them into practice." The New Frontiersmen were an eager lot. "Ask not what your country can do for you," declared their young leader, "but what you can do for your country." They were ready.

Everyone tapped for the administration's inner circle made a conscious effort to squeeze into the new President's public image: lean, cool, and incisive. Those who held old-style "soft" liberal views kept them to themselves or made sure they were expressed in tough-minded "options." Even rotund Pierre Salinger, the White House Press Secretary, set out on a 50-mile hike to prove he was physically fit enough to serve on the New Frontier. He never made it, but Salinger's blisters did little damage to the Kennedy image.

They were, however, symptomatic of a larger problem in the Kennedy years. If anything, the New Frontiersmen generated too much energy and excitement in the administration's first weeks in a display of frenetic activity. This was designed mainly to prove that, under Eisenhower's lethargic leadership, things had really become as bad as the Democrats had been saying they were. Kennedy's somber rendition of the challenges just ahead in his first State of the Union Message, only a few weeks after the inauguration, was delivered in a series of exclamations which left the speaker and his audience almost breathless: "Each day the crises multiply. Each day their solution grows more difficult. Each day we draw nearer the hour of maximum danger, as weapons spread and hostile forces grow stronger."

Kennedy's cold war rhetoric reminded one of Winston Churchill, an impression and comparison the young President seemed to encourage, as it reflected his sense that Americans were fast coming to "Their Finest Hour." Churchill had once said, at the darkest moment of World War II, that he had not become Prime Minister to preside over the liquidation of the British Empire. Kennedy put it this way in 1962: "This Administration was not elected to preside over the liquidation of American responsibility in these great years." The soldier guarding the Brandenburg Gate in Germany, said the President, the Americans now in Vietnam, and the Peace Corps men in Colombia were all guards on the watchtowers of freedom and were all there to make sure that there would be no more Cubas.

Rendezvous at the Bay of Pigs

Throughout the 1960 campaign, Kennedy and his running mate Lyndon Johnson bore down hard on Eisenhower's supposed mishandling of the Cuban revolution and Fidel Castro. It was the "loss" of China all over again, only this time the Republicans were on the receiving end. After years in the mountains with a handful of lieutenants, Castro had finally enlisted the peasant army he needed to overthrow the Cuban dictator Fulgencio Batista. American diplomats had tried to get Batista to step aside—while there was still time—in favor of a moderate reformer, but the old dictator was adamant about staying where he was to the end. American public opinion in 1958 was pro-Castro: and Castro himself, a dashing figure in army fatigues, was already being compared with Simón Bolívar.

Movie actor Errol Flynn, whose exploits against the Spanish tyrants had filled theaters for two decades, flew down to Cuba for the climactic battle in Havana against Batista's henchmen and was photographed peering around bullet-pocked walls with Castro's army. Flynn could come home, however; while American businessmen with large interests in Cuba could not. They took a much more sober view of events there. Eisenhower recalled in his memoirs that he received intelligence reports from Cuba which indicated that businessmen favored early diplomatic recognition of Fidel's government, proclaimed on January 1, 1959, lest it collapse and something worse happen.

Fidel's government did not collapse, but something worse happened anyway. Cuban-American relations deteriorated rapidly in the succeeding months, especially following Castro's promulgation of an agrarian reform law which involved large-scale expropriations of American property. Castro had complained that Cubans grew plenty of tomatoes but had to purchase their ketchup from the United States. It was a good illustration of the economics of dependence. He vowed to change that and many other more important conditions. The usual remedy for Cuban disturbances began with a warning of cuts in the United States's Cuban sugar quota, followed by whatever other action was necessary. This time Washington was stymied. Castro found the Soviet Union more than willing to offer him outlets for his sugar and full of political advice in return. He took the former and ignored the latter while building his own personalized socialist revolution. By mid-1960 Soviet Premier Khrushchev was crowing anyway that the Monroe Doctrine was a dead issue and threatening to use nuclear missiles to defend his Caribbean friend against American imperialism.

This was doubly embarrassing to the Eisenhower administration, which was already under attack from the Democrats for falling behind in missile technology. Now Kennedy had a new issue: the Republicans had permitted the establishment of a communist regime only 90 miles from our Florida coastline. The stage was thus set for a left-right combination: from the left he harangued the Republicans for supporting Batista over the years (actually the dictator had been put in power and supported by Democrats in the 1930s); from the right he charged that the administration had stood by while Castro subverted a legitimate (whatever that meant) Cuban revolution and sold it out to the Communists.

Vice President Richard Nixon, his opponent, claimed a foul—two years too late. He could not have said anything during the campaign, Nixon candidly explained in *Six Crises* (1962), because to have done so might have meant exposing the "fact that for months the CIA had not only been supporting and assisting but actually training Cuban exiles for the eventual purpose of supporting an invasion of Cuba itself." Nixon's frankness compared favorably with the Kennedy administration's later cover stories for the Bay of Pigs fiasco. Frankness out of office is a luxury, however, and a presumed asset when directed toward a display of anti-Soviet "toughness."

The former Vice President's account was incomplete, however, for it left out the fact that the CIA training camp in Guatemala had been opened long before Castro declared himself an avowed Marxist, or, more importantly, before the Soviet Union began shipping large quantities of heavy arms to Cuba. Chronology is important, because the issue then was Cuba's right to a revolution which injured American property, not the establishment of a

Soviet military base in the Western Hemisphere.

Nixon went on in *Six Crises* to add that Kennedy had known all about the clandestine preparations, since they had both received briefings on "all covert operations around the world" from the CIA director himself. Some Kennedy biographers later disputed that point, but Nixon maintained his position.

When Kennedy proposed giving aid to the Cuban exiles to help them retake their homeland, Nixon was, by his own account, put in a terrible bind. He could not reveal the secret preparations for an invasion, or his part in urging them on Eisenhower, without jeopardizing the plan. If he said nothing, on the other hand, Kennedy would walk off with the match by default. The Vice President finally solved the problem, he tells us, by reaching back to his college debating experience: he would make the best possible case against intervention. If the U.S. government followed Kennedy's foolish advice, Nixon asserted in the fourth and final television debate between the two men,

we would lose all of our friends in Latin America, we would probably be condemned in the United Nations, and we would not accomplish our objective. . . . It would be an open invitation for Mr. Khrushchev . . . to come into Latin America and to engage us in what would be a civil war and possibly even worse than that.

He had presented a good brief. Others put similar arguments to the new President after the election, but neither "hard-liner" Dean Acheson nor the skeptical Senator J. William Fulbright, the Chairman of the Senate Foreign Relations Committee, could dissuade him from going ahead with the Bay of Pigs plan.

CIA Director Allen Dulles apparently had the last word with Kennedy, telling him that he was more certain of this operation than he had been of the Guatemalan operation in 1954. Moreover, said Dulles, there was a serious "disposal" problem to consider: what would happen if the invasion were canceled and all those exiles filtered back into the United States with tales of where they had been all those months and what they had been doing? Dirty tricks were all right—as long as you never got caught at them. In a more serious light, perhaps the most disturbing aspect of the Bay of Pigs was the ahistorical perspective everyone who favored the plan brought to its planning and execution. One could not reduce the most important development in Latin America since the 1910 Mexican Revolution to a "disposal" problem without paying a heavy price—not just in Cuba, but throughout the world.

Both the logic and the logistics of the Bay of Pigs invasion proved faulty. On April 17, 1961, the 1,700-man Brigade 2506 waded ashore, expecting full air support from its American sponsors and an internal uprising against Castro. Neither showed up. One air strike had been canceled because of clouds, a second by Kennedy himself as the magnitude of the disaster began to become apparent. The whole thing lasted less than three days, ending with the death or capture of nearly every member of the brigade.

Kennedy blamed himself publicly for the fiasco, though he displayed more than a little pique in a speech to newspaper editors calling for self-censorship in this time of national peril. What more he could have expected from them at the time of the Bay of Pigs, since they had in fact covered up for the administration, was not made clear. Neither were Kennedy's future plans for dealing with the

Figure 24-1 Nixon defends nonintervention. J.F.K. came across as a super cold warrior in the TV debates with the Vice President. (*Wide World Photos*)

Cuban problem, but his words carried a message to Havana and Moscow: "Let the record show that our restraint is not inexhaustible." If the nations of the hemisphere failed to "meet their commitments against outside communist penetration," he wanted it "clearly understood that this Government will not hesitate in meeting its primary obligations which are to the security of our Nation."

In other words, the other nations of the hemisphere had been put on notice. Noninterference had its limits. Those limits had been exceeded in Cuba, and, by implication, anywhere else where Communists established themselves in power with or without

Soviet aid. To many noncommunist nationalists in Latin America, however, the Bay of Pigs and Kennedy's rhetoric were part of a long unhappy tradition which went back to 1898, when America went to war with Spain to free Cuba and stayed to impose the Platt Amendment restricting Cuban independence to American-approved standards.

The administration's efforts to justify the anti-Castro invasion on grounds that the Cuban leader had betrayed his own revolution to the Communists failed everywhere, except at home, where it caused additional political problems. The Cuban "White Paper" (authored in part by Arthur M. Schlesinger,

Jr.), far from providing a fresh wind, simply blew up the old storm of cold war rhetoric which had obscured so much in the past fifteen years. If the international communist conspiracy was responsible, reasoned Kennedy's conservative critics, why had he proved indecisive at the critical moment? Why, indeed? It was a tough question to answer without admitting there were at least some ambiguities or even contradictions in the New Frontier's definition of the world situation.

The Bay of Pigs, moreover, cast a long shadow over the Alliance for Progress, the administration's proposal for a new aid program for Latin America. Castro's success had awakened the Eisenhower policy makers to the dangers of revolution throughout Latin America and had forced a change in post-World War II attitudes about large-scale government aid to other countries in the hemisphere. At the time of the Marshall Plan in 1947, that Secretary of State had insisted that no need existed for government aid to Latin America. Private enterprise could, and would, do the job better. Embittered by the fact that wartime inflation followed by postwar deflation had damaged their raw materials-based economies, Latin American leaders had protested this attitude without success. It was said that when a Chilean diplomat went through a White House reception line, he answered President Truman's query about how things were in his country, "Rotten, sir, we can't find a damned Communist!"

Early in the Eisenhower administration a bright young man came up with an idea on how to blunt demands for land reform without alienating Latin American land owners. "A profound effect might be obtained," said a memorandum for Secretary Dulles, "by initiating discussion of programs for settlement of landless or marginal subsistence farmers on under-developed lands. United States tradition holds that farmers should own the land they till. Thus, we might demolish communist claims on land reform without alienating any economic group." But when Vice President Nixon went to Latin America in 1958, he met a barrage of rocks and rotten eggs. He was rescued by the timely intervention of police and while Eisenhower wondered anxiously what he should do: send in the Marines or try something else.

The decision was to try something else, especially after difficulties emerged with Cuba. The plan, which evolved under Kennedy, was called the Alliance for Progress. It provided for an infusion of $10 billion of government aid over a ten-year period. The Latins, for their part, were supposed to initiate genuine land-reform programs. The aim, however, was still to provide a healthy climate for foreign investment, regarded (as always) as the best means to improve the living standards of the Latin American countries.

But the Alliance for Progress depended on securing cooperation from reactionary governments who, bolstered by their American-trained military chiefs, could cite the Bay of Pigs (and American reactions to Castro in general) to argue that while the aid was needed more than ever, the times were too perilous for beginning a reform program. American investors could say, for their part, that unless something was done about Castro and Castroism throughout Latin America, the times were too perilous to risk more capital. And so on.

The Bay of Pigs, finally, damaged the President's self-image. All accounts agree that the President feared that Khrushchev must believe him a very weak man for allowing his advisers to sell him on the merits of the plan and then backing off when the crunch came. After all, the Soviet leader had not hesitated to crush the Hungarian revolution in 1956. Kennedy tried to rebuild his image quickly through military expenditures.

Of missile gaps and Green Berets

The famous "missile gap" of the 1960 campaign had closed after the election. In fact, it had never existed. Both Eisenhower and Khrushchev knew that the U-2 had provided the United States with full data on the latest developments and deployment of Soviet missiles. The information the spy plane brought back revealed that the Soviets were actually behind in every category except missile thrust capability.

The new President skimmed over that point in a special message asking Congress for additional funds for the Defense Department. The buildup in missiles finally included 1,000 Minuteman rockets, 656 submarine-based Polaris weapons, and 600 long-range bombers. In 1961, Secretary of Defense Robert McNamara later reported, the Soviets actually possessed "a very small operational arsenal of intercontinental missiles." Over the next few years, they quadrupled their missile force. But, added McNamara, the American decision and initiative, however well-justified on the basis of what the Soviets could or might do, "could not possibly have left unaffected the Soviet Union's nuclear plans."

The missile program was closely tied in Kennedy's mind not only to Soviet capabilities for nuclear war but also to the need for a special force to deal with the problems of what he and his advisers called counterinsurgency. Their aim was to develop a total weapons system which would give America absolute superiority at every level of conflict, from below guerrilla warfare to a full nuclear

exchange. "The free world's security," he told Congress,

can be endangered not only by nuclear attack, but also by being slowly nibbled away at the periphery, regardless of our strategic power, by forces of subversion, infiltration, intimidation, indirect or non-overt aggression, internal revolution, diplomatic blackmail, guerilla warfare or a series of limited wars.

Anything Harry Truman had left out in the 1947 Truman Doctrine speech was surely on this list. Aides noted that Kennedy was much impressed by Khrushchev's January 1961 speech surveying the prospects of the world communist movement. He had advised them to read it over carefully, as it seemed to him to be a declaration of war by all those means he listed in his speech to Congress.

Neither Kennedy nor any of his advisers ever clarified one point in this regard: Did Kennedy regard only Moscow-sponsored revolutions as dangerous to American security, or was a Communist revolution per se the threat? In a campaign speech on September 23, 1960, candidate Kennedy had made it plain that he saw the issue as a life-and-death struggle not with Russia alone but with a "system":

The enemy is the communist system itself— implacable, insatiable, unceasing in its drive for world domination. For this is not a struggle for the supremacy of arms alone—it is also a struggle for supremacy between two conflicting ideologies: Freedom under God versus ruthless, godless tyranny.

In any event, Kennedy developed two special forces to meet the challenge: the Peace Corps and the "Green Berets." Hundreds of idealistic young men and women were drawn into the Peace Corps, and they served in countries throughout the third world, helping people to help themselves. What they learned there sometimes led them to oppose official American policies, and this became a growing problem for the Peace Corps administrators. The Green Berets were designated a military elite corps combining knowledge of guerrilla warfare and tactics with skill in helping "native" leaders develop the "infrastructures" (a favorite New Frontier word) of their countries. Both the Peace Corps and the Green Berets were to be responsible for showing underdeveloped countries the noncommunist route to modernization.

A Marine Corps spokesman was highly skeptical of the Army's self-boosting role in promoting the Special Warfare Forces. "We need no special stress," he told a reporter. "We have been fighting guerilla wars for a long time. We learned our lessons decades ago in the banana wars in Nicaragua, Haiti and the Dominican Republic." It was a very perceptive comment, but no one along the New Frontier seemed to be listening.

Confrontation in Vienna

President Kennedy went to Vienna in the summer of 1961 to meet face-to-face with Premier Khrushchev. Still concerned about the Premier's reaction to the Bay of Pigs, Kennedy was determined to show he was no callow youth who had taken on a job far too demanding for his talents and maturity. The Soviet leader twitted him about the Cuban misadventure, as had been expected, but he kept steering the conversation around to Berlin and the two Germanys. The situation in the former Nazi capital was becoming more intolerable for the East Germans day by day. The problem, which went back to the original Big Four decisions (or lack thereof) on post-

war Germany, now centered in Berlin's anomalous role as the capital of a nation which existed only in the dreams (and nightmares) of the present generation. West Berlin was a noncommunist enclave deep within the German Democratic Republic, and as such it offered an escape hatch to the West through which thousands had fled to the Western zones, now called the German Federal Republic. Besides the loss of talents and skills involved, the population drain endangered political stability on both sides of the Iron Curtain but most especially, of course, in East Germany. To the Soviets themselves, the Western military presence was the major source of danger, since any type of disturbance might quickly escalate into an East-West military explosion. To the Americans, West Berlin represented a pledge of good faith to the German Federal Republic.

If necessary, Kennedy's "hard-line" advisers told him, the United States must be willing to seem "irrational" on the question of altering Berlin's status in the slightest degree. As it happened, this advice jibed with the President's determination not to appear indecisive or vacillating—not only where Berlin was concerned but generally. Again and again at Vienna the President returned to his favorite subject: Soviet adventurism and its danger to the equilibrium of power. Khrushchev always countered with the remark that the Soviet Union could not be held responsible for what happened when the United States persisted in backing reactionary regimes. Khrushchev did offer to neutralize Laos, thereby admitting that the Soviet Union was involved in at least one "revolutionary" situation. By agreeing to negotiate a Laotian settlement, however, Kennedy implicitly acknowledged also the U.S. involvement in a "counterrevolutionary" posture.

On the big issue, Berlin, the Soviets proposed making the city into an international trusteeship of some kind, under whatever social system its citizens desired and with guaranteed access to the outside world. Kennedy's Berlin task force saw such proposals as leading to surrender to communist demands on the installment plan. If the Americans had a better idea, said Soviet diplomats, let them present it, and negotiations could begin. The task force had some ideas but no negotiating proposals. What it most desired was to turn over the German situation exactly as it was to the next administration. Khrushchev warned that he could not wait much longer, a contention more than borne out by the steadily growing stream of East German defectors who were escaping to the West through the Berlin corridor. He would sign a treaty with East Germany at the end of the year, Khrushchev declared, unless serious negotiations were then under way.

What was so important to both sides about the signing of a Soviet-East German treaty that Khrushchev could make it sound like a momentous threat and Kennedy would treat it so? One fear centered in East German boasts that after the treaty, they would take care of the Berlin situation in their own way. The United States would either have to acquiesce or take steps which would certainly involve the Soviets. More than that, the Soviet Premier's recognition of an independent East Germany would give international status to a government which the United States insisted was illegal and which they had promised the West Germans never to recognize. Finally, the Americans feared that Khrushchev might really want to wash his hands of whatever happened. He could not get away with that, and American policy must make him understand that he could not.

"If Khrushchev wants to rub my nose in the dirt," the President told a newsman privately, "it's all over." Around Washington, the word spread that the administration regarded the next few months as the most critical for Europe and America since the summer of 1939. On July 25, 1961, Kennedy addressed the nation, beginning with the statement that Berlin had become a focal point for a confrontation between American commitments and Soviet ambitions, "the great testing place of Western courage and will." Then he announced that he was asking for $3.25 billion more from Congress for extra military appropriations, bringing the total to $6 billion in new additions to the defense budget since he took office. Draft calls were to be doubled and tripled in order to provide 350,000 additional servicemen for all branches of the military. He wanted authority to call up 150,000 reservists and to freeze those already on active duty who were scheduled for release in the next few months. And, finally, he wanted $207 million for civil defense projects such as fallout shelters.

Congress complied with every request. In the White House, contingency plans were reviewed down to the last detail. Then Khrushchev found a way out for everybody, or, better put, he found a way for the East Germans to keep their citizens in by building the Berlin Wall around the Soviet sector of the city. It was a costly project for the Soviets; once again, as in 1948, they would have to take onto themselves the onus for creating an edifice to tyranny and disregarding the most elementary human rights. But it provided a solution to a problem which could have led to nuclear war; and it cannot be said that American policy makers offered anything better toward the resolution of a crisis both sides had helped to bring about.

Kennedy's advisers were perplexed about how to meet this unexpected development. At first a few, the real hard-liners, said that he should use tanks or whatever else necessary to knock it down. Two answers were given to that proposal: first, it was already built on territory within the Eastern Zone and, second, the Russians could simply rebuild it farther back. Another suggestion was to remove the Western Military Governors' restriction on the West German constitution's clause incorporating Berlin into the Federal Republic as one of the component states. That idea was also turned down because, as some of the more cool-headed Kennedy advisers realized, Russian policy in Germany had always been justified to the world as a defense against the re-creation of the Reich with Berlin as its capital. Khrushchev also insisted that the East German drain was in large part the result of West German maneuvers to make Berlin part of their regime.

Ten years later, in 1971, the West Germans themselves would offer concrete proposals for reducing East-West tensions over Berlin, and an agreement guaranteeing the city's status as an independent (i.e., non-West German) political entity was easily reached. Dean Acheson, who had survived to become the nation's oldest active cold warrior, publicly chastised the Nixon administration for encouraging such goings on, but few remembered then that this was the issue on which America would have to appear "irrational" if necessary to redeem its pledges.

Ten days in October

From the Berlin crisis to the Cuban missile crisis of October 1962 was only a matter of months. The nation hardly had a chance to catch its breath before the onset of the most dangerous cold war confrontation yet brought the world to the edge of nuclear conflagration. In the gloomy aftermath of the Bay of Pigs, Kennedy had vowed publicly that if Cuba ever became a serious threat to the Western Hemisphere he would not hesitate to take whatever steps were necessary to eliminate the menace. American policy in succeeding months was to isolate the Castro regime from Hemisphere nations, thus producing a self-fulfilling prophecy that Cuba was linked closely to the communist world. At the January 1962 meeting of the Organization of American States (OAS), Secretary of State Dean Rusk sought and obtained a two-thirds majority vote for expelling Cuba from its councils. Only the Cuban delegate voted against the resolution, but the four most important Latin American nations abstained. The majority vote hinged on the support of the Haitian delegate, who neatly picked $5 million in Alliance for Progress funds from Dean Rusk's pocket at breakfast the morning the final vote was taken.

Castro said later that the outcome of this OAS meeting led him to ask the Soviets for sufficient military support to forestall a second Bay of Pigs invasion or something much worse. The decision to send intermediate-range ballistic missiles (IRBMs), however, was Khrushchev's. Whatever his reasons, and they would be criticized by his opponents at home and in China, the Soviet Premier had miscalculated Kennedy's willingness to go to the brink in order to force him to back down publicly by withdrawing the missiles.

Rumors of missile-site construction in Cuba had been floating around for months in unsifted intelligence reports supplied by Cuban exiles. Analysts discounted these as self-interested, but they soon became a prominent part of Republican campaign oratory, especially in New York, where Senate candidate Kenneth Keating insisted he had proof of their existence. The administration was trying to cover up, he asserted, for its unwillingness to do anything about Castro. The discovery, first confirmed by a U-2 reconnaissance plane on October 14, 1962, that the Soviets *actually were* engaged in building missile launching pads, came as a most unpleasant surprise.

However the matter was eventually settled between the United States and the Soviet Union, the "crisis" had obvious domestic political overtones. How could the administration negotiate in secret for the removal of the missiles, for example, without risking exposure and embarrassment somewhere along the line? It just would not do to be caught negotiating with the Soviets over the withdrawal of weapons the Democrats had denied existed—even if they had not existed at the time of the denials. But there was another dimension to the domestic side of the Cuban missile crisis that went all the way back to the 1898 decision to go to war to "free" Cuba. With that decision Americans made themselves responsible for Cuba's future. In those terrible days of October 1962, they confronted their own failure to make democracy work in Cuba and their inability to allow Cubans to define their own future and make their own mistakes.

Just a few days before the presence of the missiles had finally been verified, Cuban President Oswaldo Dorticos told the U.N. General Assembly that his country was ready for demilitarization if Washington gave assurances "by word and by deed" that there would be no more attempts to overthrow the Havana government by military means. Adlai Stevenson, the American Ambassador to the world security organization, replied (as Kennedy had earlier vowed): "The maintenance of communism in the Americas is not negotiable."

Still, it *was* a Soviet-American confrontation in the first instance; and, as one of Kennedy's chief assistants pointed out, it offered an opportunity to turn the tables on the Soviets for the original U-2 incidents and the Bay of Pigs. Now *they* would have to own up for pretending to the world that they had not done what Kennedy would make clear they had done, or at least intended to do, by installing "offensive" weapons on the island. Several options or "tracks" were offered to the President by his advisers, all the way from ignoring the missiles to full-scale invasion. He chose "Track D," an embargo and naval blockade against further weapons deliveries. The choice was announced to the nation on October 22, in a speech accusing the Soviets of deception and bad faith and of desiring to upset the balance of power by moving in for a close shot at North America.

For almost a week, the Cubans, like the rest of the world, watched while the two superpowers tried to find a way out of the crisis. Finally, on October 26, a message arrived from Khrushchev offering to remove the missiles if the United States pledged not to launch or participate in a military attack on Cuba. A second message arrived the next morning, offering to remove the missiles only if the United States also agreed to remove its IRBMs from Turkey. Ironically, Kennedy had ordered these weapons to be withdrawn some months earlier because they were no longer needed with the advent of intercontinental ballistic missiles (ICBMs). He could not agree to their removal in the midst of the Cuban crisis, however, without seeming to yield to Soviet pressure and thus losing whatever he hoped to gain on the domestic side of the crisis.

Kennedy's brother Robert suggested how this phase of the crisis might be managed successfully—by replying to the first letter as if the second had never arrived. But he also proposed going to the Soviet Ambassador with private assurances that American IRBMs would be out of Turkey in a few months.

Whether this combination did it, or whether Khrushchev "blinked" in an eyeball-to-eyeball showdown, as Secretary of State Dean Rusk would put it, word came on October 28 that Moscow had accepted the no-invasion pledge and would withdraw its missiles.

Thus ended the most dangerous crisis of the cold war. When it was all over, several things occurred to observers which had not been apparent in the midst of the sound and fury accompanying the crisis. What, for example, was the definition of "offensive"? Were liquid-fueled IRBMs, which required hours of prelaunch preparation, offensive like ICBMs, which could be launched with only a few minutes' preparation? How, given these differences, could an IRBM strike have been coordinated with an ICBM attack from the Soviet Union? Why were Soviet weapons in Cuba "offensive" and American missiles in Turkey "defensive"? Kennedy seemingly recognized that some further explanation was needed during a television interview on December 27, 1962. He began with a reiteration of his original interpretation of the Soviet move but quickly shifted to other grounds:

This was an effort to materially change the balance of power, it was done in secret, steps were taken to deceive us by every means they could, and they were planning in November to open to the world the fact that they had these missiles so close to the United States; not that they were intending to fire them, because if they were going to get into a nuclear struggle, they have their own missiles in the Soviet Union. But it would have politically changed the balance of power. It would have appeared to, and appearances contribute to reality.

Newspaper accounts of the administration's attitude as the crisis was in progress, back in October, never hinted at any concern except a military one. Kennedy's speech to the nation describing the dangers of the crisis discussed only the military threat to North and South America. The revelation, however offhandedly, of these political and psychological matters brought new criticism from some on the left and the right. To the left, the Cuban missile crisis had demonstrated again that the President was more concerned with style and image than substance; a man who would risk nuclear war on appearances could hardly be expected to have a profound vision of America's future. To the right, Kennedy's slick crisis management concealed the reality that although he had once declared that communism in the Western Hemisphere was not negotiable, he yielded that very point when the going got rough.

It had been a time, in Khrushchev's phrase, when the smell of burning was in the air. But, when everything is accounted for, Kennedy's risks were less than those taken by Khrushchev. The President knew, to begin with, that the United States enjoyed a substantial missile advantage in a final showdown. He, and only he, knew that he would accept an offer to exchange removal of the missiles from Cuba for a no-invasion pledge. After the crisis, Kennedy appeared to have redeemed himself in his own eyes for the Bay of Pigs. Khrushchev, on the other hand, was soon on his way out in the Soviet Union.

The longest war

Kennedy's standing in the polls reached new highs, as did his international rating. In 1963 he discovered that the "peace issue" had popular support when a partial test ban treaty was signed with the Soviet Union, marking the first significant check on the arms race. He could still be the "tough" cold warrior, as in a famous speech given at the site of the Berlin Wall when he declared that those who thought the West could get along diplomatically with the Soviets should come to Berlin to see for themselves what separated East and West.

At his death by an assassin's bullet on November 22, 1963, it was not clear which world view would have prevailed in a second Kennedy term in the White House. As the Vietnam war got worse and worse in the mid-1960s, former Kennedy advisers claimed that their fallen leader would never have taken the nation into the swamps of Southeast Asia on such a fool's errand, even had he continued to accept an outdated view of the cold war. Moreover, they insisted, there was good reason to believe he was fast shedding earlier beliefs in the months before he was struck down. Neither assertion was entirely convincing, especially coming from men who had produced that series of "contingency" plans which invariably concluded that the war in Vietnam was "winnable" with just a little more team effort here and a little more "can do" attitude over there.

To be sure, Kennedy had inherited the situation in Southeast Asia. Indeed the one area Eisenhower had warned the President-elect about at their preinaugural meeting, as far as the possibility of an early armed clash was concerned, was Laos. And Kennedy confided to an aide that Eisenhower had been able to afford to lose half of Vietnam to the Communists after Dien Bien Phu in 1954 only because of his great prestige as a military leader. But he could not lose the rest of Indochina under any circumstances. All Democrats were suspect (even in their own eyes) ever since Harry Truman "lost" China back in 1949, or so it seemed in modern political mythology.

A rule of thumb for successful political campaigning in the 1960s, noted some commentators, was never to be in a position of losing in Indochina just before the elections. As far as it went, it was a good explanation, but it should have gone much farther. How had Vietnam become so important to American security in the first place? An ingenious defense of the war policy along different lines was offered by its defenders when things got really bad: maybe Vietnam originally was not important to American security, or maybe it was—but in either case the historical issue was unimportant compared with the question of fulfilling a commitment once it was undertaken. To cut and run, went this argument, however one explained it, was to risk the future. Great powers do not go back on promises and remain great powers. International stability depended upon security pacts, and these in turn depended upon the often unpleasant job of manning the watch on the far-off bastions of freedom.

Kennedy believed this firmly until the day of his death. Even in his post-missile crisis efforts to establish a modus vivendi with the Soviets, his "realism" had severe limits when it came to dealing with revolution. The only standard of measurement that meant anything to the New Frontiersman was how close the revolutionary stood to Moscow or Peking. Doubts were always resolved in favor of too close. Moreover, appearances were deceiving: suppose Ho Chi Minh *was* a nationalist. He was a Communist as well, wasn't he? Sooner or later he would be subject to Moscow's discipline. The argument should have been received with at least some degree of skepticism by Kennedy, especially since a similar argument had been advanced by anti-Catholics in the 1960 campaign. (Sooner or later would he not be subject to Rome's discipline?)

French President Charles deGaulle tried to

explain to Kennedy that even if he found local leaders who were prepared to support American policy, intervention would become an endless undertaking. American ideology, however superior to that offered by Ho Chi Minh, would become identified with the American will to power, and as it did, the Communists would appear as the champions of national independence. "We French have had experience of it. You Americans wanted to take our place in Indo-China. Now you want to take over where we left off and revive a war which we brought to an end. I predict that you will sink step by step into a bottomless military and political quagmire, however much you spend in men and money."

Kennedy listened to the old statesman respectfully, but other voices seemed louder and more confident. Although the United States had only a few thousand "advisers" in Vietnam by mid-1963, the determination of the Kennedy administration to support an anticommunist government in Saigon was already complete enough to permit policy makers to consider how best to remove President Ngo Dinh Diem from power. Diem's brutal efforts to suppress Buddhist opposition had brought him under sharp ciritcism in the United States (and elsewhere) and was fast destroying his usefulness to American policy. Cooperation with Vietnamese generals in a coup d'état was considered, rejected, and then reconsidered. Most of all Washington was concerned that if a coup took place, it be successful. Presidential aide McGeorge Bundy cabled the American Ambassador in Saigon on October 25, 1963:

We are particularly concerned about hazard that an unsuccessful coup, however carefully we avoid direct engagement, will be laid at our door by public opinion almost everywhere. Therefore, while sharing your view that we should not be in position of thwarting coup, we would like to have option of judging and warning on any plan with poor prospects of success.

The coup took place on November 1, 1963, but Diem's overthrow and assassination did not improve things much. In fact, for a time it looked like the beginning of the end. The generals quarreled among themselves while the Vietcong closed in around Saigon itself. The most recent special mission to Vietnam was scheduled to report to President Kennedy at the conclusion of his Texas visit. Instead, it met with Lyndon B. Johnson at the end of a weekend which had begun with Kennedy's assassination.

All the way with L. B. J.

The briefing was a gloomy affair. Ambassador Henry Cabot Lodge reported that the generals suddenly seemed to lack the will to fight, let alone the ability to instill that spirit into their soldiers. Some hard decisions would have to be made—at once. Johnson's response was not clouded with a single doubt or question. "I am not going to lose Vietnam," declared the President of fourty-eight hours. "I am not going to be the President who saw Southeast Asia go the way China went."

Probably Johnson's motives were more complicated than he revealed in this instance. As the head of an earlier special mission to Southeast Asia, he had reported to President Kennedy that the choice was whether to support anticommunist governments or to "throw in the towel in the area and pull back our defenses to San Francisco and a 'Fortress America' concept." Here was an important clue to policy makers' attitudes about Indochina: what happened there would, perhaps not in domino fashion, shape the area's future—and America's role in Asia.

Johnson had never spent much time on foreign affairs. His speciality was domestic legislation; and he had made himself master of the Senate in this area by learning the strengths and weaknesses of his colleagues. His views on the cold war were highly orthodox, but he was by nature a cautious man. In 1954, ironically, at a time when Secretary of State Dulles seemed ready to risk everything on a few last-minute air strikes if Congress would support the President, he strongly opposed American intervention to save the French from defeat in Indochina.

He had had literally no time to study the strengths and weaknesses of Kennedy's foreign policy advisers before being asked to make a major decision. When he did, it was too late. Once set in motion by Johnson's decision against accepting even a "neutralist" regime in Saigon, the American policy machinery whirred along at an ever faster rate. At the center was Secretary of Defense Robert McNamara, whose Pentagon computers continued to provide optimistic printouts demonstrating that the "kill" ratio necessary for winning a guerrilla war, 10 to 1, was holding up in all sectors. What was happening, of course, was that local commanders soon learned what to feed the computers to produce such healthy results, and they supplied the fictional "body counts" on a regular weekly basis.

American troop levels rose steadily to more than 500,000 by 1968. But the real story of America's participation in the Vietnam war was air power. In World War II the United States dropped more than 2 million tons of explosives on Axis targets; by mid-1971 the total for Indochina had surpassed 5½ million tons! North Vietnamese targets were bombed again and again, but the air war inside South

Vietnam and in Laos and Cambodia also involved saturation bombing. Sorties flown against enemy supply lines in Laos, to take a specific example, averaged well over 1,000 per month for long periods of time. One Pentagon official remarked in 1967, "We seem to be proceeding on the assumption that the way to eradicate Viet Cong is to destroy all the village structures, defoliate the jungles, and then cover the entire surface of South Vietnam with asphalt."

The bombing campaign had begun in 1964 on a tit-for-tat basis following a supposed attack on American war vessels in the Gulf of Tonkin. President Johnson's dramatic appeal for a congressional resolution supporting his policy of "restraint" in responding to North Vietnamese provocations was quickly granted by the legislators. Some Democrats later said that they voted for the resolution to strengthen the President's hand against the Republicans, who had nominated the "hawkish" Senator Barry Goldwater (a brigadier general in the Air Force Reserve). Others no doubt hoped that their President would deal summarily with the North Vietnamese.

Both groups were disappointed. The first round of teach-in protests began in the spring of 1965, and these soon escalated into protest marches on Washington and civil disobedience campaigns. Johnson's determination to see it through to the end amazed former Senate colleagues who had always imagined Lyndon to be the consummate pragmatist. Instead, he became more and more peevish, taking out his frustrations on war critics.

Released from their loyalties to the late President Kennedy, the inner circle of Presidential advisers who had shaped New Frontier policies began to drift away in ones and twos. Robert McNamara remained at Johnson's side for a long time, but then he too went over to the "doves." "Don't see Bob," the President remarked to a Senator seeking information—"he's gone dovish on me." Johnson replaced McNamara with Clark Clifford, who had designed Harry Truman's winning political strategy against the doves in 1948. His cold war credentials, like those of Dean Acheson, were unchallengeable. Yet both now warned Johnson that he had to find another way out of Vietnam. The Democratic party and the country were on the edge of revolt.

On March 31, 1968, Johnson took himself out of the Presidential race, saying that he would devote the remaining months of his term in office to seeking peace. The message that went out to American diplomatic posts in Asia, however, advised that a suspension of the bombing campaign would allow for a shift in strategy, the rebuilding of the ARVN (South Vietnamese Army) and new efforts against enemy strongholds in Laos and Cambodia.

"I am going to tell you how we got in Vietnam," snapped an angry Lyndon Johnson in 1966. "We have always been in Vietnam." Sometimes it seemed that way, especially to a generation of Americans whose political consciousness had been shaped around the war and the bitter debate over its origins and conduct.

The portrait of Pax Americana

At the height of the Vietnam war, President Lyndon Johnson became, in effect, a caricature of the liberal-realist position on the cold war. Kennedy men lamented the vulgarity and lack of style in the White House, but what they were seeing was really much more disturbing, involving not Johnson alone but a portrait of an era—a portrait of Pax Americana.

In response to the first teach-ins, Johnson went to Johns Hopkins University in April 1965 to offer "unconditional discussions" to the enemy as long as the question of who ruled in Saigon was not one of the issues to be unconditionally negotiated. He also proposed an internationally financed Asian Development Bank and a TVA-like project to develop the economic potential of the Mekong River Valley. Hanoi could share in these undertakings, too, just as soon as she abandoned the effort to conquer South Vietnam. Sometimes called "welfare imperialism," this belief that the rest of the world shared, or ought to share, American assumptions about what was good for all peoples had permeated the nation's cold war policy from the beginning.

A second aspect of Pax Americana was the rationalization that anything that "worked" was justified when one faced an implacable enemy in a mortal struggle like the cold war. Only a few weeks after the Johns Hopkins speech, Johnson dispatched 23,000 troops to the Dominican Republic to suppress a revolt against the ruling military junta. Four years earlier at the time of dictator Rafael Trujillo's assassination, Kennedy had laid out the possibilities as follows: "There are three possibilities in descending order of preference: a decent democratic regime, a continuation of the Trujillo regime or a Castro regime. We ought to aim at the first, but we really can't renounce the second until we are sure that we can avoid the third." For a short time, liberal Juan Bosch had given the administration hope that the first might become a real alternative. Overthrown by the military, Bosch waited for another opportunity to take power. But the atmosphere in Washington had changed by 1965. Bosch now appeared to represent a positive threat, a nascent Castro regime. Evidence of communist involvement

Figure 24-2 The basics of war. This was a mistake; the napalm hit the "friendlies" instead of the VC. (*Wide World Photos*)

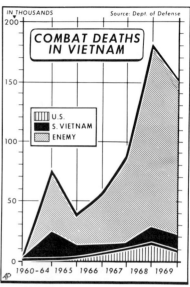

Figure 24-3 By every quantitative yardstick, "we" won the war. So what went wrong? (*Wide World Photos*)

Figure 24-4 Vietnamizing college campuses. (*Wide World Photos*)

Figure 24-5 Once more with feeling. LBJ on board AF1, and on top of the world. Then he fell off into Vietnam. (*Wide World Photos*)

in the uprising of May 1965 was flimsy, but Ambassador Stevenson gave it his best in a speech to the U.N. Security Council. "I would remind you that only 12 men went to the hills with Castro in 1956, and that only a handful of Castro's own supporters were Communists. I would also remind you that Castro, too, came into power under cover of constitutionalism, moderation, and cooperation with others."

If one took Stevenson seriously, there was literally no way change could take place in the world unless America approved. No one took him literally, not even Stevenson himself, whose growing doubts about American policy made him increasingly uncomfortable as its chief spokesman before the world.

A third point in Pax Americana was the steadfast insistence of its practitioners that the United States wanted nothing for itself except peace and security—the common goals of mankind. The United States wanted not one foot of territory in the Western Hemisphere, Woodrow Wilson had said in a famous speech in 1913 defending his intervention against Mexican dictator Victoriano Huerta. As for economic motivation, said one of Wilson's great admirers, Dean Acheson, it was simply nonexistent. Occasionally, however, policy makers spoke of America's broader national interests, as in the following instance when Walt Whitman Rostow appeared before Congress: "The location, natural resources, and populations of the under-developed areas are such that, should they become effectively attached to the Communist bloc, the United States would become the second power in the world. . . . " Earnings on American foreign investments rose from an average of $2.1 billion in 1950 to $7.8 billion per year by 1965. Perhaps more significant, in the light of Rostow's remarks to Congress, was the overall pattern that was developing in those investments.

In Latin America, American investment increased from $8.1 billion in 1959 to $9.3 billion in 1965 while profits totaled $5.3 billion. In Asia, investments increased from $2.2 billion to $3.6 billion while profits realized totaled $6.5 billion. But in Europe investments for those years rose from $5.3 billion to nearly $14 billion by 1965 while profits were only $3.7 billion. The profits drawn from two underdeveloped continents were thus providing American capitalists with the means to "colonize" the European economy and extend their holdings into Africa directly and indirectly through European-based corporations.

The American economic empire was not built according to any prearranged plan, but neither was it put together in a fit of absent-mindedness. Eugene R. Black, a former President of the World Bank, once explained how foreign aid, from the Marshall Plan to the Alliance for Progress, contributed to the national interest: "Our foreign aid programs constitute a distinct benefit to American business. The three major benefits are: (a) Foreign aid provides a substantial and immediate market for U.S. goods and services; (b) Foreign aid stimulates the development of new overseas markets for U.S. companies; (c) Foreign aid orients national economies toward a free enterprise system in which U.S. firms can prosper."

Policy makers in the cold war had little time to concern themselves with the problem which often troubles theorists and academics: the distinction between profit and power, and which motivates which. If one begins with the proposition, as Kennedy did in 1960 that "a prosperous business community is the measure of our performance," then the direction seems set: "I therefore favor expansion of our foreign trade and private investments abroad."

"Our exports," he warned, "have not been large enough." In 1962 the New Frontier presented its Trade Expansion Act to Congress. The President explained why it was necessary at a dockside speech in New Orleans on May 4, 1962:

Trade expansion will emphasize the modern instead of the weak, the new frontiers of trade instead of the ancient strongholds of protection.

And,

we cannot continue to bear the burden that we must bear of helping freedom defend itself all the way, from the American soldier guarding the Brandenburg Gate to the Americans now in Vietnam, or the Peace Corps men in Colombia. Unless we have the resources to finance those great expenditures which in the last year totaled over three billion dollars, unless we are able to increase our surplus balance of payments, then the United States will be faced with a hard choice, of either lessening those commitments or beginning to withdraw this great national effort.

That was one alternative, to raise tariffs, restrict capital investments, and pull back from the world. Then this:

This Administration was not elected to preside over the liquidation of American respon-

sibility in these great years [emphasis added].

There is a much better answer—and that is to increase our exports, to meet our commitments and to maintain our defense of freedom. I have every confidence that once this bill is passed, the ability of American initiative and know-how will increase our exports and our export surplus by competing successfully in every market of the world.

By 1968 the American empire was seriously endangered by the very policies its advocates had pursued so relentlessly in Vietnam. That war, first, had proved too costly for any benefits that might be expected from continuing it, at least in the way it was being conducted. It was endangered, second, by challenges from inside the free world itself, an adverse balance of payments and the gold drain. America's capitalist competitors, West Europe and Japan, were by design or coincidence taking full advantages of U.S. difficulties around the world to solidify their own positions. A new world view was needed, and an appropriate leader.

Selected references

Filled with inside accounts of goings-on in the Kennedy administration is Arthur M. Schlesinger, Jr.'s, massive *A Thousand Days:* *John F. Kennedy in the White House* (1965). Theodore Sorenson's *Kennedy* (1965) is also useful. On Lyndon Johnson two books are very helpful: Philip Geyelin, *Lyndon B. Johnson and the World* (1966), and Rowland Evans and Robert Novak, *Lyndon B. Johnson: The Exercise of Power* (1966). The growth of the "loyal" opposition is traced in Haynes Johnson and Bernard M. Gwertzman, *Fulbright: The Dissenter* (1968). The view from Europe is given in J. J. Servan-Schreiber, *The American Challenge* (1968).

On Latin America, start with Jerome Levinson and Juan de Onis, *The Alliance That Lost Its Way* (1970). Cuban background for the crisis is given in Maurice Zeitlin and Robert Scheer, *Cuba: Tragedy in Our Hemisphere* (1963); the crisis itself from an American point of view is covered well in Elie Abel, *The Missile Crisis* (1966), and in Robert Kennedy's own memoir, *Thirteen Days* (1969).

Literature on Vietnam is voluminous. David Halberstam's *The Best and the Brightest* (1972) surveys the world policy makers thought they knew their way and demonstrates how lost they really were. An excellent primer is George M. Kahin and John W. Lewis, *The United States in Vietnam* (1967). Tonkin is dissected in Joseph C. Goulden, *Truth Is the First Casualty: The Gulf of Tonkin Affair* (1969). A short report, *Mass Communications and American Empire* (1969), by Herbert I. Schiller ought to be on many more reading lists in American history.

TWENTY-FIVE

Camelot and After

Period covered: 1961–1971
Emphasis: National politics
Major events: Kennedy becomes President, 1961
Johnson becomes President, 1963
Great Society, 1965
Election of 1968
Nixon becomes President, 1969

486

Figure 25-1 President Kennedy at his inaugural ball. (*Photograph by Paul Schutzer for* Life *magazine*)

The Kennedy Presidency

The Kennedy administration was anything but unambitious. In his inaugural the President suggested: "Together let us explore the stars, conquer the deserts, eradicate disease, tap the ocean depths and encourage the arts and commerce." Kennedy people knew that to accomplish greatly, great power was needed. They spoke of "breaking Congress," which they saw as the chief obstacle to reform. Congress broke them instead. It refused to pass Kennedy's minimum wage and education bills and frustrated the administration on Medicare, tax revision, postal increases and long-term appropriations for foreign aid. Congress did give him a Peace Corps, and the spectacle of young American volunteers working in unlikely places around the world was popular at first. When Kennedy decided to beat the Soviet Union to the moon whatever it cost, that went down well too. Congress, so eager to save money in other areas, could hardly be restrained when voting cold war expenditures. It had little enthusiasm for education but much for arms and rockets to the moon.

Kennedy played upon cold war enthusiasms to get more missiles, though he knew the United States was already well ahead of the Soviet Union. He greatly expanded American "counterinsurgency capabilities," Defense Department jargon for the Special Forces. He also asked for newer and more expensive conventional weapons. For reasons peculiar to itself, the Pentagon decided that America should be prepared to fight two and one half wars at the same time. Thus, even before Vietnam, arms expenditures went up rapidly; in 1962 they rose above $50 billion for the first time since Korea. In three years Kennedy raised defense spending by nearly 50 percent. New cost-control systems allegedly saved billions of dollars, but these savings were blotted out by enormous cost overruns on the F-111 fighter-bomber, the C5A transport, and other fiascos.

Despite Congress, Kennedy managed a few domestic victories. When U. S. Steel raised its prices in defiance of Presidential guidelines, he made the company back down. This antagonized many capitalists, who remained antiadministration even after Kennedy sponsored tax reductions that saved corporations many billions of dollars. When violence threatened the first black student at the University of Mississippi, Kennedy sent federal marshals and then troops who saw James Meredith through to graduation. Attorney General Robert Kennedy got the Interstate Commerce Commission to end segregation in facilities related to interstate travel, though not until freedom riders had been mobbed. Although President Kennedy had said when campaigning that discrimination in federally assisted housing could be ended with the stroke of a pen, he waited years to end it. Kennedy did not do much more for civil rights than Truman or even Eisenhower, but he was infinitely more popular among blacks. This showed how much appearances count in public life. Frustration at home led Kennedy to concentrate on foreign affairs—hence the Bay of Pigs, the Cuban missile crisis, and the war in Vietnam. But Kennedy was handsome and witty, his wife beautiful, and his appointees as a group notably stylish, particularly by comparison with their stodgy predecessors. So Kennedy was much admired and greatly mourned after his assassination on November 22, 1963.

The Johnson Presidency

President Kennedy was a tough act to follow; all the more so because of the Camelot cult that sprang up after his death. Its followers held that Kennedy had begun a golden age of elegant liberalism during which all the country's problems would have been solved had he not been slain. This made things even more difficult for Lyndon Baines Johnson, who was not glamourous or even particularly likeable. Kennedy people said he was unfit for the Presidency on account of his homely Texas manners. Strangely enough, Johnson almost agreed. Overnight a new qualification for the Presidency—suaveness—had been established. All the same, Johnson was a man of immense energy and political skill who had considerable sympathy for the poor and oppressed. He had been one of the great Senate majority leaders before becoming Vice President. No one could play the Congress as he did or knew where so many bodies were buried, or was owed so many favors. Johnson used all his awesome powers brilliantly. Congress gave Johnson the very things it had denied Kennedy, beginning with a tax cut. In the late fifties and early sixties there was little inflation but also little growth. Kennedy argued that a tax cut would fix things up, but Congress preferred balanced budgets to lower taxes. In his first State of the Union message Johnson said he would reduce the budget by $5 billion. Congress was so impressed, and so expertly worked over by the President, that it gave Johnson an $11 billion tax cut and another billion in appropriations for the war on poverty he had just declared. In May, Johnson proclaimed the Great Society. In June, Congress gave him the Civil Rights Act of 1964. Together with the voting rights bill he would introduce later, this went about as far as law could go in removing injustices. Thereafter the focus would be on improving opportunity.

President Johnson took charge of government so masterfully that he had a good chance of being elected in his own right, and the Republicans gave him four more years on

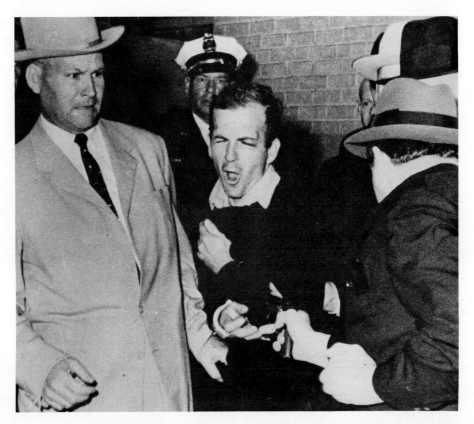

Figure 25-2 The slaying of Lee Harvey Oswald. (*Wide World Photos*)

a platter by nominating Senator Barry Goldwater. As a rule, politicians would rather be President than right, but Goldwater was an exception. The darling of Republican conservatives for his Victorian prejudices and loose tongue, he put principle above ambition and tried to campaign as a militant reactionary. He proved once again that voters are frightened by Presidential candidates who move too far from the center line. By criticizing TVA and social security and implying that he would escalate the war in Vietnam, Goldwater left Johnson with all the popular issues. Johnson, running as a humanitarian

and lover of peace, carried all but six states. There was some complaint afterward that this was unsporting, but Johnson, knowing that he would never be as strong again as he was in 1965, wanted every possible advantage to put over the Great Society then—and to a surprising extent he did. He had made a start in 1964 by getting the Manpower Development and Training Act and the Urban Mass Transit Act. They were followed by the Office of Economic Opportunity, the Voting Act of 1965, the Higher Education Act of 1965, another Urban Mass Transit Act and the Model Cities Act, both in 1966, a series of environmental bills, the Job Corps, the Teacher Corps, Medicare, Medicaid, Head Start, the Housing Act of 1968, and many more. It was the greatest outpouring of health, education, and welfare legislation since the New Deal.

These bills, often hastily written and poorly thought out, had many flaws. Some were underfinanced; others—housing acts especially—had loopholes that allowed speculators to cheat the government of millions. Yet even the Great Society's failures were instructive. Head Start showed that helping preschoolers was not enough, that aid to the disadvantaged had to take place at all levels. Welfare failures showed that the system had to be reconstructed, not simply patched up. Many other weaknesses were the product of

excessive zeal and compassion and hence far from contemptible. Johnson's biggest mistake at home was failing to raise taxes. The tax cut of 1964 had worked, stimulating the economy and reducing unemployment. Everyone was now half a Keynesian, Republicans having discovered that people did not mind deficit spending and loved tax reductions. The problem was that Keynesianism had two sides. Its attractive side was combating deflation by spending more and taxing less, but the hard side was that to fight inflation taxes had to go up and spending down. The war in Vietnam caused inflation, but Johnson feared to act, knowing that the war was tolerable only as long as it seemed not to affect living standards. As prices did

Figure 25-3 LBJ pressing the flesh. (*United Press International*)

not go up rapidly at first, Johnson avoided raising taxes when doing so would have been easy, only to find later that when tax hikes were most needed they were too hard to get.

The election of 1968

Johnson's last years in office were very different from his earlier ones. Inflation reached a point where for many workers real income declined. Casualty lists went up also, producing hostile reactions among people who normally never questioned American militarism. Large draft calls outraged students, who demonstrated and rioted until government officials dared not speak on campus or, sometimes, anywhere else in public. Secretary McNamara, when demonstrated against, shouted at students that he was tougher than they; but in time even he sickened of the war and resigned. With the Great Society flagging while liberals and minorities called for ever larger programs that could not be funded, and with political vituperation rising to levels not seen since the McCarthy era, dissident Democrats launched a dump-Johnson movement late in 1967. They asked every prominent Democratic Senator to run in the primaries, but all refused except Eugene McCarthy of Minnesota, who had no national following. Professionals laughed when he started to campaign in New Hampshire aided only by Robert Lowell, the poet; Paul Newman, the actor; and a handful of young people. Johnson men predicted McCarthy would do well to get 5 percent of the Democratic vote. Instead he got 42 percent, partly because hundreds of students worked for him, mostly because people were tired of a war that seemed likely to go on forever—a possibility underscored by the Tet offensive which got underway just before the election. Washington insisted Tet was a wonderful victory because the Communists were finally driven out of the cities they had invaded, but few outside of government took this lighthearted view.

Robert F. Kennedy now entered the race. As the most popular antiwar Democrat, it was his duty to seek the nomination. He had refused before New Hampshire and Tet, thinking Johnson was too strong to beat; But once McCarthy showed he was not, Kennedy had to come in or lose part of his following. McCarthy could not withdraw, as that would betray those people who had believed in him when things seemed hopeless. This impasse created great bitterness. President Johnson surprised everyone by bowing out just before McCarthy beat him in the Wisconsin primary. Johnson was probably strong enough to get the nomination if he wanted it and even to beat whoever the Republicans put up, but he would have been hard-pressed to govern effectively. To his credit, Johnson relished power not so much for its own sake as for what he could do with it. Once it became clear that his next term would be marked by paralyzing differences of opinion, he gave up office.

Robert Kennedy pulled ahead of McCarthy in the primaries, then he was killed in California and McCarthy struggled on alone in vain. Kennedy followers were emotional and partisan, caring more for their man and for Camelot than for any cause. They now hated McCarthy for having spoken ill of their prince and would not support him at the convention. This gave the nomination to Hubert Humphrey, once a favorite of liberals, then a Vice President who endorsed every brutal thing Johnson said or did with twice the President's gusto. While McCarthy and Kennedy were fighting in the primaries, Humphrey was conferring with party bosses. He never ran in a single primary but had the nomination sewed up by August, when the Democrats met in Chicago. Protesters railed against the politicians and were beaten in the streets while Humphrey was being nominated—all of which left the Democrats badly divided. Because many disaffected liberals now chose not to vote at all they in effect helped to elect Richard Nixon. (Though beaten in 1960 for President and in 1962 for Governor of California, Nixon came back to establish himself as the most available Republican.) The reasons for Nixon's success are mysterious. Liberal Republicans never liked him, while conservatives preferred Goldwater or Governor Ronald Reagan of California. They ended up with Nixon just the same. The Democratic civil war gave Nixon an enormous lead in the polls, but even so he nearly lost the election. Humphrey campaigned hard and picked up many estranged Democrats who, although alienated, were unwilling to stand by and see Nixon win. Had the campaign lasted a few weeks longer or had Humphrey begun to make faint antiwar noises earlier than he did, he might have won. But he did not, and the prospect of an unhealthy Democratic interregnum, as after 1948, thus vanished.

The Nixon Presidency

Of all major politicians, Nixon was the one liberal Democrats hated most. He had been a witch hunter in the 1950s—the official mud slinger in Eisenhower's cabinet. Yet his election was the best thing for Democrats and perhaps for the country. As a Republican with flawless anticommunist credentials, he could end the war in Vietnam if he wished—something no Democrat could do without being accused of selling out to the reds. He could also negotiate with China, or any communist state, whereas a Democrat probably could not. The Republican party, though in fact more hawkish than its rival, was not held responsible for the war, and so the passions which a Humphrey administration could not easily have dealt with cooled. Only a hawk could make peace, only a cold warrior could ease the cold war, only a conservative could advance the welfare state.

Few guessed Nixon would take advantage of this. The most partisan of all major politicians and—it was thought—the most conservative President since Herbert Hoover, he was expected to indulge the prejudices he was known to hold. But Nixon surprised nearly everyone. His admirers supposed him to be a fiscal conservative, an anticommunist hard-liner, a law-and-order man, and an enemy of the limited welfare state. So he may have been, but the most striking thing about how his first term began was the ease with which he exploited his strengths at the expense of his principles. Inflation was getting worse when he took over. A conservative's duty was to at least cut spending and perhaps even raise taxes during the emergency, but he did neither. In fact, spending went up, and not just for the military. As this stimulated inflation, prices and wages rose—along with budget deficits, which within a few years became the largest since World War II. They would amount to perhaps $100 billion. As inflation got worse, critics demanded a price-wage freeze. Although Nixon had said that was out of the question, he suddenly imposed one in 1971. This seemed to help, and—judging by the polls—did him little harm among the voters.

The Republican solution to the welfare "mess," conservatives thought, would be to drive cheaters and loafers off the rolls and cut down payments. Instead, Nixon proposed to federalize the welfare system and establish a minimum family income program. The blow was eased slightly by a provision that able-bodied people on welfare would have to work at specified employments, but this meant little as most people on welfare were too young or too old, sick, disabled, or mothers with preschool infants. "Do not judge us by what we say," Nixon insisted, "but by what we do," which implied that while he might pander verbally to the right, his programs would be liberal. To a degree this was clearly so, since conservatives got symbolic concessions. Nixon opposed busing to effect school segregation; William Buckley, most popular of conservative writers, was appointed to the USIA; and Southerners accused of racism, greed, or incompetence were named to the Supreme Court (when the Senate failed to confirm them, however, they were replaced by conservative Northern judges). His Attorneys General were fanatic law-and-order men. But these proconservative gestures made little difference except to the Supreme Court, which did become more conservative. Even so, by the end of 1973 it had not reversed the Warren Court significantly. The Justice Department behaved much as it had under the Democrats, which may not have been good but was not terrible either.

The Nixon paradox was not easily resolved. He was a fiscal conservative when out of office, a Keynsian when in. A lifelong anticommunist, he invited himself to China. An advocate of the Puritan ethic, he proposed sweeping welfare reforms. Beloved of big business, he also promoted mild efforts to help the environment and personally saved the Everglades from being destroyed by a jetport. He remained as square and chauvin-

istic as ever: always ready to invoke the old verities, a champion of fetuses against their abortion-minded mothers, a friend of Billy Graham and Norman Vincent Peale. His administration was the most mediocre and corrupt since Harding's.

Despite his weaknesses, and those of his administration, when the Democrats nominated George McGovern to run against him in 1972 his future seemed assured. McGovern was in reverse what Goldwater had been to the Republicans in 1964. He represented feminists, militant liberals, and racial minorities who, thanks to the very reforms in nominating procedures which McGovern had helped secure after the convention debacle of 1968, had seized control of the Democratic National Convention in 1972. The result was a campaign platform that called for tax and welfare reforms, reduced military expenditures, aid for education, and much else. These proposals, however desirable in principle, went considerably beyond what many in the white working classes who are still the backbone of the Democratic party were prepared to accept. Aided by McGovern's errors, Nixon won reelection by a handsome majority. At the beginning of 1973 he appeared to be sitting on top of the world, endowed with a great popular mandate, wreathed in glory from his negotiations with China and Russia, and able to claim that he had brought peace to Indochina, though in fact bombing continued in Cambodia until August, when a congressional deadline against further military action was reached.

Nixon was not allowed to enjoy his triumphs for long, however. On February 7, 1973, the Senate voted to form a select committee under Senator Sam Ervin of North Carolina to investigate campaign practices. The committee was especially concerned with a bizarre event the previous June when a band of robbers, led by the security director of the Committee to Reelect the President (CREEP), was found in the offices of the Democratic National Committee in the Watergate complex. At the time this was passed off as a crazy stunt confined to low-level figures in the campaign. But enterprising reporters found more and more evidence linking not only CREEP but the White House itself to the Watergate break-in and subsequent attempts to cover it up. When the Ervin committee got to work, it heard testimony implicating former Attorney General John Mitchell, head of CREEP at the time of the break-in, and his top aides. John Dean III, formerly counsel to the President, testified that Nixon himself was involved in the coverup, as were H. R. Haldeman and John Ehrlichman, the President's chief domestic advisors. Other testimony disclosed that a special group in the White House known as the "Plumbers" had burglarized the office of Daniel Ellsberg's psychiatrist, looking for material that would discredit Ellsberg, who was on trial for having released the secret Pentagon papers. It was also learned that the judge hearing the Ellsberg case had been interviewed for the position of Director of the FBI while the trial was in progress.

The entire Watergate affair is too complicated to relate here. But the hearings and numerous trials and investigations that arose from the 1972 campaign indicate that many different kinds of illegalities had been practiced. One level included the burglaries and wiretappings of the Democratic National Convention and Ellsberg's psychiatrist. Another involved large cash payments to CREEP by organizations such as International Telephone and Telegraph in return for favors. A third was a form of blackmail by which companies awaiting government decisions on, for example, airline routes, mergers, and the like were approached by CREEP members who asked for illegal contributions, the implication being that the companies would suffer otherwise. A fourth level were so-called dirty tricks, numerous crimes of a less serious nature than those related to Watergate. While the Watergate affair was still under investigation during the summer of 1973, it was learned that a grand jury in Baltimore was hearing evidence to the effect that Vice President Agnew had accepted bribes throughout most of his political career, including his first term as Vice President. Mr. Agnew strenuously denied these charges, then suddenly on October 10, 1973, pleaded no contest to tax evasion in return for immunity from prosecution on the other charges—an act known as plea bargaining or, in the vernacular, copping a plea. Thus the country learned that in 1972, while the President and Vice President were both lecturing everyone else about morality, the one was taking bribes and the other was attempting to cover up serious crimes intended to assure his reelection.

Watergate and the Agnew affair so compromised the Nixon administration that for the first time in recent memory Congress was able to take initiatives of its own, such as ending the bombing in Cambodia. Nixon's popularity, according to the polls, reached an all-time low, not only because of Watergate but also because of runaway inflation (grocery prices went up 20 percent in the month of August alone) and shortages of energy and raw materials that led to real declines in the standard of living for many people.

By the end of 1973 the administration, which earlier had looked to the future with such confidence, was in ruins. Two former cabinet officers (Mitchell and Maurice Stans, former Secretary of Commerce) were under indictment for criminal acts. Congress was refusing to confirm Nixon appointees and was regularly passing bills which the President opposed—though often his vetoes of them were sustained. His ability to conduct domestic affairs was crippled. For months the President remained in hiding, flitting from one of his expensive homes to another (on which, it was also learned, the government had spent millions of dollars for security, communications, and sometimes, it appeared, for mere comforts). The President had never been accused of venality before, but in 1973 it was extensively rumored that on annual incomes of over $200,000 a year since taking office he had paid almost no income tax. When he did begin speaking in public and meeting the press again he was on the defensive, and even though he spoke effectively at times the polls showed that a large majority of Americans believed not only that he helped cover up the Watergate affair but that he knew about it in advance—something the Ervin committee witnesses had not so much as insinuated. And nearly everyone blamed the President for high prices, the cheapened dollar, and the shortages of energy and raw materials, especially gasoline in the summer of 1973 and fuel oil the following winter.

The Nixon campaign of 1972 demonstrated that it is easy for a President to lose touch with reality altogether. But the events of 1973 proved that it is impossible to do so for long. The Plumbers and the Watergate conspirators and the CREEPs lived in a fantasy world of spies, secret meetings, and payoffs, thinking themselves above the law because they were the President's men. Yet because America was still a democracy, despite their best efforts to the contrary, in the end reality caught up with them and they were destroyed. Their collective efforts won few if any

votes for Nixon. What they did was to destroy his effectiveness as President. At the end of 1973 everyone expected three years of political stalemate during which the nation's problems would pile up. Despite Nixon's remarkable feats of diplomacy, his presidency seemed destined to go down in history with those of Grant and Harding, or even beneath them, for in no previous administration had crime and corruption reached the very highest levels. The President and his CREEPs paid a high price for their neurotic suspicions in 1972. It remained to be seen if the country would have to pay a higher one.

Selected references

A general account is William L. O'Neill, *Coming Apart: An Informal History of the 1960s* (1971). The best book on Kennedy's dministration is the intensely partisan Arthur M. Schlesinger, Jr., *A Thousand Days* (1965). There is no study of the Johnson Presidency except his own bland memoir *The Vantage Point* (1971). An excellent account of his earlier career is Rowland Evans and Robert Novak, *Lyndon B. Johnson: The Exercise of Power* (1966). A revealing study of business policy is Hobart Rowen, *The Free Enterprisers: Kennedy, Johnson and the Business Establishment* (1969). There are shrewd observations in Tom Wicker, *JFK and LBJ: The Influence of Personality upon Politics* (1968). A fine exposé of how foreign policy was made in the Johnson and Kennedy years is David Halberstam, *The Best and the Brightest* (1972). A fascinating account of the 1968 election by three English journalists is Lewis Chester, Godfrey Hodgson, and Bruce Page, *An American Melodrama* (1969). The best book on Nixon is the extraordinary Garry Wills, *Nixon Agonistes: The Crisis of the Self-Made Man* (1970).

TWENTY-SIX

Modern Times

Period covered: 1960–1971
Emphasis: Social history
Major events: Freedom rides, 1961
Civil Rights Act of 1964
Voting Rights Act of 1965
Watts riot, 1965
Murder of Martin Luther
King, Jr., 1968

Civil rights

Justice for black Americans was the great domestic issue of the 1960s, a source of turmoil and bloodshed for most of these years. Yet few could have foreseen either the greatness or the violence that was coming. When Martin Luther King, Jr., first articulated his nonviolent philosophy during the Montgomery bus boycott of 1955, it seemed strange, even to people who admired it. Drawing on Gandhi, Thoreau, and other pacifists as well as on more conventional Christian teachers, the Reverend Dr. King urged blacks to meet hate with love and violence with nonviolence. His aim was not simply to disobey unjust laws but to convert the oppressor. The power of this doctrine and the strategies it called forth were not immediately apparent. The bus boycott was won, but little else seemed to change. Then, on February 1, 1960, four black students in Greensboro, North Carolina, refused to leave when denied service at a white lunch counter. This small first step led to the sit-in movement which affected 100 communities that year and remained a favorite tactic of protesters for years to come.

Sit-ins demonstrated that nonviolence worked. Segregated facilities were opened throughout the South. In 1961 members of the Congress of Racial Equality went on "freedom rides" to challenge segregated restaurants, waiting rooms, and toilets. They were mobbed and a bus was burned. This led the Interstate Commerce Commission to prohibit segregation in all facilities relating to interstate travel. CORE, Dr. King's Southern Christian Leadership Conference (SCLC), and the Student Nonviolent Coordinating Committee (SNCC or "Snick") transformed American race relations. The pressure they generated led to the abandonment of laws and customs that had humiliated blacks for a century. The federal government was persuaded to enact and enforce legislation that gave Southern blacks the vote, which in practice had long been denied them despite the Constitution. Nearly all the numerous programs, on every level of government, aimed at solving black problems were a consequence of the nonviolent civil rights movement. Leaders like Dr. King and James Farmer of CORE were heroes not only to blacks but also to white liberals and especially the young.

Though successful beyond belief, nonviolence was unable to hold the affections of many, who, by 1964, were complaining that it did not work. Of course it did work. No other movement ever got such speedy results, except perhaps labor in the 1930s. But desegregation and even the Civil Rights Act of 1964 and the Voting Rights Act of 1965 were not enough. Change generated an appetite for more change. When black incomes did not shoot up instantly and housing patterns failed to improve much, young militants declared that nonviolence had failed. What they meant was that the effort to remain nonviolent had failed. While nonviolence was effective, it exacted a very considerable psychic cost. The strain of bearing insults and assaults was greater than many could bear. Black militants, denied other outlets for their rage, first expressed it in fights among themselves and then by open expressions of hostility toward whites. White members were driven out of SNCC, which adopted the cry of Black Power. As blacks had little power this made little sense except psychologically, because it permitted the release of hatreds long denied.

Even when nonviolence was most popular, it had black critics. The "Black Muslims" who followed Elijah Muhammad referred to white people as devils and condemned blacks who cooperated with them. (They were also the first to call themselves blacks instead of Negroes or Afro-Americans, terms that had come into use as polite substitutes for "black" and "colored."). Muslims defended themselves against police harassment, which was common in the early sixties but declined in a few years, after authorities realized that the Muslims were a conservative social force, their violent rhetoric notwithstanding.

Malcolm X, the most famous Muslim and one who later founded a separate movement, also used extravagant language. Although he had few followers when he was murdered in 1965, he was canonized by militants who misread his teachings or more likely ignored them. Malcolm was tough, but he was also practical. After breaking with the Muslims he urged blacks to unite with those whites who also wanted radical change. Black militants frequently praised Malcolm X while expelling white allies, as did SNCC and—to a lesser extent—CORE in the mid-sixties. This deprived them of much financial support, and in a few years' time both organizations counted for little.

In the late sixties blacks began to turn away from violence, not so much from principle as because it clearly had failed. Black power organizations like SNCC and the Black Panther party were weakened by a combination of police repression and declining revenue. Their judgment had been impaired by the great riots which wracked major cities from 1965 through 1968. (White radicals were intoxicated also. Tom Hayden of Students for a Democratic Society excitedly described the Newark riot as "the people making history," which was true but fatuous.) The riots led some younger leaders to call for urban warfare and to depict themselves as black Che Guevaras. Though stimulating, the riots were costly and unproductive. Scores of blacks died in riots like those in Watts in 1965, in

Figure 26-1 The great march on Washington, high point of the nonviolent civil rights movement. (*Wide World Photos*)

Figure 26-2 Detroit burns, 1967. (*United Press International*)

Newark and Detroit in 1967, and in a hundred towns and cities after Martin Luther King was murdered in 1968. Thousands of homes and businesses were destroyed. Thousands of jobs were lost in ghettos, often for good when white businessmen failed to rebuild. Government money was spent in the ghettos after each riot, but nowhere did aid come near equaling what the black community lost in jobs and property, still less in lives. The riots may have elated militants, but street blacks soon grasped the basic arithmetic. There were no great riots after 1968, and most black extremists soon dropped from sight. Stokely Carmichael of SNCC moved to Africa; H. Rap Brown, who succeeded Carmichael, went in for banditry and was captured after hitting a black bar in New York City, for selfless reasons undoubtedly. The Black Panther party survived, though many members were imprisoned, deescalating its rhetoric and getting into local politics in Oakland, California.

Nonviolence did not make a comeback on account of this. After King's death the SCLC declined. Black leaders seldom enjoined people to love their enemies, and no one seemed to believe that the oppressor would be redeemed through inspiring example. All the same, hardly anyone thought that arming blacks would improve their condition. The style of black protest remained harsh and abrasive, but it became more realistic. Le Roi Jones symbolized the change in black tactics. He was among the first black intellectuals to exploit liberal white masochism. Jones wrote plays, showing whites to be hopelessly vile, that were given high marks by liberal critics. In 1963 he called Martin Luther King an Uncle Tom, and when the novelist Philip Roth disliked his play *Dutchman,* Jones said Roth was a racist. These manners soon became the style among black intellectuals, who for a time found it easy to insult white audiences for fun and profit. Jones went beyond this however. He moved to Newark, divorced his white wife, renamed himself Imamu Baraka, and founded a movement devoted to politics and black culture. He helped elect the first black mayor of Newark and achieved real political power, almost the only black militant to do so. Baraka was unique, but his evolution from white baiting to serious politics symbolized the history of black militancy in the 1960s. Those who lived to be effective all came to terms with the American environment. Blacks would not get power on demand, still less by threatening bodily harm to those who possessed it. But there was power in the ballot box, as many discovered.

In 1960 the median income of black families was $3,000. By 1972 that figure had risen to $6,440—an impressive gain. Yet white incomes went up too, so that while average black family income as a percentage of white family income had risen, the dollar gap between white and black incomes was wider also. About a third of all black families lived below the poverty line in 1972. Blacks had good reason to be angry but little ground for despair. In income, education, and political influence, they had made great gains in the 1960s; and if much remained to be done, their position in American society was still stronger than it had ever been before.

The new left

In 1960 the dominant age group was composed of people between thirty-five and forty years of age. Then suddenly, that is to say, within five years, the population's center of gravity became youthful. In 1964 seventeen-year-olds outnumbered all other ages. From 1964 to 1971 the number of people who turned seventeen increased each year. Col-

lege enrollments doubled in the sixties. Never before had there been so many of college age, never had so many been in college and hence without responsibilities. Students were supported by parents, either wholly or in part, which made little difference when they were few but became very important in the 1960s when they were many.

In 1964 the Free Speech Movement (FSM) erupted at the University of California, proving that the new, large student population would not be so docile as the old, small one. The uprising's proximate cause was that Berkeley students were very involved in the civil rights movement while the university was against political activity on campus. Officials tried to suppress it by eliminating tables on a sidewalk where student organizations of all kinds liked to propagandize and solicit funds. This led to great demonstrations, sit-ins, wholesale arrests, and worse, even after the free speech issue was resolved in the students' favor. California's President Clark Kerr was later forced out of office on account of these uprisings, and they helped elect Ronald Reagan Governor of California.

Most adult Americans disliked the FSM, and they disliked its aftermath even more. But opinions varied as to what caused them. One view was that Berkeley was unique because the San Francisco Bay area had long been a magnet for radicals, but subsequent demonstrations on other campuses disposed of this theory. Another explanation was that Berkeley was too big and impersonal, and that hence students were compelled to band together against the university to preserve their humanity. This argument appealed to students and was pushed hard by *The New York Times*. The problem with it was that surveys taken during the FSM period showed that most students liked "Cal" and had come to the U.C. campus at Berkeley precisely because it was large and exciting. After all, Californians, and students in other states too, had a choice of schools. If the university, or multiversity as Kerr called it, was too big, there were always state or private colleges. Nearly everyone at universities like Berkeley was there by choice. Why should students have complained of the very things which attracted them?

Demonstrations and sieges took place at a great many colleges and universities thereafter. Sometimes the issues were racial: usually demands that more black students be admitted and subsidized, often that a black studies department be created. Students protested the Vietnam war, ROTC, recruiting by the military and by defense contractors on campus, and dormitory rules. More and more complex ideas were offered to account for these acts. Some argued that generational conflict, a feature of all modern societies, was at the root of youthful discontent. Theories of postindustrial social dysfunctions, alienation, affluence, loss of identity, and all the invisible maladies social critics had diagnosed in the 1950s were now applied to campus uprisings. Conservatives blamed the uprisings on permissive child-rearing practices, usually the fault of Dr. Spock, Communists, outside agitators, nonstudents, and other sinister elements.

Though overdrawn, these charges were not altogether fanciful. In 1962 a handful of radicals, calling themselves Students for a Democratic Society (SDS), had issued a manifesto called the "Port Huron Statement" which claimed that intellectuals and students were potential forces for change. No one had heard of SDS at the time, and its ideas were widely ignored. But after the FSM and after the Vietnam war was escalated in 1965, SDS grew rapidly. Other radical groups blossomed also, though some faded as quickly as

they had arisen. Organizations like the May Second Movement perished before most people even knew they were alive. All the new organizations were known collectively as the new left. SDS, by far the largest of them, went through several phases. In the mid-sixties it worked to little effect, at organizing poor communities in the North. Then it was caught up in antiwar demonstrations almost despite itself. As antiwar feelings intensified and people became more frustrated, the mood of SDS soured. In its early stages SDS was democratic and analyzed problems in sociological as well as ideological terms. Events made it more romantic, more violent, more impressed with third-world revolutionary movements. Some in SDS became anarchists who believed that shocking the bourgeoisie with rough language and sexual freedom was revolutionary. Others came to think that the only way American radicals could be of use to the worldwide struggle against imperialism was by terrorism. Calling themselves Weathermen, they physically assaulted Chicago policemen in 1969 and then went underground. They blew up what they took to be elements of the imperialist system and sometimes themselves as well. After a time they burrowed so far underground that nothing was heard from them at all. SDS had self-destructed.

Campus protest and open new left activities declined sharply after 1969. They revived briefly during the Cambodian invasion of 1970 but then faded from view again. The new left was soon forgotten. Students became silent once more. The whole new-left–student-protest era was so short that it raised doubts about the grand theories that had been used to explain it. Perhaps there were homelier reasons why young people had become rebellious. One reason surely was that restrictions on student conduct had become anachronistic. Masses of self-confident students in an age of libertarian ideas and aggressive sexuality could no longer be treated as children, and most important colleges and universities soon gave up the effort. Thus, by the late 1960s, *in loco parentis,* the doctrine that university administrations stood in the same relation to students as their parents did, was abandoned. This reduced discontent, as did the efforts most schools made to recruit and assist blacks. Another response was to make academic work easier. In the early 1960s students were afflicted with the post-Sputnik backlash which led institutions to stiffen requirements, a process made easier by the surge in applications. Once students began to demonstrate, protest, and call for educational "reforms," the colleges slackened off. Requirements were eased and grades went up. Students claimed to want the grading system abolished because it did not measure true intellectual progress and stimulated an unhealthy competition. Insead, the grading system was subverted, and "grade inflation" raised averages everywhere. This was a successful compromise, though it was never presented as such. Easier requirements and social freedom, including often coeducational dormitories, reduced tensions.

Larger economic changes were important too. During the sixties students believed that whatever they did they would find good jobs if they wanted them. A student might drop out, but he could always drop in again later. Students worried less about what effect making trouble might have on their futures; general affluence was one reason for thinking this way. Whereas per capita income had risen in the 1950s by only about $100 a year, in the Kennedy-Johnson era it went up by about $250 annually. And teaching, the single most important occupation for college graduates, generated many new jobs. This was not only

because there were more schoolchildren but also because the largest number of practicing teachers had been hired in the 1920s, and most of these died or retired in the late 1950s and 1960s. Five million new teachers were hired in this period.

After 1970, demography and economics began working against the young. The declining birthrate and the fact that schoolteachers now had the lowest average age of any professionals meant that in the seventies perhaps only 1 million new teaching positions would open. Yet colleges were still turning out graduates at the old high rates and would go on doing so for years. Inflation ate up capital, so that after 1968 there was little real capital surplus—yet it took about $20,000 worth of investment to create each new job. Moreover, the areas where employment did increase—computer programming, medical technology, etc.—absorbed few college graduates. Unless more capital became available for investment in professional and managerial jobs and unless productivity in these fields went up, there was not much likelihood that the horde of new graduates could earn the increased salaries they had come to expect.

The new sobriety on campus was partly a function of grievances having been met; but even more, perhaps, it stemmed from awareness that the carnival was over. There was a growing sense that one could not have his cake and eat it too, revile the establishment and break its rules while expecting at the same time to be supported by it. When the student movement began, many liberals claimed that it showed students to be more high-minded—"idealistic," as was said—than any before them. But the movement always had an element of self-interest. Students worked to make life on campus more comfortable, and antiwar protests declined sharply when draft calls did, showing that what drove students was as much fear of induction as any abstract sympathy for the Vietnamese. And students were buoyed up by the comforting knowledge that the economy would always need college graduates, however troublesome. This is not to make light of students, only to say that they were one with the rest of mankind—selfless at times, but selfish too. They had no special virtues denied others, as used to be said, and no immunity from the workings of history.

The counterculture

As with the new left, so with the counterculture, which arose at the same time and had a parallel history. In the 1950s the young had their own culture, but it was not so much antagonistic to adult values as a parody of them. If the adult world tended to make sex objects of women, in the youth culture girls had almost no other role. Adults admired hard work and competition. The young applied these chiefly to athletics, and with a vengeance. The young consumed less than adults, having less money; but they were preoccupied with consumption to a far greater degree and, as they had more leisure, recreation was also more important to them. Adults complained of the youth culture, but as it mirrored their own values, they did so without much heat.

Then, in the mid-sixties, youngsters began singing stranger tunes. They announced that adults were eaten up with hate, envy, competition, materialism, and other noxious traits. Youngsters claimed to practice love, sharing, and the free life, unencumbered by possessions and status anxieties. They were enjoined by Timothy Leary and other gurus to drop out of society and turn on with drugs,

which would impart truths unknown to the world of reason. Many youngsters came to New York and San Francisco, where they patronized rock musicians and folk artisans. But the "flower children," as they were sometimes called, did not last long. Drug dealing was dangerous. They were preyed on by criminals and suffered from disease. "Flower power" lasted but a short time.

Yet though the community of love failed, the ethic remained attractive and many young people tried living together in various combinations—in rural and urban areas alike. Most of their "communes" were transient, since population turnover and rates of failure were high. The dropout style was popular all the same, and millions of youngsters who did not drop out looked as if they did, smoking pot on weekends and dressing in beads and blankets. Fellow traveling adults wrote inane best-selling books claiming that the truer values of the young would save civilization by abolishing it, and that intuition and handicrafts would replace science and industry.

Though attractive, the counterculture was not very durable. Most people were unwilling to live in poverty—not to mention squalor—as most dropouts did. The dropout culture depended heavily on welfare payments, thus presupposing that most people would remain taxpayers. The higher products of countercultural activity, like rock and spontaneous theater, were disappointing also. Rock bands, even ones that espoused dropout values, became commercial successes. Once rich, they found it hard to pose as alternatives to a system from which they profited so greatly. The counterculture, being more fun than the new left, seduced many of its members; but it was not so much a critique of advanced capitalism as a product of it. The counterculture was possible because society was so wealthy that it could support marginal elements, even hostile ones. The counterculture claimed to be virtuous but offered little evidence of it. Traditionally, holy men who criticized society displayed their virtue by self-denial and good works. whereas, members of the counterculture were self-indulgent and performed few charitable deeds, except for their companiőns. In claiming that promiscuity was better than chastity, marijuana ahead of alcohol, free association superior to discipline, and the pleasure principle greater than the work ethic, they merely placed one set of values in opposition to another. Proof that their system had higher values was seldom forthcoming, and they produced little in the way of art or intellect. The counterculture's characteristic artifact was a crudely made sandal; its characteristic intellectual achievement an unintelligible polemic. In short, it hardly ever rose above manual mediocrity in handicrafts or sloppyness in journalism. Little was heard of it after 1970, though youngsters went on dressing and speaking as before. This created the illusion of a vitality that was no longer there.

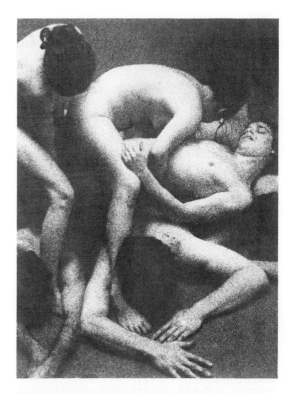

Figure 26-3 A scene from the Off-Broadway hit *Dionysus in 69.* They took off all for art. *(© 1969. Photograph by Max Waldman)*

Women's liberation

Feminism was the only social movement that did not decline after 1968 or 1969, partly because it had gotten off to a late start. Though Betty Friedan wrote *The Feminine Mystique*, the first important new feminist tract, in 1963 and founded the National Organization for Women (NOW) in 1966, it was not until 1968 that most Americans became conscious of women's liberation, and then almost by accident. A group of feminists decided to picket the Miss America Pageant in Atlantic City, charging it with the degradation of women. For some reason they got much publicity, most of it negative (and sometimes even wrong, as when it was said that bras were burned—a notion discussed but never implemented). But thereafter, while frequently ridiculed and denigrated as "women's lib," the movement was never out of sight for long. Soon women were officially certified as victims. The Civil Rights Act of 1964, which protected women as well as minorities, became a tool for women's rights, and Congress passed, though the states have yet to ratify, a constitutional amendment prohibiting all forms of sexual discrimination.

The new assertiveness of women had some relation to the fact that everyone else— blacks, Indians, the young, welfare recipients, homosexuals—appeared to be complaining too. Some women had been new leftists before joining the women's movement, but the sexual chauvinism of male radicals persuaded them that in order to help others they must first help themselves, precisely the conclusion arrived at by the first generation of feminists in the 1830s and 1840s. Women had good reasons for their discontent. They were a smaller proportion of all college students in 1960 than in 1920, women earned a smaller proportion of advanced degrees than in 1930, and certain desirable employments were closed to them by "protective legislation." Women were rarely found in professional or managerial occupations, and they were discriminated against economically at all levels. In 1970 women earned only 62 percent of the wages paid men in similar occupations; even in professional and technical fields they earned only 66 percent of what men did. Women were an increasing part of the work force—in 1940 only 26 percent of women over age fourteen were employed; in 1970, 40 percent were—yet women were concentrated in low-paying fields. Between 1960 and 1970 the percentage of employed women who worked in professional and technical jobs

rose by 2 percent, while the percentage of men in such jobs, already much larger, rose by half again as much.

These figures suggest why women were angry and also why they were more willing to express their feelings. Women once used to work almost entirely at home, but now four of every ten employees were female. Women used to be a minority of the population, but in 1970 there were 100 women for every 95 men. Demographically and economically women were more important than ever, but their status did not reflect this. The discrimination against women was not only unjust but archaic, an echo of times past when conditions had been very different. Yet though women were more prominent, most were not willing to claim what was owed them—partly, perhaps, because they were conditioned from birth to serve and nurture. Having spent their lives in subordinate roles, older women frequently resented feminists for saying, in effect, that the values they had lived their whole lives by were false. And though the younger woman did not have a lifetime to defend, she often believed that the way to get ahead was to marry a man who would take her with him. Because girls were not formally discriminated against in school, it was hard for them to understand that, once graduated, their status would decline. Caught up in the dating game and the sex play game, it was not easy for them to see that what was fun at twenty might well be fatal to their ambitions at forty. And some young women failed to realize that sexual freedom did not mean freedom from the consequences of sex. Although some women came to think of premarital intercourse as usual and commonplace, when things went wrong it was still women, not men, who got pregnant and either had to bear children or seek abortions.

The feminists found their attempts to change conventional attitudes and practices

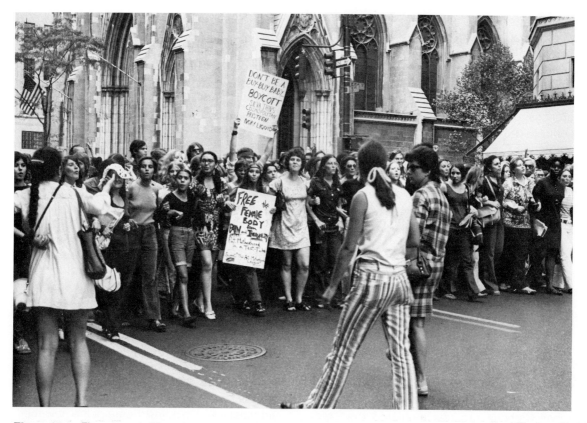

Figure 26-4 The women's liberation movement. (*Paul Kirouac*)

to be uphill work. And it was difficult to advance a movement subject to so much ridicule and denigration—hazards unique to feminism. Sometimes feminists reacted eccentrically, as when lesbianism was proclaimed the only road to freedom or obscure psychological abuses were made much of. Nevertheless, the movement grew as more women came to feel their lives could be changed. Women's position was further enhanced by the trend toward small families. The baby boom years had left women with little time or strength to advance themselves. But by 1971 mothers were bearing an average of only 2.1 children apiece, and the median age at marriage for women was twenty-one, which meant that most saw their youngest child off to school by the time they were thirty. Demography and feminism both worked to strengthen the women's case, and odds were it would get stronger still in years to come.

Other excitements

The 1960s was a great time for enthusiasms. In the fifties people had striven to be "cool," as was said. In the sixties people wanted to be hot, turned on, involved—and few areas of life escaped these attentions. The Catholic Church was shaken by rebels of all ages, and Pope John XXIII, who died on June 1, 1963, promoted reform in the church, which had long been especially rigid and conservative in America. It turned out that once begun, the process of self-examination was not easily controlled. Not only liturgy but doctrine was challenged. Priests demanded the right to marry and, when denied it, left the church in growing numbers—frequently to wed nuns, who also asked to live more normal lives despite their holy calling. Pope Paul VI upheld celibacy to little avail. Laymen demanded the right to use contraceptives, but while the Pope insisted contraception was practically murder, polls showed that 70 percent of American Catholic laymen believed in birth control despite the church's stand and 50 percent of Catholic priests agreed. Pope Paul reaffirmed the doctrine of papal infallibility, but hardly anyone seemed to be listening. Not only did American Catholics show more independence, some of them became radical witnesses. The Fathers Berrigan and other Catholic radicals mutilated draft records and went to jail for a faith that was real, but they seemed to have little in common with the Pope in Rome who was fighting hard to save his medieval prerogatives.

Liberal Protestant churches were less affected by the new freedom of the sixties. They were pretty free to begin with and had a long tradition of social activism. Trendy theologians toyed with the idea that God was dead, then espoused the "theology of hope." Young enthusiasts disregarded formal theology in favor of the ecstatic religion of "submarine churches," informal bodies often composed of "Jesus freaks" who used the language of hip youth to push old Christian ideas. Pentecostalism with its emphasis on mysticism, direct contact with God, and speaking in tongues attracted youngsters who found Eastern mysticism and contemporary Christianity equally unsatisfying. In one sense this was reactionary, a throwback to preindustrial religion, but in another sense it was very modern, for the young were rebelling against science and reason in many different ways and there was no reason for rational Christianity to be spared.

Few adults went to the extremes that Jesus freaks, some new leftists, and counterculture enthusiasts did. But they too felt their lives to be incomplete and suffered from anxieties that science and technology did little to abate. Many joined new therapy groups like the encounter groups, T-groups, nude group therapy, and other approaches that ignored the conventions of psychotherapy and were becoming increasingly popular. The Esalen Institute in California was a multimillion dollar enterprise that combined the features of a hip spa, a mental health clinic, and a religious center. Its formal program was based on Gestalt therapy, but Esalen was open-minded and encouraged dialogues between social scientists and mystics. Some of the new therapies were intellectually complex and demanding, others simple-minded, perhaps even exploitative, but all demonstrated a felt need for more rewarding human experiences. This was hardly new. Modern history is one long sequence of cults, mind-cure religions, and similar fads promising happiness and personal integration. The difference was that whereas dissatisfied people in earlier times would have gone to someone like Aimee Semple McPherson, they now flocked to Esalen. Therapy was displacing religion among certain adults, even as religion pushed out other enthusiasms among some of the young.

While the sixties were a hot time, people could stand the heat for only so long. Nixon's election was not only a symbol of the turn toward order, regularity, predictability, and low affect but also a cause of it. Politics became less emotional, as did life in general. T-groups, Jesus freaks, the sexual revolution, and other excitements continued, but they were noticed less. The new left disintegrated, the counterculture became less conspicuous, and even rock music was, as one critic put it, "Nixonized." These changes brought relief to many, but they aroused fears that the seventies would be as boring as the fifties. Time alone would tell.

America in the early 1970s

Perhaps the most important feature of the sixties and the most taken for granted was the demographic and economic tilt in favor of suburban areas. The suburbs had been growing rapidly ever since the war, but now they began to overtake the central cities in almost every respect. More people lived in the suburbs than anywhere else in 1970, 76 million compared with 64 million in the cities and 63 million outside metropolitan areas. Surprisingly, more also worked in suburban areas than in the cities. In 1960 central cities had about 12 million jobs and suburbs about 7 million. In 1970, by comparison, central cities had only 52 percent of all metropolitan jobs and in 1972 slightly less than 50 percent. Except in New York City and Texas, where local law allowed cities to annex their suburbs, the common pattern was now for the suburban dweller also to work in the suburbs. The new imbalance was partly a matter of jobs being added in suburbs but also of jobs being subtracted from cities. Nine of the fifteen largest central cities suffered a net loss in jobs during the sixties.

Other changes were less striking. Black migration continued, though at a slower rate.

In 1940, of all blacks, 77 percent lived in the South. By 1970 the proportion had dropped to 53 percent. By 1970, however, 58 percent of blacks lived in central cities compared with 28 percent of the white population. In nine cities over 40 percent of the population was black, and four cities had black majorities. Everyone was now better educated, though not all groups shared equally in these gains. The median number of school years completed in 1970 for all adults was 12.1. For the first time in world history an absolute majority of a major country's adult population were high school graduates. Blacks, however, did not do so well, since only 35 percent of urban blacks were high school graduates and only 25 percent of rural blacks. But as noted earlier, average black income as a proportion of white income improved slightly. One reason for this was the rapid decline of poorly paid domestic workers. In 1970 there were fewer than two-thirds as many private household workers as there had been in 1960. The servant population, which was mostly black, now numbered only a little more than a million. If this trend continued, as seemed likely, in another fifteen years the servant population would have vanished to all intents and purposes. The abolition of domestic service was unplanned, even unwanted. All the same, it did more to promote human dignity than almost any act since the slaves were freed.

There was considerable question about the country's demographic future. Birthrates had been declining since 1957, and in the early seventies they fell even more sharply, though the number of women of childbearing age kept going up. In 1972 the decline was so great that the actual number of live births was lower than the year before. This did not mean zero population growth (ZPG), which those afraid of overpopulation wanted, but it did mean that if rates remained at low levels ZPG would be reached in seventy years. No one was willing to bet on this. In the past population changes were reasonably easy to forecast since, barring minor irregularities caused by wars and depressions, the age of marriage tended to rise and the birthrate to fall. By the 1930s birthrates were thought to have reached a permanently low level. Then came the great baby boom, after which experts predicted that the population might double in a few generations. As late as 1970 in fact, it was thought the country's population in the year 2000 would be about 320 million. But the low birth rates of 1970 and 1971 led to a new projection of about 270 million.

But no one knew any longer what to expect. Demographic projections were useful when conception was hard to regulate, as it had been before about 1920, when self-restraint was the only sure way to avoid it. After 1920, however, improved prophylactics made birth control easier. Then in 1960 the birth control pill became available, and soon abortions were easier to get. As a result, the birthrate now responded to short-term pressure where before only large movements had affected it. Having become a matter of individual choice, births were virtually unpredictable. In this respect technology, far from reducing the power individuals had over their lives, enhanced it.

Here as elsewhere the lie was given to charges that in the mass society people were ciphers with no voice in their own destinies. As far as it could be measured, the affluent mass society gave people more autonomy in the areas that counted. Things like dress, speech, recreation, and foodstuffs became more standardized. People of the same ages and backgrounds looked, ate, and played the same everywhere in America. These were largely matters of taste. When people wished

to differ on serious matters they found it easier than ever before. Whether married, single, or homosexual, people had more sexual options. Better transportation meant that the job did not also dictate the homesite, as it used to. Higher incomes had the same effect, allowing more choice not only on where one lived but also on how one lived.

In 1900, when three-fifths of the population lived in poverty, there were few real choices open to most Americans. But in the seventies they had a considerable voice in their own affairs. Perfect freedom was still distant. New opportunities brought new problems. The people, though better off, were always letting their critics, both radical and conservative, down. They lived more richly anyway, not only because they owned more but especially because more was open to them. This was no small thing. The promise of American life was still to be realized, but that life was worth living just the same.

Selected references

As a new book on some aspect of the black experience appears every twenty-seven seconds, it is impossible even to begin listing them. Martin Luther King, Jr., *Stride Toward Freedom* (1958), is a clear statement of his beliefs. A sound history is C. Eric Lincoln, *The Black Muslims in America* (1961). Anthony Lewis, *Portrait of a Decade: The Second American Revolution* (1964), is good on the pre-black power civil rights era. The best book to come out of the great riots is John Hersey, *The Algiers Motel Incident* (1968). Seymour Martin Lipset and Sheldon S. Wolin (eds.), *The Berkeley Student Revolt* (1965), is interesting. A typical anthology of literature generated by the movement is Arthur Lothstein, "*All We Are Saying* . . . " (1970); though as it concerns theory it is more literate and difficult than most. Lewis S. Feuer, *The Conflict of Generations* (1969), is the most ambitious effort to explain the historic and social origins of the student movement. The most respectable book by an enthusiast on its subject is Theodore Roszak, *The Making of a Counter Culture* (1969). A comprehensive account of the new woman movement is Judith Hole and Ellen Levine, *Rebirth of Feminism* (1971). On these and other social developments see again William L. O'Neill, *Coming Apart.*

TWENTY-SEVEN

The Appropriate Man: Richard Milhous Nixon and the Cold War

Period covered: 1968–1973

Emphasis: Diplomacy

Major events: Tet offensive, 1968

Nixon elected, 1968

Vietnamization introduced, 1969

Cambodian incursion, 1970

Laos invasion, 1971

Berlin Accord signed, 1971

Nixon visit to China, 1972

Signing of Strategic Arms Limitation Agreement, 1972

Vietnam Accord signed, 1973

It was unbelievable—even, so it seemed, to Nixon himself. Sometimes late at night in the White House, he told a group of American clerics, he would half wake up, troubled by a problem that he ought to speak to the President about. "Then, when I am fully awake, I realize that I am the President." Looking back on the sequence of events leading to Richard Nixon's election in 1968, no matter how one juggled possibilities and coincidences, it was *still* unbelievable.

The reincarnation of Richard Nixon

Discarded by the voters of California in the gubernatorial race of 1962, the former Vice President had pronounced his own political obituary at the end of a rambling soliloquy before the press. "You won't have Nixon to kick around anymore, because, gentlemen, this is my last press conference. . . . " Almost at once, however, he decided he had been a bit hasty. The Eastern Republican "establishment" did not agree. They were ready to see to it that Nixon stayed buried when he moved to New York City. It was even difficult for the friends of the Vice President to get together a list of notables for a Nixon dinner party. But the snub did little damage, primarily because Nixon expected, indeed welcomed, the challenge. If there was to be a *new* Nixon, he would have to emerge here, on the "fast track" run by the corporate "500" in New York.

Nixon's cold war views were now regarded by sophisticates as very definitely "middlebrow," especially as he continued to publish them in places like the *Reader's Digest*. In one article he challenged the new Kennedy image, pointing out that for all the credit the President had received for his handling of the Cuban missile crisis, the fact was that Castro was still in power and the Communists were still only 90 miles from Florida. In another, he assailed the advocates of "accommodation," "disengagement," and of any "other devices which add up to our approval of Soviet domination of Eastern Europe." "The communist goal is to impose slavery on the free world," he concluded in Dulles-style rhetoric. "Our goal must be nothing less than to bring freedom to the communist world."

On Vietnam, the 1964 Nixon was every bit as militant as Republican candidate Barry Goldwater—perhaps more. Victory in South Vietnam, he wrote, was "essential to the survival of freedom. . . . All that is needed . . . , is the will to win—and the courage to use our power—*now*." As the war escalated, Nixon kept several rungs above other "hawks" in Washington; and as others became nervous about how high America had already gone, Nixon remained publicly committed to a worldwide anticommunist policy. "I completely reject the idea that there are so-called peripheral areas, collateral areas—like Cuba and Vietnam—that are not important."

Nixon's reliability even comforted Democrats who were having second thoughts about Vietnam and other policies. If *he* was upset, then Kennedy (and later Johnson) was probably just about on course. Aside from the crudity of the former Vice President's anticommunism, there was his lack of selectivity. He was still a McCarthyite, wasn't he? His support of a New Jersey gubernatorial candidate who wanted to fire a college professor for speaking out in favor of a Vietcong victory was proof of that. So while liberals took comfort in Nixon's critical broadsides and reassured themselves about their Presidents' foreign policy, the war got worse and still worse.

Yet something new was happening to Nixon. The former Vice President's New York surroundings began to rub off on him. Twice a week he lunched at the Recess, an appropriately named club frequented by the top echelon of Wall Street lawyers. Nixon's current speciality was international trade, and this was already the era of the multinational corporation. The multinationals were being touted as the solution to several age-old economic problems: By bringing together capitalists from several countries, the multinationals would reduce friction between industrial nations; they would also, by spreading the risk, make investments in the underdeveloped world safer—and more profitable. They would decrease complaints of British colonialism or "Yankee imperialism." And so on.

Nixon also found time to do some serious reading in American history, especially in the careers of Theodore Roosevelt and Woodrow Wilson. These men came to epitomize for Nixon the proper balance between thought and action; they also represented that "great dynamic drive and ability to mobilize a young country and make it a responsible world power."

As he read and listened to his luncheon companions, Nixon began to put together a new vision out of Wilson's old dream. "It is a time when a man who knows the world will be able to forge a whole new set of alliances," he told an interviewer, "with America taking the lead in solving the big problems. We are now in a position to give the world all the good things that Britain offered in her Empire without any of the disadvantages of nineteenth-century colonialism."[1] All vintage Wilson. And all straight out of the table talk of men who saw the world as a place where the sun never set on the multinational corporation.

Richard Nixon had come too far with an-

---

[1]Garry Wills, *Nixon Agonistes: The Crisis of the Self-Made Man*, Houghton Mifflin Co., Boston, 1970, p. 20.

ticommunism to throw it over all at once, even as he witnessed the splintering of the Democratic party coalition over Vietnam. That coalition, as he knew full well, had, with the exception of the Eisenhower years, ruled the nation since 1933. And he also knew very well that a new Republican majority could be chopped to bits by conflict over Vietnam. Here was a major dilemma not only for Nixon but for the nation as well.

The road away from war?

Instead of heightening Soviet-American tensions, however, the deepening crisis in Vietnam clearly produced greater yearning in policy-making elites (in Moscow as well) for an end to the cold war. Nixon sensed this better, and was freer to act upon the insight, than Vice President Hubert Humphrey, the likely opponent in 1968. While Humphrey was appealing for support for Lyndon Johnson's war policies before 3,000 workers in Pennsylvania, Nixon was addressing the opinion-making readers of *Foreign Affairs Quarterly,* assuring them that he looked beyond the immediate situation to future opportunities. Humphrey loudly shouted old slogans, saying, for example, "Make no mistake about it. Communist China has failed in its attempt to overrun Southeast Asia because we are there resisting aggression." Nixon, on the other hand, quietly balanced his judgments, agreeing that one had to meet the present danger, yet, taking "the long view, we simply cannot afford to leave China forever outside the family of nations, there to nurture its fantasies, cherish its hates and threaten its neighbors."

The article proved to the foreign policy elite that Nixon was adept at turning out something more than cold war-isms. More than that, he updated T. R.'s *Winning of the*

Figure 27-1 A cold war career is launched. Representative Richard Nixon informs the press that Whittaker Chambers has testified that Alger Hiss gave him "restricted" documents. Nixon's career as a scourge of subversives won him second place on the 1952 presidential ticket. (*Wide World Photos*)

Figure 27-2 The politician and the general. Eisenhower took the high road to the White House. Nixon went along for the ride with great expectations. (*Wide World Photos*)

Figure 27-3 Dick on TV. A crisis moment in the nominee's road to the Vice Presidency. He got over the hurdle with a brilliant speech on television defending his California friends and himself from any financial wrongdoing. (*Wide World Photos*)

Figure 27-4 A political miracle. Once thought dead after the 1962 California gubernatorial race, Nixon returned from the political grave to capture the Presidency in 1968 from a hapless Hubert Humphrey, saddled to past mistakes in Southeast Asia. (*Wide World Photos*)

Figure 27-5 Dick and Henry and Bill. Nixon needed Kissinger to reassure the Establishment and to work out in practice his own theories about the post-cold war world. Bill was there too. (*Wide World Photos*)

Figure 27-6 Where's Alger Hiss? No one seems to care. In the most dramatic turnabout in the cold war, President Nixon went to China to begin the "normalization" of U.S.-Chinese relations. (*Wide World Photos*)

West and gave it a twist sure to appeal to corporate leaders with the following: "In a sense it could be said that a new chapter is being written in the winning of the West: in this case, a winning of the promise of Western technology and Western organization by the nations of the East." The article, "Asia After Viet Nam," was the product of close teamwork with writers Nixon brought together for the presidential campaign of 1968. As yet they still had no ready answer for the candidate on the immediate question: how to go about getting out of Vietnam—without getting out of Asia?

As it turned out, Nixon did not need an answer. In the aftermath of the February 1968 Tet offensive, the council of wise men Lyndon Johnson summoned to the White House in late March 1968—a veritable who's who of the American foreign policy establishment—concluded that the President had better start looking for another way to get the war settled. The results of the New Hampshire Democratic primary confirmed the impression that Johnson was in deep trouble, even within his own party. On March 31, 1968, the President told a surprised nation that he would not run for reelection so that he could carry on the search for peace in Vietnam outside the domestic political arena. All Nixon had to do was to agree—and say that he would do nothing to undermine Johnson's noble quest by advancing alternative peace proposals for narrow political gain.

Old and new in the White House

Nixon's selection of Harvard Professor Henry Kissinger as his chief foreign policy adviser further reassured those who had been concerned that the President-elect might not know how to run the shop he would inherit from Kennedy and Johnson. Kissinger's "balance of power" concepts fit in perfectly with the new Nixon version of the Pax Americana, and his self-assured status in the foreign policy elite enhanced the new administration's credibility abroad. But Nixon had himself already decided the general outlines of his foreign policy. He wanted to begin by reestablishing close relations with Western Europe, especially Gaullist France. At a NATO Council meeting on April 10, 1969, the new American leader sounded the keynote of his foreign policy: "As men of the Old World and of the New World, we must find ways of living in the real world." In the real world, Nixon continued, the Western "partners" had already agreed on the need for strategic arms control talks with the Soviet Union, and so had the United States. But they all had to recognize and deal with the likely results of such negotiations, which would codify a nuclear balance between East and West.

On the assumption that these results would be far-reaching politically as well as militarily, the President's concern to "forge new bonds to maintain our unity" appeared to have several sources: First, and most obvious, he needed a common Western policy to assure the success of any strategic arms limitations talks (SALT) with the Soviet Union; beyond that, he wanted to reshape the NATO alliance to deal with future problems; third, and increasingly important in American calculations, he was anxious to avoid a new German "problem." West Germany had found a "home" in NATO. A detente with the Soviet Union could not be negotiated over the heads of West European leaders lest it set off family quarrels of the type that had caused two world wars. The likelihood of a new war was not great, obviously, but there were other dangers. Chief among these was that excessive rivalry in the West would allow the Soviets "to offer selective detente, smoothing relations with some Western nations but not others." And nothing would disturb Europe more than the prospect of West German-Soviet bargaining outside the frame work of the Atlantic Alliance.

The German issue resolved

Nixon had moved to minimize this danger even before he discussed the real world with the NATO Council. The focal point of East-West tensions over Germany (and within Europe as well) had always been Berlin. Deep within the Soviet occupation zone, the former German capital had been subdivided into four occupation zones. The Western sectors were regarded by the United States and its allies as an "outpost of freedom" behind the Iron Curtain. To the Soviets, Berlin symbolized something quite different, the ever-present danger of resurgent German nationalism. Twice those tensions reached a crisis point, first in 1948–1949 with the Berlin blockade and again in 1959–1961 when Nikita Khrushchev threatened to impose a unilateral solution but finally settled for a wall sealing off the Eastern sector. On a visit to West Berlin in February 1969, Nixon called for an end to tensions over the city.

So had his predecessors, but this former cold warrior said he was prepared to put aside what he now down-played as "arguments" over the "juridical status of the city" in favor of practical agreements. On September 3, 1971, a Four-Power Agreement on Berlin was signed. It provided for firm guarantees that civilian traffic between West Berlin and the Federal Republic of Germany (West Germany) would not be impeded by Soviet or East German actions in exchange for Western assurances that West Berlin would not be incorporated into the Federal Republic. In addition, the Soviets agreed that where the "security and status of the city" was not involved, international agreements entered into by the Federal Republic could be extended to the Western sectors of Berlin.

The Four-Power agreement did not put an end to the cold war in Europe or to concern about a German-Soviet "understanding" at some future date which would reduce American influence on the Continent, but it was a beginning to the first and it reduced the dangers of the second.

Vietnam still

These rather remarkable developments in Europe were overshadowed, however, by the continuing war in Southeast Asia. It soon became apparent that the new President had no clear idea or plan to end the war. Beginning with a small reduction of 25,000 in May 1969, he did start removing American troops from Vietnam. By December 1972 he had withdrawn all but 25,000 of the more than 568,000 soldiers Kennedy and Johnson had sent to "advise" the succeeding rulers in Saigon and who had wound up fighting their war. He also announced a so-called "Nixon Doctrine" after touring Asia in the summer of 1969. According to this doctrine, the United States would supply a nuclear shield for nations threatened by big power aggression, and she would supply military and economic assistance to those threatened by "other types of aggression." But for the future, "we shall look to the nation directly threatened to assume the primary responsibility of providing the manpower for its defense." It was an ambiguous statement, to be sure, and critics pointed out that no one had intended to get bogged down in Vietnam either when we started giving military aid. Yet by June 1971, more than 57,000 troops had been withdrawn from other Asian areas, South Korea, Thailand, Japan, and the Philippines.

Lacking a plan to end the war, Nixon improvised as he went along and called it "Vietnamization." The general idea, it became obvious to everyone, was to turn over the fighting to the South Vietnamese in a step-by-step process—as they proved they could "hack it" alone. It was not a new idea. John Foster Dulles had proposed the essentials of the scheme in the 1950s as the working premise of the Southeast Treaty Organization. And Lyndon Johnson advised American diplomats in Southeast Asia, at the time he ordered a halt to the bombing of North Vietnam, that the major emphasis would now be put on equipping and training the South Vietnamese Army. The "Nixon Doctrine" amounted to the same thing.

The incursion route

A survey of various policy-making agencies conducted by Henry Kissinger in early 1969 produced a gloomy assessment of the situation, no matter what policy the new administration might choose. The word was out that all Nixon wanted was a "decent interval" to allow him to withdraw his ground forces in a way that would not make it appear that Vietnam was a military defeat for the United States.

Whenever he addressed the American public, however, the President gave no indication of being willing to settle for something that small. Recounting fifteen years of resistance to communist aggression, Nixon warned that no matter how historians judged the decision to go into Vietnam, the most important question facing us today was how the United States got out of Vietnam. "For the United States, this first defeat in our nation's history would result in a collapse of confidence in American leadership not only in Asia but throughout the world."

There was some justice in his complaint that critics too often overlooked that point. But their position was that it was equally important to recognize that the way the United States got into Vietnam had a lot to do with the way it would have to get out. If, as they contended, it was not a case of meeting communist aggression but of attempting to thwart powerful nationalistic forces, the final day of reckoning was already upon us—and upon the American empire everywhere.

Until the Cambodian "incursion" of May 1970, Nixon managed the antiwar protest with consummate political skill. After that it was Nixon's war. And the Democrats rejoiced that they had the old Nixon back; the burden of guilt having been lifted, the new doves flew out, shedding their hawk's feathers as they flocked to join the protest marches on Washington. Once again, everyone had underestimated Richard Nixon, who took the momentum out of the protest by promising that American troops would be withdrawn from Cambodia within six weeks. They were; and this gave a measure of credibility to his assertion that the maneuver had denied the North Vietnamese and Vietcong a chance for an easy victory in both countries. To a nation sorely disturbed by the war, the keeping of even this promise seemed to be a good sign.

American military leaders had wanted to clean out the communist "sanctuaries" in Cambodia for a long time, but the decision to go into that country reflected Professor Kissinger's belief that the only hope for salvaging anything out of the situation was to create new problems for the other side by taking the initiative at a number of points. The Cambodian "incursion" at least did no harm argued the President's supporters, whatever else it accomplished militarily. A similar thrust into Laos in the spring of 1971, touted by the administration as a test of South Vietnam's ability "to hack it alone," was little short of disastrous. With the pace of troop withdrawals being stepped up, about the only thing left was to go back to air and sea bombardment.

The big turnabout

Nixon was down to the bottom of the "Vietnamization" barrel, but he was about to pull the lid off a much bigger one. And no one, except Nixon, seemed to know what he would find there. On July 15, 1971, the President made a brief evening appearance on national television to announce that he had accepted the invitation of Chairman Mao Tse-tung to visit the People's Republic of China. He later explained that he had had China "very much in mind" as he delivered his inaugural address on January 20, 1969, especially in these sentences:

After a period of confrontation, we are entering an era of negotiation.
Let all nations know that during this Administration our lines of communication will be open.
We seek an open world—open to ideas, open to the exchange of goods and people—a world in which no people, great or small, will live in angry isolation.
We cannot expect to make everyone our friend, but we can try to make no one our enemy.

The first steps toward reopening the door to China were taken in July 1969, each one

deliberately chosen so that it could be ignored or quietly accepted. In April 1971 came the response Washington had been waiting for, in the form of an invitation to a U.S. table tennis team to visit China after it finished competing in the world championship matches then underway in Japan. Nixon had planted the idea of *his* visiting the People's Republic with the Rumanians in early 1969, and this was the first sign it had taken root. American trade restrictions, in force for twenty-one years, were lifted on June 10, 1971. By the President's own account, "The stage was thus set for Dr. Kissinger's secret visit to Peking."

Kissinger's weekend jaunt to Peking on July 9 to 11 finalized details of the invitation. Chinese Premier Chou En-lai readily offered his interpretation of the change in American policy to anyone, especially Americans, who was willing to listen. It was really quite simple, Chou told a *New York Times* editor—the United States was concerned about Japan. Referring to a number of American statements on Japan's resurgence as a powerful economic competitor, the Premier called special attention to the President's August 6, 1971, warning in Kansas City that "four other powers [Russia, Western Europe, China, and Japan] have the ability to challenge us on every front."

The economic challenge was already clear. Government economists were predicting a more than $2 billion overall trade deficit for 1971, the first since 1893. In 1972, it reached $6 billion. Trade with Japan alone was also projected to show a more than $2 billion deficit. More important than those figures, however, was the pattern of Japanese-American trade, which government experts complained was asymmetrical. The bulk of Japan's imports from the United States were agricultural products and industrial raw materials; its exports were increasingly concentrated in sophisticated industrial products. Japan's overall trade balance with the rest of the world showed a surplus of $4 billion in 1970, $6.6 billion in 1971, and was projected to reach $11 billion by 1975.

Nixon's NEP

Exactly one month after announcing his forthcoming visit to China, the President once again startled the nation, this time with a speech on international economic policy. America's New Economic Policy, Nixon said, would be launched with a series of steps such as a temporary surtax on imports, which would continue until other nations agreed to cooperate in reducing barriers against American trade and took their own steps to correct unfair dollar exchange rates which gave them an advantage in the U.S. domestic market. The United States, having helped the economies of the major industrial nations to get on their feet, would no longer compete "with one hand tied behind her back."

Speaking to the Veterans of Foreign Wars not long after his announcement of the New Economic Policy, the President explained that "Peace itself, as William James discovered, brings new challenges of its own. . . . Here we are, 25 years after World War II, we have been through Korea, we are finishing Viet-Nam. We are looking toward the time when we will have peace. And the question for America is far more serious than the challenge that we confronted even in the dark days of Pearl Harbor."[2]

---

[2]"A Strong Economy and a Strong National Defense," speech before national convention of the VFW, August 19, 1971, *Department of State Bulletin*, Sept. 13, 1971, pp. 273–276.

To put the matter another way, the cold war world view that Richard Nixon had once helped to formulate was simply no longer capable of sustaining either American power or prosperity. The visit to China took place in February 1972 and marked the beginning of the post-cold war era. F. D. R. had never met Mao Tse-tung or Chou En-lai, the men he supposedly wanted to run China when he sold Chiang out. That, of course, had been Nixon's line in the late 1940s; now, inside the Great Hall of the People in Peking, President Nixon toasted the Chinese leadership with a quotation from Chariman Mao: "So many deeds cry out to be done, and always urgently. The world rolls on. Time passes. Ten thousand years are too long. Seize the day, seize the hour."

A conservative journalist in the President's entourage grumbled that Nixon would even have toasted Alger Hiss that evening if he had found him in the crowd. It was an insider's story: Richard Nixon had begun his rise to national prominence back in 1948 as a first-term Congressman from California by exposing Alger Hiss as a key leader in the supposed "Communist conspiracy" within the State Department, which, according to some Republicans, had sold out Nationalist China to the Reds. By 1972 no one cared anymore.

The world *had* rolled on. Time *had* passed. And Richard Milhous Nixon was the most appropriate man to seize the day. His talks with Chinese leaders produced a series of agreements on issues long thought to be beyond diplomacy. The two nations agreed, to begin with, to proceed with the "normalization" of their diplomatic relations. That was a big step in itself. But they also agreed to discuss the "progressive development of trade between their two countries." For their part, the Chinese declared that Taiwan was the most important question in Sino-American relations. American spokesmen affirmed in response that their "ultimate objective" was the withdrawal of all U.S. forces and military installations from Taiwan. Eisenhower and Dulles had once been ready to go to war for two offshore islands between Taiwan and the Chinese mainland simply to demonstrate American determination not to abandon Chiang or to remove the American military presence from his island bastion. It was a week in which the cold war finally became history.

Vietnam yet again

The visit had several liberating effects on Nixon's foreign policy. He was now able to take maximum advantage of the Sino-Soviet split and to exploit it at every possible opportunity. In Vietnam, for example, American policy makers had wanted to bomb Hanoi and mine the Haiphong Harbor since at least 1967, but they had always concluded that the risks were too great. Such a move might drive the Chinese and Soviets together and lead to a much wider war. When the North Vietnamese offensive of April 1972 threatened to divide South Vietnam in two along a line south of Hue, Nixon gambled that he could get away with the mining of Haiphong and won. Even so, he was still a long way from winning the war or even from securing a "decent interval" before the Saigon government collapsed.

The President had scheduled a visit the Soviet Union in May. His aides commented that he could never negotiate the final stages of a SALT agreement desired by both sides if communist forces were swarming into Hue at the same moment. The Soviet response to the blockade was far milder than anyone could have expected. Whatever countereffect the Sino-American talks had on the Kremlin, the

Soviet leadership behaved as if nothing unusual had happened in Vietnam when Nixon arrived in Moscow. A SALT agreement was duly signed, giving the Soviets a quantitative edge in certain categories of long-range missiles, and setting a limit on antiballistic missile systems (ABMs) in both countries. With limits established on the Soviet Union's defense systems, American leaders were satisfied that their qualitative edge more than balanced the numbers of Soviet missiles.

The Nixon administration, and the President himself, used the "backgrounder" news conference with great skill to convey a point of view or a conclusion without taking responsibility for specifics. In such a meeting with newspaper editors at Hartford, Connecticut, on October 12, 1970, the President explained that the United States and the Soviet Union were both interested in an arms agreement to reduce defense expenditures but that the Soviets were more concerned because a higher percentage of their gross national product went for weapons. Both countries, he stressed, were interested in expanding trade.

The Soviet Union and China offered potentially huge markets for technology-intensive products, the goods that Japan and Western Europe were exporting to the world with increasing success, often at American expense. If the great China market was at last about to materialize *and if* there was also to be a great Russian market, it was essential for the United States to get in early and not come trailing after other industrial powers. These were long-range considerations, however; more immediately, President Nixon seemed determined to maintain the American empire while at the same time dismantling its worn out cold war superstructure. A convert to the balance-of-power system, he remained "totally unwilling to cede U.S. influence in any part of the world where it exists."[3] Indeed, as the President maintained on several occasions, he expected his policies to result in an *expansion* of American influence into new areas formerly shut off by cold war considerations.

A central purpose in the new China policy, he reported to Congress early in 1972, was to encourage the People's Republic to "play its appropriate role in shaping international arrangements that affect its concerns. Only then will that great nation have a stake in such arrangements; only then will they endure." It was classic conservative doctrine, but perhaps Nixon was right. Perhaps it was a time when "a man who knows the world" could forge a new set of alliances, despite ideology, and enlist his new partners, however reluctantly, in defense of the status quo.

Whether Richard Nixon could "get it all together" was still an open question. He proceeded on the assumption that he could, announcing a much tougher policy towards foreign expropriations of American investments under which the United States would use its influence in multilateral development banks to deny loans to less developed countries which took over properties without making "reasonable provision" for compensation. America would take the lead, he said, to develop and support a framework of international law which would enable the developed nations "to provide increasing support for the aspirations of our less developed neighbors around the world." As one observer put it, Nixon seemed to be offering China and the Soviet Union junior partnerships in the Pax Americana in place of the cold war. Maybe that was not quite accurate, but the combina-

[3]The conclusion is that of Rowland Evans, Jr., and Robert Novak in *Nixon in the White House: The Frustration of Power,* Random House, New York, 1971, p. 79.

tion of Sino-Soviet divisions and fears—and the inducements the President offered each separately—had already changed the course of history.

Postlude and prelude

The last President who had talked about integrating China into a stable postwar world order had been Franklin D. Roosevelt, Nixon's favorite target in the early cold war. The last President who had talked about settling the Soviet Union's World War II Lend Lease debt had been Harry S. Truman, another Nixon target. Truman had never really wanted to talk with the Soviets about the debt; it was a useful cold war device to demonstrate—once again—that the Soviets had no sense of legal or moral obligation to the capitalist world. In 1972 Nixon's aides negotiated a settlement calling for a Soviet payment of $500 million, which would be taken as a final settlement for their more than $12 billion obligation. Once the Lend Lease debt was cleared away, Russia would become eligible for export credits on a long-term basis to pay for U.S. goods.

Nixon economic aide Pierre A. Rinfret wrote on the eve of the 1972 election:

I believe that we are witnessing a new alignment in world trade. The willingness to sell food and nonstrategic goods to Russia and China puts us in competition with the rest of the world, which has had a monopoly on trade with China and Russia for a little too long.

We have, in my judgment, dealt ourselves a new hand in world trade and done it with a trump card. . . . It is truer than most people realize that our position of leadership in the world is based on our economic superiority.

Also on the eve of the election, Henry Kissinger announced at a press conference that "peace was at hand" in Vietnam. Only a few minor details remained to be worked out. The reason for this optimism, he continued, was that the North Vietnamese had taken the initiative with a new peace plan. For the first time they had removed their insistence that military questions and political questions be taken up simultaneously. That is, they had agreed that the question of a truce could be separated from the question of who (or what) was to rule in Saigon after the war ended.

Critics charged that the actual truce terms cited by Kissinger only revealed that the United States could have had peace in 1969 had Nixon been willing to accept something less than victory. These other terms included an apparent willingness of the United States to accept a truce with North Vietnamese troops, more than 100,000 of them, still in place in the South. They also included a willingness to accept a provisional coalition arrangement to supervise the truce and work out the details for new elections. Saigon's President Thieu objected sharply to these terms, whether or not the United States could have obtained them in 1969, and soon proved to be more than a "minor detail" in the North Vietnamese-United States talks that followed.

Previous elections in South Vietnam (and in the North, of course) were determined by those who occupied the territory in which the elections were held. When the talks broke down in December, Kissinger stated that the real reason was that the North Vietnamese representatives had reneged on the question of the size and duties of an international truce team. But he also pointed out that there was still the question of whether Saigon would exercise authority over areas where the North Vietnamese troops remained. That was the crux of the dispute. A stalemate now?

Apparently Nixon was unwilling to risk a stalemate on those terms. In mid-December a resumption of the bombing was ordered. Heavy damage was done to North Vietnam, but the United States incurred heavy losses in the process. A new round of talks in January actually produced a truce settlement, which both sides promptly labeled a victory. The draft accord of October 1972 had as its first article: "The United States respects the independence, sovereignty, unity and territorial integrity of Vietnam as recognized by the 1954 Geneva agreements." Chapter I, Article I of the final agreement read: "The United States and all other countries respect the independence, sovereignty, unity and territorial integrity of Vietnam as recognized by the 1954 Geneva Agreements on Vietnam." The slight changes here and there in the two documents may have been worth the added pain caused to both sides by the bombing. Additional restraints may have been imposed on North Vietnam in the postwar era, yet the essential fact is that the United States had finally recognized the legitimacy of the original Geneva agreement on Vietnam. And although Vice President Spiro Agnew dutifully insisted on his official postagreement tour of Asia that the United States recognized only the Saigon regime as the legitimate government of South Vietnam, the document itself spoke of "the two South Vietnamese parties," not of governments, and obliged them to set up a "National Council of National Reconciliation and Concord" to organize "free and democratic general elections."

North Vietnam did not get what it wanted—the immediate resignation of the Thieu government, but Americans had been fighting for a decade to prevent recognition of the Vietcong on an equal basis with the Republic of Vietnam. The outlook was for a resumption of the fighting between the Vietnamese themselves unless changes of the magnitude of those that brought Nixon to Peking took place in the jungles of Indochina. Nothing seemed impossible anymore, however, as the world was in a state of flux.

Nixon had promised the American people that his quest for peace with honor would not be in vain. He would not, he said, permit the United States to be guilty of an elegant bug-out in Southeast Asia. The future was too important to risk the consequences of not living up to national commitments. Those who analyzed the truce agreement, and the bombing that preceded it, remained skeptical. Nixon was backing out of the saloon with his six-shooters blazing, said some, even before the final accord was signed. If so, said others, the cold war was still over, and what we were witnessing was the prelude to a new foreign policy. Still others insisted that it was the final, climactic scene of the old, and it was too soon to tell what would follow. History inevitably reaches the present and waits to have the last word on the future.

A summer of reversals

Some say that history reaches the present only by going in circles. But the events of the summer and fall of 1973 suggest that while it may go round clockwise for a long time, history can reverse itself without warning and race around counterclockwise. Consider these developments:

1. After difficult negotiations, the United States had succeeded in making large grain sales to both the Soviet Union and communist China. American officials openly talked of the importance of agricultural exports to communist nations in redressing the persistent balance of trade problems encountered since the end of the 1960s. Often before, agricultural exports had bailed out the industrial sector. Why not again? Congress soon

learned why from several sources. Farmers complained that speculators had grabbed off the profits from the Russian deal; consumers connected large farm exports with rising food costs at home. Since World War II (indeed, since the Great Depression) the nation's only agricultural problem had been overproduction. At the same time that Secretary of the Treasury George Shultz was proclaiming agricultural exports as the solution to America's international financial problem, U.S. Agriculture Department officials were talking about an era of food scarcity and high farm prices.

2. Throughout the cold war, American officials had attempted to boycott Russian trade and thereby slow the development of the Soviet economy and war-making potential by various trade mechanisms. As part of its general reassessment of the world situation, the Nixon administration negotiated a new trade plan with Moscow in January, 1973 which would allow Russia access to the American market on the same terms granted to all other nations. Liberal critics of the cold war had held in recent years that increased trade with the Soviet Union, and the elimination of other obstacles to closer relations, such as Radio Free Europe should be accomplished at once. Nuisance trade barriers harmed no one, they argued, except the United States. Messages from Radio Free Europe tweaked Russian noses but had not stopped the suppression of the liberal Czechoslovakian regime in 1968. Yet in the summer and fall of 1973, a self-proclaimed conservative administration found itself under attack from many of these same liberals for wishing to grant the Soviets trade equality.

Congress, however, stung by accusations of Soviet dissidents Alexander Solzhenitsyn, Andrei Sakharov, and other intellectuals that the West was sacrificing them to the cause of *détente*, disturbed by the plight of Soviet Jews wishing to emigrate to Israel, and perhaps afraid of going too far too fast in the new Russian policy, balked at the Nixon pact as written and demanded assurances that efforts would be made to help those oppressed inside the Soviet Union.

In between these positions some argued for continued negotiations with the Russians on military and political issues while bringing pressure to bear on economic questions. After all, it was argued, the Soviets needed economic aid as much as, or more than, we needed new markets and sources of raw materials. But in early October 1973 a Russian trade official blandly remarked that while his country wanted equal status with others exporting to the United States, it was not essential—everyone wanted to trade with the Soviet Union. "You need more and more raw materials," he said of the United States. "If you want to be out of step, it's up to you. It's a matter that concerns your Congress alone."

Russian officials had misjudged American ideological attitudes and idealist forces before during the cold war. Perhaps they would start off the post-cold war era in the same way. Nevertheless, American capitalists stood ready to invest $5 billion in the development and production of natural gas inside the Soviet Union in the fall of 1973, and President Nixon had just announced a compulsory allocation program for fuel oils to tide the nation over the winter season—the first such rationing of petroleum products since World War II. Like the turnabout in agricultural outlook, this news that energy resources were not unlimited seemed to have a crucial bearing on foreign policy questions, not only with the Russians but throughout the world. The energy issue, in this form, was relatively new in foreign policy. In the past, nations had struggled for comparative advantage and cheap supplies. Now the stakes were higher. By the end of of 1973, it was predicted, the United States could be one of the largest traders with the Soviet Union and communist China.

Historians are usually bad prophets. Even with full access to the "sources," the writing of history remains, as Charles Austin Beard once said, an act of faith, a belief that it does not, after all, come down to chasing in circles. Looking backward will not help you deal with the future in a direct way. Nothing can. It may help you to decide whether we are talking about circles or something else, whether history is a spectator sport or not.

Selected references

Gary Wills's *Nixon Agonistes* (1970) is far more than a good political biography. It is a study of a man and his times almost without peer in recent writing. Nixon's foreign policy has received its first critical analysis in Rowland Evans and Richard Novak, *Nixon in the White House* (1971). The background for the time of reckoning in economic diplomacy is filled in by Michael Hudson, *Super Imperialism* (1972). A Japanese view is presented in great detail in *The Pacific Rivals* (1972), written by the editors of *Asahi*.

On Kissinger, consult his own work, *Nuclear Weapons and Foreign Policy* (1957), and David Landau, *Kissinger: The Uses of Power* (1972). The multinational corporation will be the subject of many books in the future. Right now one of the best is Louis Turner, *Invisible Empires* (1971). A general survey of American diplomatic history down to the Vietnamese truce is Lloyd C. Gardner, Walter F. LaFeber, and Thomas J. McCormick, *Creation of the American Empire* (1973).

INDEX